OXFORD EC LAW LIBRARY

General Editor: F. G. Jacobs
Advocate General, The Court of Justice
of the European Communities

DIRECTIVES IN EC LAW

Second, Completely Revised Edition

OXFORD EC LAW LIBRARY

The aim of this series is to publish important and original studies of the various branches of EC Law. Each work provides a clear, concise, and original critical exposition of the law in its social, economic, and political context, at a level which will interest the advanced student, the practitioner, the academic, and government and Community officials.

Other Titles in the Library

The European Union and its Court of Justice
Antony Arnull

The General Principles of EC Law
Takis Tridimas

EC Company Law
Vanessa Edwards

EC Sex Equality Law
second edition
Evelyn Ellis

EC Competition Law
fourth edition
Daniel G. Goyder

EC Agricultural Law
second edition
J.A. Usher

Intellectual Property Rights in the EC Volume 1 Free Movement and Competition Law
David T. Keeling

External Relations of the European Union Legal and Constitutional Foundations
Piet Eeckhout

EC Employment Law
second edition
Catherine Barnard

EC Customs Law
Timothy Lyons

The Law of Money and Financial Services in the EC
second edition
J.A. Usher

EC Securities Regulation
Niamh Moloney

Workers, Establishment, and Services in the European Union
Robin C.A. White

Directives in EC Law

Second, Completely Revised Edition

SACHA PRECHAL

OXFORD
UNIVERSITY PRESS

*This book has been printed digitally and produced in a standard specification
in order to ensure its continuing availability*

OXFORD

UNIVERSITY PRESS

Great Clarendon Street, Oxford OX2 6DP

Oxford University Press is a department of the University of Oxford.
It furthers the University's objective of excellence in research, scholarship,
and education by publishing worldwide in

Oxford New York

Auckland Cape Town Dar es Salaam Hong Kong Karachi
Kuala Lumpur Madrid Melbourne Mexico City Nairobi
New Delhi Shanghai Taipei Toronto
With offices in
Argentina Austria Brazil Chile Czech Republic France Greece
Guatemala Hungary Italy Japan South Korea Poland Portugal
Singapore Switzerland Thailand Turkey Ukraine Vietnam

Oxford is a registered trade mark of Oxford University Press
in the UK and in certain other countries

Published in the United States
by Oxford University Press Inc., New York

© S. Prechal, 2005

ISBN 0-19-826832-7

For Alex

General Editor's Foreword

In the twenty-five Member States of the European Union, a very high proportion of social and economic legislation now has as its essential purpose the implementation of EC directives. This is the case in many areas of employment law, of environmental law, of fiscal law, of company law, of intellectual property law, and in a variety of other fields. By far the greater part of the Community's internal market legislation consists of directives. Increasingly, courts and tribunals in all the Member States, and lawyers advising their clients, have to look beyond their national legislation to the Community directives on which it is based.

Yet the nature of the directive, as a legal instrument, gives rise to fundamental difficulties even today, and it seems to have no true analogue in any other legal system. The distinction drawn by Article 249 of the Treaty between the two principal forms of Community legislation may have seemed reasonably clear at the outset: a regulation has general application, is binding in its entirety, and is directly applicable in all Member States, while a directive is binding on Member States as to the result to be achieved, but leaves to the national authorities the choice of form and methods. The fundamental distinction remains that regulations are directly applicable while directives must be transposed into national law. But beyond that, the dichotomy is increasingly uncertain. The Community's legislative practice has been such that directives are not only binding 'as to the result to be achieved', but impose very specific obligations on the legislatures of the Member States. Indeed, because of the detailed drafting of directives, the 'choice of form and methods' has often proved illusory.

In consequence, issues of great theoretical, practical, and even political importance have arisen: by way of example, the extent to which directives are directly enforceable in the courts of Member States in the absence of implementing national measures; the scope of the national courts' obligation to interpret national legislation so as to give effect to directives; and the extent of Member States' liability in damages where individuals are caused loss by non-implementation. On all these issues the abundant case law of the Court of Justice, which is authoritative for the national courts and tribunals, is still evolving, and many problems remain unresolved or have indeed become more complex—not least the concepts of the vertical, horizontal, or even diagonal effect of directives. The author also addresses questions of even wider concern, notably the whole range of substantive and procedural questions raised by the enforcement of Community law in the national courts.

This new edition is substantially a new book. It retains however the merits of the first edition. It draws on an exceptionally wide range of materials, both judicial decisions and scholarly writing; it maintains a lucid and cogent argument throughout; and it certainly achieves its author's aim of writing a book accessible to lawyers from different legal cultures.

This volume is also very well suited to the Oxford EC Law Library. While many other books in this series deal with specific areas of substantive law, the present volume addresses the nature and effect of Community legislation itself. Not only will the work appeal to scholars, practitioners, and officials and all interested in the Community legal system and its relationship with national law; it also forms a valuable complement to other books in the series covering those areas of substantive law, such as company law, tax law, intellectual property law, and financial services law, which are themselves the subject of directives. In this way the book will illuminate and be of practical value in many areas of substantive Community law.

Francis G. Jacobs
September 2004

Preface

How does one prepare a second edition after a period of nearly ten years? The well-meaning and wise advice was: bring it up to date but do not rewrite it. I am afraid that I have done exactly the latter. Partly, indeed, because the law has evolved considerably since the previous edition. This is particularly true for the area of State liability: the first edition could take into account only the judgment in *Francovich*. However, in other respects too the emphasis in academic discussions, legal practice, and case law has shifted. The continuous debate on horizontal direct effect of directives refocused towards the horizontal side effects, often also called incidental effects. Certain tendencies spotted in the first edition of this book became more perceptible (but not always less confusing): direct effect as a matter of legality review, the obligations resulting from Community law for national (e.g. administrative) authorities, the question of 'creation of rights' and the emphasis on application and enforcement of the rules originating in directives instead of the sometimes legalistic focus on proper transposition of directives in national law. The relationship between national procedural and remedial law went through a whole cycle, with the inevitable ups and downs, both in terms of scholarly comments and of jurisprudential developments. On the other hand, some issues have lost topicality, at least for the time being. The question of what is an 'emanation of the State' did not evolve much since the judgment in *Foster*. Neither did the doctrine of consistent interpretation lead to really new insights, in particular as far as its limits are concerned. Yet, the absence of revealing judgments from the Court of Justice does by no means exclude that on a national level interesting things may happen!

For another part I have also substantially revised the text in order to make it look less like a doctoral thesis, which it originally was. Most remarkably, for both some clear and some less clear reasons, preparing the second edition proved to be a more difficult enterprise than writing the thesis. At a certain moment I even feared to engage in legal history, with the Draft Constitution coming up and the directive disappearing!

This said, I have to thank many people for their support, understanding and patience, in particular during the final stages of the project. In chronological order, my former colleagues and the former student-assistants from the Department of European and International Public Law of the University of Tilburg and, since December 2003, my colleagues at Utrecht University, in particular those of the Section of International and European Institutional Law. I am especially grateful to my colleague Kamiel Mortelmans, for his willingness to read the draft chapters and for his valuable comments and suggestions. Ekram Belhadj, you have done a great job by checking all the references to the case law and literature. Finally, I am greatly indebted to Marlon Steine, for her language and other editing work and, in particular, for giving me the feeling, during the last hectic weeks, that this time I will meet the deadline.

And the home front? I hope the dedication says it all.

Sacha Prechal
Utrecht, June 2004

Contents

Table of Cases

European Court of Justice

Pending Cases

Opinions

Court of First Instance

European Court of Human Rights

National Courts

France

Germany

The Netherlands

United Kingdom

Abbreviations

AA	Ars Aequi
AJDA	Actualité Juridique. Droit Administratif
Anglo-Am L Rev	Anglo-American Law Review
AöR	Archiv des öffentlichen Rechts
Bull EC	Bulletin of the European Communities
CDE	Cahiers de Droit Européen
CJEG	Cahiers juridiques de l'electricité et du gaz
CLJ	Cambridge Law Journal
CMLR	Common Market Law Reports
CMLRev	Common Market Law Review
DöV	Die öffentliche Verwaltung
DVBl	Deutsches Verwaltungsblatt
ECHR	European Convention on Human Rights
ECR	European Court Reports
ECrtHR	European Court of Human Rights
EELR	European Environmental Law Review
EHRR	European Human Rights Reports
ELR	European Law Review
EPL	European Public Law
ERPL	European Review of Private Law
EuGRZ	Europäische Grundrechte-Zeitschrift
EUI	European University Institute
EuR	Europarecht
EuZW	Europäische Zeitschrift für Wirtschaftsrecht
EWS	Europäische Wirtschafts- und Steuerrecht
FED	Fiscaal-Economische Documentatie
ICCRR	International Covenant on Civil and Political Rights
ICLQ	International and Comparative Law Quarterly
ILJ	Industrial Law Journal
JB	Jurisprudentie Bestuursrecht
JBL	Journal of Business Law
JCMS	Journal of Common Market Studies
JöR	Jahrbuch des öffentlichen Rechts der Gegenwart
JZ	Juristenzeitung
LIEI	Legal Issues of European Integration
LJIL	Leiden Journal of International Law

LQR	Law Quarterly Review
MJ	Maastricht Journal of European and Comparative Law
MLR	Modern Law Review
OJ	Official Journal of the European Communities
NJ	Nederlandse Juriprudentie
NJB	Nederlands Juristenblad
NJCM-Bulletin	Nederlands Juristen Comité voor de Mensenrechten Bulletin
NJW	Neue Juristische Wochenschrift
NTB	Nederlands Tijschrift voor Bestuursrecht
NuR	Natur und Recht
NVwZ	Neue Zeitschrift für Verwaltungsrecht
RabelsZ	Rabels Zeitschrift für ausländisches und internationals Privatrecht
RBDI	Revue Belge de Droit International
RFDA	Revue Française de Droit Administratif
RIW	Recht der Internationalen Wirtschaft
RMC	Revue du Marché Commun
RTDE	Revue Trimestrielle de Droit Européen
RW	Rechtskundig Weekblad
SEW	Sociaal-Economische Wetgeving
TBP	Tijdschrift voor Bestuurswetenschappen en Publiekrecht
TPR	Tijdschrift voor Privaatrecht
WFR	Weekblad voor Fiscaal Recht
YEL	Yearbook of European Law
ZaöRV	Zeitschrift für ausländisches öffentliches Recht und Völkerrecht
ZeuP	Zeitschrift für Europäisches Privatrecht
ZGR	Zeitschrift für Unternehmens- und Gesellschaftsrecht
ZIP	Zeitschrift für Wirtschaftsrecht und Insolvenzpraxis
ZÖR	Zeitschrift für öffentliches Recht
ZRP	Zeitschrift für Rechtspolitik

1

Introduction

1.1 Controversies about directives

'... il [est] difficile d'imaginer acte plus clair que l'article 189 [249]'[1] wrote Boulouis in 1979 in a comment on the notorious *Cohn-Bendit* case[2] which still haunts the corridors of the *Conseil d'Etat* and perhaps even those of the Court of Justice of the EC.[3] If one considers the quantity of publications on Article 249 of the EC Treaty[4] and, in particular, on its third paragraph giving the legal definition of directives, this statement could seem rather bold. All the acts described in Article 249 have received considerable attention in the (Community law and other legal) literature; it is, however, the directive in particular which has exercised learned minds. In the past there were three main reasons for this special interest.

Firstly, there is the impossibility of 'capturing' the directive in terms of legal acts existing in national and international law. Although it was very quickly recognized that directives have no equivalent under either national or international law,[5] this realization in no way facilitated legal analysis. Some authors attempted to overcome this difficulty somewhat by drawing parallels with framework legislation but this also failed to elucidate the matter.[6]

Secondly, the deficient definition[7] given in Article 249(3) provoked a whole series of questions, leading some authors to propose the abolition of this instrument, which they believed to be rather a failure. The Commission itself even described

---

[1] Boulouis 1979, 107.

[2] *Conseil d'Etat* 22 December 1978 [1980] 1 CMLR 543. In this case the *Conseil d'Etat* held that directives cannot be relied upon by individuals in actions for annulment of individual administrative decisions failing general implementing measures by the Government. Meanwhile, Cohn-Bendit himself haunts the corridors and assembly rooms of the EP.

[3] Despite some new developments in its case law, the *Conseil d'Etat* still seems to hold the same position. Cf Cassia, 2002, 30–1. As to the Court of Justice, in Case C–91/92 *Faccini Dori* [1994] ECR I–3325, it based the absence of horizontal direct effect of directives on an argument relating to the competence of the Community. A comparable argument was also invoked by the *Conseil d'Etat*; cf Boulouis 1979, 106.

[4] And indeed, its predecessor, Art 189 EEC, later EC Treaty. As the present study is limited to EC context, I will hardly refer to the broader EU context. Furthermore, I will refer to the current numbering of the EC Treaty. Only where relevant for proper understanding or in case of a quotation, I will use the old numbering, followed by the new one in brackets.

[5] Cf Ipsen 1965, 69 and 71, Boulouis 1975, 197, Kapteyn and VerLoren van Themaat 1998, 326.

[6] Cf Louis 1993, 503, Ophüls 1966, 10.   [7] See below, Chapter 2, Section 2.1.

directives as an *'instrument hybride, et de statut ambigu'*.[8] Others, however, considered the directive to be an 'ideal' or 'original' instrument, fit to fulfil the functions it was designed to have within the system of the EC Treaty.[9]

Thirdly, at a relatively early stage a good deal of effort was invested in the consideration of whether directives could produce direct effect.

The controversies and ambiguities surrounding directives as legal instruments of Community action are certainly not things of the past. In particular, the discussion on replacing the directive by a different Community act has on occasions been sparked off again, also in more recent times. In the European Parliament's Draft Treaty for European Union (1984)[10] the directive disappeared as a separate legal act, not least for reasons related to uncertainties as to the effects it could produce within the national legal order. On the other hand, however, because the new 'law of the Union',[11] a directly applicable act, should have the character of framework legislation which in principle needs further implementation either by the Union institutions or by the Member States, the nature of this law was to an extent comparable to that of a directive.[12]

During the preparations for the Intergovernmental Conference on European Union proposals were made which broke with the typology of existing Community acts as defined in the old Article 189 of the EEC Treaty, the main purpose being to introduce a clear hierarchy of norms.[13] The directive again disappeared but its essence would be retained in a new legal instrument, 'the law', establishing the basic principles and leaving the Member States considerable discretion with respect to its implementation. At the end of the day, however, the proposed changes were not adopted. Instead, a Declaration on the Hierarchy of Community Acts was annexed to the Maastricht Treaty, providing that

the Intergovernmental Conference to be convened in 1996 will examine to what extent it might be possible to review the classification of Community acts with a view to establishing an appropriate hierarchy between the different categories of acts.

In another document it was recommended that directives be converted into directly applicable regulations, after a satisfactory degree of approximation of national laws by means of directives had been achieved. The conversion of directives into regulations would constitute an important contribution to legal certainty and transparency of Community legislation, in particular towards meeting the need on the part of individuals and national enforcement authorities to have a single point of reference throughout the Community as far as the applicable Community

---

[8] See Snyder 1993, 41, n 127. For a less negative, although not enthusiastic appreciation of the directive by the Commission see its Report on European Union, Bull EC Supp 5/75, 13. Cf also Louis 1976, 484–6.   [9] See Ipsen 1965, 69 for further references. Cf also Boulouis 1990, 167.
[10] [1984] OJ C77/41.   [11] Art 34 of the Draft.
[12] Cf Jacqué 1985, 37, Constantinesco 1985, 50–3, Capotorti 1988, 157.
[13] See e.g. the Resolution of the EP on the nature of Community acts [1991] OJ C129/136 and *Intergovernmental Conferences: Contributions by the Commission*, Bull EC Supp 2/91, 117–23. Cf also Snyder 1993, 41, Curtin 1993, 39–41.

legislation is concerned. Similarly, uniform application of rules would be better safeguarded.[14]

The main reasons for the dissatisfaction with directives are arguably no longer of a conceptual nature. More practical considerations undoubtedly also lie behind the proposals to replace them.[15]

Finally, even in more recent legal writing the discussion about directives has certainly not abated. Problems encountered with respect to their implementation and, in particular, their enforcement by national courts have generated an impressive list of publications.

1.2 Functions of directives within the EC Treaty

Article 249 alone says nothing about the function of directives within the system of the EC Treaty. From the first paragraph one merely learns that the European Parliament, acting together with the Council, the Council and the Commission shall issue directives in order to carry out their task and they must do this in accordance with the provisions of the Treaty. This implies that an inquiry into the role of directives within the Community law system should primarily focus on the specific Treaty Articles authorizing the Council, the European Parliament, and the Commission to adopt directives.

In legal writing it was observed at a relatively early stage, on the basis of an analysis of the Articles of the then EEC Treaty in which the directive is the only instrument prescribed, that directives will be used in particular in those areas where existing national law is rather complex and voluminous and needs to be adapted for the purposes of the Treaty.[16] From these Treaty provisions alone it already followed that the most important field of activities in which directives will be used as a means of Community intervention will be the harmonization of laws.[17] This view was entirely confirmed in practice, under both provisions designating directives as the only instrument of action and provisions leaving the institutions the choice of instrument.[18]

However, more recently the EC started to use directives as instruments for liberalization, particularly in the field of public utilities, such as communication, electricity, and gas. The objective of these directives is not primarily harmonization but the (re-)regulation of the markets. This process aims at creating or, at least, facilitating the

---

[14] *The Internal Market after 1992*, Report to the EEC Commission by the High Level Group on the Operation of Internal Market (hereafter: *Sutherland Report*), Brussels 1992, 33–4. Cf also Timmermans 1997, 6 and White Paper on European Governance, COM (2001) 428 final, 20. As to the distinction between regulations and directives and how to use it in practice see, for instance, Koopmans 1995.

[15] See below, Section 1.3, in particular the problems relating to timely and correct implementation. Cf also Hilf 1993, 19–22.

[16] Cf Kapteyn and VerLoren van Themaat 1998, 327–8. For an 'early' examination see e.g. Oldenkop 1972, 63–71, Fuß 1965, 379–80.   [17] See Oldenkop 1972, 64.

[18] Cf e.g. Lauwaars and Maarleveld 1987, 60–1, Manin 1990, 669, Nettesheim 2002, 45.

conditions for competition and, subsequently, policing the functioning of the markets. This type of intervention through directives reaches deeply into the economies and administrative and other structures of the Member States. In other words, the directive becomes in this context an instrument of regulation rather than harmonization.[19]

Without entering into the discussion of what 'harmonization' exactly means, or whether there is or should be a difference between harmonization, approximation, co-ordination, unification, etc. of laws,[20] for the purpose of this Chapter it is sufficient to observe that harmonization represents, at least as it was conceived under the Treaty and in contrast to the introduction of common (uniform) rules, a form of limited intervention. The Member States are required to adapt their laws only to a certain extent, namely as far as necessary for achieving the objectives set out in the relevant Treaty provision which serves as the legal base for the directive.[21] The directive is an instrument which corresponds very well with this idea of limited intervention. Being binding 'as to the result to be achieved' but leaving the Member States the choice of 'form and methods', it is by its nature very suitable for bringing about the necessary changes in national laws while respecting as far as possible the national legal systems, with their own conceptions and terminology.[22] Not surprisingly, in the Declaration on Article 100a [95] of the then EEC Treaty annexed to the Single European Act, the Member States expressed their preference for directives as instruments of harmonization of laws above the use of regulations. Similarly, more recently, at the Edinburgh Summit the Member States agreed that the principle of proportionality codified in Article 3B [5] (third paragraph) of the EC Treaty should imply that wherever legislative intervention by the Community is required, preference should be given to directives above regulations and to framework directives above detailed measures.[23]

Looking at the directive from a different angle, namely not as a means of limited intervention but rather as a new form of decision making, Boulouis explained the specific function of the directive by referring to the technical difficulty of concentrating the exercise of decision-making power in one single normative act.[24] In his view, a directive aims at restricting and directing the behaviour of a subordinated body according to orientations laid down by a hierarchically higher body. Apart from political considerations,[25] it is notably the need for new organization of decision making,

---

[19] Cf on this process e.g. Bavasso 2004.

[20] For a discussion of these concepts see Lauwaars and Maarleveld 1987, 7–11 and 45–9 and, briefly, Slot 1996, 379.

[21] Kapteyn and VerLoren van Themaat (1998, 327) point out in this respect that the directive serves to fetter the law-making power of the Member States on certain points.

[22] Cf Kooijmans 1967, 128, Lauwaars and Maarleveld 1987, 62, Timmermans 1979, 542, Oldenkop 1972, 61–2.

[23] *Edinburgh European Council*, Bull EC 12–1992, 15, confirmed in the Protocol on subsidiarity and proportionality to the Treaty of Amsterdam, in point 6 and, by the Commission, in the White Paper on European Governance, COM (2001) 428 final, 20.

[24] Boulouis 1975, 197. It should be noted that Boulouis' contribution does not concentrate on the Community directive only but also upon the phenomenon of directives in general.

[25] Namely to respect as far as possible the sovereign powers of the Member States and, in particular, the position of national parliaments. Cf Bleckmann 1997, 163.

both within the Community and in any other State administration, that has inspired the directive as a specific act of the institutions. The main reasons for this are the diversity, changeability, and complexity of the situations to be dealt with, aspects which the central body is unable to oversee. It is therefore better if the more concrete actions are taken at a lower level. However, the coherence of the actions is safeguarded by the orientation laid down in the directive. From this point of view, the directive has a decentralizing function within the decision-making process.[26]

The limited intervention concept and the directive as a means of decentralization have one important feature in common: they should contribute to smooth achievement of the result desired by the directive within the national legal orders. Similarly, by virtue of these characteristics, the directive seems to go hand-in-glove with the principle of subsidiarity.[27]

This, as such, does not mean that the directive is always perceived as a smoothly operating instrument, which perfectly integrates into national law. There is, for instance, a growing criticism from, especially but not only, private law which concerns the disharmonizing or even disruptive effects the implementation of directives has on the domestic legal system and dogmatics.[28]

1.3 The implementation process and the types of non-compliance

Article 249(3) obliges the Member States to achieve the result prescribed by the directive. Consequently, the actual obligations which are imposed upon the Member States will depend on the content of the directive concerned.[29]

The entire process by which obligations under Article 249(3) are fulfilled can be denoted by the term *implementation*. This process can be broken down into a number of separate stages, depending on the obligations imposed.[30]

A prototypical directive must, in the first stage, be *transposed* into national law; this requires the adoption of general measures of a legislative nature. In other words, *transposition* of directives denotes the process of transforming directives into

---

[26] Cf e.g. Mertens de Wilmars 1991, 393, Louis 1993, 502, Gaja, Hay and Rotunda 1986, 126–8. However, as Capotorti (1988, 156–7) has pointed out, practice is often different: especially owing to the detailed description of the result to be achieved, directives attain a considerable degree of centralization. Another side of the coin is that decentralization poses, in turn, new problems, namely the coordination between EC and decentralized level and the Member States *inter se*. The remedy for this is then sought in the setting up of networks or committees.

[27] Cf Snyder 1993, 41, Hilf 1993, 2, Timmermans 1997, 4–5 and Simon 1997, 11–12, as well as *Commission's Communication on the principle of subsidiarity*, Bull EC 10–1992, 123–4 and the *Edinburgh Guidelines*, Bull EC 12–1992, 15. As to 'framework laws' and subsidiarity cf Lenaerts and Desomer 2003, 126.

[28] Cf Basedow 2001, 35, Van Gerven 2001, 485 (in particular on 'the dark side of harmonisation'), Pfeiffer 2001, Jung 2001 and, more general, Steyger 1996.   [29] For a detailed discussion see Ch 3.

[30] For a distinction of the various stages see, e.g. Krislov, Ehlermann and Weiler 1986, 61–2, Capotorti 1988, 158, Macrory 1992, 348, Snyder 1993, 21–7, Curtin and Mortelmans 1994, 426–9, Siedentopf and Ziller 1988, 27 ff.

provisions of national law by the competent national legislative body or bodies.[31] Yet, this should not be understood too strictly. Transposition may also involve the empowerment of certain bodies for application of the transposed rules, such as in the case of national regulators under the telecommunication directives.[32] Moreover, it must be noted that not every (provision of a) directive requires transposition in this sense. Some (provisions of) directives may require some factual conduct, for instance, sending certain data to the Commission. In this context it is, in my view, not appropriate to use the term transposition: it is better simply to talk about implementation.

The second stage is the *application* of directives, i.e. the administration of directives in a concrete case. Strictly speaking, this expression should in principle refer to the application of the national measures transposing the directive. However, in some situations it is the directive as such which is applied, namely where it is directly effective and there are no appropriate transposition measures. Furthermore, it must be observed that both scholars and Community institutions use the term 'application of directives', even in cases where they are actually referring to the application of the national measures transposing them.

In the third stage, directives (or often, again, the measures transposing them) must be *enforced*. Enforcement of directives refers to the process of compelling observance of the directive, either as such or as the national measures transposing it.

> Although the implementation process of a directive can thus be divided into several stages, the major problem one encounters in this respect is that neither the EC institutions, including the Court of Justice, nor many scholars follow a coherent terminology (or terminology which they define in advance) to designate the various stages. Furthermore, matters are even more complicated when one compares the terms used in the different languages.[33] In particular, the term 'implementation' is often used as equivalent to transposition. In other cases, however, it may denote in general the course of action (to be) adopted by Member States in order to achieve the result prescribed by the directive. It is not my intention to cause a small upheaval in familiar (though unprecise) terminology in this respect. Neither shall I slavishly adhere to the distinction made above between implementation and transposition, in which the former encompasses the latter. Moreover, it is often immaterial, either for the subject under discussion or for proper understanding of the text, to differentiate between the two. I shall therefore frequently use the term implementation (or implementing measures) either as a synonym for transposition (but not *vice versa*) or, where this is irrelevant, in the broader meaning indicated above.

The phased character of the implementation process entails that non-compliance with the obligations under Article 249(3) can take forms which correspond with the different stages: non-transposition/inadequate transposition (or implementation

---

[31]   Indeed, this relates not only to bodies enacting primary legislation, but also to any other body which may be competent to enact generally binding rules, such as delegated legislation.

[32]   Cf the more detailed discussion below, in Ch 3, Subsection 3.2.1 and Ch 4, Section 4.3.

[33]   Cf Curtin and Mortelmans 1994, 425–7.

in the stricter sense), non-application/inadequate application and non-enforcement/inadequate enforcement.

The non-implementation of directives within the time limits set or implementation which is not adequate, like partial and incorrect implementation, is one of the major and by now well-known problems in Community law.

> The figures and overviews produced by the Commission in its annual reports to the European Parliament on monitoring the application of Community law provide some useful indications in this respect. The (latest) 20th Report, which covers 2002, reveals that at the end of 2002, 2,240 directives were in force.[34] The average notification rate in 2002 was ample 98 per cent. Nevertheless, the Commission started in 2002, 607 proceedings for the failure to notify transposition measures. Apart from non-notification, the Commission's Report gives detailed tables of proceedings started for inadequate implementation and for incorrect application.

As such, it is relatively simple to initiate infringement procedures more or less automatically as soon as the period provided for implementation has expired if no national implementing measures have been notified. Yet, if they have been notified, nothing is said about either their quality or their application and enforcement in practice. Without much exaggeration it can be said that there is a large area of 'hidden failures' by the Member States which the Commission is not able to deal with in the more systematic fashion which a successful strategy for safeguarding compliance would require.[35] In this respect, especially individual complaints from the Member States play an important role in discovering the (potential) failures.

As was stressed in the Declaration on the implementation of Community law annexed to the Maastricht Treaty, full and accurate transposition of directives into national law within the period prescribed 'is central to the coherence and unity of the process of European construction', it therefore remains one of the major concerns. Nevertheless, there is also another development, namely the increased focus on application and enforcement at national level. A number of documents have emphasized the importance of these two last stages of the implementation process.[36] Similarly, in the above-mentioned Declaration it was considered essential for the proper functioning of the Community that Community law is applied with the same effectiveness and rigour as national law.

One of the important factors causing the shift in emphasis is undoubtedly the completion of the Internal Market. Clearly, after the 'legislative stage', comprising

[34] Com (2003) 669 final. Cf further, for instance, Azzi 2000 and Mastenbroek 2003.

[35] Cf Curtin 1990b, 709–12, Ehlermann 1987, 210–12, Timmermans 1994, 395–400.

[36] E.g. Council Resolution of 7 December 1992 on making the Single Market work [1992] OJ C334/1, Council Conclusions of 21 December 1992 on effective implementation and enforcement of Community legislation in the area of social affairs [1993] OJ C49/6, Sutherland Report, 14–17 and 42–51, Reinforcing the effectiveness of the Internal Market, COM (93) 256 final, in particular 13–20, Council Resolution of 29 June 1995 on the effective uniform application of Community law and on the penalties applicable for breaches of Community law in the internal market [1995] OJ C188/1, and the Commission Communication Better Monitoring of the Application of Community Law, COM (2002) 725 final.

the transposition of some 200 directives, had been completed, the next major concern was the actual application and enforcement of the rules. Furthermore, more recently, the concerns about the capacity of the 'new' Member States to apply and enforce Community law added a new dimension to the problem.[37]

Another factor is the increasing attention paid to decentralized enforcement of Community law through national courts.[38] As explained above, the control of adequate and timely implementation of directives on Community level is an activity which consumes a good deal of time and (human or other) resources. Moreover, there still remains a considerable risk that the directives are not complied with fully and correctly, owing not only to the limited enforcement capacity of the Commission but also to the inherent limitations of the infringement proceedings.[39] Not surprisingly, decentralized enforcement through national courts provides a viable alternative, or rather a crucial complement, to enforcement at Community level.[40] Especially in relation to directives, the case law of the Court of Justice has proved to be a vital source of material for construing a system for their enforcement in national courts.

1.4   Directives in the Court's case law: two levels, four lines, and several questions

Levels

The Court's case law relating to problems of non-implemented or (allegedly) inadequately implemented directives can be situated at two different levels.

The first level is that of infringement proceedings or, to put it differently, the Community level of enforcement. Since the mid-seventies the Commission has been bringing an increasing number of cases for non-implementation or inadequate implementation of directives. Today these types of cases form a considerable part of Article 226 actions brought before the Court.[41] Although cases concerning non-implementation are not very spectacular, they have enabled the Court to rule on several kinds of excuses which the Member States have invoked to justify their failure to implement directives in due time. In cases concerning (alleged) inadequate implementation the Court has developed a set of increasingly strict requirements which adequate implementation must satisfy. On the whole, the case law provides

---

[37] Cf e.g. Nicolaides 2003.

[38] See e.g. Ehlermann 1987, Langenfeld 1991, Curtin 1992, as well as FIDE Reports 1992 and FIDE Reports 1998.   [39] Cf Ehlermann 1987, 210–13, Timmermans 1994, 379–400.

[40] Cf Joined Cases C–106/90, C–317/90, and C–129/91 *Emerald Meats* [1993] ECR I–209, para 40. The role of national courts is also important in the light of the priority criteria for bringing infringement proceedings which the Commission has recently developed. See the Commission Communication Better Monitoring of the Application of Community Law, COM (2002) 725 final, 10–12.

[41] Of the 91 infringement proceedings decided by the Court in 2002, 65 related to non-implementation or inadequate implementation of directives.

several vital elements concerning the characteristics of the directive and the consequences which the adoption of a directive has for the Member States. Moreover, in some cases the Court has also indicated the (possible) effects of its judgment establishing that a Member State has failed to implement a directive either in due time or adequately.

The second level is that of decentralized enforcement, i.e. enforcement of non-implemented or inadequately implemented directives in national courts. In preliminary proceedings the Court of Justice has elaborated a wealth of case law on the various effects that directives may produce within the national legal order and, particularly, on the role national courts are supposed to play in this context. This case law has developed along four different lines.

Lines

The first and oldest line is that of direct effect. As from 1974,[42] it became more or less definitively clear that, following the line set out in the case law for Treaty provisions and regulations, directives may have direct effect. This concept is often defined in terms of creation of rights for the benefit of individuals which the national courts must protect, or as the possibility for individuals to rely on directives and the corresponding duty of national courts to apply them. Direct effect has proved to be an important device both for protecting the legal position which individuals derive from directives and for combatting the inertia in implementation on the part of the Member States. Obviously, over the years the doctrine of direct effect of directives has been further refined by the Court of Justice. One of the major setbacks in this development has been the refusal of the Court to recognize horizontal direct effect, i.e. the possibility for an individual to rely on the directive against another private individual.[43] Arguably in order to obviate this setback as far as possible, the Court has expanded considerably the category of bodies against which the directive can be relied upon by giving an extensive interpretation to the concept of 'the State'. In this way, the relationship at issue could still be dealt with within the scope of vertical direct effect, i.e. the possibility for an individual to rely on the directive as against the State.

The second line which can be discerned in the Court's case law is that of inter-pretation of national law in conformity with the directive. In 1984[44] the Court of Justice laid down an obligation for all the authorities of the Member State, and especially for the courts, to proceed to such 'consistent interpretation'. Although this obligation had been formulated by the Court some two years before the explicit denial of horizontal direct effect of directives and, from this perspective, it would not seem entirely correct to maintain that the obligation to follow this method of interpretation

---

[42] Case 41/74 *Van Duyn* [1974] ECR 1337.   [43] Case 152/84 *Marshall I* [1986] ECR 723.
[44] Case 14/83 *Von Colson* [1984] ECR 1891.

was intentionally designed to palliate the problems caused by the absence of horizontal direct effect of directives, in practice it does actually often function in this way. However, the scope of the obligation of consistent interpretation is more ample than this. It can, for instance, also bring relief in cases where there is no direct effect at all.

Simultaneously but independent from these two developments, another (third) line in the Court's case law was taking shape: the—what I will call—'effective judicial protection line'. This case law, which is in no way limited only to directives, is characterized by increasing interference by the Court with the standards of judicial protection available within the Member States. As from 1986,[45] the Court started to impose increasingly unambigous Community law requirements which national systems of judicial protection must satisfy. These requirements concern a whole range of different issues, such as access to the courts, rules of evidence, time limits for bringing action and, last but not least, the type of redress which must be available for individuals bringing actions with a view to protecting the position accorded to them by Community law. Although, seen over a longer period of time, the Court's approaches in this area fluctuate between a 'hands-off' policy on the one hand to severe intrusiveness on the other, the overall impact of this cannot be underestimated.

The fourth line in the developments can be considered as the natural continuation of the 'effective judicial protection' case law. Using the necessity of effective judicial protection as one of the two main arguments, the Court decided in 1991[46] that a Member State is in principle liable for harm caused to individuals by breaches of Community law, including the non-implementation of directives. It has been suggested that the Court intentionally denied direct effect of the directive at issue with a view to establishing the liability of the State as a remedy which did not depend on direct effect.[47] In this way, especially the problems arising from the absence of horizontal direct effect of directives can be circumvented.

Questions

In the light of these developments it cannot be denied that the enforcement of directives at decentralized level has become a complex matter. In particular, if one takes into consideration the various conditions and limits governing these different routes to enforcement, it may be asked whether these developments have not reached such a degree of sophistication that the system—if there is any[48]—has become unworkable for the national courts and entirely opaque for the individual.[49]

---

[45] Case 222/84 *Johnston* [1986] ECR 1651.

[46] Joined Cases C–6/90 and C–9/90 *Francovich and Bonifaci* [1991] ECR I–5357.

[47] Steiner 1993, 9. Such a point of view was, however, doubted by e.g. Geiger 1993, 470.

[48] Some have characterized the case law as a '*bateau ivre*': see Emmert and Pereira de Avezedo 1993.

[49] For a critical review of the case law see e.g. Hilf 1993, Manin 1990, and Emmert 1992. More recently, the criticism especially concentrates on the Court's case law about horizontal side effects and the State liability as a 'default option'. For a detailed discussion see below, Ch 8, Section 8.6, Ch 9 Subsection 9.5.3 and Ch 10, Section 10.6.

The picture becomes even more complicated if the developments at the first level, the case law at Community level of enforcement, are taken into account. In the past it was to a large extent possible to consider cases decided under Article 226 and the case law developed in preliminary proceedings as two separate matters, particularly since the two types of proceedings serve different purposes. However, on closer consideration, certain links can be discerned between the requirements as to adequate implementation and some elements of the case law developed in preliminary proceedings (and *vice versa*). Furthermore, as regards the characteristics of the directive, the case law as a whole must be taken into consideration.

It will certainly not come as a surprise that directives, and especially their enforcement at both Community and national levels, give rise to complex issues, many of which are as yet far from resolved.

The first and most important group of problems relates to the four different lines of development considered separately: what is the content of the concepts, what are the conditions for their application, what are their limits and effects? Can the developments within the separate lines of case law be considered as consistent? Obviously the answers differ, not least because some concepts, like direct effect, are relatively old and already elaborated, while others, like State liability, are of a more recent date.

The way in which the developments take place could suggest that the Court reacts to individual problems in an *ad hoc* fashion, and thus hardly in a systematic manner. The next question is therefore whether and, if so, to what extent there exists coherence between the distinct lines. Two different aspects can be discerned in this connection. Firstly, there is the question whether and, if so, in what way the four lines elaborated within the decentralized enforcement context are interrelated. Secondly, there is the question as to the relation or interaction of the elements of the case law developed in infringement proceedings and those developed in preliminary proceedings.

Finally, it may be asked: to what extent have the various elements of the Court's case law clarified or perhaps even expanded the definition of directives given in Article 249(3)?

1.5   What is the rest of this book about?

The purpose of this book is to examine in detail the multiple aspects of directives outlined in the previous Section. The analysis will not, however, entirely follow the sequence of the questions formulated above. Moreover, it will primarily be conducted from a particular viewpoint, namely the judicial protection of rights which individuals allegedly derive from Community directives.

The book concentrates on three central themes. The first theme concerns the main characteristics of directives. Therefore, the next four Chapters respectively focus on the binding force of the Directive and its implications; the result to be achieved, which involves a scan of the content of directives; the addressees of directives, not only the formal addressees, i.e. the Member States, but also the indirect addressees, the persons to be ultimately bound by the Directive. In this context, attention will also be given to the problems which arise because directives are binding on all public authorities and all emanations of the State. Finally, the freedom to choose the form and methods of implementation will be discussed. It is particularly—but not exclusively—in Chapter 5 that the various elements of the 'Article 226 case law' pass in review. The respective Chapters examine all these issues in a practical rather than a theoretical manner, i.e. drawing heavily upon the relevant case law of the Court and upon the actual texts of several directives.

The second theme considers the directive as an integral part of national legal orders and the implications this has for national courts. Chapter 6 focuses on the directive as a source of law valid within the Member States as well as a source of individual rights. The various meanings of the concept of 'rights' as they appear in the Court's case law are explored and the possible parameters of when legal rules do create a right will be discussed. Next, the role national courts are supposed to play in protecting these rights, or in providing judicial protection more in general, will also be addressed in detail. This second component of this theme, Chapter 7, corresponds mainly with the 'effective judicial protection line' mentioned above and analyses the inroads Community law makes into the 'national procedural and remedial autonomy'.

The last theme focuses, in three Chapters, on the three mechanisms available to national courts for enforcement of directives: the concept of consistent interpretation, the doctrine of direct effect and the principle of State liability will be examined in detail. The content of the three mechanisms, the conditions for their operation, their effects and their limits will be discussed in particular.

In Chapter 11, the final Chapter, I shall bring together a number of aspects resulting from the foregoing analysis.

The materials used for this study comprise various directives, judgments of the Court of Justice, opinions of Advocates General and legal literature, as well as a number of Community documents. The text, as far as possible, reflects the materials available at the close of April 2004.[50]

Finally, the book concentrates primarily on the Community law dimensions of the subject. It is very difficult and, it is submitted, even erroneous, especially with respect to a subject like this, to divorce entirely the Community law and national law sides of the problems. However, within the limited scope of one single book it is not feasible to integrate the two. Therefore, it is only in order to illustrate the amplitude of the issues and the interrelationship of Community law and national law, or with a view to clarifying certain contentions, that minor excursions into national law of some of the Member States are be made.

---

[50] Important exceptions are the Cases C–397/01 to C–403/01 *Pfeiffer*, judgment of 5 October 2004, nyr in ECR, Case C–127/02, *Landeiÿke Vereniging tot Behond van de Waddenzee*, judgment of 7 September 2004, nyr in ECR, and Case C–222/02 *Peter Paul*, judgment of 12 October 2004, nyr in ECR, which I have squeezed into the text at the proof stage.

2

Directives as binding instruments of legislative action

2.1 The main characteristics

The distinguishing elements in the definitions of binding Community acts given in Article 249 are the subjects to whom the acts can be addressed, the scope of their binding force, and the effects they may produce in the internal legal orders of the Member States.

With the statement that regulations shall have 'general application', the Treaty Article is saying that a regulation applies to abstract categories of persons. It lays down general rules which affect the legal position of general classes of persons. Furthermore, the Court of Justice has emphasized that these terms entail the applicability of the regulation to 'objectively determined situations'.[1] Decisions on the other hand can be directed to a definite number of addressees, i.e. Member States and private parties, and they only affect specific legal subjects.[2] Both acts are binding in their entirety.

Like a decision, a directive can be addressed to a limited number of subjects, namely one or more Member States, and it too is binding, although in a limited way, namely 'as to the result to be achieved'.

We also learn from Article 249 that the national authorities have the choice of form and methods for the realization of the result prescribed by a directive.

Finally, Article 249 indicates that regulations are directly applicable *in* all Member States. No comparable indication as to the effect of the acts is given with respect to directives and decisions. The wording of the definition of the two latter acts could indeed suggest that they should not produce legal effects other than between the author and the addressee.[3]

It is not at all surprising that such a rudimentary description[4] of the most important Community instruments and their delimitation has generated an impressive literature in the attempt to fathom the nature of the different acts.

---

[1] See e.g. Case 6/68 *Zuckerfabrik Watenstedt* [1968] ECR 409.
[2] See e.g. Joined Cases 16 and 17/62 *Fruit et Légumes* [1962] ECR 471.
[3] Cf De Ripainsel-Landy and Gérard 1976, 44, Ophüls 1966, 6.
[4] Cf Ipsen 1965, 70, De Ripainsel-Landy and Gérard 1976, 37.

One of the most problematic areas with regard to directives has been their delimitation *vis-à-vis* regulations.[5] This has particularly been caused by a number of practical and jurisprudential developments, namely: the case law of the Court of Justice on direct effect of directives; the facts that, although regulations require no incorporation into national legal order, in practice adoption of national rules is often necessary in order to make them fully operative and that, in this respect, some discretion may be left to the Member States;[6] the fact that the *content* of directives is largely normative in nature;[7] and, finally, the reality that directives have become quite detailed.[8]

The last of these issues in particular has given rise to differences of opinion in legal writing and has also created discord in practice.[9] In any case, from Article 249(3) it appears that the Member States must have a certain amount of freedom in choosing the form and methods. If they do not, the instrument which is adopted loses the character of a directive. In practice, however, the content of a directive may considerably curtail this freedom, being so detailed that in fact the Member States are left with very little latitude.

The crux of the problem is that the definition of Article 249(3) as such provides little help when determining the extent to which directives may go into detail. Despite some attempts in this direction, doctrine eventually recognized that an abstract analysis of Article 249(3) alone was doomed to fail.[10] A more concrete analysis, however, also reveals that the relationship between 'result' and 'form and methods' shows fluctuations.[11] If the provision constituting the legal basis of the directive is examined in a number of concrete cases, it will become apparent that in some cases detailed rules may be necessary for the accomplishment of the objective pursued, while in others the Community institutions may confine themselves to more general indications. In this respect as well, therefore, no general rule can be given.[12]

Today, although not without criticism, it is generally accepted, both by doctrine[13] and the Court of Justice,[14] that a directive may give a detailed description of the result to be achieved, provided that it is necessary for effective realization of the objective pursued.[15] Every case must be assessed individually in this respect and the resulting assessments can, if necessary, be submitted to the control of the Court of Justice or

---

[5] For a discussion of the delimitation of directives and regulations or directives, regulations, and decisions see e.g. Kooijmans 1967, 130–1 and 136, Capotorti 1988, Galmot 1990, Scherzberg 1991. For a 'contemporary' and general discussion of Art 249 and the legal instruments defined therein see Bast 2003.

[6] Cf De Ripainsel-Landy and Gérard 1976, 46 and 88, Lauwaars 1983.

[7] Cf Bleckmann 1997, 170, De Ripainsel-Landy and Gérard 1976, 88.

[8] Cf Monaco 1987, 471, Kooijmans 1967, 134, Galmot 1990, 74, Capotorti 1988, 154, Bast 2003, 11.

[9] For a more detailed discussion see the first edition of this book, 16–17. See also e.g. Winter 1996, 488–90, Simon 1997, 18–20, Timmermans 1997, 4–6.

[10] Cf Beyerlin 1987, 127, Oldenkop 1972, 78–92, Bleckmann 1997, 165–7.

[11] Kapteyn and VerLoren van Themaat 1998, 329.

[12] Cf Louis 1993, 500, Fuß 1965, 380–1, Bleckmann 1997, 165–6.

[13] Cf e.g. Everling 1984, 112, Lauwaars 1973, 30, Timmermans 1971, 621, Easson 1981, 10, Mertens de Wilmars 1991, 394, Winter 1996, 489–90, Bast 2003, 11.

[14] Case 38/77 *Enka* [1977] ECR 2203.   [15] Cf for instance Nettesheim 2002, 47.

the Court of First Instance, where appropriate.[16] It is similarly accepted, however, that Article 249(3) sets a limit: a directive as a whole must leave some latitude to the Member States as far as the form and methods of implementation are concerned. It certainly cannot oblige a Member State simply to introduce an exhaustive set of rules with no consideration of the law existing within the national legal order.[17]

During the 1990s, partly as a reaction to the detailed character of many directives, a new term became fashionable: the framework directive. This is an unknown instrument in the typology of the EC Treaty and it is, in fact, not clear what it exactly refers to. One of the characteristics of a framework directive seems to be that it lays down only basic and general principles. From this perspective, it is believed that the Member States have more latitude in relation to the implementation of these directives.[18] However, much depends on how this framework is further completed. Quite a few directives known as 'framework directives' are implemented further through so-called 'daughter directives' or 'individual directives' which may be rather detailed.[19]

The Dutch Council of State has indicated in its Annual Report of 1999, that framework directives must be distinguished from the so-called basic directives. The latter delegate powers to adopt implementing legislation to, as a rule, the Commission. The power to adopt individual directives in order to 'flesh out the framework' is based directly on the Treaty. However, the terminology seems far from settled. Some use the term framework directive for the 'new-approach' directives which lay down the essential requirements and the businesses have a choice as to the way in which they comply with these obligations. In other words, it is a combination of a legislative framework and self-regulation.[20]

In relation to the last point another rather recent phenomenon should be mentioned, namely directives which are in fact 'hiding' framework agreements between the social partners adopted under Article 139(1) EC and which are 'implemented' by the Council in accordance with the procedure provided in Article 139(2) EC.[21]

The essential difference between directives and regulations is 'the structural necessity'[22] to enact national transposition measures in order to give them full legal

---

[16] Cf Kooijmans 1967, 134.

[17] Cf Kapteyn and VerLoren van Themaat 1998, 329, Louis 1993, 501, Lauwaars 1973, 30–1, Hilf 1993, 7. Nettesheim 2002, 47, however, seems to accept that directives may leave no latitude at all, provided that it is necessary for the achievement of the objective pursued.

[18] In particular for that reason the Protocol on the application of the Principles of Subsidiarity and Proportionality (annexed to the EC Treaty by the Treaty of Amsterdam), in para 6, gives preference to framework directives over detailed directives. Cf also Timmermans 1997, 6–7.

[19] Examples of directives which are called framework directives are Directive 75/442 (waste) [1975] OJ L194/39 (as amended by Directive 91/156 [1991] OJ L78/32), Directive 76/464 (pollution of aquatic environment) [1976] OJ L129/23, Directive 89/391 (safety and health at work) [1989] OJ L183/1, Directive 96/62 (air quality assessment) [1996] OJ L296/55 and Directive 2000/60 'establishing a framework for Community action in the field of water policy' [2000] OJ L327/1.

[20] Cf The legal instruments: present system, CONV 50/02 and Simon 2001, 325.

[21] Cf e.g. Directive 1999/70 (fixed-term work) [1999] OJ L175/43. On this topic see Franssen 2002.

[22] Capotorti 1988, 156.

effect. In this respect the terms 'two-stage legislation'[23] or 'indirect legislation'[24] are often used. In the first—Community—stage the intended result of a directive is laid down in an act which is binding for the Member States. In the second—national—stage the Member State effectuates the content of the directive by transposing it into national law and thus turning it into a normative act with an effect *erga omnes*.

Directives as such address a definite number of subjects, i.e. the Member States, and to this extent they may be seen as decisions. As far as their content is concerned, however, they are usually intended to regulate objectively determined situations and to produce effects with regard to general and abstract categories of persons.[25] In general, directives require further national legislation in order to realize entirely their normative content. Directives therefore, unlike regulations, are not immediately generally applicable. Nevertheless, they are regarded as a piece of legislation. The Court of Justice in particular seems to consider them, without further ado, as legislative acts or as acts of general application.[26] The fact remains, however, that their general applicability is in principle an indirect one.[27]

2.2 Article 249(3): the basis of Member States' obligations

Article 249(3) imposes upon the Member States an obligation to achieve the result required by the directive. The fact that Article 249(3) leaves the Member States free to choose the form and methods of implementation in no way affects this obligation.[28] The provisions of a directive have no less binding an effect than those of any other rule of Community law.[29]

The obligation to achieve the result envisaged by the directive follows from Article 249(3), since it is by virtue of this provision that directives are binding. The concrete content of the obligation is in turn spelled out in each individual directive. In this respect it must be noted that, in general, when a Member State has not implemented a directive within the time limit or has not implemented it properly, the Court will

---

[23] See e.g. Hilf 1993, 4, Capotorti 1988, 154.

[24] See e.g. Pescatore 1980, 171, Capotorti 1988, 156, Fuß 1965, 379, Lauwaars 1973, 29. Cf also Case C–298/89 *Gibraltar* [1993] ECR I–3605 para 16 and C–10/95 P *Asocarne* [1995] ECR I–4149, para 29.

[25] Cf e.g. Case 160/88 *Fedesa* [1988] ECR 6399. Cf Von Bogdandy, Bast and Arndt 2002, 99, who point out, in this respect, that there is in principle not much difference between decisions directed at Member States and directives.

[26] As early as Case 41/74 *Van Duyn* [1974] ECR 1337 the Court designated directives as 'legislative acts'. See further Case 160/88 R *Fedesa* [1988] ECR 4121, Case C–298/89 *Gibraltar* [1993] ECR I–3605 and Case C–63/89 *Assurances du Crédit* [1991] ECR I–1799 and Joined Cases T–172/98, T–175–177/98 *Salamander* [2000] ECR II–2487, paras 28–29.

[27] Cf Capotorti 1988, 156. See, however, also below, Ch 9.

[28] Cf Case 14/83 *Von Colson* [1984] ECR 1891.

[29] See Case 79/72 *Commission v. Italy* [1973] ECR 667 and Case 52/75 *Commission v. Italy* [1976] ECR 277.

state in fairly neutral terms that the Member State concerned has failed to fulfil its obligations under the EC Treaty,[30] i.e. under Article 249(3).[31] The Court's case law, however, shows little consistency in this respect. In some cases the Court has found that a Member State had not fulfilled its obligations under the directive at issue, while in other cases a similar infringement has amounted to non-fulfilment under the Treaty or under both the Treaty and the directive.[32] In my view, the difference is not relevant, since it is more a matter of formulation.[33] Any failure to comply with a specific (provision of a) directive implies *eo ipso* a violation of Article 249(3).

Directives usually stipulate explicitly that the Member States shall bring into force the laws, regulations, and administrative provisions which are necessary to comply with the directive, or that they shall take the necessary measures and so on. In this way they reiterate the obligation already laid down in Article 249(3).

The obligation to achieve the result prescribed by a directive also follows from the more generally worded Article 10 of the EC Treaty, i.e. the duty of the Member States to take all appropriate measures to ensure fulfilment of the obligations arising out of the Treaty or resulting from an act of an institution. In practice, this cumulation of obligations has no special significance. According to the Court of Justice the mere non-fulfilment of specific obligations arising under a directive makes unnecessary an inquiry into the question whether a Member State has also failed its obligations under Article 10.[34] Only if a breach *distinct* from non-compliance with Article 249(3) or the directive can be established will Article 10 play a part as an independent standard for review.[35] This does not mean, however, that Article 10 is entirely irrelevant for the obligation at issue. As the case law shows, the Court uses Article 10 as an additional argument for a certain interpretation of Article 249(3), and thus to reinforce the obligations arising therefrom.[36]

The binding force of directives further requires not only that directives *are* implemented, but that they are also implemented in due time and *correctly*. The underlying reason is the uniform and (thus) simultaneous application of

[30] See e.g. Case 235/84 *Commission v. Italy* [1986] ECR 2291 and Case C–131/88 *Commission v. Germany* [1991] ECR I–825.   [31] Cf Case 145/82 *Commission v. Italy* [1983] ECR 711.

[32] For reference to a directive only see e.g. Case 235/85 *Commission v. the Netherlands* [1987] ECR 1471 and Case C–45/89 *Commission v. Italy* [1991] ECR I–2053. For reference to the Treaty see e.g. Case 420/85 *Commission v. Italy* [1987] ECR 2983 and Case C–290/89 *Commission v. Belgium* [1991] ECR I–2851. For reference to the Treaty and a directive see e.g. Case 107/84 *Commission v. Germany* [1985] ECR 2655 and Case C–293/91 *Commission v. France* [1993] ECR I–1.

[33] See e.g. Case 415/85 *Commission v. Ireland* [1988] ECR 3097 and Case 416/85 *Commission v. UK* [1988] ECR 3127 in which the Court stated explicitly that the Member States concerned, by having contravened the provisions of the directive at issue, had therefore failed to fulfil their obligations under the Treaty.   [34] Case C–48/89 *Commission v. Italy* [1990] ECR I–2425.

[35] Cf Case C–374/89 *Commission v. Belgium* [1991] ECR I–367 and Case C–382/92 *Commission v. United Kingdom* [1994] ECR I–2435. Cf also Due 1992, 356–7 and Prechal 1992, 374–7. Incidentally the Court finds that the directive at issue, Art 249(3) and Art 10 have been violated: Case 239/85 *Commission v. Belgium* [1986] ECR 3645.

[36] Cf Due 1992, 357. In particular, Art 10 reinforces Art 249(3) as a basis for consistent interpretation and direct effect. See below, Ch 8, Section 8.1 and Ch 9, Subsection 9.2.1.

Community law, which is the very essence of the Community legal order. As the Court has explained

[i]n permitting Member States to profit from the advantages of the Community, the Treaty imposes on them also the obligation to respect its rules. For a State unilaterally to break . . . the equilibrium between advantages and obligations flowing from its adherence to the Community brings into question the equality of Member States before Community law and creates discriminations at the expense of their nationals, and above all of the nationals of the State itself which places itself outside the Community rules. This failure in the duty of solidarity accepted by Member States by the fact of their adherence to the Community strikes at the fundamental basis of the Community legal order.[37]

In a declaration annexed to the Maastricht Treaty, the Member States underlined

that it is central to the coherence and unity of the process of European construction that each Member State should fully and accurately transpose into national law the Community Directives addressed to it within the deadlines laid down therein.[38]

2.3   The obligation to implement the directive in due time: the relevance of deadlines

From the old Article 191(2) of the EEC Treaty it followed that the obligation to implement started to run as from the day on which the directive was notified to the Member States concerned. Since the entry into force of the Treaty on European Union,[39] directives adopted in accordance with the co-decision procedure[40] and those directed to all Member States enter into force after publication and on the date specified in them. In the absence of such a specification, they enter into force on the twentieth day following that of their publication.[41] For the remaining category of directives it is still on the day of notification that they enter into force. Yet directives do allow the Member States a certain period, varying from a few months to several years, within which the directive must be implemented. The deadline for implementation will usually be uniform for all addressees. However, directives may sometimes fix different deadlines for certain Member States, as with Directive 89/654 (health and safety at the workplace) for Greece and Directive 92/13 (public contracts—excluded sectors) for Greece, Portugal, and Spain.[42] According

---

[37] Case 39/72 *Commission v. Italy* [1973] ECR 101, paras 24–25.

[38] *Declaration on the Implementation of Community Law.* Cf also White Paper on European Governance, COM (2001) 428 final, 25. Since the early 1990s, problems relating to, *inter alia*, the 'full and accurate transposition' of directives became part of a much broader discussion about the quality of EC legislation. Cf below, Ch 11, Section 11.8.   [39] 1 November 1993.

[40] Art 251 EC Treaty.

[41] Publication is now provided for in Art 254 EC Treaty. Under the EEC Treaty there was no obligation to publish directives in the OJ.

[42] Arts 10(1) and 13(1) respectively; [1989] OJ L393/1 and [1989] OJ L76/14.

to Article 12(1) of Directive 86/613 (equal treatment of the self-employed) a different deadline applies for those Member States which, in order to comply with it, have to amend their legislation on matrimonial rights and obligations.[43] In some cases the deadline may be postponed[44] or must still be decided upon by the Council.[45] Furthermore, it must be noted that certain directives provide for different implementation periods: a shorter period for the adoption of transposition measures and a longer one within which the factual situation must be achieved, i.e. for their application.[46]

Although the Treaty is silent on this point, and thus appears not to exclude *eo ipso* the entry into force of the directive coinciding with the date at which the measures necessary for its implementation must be adopted,[47] it has been argued in legal literature[48] that such a coincidence would not be in accordance with the nature of the directive.

Firstly, the fact that there is choice of form and methods of implementation makes a certain lapse of time necessary.

Secondly, a period for implementation is necessitated by the very purpose of the directive, i.e. to compel the Member States to take measures within their internal legal order.

Whatever the theoretical considerations may be, it is clear that the inclusion of time limits for the implementation of a directive bears witness to a healthy realism. In this respect the time limit can be compared to the transitional periods in the EEC Treaty or in Acts of Accession.

The dissociation of the entry into force of a directive and the required entry into force of the implementing measures raises a number of questions as to the effects produced by the obligation during this interval of time.

Obviously, during the period provided for implementation the Member States should consider and prepare the national measures which must be taken to enable them to comply with their obligation in due time.[49] It was for this reason that the Court of Justice denied the possibility to rely in national courts on a directive

---

[43] [1986] OJ L359/56.

[44] E.g. Directive 89/104 (trade marks), Art 16 (2) [1989] OJ L40/1. See for this postponement Council Decision 92/10 [1992] OJ L6/35. Cf also Directive 80/778 (drinking water), Art 19 [1980] OJ L229/11: Commission may grant an additional period. Furthermore it must be noted that Member States may not unilaterally or *de facto* postpone the deadline through, for instance, national transitional measures. See Case C–396/92 *Bund Naturschutz in Bayern* [1994] ECR I–3717.

[45] E.g. Directive 80/217 (classical swine fever), Art 19 [1980] OJ L47/11.

[46] E.g. Directive 76/760 (bathing water) [1976] OJ L31/1: two years for legislative and other measures and ten years for achievement of the prescribed marginal values. Cf e.g. also Directive 86/378 (equal treatment in occupational social security schemes) [1986] OJ L225/40 or Directive 96/98 (marine equipment) [1997] OJ L46/25. See also below, Ch 3, Section 3.3.

[47] And must, as a rule, also enter into force in the national legal order. For the sake of clarity it must be observed that the term 'entry into force of the directive' should refer, in my opinion, to the moment that the directive becomes binding upon the Member States and *not* to the entry into force of the implementing measures.   [48] De Ripainsel-Landy and Gérard 1976, 54.

[49] Cf Kooijmans 1967, 141 and Lauwaars and Maarleveld 1987, 191.

before the deadline for implementation expires.[50] However, it has been argued in the legal literature that the binding force of a directive as from the time it enters into force entails nevertheless certain more far-reaching effects, even before the expiry of this deadline.

Firstly, a question addressed both in legal writing and in practice concerns the problem whether, during the period provided for implementation, Member States may take measures which, when compared with the directive at issue, entail a retrograde step.[51] The Court of Justice has addressed this issue in *Inter-environnement Wallonie*,[52] a reference from the Belgian *Conseil d'État*. The Court held that the Member States cannot be faulted for failing to transpose a directive before the period prescribed for its transposition, because the purpose of that period is to give the Member States the necessary time to adopt transposition measures. On the other hand, Article 10(2) in conjunction with Article 249(3) and the directive itself require that the Member States must refrain from taking any measures liable to seriously compromise the result prescribed by the directive. The Court went on to give some guidance to the national courts as to when a measure taken in this period would be liable seriously to compromise the result prescribed. If, for instance, the provisions in question are intended to constitute full and definitive transposition of the directive, their incompatibility with the directive may give rise to the presumption that the result will not be achieved in time. Yet, where the measures are of a transitional nature, their incompatibility with the directive would not necessarily compromise the result prescribed, since the Member States are entitled to take transitory measures or to implement the directive in stages. The same considerations apply where certain provisions of a directive have not been transposed at all during the period provided for implementation.

Secondly, there is the question as from which moment the obligation of consistent interpretation applies. Some authors read the judgment of the Court in

---

[50] See e.g. Case 148/78 *Ratti* [1979] ECR 1629 and, more recently, Joined Cases C–140/91, C–141/91, C–278/91, and C–279/91 *Suffritti* [1992] ECR I–6337. For a brief discussion of some speculations as to whether a person should perhaps be entitled to rely on a directive which has been implemented before the deadline but the implementation of which proved inadequate see AG Jacobs in Case C–156/91 *Mundt* [1992] ECR I–5567, paras 18–22. For the sake of clarity it must also be pointed out that the opportunity to plead the invalidity of a directive before national courts is not conditional upon it actually having been transposed or the expiry of the deadline for transposition. See Case C–491/01 *British American Tobacco* [2002] ECR I–11453.

[51] See Lauwaars and Maarleveld 1987, 191, referring to Commissioner Richards, who announced that the Commission may start infringement proceedings whenever a Member State takes retrograde steps during the period provided for implementation of Directive 79/7 (equal treatment in statutory schemes of social security) [1979] OJ L6/24. Cf also for some explicit safeguards against retrograde steps after notification Directive 64/221 (public policy and public health), Art 4(3) [1963–1964] OJ English Spec Ed 177. Another form of safeguard against reducing the level of protection existing at the time of adoption of the directive can be found in Art 1(3) of Directive 92/85 (pregnant workers) [1992] OJ L348/1.

[52] Case C–129/96 *Inter-environnement Wallonie* [1997] ECR I–7411. See also Case C–14/02 *ATRAL* [2003] ECR I–4431 and Case C–157/02 *Rieser*, judgment of 5 February 2004, nyr in ECR. For a more extensive discussion see Kaczorowska 1999, Sevón 2003 and Ehricke 2001.

Kolpinghuis[53] as implying an obligation for the national courts to interpret national law in conformity with the directive concerned actually before the expiry of the time limit.[54] In other words, in their view, there is an obligation to 'anticipatory interpretation' of national law in conformity with the directive at issue. In my opinion, however, the judgment is not as clear as some would claim. In fact, in this judgment the Court only addressed the question of the *limits* which Community law may impose on the obligation or power of the national court to interpret national law in conformity with the directive. In this particular respect it was held to be irrelevant whether or not the period for implementation has expired.[55] In my view, this consideration is in no way conclusive as to the said obligation.[56]

The issue remains controversial.[57] While in one instance the Court of Justice seems to have suggested that the obligation of consistent interpretation starts to run as from the expiry of the time limit for transposition,[58] the case is not clear and, moreover, it remains isolated.[59]

In my opinion, since the obligation contained in a directive is an obligation to act *within a stated period* and 'the purpose of that period is . . . to give the Member States the necessary time to adopt transposition measures',[60] it is difficult to understand why national courts should be bound by an obligation which must be complied with at some point in the future. The duty to interpret national law in conformity with the directive concerned exists for national courts in their capacity of 'national authorities of the Member States'.[61] Therefore, as long as a Member State has not adopted any transposition measures, there is no obligation for national courts to proceed with consistent interpretation. Matters are different, however, if the Member State implements the directive before the deadline, i.e. in a case of 'premature' implementation. Arguably, in such a situation the implementing measures, a narrower category than national law in general, must be interpreted in accordance with the directive from the date of the actual implementation. This follows, in my view, also from the judgment in *Inter-environnement Wallonie*, since an interpretation of the implementing measures at issue which is not consistent with the underlying directive would involve a risk of compromising the result to be

---

[53] Case 80/86 [1987] 3969.

[54] E.g. Timmermans 1988, 333, Lenz 1990, 908, Prechal and Burrows 1990, 36. Cf also, for instance, the Opinion of AG Darmon in Case C–236/92 *Comitato* [1994] ECR I–483, para 27 and the opinion of AG Jacobs in Case C–295/90 *European Parliament v. Council* [1992] ECR I–4193, para 43. AG Jacobs did, however, take a more balanced position in Case C–156/91 *Mundt* [1992] ECR I–5567, paras 23–27.

[55] Para 15 of the judgment. The limits concerned were the general principles of law, in particular legal certainty and non-retroactivity. For a detailed discussion of the limits see below, Ch 8, Section 8.5.3.

[56] Cf also Dommering-Van Rongen 1991, 36, De Burca 1992, 218, n 24, Götz 1992, 1854, AG Jacobs in Case C–156/91 *Mundt* [1992] ECR I–5567, para 26.

[57] See e.g. Jarass 1991a, 221, Hilf 1993, 15, Timmermans 1997, 11–12, Ehricke 1995, 621–2 and Ehricke 1999, 554–7. Cf also *Colloque des Conseils d'État 1996, Rapport général*, 22–4.

[58] Case C–456/98 *Centrosteel* [2000] ECR I–6007.   [59] Cf Betlem 2002, 85–8.

[60] Case C–129/96 *Inter-environnement Wallonie* [1997] ECR I–7411, para 43.

[61] E.g. Case 14/83 *Von Colson* [1984] ECR 1891, para 26.

achieved once the deadline for implementation expires.[62] All this does not necessarily mean, of course, that the courts are not entitled to proceed to an anticipatory interpretation if the latter is possible as a matter of national law.[63]

The duty to interpret national law in conformity with the directive concerned does not exist solely for national courts, but, as was already remarked here above, for all national authorities of the Member States. Basing their arguments on *Kolpinghuis*, some writers submit that an obligation to this type of anticipatory interpretation exists for other national authorities as well.[64] Yet the same considerations as presented above with respect to such an obligation for national courts also militate, in my opinion, against an obligation of anticipatory interpretation on the part of other national authorities.

In short, in my view and for the reasons stated above, there is no Community law obligation for national authorities and national courts to comply with a directive before the deadline for implementation has expired.

Thirdly, one may wonder whether what is known as the '*Sperrwirkung*' (blocking effect) of directives produces effects after the entry into force of the directive but before the time limit for implementation has expired. Briefly, 'blocking effect' means that the enactment of directives entails a change in the division of powers between the Member States and the Community in the sense that it causes a transfer of legislative power from Member States to the Community.[65] *Sperrwirkung* is often discussed when considering the problem of amendments to harmonized national law made for the purpose of adapting it to socio-economic developments, and thus after the deadline for implementation has expired. It is accepted that national legislature lacks competence in this respect, unless and in so far as the directive concerned provides otherwise. Any necessary changes can be initiated only by a new directive.[66] From the concept of *Sperrwirkung*, however, it also follows that a directive produces the stated effect from the moment of its entry into force.[67] The only legislative competence the Member States retain with respect to the issues covered by the directive is to enact the measures necessary for its implementation. The logical consequence of this blocking effect of directives would arguably be that once the directive has entered into force, it prohibits the adoption of measures contrary to its provisions, even during the implementation period.[68] Yet, the theory of blocking

---

[62] Cf also Case C–165/98 *Mazzoleni* [2001] ECR I–2189 where the Court has refused to interpret a directive '[s]ince the period prescribed for the implementation . . . had not in fact expired and the Directive had not been transposed into national law at the material time . . . ' (para 17).

[63] Cf Winter 1996, 491.

[64] Cf Curtin and Mortelmans 1994, 444 and Hilf 1993, 7, who, however, points out that the situation is unclear. Cf also for a comparable reasoning already Ipsen 1965, 77. Cf also Kooijmans 1967, 141.

[65] Cf Ipsen 1972, 267 and 701, Timmermans 1979, 551–3, Constantinesco 1977, 624, Lauwaars and Maarleveld 1987, 189.

[66] Cf Lauwaars and Maarleveld 1987, 188. See also e.g. Scherzberg 1991, 38 and Oldenkop 1972, 100.

[67] Cf Timmermans 1979, 551, Hilf 1993, 7, Bebr 1981, 588. According to some scholars blocking effect exists even before the adoption of the directive. For further discussion and references see Lauwaars and Maarleveld 1987, 190. Contra: Hilf 1993, 7.

[68] Cf AG Mancini in Case 30/85 *Teuling* [1987] ECR 2497, para 7, and Hilf 1993, 7.

effect of directives is far from a generally accepted matter and, therefore, it does not constitute a firm basis for the obligation to proceed to consistent interpretation before the deadline for transposition has expired.[69]

2.4 The rigour of the obligation to implement the directive in due time

The obligation to adopt the measures for implementation of a directive and to do so within the period prescribed by the directive at issue is an extremely rigorous obligation. With respect to the failure to enact the necessary measures within the specified time, various excuses have been offered by the Member States, but they have not been accepted by the Court of Justice. According to established case law a Member State may not plead provisions, practices, or circumstances existing in its internal legal system or, more generally, practical, financial, and administrative difficulties in order to justify non-compliance with the obligations and time limits.[70] Neither does the argument help that the Directive was in any case applied by the authorities.[71] Similarly, the fact that a directive may pose serious problems of interpretation cannot constitute a valid excuse for failing to implement it within the required time.[72] The view of the Court is that since the governments of the Member States participate in the preparation of a directive, they must be able to draft the necessary measures within the period allowed for implementation.[73] Moreover, if the said period nevertheless proves to be too short, the Member State

---

[69] Cf Also Timmermans 1997, 12–13, who points out that the Court did not argue the *Inter-environnement Wallonie* case in terms of the doctrine of blocking effect. Such an approach would have much more radical consequences. For a brief discussion see also the opinion of AG Jacobs in *Inter-environnement Wallonie*, paras 37–50. In this context it must also be noted that there is no clear-cut distinction between 'Sperrwirkung' and the obligations under Art 10(2). Some authors see as the basis for 'Sperrwirkung' the principle of supremacy of Community law (e.g. Ipsen 1972, 267, Pieper 1990, 685, Nettesheim 2002, 54, Lauwaars and Timmermans 2003, 33), while according to others the basis lies in Art 10(2) (e.g. De Ripainsel-Landy and Gérard 1976, 53). According to Oldenkop 1972, 100, 'Sperrwirkung' is to be considered as a secondary 'negative' obligation resulting from the primary 'positive' obligation under Art 249(3). In Case 30/85 *Teuling* [1987] 2497, para 7, Mancini linked blocking effect and Art 10(2).

[70] See e.g. Case 163/78 *Commission v. Italy* [1979] ECR 771, Case 390/85 *Commission v. Belgium* [1987] ECR 761, Case 419/85 *Commission v. Italy* [1987] ECR 2115, Case 42/80 *Commission v. Italy* [1980] ECR 3635, Case 100/81 *Commission v. the Netherlands* [1982] ECR 1837, Case C–42/89 *Commission v. Belgium* [1990] ECR I–2821, Case C–351/01 *Commission v. France* [2002] ECR I–8101 and Case C–22/02 *Commission v. Italy* [2003] ECR I–9011. The arguments put forward relate, for instance, to government crises, the complexity of national procedures, the dissolution of parliament, and the need to hear advisory bodies. In Case C–45/91 *Commission v. Greece* [1992] ECR I–2509 the Greek government invoked opposition of the local population against the implementation of the directive concerned.   [71] Case C–348/01 *Commission v. France* [2002] ECR I–10249.

[72] Case 301/81 *Commission v. Belgium* [1983] ECR 467.

[73] See e.g. Case 136/81 *Commission v. Italy* [1982] ECR 3547, Case 361/85 *Commission v. Italy* [1987] ECR 479 and Joined Cases C–178/94, C–179/94, C–188/94, C–189/94, and C–190/94 *Dillenkofer* [1996] ECR I–4845 at para 54.

concerned must take the appropriate initiatives within the Community in order to obtain an extension of the period by either the Council or the Commission.[74]

Apart from these excuses of—what one may call—a predominantly practical nature, other types of justifications have also been put forward by the Member States. These justifications actually all reduce to the argument that implementation was not necessary because, for instance, the directive had direct effect or because the objective of the directive had already been fully realized in the legal order of the Member State concerned.[75] In one case a government even suggested that the directive itself was superfluous, arguing that the failure to implement it had no adverse effect on the functioning of the Common Market.[76] Furthermore, since each Member State is responsible for its own default, it may not justify its failure by stating that another Member State has also failed to comply with the obligation to implement the directive in due time.[77] Finally, Member States are in principle obliged to implement the directive even if there is doubt about its validity.[78]

The strictness of the Court with respect to implementation of directives within the period provided can be explained by the following arguments. A non-simultaneous implementation may result in discrimination[79] and endangers the uniform application of Community law within all Member States.[80] Indeed, the harmonizing effect of directives requires entry into force of the implementing measures from the same date, since the very purpose of a directive would otherwise be seriously compromised.[81]

As mentioned above, no excuses for delayed implementation have as yet been accepted by the Court of Justice. In my view, however, one cannot maintain that the obligation is absolute.[82] It is conceivable that in certain situations a Member State could invoke particular circumstances which could free it, at least for a certain period, from the obligation to implement a directive. In this respect at least two types of situations can be distinguished.

The first is a situation of practical difficulties connected with serious internal disturbances, such as a state of emergency, (imminent) war, and so on. After all, it can hardly be expected of a Member State to implement a directive on the

---

[74] See e.g. Case 52/75 *Commission v. Italy* [1976] ECR 277, Case 301/81 *Commission v. Belgium* [1983] ECR 467. Under certain directives, the Commission may grant an additional period on special request: see e.g. Art 19 of Directive 80/778 (drinking water) [1980] OJ L229/11 and Case C–42/89 *Commission v. Belgium* [1990] ECR I–2821.

[75] The argument drawing upon 'direct effect' was rejected by the Court in e.g. Case 102/79 *Commission v. Belgium* [1980] ECR 1473 and Case C–207/96 *Commission v. Italy* [1997] ECR I–6869. The second argument is related to the question as to what constitutes adequate implementation; this subject will be discussed below, in Section 2.6 and in Ch 5.

[76] Case 95/77 *Commission v. the Netherlands* [1978] ECR 863.

[77] See e.g. Case 52/75 *Commission v. Italy* [1976] ECR 277. Cf also Case C–38/89 *Blanguernon* [1990] ECR I–83.   [78] See below, Section 2.7.

[79] Case 52/75 *Commission v. Italy* [1976] ECR 277.

[80] Case 10/76 *Commission v. Italy* [1976] ECR 1359.

[81] See e.g. Case 79/72 *Commission v. Italy* [1973] ECR 667 and Case 52/75 *Commission v. Italy* [1976] ECR 277. Cf also Marescau 1980b, 659.   [82] Cf Curtin 1990b, 714, Morris 1989, 238.

marketing of vegetable seed, for instance, while a war is going on. It is uncertain whether Article 297 EC Treaty could be relied on since this Article is limited to *measures taken* by a Member State 'in the event of serious internal disturbances affecting the maintenance of law and order' and so on. This problem was touched upon in *Johnston*,[83] albeit in a different context. The circumstances of the case, however, caused the Court to decide that the question whether Article 297 may be relied upon by a Member State in order to avoid compliance with the obligations imposed by Community law and in particular by the directive at issue did not arise. Furthermore, in the same case the Court also decided that the Treaty does not contain a general proviso covering all measures taken for reasons of public safety.[84]

Another, more common sense argument could be a plea of *force majeure* or comparable circumstances. In Case 101/84 (*Statistical Returns*)[85] the Court accepted in principle that a bomb attack may constitute a case of *force majeure*.[86] In this case, however, it was of no avail for the Italian government, as the Court found that the government could not rely on this event to justify continuing failure to comply with the directive concerned several years after the bomb attack had occurred.

The second type of situation is concerned with obligations of the Member States under international law: namely, that the implementation of a directive may entail a violation of an obligation resulting from a bilateral or multilateral treaty. This was the background to the *Stoeckel* and *Levy* cases,[87] for instance.

Article L 213–1 of the French Labour Code prohibiting nightwork of women was enacted in order to give effect to ILO Convention no. 89,[88] ratified by France in 1953. Directive 76/207 (equal treatment at work),[89] however, as interpreted by the Court, prohibits discrimination between men and women with respect to working conditions and access to employment, including nightwork. The prohibition of nightwork by women only was therefore contrary to the said directive. Yet as France had not denounced the Convention (which was only possible at intervals of 10 years), a conflict arose between the Community obligations on the one hand and the obligations under the ILO Convention on the

---

[83] Case 222/84 [1986] ECR 1651.

[84] Cf also Joined Cases C–19/90 and C–20/90 *Karrella and Karrellas* [1991] ECR I–2691. Cf however also Case C–57/89 *Commission v. Germany* [1991] ECR I–883, which suggests that, exceptionally, Member States may deviate from a directive for reasons based on general interest which is superior to the interest represented by a directive (paras 21 and 22) and Case C–186/01 *Dory* [2003] ECR I–2479.

[85] *Commission v. Italy* [1985] ECR 2629.

[86] Which may in this context be defined as 'a temporary absolute impossibility to implement due to an unforseeable and irresistible event'. Cf also Case C–56/90 *Commission v. United Kingdom* [1993] ECR I–4109, in particular para 46 (absolute physical impossibility to carry out the obligations imposed by the directive) and Case C–74/91 *Commission v. Germany* [1992] ECR I–5437, para 12 (absolutely impossible for [the Member State] to implement).

[87] Case C–345/89 [1991] ECR I–4047 and Case C–158/91 [1993] ECR I–4287. Cf also Case C–13/93 *Minne* [1994] ECR I–371.

[88] Convention concerning Nightwork by Women Employed in Industry of 9 July 1948.

[89] [1976] OJ L39/40.

other. By virtue of Article 307 of the EC Treaty, France's obligations under the Convention could not be affected by Community law. Indeed, under the second paragraph of Article 307 France was only obliged to take 'all appropriate steps to eliminate the incompatibilities', i.e. to denounce the Convention in due course in order to be able to meet its obligations under the directive. The deadline for implementation of the directive was 14 February 1980, but the Convention could not be denounced before 27 February 1981 at the earliest. In *Stoeckel* the Court did not address this problem. In *Levy*, however, the Court found that national courts are under a duty to ensure that Article 5 of Directive 76/207 is fully complied with by leaving unapplied any contrary provisions of national legislation, unless the application of such a provision is necessary in order to ensure the performance by the Member State concerned, pursuant to Article 307 of the Treaty, of obligations arising from agreements concluded with third countries before the entry into force of the Treaty.[90]

Although the *Levy* case was decided under Article 234, in my view on the basis of the judgment it could be argued that the same reasoning will also apply in an infringement procedure, the obligation under international law being a sufficient argument to excuse temporarily the Member State's failure to comply with its obligation. This case illustrates nicely how an international agreement may block the implementation of a directive within the period prescribed.

There is another important element to be taken into account in the present discussion, namely the nature of the Article 226 procedure. It is generally accepted that this procedure aims at an *objective* finding of a failure to fulfil the obligations under the Treaty, which should clarify the law and enable the Member States to know the exact scope of their obligations.[91] The procedure is, as expressed by AG Roemer,

intended to establish whether a specified national legal situation or administrative practice is in harmony with Community law, that is, a procedure which in principle excludes any considerations of fault.[92]

The judgment of the Court is declaratory; it formally establishes the violation, which, with all its legal consequences, existed as from the date it was committed. Moreover, it lacks executory force and no national measures being thereby annulled.[93] From this viewpoint it is understandable that the Court accepts no excuses for belated (or incorrect) implementation.

---

[90] Case C–158/91 [1993] ECR I–4287, para 22.

[91] Cf Kapteyn and VerLoren van Themaat 1998, 449. See also Case 301/81 *Commission v. Belgium* [1983] ECR 467.

[92] Case 8/70 *Commission v. Italy* [1970] ECR 961 at 970. Cf also Case C–73/92 *Commission v. Spain* [1993] ECR I–5997 and Case C–226/01 *Commission v. Denmark* [2003] ECR I–1219, where the Court held that the infringement exists regardless of the frequency of the scale of the circumstances complained of. Similarly, the finding of a failure is not tied up with a finding as to the damage flowing therefrom (Joined Cases C–20/01 and C–28/01 *Commission v. Germany* [2003] ECR I–3609).

[93] Cf Brown and Jacobs 2000, 130.

The declaratory nature of the judgment, however, does not imply that it has no consequences.

Firstly, pursuant to Article 228 EC, the Member State concerned is obliged to terminate the violation; all its institutions, including the courts, must draw the necessary inferences from the judgment.[94] The finding that a Member State has not complied with its obligations entails for its authorities a prohibition against applying a national rule recognized as incompatible with the Treaty and, if the circumstances so require, they are obliged to take all appropriate measures to enable Community law to be fully applied.[95] These effects apply *ex tunc*, i.e. from the time the breach occurred.[96]

Secondly, the judgment can form the basis for 'responsibility that a Member State can incur as a result of its default, as regards other Member States, the Community or private parties'.[97]

Thirdly, the judgment can generate, albeit indirectly and in limited fields, negative financial consequences.[98]

Fourthly, since the entry into force of the Maastricht Treaty, lump sum or penalty payments can be directly imposed in cases of failure to comply with Article 228 EC. A judgment declaring that a Member State has failed to fulfil its obligations constitutes quite obviously a condition precedent to the bringing of proceedings under Article 228.[99] On the basis of this new provision the Court has, for instance, imposed a penalty payment of 20,000 euro a day on Greece for not taking the necessary measures to ensure that toxic waste is disposed of without endangering human health and without harming the environment.[100] The failure to do so was already established in an earlier judgment.[101]

In summary, on the one hand, a judgment under Article 226 *as such* has no legal effects; the latter result from the Treaty itself. On the other hand, these effects may be considerable. Since the judgment and the effects are two different matters, a careful distinction should be made between the fact that the Court is in principle

---

[94] Joined Cases 314 to 316/81 and 83/82 *Waterkeyn* [1982] ECR 4337.

[95] See e.g. Case 48/71 *Commission v. Italy* [1972] ECR 527 and Case C–101/91 *Commission v. Italy* [1993] ECR I–191.

[96] Cf Schermers and Waelbroeck 2001, 641. Cf also the Opinion of AG Slynn in C–293/85 *Commission v. Belgium* [1988] ECR 305 where the possibility of limiting the retroactive effects of a judgment given under Art 169 is discussed: 342–4.

[97] E.g. Case 39/72 *Commission v. Italy* [1973] ECR 101 and Case C–229/00 *Commission v. Finland* [2003] ECR I–5727. See also below, Ch 10, Section 10.1.

[98] E.g. payments out of the European Guidance and Guarantee Fund for Agriculture or other Structural Funds. Cf Ehlermann 1987, 214–15.

[99] E.g. Case C–365/97 *Commission v. Italy* [1999] ECR I–7773.

[100] Case C–387/97 *Commission v. Greece* [2000] ECR I–5047. Cf also Case C–278/01 *Commission v. Spain*, judgment of 25 November 2003, nyr in ECR with a detailed reasoning as to the calculation of the penalty to be imposed.

[101] Case C–45/91 *Commission v. Greece* [1992] ECR I–2509. Cf also Case *Hornsby v. Greece*, ECrtHR 19 March 1997, 24 EHRR 250 (the non-execution of a judgment by which the Greek Supreme Administrative Court gave effect to an ECJ judgment under Art 226 EC, constituted a violation of Art 6 ECHR)

not willing to accept excuses in an infringement procedure and the possibility that excuses may play a part when the effects come under consideration. In particular, in my view, certain types of justifications could be relevant once the questions of direct effect and of liability of the State for damages resulting from non-implementation are addressed. The Court's strict attitude in Article 226 proceedings with respect to possible justifications cannot in fact be transposed to these issues when they emerge within the context of procedures of a different nature.[102]

2.5 Delays in implementation, retroactive legislation, and transitory measures

Although, as stated above, the obligation to implement directives in due time should not, in my opinion, be considered to be absolute, in principle the Court of Justice vigorously upholds the observation of the time limits for implementation by the Member States. It is, however, no secret that the deadlines are frequently not respected. The next question is therefore how the national implementing measures can minimize the detrimental effects of belated implementation.

It appears from the judgment in *Dik*[103] that if national implementing measures are adopted after the expiry of the period for implementation 'the simultaneous entry into force of [the directive concerned] in all Member States is ensured by giving such measures effect retroactively as from [the date for implementation]'.[104] The Court added an important proviso to this: that in such a case the rights which the directive confers on individuals in the Member States must be respected as from the expiry date of said period.[105]

In other cases the Court held that retroactive application of the measures implementing the directive enables, in principle, the harmful consequences of the breach to be remedied, provided that the directive as been transposed properly.[106]

Arguably, a defaulting Member State is in principle under the duty to implement the directive with retroactive effect.[107] However, in that case another problem arises, namely the admissibility of retroactive legislation. Only if the sole effect of the directive and, therefore, also the implementing measures is to confer a benefit on

---

[102] Cf also Ch 10, Subsection 10.4.3.   [103] Case 80/87 [1988] ECR 1601.

[104] Strictly speaking it should be 'entry into force of the implementing measures'. See above, n 47.

[105] The directive at issue 'conferred rights' by virtue of direct effect. Cf also Case C–343/92 *Roks* [1994] ECR I–571.

[106] Joined Cases C–94/95 and C–95/95 *Bonifaci* [1997] ECR I–3969 and Case C–373/95 *Maso* [1997] ECR I–4051. See also e.g. Case C–371/97 *Gozza* [2000] ECR I–7881. For a discussion of the relationship between State liability and retroactive application of implementing measures, see Anagnostaras 2000.

[107] Cf the Opinion of AG Cosmas in Joined Cases C–94/95 and C–95/95 *Bonifaci* [1997] ECR I–3969, paras 56–59.

private persons, there is in principle, no problem. In other cases the lawfulness of retroactive measures must be determined.

In *Dik* Advocate General Mancini remarked that such a review has to be done on the basis of national law.[108] Here national general principles of law and, in particular, the prohibition of retroactive application of legislation, will come to the fore. According to well-established case law, the Court allows the application of general principles of law which are part of the legal order of the Community; the application of the same or similar principles at national level can therefore not be considered contrary to that same legal order.[109] Yet, the application of these principles is not unlimited. For instance, the national principle of non-retroactivity cannot go beyond what that principle requires under Community law.[110] It is their interpretation and application which is ultimately submitted to the control of the Court of Justice.

Thus, for instance, from *Kent Kirk*[111] it follows that national measures imposing criminal sanctions with retroactive effect are incompatible with Community law: the principle of non-retroactivity of criminal provisions is a principle common to all the legal orders of the Member States and is enshrined in Article 7 of the European Convention for the Protection of Human Rights. As such it occupies a place among the general principles of law whose observance is ensured by the Court of Justice. In *Zuckerfabrik Franken*[112] the Court considered it necessary to examine whether certain German measures taken in execution of a regulation were compatible with superior rules of Community law, in particular with the principles of legal certainty and proportionality.

In brief, in so far as national provisions and general legal principles, such as *nulla poena sine lege* and legal certainty, should make implementation of directives with retroactive effect impossible, the limitations must be appreciated in the context of Community law, taking into account the limits imposed by the Court upon the application of such principles.

Some lessons can be learned in this respect from the Court's case law on retroactive effect of Community legislation. In this area the principle laid down by the Court is that retroactivity is allowed in exceptional cases only, since the principle of legal certainty militates against such an effect.[113] If Community legislation, including directives, 'must be unequivocal and in its application must be predictable for those who are subject to it'[114] and, moreover, a directive cannot impose on Member

---

[108] Case 80/87 [1988] ECR 1601, para 3.

[109] E.g. as one from the many cases C–5/89 *Commission v. Germany (Bug-Alutechnik)* [1990] ECR I–3437.   [110] AG Mischo in Case C–403/98 *Monte Arcosu* [2001] ECR I–103, para 73.

[111] Case 63/83 [1984] ECR 2689.

[112] Case 77/81 [1982] ECR 681. Cf also Case C–107/97 *Rombi* [2000] ECR I–3367, in particular para 65.

[113] Cf e.g. the Opinion of AG VerLoren van Themaat in Case 70/83 *Kloppenburg* [1984] ECR 1075, Sections 5 and 6. For a detailed discussion of retroactive (community) legislation see Heukels 1991, in particular Chs II and III. Cf also Tridimas 1999, 170–86.

[114] Case 70/83 *Kloppenburg* [1984] ECR 1075, para 11.

States an obligation to adopt measures which conflict with the principle of legit-imate expectations and the principle of non-retroactivity of penal provisions,[115] it follows, in my opinion, *a fortiori* that implementing measures adopted by the Member States must satisfy the same requirements, particularly if the result of those measures is to impose obligations on individuals.[116]

To some extent this discussion is mainly theoretical since belated transposition of directives into national law is usually not retroactive.[117] Similarly, the Commission does not open or continue a procedure under Article 226 in order to enforce transposition with reverse effects. There are only very few exceptions, like the *Minerval* case against Belgium[118] and a case on equal treatment of men and women against Greece.[119] Private parties who have suffered loss because of the belated transposition must seek legal protection through national procedures, *inter alia*, via the route of State liability.[120]

More current are problems which relate to belated implementation in combination with the non-observance of transitory measures provided for in a directive itself. As was already observed above,[121] some directives differentiate between the date before which transposing legislation should be adopted and a later date before which this legislation should enter into force.

In any case a Member State is not allowed to postpone the transposition of a directive until the end of the second, transitional period.[122] Similarly, Member States may not postpone the time limit laid down in a directive for the entry into force of the transposition measures, even if the directive is not transposed in due time.[123] Even where the Member States are left some discretion as to how to design the transitory measures, a short time limit, due to belated transposition, which does not enable the persons involved to adapt to the new circumstances, may be in breach of the principle of proportionality.[124] In the Netherlands, problems of this kind occurred in relation to Directive 89/622/EEC (labelling of tobacco products) which had to be transposed by 1 July 1990.[125] The transposition measures should enter into force on 31 December 1991 at the latest. Furthermore, the Directive permitted, *inter alia*, the sale of products which did not comply with its requirements until 31 December 1992. These two transition periods were intended to accommodate the interests of private parties who had to adapt their business to the

---

[115] See Case C–331/88 *Fedesa* [1990] ECR I–4023.

[116] Rights which individuals derive from directives are safeguarded under the 'Dik construction', at least for the period between the deadline provided for implementation and the actual (but belated) implementation itself. There is, however, no such guarantee for the future. See Case C–343/92 *Roks* [1994] ECR I–571.   [117] Barav 1998, 422.

[118] Case 293/85 *Commission v. Belgium* [1988] ECR 305.

[119] Case C–187/98 *Commission v. Greece* [1999] ECR I–7713.   [120] Cf Timmermans 1997, 15.

[121] Section 2.3.   [122] Case C–157/91 *Commission v. Netherlands* [1992] ECR I–5899.

[123] Case C–307/94 *Commission v. Italy* [1996] ECR I–1011.

[124] Case C–2/97 *Borsana* [1998] ECR I–8597.

[125] [1989] OJ L359/1. Cf Donner *et al.* 1998, 339. See on the problem of transitory measures also *Colloque des Conseils d'État* 1996, *Rapport général*, 10–11.

requirements of the new legislation. Due to belated transposition, the Dutch legislator extended both these periods of adjustment by setting later dates. This way of transposing a directive is clearly contrary to Community law. However, it also illustrates the key problem: how to protect private individuals in case of belated transposition where the transition periods serve their interests. In my view, a 'catching-up' operation by the national implementing authorities must take these interests and, therefore, the purpose of the transition periods at issue duly into account.[126]

2.6   The obligation to implement the directive correctly: a preliminary inquiry

By comparison with the problem of implementation of directives in due time, correct implementation is a considerably more complex matter. It is 'intellectually much more demanding', as one author expresses it,[127] since it 'requires both understanding of the legal meaning of the provisions of the directive and ability to interpret the meaning of national legislation in the light of the Member State's own legal and administrative practice'.[128]

It is obvious that the national implementing measures must correspond to the internal substance of the directive concerned. For instance, a directive requiring equal pay for men and women for 'work of *equal value*' is not adequately implemented by national provisions providing for equal pay for 'the *same* work';[129] if a directive contains exhaustive rules as to the obligation of traders to give notification of the placing on the market of certain new substances, the Member States cannot, in their legislation adopted to implement the directive, widen or restrict the obligation at issue;[130] a provision of a directive exempting from VAT the care administered to persons in the exercise of the medical and paramedical professions may not be implemented as exempting veterinary surgeons from taxation;[131] neither can a Member State limit itself to partial transposition only.[132]

Since a directive imposes upon the Member States an obligation of result, the measures taken by the Member States must be such as to ensure that the directive

---

[126] This may give rise to complex questions as there will often be another category of individuals which may complain about, for instance, distortion of conditions of competition. In some cases damages may bring a solution. Cf also Van de Gronden 1997.

[127] Macrory 1992, 354. Cf also Timmermans 1997, 13–14, who points out that while for the surveillance of non-transposition there are standard—more or less automatic—procedures, for non-conformity of national law the Commission often depends on complaints by individuals. As to the improvements in monitoring non-transposition, see the Eighteenth annual report on monitoring the application of Community law, COM (2001) 309 final, 10–11.   [128] Ibid. Cf also Easson 1981, 31–2.

[129] Case 143/83 *Commission v. Denmark* [1985] ECR 427.

[130] Case 278/85 *Commission v. Denmark* [1987] ECR 4069.

[131] Case 122/87 *Commission v. Italy* [1988] ECR 2685.

[132] Case C–236/95 *Commission v. Greece* [1996] ECR I–4459.

is 'fully effective, in accordance with the objective which it pursues'.[133] This means that the obligation arising from Article 249(3) goes further than the actual text of the directive at issue and the mere transposition of this text into national law. It imposes certain requirements as to the nature of the implementing measures (i.e. the legal effects they produce) and, moreover, it requires that these measures are applied and enforced in practice in an effective manner.[134]

In other words, the question of correct implementation comprises three closely related but nevertheless distinguishable issues. The first concerns the requirements regarding the *content* of the measures adopted with a view to implementation, the second relates to the requirements regarding the *nature* of the measures, and the third relates to their *effective application* and *enforcement in practice*. These requirements actually appear to interfere with the freedom ostensibly enjoyed by the Member States with respect to the 'form and methods' of implementation under Article 249(3). The scope of these requirements and the reasons for imposing them will be discussed in more detail in Chapter 5.

At this point, I would like to continue by addressing two more general issues related to the proper implementation of directives, which have much in common with some of the problems discussed above in Sections 2.4 and 2.5 on belated implementation. They concern the possible justifications for incorrect implementation and the measures a Member State should take once it has been established that the directive has not been implemented properly.

When enacting the measures necessary to meet their obligations under Article 249(3), the Member States have the choice of different modalities of implementation, lying anywhere between verbatim transposition of the directive's provisions into national law at one end of the spectrum and a 'translation' of the directive into the terminology and concepts of their national legal system at the other.[135]

Verbatim reproduction may have the advantage that, at least at first sight, the Member State has complied with its obligation. The obvious disadvantage is then, however, that national legislation may be using unfamiliar terms. Consequently, there is no guarantee that the implementing measures will be understood, interpreted, and applied correctly.[136]

Although it may be preferable and may correspond more with the character of the directive, implementation by way of 'translation' of the directive into national legal equivalents is also not unproblematic. In the first place, it may be that equivalent national concepts and terms simply do not exist or that their equivalence is only one of appearance. In *CILFIT*,[137] the Court of Justice indicated this danger very clearly when it held that Community law uses terminology which is peculiar to itself: its legal concepts do not necessarily have the same meaning as they have in

---

[133] Case 14/83 *Von Colson* [1984] ECR 1891, para 15.   [134] Cf Ch 3, Section 3.3.

[135] Cf Easson 1981, 34–5 and Samuels 1998. See also below, Ch 5, in particular Subsection 5.2.1.

[136] Cf for instance Case C–185/00 *Commission v. Finland* judgment of 27 November 2003, nyr in ECR, where the Court and the AG disagreed on the issue whether *verbatim* transposition was necessary or not.   [137] Case 283/81 [1982] ECR 3415.

the law of the various Member States; moreover, every provision of Community law must be placed in its context and interpreted in the light of the provisions of Community law as a whole. Although this case was concerned with, *inter alia*, the application of the doctrine of '*acte clair*' by national courts, the same considerations apply equally with respect to the problem of proper implementation of directives.

Furthermore, directives themselves are often vague and open to a variety of interpretations, since they must accommodate different national legal concepts and constructions. Their vagueness may also be the result of political compromise within the Council. And possibly both of these aspects play a part respectively. Combined with the facts that they may be quite complicated, may have a structure of their own which does not necessarily correspond with the structure of the national law which is to be adapted,[138] and may be internally inconsistent or incompatible with other provisions of Community law,[139] this means that their implementation is often not an easy task.[140]

Although the COM documents which usually accompany a draft directive may be of some help towards a better understanding of its provisions, the final outcome of the Community decision-making process can differ considerably from the original draft.[141] Yet the only explanatory text the implementing authorities can rely on is the directive's preamble, often expressed in non-committal terms. A partial remedy for this unsatisfactory situation could in fact be a detailed explanatory memorandum drafted by the Council—in case of co-decisions together with the European Parliament?—to be released at the time of the adoption of the directive[142] or a substantive expansion of the preamble. The latter happens to some extent already. Yet, it also illustrates the problem that occurs next: such explanatory memoranda, like some of the more extensive preambles,[143] become themselves a subject of further negotiation, which is certainly not a guarantee for more clarity. Moreover, from a Community point of view, 'constructive ambiguity' has undoubtedly also certain virtues!

[138] Cf Kortmann 1991, 48.

[139] Cf *Sutherland Report*, 35–6 and e.g. the consequences resulting from Case C–262/88 *Barber* [1990] ECR I–1889 for Directive 86/378 (equal treatment in occupational social security schemes) [1986] OJ L225/40.

[140] For further references on the quality of EC legislation, see below, Ch 11, Section 11.8. On the relationship between the quality of EC legislation, and problems with its interpretation, both in context of implementation and application by the domestic courts, see the reports for the 19th colloquium of the Association of the Councils of State and Supreme Administrative Jurisdictions of the European Union, available at www.raadvst-consetat.be.

[141] For a rather rare example, where the Court looks in detail at the history of the relevant directives, see Case C–324/98 *Teleaustria* [2000] ECR I–10745, in particular paras 45–51.

[142] Cf Hilf 1993, 8.

[143] E.g. Directive 2001/37 (manufacture, presentation and sale of tobacco products) [2001] OJ L194/26, Directive 95/46 (processing of personal data) [1995] OJ L281/31, Directive 2000/31 (electronic commerce) [2000] OJ L178/1 and Directive 2003/6 (insider dealing and market manipulation) [2003] OJ L96/16.

Another suggestion is to involve the Commission more closely in the process of implementation of directives.[144] This may nowadays happen in the context of *ad hoc* organized meetings between the Commission and the national authorities responsible for the implementation of a certain directive.[145] The problem is, however, that sometimes the Commission itself also does not understand the exact meaning of a directive's provisions and especially their concrete implications.[146]

The fact that the Commission is also far from certain of the exact meaning of a directive's provisions and what should be considered as adequate implementation in a concrete case is perhaps best illustrated by the withdrawal of its complaints during the administrative or judicial stage of Article 226 proceedings. It is well known that the administrative stage in particular often has more the character of negotiations between the Commission and the Member States than that of straightforward control by the Commission or a mutual exchange of views on points of law.[147] If the Commission and the Member State concerned fail to reach an agreement on the divisive issues, and the Commission decides to bring the case before the Court of Justice, even then it is not unusual for the Commission to withdraw some of its complaints or even the entire case. The reasons for such a withdrawal may vary. In some cases the Member State eventually complies with Community law provisions as interpreted by the Commission. In other cases, however, it is the Commission which admits that it was mistaken.[148] Finally, in one case it appeared that the Commission was so utterly confused about the application of

---

[144] Cf *Sutherland Report*, 33–4. This view is also endorsed by the Commission. See e.g. the *Eleventh annual report to the European Parliament on monitoring the application of Community law*, [1994] OJ C154/1, 7–8. From the FIDE 1998 national reports it transpires that the Commission is rarely consulted. See Barav 1998, 425. In this context it is interesting to mention that for instance the Councils of State in a number of Member States contemplate to co-operate more closely in the area of implementation of directives. See the web site of the Associations of the Councils of State and Surpeme Administrative Jurisdictions of the European Union at www.raadvst-consetat.be. In some sectors the Commission tries to steer the implementation by issuing 'notes for implementation'. See e.g. 'Notes for the implementation of the Electricity directive 2003/54/EC and the Gas directive 2003/55/EC' at http://europa.eu.int/comm/energy/electricity/legislation/notes_for_implementation_en.htm.

[145] Cf also Commission Communication 'Better Monitoring of the Application of Community Law', COM (2002) 725 final, in particular 6–8.

[146] Cf Case 291/84 *Commission v. the Netherlands* [1987] ECR 3483, para 6, Case C–58/89 *Commission v. Germany* [1991] ECR I–4983, para 8. In case C–13/96 *BIC* [1997] ECR I–1753 the Court overruled the Commission's interpretation of the term 'technical requirement' in the sense of Directive 83/189.

[147] Cf Snyder 1993, 27–31.

[148] See e.g. Case 274/83 *Commission v. Italy* [1985] ECR 1077, para 12, C–190/90 *Commission v. the Netherlands* [1991] ECR I–3265, para 8. As regards the administrative stage of Art 226 proceedings, which is confidential, it is indeed difficult to determine the exact reasons for the Commission's withdrawal of certain complaints. The Commission's policy of transparency in Art 226 proceedings has, however, improved to an important extent since the reform of the working methods in relation to infringement proceedings in 1996. See the *Fourteenth annual report on monitoring the application of Community law* [1997] OJ C332.

a directive in a Member State that it did not even know what the precise complaint should be.[149]

It is against this—roughly sketched—background of frequently complicated questions on the interpretation of both Community and national law, to which neither the Commission nor the Member State concerned will instantly know the answer, that the problem of possible justifications for inadequate implementation must be considered.

The solution to the problem seems to be rather simple: in principle no excuses from the Member States are accepted for incorrect implementation. As in the case of justifications presented for delays in implementation, practical difficulties and serious problems of interpretation cannot constitute valid excuses for deficient implementation. Indeed, difficulties which may be encountered by the implementing authorities during the implementation phase can be overcome to a large extent by, for instance, proper information from those who participated in the negotiations about the directive or by involving those who will be responsible for the implementation from the very beginning of the decision-making process.[150]

Furthermore, since the Member States themselves participate in the elaboration of a directive, they are, in a way, also at the source of the difficulties which the directive may pose at a later stage. Under these circumstances it is difficult to accept the vagueness and obscurity of its terms as a valid argument.[151] In this context it should also be noted that the Member States cannot rely upon declarations in the Council minutes for the interpretation of a provision of a directive. The true meaning can be derived only from the actual wording and the directive itself.[152]

Ultimately, however, after having submitted the implementing measures to the Commission and after being informed that the Commission is satisfied with the measures at issue, can a Member State believe with reason that it has implemented the directive correctly?

In this respect at least two situations must be distinguished. The very first examination by the Commission after notification of the implementing measures by the Member States cannot really give rise to such expectations, since this examination is very general in nature and mainly serves the purpose of ascertaining whether implementing measures have been enacted at all.[153]

---

[149] Case C–52/90 *Commission v. Denmark* [1992] ECR I–2187, in particular para 21. Cf also Case C–43/90 *Commission v. Germany* [1992] ECR I–1909, where the Commission argued that Germany had not complied with certain obligations under Directive 79/831 (labelling of dangerous substances) [1979] OJ L259/10, although, with the best will in the world, these could not be found in the Directive concerned.

[150] Cf on this practice in the UK Jeffreys 1991.

[151] See, however, the—rather exceptional—judgment in Case 26/69 *Commission v. France* [1970] ECR 565: 'bearing in mind the equivocal nature of the situation thus brought about, the French Republic cannot be accused of any failure to fulfil its obligations' (para 32).

[152] See e.g. Case 237/84 *Commission v. Belgium* [1986] ECR 1247. Cf also Case 429/85 *Commission v. Italy* [1988] ECR 843.   [153] Cf Case 96/81 *Commission v. the Netherlands* [1982] ECR 1791.

The situation could be different after the implementing measures have been more closely scrutinized, or if the Commission has given an unequivocal opinion on a particular problem of implementation at the request of the Member State concerned. Depending on the formulation of the views expressed by the Commission or perhaps also in cases of sustained and tacit tolerance of a certain way of implementation, the possibility should not be excluded that a Member State might derive *some protection* from the Commission's conduct. This will, in principle, not be the case with infringement proceedings, due to its objective character.[154] However, the matter is different if the possible legal effects of non-compliance are at issue: the Member State may be protected by the principle of legitimate expectations or other related principles. As the Court's case law shows, the Commission's point of view or its inaction may serve, in exceptional circumstances, as grounds for applying a time limit to the Court's judgments. The ratio behind this *démarche* by the Court is the principle of legal certainty, including the protection of legitimate expectations.[155] Similarly, in the context of its case law on State liability the Court recognizes that a position taken by a Community institution may be one of the factors to be taken into account when considering the sufficiently serious character of the breach of Community law.[156]

Once it has been established that a Member State has not implemented a directive properly, how should it remedy the situation? In my view, the same requirements as in the case of belated implementation must apply:[157] i.e. reparation with retroactive effect with, however, possible limitations by general principles of law. Moreover, the rights which individuals might have derived directly from the directive at issue must also be observed. From the point of view of Community law there is no difference between delayed and incorrect implementation. In both cases, the legal situation prescribed by the directive has not been achieved, to the detriment of uniform and simultaneous entry into force of the directive's content within the national legal orders of the Member States.

---

[154] Cf above, Section 2.5. There are several cases in which the Court did not accept justifications based on the behaviour of the Commission as, in principle, the Commission may not give guarantees as to the compatibility of specific practices with Community law. See e.g. Case 288/83 *Commission v. Ireland* [1985] ECR 1761, Case C–317/92 *Commission v. Germany* [1994] ECR I–2039, Case C–56/90 *Commission v. United Kingdom* [1993] ECR I–4109 and Case C–340/96 *Commission v. United Kingdom* [1999] ECR I–2023.

[155] See in particular Case 43/75 *Defrenne II* [1976] ECR 455 and Case C–163/90 *Legros* [1992] I–4625. Cf also Report of the hearing in Case C–9/91 *EOC* [1992] ECR I–4297, at I–4313: 'The Commission has to concede that its silence . . . may have reinforced the United Kingdom's view that the difference in contribution requirements as between men and women was permitted by Article 7(1) of directive 79/7', and the Opinion of AG Alber in Case C–63/01 *Evans*, judgment of 24 October 2001, paras 119–120, nyr in ECR.

[156] Joined Cases C–46/93 and C–48/93 *Brasserie du Pêcheur* [1996] ECR I–1029, para 56. Cf also below, Ch 10, Section 10.4.3.   [157] See above, Section 2.5.

2.7   An end to the obligations?

The obligation to achieve the result prescribed by the directive exists for the Member States as long as the directive is in force.[158] Directives are not however written for eternity. Accordingly, the obligations may change or cease to exist. Essentially, in this respect the following situations may arise:

The directive itself is limited in time, as with the Sixth Directive on summertime arrangements, which concerns only the years 1993 and 1994.[159]

The provisions of a directive are amended by a later directive[160] or by an Act of Accession,[161] which can involve a number of possibilities, such as repealing or replacing (parts of) Articles of the old directive, inserting new Articles or parts of text, adding or updating (technical) annexes, etc. This will consequently change the content of the Member State's obligation.[162]

Similarly, an entire directive may be repealed (and at the same time replaced) by another directive, as happened in the fields of driving licences and public works contracts,[163] for instance, or by a regulation.[164]

Another—far less common—way to terminate the existence of the obligation occurs as a rule when the directive is tainted with illegality, i.e. the directive itself or the way in which it was adopted is in violation of the law. Yet in this respect a further distinction must be made as to the consequences of such a finding. The issue of illegality can be raised in several different types of proceedings; the consequences of the challenge will vary according to the proceedings under which it was brought.

---

[158] Cf Case C–310/89 *Commission v. the Netherlands* [1991] ECR I–1381 where the Court pointed out that 'the Member States are bound to comply with all their obligations under an existing directive . . . In any event, the binding force of a directive may not be challenged as long as it has not been abrogated or amended' (Summary publication, para 2 of the summary). Cf also Case C–137/92 P *Commission v. BASF* [1994] ECR I–2555, in particular para 48.   [159] Directive 92/20 [1992] OJ L89/28.

[160] E.g. Directive 71/305 (public works contracts) [1971] OJ English Spec Ed (II) 682 by Directive 89/440 [1989] OJ L210/1, Directive 82/606 (surveys of earnings of workers in agriculture) [1982] OJ L247/22, by Directive 91/534 [1991] OJ L288/36, Directive 69/169 (tax-free allowances for travellers) [1969] OJ English Spec Ed (I) 232, by Directive 91/191 [1991] OJ L94/24.

[161] E.g. Directive 71/305 (public works contracts) [1971] OJ English Spec Ed (II) 682, by the Act of Accession of Spain and Portugal.

[162] Member States are, however, not allowed to invoke the pending amendments in order to justify their failure to implement the directive at issue fully and correctly. Cf Case 306/84 *Commission v. Belgium* [1987] ECR 675.

[163] Cf Directive 91/439 (driving licences) [1991] OJ L237/1, repealing Directive 80/1263 and Directive 89/440 (public works contracts), [1989] OJ L210/1, repealing Directive 77/277. For a regulation repealing a directive see e.g. Regulation 259/93 (shipments of waste) [1993] OJ L30/1.

[164] Cf Regulation 259/93 (shipments of waste) [1993] OJ L30/1, replacing Directive 84/631 [1984] OJ L326/31.

In an action for annulment under Article 230, a directive (or a provision of a directive) will be declared void[165] with an effect *erga omnes* and *ex tunc*, unless the Court decides, by applying Article 231, to uphold (some of) the effects of the directive.[166] In a preliminary procedure the Court may declare the directive to be invalid.[167] Likewise, a judgment in an action for damages may give the necessary indications as to the illegality of the directive at issue, even if the action is not ultimately successful as far as the claim for damages is concerned.[168] While this has not yet been entirely settled, it is conceivable that the illegality of a directive could be raised under Article 241,[169] although this would mean that the directive is merely inapplicable in the concrete case before the Court of Justice.

In theory, in the last three types of actions the directive will be made inoperative only in the particular case. There is thus no effect *erga omnes*. Yet in practice the finding that the directive is invalid or illegal or inapplicable has a much wider scope, as it will *de facto* compel the institutions to replace the act.

According to the Court, a national court should regard an act which has been declared invalid in another preliminary procedure as invalid for the purposes of a judgment to be given by this court.[170] The much broader practical effect of a declaration of invalidity is likewise underlined by the apparent need to limit the effects of such a declaration by applying Article 231 by analogy.[171] A finding under Article 288 and Article 241 does not as such affect the validity of the act. Nevertheless, in order to prevent the illegality being raised repeatedly before the Court of Justice, the best policy is to amend, withdraw, or replace the act at issue.

If it results from a judgment of the Court under Articles 230 or 234 that a directive or a provision of a directive is declared void or illegal, the obligation at issue

---

[165] See e.g. Case C–202/88 *France v. Commission* [1991] ECR I–1223. For an effort—yet in vain for reasons of limited standing under Art 230 for individuals—see Joined Cases T–172/98, T–175–177/98 *Salamander* [2000] ECR II–2487.

[166] Cf for instance Case C–295/90 *European Parliament v. Council* [1992] ECR I–4193 and Case C–157/02 *Rieser*, judgment of 5 February 2004, nyr in ECR.

[167] As regards preliminary questions concerning the validity of a directive (provision) see e.g. Case 5/77 *Tedeschi* [1977] ECR 1555, Case 21/78 *Delkvist* [1978] ECR 2327, Case C–331/88 *Fedesa* [1990] ECR I–4023, Case C–491/01 *British American Tobacco* [2002] ECR I–11453 and Case C–25/02 *Rinke* [2003] ECR I–8349.   [168] See e.g. Case T–210/00 Biret [2000] ECR II–47.

[169] It is, in particular, uncertain whether a Member State in an infringement proceedings may rely on Art 241. See Kapteyn and VerLoren van Themaat 2003, 386–7. In Case C–74/91 *Commission v. Germany* [1992] ECR I–5437, the Court held that 'a Member State cannot . . . properly plead the unlawfulness of a decision addressed to it as a defence in an action for a declaration that it has failed to fulfil its obligations arising out of its failure to implement that decision . . . Nor can it plead the unlawfulness of a directive which the Commission criticizes it for not having implemented' (para 10). Yet, Germany did not rely explicitly on Article 241. It could also be deduced from Case C–241/01 *National Farmer's Union* [2002] ECR I–9079 that a Member State cannot argue the invalidity of a directive in the context of a preliminary procedure.   [170] Case 66/80 *ICC* [1981] ECR 1191.

[171] See e.g. Case 4/79 *Providence Agricole* [1980] ECR 2823 and Case 41/84 *Pinna I* [1986] ECR 1.

ceases to exist.[172] The condition is, however, that there has been a judgment of the Court, since the latter has made clear that a Community act must be presumed to be valid until it has been held to be invalid (or declared void, as the case may be) by a competent court, i.e.—since *Foto-Frost*[173]—the Court of Justice itself; if there has not been such a judgment, national authorities are obliged to apply the rules of Community law.[174] Clearly it is not for the Member States to decide on the validity of a Community act, in the same way as it is not for the national courts to declare such an act invalid.[175]

On the other hand, illegality established under Article 288 and, in so far as this is conceivable, under Article 241, does not appear to be sufficient to release the Member States from their obligations resulting from Article 249(3). Similarly, in a preliminary judgment the Court of Justice may give an interpretation of a Treaty Article which makes it clear that a directive is (on certain points) incompatible with the Treaty.[176] Formally, the directive is not declared to be invalid or void and the Member States will have to comply with their obligation to implement the directive. However, from a more practical point of view, obliging them to implement a deficient directive shows little common sense.[177] Obviously, in such a situation a prompt intervention of the Community legislature is highly desirable for the sake of legal certainty.

---

[172] Complex issues may then arise as to the status and effects of national measures implementing the directive concerned. For a detailed study see Vandamme 2005.

[173] Case 314/85 [1987] ECR 4199.

[174] See Case 101/78 *Granaria* [1979] ECR 623. Cf also Case C–310/89 *Commission v. the Netherlands* [1991] ECR I–1381. For a recent confirmation of this 'presumption of legality principle' see e.g. Case T–120/99 *Kik* [2001] ECR II–2235, para 55.

[175] Cf Case 314/85 *Foto-Frost* [1987] ECR 4199 and, for further support, Case C–217/88 *Commission v. Germany* [1990] ECR I–2879.

[176] Cf the whole line of 'pension cases' on interpretation of Art 141EC, which started with Case C–262/88 *Barber* [1990] ECR I–1889.

[177] Cf Easson 1981, 25. Furthermore it must be noted that the Court is prepared to accept an exception to the presumption of legality of Community acts in case of 'acts tainted by an irregularity whose gravity is so obvious that it cannot be tolerated by the Community legal order', Case C–137/92 P *Commission v. BASF* [1994] ECR I–2555, para 49. On such non-existent acts, which need not be implemented, see also Case C–74/91 *Commission v. Germany* [1992] ECR I–5437, para 11.

3

On the content of directives

3.1 Introduction

By stating that directives are binding as to the result to be achieved, Article 249(3) may suggest that they lay down in fairly general terms certain objectives which are to be accomplished. In particular the German version of the Treaty, which employs the term 'Ziel' (objective), has given rise to considerable speculation as to its meaning *and* its implications for the content of a directive. For instance, it was suggested that a directive should restrict itself to a description of the essential elements of the measures proposed.[1] However, today it is understood that the result to be achieved is determined by the content of the directive at issue. Similarly, as pointed out above,[2] it is generally accepted that directives may go into detail. Consequently they may meticulously spell out the result to be achieved.[3] Since, in this way, the result to be achieved depends on and varies according to the content of a directive, any definition of the term 'result' must remain abstract and rather general. It is often defined, notably in German literature, as a general legal, economic, or social situation[4] or 'a legal or factual situation which does justice to the Community interest which, under the Treaty, the directive is to ensure'.[5] In other words, the result may concern both the state of affairs in law and in fact and must be situated within one or more objectives of the Treaty.[6]

From the foregoing it clearly follows that a search for more concrete indications as to the result to be achieved boils down to an analysis of every individual directive.[7] This is quite beyond the scope of this book. Likewise, I am not going to discuss the various differences which exist between directives depending on the subject matter area to which they relate. Directives adopted for the purposes of harmonization in the internal market differ indeed from directives aiming at social protection or at environmental protection. The character of directives adopted for the liberalization of the market is again different, etc.

---

[1] For a more detailed account of this discussion see the 1st edition of this book, 44–5.
[2] Ch 2, Section 2.1.
[3] Cf e.g. Fuß 1965, 380, as well as Schmidt 2004, 786.
[4] Cf Schmidt 2004, 786. Cf also Bleckmann 1997, 164, making reference to Oldenkop.
[5] Kapteyn and VerLoren van Themaat 1998, 328.
[6] This actually already follows from the structure of the Treaty and the system of conferred powers ('*compétences d'attribution*').   [7] Cf Easson 1981, 27.

However, some general remarks on the *type* of provisions a directive will usually contain may be helpful in comprehending *what*—in general terms—can be the content of the obligation a directive may impose. At first sight, the following analysis may perhaps seem a somewhat obsolete exercise. However, to gain insight into what the content of a directive may be and, consequently, what type of obligations a directive may contain is vital for a whole range of subsequent questions and problems. It is, for instance, highly relevant for the question whether and if, how a directive has to be implemented, both for the question of State liability in case of non- or inadequate implementation and for the issue of direct effect. It also tells us about the nature of directives and how they differ or not from regulations.[8]

3.2 Different types of provisions which a directive may contain

3.2.1 The 'hard core' rules

The 'hard core' of a directive is its substantive rules spelling out the matters to which the directive relates, thus defining its scope, and often indicating its purpose, thus setting the framework for implementation. The substantive rules also contain provisions which describe, often in a very precise manner, the legal and/or factual situation which the Member States are required to bring about, and which often indicate the ways in which the desired situation must be realized. Obviously, the substantive rules are as varied as is the area of intervention by the Community.

In some cases it is immediately clear from the directive that it is aiming at the introduction of national legal rules, and thus at changing or establishing a legal situation. However, even a directive which at first sight obliges the Member States to establish a factual situation will actually in the majority of cases require national legal provisions to be changed or introduced in order to achieve the situation prescribed. The question whether legal provisions must be adopted or not is, however, a matter concerning the choice of form and methods covered below in Chapter 5, Section 5.2.

The hard core substantive rules of a directive may concern both substantive national law and procedures, including those before national courts.

An example of the first category is Article 9 of Directive 2000/31 (electronic commerce)[9] according to which Member States must ensure that their legal system allows contracts to be concluded by electronic means; in pursuance of Directive 91/671 (use of safety belts)[10] the driver and passengers travelling in a certain type of vehicle on the road must wear safety belts; Directive 92/28 (advertising of medicinal products)[11] prohibits advertising to the general public of medicinal products available only on medical prescription.

[8] Cf above, Ch 2, Section 2.1.   [9] [2000] OJ L178/1.   [10] [1991] OJ L373/26.
[11] [1992] OJ L113/13.

Examples of directive provisions relating to procedures are Directive 91/263 (telecommunication terminal equipment)[12] providing for a procedure of conformity assessment; Directive 2003/48 (taxation of interest),[13] providing, *inter alia*, for an exchange of information by the 'paying agent' and the authorities of the State of establishment of the person concerned; Article 5 of Directive 2003/86 (family reunification)[14] spells out the Member States' obligations in relation to the submission and examination of the application. Increasingly, directives also stipulate explicitly that the persons concerned must be enabled to defend their rights as laid down in the directive before a national court;[15] this may in fact entail an adjustment of national procedural rules.

A relatively new phenomenon are directives providing for national regulatory authorities. Under these directives, which aim at the liberalization or, basically, the (re-)regulation of the markets in the area of public utilities, the national regulatory authorities must be given rather far-reaching powers to regulate (and supervise) the market at issue. This often happens under the direct control of and in close cooperation with the Commission.[16] The result is that, in fact, a sort of 'third layer' of enforcement or regulation is created, situated between the Commission and the Member States.

For the purposes of implementation, it makes no difference whether the directive's provisions concern substantive law or whether they are provisions relating to procedures.[17] In both respects the directive must be fully transposed into national law. Furthermore, it is not only procedures involving the direct participation of private individuals which have to be implemented into national law. A transposition of provisions concerning the Member States *inter se*, for instance those imposing a consultation procedure between two or more Member States prior to adoption of certain measures, must also, under certain circumstances, be laid down in national law.[18]

The various obligations can be formulated in a negative way, as prohibitions of particular activities, or—more often—in a positive way, prescribing certain conduct.[19]

The obligations formulated *in the substantive provisions of the directive*, i.e. as opposed to the fact that a directive *as a whole* is addressed to the Member States, are addressed either to the Member States or to persons or bodies they will ultimately

[12] [1991] OJ L128/1.   [13] [2003] OJ L157/38.   [14] [2003] OJ L251/12.
[15] Cf e.g. Directive 64/221 (public policy and public health), Art 8 [1963–1964] OJ English Spec Ed 117, Directive 76/207 (equal treatment at work), Art 6 [1976] OJ L39/40, Directive 92/59 (product safety), Art 14 [1992] OJ L228/4, Directive 91/533 (conditions of employment relationship—information of employees), Art 8 [1991] OJ L288/32, Directive 92/28 (advertising of medicinal products), Art 12 [1992] OJ L113/13, Directive 2003/6 (insider dealing and market manipulation), Art 15 [2003] OJ L96/16, Directive 2000/43 (non-discrimination on grounds of race), Art 7 [2000] OJ L180/22. See also below, Ch 5, Section 5.4 and Ch 7, Subsection 7.2.1.
[16] Cf for instance Directive 2002/21 (electronic communications networks and services) [2002] OJ L108/33.   [17] Cf e.g. Case C–131/88 *Commission v. Germany* [1991] ECR I–825, para 61.
[18] Cf Case C–186/91 *Commission v. Belgium* [1993] ECR I–851.
[19] Cf e.g. Directive 97/67 (postal services), Art 3 [1998] OJ L15/14, 'Member States shall ensure that users enjoy the right to a universal service . . . '; Directive 2003/6 (insider dealing and market manipulation), Art 5 [2003] OJ L96/16, 'Member States shall prohibit any person from engaging in market manipulation'.

concern once the directive is implemented. To put it another way, a directive may 'double' the obligations for the Member States in the sense that the instrument is addressed to them and so too are the separate substantive provisions; or it may be that the instrument is addressed to them but the separate substantive provisions are formulated in terms of obligations of (some) individuals or bodies. The difference is in fact merely one of drafting technique.

Thus for instance, on the one hand, Article 7 of Directive 83/189 (technical standards)[20] provided that 'Member States shall take all appropriate measures to ensure that their standard institutions do not draw up or introduce standards . . .'; according to Article 3(3) of Directive 91/296 (transit of natural gas through grids)[21] 'Member States take the measures necessary to ensure that the entities under their jurisdiction . . . open negotiations on the conditions of the natural gas transit requested'; Article 10 of Directive 95/46 (processing of personal data)[22] stipulates 'Member States shall provide that the controller or his representative must provide a data subject . . . with at least the following information . . . '.

On the other hand, Article 3 of Directive 97/5 (cross-border credit transfers)[23] provides that '[t]he institution shall make available to their actual and prospective customer . . . information on conditions for cross-border credit transfer'; Article 22 of Directive 77/388 (Sixth VAT Directive)[24] lays down that 'every taxable person shall state when his activity as a taxable person commences, changes or ceases'; according to Article 12 of Directive 2002/8 (access to justice in cross-border disputes)[25] '[l]egal aid will be granted or refused by the competent authority of the member State in which the court is sitting . . . '; according to Article 3(2) of Directive 92/59 (product safety)[26] ' . . . producers shall . . . provide consumers with the relevant information . . . ' and according to Article 6(1) of Directive 98/24 (chemical agents at work)[27] ' . . . the employer shall ensure that the risk from a hazardous chemical agent . . . is reduced to the minimum'.

A directive will also often contain provisions which leave it to the discretion of the Member States to derogate from its contents[28] or to give their own interpretation to certain concepts,[29] thus allowing them room to manoeuvre. In some cases, however, the exercise of the discretion which is left to the Member States may be submitted to a special procedure; it may be made conditional upon permission of another body[30] or it may be submitted to periodical assessment by the Member States themselves.[31]

---

[20] [1983] OJ L109/8.   [21] [1991] OJ L147/37.   [22] [1995] OJ L281/31.

[23] [1997] OJ L43/25.   [24] [1977] OJ L145/1.   [25] [2003] OJ L26/41.

[26] [1992] OJ L228/24.   [27] [1998] OJ L131/11.

[28] Usually by providing that the directive 'does not prevent the Member States from' [applying different provisions], or that the directive is 'without prejudice to the right of the Member States to . . . ', or that 'the Member States may . . . '.

[29] Cf e.g. Art 20(4) of Directive 77/388 (Sixth VAT Directive) [1977] OJ L145/1, or Art 2 of Directive 74/562 (road passenger transport operators) [1974] OJ L308/23.

[30] See below, Subsection 3.2.2.

[31] Under the ultimate control of the Commission. See below, Subsection 3.2.2. Cf also Case 248/83 *Commission v. Germany* [1985] ECR 1459.

Finally, the method of harmonization is also relevant. The extent to which Member States may act depends also on the method used.[32] In case of total harmonization the relevant field is exhaustively regulated, with no room for independent action for the Member States, unless provided for it in the directive itself. On the other hand, where the Community has opted for minimum harmonization, the Member States are still free to maintain or adopt more stringent standards. However, the latter must be compatible with other Community law, in particular the Treaty. In other words, the Member States are free to maintain or adopt national measures, with the directive as the floor and the Treaty as the ceiling.

To summarize, the content of the result to be achieved, i.e. the content of the national implementing measures is determined by the substantive rules of the directive at issue. This does not necessarily mean that no latitude is left to the Member States, since a directive may give them an option for derogations or require them to 'fill in' certain concepts. However, if the directive does this, it goes without saying that the measures taken may not go beyond the limits set forth in the directive.[33]

3.2.2   Ancillary obligations for the Member States

Directives also contain other types of provisions formulating obligations for the Member States. These can be designated as ancillary, as completing 'hard core' provisions just briefly discussed in the previous Subsection. This is certainly not to suggest that they are less binding or less important.[34] Their function, however, is different.

In the first place, there is the *vital* provision laying down the period allowed for implementation, thus specifying the date from which the substantive content of the directive must be a reality achieved in law and in fact within the Member States.[35]

Secondly, directives require the Member States to adopt laws, regulations, and administrative provisions or, in more neutral terms, to take the measures necessary in order to comply with the directive.[36] As argued above,[37] this should be seen as an explicit restatement of the obligation under Article 249(3) and the more general obligation under Article 10 of the Treaty. Moreover, since 1991, directives have required the

---

[32] On harmonization methods see, for instance, Slot 1996.

[33] Cf e.g. Case 815/79 *Cremonini* [1980] ECR 3583, in particular para 6, Case 51/76 *VNO* [1977] ECR 113, Case 415/85 *Commission v. Ireland* [1988] ECR 3097 and Case C–72/95 *Kraaijeveld* [1996] ECR I–5403. See however also Case C–468/93 *Emmen* [1996] ECR I–1721 where the fleshing out of a definition was entirely left to the Member States.

[34] Cf Case 274/83 *Commission v. Italy* [1985] ECR 1077: in particular from the Opinion of AG Lenz it appears that the Italian government suggested that an obligation to notify the Commission of the implementing measures is of minor importance. The Court found, however, as with respect to any other provision of the directive, that Italy had failed to fulfil its obligations.

[35] As to the vital character of this type of provision see Ch 2, Sections 2.3 and 2.4.

[36] Exceptionally this may not be so, depending on the substance matter of the directive concerned. See e.g. Directive 90/684 (aid to shipbuilding) [1990] OJ L380/7 and Directive 91/675 (setting up an Insurance Committee) [1991] OJ L374/32.   [37] Ch 2, Section 2.1.

Member States, when adopting the implementing measures, to include a reference to the directive concerned or to accompany the measures by such a reference on the occasion of their official publication (the so-called 'interconnection clause'). The way in which the reference is made is left to the discretion of the Member States. The purpose of such a reference is to make the Community origin of the implementing measures explicit. This will make transparent the relationship between a piece of national legislation and the underlying directive, which is of particular importance for the judicial protection of individuals and for the control and interpretation of the implementing measures by national courts or national authorities, where appropriate. The problem is, however, that if for instance the rules are later amended or if the provisions at issue form only a small part of an existing code (e.g. the Civil Code) in which they have to be inserted, the clause becomes invisible again.[38]

Thirdly, directives oblige the Member States to inform the Commission of the measures adopted in order to comply with the directive in question. The Court has explained that this duty must be seen in the light of Article 10 of the Treaty, which obliges the Member States to facilitate the achievement of the Commission's tasks under Article 211. According to the latter the Commission must, *inter alia*, ensure that the provisions of the Treaty and the measures adopted by the institutions pursuant thereto are applied.[39] This obligation also extends to cases where, in the opinion of the Member State concerned, no specific implementing measures need to be enacted.[40] The Court has further stated that, in order to be effective for the purposes for which it is required, the information must be clear and precise, indicating unequivocally the measures which have been adopted. Failure to provide the information required or providing information of poor quality will mean that the Commission will be unable to ascertain whether the Member State has effectively and completely implemented the directive;[41] even if the Commission becomes aware of the implementing measures through other channels, this does not release the Member State concerned from its duty to notify the Commission officially of the measures adopted.[42]

Fourthly, directives may contain provisions requiring the Member States to submit to the Commission the texts of the main national legal measures which they are planning to adopt in the field governed by the directive. The purpose of this type of obligation is probably to ensure that the Commission is able to monitor the conformity of national measures adopted after the actual implementation of the directive and to intervene wherever the subsequent national measures are incompatible with the directive at issue.

---

[38] Cf Timmermans 1997, 9–8, who also suggests that legislation transposing a directive should be accompanied by transposition tables, indicating for each directive article the corresponding national provisions.

[39] Cf e.g. Case 96/81 *Commission v. the Netherlands* [1982] ECR 1791, Case 97/81 *Commission v. the Netherlands* [1982] ECR 1819, and Case C–33/90 *Commission v. Italy* [1991] ECR I–5987.

[40] Cf Case C–69/90 *Commission v. Italy* [1991] ECR I–6011.

[41] Cf Case 96/81 *Commission v. the Netherlands* [1982] ECR 1791 and Case C–33/90 *Commission v. Italy* [1991] ECR I–5987.   [42] Cf Case 274/83 *Commission v. Italy* [1985] ECR 1077.

In the fifth place, an obligation of notification, information, or consultation may exist with respect to national measures adopted within the margin of discretion left to the Member States or with respect to national draft measures before their final adoption in general. The implications of the obligation may differ and their non-observance may have legal effects.

At the one end of the spectrum, there are obligations which involve only a simple information or consultation procedure. For instance, notification of national draft measures under Article 3(2) of Directive 75/442 (waste)[43] has no legal consequences. It is merely intended to ensure that the Commission is informed of any plans for national measures. This should enable it, *inter alia*, to consider whether (further) Community harmonization is necessary.[44] At the other end of the spectrum, there are notification obligations which may have far-reaching consequences if not complied with, such as the notification obligations under Directive 83/189 (technical standards).[45] This Directive requires the Member States to notify the Commission of draft technical standards or measures and to refrain from applying them pending the Commission's examination of their compatibility with Community law. According to 'settled case-law',[46] a failure to observe the notification obligation constitutes a substantial procedural defect which renders the technical regulation in question inapplicable and therefore unenforceable against individuals. In the much debated *CIA Security* case[47] the Court has based this finding on the purpose of the Directive, i.e. the protection, by means of preventive Community control, of the freedom of movement for goods and the effectiveness of that control. The Court has explicitly contrasted this outcome with the one in *Enichem* by pointing out that the aim of Directive 83/189 is not simply to inform the Commission, but to eliminate obstacles to trade. Furthermore, in the context of the procedure for Community control of draft national measures their entry into force is made subject to the Commission's agreement or lack of opposition.[48]

In the sixth place, different types of collaboration, mutual consultation, and exchange of information between the Member States (or their 'competent authorities')[49] and/or between the Member States (or their 'competent authorities')

---

[43] [1975] OJ L194/47.

[44] Cf Case 380/87 *Enichem* [1989] ECR 2491. See e.g. also Art 4 (3) of Directive 80/987 (protection of workers—insolvency of employers) [1980] OJ L283/23.

[45] [1983] OJ L109/8, now replaced by Directive 98/34 [1998] OJ L204/37. Indeed, there are many notification obligations 'in-between'. Their effect will depend on their wording and purpose and may vary considerably.   [46] Case C–159/00 *Sapod* [2002] ECR I–5031, para 49.

[47] Case C–194/94 [1996] ECR I–2201.

[48] Confirmed in Case C–159/00 *Sapod* [2002] ECR I–5031. Cf also Case 5/84 *Direct Cosmetics* [1985] ECR 617 and Case C–97/90 *Lennartz* [1991] ECR I–3795, which show that national provisions derogating from the Sixth VAT Directive cannot be relied upon by national tax authorities to the detriment of taxable persons if the procedure provided for in Art 27 (notification and authorization) has not been followed. For a more detailed discussion of this '*CIA Security* case law' and its consequences see below, Ch 6, Subsection 6.3.2, Ch 9, Subsection 9.3.5 and 9.5.3, and Ch 10, Subsection 10.4.2.

[49] Often to be entrusted by the Member States with specific tasks under the directive concerned.

and the Commission are provided for under various directives.[50] The information to be exchanged may concern a variety of matters, such as the national authorities designated to act in pursuance of the directive,[51] or installations, undertakings, etc. which have a specific task under the directive,[52] or the experiences acquired concerning the application of the directive at issue.[53] A directive may likewise oblige Member States to set up information networks.[54]

In the seventh place, some directives request the Member States to undertake certain assessments or studies.

For instance, Directive 76/207 (equal treatment at work) and Directive 79/7 (equal treatment in statutory schemes of social security)[55] require the Member States to periodically assess whether certain exclusions allowed for under the respective Directives remain justified; they must inform the Commission of the results of these assessments. As the Court pointed out in Case 248/83 *(equal treatment in public service)*[56] these provisions provide for supervision in two stages: firstly by the Member States themselves and secondly by the Commission, enabling it to exercise effective supervision of the application of the Directive, in pursuance of Article 211 of the Treaty.[57]

Finally, Member States may be obliged to draft and submit regular reports on the application of the directive at issue.[58] The directive concerned will normally specify the type of information which must especially be included in the reports.

3.2.3 Provisions regarding the institutions

Although according to Article 249(3) directives are addressed to the Member States, they often also contain provisions directed to Community institutions, usually the Council and the Commission.

---

[50] Cf e.g. Art 13 and Art 33 of Directive 73/239 (insurance other than life assurance I) [1973] OJ L228/3, Art 6 of Directive 77/489 (transport of animals) [1977] OJ L200/10, Art 9 (1) of Directive 89/48 (mutual recognition of diplomas) [1989] OJ L19/16, Art 14 of Directive 95/21 (port State control) [1995] OJ L157/11, Art 19 of Directive 2000/31 (electronic commerce) [2000] OJ L178/1, and Art 17 of Directive 2000/43 (non-discrimination on grounds of race) [2000] OJ L180/22.

[51] Cf e.g. Art 9 of Directive 89/48 (mutual recognition of diplomas) [1989] OJ L19/16.

[52] Cf e.g. Art 12 of Directive 84/631 (transfrontier shipment of hazardous waste) [1984] OJ L326/31.

[53] Cf e.g. Art 11 of Directive 85/337 (environmental impact assessment) [1985] OJ L175/40 or Art 8 of Directive 2003/4 (access to environmental information) [2003] OJ L41/26.

[54] Cf e.g. Art 13(3) of Directive 91/477 (arms control) [1991] OJ L256/51.

[55] [1976] OJ L39/40 and [1979] OJ L6/24.   [56] *Commission v. Germany* [1985] ECR 1459.

[57] See further e.g. Art 8 of Directive 86/613 (equal treatment of the self-employed) [1986] OJ L359/56, Art 22(1) of Directive 92/43 (natural habitats) [1992] OJ L206/7.

[58] Cf e.g. Art 11 of Directive 89/48 (mutual recognition of diplomas) [1989] OJ L19/16, Art 8 of Directive 91/689 (hazardous waste) [1991] OJ L377/20 and Art 39 of Directive 92/50 (public service contracts) [1992] OJ L209/1 and Art 15 of Directive 98/24 (chemical agents at work) [1998] OJ L131/11. Cf e.g. Case C–406/02 *Commission v. Belgium*, judgment of 12 February 2004. See also Case C–72/02 *Commission v. Portugal* [2003] ECR I–6597, concerning reports to be sent to the Commission. According to the Court, the obligation at issue concerned only the relations between the Member States and the Commission.

Directives may provide for further decision making which is necessary for their implementation and which may concern a considerable variety of issues. In the majority of cases it is the Commission which is empowered by the Council to adopt measures for this purpose.[59] The Commission's power in this respect is often delineated by procedures for consultation with the Member States, various committees or the Council;[60] not infrequently, a management committee type of procedure must be followed.[61]

Adjustments of the provisions of a directive, particularly with respect to technical progress, are also often left to the Commission.[62]

Some directives include a provision stating that the Council will in the future adopt other directives or measures related to the subject matter of the directive at issue,[63] or that it will re-examine or review the directive in question within a certain period.[64]

Directives quite often request the Commission to draw up a report on the application of the directive and submit it to the Council,[65] to the Council and the European Parliament,[66] or to both of these and the Economic and Social Committee.[67] Similarly, the Commission may be requested on this occasion to submit proposals for improvement.[68]

Finally, to give just a few examples of the other types of provisions which directives may contain, the Commission may be requested to draw up practical (and usually non-binding) guidelines[69] or encourage (together with the Member States)

[59] Cf Arts 202 and 211 of the EC Treaty.

[60] Cf e.g. Art 13 of Directive 91/263 (telecommunications terminal equipment) [1991] OJ L128/1, and Art 3 of Directive 92/85 (pregnant workers) [1992] OJ L348/1 and Art 17 of Directive (2003/6 (insider dealing and market manipulation) [2003] OJ L96/16.

[61] On conditions governing the exercise of powers delegated to the Commission in general, see Council decision of 13 July 1987 (comitology) [1987] OJ L197/33, replaced by Council decision of 28 June 1999 [1999] OJ L184/23.

[62] Cf e.g. Art 10 of Directive 91/157 (batteries containing dangerous substances) [1991] OJ L78/38, Art 13(1) of Directive 92/85 (pregnant workers) [1992] OJ L348/1; a 'management committee type' procedure may be provided for in this respect as well: see Art 17 of Directive 89/391 (health and safety of workers) [1989] OJ L183/1. In other cases it will be for the Council to adjust the directives. See e.g. Art 21 of Directive 92/46 (milk products) [1992] OJ L268/1 and Art 4 of Directive 91/441 (emissions from motor vehicles) [1991] OJ L242/1.

[63] Cf e.g. Art 16 of Directive 89/391 (health and safety of workers) [1989] OJ L183/1, and Art 1(2) of Directive 76/207 (equal treatment at work) [1976] OJ L39/40.

[64] Cf e.g. Art 11 of Directive 86/613 (equal treatment of the self-employed) [1986] OJ L359/56, Art 18 of Directive 80/217 (classical swine fever) [1980] OJ L47/11, and Art 14(6) of Directive 92/85 (pregnant workers) [1992] OJ L348/1.

[65] Cf e.g. Art 12(2) of Directive 86/378 (equal treatment in occupational social security schemes) [1986] OJ L225/40.

[66] Cf e.g. Art 4 of Directive 90/364 (right of residence) [1990] OJ L180/26.

[67] Cf e.g. Art 10 of Directive 89/654 (health and safety at work) [1989] OJ L393/1.

[68] Cf e.g. Art 7 of Directive 91/671 (use of safety belts) [1991] OJ L373/26, Art 9 of Directive 79/7 (equal treatment in statutory schemes of social security) [1979] OJ L6/24, Art 13 of Directive 89/48 (mutual recognition of diplomas) [1989] OJ L19/16, Art 33 of Directive 95/46 (processing of personal data) [1995] OJ L281/31, Art 17 of Directive 97/7 (distance contracts—protection of consumers) [1997] OJ L144/19, and Art 21 of Directive 2000/31 (electronic commerce) [2000] OJ L178/1.

[69] Cf e.g. Art 12 of Directive 98/24 (chemical agents at work) [1998] OJ L131/11.

the drawing up of codes of conduct,[70] examine information submitted by the Member States,[71] communicate certain information to the Member States,[72] or the directive may set up a body entrusted with specific tasks.[73]

3.2.4 Conclusions concerning the various types of provisions

What lessons can be learned from this brief anthology of the various types of provisions which may be contained by a directive, as regards the subject under discussion here?

It would seem that directives comprise *more* binding elements than simply the 'hard core provisions', as I have termed them, which describe (in more or less detail) the content of the adjustment of national law or of the factual situation to be brought about by the Member States in their respective legal orders and which are the primary purpose of a directive.

To a large extent directives impose ancillary obligations upon the Member States which by their very nature do not lend themselves to transposition into national law. This applies particularly for provisions laying down obligations of the Member States *vis-à-vis* the Commission (or other Community institutions, as the case may be) or for certain obligations for the Member States *inter se*.[74]

It would also seem, from the foregoing paragraphs, that these provisions serve several purposes.

Some of them curtail (with varying degrees of intensity of Community interference and, in particular, with varying legal consequences) the discretion left to the Member States under the directive in question, thus providing for different forms of supervision of the exercise of discretion.

Other provisions are to enable the Commission to supervise effectively, according to its duty under Article 211 of the Treaty, the transposition of the directive into national law or to monitor the actual application of the rules laid down in the directive: depending on the experience gained with the application of the rules, the Commission may consider whether further Community interference in the matter concerned is necessary.

Provisions on collaboration, mutual exchange of information, or various types of consultation between the Member States or the Member States and the Commission are often indispensable for effective operation of the system provided for.

Studies and ostensibly non-committal examinations by the Member States usually relate to issues which are relevant as such for the subject matter of the

---

[70] Cf e.g. Art 16 of Directive 97/5 (cross-border credit transfers) [1997] OJ L43/25.
[71] Cf e.g. Art 9 of Directive 76/630 (surveys of pig production) [1976] OJ L223/4.
[72] Cf e.g. Art 4 of Directive 76/491 (information on oil prices) [1976] OJ L140/4.
[73] Cf e.g. Art 9(2) of Directive 89/48 (mutual recognition of diplomas) [1989] OJ L19/16.
[74] However, as case C–186/91 *Commission v. Belgium* [1993] ECR I–851 shows, mutual consultation between the Member States prior to introduction of certain measures has to have been provided for in national legislation. A careful approach is therefore necessary in this respect. The same holds true for obligations relating to notification: Case C–237/90 *Commission v. Germany* [1992] ECR I–5973.

directive but which, for a number of reasons (not uncommonly political), are not yet suitable for Community rule.

Together the substantive and ancillary provisions constitute the inseparable entity of the system of rules laid down by a directive. They must therefore be seen as the result the Member States are required to achieve and, consequently, they are equally binding upon the Member States. Non-observance of ancillary obligations, such as failing to provide the Commission with information or a unilateral derogation from the directive, which in fact required a particular procedure to be followed, amounts to infringement of Article 249(3) with possible implications for the judicial protection of individual citizens.[75]

As regards the provisions concerning Community institutions, at first sight they may appear rather peculiar. According to Article 249(3) directives are addressed to the Member States and by virtue of this Article they are binding upon them. Provisions which are directed to the Commission or the Council or which concern some committee that is to be established or which operate at Community level therefore look rather inappropriate and cannot be considered as binding upon the institutions in pursuance of Article 249(3). In fact, these provisions raise a number of intricate questions as to their legal nature. One of these questions is whether they should be considered as decisions *sui generis*[76] which are binding for the institutions concerned. Or are they merely the expression of (political or other) intentions with no binding effect whatsoever?[77] The discussion of these problems is actually beyond the scope of this book. It should be noted, however, that the legal literature does not exclude the possibility of the provisions at issue, or at least some of them, being obligatory for the institutions.[78]

As far as their function is concerned, it becomes clear upon closer consideration of the directive as an instrument of Community intervention, laying down a system of rules aimed at regulating a certain subject matter, that this type of provision is also intimately linked with the objective a directive seeks to achieve, which is not necessarily a static situation.

---

[75] Although not every violation of Art 249(3) and, in particular, a violation consisting of non-observance of ancillary provisions, will be equally relevant for individuals who may try to invoke this fact in national courts. See above, Section 3.2.2 and below, Ch 6, Subsections 6.4.3 and 6.4.4, Ch 9, Subsections 9.3.5 and 9.5.3 and Ch 10, Subsection 10.4.2.

[76] I.e. *not* decisions in the sense of Art 189(4); as to the terminological confusion see Lasok 2001, 155–7. Cf also Louis 1993, 518–20.

[77] Cf Joined Cases 90 and 91/63 *Commission v. Luxembourg and Belgium* [1964] ECR 625: Resolution to set up a common organization of markets for dairy products by a certain date was not binding and therefore could not constitute an obligation for the Council.

[78] Cf Schmidt 2004, 775, according to whom regulations, directives and decisions '*werden zwar häufig, wenn nicht stets, auch Befugnisse und Verpflichtungen ihrer Urheber oder anderer Gemeinschaftsorgane und -hilfsorgane normieren*'. Much will of course depend on the content and purpose of the provisions concerned. Delegation of powers, for instance, is not only a matter of the legal relationship between the Commission and the Council; it also has external effects: lack of competence can be invoked by third parties. Cf also Case C-212/91 *Angelopharm* [1994] ECR I-171. Furthermore, it should not be ruled out that in some cases the institutions might be bound on the basis of '*patere legem quam ipse fecisti*'.

To make the rules work effectively in practice and to ensure that they remain up-to-date, it may be necessary to delegate powers to (usually) the Commission enabling it to lay down further implementing rules; adjustments or amendments are indispensable if Community rules are not to become outdated, which would potentially frustrate rather than promote the achievement of the objective. Permanent monitoring at Community level of the operation of the rules in practice should ensure surveillance of their effectiveness and may give rise to their improvement or to further Community action.

A review or examination of directives should be seen in the same light. Another factor which may play a part in this respect will often be that a directive may be the result of a highly political compromise at a particular point in time; provisions for review or re-examination will make it possible to reconsider certain issues governed by the directive when the political climate has changed.

In summary, directives lay down a frequently complex system of different rights and duties for different legal subjects of Community law, not only for the Member States and their national authorities, but also, where appropriate, for Community institutions and, particularly through transposition into national law, for individuals.[79] Although the primary purpose of most directives is the obligation for the Member States to transpose the content of the directive into national law, in so far as the directive provisions concerned lend themselves to such transposition, for an actual and effective achievement of the objective pursued a directive may often require that the obligations imposed go far beyond a 'simple' transposition by the Member States.[80]

In the light of these many considerations it is submitted that *the result to be achieved under a directive is both a legal and a factual situation as determined by the substantive and ancillary provisions* of the directive at issue. Provisions directed at the institutions are obviously not a part of the 'result' in the sense of Article 249(3). For the correct operation of the entire system envisaged by a directive, however, they are of great importance.

It is striking that, until relatively recently, the 'factual component' of the obligation was paid little attention, both in the legal literature and the case law of the Court. This issue will be discussed in more detail in the following Section. It is, *inter alia*, an important element for the discussion what type of breaches may be relied upon by individuals in national courts, either for the purposes of direct effect or for the purposes of State liability.

3.3   The result to be achieved: in law and in fact

As indicated in Subsection 3.2.1 above, in the vast majority of cases the Member States have to enact national legal measures in order to comply with the obligations resulting from the substantive rules of a directive. The Court of Justice has repeatedly held that the Member States must secure full implementation of directives in law and

---

[79] See below, Ch 6, Section 6.2.
[80] Cf De Ripainsel-Landy and Gérard 1976, 52–3. See also below, Section 3.3.

not only in fact.[81] However, the opposite is equally true. In principle, the ultimate purpose of the rules laid down in a directive is, just like the purpose of *any* legal rule,[82] to influence the behaviour of legal subjects.[83] The transposition of the terms of a directive is therefore not an end in itself but rather a means to bring about a certain situation. Consequently, the obligations imposed by a directive are not fulfilled merely by the fact that national rules have been enacted. The rules must then be applied and enforced in practice. Thus even after the adoption of national rules a continous obligation is incumbent upon the Member States. As Mertens de Wilmars put it:

La directive implique . . . l'obligation, puisque L'Etat membre a assumé une obligation de résultat, de veiller à l'application efficace de la législation nationale à l'objectif communautaire.[84]

Although the problem of non-application or insufficient enforcement of Community law, including directives,[85] is certainly not new,[86] it is only since the last decade that particular attention has been paid to it.[87] Similarly, the majority of cases brought by the Commission before the Court of Justice in infringement proceedings have for a long period of time concerned the absence or the inadequacy of national rules transposing a directive, and not the issue of effective application and enforcement. Nevertheless, more recently, there has been case law from which it can be deduced that application and enforcement *in practice* are just as important as the enactment of the rules.

In several preliminary rulings the Court has held that the third paragraph of Article 249 requires the Member States to adopt in their national legal systems all the measures necessary to ensure that the provisions of the directive at issue are fully effective.[88] This is, according to the Court, a general obligation of the Member States.[89] From the context of the cases it appears that the main concern of the Court is that provisions of directives will not remain a dead letter but will be given practical effect.

An interesting example in this respect is provided by the *Marks & Spencer* case.[90] In that case the referring court apparently proceeded on the premiss that if a Member State has correctly implemented the provisions of a directive in national law individuals can no longer rely on the directive at issue before domestic courts. Yet, the Court made clear that correct transposition does not exhaust the effects of the directive at issue. Since the Member States remain bound to actually ensure full application of the directive even after the adoption of those measures, individuals are entitled to rely on the relevant

---

[81] Cf e.g. Case C–361/88 *Commission v. Germany* [1991] ECR I–2567, para 24.

[82] Unless the legislation is merely 'symbolic'.

[83] Cf Capotorti 1988, 157. Yet, the requirement that a directive is implemented both in law and in fact does not imply that, in order to prove that a transposition is inadequate, the actual effects of the legislation transposing the directive have to be established. See Case C–392/96 *Commission v. Ireland* [1999] ECR I–5901.   [84] Mertens de Wilmars 1991, 393; cf also Capotorti 1988, 160.

[85] More properly expressed: the national measures transposing the directive. See above, Ch 1, Section 1.3.   [86] Cf Krislov, Ehlermann, Weiler 1986, 59 ff.

[87] Cf above, Ch 1, Section 1.3.

[88] Cf Case 14/83 *Von Colson* [1984] ECR 1891 and Case C–271/91 *Marshall II* [1993] ECR I–4367.

[89] Cf Case C–143/91 *Van der Tas* [1992] ECR I–5045.   [90] Case C–62/00 [2002] ECR I–6325.

provisions of a directive before national courts whenever the full application of the directive is not in fact secured. For instance, where the national measures correctly transposing the directive are not being applied in such a way as to achieve the result sought by it.

Furthermore, as will be shown in Chapter 5, in infringement proceedings the same concern lies behind the requirements imposed by the Court upon the Member States with respect to the implementing measures they adopt.[91] In Case 29/84 (nurses), for instance, the Court stressed that the principles of constitutional and administrative law relied on by the German government as a means of implementation 'must guarantee that the national authorities will in fact apply the directive'.[92]

In several cases brought under Article 226 the Court now addressed the issue of practical application more explicitly, i.e. without focusing on the adequacy of the rules enacted pursuant to a directive.

For instance, in two cases brought by the Commission against Italy the Italian government was found to be in breach of Directive 71/305 (public work contracts)[93] because two bodies awarding a public work contract failed to publish a notice in the Official Journal.[94]

In Case C–42/89 (*water supply Verviers*) the Belgian government failed to fulfil its obligations under the Treaty because the Verviers water supply did not accord with the parameters of Directive 80/778 relating to the quality of water intended for human consumption.[95] This failure was not caused by inadequate (regional) legislation but rather the costs and complexity of the construction work at the water treatment station which was necessary for providing Verviers with 'good water'.

---

[91] A clear example in this respect is case C–361/88 *Commission v. Germany* [1991] ECR I–2567 concerning the proper implementation of Directive 80/779 (air quality) [1980] OJ L29/30, which requires, among other things, the Member States to take appropriate measures so that the concentration of sulphur dioxide in the air does not exceed certain limit values. The Court held that mandatory rules are necessary under which the administrative authorities are required to adopt measures in all the cases where the limit values of the Directive are likely to be exceeded. In other words, putting the values into a piece of legislation is not sufficient. The authorities must be obliged to take action where necessary.

[92] *Commission v. Germany* [1985] ECR 1661, para 23.   [93] [1971] OJ English Spec Ed. II 682.

[94] Case 199/85 *Commission v. Italy* [1987] ECR 1039 and Case 194/88 R *Commission v. Italy* [1988] ECR 5647. Ever since then, several of the public procurement cases were brought by the Commission for incorrect application of the rules rather than for incorrect transposition. Cf e.g. Joined Cases C–20/01 and C–28/01 *Commission v. Germany* [2003] ECR I–3609.

[95] [1980] OJ L229/11; *Commission v. Belgium* [1990] ECR I–2821. Here again, there is a clear trend to initiate proceedings against Member States where they do not meet quality or other environmental standards or related obligations. See e.g. Case C–316/00 *Commission v. Ireland* [2002] ECR I–10527 (again on the quality of water for human consumption), Case C–337/89 *Commission v. UK* [1992] ECR I–6103, which concerned (partly) the non-achievement of a factual situation, namely an excessively high concentration of nitrates in drinking water, Case C–56/90 *Commission v. UK* [1993] ECR I–4109 on quality of bathing water, Case C–147/00 *Commission v. France* [2001] ECR I–2387 and Case C–368/00 *Commission v. Sweden* [2001] ECR I–4605, both concerning the frequency of sampling, and Case C–103/00 *Commission v. Greece* [2002] ECR I–1147 (protection of sea turtles).

Interestingly, in the *Grosskrotzenburg* case[96] the German government
challenged the admissibility of the action, arguing that only non-transposition,
rather than non-compliance in individual situations may be brought by the
Commission under Article 226. The Court dismissed this argument, stating
that the Commission is entitled to bring a case where a Member State has
allegedly failed to fulfil its obligations by not having achieved in a specific case
the result intended by the directive.

A comparable defence was raised by the Italian government in the *San Rocco*
case,[97] where it argued that the Commission was only entitled to review the
correct transposition of a directive. Yet the Court allowed the Commission to
seek a declaration that Italy had infringed the directive at issue by not taking
the necessary measures to ensure that waste was disposed of without endangering human health and without harming the environment. A significant element
was that the competent authorities had recently allowed waste disposal in the
San Rocco valley, thus creating a persistent situation which led to a significant
deterioration of the environment.

Another patent example, from an entirely different area, is the judgment of the
Court in Case C–287/91 (*reimbursement of VAT*):[98] Italy in fact correctly transposed the Eighth VAT Directive[99] concerning the relevant point but in practice
the fiscal authorities did not observe the six-month period within which VAT
has to be reimbursed to certain categories of persons. The Court recalled its
established case law according to which the Member States must guarantee that
directive provisions are fully applied, and it found that Italy was in breach of said
directive as it allowed the Ministry of Finance to disregard the time limits for
refunds of VAT, without intervening from the outset to remove the consequent
prejudice to Community law.[100]

In brief, it appears that the Court and, in particular, the Commission, when bringing cases under Article 226 against the Member States for their failure to comply with
the obligations under Article 249(3), no longer concentrate almost exclusively on the
extent to which there is conformity between the directive and the national legal texts
which transpose it. There has been a discernible shift in attention towards situations
concerning the non-application of the directive which has, as such, been correctly
transposed.[101] This tendency fits in with the concerns of the Community relating to
the application and enforcement of Community law mentioned in Chapter 1.

---

[96] Case C–431/92 *Commission v. Germany* [1995] ECR I–2189. See on this case also below, Ch 4, Section 4.4.

[97] Case C–365/97 *Commission v. Italy* [1999] ECR I–7773. See also below, Ch 9, Subsection 9.4.3.

[98] *Commission v. Italy* [1992] ECR I–3515. A similar action was again recently announced in Agence
Europe, 23 July 2003, no 8509, 14. See also, for yet another area e.g. Case C–229/00 *Commission v. Finland*
[2003] ECR I–5727.   [99] Directive 79/1072 [1979] OJ L331/11.

[100] Cf also Case C–229/00 *Commission v. Finland* [2003] ECR I–5727.

[101] It is also interesting to note that the latest three Annual reports on monitoring the application of
Community law, i.e. the Eighteenth (Com (2001) 309 final), the Nineteenth (COM (2002) 324 final)
and the Twentieth (COM (2003) 669 final) distinguish between the notification of national measures
implementing directives, infringements for non-conformity, and infringements for incorrect application
of national measures implementing the directives.

4

The addressees of a directive

4.1   No obligations for individuals

From Article 249(3) it follows that a directive can be addressed to and is binding upon Member States alone. Unlike ECSC recommendations,[1] an EC directive cannot be addressed to subjects of Community law other than the Member States. Although directives may be directed to one Member State or to a certain number of Member States,[2] in practice they are usually addressed to all of them.[3] Furthermore, the fact that according to the terms of Article 249(3) the binding force of a directive exists only in relation to the Member State to which it is addressed has led the Court of Justice to decide that a directive cannot impose obligations on an individual.[4] This finding of the Court merits particular attention, notably because it forms the basis for denying both horizontal direct effect of directives, i.e. that a provision of a directive may not be relied upon by an individual against another individual, and inverse vertical direct effect, i.e. that a Member State may not rely upon a provision of a directive against a private individual.[5]

As was already briefly discussed above,[6] several obligations may devolve upon individuals from the text of a directive, but these individuals are in principle bound by the obligation only from the moment the directive is implemented into national law. In *Marshall I*[7] the Court made clear that a directive may not *of itself* impose obligations upon individuals and, therefore, it may not be relied upon *as such* against

---

[1] Art 14 of the late ECSC Treaty.

[2] Cf Ipsen 1965, 75, Lauwaars 1973, 28, Schmidt 2004, 785.

[3] Cf Capotorti 1988, 153. Interestingly, as a consequence of Art 286 (1) of the EC Treaty certain directives, such as Directive 95/96 (processing of personal data) [1995] OJ L281/31, the EC institutions and other bodies are to be considered as addressees of the directive. Cf on this reference Haratsch 2000.

[4] Cf Case 152/84 *Marshall I* [1986] ECR 723, Case 80/86 *Kolpinghuis* [1987] ECR 3969 and Case C–91/92 *Faccini Dori* [1994] ECR I–3325.

[5] For a detailed discussion of horizontal and inverse vertical direct effect of directives see Ch 9, Subsections 9.5.2 and 9.5.3.   [6] Ch 3, Subsections 3.2.1 and 3.2.4.

[7] Case 152/84 [1986] ECR 723, since then confirmed in a whole line of cases. In the Netherlands, the question as to whether VAT Directives can be relied upon by the tax authorities against an individual was answered in the negative before *Marshall I* by the *Hoge Raad* (20 February 1985, BNB 1985 no 128) without the case being referred to the Court of Justice. See for discussion of the case Bijl 1986 and Kortenaar 1985. Cf also the Opinion of AG VerLoren van Themaat in Case 89/81 *Hong Kong Trade* [1982] ECR 1277, Section 4 of the Opinion.

such a person. Some twenty years after *Marshall* and a number of efforts by the Court
to confirm this judgment, the debate on the possible obligations for individuals
which may result from directives has still not been settled. The Court's case law,
which seems to accept certain side effects of vertical direct effect, imposing a burden upon individuals, is one of the main causes.[8] Similarly, the obligation to interpret national law in conformity with the directive at issue regularly gives rise to the
question whether it does result in imposing a new obligation on individuals and,
therefore, should be equated to horizontal or inverse vertical direct effect, which is
not allowed under *Marshall*.[9]

However, there are also other, more subtle techniques for coping with the limitations resulting from the denial of horizontal and inverse vertical direct effect of
directives.[10] For instance, in his opinion in *Barber*, Advocate General Van Gerven
suggested that a provision of international law, in this particular case the prohibition
of (sex) discrimination in the UN Covenants,[11] could possibly of its own accord
take effect between individuals in the Community legal order. A directive should
then be seen as rendering a provision of international law more precise and thus
removing a possible obstacle to horizontal direct effect of the provision.

Another alternative is to read a directive together with a directly effective
provision of the Treaty which a directive merely implements but does not expand.[12]
It is generally accepted that certain Treaty provisions may impose obligations upon
individuals.[13] If a provision of a directive implements a provision of the Treaty which
imposes an obligation on individuals, the former should also be capable of imposing
an obligation.

> Directives may contain provisions designed to facilitate the practical applica-
> tion of a Treaty Article while in no way altering its content or scope. This is,
> for instance, the case in relation to Article 141 and Article 1 of Directive 75/117
> (equal pay for men and women).[14] In *Defrenne II*[15] the Court denied direct effect
> (and thus the possibility of it being binding on individuals) of Article 141 if the
> discrimination cannot be identified using the criteria 'equal work' and 'equal
> pay'. In such cases more explicit implementing provisions of a Community or
> national character would first have to be adopted for the purposes of such an
> identification. Now, Article 1 of Directive 75/117 undoubtedly contains a

---

[8] For a detailed discussion see Ch 9, Subsection 9.5.3.
[9] For a detailed discussion see Ch 8, Section 8.6.
[10] For a more detailed discussion see the first edition of this book, 62–5.
[11] Case C–262/88 [1990] ECR I–1889, para 53 of the Opinion.
[12] Cf Wyatt 1983, 245–6, Easson 1979b, 78 and Easson 1981, 40–1. This was apparently also what the
referring court had in mind in Case C–192/94 *El Corte Inglés* [1996] ECR I–1281 when it wanted to
'couple' Directive 87/102 and Art 153 EC Treaty (then Art 129A).
[13] Cf Case 43/75 *Defrenne II* [1976] ECR 455, Case 36/74 *Walrave and Koch* [1974] ECR 1405 and
Case C–281/98 *Angonese* [2000] ECR I–4139.
[14] [1975] OJ L45/19. On the relationship see e.g. Case 96/80 *Jenkins* [1981] ECR 911.
[15] Case 43/75 [1976] ECR 455.

'more explicit implementing provision' of this kind, providing that job classification systems must be based on the same criteria for both men and women and must be drawn up in such a way as to exclude any discrimination on grounds of sex. In cases of discrimination in job classification systems Article 141 is directly applicable since Article 1 of the Directive now provides sufficient guidance for the identification of discrimination.[16] From the point of view of a private employer, this result could be considered as imposing an obligation. However, since Article 1 of Directive 75/117 is considered not to alter the content or scope of Article 141, it must be assumed that the employer concerned is bound by the obligation which results from Article 141 but is made explicit in the Directive.

Another legacy of the Court's persistent denial of horizontal direct effect is the broad definition of the concept of 'the State'. As is well-known, an individual may in principle always rely on the provisions of a directive against a 'Member State'.[17] However, since in legal relationships within the national legal order an individual does not usually deal with the Member State as such but rather with one of its organs, bodies, agents etc., the crucial question arises as to how far, for the purposes of direct effect, the concept of 'the State' reaches. I will deal with this issue in Section 4.2.

This is, however, not the end of the story. The binding force of a directive upon the Member States has a number of further—complex and barely explored—implications. In this context, it must be noted that the Court has gone beyond the abstraction, in itself not very revealing, that directives are binding upon the Member States, by considering explicitly that

the Member States' obligation arising from a directive to achieve the result envisaged by the directive and their duty under Article 5 [Article 10 New] of the Treaty to take all appropriate measures . . . to ensure the fulfilment of that obligation, is binding on all the authorities of Member States including, for matters within their jurisdiction, the courts.[18]

In its judgment in *Melgar*, the Court slightly changed this classic point, by stating that the obligation 'is binding on all the authorities of Member States, including decentralized authorities such as municipalities'.[19]

The Court's finding gives rise to at least two questions. Firstly, in a concrete case, which authorities are bound by the obligation laid down in a directive? In other words, who are the *actual* addressees within the Member State of a particular directive? Secondly, what are the implications of the fact that the obligation is

[16] Cf Case 109/88 *Danfoss* [1989] ECR 3199 concerning the interpretation of the equal pay directive and Case C–184/89 *Nimz* [991] ECR I–297, which refined *Danfoss* but was decided under Art 119.
[17] Indeed, provided that the conditions for direct effect are met.
[18] Case 14/83 *Von Colson* [1984] ECR 1891. Since then it has become established case law. Cf also Grabitz 1971, 5, who already argued that the '*Zurechnungsendpunkte*' of directives are not Member States as such but their organs.   [19] Case C–438/99 *Melgar* [2001] ECR I–6915, para 32.

binding upon *all* national authorities? I will address these questions in Sections 4.3 and 4.4.

4.2   The concept of 'the State'

The answer to the question whether, in a specific setting, a certain entity or person is *directly* bound by an obligation laid down in a directive,[20] with all the consequences resulting therefrom, will depend on the definition of the term 'State' given for this particular purpose.

As mentioned above, this problem arose in relation to the question concerning the parties against which an individual may rely on a provision of a directive, i.e. within the context of direct effect.[21] In this respect it must be pointed out that the terminology used by the Court is rather loose. It uses the terms 'State', 'organ of the State', 'emanation of the State', 'State authority' and 'public authority' interchangeably.

The problem of designating an entity as a part of the State, a public authority or any other synonym is certainly not new, the notions being involved in several areas of Community law.[22] The general approach of the Court is to interpret the concept of 'the State' in the way which best achieves the objectives of the measure at issue.[23] For those familiar with the Court's methods of interpretation, this will hardly come as a surprise. At the same time, however, it means that there is no generic definition at Community level of the types of entities which should be assimilated to the State. The approach of the Court is highly functional, i.e. the interpretation is related to the objective pursued by the rules within which the concept figures and, moreover, the interpretation is more or less tailored to the factual situation of the entity in question.[24]

For the purposes of deciding whether a particular body is directly bound by a directive, a *specific* frame of reference is lacking. If the obligations upon the Member States result from the binding nature which Article 249(3) confers on the directive *in general*, the objective of a particular directive is irrelevant and, therefore, it is arguable that the directive as such will be of no avail in this respect.

The problem of the criteria to be applied in order to find out whether a directive imposes obligations upon a certain body or, in other words, whether the body concerned should be regarded as falling within the concept of 'the State', was submitted to the Court of Justice in *Foster*.[25]

---

[20] I.e. whether the directive imposes an obligation without the intercession of national rules.

[21] See above, Section 4.1.

[22] For a discussion of several examples see the first edition of this book, 77–9.

[23] Cf also the Opinion of AG Van Gerven in Case C–188/89 *Foster* [1990] ECR I–3313, para 11.

[24] Cf on this subject in general Hecquard-Theron 1990 and as regards direct effect of directives in particular, Curtin 1990a.   [25] Case C–188/89 [1990] ECR I–3313.

In *Foster*, basically two types of tests were discussed in the written observations and, subsequently, at the hearing.

The first of these was a *functional test*, involving consideration of the activities in which the body is engaged. A body carrying out a public function on behalf of the State or a body entrusted with a public duty by the State, should be considered as a part of the State.

The second was an approach based on the existence of *control* on the part of the State in relation to the entity concerned. Within this test, two forms of possible control were identified. The first form was regulation by the State by means of binding directions or specific legislation. The second form of possible control was based on 'economic reality', that is to say on the possibility of controlling a body by means of ownership of shares in the body or through financial means, such as funding by the State. There was, however, a disagreement about which test should apply. Furthermore, problems arose with respect to the functional test in that there was uncertainty as to the kind of activities which should be considered as public functions; and with respect to the control test in that it was not clear how far the control should go and what kind of control should be required.[26]

In *Foster*, the Court did not define the concept of 'the State' in the abstract but gave guidelines which seem to be written for the particular situation of the BGC, at the material time, a nationalized gas undertaking. Subsequently, the Court referred to its case law on direct effect of directives, stressing that 'it is necessary to prevent the State from taking advantage of its own failure to comply with Community law'. As to the question concerning the entities against which a directive can be relied on, the Court summarized its position as follows: a provision of a directive meeting the requirements of direct effect

could be relied on against organizations or bodies which were subject to the authority or control of the State or had special powers beyond those which result from the normal rules applicable to relations between individuals.[27]

The bodies in question were tax authorities,[28] local or regional authorities,[29] constitutionally independent authorities responsible for the maintenance of public order and safety,[30] and public authorities providing public health services.[31]

---

[26] For a discussion of the separate criteria see AG Van Gerven in Case C–188/89 [1990] ECR I–3313, paras 17–20 and Prechal 1990, 457–9. According to AG Van Gerven, the rationale is that a Member State may under no circumstances benefit from its failure to implement the relevant provision of a directive, so obviously the term 'State' must be given a broad scope. Next, the Advocate General has streamlined the control test by linking it to the subject matter of the directive in question.

[27] Case C–188/89 *Foster* [1990] ECR I–3313, para 18.

[28] Case 8/81 *Becker* [1982] ECR 53 and Case C–221/88 *Busseni* [1990] ECR I–495.

[29] Case 103/88 *Costanzo* [1989] ECR 1839.   [30] Case 222/84 *Johnston* [1986] ECR 1631.

[31] Case 152/84 *Marshall I* [1986] ECR 723.

Consequently the Court held that

a body, whatever its legal form, which has been made responsible, pursuant to a
measure adopted by the State, for providing a public service under the control of the State
and has for that purpose special powers beyond those which result from the normal rules
applicable in relations between individuals is included in any event among the
bodies against which the provision of a directive capable of having direct effect may be
relied upon.[32]

The four criteria laid down in *Foster* seem to relate both to the possibility of
control and the functions performed. On the one hand, the performance of the
activities of the body concerned was subject to the control of the State and, moreover, this performance stemmed from the authority of the State (BGC was made
responsible 'pursuant to a measure adopted by the State'). On the other hand, the
Court emphasized both the nature of the activities (providing a public service) and
the conditions under which the activities were pursued (special powers possessed
by the BGC).

   However, from a later judgment it transpires that reference to the fact that the
body provides a public service was related to the specific circumstances of the *Foster*
case. In *Kampelmann* the Court held that a directive may

. . . be relied on against organizations or bodies which are subject to the authority or control
of the State *or* have special powers beyond those which result from the normal rules applicable
to relations between individuals, *such as* local or regional authorities or other bodies which,
irrespective of their legal form, have been given responsibility, by the public authorities and
under their supervision, for providing a public service.[33]

In other words, the test to be applied seems to be either 'authority or control of the
State' or 'special powers' on behalf of the body concerned. Having been made
responsible for providing a public service would seem inessential. However, in a
more recent judgment the Court again applied the 'full' *Foster* test.[34] In any case, the
judgments testify that the Court is willing to apply a broadbrush approach which
covers the whole panoply of bodies which exercise public authority in one way or
another, through which the State pursues its policies, whether in its regulatory
capacity or in its interventionist capacity or where the State operates as a market
participant. Since the legal form of the bodies or their status under national law is
irrelevant, the approach cuts through the existing dividing lines between the various
kinds of bodies applicable within the Member States.[35] It must be assumed that

---

[32] Para 20.
[33] Joined Cases C–253/96 to C–258/96 *Kampelmann* [1997] ECR I–6907, para 46 (emphasis added).
[34] Case C–157/02 *Rieser*, judgment of 5 February 2004, paras 24–28. On the other hand, there are
clear indications that the test in not exhaustive. The bodies meeting the *Foster* criteria are '*included in any
event* among the bodies against which [a directive may be relied upon]' (emphasis added).
[35] Dividing lines which are often far from clear in national law itself. For a discussion of some national
case law dealing with the classification of different bodies see Curtin 1990a.

precisely due to this broadbrush approach the application of the *Foster* test did not give rise to any questions of such complexity, that new references to the Court were necessary.[36]

Finally, mention should be made of one possibly far-reaching consequence of *Foster* and *Kampelmann*. The judgments suggest that the application of the test should take place independently of the directive at issue. More *in concreto*, this means that once the body in question has satisfied the test ('control of the State' or 'special powers') it must be regarded as being bound by the obligations laid down in the directive—if this is relevant for its conduct—even in those areas which are beyond its control or which fall outside the scope of the activities causing the body to be considered a part of the State, such as in the case of BGC which had to comply with an EC equal treatment directive.[37]

4.3 The actual addressees of a directive

As was already observed above,[38] behind the term 'Member State' in Article 249(3) hides a wide range of national authorities, which are bound by the directive. When considered from the point of view of different functions, the obligations imposed on Member States by Article 249(3) concern legislative, executive, and judicial authorities. Likewise, when considered from a geographical angle, they concern both central and decentralized bodies.[39]

There are, in the first place, the authorities responsible for implementation. Proper implementation of directives will usually require the enactment of binding rules of general application.[40] It is therefore generally assumed that the organ which

---

[36] For a general overview of the application of the *Foster* test in various Member States see e.g. the national reports to the FIDE Congress 1998, vol I.

[37] Another example is Case 271/82 *Auer II* [1983] ECR 2727, where the National Society of Veterinary Surgeons of France was bound by Directive 78/1026 (veterinary surgeons—recognition of qualifications) because it was exercising public powers conferred on it by national law and consequently the Society was to be considered an 'emanation of the State'; the Society shall also have to observe other directives, relating to areas in which no public powers had been conferred to it, like employment of its own staff. Cf also *Marshall I*, Case 152/84 [1986] ECR 723, where the Health Authority in question was, in functional terms, operating at arm's length from the government in the field of national health care. However, it is at least arguable whether its employment policy was under the control of the State, the Authority had to comply with the obligations resulting from Directive 76/207 (equal treatment at work) [1976] OJ L39/40.   [38] Section 4.1.

[39] Cf Case 103/88 *Costanzo* [1989] ECR 1839, Case C–224/97 *Ciola* [1999] ECR I–2517, and C–438/99 *Melgar* [2001] ECR I–6915. See also Schmidt 2004, 789 and Hessel and Mortelmans 1993, in particular 916.

[40] Cf Ch 5, Subsection 5.3.1. However, in certain cases also other types of actions may be required. Cf the various types of obligations discussed in Ch 3.

is *primarily* concerned by a directive is the legislator.[41] In other words, it is first and foremost the responsibility of the respective authorities which exercise legislative power to draw, within the field of their competence, the inferences from a directive, i.e. to adopt the necessary rules. Which authorities these are in a concrete case, is a matter left to the Member States.

In principle, Community law is said not to be concerned with the question of which authorities take the necessary measures in order to fulfil the Member State's obligation. In this respect Community law maintains the traditional rule of international law that the State as such and not its individual organs bears responsibility in international relations, and that it is up to the Member State concerned to decide on the way it will realize its international obligations within its own legal order.[42] In *International Fruit Company II* the Court of Justice stated in unequivocal terms that

> when provisions of the Treaty or of regulations confer power or impose obligations upon the States for the purposes of the implementation of Community law the question of how the exercise of such powers and the fulfilment of such obligations may be entrusted by Member States to specific national bodies is solely a matter of the constitutional system of each State.[43]

In a number of cases this principle of institutional autonomy has also been explicitly confirmed with respect to directives. The Court held that each Member State is free to delegate such powers to its authorities as it considers fit, and to implement directives by means of measures adopted by regional or local authorities.[44] Likewise,

---

[41] Cf e.g. Pescatore 1971, 90, Wyatt 1983, 247, Lutter 1992, 594 and the Opinion of AG Cruz Vilaça in Case 412/85 *Commission v. Germany* [1987] ECR 3503, para 19. Both legislature and the executive in its rule-making capacity. Depending on the subject matter of the directive at issue, the competence of the respective bodies and the state of national law of which the provisions of the directive will be a part, the organ actually adressed for the purposes of implementation will not necessarily be the one responsible for primary legislation. As to the tendency to transpose directives by means of secondary legislation see Siedentopf and Ziller 1988, 44. Cf also Case C–339/87 *Commission v. the Netherlands* [1990] ECR I–851, in which the Court of Justice accepted as proper means of implementation a combination of a Law and ministerial regulations (generally binding instruments under Dutch law).

[42] Cf Bleckmann 1984, 776 and Hessel and Mortelmans 1993, 929.

[43] Joined Cases 51–54/71 [1971] ECR 1107, para 4. Confirmed in Case 240/78 *Atalanta* [1979] ECR 2137. More recently the Court found in Case C–8/88 *Germany v. Commission* [1990] ECR 2321, that '. . . it is not for the Commission to rule on the division of competences by the institutional rules proper to each Member State, or on the obligations which may be imposed on federal and Länder authorities respectively' (para 13). Cf also Case C–302/97 *Konle* [1999] ECR I–3099, paras 62–63, briefly discussed below, Ch 10, Subsection 10.5.2. On the implementation in a federal context see e.g. Egger 1998 and Haslach 2001.

[44] Cf Case 96/81 *Commission v. the Netherlands* [1982] ECR 1791, Case 97/81 *Commission v. the Netherlands* [1982] ECR 1819, Joined Cases 227–230/85 *Commission v. Belgium* [1988] ECR 1, Case C–156/91 *Mundt* [1992] ECR I–5567 Case C–435/92 *Association pour protection des animaux sauvages* [1994] ECR I–67, Case C–225/96 *Commission v. Italy* [1997] ECR I–6887 and Case C–236/99 *Commission v. Belgium* [2000] ECR I–5657. Cf also Hessel and Mortelmans 1993, 916.

in the legal literature it is generally accepted that a directive does not interfere with the institutional structure of the Member States. It therefore does not authorize an organ of the State to take the necessary measures if this organ is not competent to do so under national law. In other words, it does not constitute an independent source of power for the authorities concerned.[45] The Court's finding, quoted in Section 4.1, that the obligations imposed on Member States by Article 249(3) and Article 10(1) are equally binding on all the authorities of the Member States, does not seem to change the matter, at least on the face of it. The proviso added with respect to the obligations for the courts, namely 'for matters within their jurisdiction', can be understood as indicating that the obligations are binding for those authorities which already possess the necessary powers by virtue of national law.[46]

From the above it follows that the answer to the question of which organ or authority of a Member State is actually bound by a directive will, depending on the subject matter of the directive at issue, vary from Member State to Member State, according to the internal distribution of tasks and competences.[47]

Similarly, the foregoing suggests that the Member States are free to decide which organ or authority will be entrusted with the actual implementation of a particular directive.[48] This is however true only to a certain extent. As pointed out above (and discussed in more detail below),[49] Community law imposes certain requirements as to the nature of the implementing measures. This limitation of the freedom to choose the measures will also entail a limitation as to the choice of the organ or authority.[50] Thus, for instance, where a proper implementation of a directive requires transposition by primary legislation, collaboration of the Parliament will be necessary. In other cases implementation by secondary legislation may suffice and consequently, other bodies with appropriate legislative competences will be involved.

Another factor with implications for the principle of institutional autonomy and the internal structure of a Member State is the *indifference* of Community institutions, and the Court of Justice in particular, with regard to the internal state order.

---

[45] Cf Ipsen 1965, 76, Kooijmans 1967, 137, Lauwaars 1973, 28, Monaco 1987, 466–8, Kortman 1991, 47, Nettesheim 2002, 56, Everling 1992b, 378. For another view, i.e. that a directive as such can serve as a direct source of powers enabling national authorities to act even if they do not have the necessary powers under national law, see Van Emde Boas 1965, 148–9 and Temple Lang 1998, 126–8.

[46] Cf Everling 1992b, 380, Schmidt 2004, 789, Jarass 1991, 216. Cf also the opinion of A–G Mancini in Joined Cases 227–230/85 *Commission v. Belgium* [1988] ECR 1, para 2 and Case C–8/88 *Germany v. Commission* [1990] ECR 2321, para 13: 'it is for all the authorities of the Member States, whether it be central authorities of the State or the authorities of a federated State, or other territorial authorities, to ensure observance of the rules of Community law *within the sphere of their competence*' (emphasis added). See, however, below, Section 4.4.

[47] Or, as Pescatore put it (1971, 91): '*dire que la directive s'adresse aux Etats Membres cela signifie concrètement qu'elle engage les organes des Etats Membres dont l'action peut être requise pour la mise en application de la directive. Quels sont ces organes? Ceci dépend des circonstances de chaque cas: tantôt ce sera le pouvoir législatif; tantôt le gouvernement en tant qu'il est investi du pouvoir réglementaire et de la haute direction de l'administration nationale.*'

[48] Cf the term national authorities in Art 249(3).   [49] See Ch 2, Section 2.6 and Ch 5.

[50] Cf Kortman 1991, 47.

Although, on the one hand, the Court demonstrates that it is willing to look beyond the abstraction of the 'Member State' when it says that all national authorities are bound by the obligation to achieve the result prescribed by a directive, on the other hand, it is the Member State as such that is responsible for the transposition and application of Community law in the national legal order.[51]

The most obvious example of this can be found in the case law of the Court in infringement proceedings: a Member State is liable under Article 226 of the Treaty, irrespective of which State authority has occasioned the infringement through its act or its omission, even if it is a constitutionally independent body.[52] The same principle also applies in full with respect to directives. According to the Court's established case law 'a Member State may not plead provisions, practices or circumstances in its internal legal system to justify failure to comply with obligations under Community directives'.[53] These internal provisions, practices, or circumstances include the division of powers, the different competences of Member State's organs, their mutual relationships, a Member State's federal structure etc. Whatever they might be, these factors cannot release the Member States from their obligation to ensure that the provisions of a directive are properly implemented in the national legal order.[54] Arguments based on the fact that a government does not have the necessary powers at its disposal to compel other organs to implement a directive are of no avail.[55] Consequently, the Member States may be obliged to provide for a mechanism by means of which national authorities, whatever their place in the institutional structure might be, are induced to comply with the obligations arising from a directive.[56]

Similarly, if *ratione materiae* competent organs do not have the appropriate powers at their disposal to adopt the measures necessary for full compliance with the obligations, or where there is no competent organ at all, it is up to the

---

[51] Thus not the government; the latter only represents the State *vis-à-vis* the Community institutions and *vis-à-vis* other Member States.

[52] Cf Case 77/69 *Commission v. Belgium* [1970] ECR 243 and Case 8/70 *Commission v. Italy* [1970] ECR 961. Cf also Arts 1993, 508. Indeed, more recently, this conception of liability of the State as a single entity reappeared in the context case law on the so-called '*Francovich* liability', to be discussed in detail below, in Ch 10.

[53] Cf Case 68/81 *Commission v. Belgium* [1982] ECR 153, para 5; cf also above, Ch 2, Section 2.4.

[54] Cf e.g. Case C–33/90 *Commission v. Italy* [1991] ECR I–5987, Case C–301/95 *Commission v. Germany* [1998] ECR I–6135, Case C–274/98 *Commission v. Spain* [2000] ECR I–2823, Case C–236/99 *Commission v. Belgium* [2000] ECR I–5657, Case C–417/99 *Commission v. Spain* [2001] ECR I–6015 and C–383/00 *Commission v. Germany* [2002] ECR I–4219.

[55] Cf e.g. Joined Cases 227–230/85 *Commission v. Belgium* [1988] ECR 1 and Case 1/86 *Commission v. Belgium* [1987] ECR 2797. See also Case C–237/90 *Commission v. Germany* [1992] ECR I–5973, where the German government argued that it was not necessary to compel the *Länder* by an explicit provision since the principle of '*Bundestreue*' constituted sufficient guarantee.

[56] Cf Winter 1991a, 54. On possible sanctions against decentralized authorities which do not comply with Community law in general see FIDE Reports 1992.

Member State, i.e. usually the legislature, to create the powers or organs respectively. In some cases, directives may contain explicit and rather detailed provisions in this respect, as was, for instance, the case with national regulatory authorities to be set up in the fields of energy and (tele)communication.[57]

In brief, as follows from the foregoing, a directive may in fact have consequences for the institutional structure of the State, despite the professed institutional autonomy.

However, this is not the end to the matter. There are still other inferences to be drawn from the fact that, according to the Court, the obligations imposed on Member States by Article 249(3) and Article 10(1) are binding on *all* national authorities. These become particularly manifest in situations of not timely or incorrect implementation of a directive. The Court's statement has some rather less expected implications for the judiciary and, in particular, for the administration (acting as the executive), which are responsible for the application and enforcement of the rules of the directive in their respective areas of competence.

It is not the purpose of this Section to anticipate the subsequent Chapters which will cover in detail interpretation in accordance with the directive, direct effect of directives and the particular role played by national courts in the enforcement of Community directives.[58] However, with respect to the administration, which will not be the focal point of the analysis in the following Chapters, a number of consequences should be discussed here.

4.4 Administrative compliance

The obligations imposed on administrative authorities by Article 249(3) and Article 10 of the EC Treaty have, in contrast to the implications for national courts, received little interest in scholarly writing.[59] Similarly, the cases that are directly relevant for this subject are only few in number. This is remarkable, since further reflection on the subject reveals that what we are facing here amounts to 'a constitutional enormity'.[60]

The most important duties of national authorities that follow from those two articles are the obligation to interpret national law in conformity with the directive, to set aside any national laws conflicting with a (directly effective) provision of a directive and to apply, where appropriate, the latter provision instead.[61]

These requirements may not seem very revolutionary when compared with the Court's case law on the effects of a judgment under Article 226 of the E(E)C Treaty. In 1972 the Court explained that a judgment of this kind entails

---

[57] Cf e.g. Directive 2002/21 (electronic communications networks and services), [2002] OJ L108/33.

[58] Chapters 7, 8, and 9 respectively.

[59] For a general and relatively recent discussion see Alberton 2002.   [60] De Witte 1999, 193.

[61] The binding effect which Art 249(3) ascribes to directives, together with Art 10(1), is the basis for the obligation to interpret national law in conformity with the directive at issue and it is the basis for direct effect of directives. For other duties of national authorities see e.g. Temple Lang 1998.

a prohibition having the full force of law on the competent national authorities against applying a national rule recognized as incompatible with the Treaty and, if the circumstances so
require, an obligation on them to take all appropriate measures to enable Community law to
be fully applied.[62]

The Court reaffirmed this principle in Case C–101/91 (exemption from VAT).[63]
The principle may indeed involve direct application of the rules of the directive
when they are suitable for such application and to proceed with consistent interpretation in order to remedy as much as possible the failure. The binding force of
the judgment upon all the national authorities results in these cases from the authority attached to the judgment (*res judicata*).[64] This has also an important advantage in
that there is an authoritative court decision on what the law is. As will be discussed
below, in the context of the obligations of national authorities, there is not always
such 'judicial guidance'.

The duty for national authorities to interpret and where appropriate apply
national law in conformity with the relevant directive is vital. As was explained
above,[65] it is by no means sufficient to merely transpose directives into national law.
The directives, or more precisely, the national implementing provisions, must be
applied and enforced by the competent administrative bodies. When carrying out
this task the administration is bound, by virtue of the obligation to interpret national
law in conformity with the directive, to interpret and apply this law in a way which
corresponds closely with the provisions of the underlying directive.[66] The more
discretion is left to the administration, the more important is this obligation.
Moreover, as will be explained in Chapter 8, the obligation is not limited to national
rules actually implementing the directive. It applies to *all* national law suitable to
achieve the objective pursued by the directive.

Interpretation of national law in conformity with a directive may often help to
overcome inconsistencies between national law and the directive at issue. Whenever
this method does not work for some reason, national administrative authorities will be
required to directly apply the provisions of the directive wherever those provisions
lend themselves to such application and to set aside conflicting national legislation.

As was already observed, traditionally, obligations resulting from directly effective
provisions of directives were approached both in the literature and the Court's case
law from the point of view of the judiciary: what must the national court do if an

---

[62] Case 48/71 *Commission v. Italy* [1972] ECR 527, para 7.

[63] *Commission v. Italy* [1993] ECR I–191.

[64] Cf Joined Cases 314–316/81 and 83/82 *Waterkeyn* [1982] ECR 4337. Furthermore, it must be
observed that in this Case the Court held that 'all institutions of the Member State concerned must
. . . ensure *within the fields covered by their powers* that the judgments of the Court are complied with'
(emphasis added).   [65] Ch 3, Section 3.3.

[66] See e.g. Case 14/83 *Von Colson* [1984] ECR 1891. Cf also Steyger 1991 and Wissink 2001, 37.
Although it may be argued that the interpretative obligation is particularly addressed to the courts, this
of course does not imply that the executive should not be bound in the same way. Cf Case C–218/01,
Henkel, judgment of 12 February 2004, nyr in ECR, para 60.

individual relies in a case before it on directly effective provisions? In the past only a few authors have explicitly addressed the question whether, in cases of belated or incorrect implementation, the administration must apply directly effective provisions of a directive and whether, if appropriate, they must disapply national provisions which are incompatible with it. The question was answered in the affirmative by Grabitz[67] and—although with some hesitation—by Everling.[68] Other authors have denied such an obligation on the part of the national administration.[69]

The Court's solution to the problem was uncompromising. In *Costanzo* it held that administrative authorities are under the same—general—obligation as a national court to apply provisions which have direct effect and to refrain from applying conflicting provisions of national law.[70]

> The Court gave two arguments for this finding. Firstly, it recalled that an individual may rely against the State on directly effective provisions of a directive in proceedings before the national courts *because* the obligations arising under these provisions are binding upon all administrative authorities of the Member States. Furthermore, it would be contradictory to rule, on the one hand, that an individual may rely upon directly effective provisions in national proceedings seeking an order against administrative authorities and, on the other hand, to hold that these authorities are under no obligation to apply the provisions concerned and refrain from applying conflicting provisions of national law.

The judgment in *Ciola*[71] has added a new element to this case law. The Court pointed out that the obligation to set aside conflicting provisions of national law does not relate only to general and abstract rules but also to specific individual decisions.[72]

Another though related question is whether the administration has to give effect to these obligations of its own motion i.e. without the individual concerned relying on them. It seems to be a quite logical consequence of the *Costanzo* obligation.[73] In contrast with court proceedings, there is usually no dialogue with the administration. Neither is it always possible to go back and ask for a new decision, taking into account Community law provisions. Much depends on how the administration is organized. The *Grosskrotzenburg* case, about the non-application of the Environmental Impact Assessment Directive, seems to confirm this point of

---

[67] Grabitz 1971, 21. Cf also Klein 1988, 29 and Oldenbourg 1984, 30. For Community law in general see Bebr 1981, 559.

[68] Everling 1983, 108 and, with even more hesitations, Everling 1993, 215.

[69] Cf Seidel 1983, 19 and further references by Oldenbourg 1984, 30.

[70] Case 103/88 [1989] ECR 1839. In relation to Art 81 EC Treaty see Case C–198/01 *CIF* [2003] ECR I–8055. In my view, the latter judgment underlines the general character of the obligation.

[71] Case C–224/97 [1999] ECR I–2517, which did not concern a directive but Art 49 of the Treaty.

[72] This gives rise to another issue, namely in how far there exists an obligation or at least a possibility to call into question decisions which became final but which are incompatible with Community law. Cf on this Case C–453/00 *Kühne*, judgment of 13 January 2004, briefly discussed in Ch 7, Subsection 7.3.2.

[73] Cf Jarass 1994, 81.

view.[74] In that case, Germany argued that provisions of Community law must be invoked before the administration, otherwise it is not obliged to apply them. This argument was dismissed by the Court. Therefore, it may be argued that implicitly, the Court has accepted that there is an obligation on the part of the administration to apply the Directive of its own motion.

While perhaps logical from a Community law perspective, the effect of *Costanzo* and related cases reaches far, so far that it may amount to 'constitutional heresy'.[75] If the national administration has to decide on its own on the direct effect of a directive provision and on its interpretation, it must do so without any intervention from a court and without assistance from the Court of Justice in preliminary proceedings; obviously, this may seriously compromise *legal certainty*. To this one might add that such a situation is at odds with the prohibition to disapply secondary Community law as long as the Court of Justice has not declared it invalid.[76]

> This problem was partly discussed by Advocate General Lenz in *Costanzo*.[77] In his view only proper implementation by the legislature can create the obligation for the administration to give effect to a legal situation consistent with the directive. National administrative authorities cannot be obliged to make a decision in conformity with Community law by directly applying a provision, because they have no possibility to obtain a ruling from the Court of Justice on the direct effect and interpretation of the provision at issue. In this respect they would lack the necessary endorsement of the Court, which the Advocate General sees as a form of requisite legal protection of the authorities concerned.
>
> On the other hand, according to the Advocate General, national administrative authorities are entitled to apply a provision of a directive if its direct effect and meaning are beyond doubt. This will particularly be the case if a prior ruling on the issue already exists: the conflict of rules being resolved *in abstracto*, the administration cannot be prevented from applying the directly effective provision *in concreto*.

However, there are more fundamental questions behind all this. Under national constitutional law, administrative authorities are, first, bound by the law[78] and, second, administrative action needs, in principle, a legal basis.[79] Yet, by accepting that administrative authorities are entitled to apply a directly effective provision of a directive and to disapply conflicting national rules, one rejects another argument

---

[74] Case C–431/92 *Commission v. Germany* [1995] ECR I–2189.
[75] De Witte 1999, 192.   [76] Case 101/78 *Granaria* [1979] ECR 623.
[77] Case 103/88 [1989] ECR 1839, paras 28–36.   [78] I.e. the law adopted by the legislature.
[79] At least in the sense that no legally binding obligations can be imposed without there being a foundation in the law for that. Indeed, there exist quite some differences between the Member States regarding the requirements of the principle of rule of law or legality or '*Gesetzmäßigkeit*' in this respect. For a brief discussion of the Dutch situation see Jans *et al.* 2002, 46–53.

against the obligation of administrative authorities to apply these national provisions, namely that the *subordination of the executive power to the legislative power* should
prevent the administration from refusing to apply the law.[80]

Furthermore, and in the same vein, these obligations imply that the administrative
authorities concerned, by virtue of Article 249(3) and Article 10(1), must—if
necessary—disregard their respective competences[81] and apply the provision of the
directive regardless of the fact that there might be *no legal basis in national law* for such
application.

> In relation to this, problems may for instance occur where a directive requires
> to set up a competent body, such as a national regulatory authority, and give
> it the necessary supervisory or otherwise powers,[82] but the Member State fails
> to do the latter.[83] Under Community law, these authorities are obliged to exer-
> cise the powers resulting from the directive. However, can a directive be con-
> sidered as a sufficient basis for direct empowerment?

To that one might also add that administrative organs—in particular individuals in
their capacity of an administrative organ—may incur disciplinary measures if they do
not comply with the instructions of a superior or hierarchically higher placed organ.[84]

In legal writing it has been argued that, in this respect, Community law confers
new competences upon national authorities.[85] Yet, in particular from a national
constitutional law point of view, this is a controversial matter and it is far from clear
what exactly the basis for this empowerment should be.[86]

> The judgment of the Court in *Dorsch Consult* may be understood to imply that
> the Court is not willing to go that far.[87] In *Dorsch Consult*, a public procurement
> procedure, the national administrative review body considered that it had no
> power to review the award of services contract at issue, since the relevant
> directive, Directive 92/50 (public service contracts),[88] had not yet been trans-
> posed in Germany. According to Dorsch Consult, the body competent to review
> awards under Directive 89/665 (public supply and public works contracts)[89] was
> also competent to hear appeals under Directive 92/50. The Court reminded that
> it is for the legal system of each Member State to determine which court or
> tribunal has jurisdiction and it found that the conclusion suggested by Dorsch

---

[80] See the observations of *Comune di Milano* in *Costanzo*, 1849–50 and the Opinion of AG Lenz on
this. Cf also for further discussion Seidel 1983, 19 and Winter 1991b, 660, Pieper 1990, 688, Jarass 1994,
102–5, Pietzcker 1995 *passim*, and, briefly, Riechenberg 1999, 765.

[81] Cf Winter 1991b, 666 and Everling 1992a, 380.

[82] Cf e.g. Art 12 of Directive 2003/6 (insider dealing and market manipulation) [2003] OJ L96/16 or
Art 11–13 of Directive 2002/21 (electronic communications networks and services) [2002] OJ L108/33.

[83] Cf Case C–221/01 *Commission v. Belgium* [2002] ECR I–7793.

[84] Cf Jans *et al.* 2002, 105–6 and Riechenberg 1999, 766.

[85] Curtin and Mortelmans 1994, 457. Cf also Temple Lang 1998 and Riechenberg, 1999.

[86] Cf also below, Ch 7, Subsection 7.4.1. This aspect has also been briefly touched upon in a number
of the national reports (e.g. Austrian, Spanish, French, and Swedish) to the FIDE Congress 2002.

[87] Case C–54/96 [1997] ECR I–4961.   [88] [1992] OJ L209/1.   [89] [1989] OJ L395/33.

Consult could not be drawn on the basis of the Directive. Although Article 41 of the Directive required the Member States to adopt measures necessary to ensure effective review in the field of public service contracts, Directive 92/50 neither indicated which national bodies had jurisdiction in the area concerned, nor that the bodies designated in the field of public supply and public works contracts should be considered the competent bodies for the purposes of Directive 92/50. In other words, the review body for 'supply and works' could not derive the power to review the award of a services contract directly from Directive 92/50. Subsequently, the Court went on and pointed out that national law had to be interpreted as far as possible in conformity with Directive 92/50. Here, however, the basis for the power to review the award of the service contract lies in national law.

Another confusing and uncertain—though perhaps also mitigating—factor is the regular reference by the Court to the sphere of the authorities' competence or to matters within their jurisdiction. In *Kühne*, for instance, the Court pointed out that administrative bodies must '*within the sphere of their competence*'(emphasis added) apply Community law provisions.[90] Yet, as will be discussed below, it is not clear whether this refers to subject matter competence or also to competence in terms of what the authorities are allowed to do as a matter of constitutional law.[91]

While the technique of consistent interpretation seems to bring about more acceptable outcomes, even then there is a risk that it may result in national authorities exceeding the various powers given to them by national law.[92]

Thus, for instance, it is highly questionable whether a (quasi-judicial) administrative body, hearing and examining complaints about sex discrimination in pay, may broaden, by interpretation, its own competence to the field of occupational pensions for the simple reason that according to the Court of Justice the Community concept of pay includes occupational pensions as well.[93]

In *Ciola*, the Court pointed out that the case law on obligations of administrative authorities is in fact a refinement of *Simmenthal*.[94] From a more recent case, it would seem that *Simmenthal* is indeed transposed to the obligations of administrative authorities in all its respects—even the more controversial ones—namely in so far as it extends to national procedural or constitutional rules which would prevent domestic courts from giving effect to EC law. As will be discussed below,[95] the

---

[90] Case C–453/00 *Kühne*, judgment of 13 January 2004, nyr in ECR, paras 20 and 22.

[91] This is an ever recurring question, which also arises in relation to the competence of national courts. See Ch 7, Subsections 7.2.1 and 7.4.1, and Ch 8, Subsection 8.5.2.

[92] Cf e.g. Everling 1992a, 380 and Jarass 1991, 216.

[93] *Commissie gelijke behandeling van mannen en vrouwen bij de arbeid* 3 April 1991, no 143-91-15 and 27 April 1993, no 340-93-15.   [94] Case 106/77 [1978] ECR 629.

[95] Ch 7, Subsection 7.4.2.

difficulty lies, *inter alia*, in how to reconcile these 'procedural' obligations with the procedural autonomy of the Member States.[96] In *Gervais Larsy*,[97] the First Chamber of the Court confirmed that national administrative authorities (in this case a Belgian social security authority) are, like national courts, under an obligation to set aside *any* national rules which may restrict them from giving full effect to Community law.[98] The question is indeed whether the obligations of administrative authorities go that far. From an opinion of Advocate General Léger it transpires that there is a role to play for procedural autonomy. While the Advocate General grafted the *existence* of the national authorities' obligation to disapply national law on the same principles as those of the domestic courts, as far as the *exercise* of the obligation is concerned, he has accepted the mitigating effects of procedural autonomy.[99] On the latter point, the Advocate General was followed by the Court.[100]

In brief, according to the case law discussed here, national administrative authorities—decentralized or not—are, in a way comparable to national courts, under the obligation to disapply national legal provisions which are not compatible with EC law, to apply directly the relevant Community law provisions at issue or to proceed to consistent interpretations of national law. They are supposed to do so, even where national law would restrict their powers in this respect or where there is no legal basis in national law for such (dis)application at all. In contrast to what was stated above,[101] it seems possible that a directive may interfere with the internal division of powers within a Member State. From a national constitutional law perspective the ultimate consequence is that the constitutional position of the administrative authorities changes; the authorities become more autonomous and instead of what they are supposed to do, i.e. apply the law, they are supposed to review it and where necessary disapply it.

These implications are enforced even further if one takes *Foster* into account. It has been explained above, that once the body in question has satisfied the *Foster* test it must be regarded as being bound by the obligations laid down in the directive and this also in those areas which are beyond its control.[102] If this interpretation of *Foster* is correct, the category of entities which must comply with the terms of a directive and which might, where appropriate, be called upon to apply the directive,[103] greatly expands, far beyond the bodies which are, under national law, responsible in some way or other for the implementation of the directive at issue. This would only be

---

[96] For a discussion of this concept see also below, Ch 7, Section 7.2.1.

[97] Case C–118/00 [2001] ECR I–5063.

[98] The problem of the social security authority was that it was not allowed to review its former decision with full retroactive effect.

[99] I.e. allowing the application of national procedural rules under the proviso that the principles of equivalence and effectiveness are met. Cf Opinion of 17 June 2003 in Case C–453/00 *Kühne*, nyr in ECR.

[100] Cf below, Ch 7, Subsection 7.3.2. Cf also Case C–201/02 *Wells*, judgment of 7 January 2004, nyr in ECR, para 65, where the Court explicitly refers to the procedural autonomy of, in this case, national administrative authorities.   [101] Section 4.3.

[102] Section 4.2.   [103] Cf also Fischer 1992b, 636.

otherwise if one were to assume that the *Foster* approach is relevant solely as regards the question whether an individual may rely on the directive against such a body.

In my opinion, it should be taken into account that the position of administrative bodies is fundamentally different from that of national courts, which have, in the majority of the Member States, the power to review and, where necessary, set aside national law and to refer preliminary questions to the European Court of Justice. Therefore it may be questioned whether the Court's 'transplant' of the obligations at issue from courts to national administrative authorities is fortunate and realistic. It is submitted that a more balanced approach to the '*Costanzo* obligation' needs to be developed. Proper consideration should be given, in this respect, to the mitigating influence of procedural autonomy and the principles of equivalence and effectiveness.

5

Implementation of directives

5.1 The freedom with respect to form and methods

By making the distinction between that which is imperative, i.e. the result to be achieved, and that which is left to the discretion of the Member States, i.e. the choice of form and methods, Article 249(3) indicates what is within the competence of the Community and what remains within the competence of the Member States.[1] It also follows from this Article that the choice is limited to the *kind* of measures to be taken; their *content* is entirely determined by the directive at issue.[2] Thus the discretion as far as form and methods are concerned does not mean that Member States necessarily have a margin in terms of policy making.

The reasons for leaving the Member States the freedom to choose form and methods are twofold. On the one hand the need for the discretion was inspired by the concern to respect as far as possible the sovereignty and law-making power of the Member States and, in particular, the position of national parliaments. On the other hand, the freedom to choose form and methods gives the Member States a certain latitude and consequently enables them to take into account national (legal or other) peculiarities and economic, social, and other circumstances when implementing a directive.[3] This allows the Member States to insert the content of a directive into their national legal order, particularly into pre-existing national legislation related to the same matter, and to do so by means of the most appropriate and familiar legislative techniques. This latter aspect in particular is now considered to constitute the very essence of a directive.[4]

The exact meaning of the term 'form and methods' gave rise to some debate in earlier legal writing,[5] but it was not really conclusive. Therefore, it is not surprising that several authors restrict themselves, when discussing the freedom to choose form and

---

[1] Cf Kovar 1987, 365, De Ripainsel-Landy and Gérard 1976, 47. Although, as was pointed out by, for instance, Capotorti 1988, 153, the boundary between the mandatory results and the means implying a margin of appreciation is far from clear.

[2] Cf above, Ch 3, Section 3.2. See also Ipsen 1965, 74.

[3] Cf Fuß 1965, 379 and 381, Green 1984, 302, Bleckmann 1997, 163. What measures will be taken also depends on the 'state of the law' within the Member State concerned. Cf Capotorti 1988, 160 and Pescatore 1971, 92, who points out that in some cases national law will require a *'réforme profonde'* while in others a *'retouche à la legislation'* will suffice. [4] Cf Everling 1992a, 380.

[5] For a more detailed discussion see the first edition of this book, 86–8.

methods, to simply pointing out that it is the ways, or the different legal constructions,[6] that are left to the discretion of the Member States. The Court of Justice apparently also does not see the two terms as problematic, usually confining itself to their simple restatement or sometimes using slightly different words, like 'ways and means'.[7]

The choice of form and methods is left to the Member States, or more precisely, according to the terms of Article 249(3), to the national authorities. As explained above, in Chapter 4, Section 4.3, Community law is in principle not concerned with the question of which authorities enact the necessary measures, and it does not interfere with the internal structure of the Member States. Thus the choice of the measures, like the choice of the competent authority, is made within the framework of national constitutional law.[8] This is the purpose *and* consequence of the discretion which is left by Article 249(3) and the division of powers between the Community and the Member States which is entailed in it.[9]

The directive was designed as a relatively 'mild' instrument of Community intervention, leaving the Member States considerable leeway with respect to the measures to be taken for implementation. However, this freedom of the Member States is far from absolute. Firstly, as mentioned above,[10] directives can be extremely detailed. It is fairly obvious that the more precise and detailed the content of a directive, the less room for manoeuvre is left for the implementing authorities, with respect not only to the substance of the measures but also to the mode of implementation.[11]

Secondly, the scope of the Member States' discretion has been considerably curtailed by the Court of Justice. Following a somewhat hesitant start[12] the Court's case law began to develop rapidly after 1980. In Case 102/79 (tractors)[13] it held that a particular mode of implementation, depending on the content of the directive, may be necessary. In this particular case the directives at issue had to be converted into provisions of national law with the same legal force as those applicable in the Member State with regard to the subject matter of the directives. Likewise, later amendments of national implementing measures pursuant to a directive amending a preceding directive must be transposed by provisions of domestic law with the same legal force as the national provisions to be amended.[14] The Court also stressed

---

[6] Cf Kooymans 1967, 135 and Mertens de Wilmars 1991, 393.

[7] Cf Case 14/83 *Von Colson* [1984] ECR 1891, also in other languages ('*voies et moyens*'; '*Mittel and Wege*').   [8] Cf e.g. Capotorti 1988, 160 and Nettesheim 2002, 56.

[9] Cf also the Protocol on the Application of the Principles of Subsidiarity and Proportionality, attached to the Treaty of Amsterdam, stressing the need to respect as much as possible the Member States' internal organization and working of the legal system.   [10] Cf Ch 2, Section 2.1.

[11] Cf Capotorti 1988, 154 and Pescatore 1971, 92, who points out that a directive may restrict itself to the simple formulation of the objective to be achieved but equally it may impose upon the Member States a sort of '*loi modèle*'. Furthermore, the Member States scope for manoeuvre may also be limited by the 'notes for implementation' which the Commission issues in certain sectors. See e.g. http://europa.eu.int/comm/energy/electricity/legislation/notes_for_implementation_en.htm.

[12] Cf Case 48/75 *Royer* [1976] ECR 497 and Case 38/77 *Enka* [1977] ECR 2203.

[13] *Commission v. Belgium* [1980] ECR 1473.

[14] Cf Case 116/86 *Commission v. Italy* [1988] ECR 1323 and Case C–207/96 *Commission v. Italy* [1997] ECR I–6869.

that each Member State 'should implement the directives in question in a way which fully meets the requirements of clarity and certainty in legal situations which the directives seek . . . '.[15]

As the case law now stands, the way in which a directive is implemented must guarantee that the national authorities will in fact apply the directive fully and that, where the directive is intended to create rights for individuals, [their] legal position . . . is sufficiently precise and clear and the persons concerned are made fully aware of their rights and, where appropriate, afforded the possibility of relying on them before the national courts.[16]

The same applies *a fortiori* where a directive aims at creating obligations for individuals: the persons concerned must also be able to ascertain the full extent of their obligations.[17]

The central notions of this case law are the two intertwined principles of full effect[18] and legal certainty. On the basis of these two principles the Court has formulated a number of more specific requirements which the implementing measures must satisfy, namely the binding nature of these measures, specificity, precision, and clarity.[19] The requirements are, for their part, crucial for the opportunity of affected individuals to enforce their rights in national courts.[20] This principle of effective judicial protection is another central *Leitmotif* of the Court's case law.[21]

The concrete application of these principles may differ from case to case. Indeed, the approach of the Court is casuistic and cannot be otherwise. The evaluation of whether the requirements are met depends, on the one hand, on the provisions of the directive at issue and, on the other hand, on the implementing measures adopted by the Member States concerned; in every single case these two aspects must be compared with each other. Nevertheless some general lessons can also be drawn from this case law.

[15] Case 102/79 *Commission v. Belgium* [1980] ECR 1473, para 11. For a critical comment of this early case law see Green 1984, 298–300.

[16] Case 29/84 *Commission v. Germany* [1985] ECR 1661, para 18. Reiterated in a whole line of subsequent cases. See e.g. Case C–131/88 *Commission v. Germany* [1991] ECR I–825, Case C–58/89 *Commission v. Germany* [1991] ECR I–4983, Case 363/85 *Commission v. Italy* [1987] ECR 1733, Case C–96/95 *Commission v. Germany* [1997] ECR I–1653, Case C–144/99 *Commission v. the Netherlands* [2001] ECR I–3541, and Case C–455/00 *Commission v. Italy* [2002] ECR I–9231.

[17] Cf Case C–58/89 *Commission v. Germany* [1991] ECR I–4983, Case C–13/90 *Commission v. France* [1991] ECR I–4327, Case C–59/89 *Commission v. Germany* [1991] ECR I–2607, Case 257/86 *Commission v. Italy* [1988] ECR 3249, and Case C–366/89 *Commission v. Italy* [1993] ECR I–4201.

[18] In particular in the sense of producing effects in practice. Cf above, Ch 3, Section 3.3. Cf also e.g. Case C–340/96 *Commission v. UK* [1999] ECR I–2023.

[19] Cf Case C–361/88 *Commission v. Germany* [1991] ECR I–2567, Case C–58/89 *Commission v. Germany* [1991] ECR I–4983, Case 291/84 *Commission v. the Netherlands* [1987] ECR 3483, Case C–197/96 *Commission v. France* [1997] ECR I–1489, and Case C–455/00 *Commission v. Italy* [2002] ECR I–9231.

[20] This holds all the more true where the directive concerns rights of individuals of other Member States. Cf Case C–478/99 *Commission v. Sweden* [2002] ECR I–4147.

[21] Cf Case 29/84 *Commission v. Germany* [1985] ECR 1661, Case C–131/88 *Commission v. Germany* [1991] ECR I–825, Case C–360/87 *Commission v. Italy* [1991] ECR I–791, Case C–58/89 *Commission v. Germany* [1991] ECR I–4983, Case C–13/90 *Commission v. France* [1991] ECR I–4327, Case C–340/96

As pointed out above in Chapter 2, Section 2.6, three different problem areas can be distinguished with respect to the proper implementation of directives. These are the content of the measures, the nature of the measures, and the application and enforcement of the measures in practice. The principles described above have implications for all three of these areas.[22]

Following this trichotomy, the next three Sections aim to give a general overview of the requirements of adequate implementation as laid down in the case law of the Court of Justice.[23] They will not address the implementation policy and the problems related thereto within the Member States.

In the majority of cases the Court's case law concerns directives which, pursuant to their content, had to be *transposed* into national law. However, for the sake of comprehensiveness, I will in principle use the 'umbrella' term *implementation/ implementing measures*.[24]

5.2   The content of the measures implementing the directive

5.2.1   Clear and precise implementing measures

As regards the content of the measures, it was mentioned above that this must correspond with the directive to be implemented.[25] It was also noted that the Member States have in principle the choice between verbatim transposition on the one hand, and 'translation' of the directive into national legal concepts and terminology on the other (plus all the possible variations lying between these two extremes).[26]

According to the Court, the implementation of a directive does not in fact necessarily require that its provisions be transposed literally.[27] Neither is there a

---

Commission v. UK [1999] ECR I–2023, and Case C–478/99 *Commission v. Sweden* [2002] ECR I–4147. Cf also Everling 1992a, 382, Kovar 1987, 367 and Curtin 1990b, 716.

[22] Another limiting and important factor is indeed that implementing measures must comply with fundamental rights and primary community law. Cf Case 5/88 *Wachauf* [1989] ECR 2609 and Joined Cases C–20/00 and C–64/00 *Booker Aquaculture* [2003] ECR I–7411 and Case C–410/96 *Ambry* [1998] ECR I–7875.

[23] For overviews of the Court's case law see e.g. Heukels 1993, 63–70, Curtin 1990b, 714–18, Beyerlin 1987, 127–35, Kovar 1987, 365–72, Everling 1992a, 380–1 and Brent 2001, 109–29 and, in the area of environmental law, Somsen 2003, 1418–24. Cf also the Opinion of AG Van Gerven in Case C–131/88 *Commission v. Germany* [1991] ECR I–825, paras 6–11.

[24] For the distinction see above, Ch 1, Section 1.3.

[25] See above, Ch 2, Section 2.6. Cf also Case C–9/92 *Commission v. Greece* [1993] ECR I–4467.

[26] Ibid. Cf also Capotorti 1988, 161, who gives a brief overview of 'implementation techniques'.

[27] Cf Case C–131/88 *Commission v. Germany* [1991] ECR I–825, Case 363/85 *Commission v. Italy* [1987] ECR 1733. However, the national terminology must correspond with the terms employed by the directive; cf Case 412/85 *Commission v. Germany* [1987] ECR 3503, Case 247/85 *Commission v. Belgium* [1987] ECR 3029, Case 363/85 *Commission v. Italy* [1987] ECR 1733, and Case C–96/95 *Commission v. Germany* [1997] ECR I–1653.

requirement that the implementing measures must follow the structure of the directive.[28] However, the content of the implementing measures must be clear and precise, particularly when the directive is intended to create rights and duties for individuals.[29] Ambiguous provisions or provisions which are too generally worded[30] would leave the individuals uncertain both as to their rights and duties and as to the possibility of enforcing them in a court. Similarly, even if the directive is not intended to create such rights and duties, if the implementing measures are unclear and vague, the mere risk of their misapplication by domestic authorities may justify the requirements of clarity and precision being imposed.[31] Depending on the subject matter of the directive in question, a particularly precise and detailed transposition may be required for specific reasons, such as the absence of economic incentive for respecting the rules and the difficulties which effective monitoring of compliance with the rules in practice may pose.[32]

Usually, in order to satisfy these criteria, enactment of *specific* legislation will be necessary, since it is not very likely that pre-existing legislation will correspond with the (terminology of) the directive to be implemented. Yet according to the Court, a *general* legal context may be sufficient in certain circumstances, namely if it ensures the full application of the directive in a sufficiently clear and precise manner.[33] Thus the combination of existing (general) rules of national law, including general

---

[28] Thus the transposition of one single directive may be effectuated by amending several different national statutes and other pieces of (secondary) legislation. Cf Case C–190/90 *Commission v. the Netherlands* [1992] ECR I–3265.

[29] Cf Case C–131/88 *Commission v. Germany* [1991] ECR I–825, Case C–59/89 *Commission v. Germany* [1991] ECR I–2607, Case C–306/91 *Commission v. Italy* [1993] ECR I–2133, Case C–96/95 *Commission v. Germany* [1997] ECR I–1653, and Case C–144/99 *Commission v. the Netherlands* [2001] ECR I–3541. In Case C–356/00 *Testa* [2002] ECR I–10797 the Court observed that when Member States extend the application of a directive beyond Community law, in order not to create confusion, it must be clear that such legislation does not constitute the transposition of that directive.

[30] Cf Case 116/86 *Commission v. Italy* [1988] ECR 1323, Case C–360/87 *Commission v. Italy* [1991] ECR I–791, and Case C–455/00 *Commission v. Italy* [2002] ECR I–9231.

[31] Cf Case C–339/87 *Commission v. the Netherlands* [1990] ECR I–851, Case 247/85 *Commission v. Belgium* [1987] ECR 3029, and Case 262/85 *Commission v. Italy* [1987] ECR 3073. In the last case the Italian law implementing the directive at issue did not guarantee that regions, in their regulations, will fully comply with the obligations resulting from the directive, as the law itself was not sufficiently clear. Consequently, the regions were left in a state of uncertainty as to the scope of their obligations. Cf also Case C–324/01 *Commission v. Belgium* [2002] ECR I–11197.

[32] Cf the opinion of AG Van Gerven in Case C–131/88 *Commission v. Germany* [1991] ECR I–825, para 9. In Case 252/85 *Commission v. France* [1988] ECR 2243 and Case 236/85 *Commission v. the Netherlands* [1987] ECR 3989, for instance, the Court emphasized the need for faithful implementation because the directive concerned 'entrusted the management of a common heritage' to the Member States in their respective territories.

[33] Cf Case C–131/88 *Commission v. Germany* [1991] ECR I–825, Case C–360/87 *Commission v. Italy* [1991] ECR I–791, Case 252/85 *Commission v. France* [1988] ECR 2243, Case C–96/95 *Commission v. Germany* [1997] ECR I–1653, Case C–102/97 *Commission v. Germany* [1999] ECR I–5051, and especially Case C–190/90 *Commission v. the Netherlands* [1992] ECR I–3265, in which the Court accepted that a whole complex of rules (in particular a combination of legislative provisions and a system of permits) satisfied the requirements for adequate implementation.

principles of constitutional or administrative law,[34] and their application and interpretation, or the combination of general provisions and specific provisions enacted for the purposes of transposition of the directive[35] may suffice, provided that the necessary clarity and precision is guaranteed and that there is no practical or theoretical risk of misapplying the rules.[36] A combination of (pre-existing) imprecise provisions and administrative practice does not however satisfy these criteria.[37] Since administrative practices are often not given adequate publicity (e.g. administrative circulars that are not available), and do not allow individuals to become acquainted with their legal position, they cannot meet the requirement of legal clarity.[38]

In relation to these requirements of clarity, in particular in the sense of cognizability, and legal certainty the practice of transposition 'by reference' is questionable. In such a case national legislation is not translating or repeating the provisions as such but merely declares the ('hard core') provisions applicable within the national legal order. Such technique has as a serious shortcoming that the rules at issue are not always easily accessible.[39] Furthermore, it seems only acceptable when the provisions of the directive are sufficiently clear, precise, and detailed and need no further implementation.[40]

Finally, the requirement of clear and unambiguous legal situations also entails that all conflicting legislation must be repealed.[41]

5.2.2   Relevance of national case law

An integral part of the general legal context is the interpretation and application of national law by the national courts. As the Court of Justice has pointed out, the scope of national legal provisions must be assessed in the light of the interpretation given

---

[34] Cf Case 29/84 *Commission v. Germany* [1985] ECR 1661, Case 248/83 *Commission v. Germany* [1985] ECR 1459. Cf however also Case C–187/98 *Commission v. Greece* [1999] ECR I–7713, where Greece relied in vain on the direct effect of national constitutional provisions since the latter were apparently not sufficiently effective.

[35] Cf Case 163/82 *Commission v. Italy* [1983] ECR 3273. Cf also Case C–339/87 *Commission v. the Netherlands* [1990] ECR I–851 relating to a combination of a statute and ministerial regulation.

[36] Cf 363/85 *Commission v. Italy* [1987] ECR 1733 and Case C–96/95 *Commission v. Germany* [1997] ECR I–1653.

[37] Cf Case 29/84 *Commission v. Germany* [1985] ECR 1661, Case 116/86 *Commission v. Italy* [1988] ECR 1323, and Case 429/85 *Commission v. Italy* [1988] ECR 843.

[38] Cf Case 29/84 *Commission v. Germany* [1985] ECR 1661, Case C–131/88 *Commission v. Germany* [1991] ECR I–825; on administrative practices and their non-binding nature see below, Subsection 5.3.1.

[39] This is in particular problematic when the technique of 'dynamic reference' is used, which also covers the future amendments of the directive at issue. Cf for instance Klindt, 1998.

[40] Cf Timmermans 1997, 8–9, *Colloque des Conseils d'État 1996, Rapport général*, 21 and, for the area of public procurement, Arrowsmith 1998. On legislation by reference in general cf Haratsch 2000.

[41] Cf Case 169/87 *Commission v. France* [1988] ECR 4093, Case 74/86 *Commission v. Germany* [1988] ECR 2139, and Case C–259/01 *Commission v. France* [2002] ECR I–11093. For an application of the *lex posterior* rule in this context see Case C–145/99 *Commission v. Italy* [2002] ECR I–2235. See also Easson 1981, 30 and the Opinion of AG Darmon in Case C–338/91 *Steenhorst-Neerings* [1993] ECR I–5475, paras 49–50.

to them by the courts.[42] Therefore, in the absence of national case law, it is in principle difficult to determine whether a directive has been incorrectly transposed. In Case C–300/95 (product liability), for instance, the Commission was not able to refer to any national judicial decision which interprets the domestic provision at issue inconsistently with the directive, neither was there any evidence that the UK courts would not interpret national implementing provisions in concordance with the wording and purpose of the directive.[43] Consequently, its claim against the UK was dismissed. Conversely, in Case C–361/88 (*TA-Luft*)[44]the existence of case law could have assisted the German government: the Court did not accept the '*technical circular "air"* ' as an appropriate means of implementation *because* the government had not produced any *national cases* establishing that the circular had external effects *vis-à-vis* third parties instead of being binding only for the administration.[45] In brief, the question whether the general legal context can be considered as ensuring appropriate implementation of a directive will also depend on national case law.

This actually raises a more general problem: to what extent can case law be considered a proper means of implementation?[46] As far as the subject matter of this Subsection is concerned, the concrete question is whether a combination of an imprecise provision and its construction by national courts will satisfy the requirement of precision and clarity; provided, that is, that the construction itself is compatible with the directive at issue.[47] It is difficult to give a general answer to this question. On the one hand, construction of national law is an inevitable everyday business of the courts. On the other hand, vaguely formulated national provisions which must first be substantiated by case law will as such scarcely meet the requirements. The matter will thus first of all depend on the degree of imprecision. Secondly, a combination of a vague provision and its interpretation by the courts could possibly be accepted if the case law is adequately publicized and sufficiently predictable.[48]

---

[42] Cf e.g. Joined Cases C–132/91, C–138/91, and C–139/91 *Katsikas* [1992] ECR I–6577 and Case C–300/95 *Commission v. UK* [1997] ECR I–2649.

[43] Case C–300/95 *Commission v. UK* [1997] ECR I–2649. Cf also Opinion of AG Alber of 24 October 2002 in Case C–63/01 *Evans* (judgment of 4 December 2003, nyr in ECR), where, *inter alia*, the fact that national courts were not able to interpret national law in conformity with the directive made the AG decide that the UK had failed to implement the directive at issue properly. The Court did not share this view. See also below, Subsection 5.3.2 and Ch 8, Section 8.2.

[44] *Commission v. Germany* [1991] ECR I–2567.

[45] On external effects see below, Subsection 5.3.1.

[46] Cf Easson (1981, 29) who, thinking of the common law system, raised the problem of the subject matter of a directive being governed by case law rather than by statute. He wondered whether such a situation meets the requirement of maximum clarity. Cf also Ehricke 1999, 557–9 and *Colloque des Conseils d'État* 1996, *Rapport général*, 13–14.   [47] Cf e.g. Siems 2002.

[48] Cf in this respect the case law of the ECHR on judge-made rules of common law which may restrict certain rights and freedoms under the European Convention. In the *Sunday Times* case the European Court accepted that judge-made law may restrict Art 10(1) of the Convention. However, the law must be adequately accessible (the citizen must be able to have an indication that is adequate in the circumstances of the legal rules applicable in a given case) and it must be formulated with sufficient precision to enable the citizen to regulate his conduct. This case law is inspired by concerns of legal certainty comparable to those inspiring the case law of the ECJ (judgment of 26 April 1979, 2 EHRR 245, 271).

The first element may indeed pose problems, as the 'culture' of publishing courts' decisions differs from Member State to Member State. Moreover, the objection can be raised that nationals from a different Member State are normally not aware of case law existing within another Member State.[49]

There is indeed also a mirror image to this question of 'when can case law be considered a proper means of implementation?', namely, 'in what circumstances does national case law amount to an infringement?' This will have, in turn, consequences for the legislation. In infringement proceedings against Italy, the Court found that widely held judicial constructions which are not compatible with Community law and which, moreover have been confirmed by a supreme court, show that the relevant legislation is not sufficiently clear to safeguard its application in a way which is in conformity with Community law.[50]

The second condition could perhaps be satisfied once there exists established case law of a supreme national court.[51] In Case 235/84 (transfers of undertakings),[52] for instance, the Commission lost the case since it did not establish that Italian law failed to provide the protection required by Directive 77/187 (transfers of undertakings—protection of employees' rights),[53] in particular by not refuting the Italian government's argument that the protection was safeguarded by established case law of the *Corte Suprema di Cassazione*. On the other hand, in Case C–144/99 (unfair terms in consumer contracts)[54] the Court found that even where there is settled case law interpreting national law in a manner consistent with the directive, it cannot achieve the clarity and precision needed to meet the requirement of legal certainty.[55] Another relevant factor could also be the authority possessed by judicial decisions within the national legal system.[56] However, the risk that a (supreme) court will depart from its case law will remain.[57]

Unfortunately, the matter is even more complicated because the Court of Justice does not accept that interpretation of national law in conformity with a directive,

---

[49] Cf *mutatis mutandis* Case 29/84 *Commission v. Germany* [1985] ECR 1661 and Case C–478/99 *Commission v. Sweden* [2002] ECR I–4147.

[50] Cf Case C–129/00 *Commission v. Italy*, judgment of 9 December 2003, nyr in ECR, paras 32–33. See also the Opinion of AG Geelhoed of 3 June 2003, in particular paras 62–67.

[51] Cf the Opinion of AG Van Gerven in Joined Cases C–132/91, C–138/91, and C–139/91 *Katsikas* [1992] ECR I–6577, para 20. Isolated cases decided by lower courts do certainly not suffice. See Case C–58/02 *Commission v. Spain*, judgment of 7 January 2004, nyr in ECR.

[52] *Commission v. Italy* [1986] ECR 2291. Cf also Case C–382/92 *Commission v. United Kingdom* [1994] ECR I–2435.   [53] [1977] OJ L61/26.

[54] *Commission v. the Netherlands* [2001] ECR I–3541.

[55] However, it could be that this finding has been highly influenced by the fact that there was quite some disagreement about the existence of well-established and consistent case law in the Netherlands. See on this the Opinion of AG Tizzano, paras 22–37.

[56] In particular whether it constitutes a 'binding precedent' or not.

[57] Cf the Opinion of AG Darmon in Case C–338/91 *Steenhorst-Neerings* [1993] ECR I–5475, para 48. Cf also Ehricke 1999, 558, who points out, *inter alia*, that under the German Basic Law courts can always depart from previous case law (of higher courts).

in accordance with the obligation laid down in *Von Colson*,[58] can expunge incorrect implementation.[59] This raises the question of the delimitation of two concepts. On the one hand there is what I shall call '*interpretation within the context of judicial implementation*', denoting the interpretation by the courts of national law which, as such, constitutes correct implementation of the directive, although for the purposes of application of the rules in the concrete case further interpretation of the—by their very nature—abstract terms is necessary. On the other hand there is '*remedial interpretation*', i.e. interpretation of national law with a view to temporarily palliating the Member State's failure to implement the directive at all or to implement it correctly. I shall address these issues in more detail in Chapter 8. Nevertheless, it should be pointed out here that interpretation *contra legem* by the courts, a very farfetched interpretation or national case law consistently disapplying a national legal provision can certainly not result in national law being considered to be in conformity with the directive concerned.[60] The basic requirement of the Court's case law on proper implementation of directives is that individuals must be able to ascertain their rights and duties *from the legislative text itself*. It seems to me that the situation just described will draw too heavily on an individual's knowledge of the law.[61]

5.3 The nature of the implementing measures

5.3.1 Legally binding measures

The principles of full effectiveness, legal certainty, and effective judicial protection are also normative for the nature of the implementing measures.

On several occasions the Court has stressed that full implementation of directives must be secured not only in fact but also in law.[62] Absence of incompatible practice or the fact that a practice is consistent with the directive in question does not discharge the Member State concerned from the obligation of actually and fully

---

[58] Case 14/83 [1984] ECR 1891.

[59] Cf Everling 1992a, 380, Jans 1994, 252, the Opinion of AG Cruz Vilaça in Case 412/85 *Commission v. Germany* [1987] ECR 3503, para 19 and Case C–236/95 *Commission v. Greece* [1996] ECR I–4459.

[60] Cf the Opinion of AG Darmon in Case C–338/91 *Steenhorst-Neerings* [1993] ECR I–5475, para 47 concerning an application *contra legem* of a national social security provision in pursuance of Art 26 of the ICCPR by the *Centrale Raad van Beroep*. The Court's judgment in this case also makes plain that the judicial practice at issue did not amount to correct implementation. See in particular paras 33 and 34. Cf also Jans 1994, 253 and Case C–236/95 *Commission v. Greece* [1996] ECR I–4459.

[61] Cf also case law which makes clear that direct effect of the provisions at issue does not expunge inadequate implementation or non-implementation: Case 102/79 *Commission v. Belgium* [1980] ECR 1473. See also Case C–208/90 *Emmott* [1991] ECR I–4269.

[62] Cf Case C–339/87 *Commission v. the Netherlands* [1990] ECR I–851.

implementing the directive.[63] The basic requirement is that the measures giving effect to a directive must be *legally binding*.[64]

According to the Court's case law the choice of form and methods, which is left to the Member States, depends upon the result intended by the directive, and thus on the content of the directive.[65] The content should therefore be examined first. The central question to be answered seems to be whether the directive is intended to create rights and duties for individuals,[66] not only between national authorities and those directly concerned but also with respect to third parties.[67] As will be argued below,[68] the Court is quite readily disposed to accept that they do. However, in a number of cases the Court has held that directives must be implemented by national provisions of a binding nature, without addressing explicitly the issue of an individual's rights and duties or without addressing it at all.

In Case C–186/91 (consultations on nitrogen dioxide)[69] the Court found that in order to ensure complete and effective protection of the atmosphere against excessive concentrations of nitrogen dioxide it was indispensable that the Member State concerned should lay down explicitly in its legislation that consultations with the neighbouring Member State, provided for in Directive 85/203 (air quality— nitrogen dioxide),[70] must take place before certain limit values of nitrogen dioxide can be fixed in a border region. Although the Commission argued that Article 11 of the directive created rights and duties with regard to individuals, the Court disregarded this argument. Apparently the very purpose of the directive (and indeed the fact that concentrations of nitrogen dioxide do not observe borderlines) was sufficient grounds for the obligation at issue.[71]

---

[63] Cf Case C–131/88 *Commission v. Germany* [1991] ECR I–825 and Case C–366/89 *Commission v. Italy* [1993] ECR I–4201.

[64] Cf Mertens de Wilmars 1991, 397, Heukels 1993, 64, Capotorti 1988, 160.

[65] Cf Case 102/79 *Commission v. Belgium* [1980] ECR 1473; more recently, see e.g. Case C–59/89 *Commission v. Germany* [1991] ECR I–2607. According to Case C–190/90 *Commission v. the Netherlands* [1992] ECR I–3265, consistent case law.

[66] Cf Case 29/84 *Commission v. Germany* [1985] ECR 1661; more recently e.g. Case C–131/88 *Commission v. Germany* [1991] ECR I–825. According to Case C–306/89 *Commission v. Greece* [1991] ECR I–5863 and Case C–190/90 *Commission v. the Netherlands* [1992] I–3265, consistent case law.

[67] Cf the Opinion of AG Van Gerven in Case C–131/88 *Commission v. Germany* [1991] ECR I–825, para 7: environmental groups or neighbouring residents, for instance. However, an obligation for the Member States to provide regularly certain information or reports to the Commission may be of such a nature, that compliance with that obligation does not require the adoption of specific implementing measures in national law at all. Cf Case C–72/02 *Commission v. Portugal* [2003] ECR I–6597. The obligation at issue concerned only the relations between those Member States and the Commission.

[68] Cf Ch 6, Subsection 6.3.4.   [69] *Commission v. Belgium* [1993] ECR I–851.

[70] [1985] OJ L87/1.

[71] In this case explicit provision obliging the regions to consult neighbouring Member States was probably the more necessary since the subject matter was within their legislative competence. For a requirement to impose a duty of notification explicitly upon a decentralized body see Case C–237/90 *Commission v. Germany* [1992] ECR I–5973.

Furthermore, the Court categorically and particularly rejects administrative practices and circulars as a means of adequate implementation.[72]

In Case C–131/88 (German groundwater),[73] after having considered that the provisions in question had to be transposed with the precision and clarity necessary to satisfy fully the requirement of legal certainty because they were intended to create rights and obligations for individuals, the Court added that mere administrative practices, which are alterable at the will of the administration and are not given adequate publicity, cannot be regarded as constituting adequate implementation.[74]

As a rule, directives are enacted in order to harmonize the laws of the respective Member States and will, therefore, usually have implications for the legal position of individuals. Moreover, harmonization of laws, i.e. legally binding acts, cannot be properly assured by an instrument which does not have the same legal nature as the one to be harmonized. Consequently, it is not surprising that *in principle* the Court requires that provisions of directives are turned into binding rules of national law[75] or that the Member States establish a precise legal framework.[76]

The binding nature of provisions implementing a directive is of crucial importance in several respects. In the first place, administrative practices which may be changed as and when the administration pleases cannot guarantee the necessary legal certainty and will jeopardize the continuity of full application of the rules laid down in the directive. However, even if, by virtue of general principles of national (constitutional or administrative) law or specific instruments such as circulars, the rules are binding for the administration as such,[77] this is in principle not sufficient. Since the

---

[72] Cf Case 116/86 *Commission v. Italy* [1988] ECR 1323, Case 236/85 *Commission v. the Netherlands* [1987] ECR 3989, Case 239/85 *Commission v. Belgium* 1986] ECR 3645, Case 160/82 *Commission v. the Netherlands* [1982] ECR 4637, Case C–13/90 *Commission v. France* [1991] ECR I–4327, Case C–381/92 *Commission v. Ireland* [1994] ECR I–215, Case C–197/96 *Commission v. France* [1997] ECR I–1489, Case C–96/95 *Commission v. Germany* [1997] ECR I–1653, Case C–145/99 *Commission v. Italy* [2002] ECR I–2235, and Case C–259/01 *Commission v. France* [2002] ECR I–11093, in relation to practices which have been adopted by economic operators of a certain sector.

[73] *Commission v. Germany* [1991] ECR I–825, para 61.

[74] Similarly, provisions in general conditions for contracts issued by a (semi-public) undertaking do not satisfy these requirements. Cf Case C–220/94 *Commission v. Luxembourg* [1995] ECR I–1589. The requirement of implementing measures being binding and properly published entails also another important feature: it involves a degree of transparency which enables the Commission to control whether and how a directive has been transposed in national law. Cf the Opinion of AG Slynn in Case 29/84 *Commission v. Germany* [1985] ECR 1661, 1666.

[75] Cf Case 102/79 *Commission v. Belgium* [1980] ECR 1473, Case 96/81 *Commission v. the Netherlands* [1982] ECR 1791, Case 97/81 *Commission v. the Netherlands* [1982] ECR 1819, and Case C–361/88 *Commission v. Germany* [1991] ECR I–2567.

[76] Cf Case C–131/88 *Commission v. Germany* [1991] ECR I–825, Case C–339/87 *Commission v. the Netherlands* [1990] ECR I–851, Case C–13/90 *Commission v. France* [1990] ECR I–4327, Case C–64/90 *Commission v. France* [1991] ECR I–4335, and Case C–340/96 *Commission v. UK* [1999] ECR I–2023.

[77] For instance by virtue of the doctrine of 'self-binding of the administration' as it exists in German law or because it results from the hierarchic structure of the administration. Cf Case C–13/90 *Commission v. France*

ratio for demanding implementation by binding measures is often the rights and obligations a directive is intended to create for individuals, the binding force must produce *external* effects,[78] i.e. the measures must bind the administration *vis-à-vis* private individuals (and *vice versa* in the case of obligations).[79] It is also important in this respect that legally binding measures are given appropriate publicity.

For individuals, the binding nature of the implementing measures is significant from two points of view: from the point of view of legal certainty, since it enables them to ascertain in a sufficiently predictable manner the extent of their rights and duties, and from the point of view of effective judicial protection, since it gives them a defined legal position.

Thus *full* (i.e. internally and externally) binding force of implementing measures is essential for both the application of the rules by the administration and the position of those subjected to them. It is for these reasons that the Court requires, *inter alia*, that prohibitions and possible derogations from them, or conditions for granting, refusing, or withdrawing of permits, must expressly be laid down in national legal provisions.[80]

The requirement of being binding in nature must, in the first place, be satisfied by the measures specifically enacted for the purpose of implementation. Secondly, if the Member State concerned argues that the rules of the directive are guaranteed by the general legal context, this combination of rules and their application must similarly produce the desired legal effects. In Case C–339/87 (wild birds) the Court accepted that implementation can be effected by a legislative provision serving as the basis for the adoption of administrative measures, provided that the latter are officially published, general in scope, and capable of creating rights and obligations for individuals.[81] In Case 248/83 (equal treatment in public service) the Court found that since the relevant provisions of the German Basic Law are intended to be directly applicable and there is an existing system of judicial remedies, including the possibility of instituting proceedings before the Constitutional Court, the legal context constitutes an adequate guarantee for implementation.[82]

[1991] ECR I–4327: according to the full text of the judgment (summary publication only in ECR) the circular at issue '*contient des instructions et recommandations qui s'imposent, en vertu du pouvoir hiérarchique, aux commissaires de la République*' (para 10). Cf also the Opinion of AG Slynn in Case 29/84 *Commission v. Germany* [1985] ECR 1661, 1666, who pointed out that in the case of binding force by virtue of general principles of law a change is possible without intervention of the legislator.

[78] According to Everling 1992, 383 the lack of external effects was decisive in the *TA-Luft* case (Case C–361/88 *Commission v. Germany* [1991] ECR I–2567). There was hardly any doubt about the binding force upon the administration as such. Cf also Case C–9/92 *Commission v. Greece* [1993] ECR I–4467.

[79] Cf Case C–361/88 *Commission v. Germany* [1991] ECR I–2567, Case C–131/88 *Commission v. Germany* [1991] ECR I–825, and Case C–190/90 *Commission v. the Netherlands* [1992] ECR I–3265.

[80] Cf Case 252/85 *Commission v. France* [1988] ECR 2243, Case C–339/87 *Commission v. the Netherlands* [1990] ECR I–851, Case 300/81 *Commission v. Italy* [1983] ECR 449, and Case 291/84 *Commission v. the Netherlands* [1987] EC 3483.

[81] Case C–339/87 *Commission v. the Netherlands* [1990] ECR I–851. Cf also Case C–435/92 *Association pour la protection des animaux sauvages* [1994] ECR I–67.

[82] Case 248/83, *Commission v. Germany* [1985] ECR 1459.

In general, however, the Court is not easily satisfied in this respect.[83] In particular, binding force through the application of general principles of constitutional or administrative law is closely scrutinized and is not readily accepted, since the effects of these are not often undisputed.[84]

5.3.2   Implementation by agreements

So far, the discussion has focused on the implementation of directives dealing with— what can be called—'vertical relationships', i.e. directives concerning primarily the relationship between national authorities and individuals. However, a considerable number of directives purport to regulate legal relationships between natural or legal persons. In other words, they are intended to create rights and obligations for individuals *inter se*. The need to implement this type of directive by binding rules of national law is quite evident. Yet comparable problems concerning the binding nature of the measures may occur in this area as well. Particularly in the field of labour law, the question has been raised whether directives can be implemented by means of collective agreements instead of being transposed into national legislation.[85] Although the Court considered that the implementation of certain issues of labour law may in the first instance be left to the representatives of management and labour,[86] it does not however release the Member States from their obligation of ensuring, by appropriate legislative and administrative provisions, that the rules of the directive are fully transposed and applied. This means firstly that, in terms of their content, collective agreements must fully correspond with the directive at issue. The Member States must be able to intervene by appropriate measures against inadequacies resulting from collective negotiations.[87]

However, in so far as relevant for the purpose of this Subsection, the major problem with collective agreements is that—even when taken as a whole—they do not necessarily cover all the persons protected by the directive in question, as they are only binding for the members of the trade unions and the employers who are party to the agreement; if, indeed, they are legally binding at all.[88] In such a case the Member States

---

[83] Cf Case C–361/88 *Commission v. Germany* [1991] ECR I–2567, in particular para 20 and Case C–187/98 *Commission v. Greece* [1999] ECR I–7713.

[84] Cf Case 29/84 *Commission v. Germany* [1985] ECR 1661, in particular paras 28–32. Cf also the observations on judicial construction as a part of the general legal context made above in Subsection 5.2.2.   [85] Cf Adinolfi 1988 and Heukels 1993, 65.

[86] Sometimes this is explicitly provided for in certain directives. See e.g. Directive 91/533 (conditions of employment relationship—information of employees) [1991] OJ L288/32, Art 9, Directive 92/56 (collective redundancies) [1992] OJ L245/3, Art 2, Directive 92/85 (pregnant workers), [1992] OJ L348/1, Art 14, and Directive 2000/43 (non-discrimination on grounds of race), [2000] OJ L180/22, Article 16. Cf further Case 235/84 *Commission v. Italy* [1986] ECR 2291, Case 91/81 *Commission v. Italy* [1982] ECR 2133, and Case 143/83 *Commission v. Denmark* [1985] ECR 427.

[87] Cf Case 312/86 *Commission v. France* [1988] ECR 6315, Case 165/82 *Commission v. UK* [1983] ECR 3431.

[88] In the UK, for instance, the legal status of collective agreements is controversial and, in particular, they are not enforceable in the courts. Cf Adinolfi, 1988, 310. Cf also Case 165/82 *Commission v. UK* [1983] ECR 3431.

are obliged to secure the application of the agreement(s) to all the persons falling within the personal scope of the directive, for instance by extending them *erga omnes*,[89] or they must 'fill the gaps' by appropriate additional binding measures.[90] The result is then implementation through a combination of legislation and collective agreements.

The approach of the Court of Justice is reflected in Article 137(4) of the EC Treaty. This Article provides that management and labour may be entrusted with the implementation of certain directives, but the Member States must ensure that the social partners have introduced the necessary measures no later than the date on which the directive in question had to be transposed. Moreover, the Member States are required to take any necessary measures enabling them at any time to be in a position to guarantee the results imposed by the directive.[91]

In the field of environmental law, certain directives may be transposed by so-called environmental agreements, i.e. agreements between national authorities and other parties concerned, like certain branches of industry, which aim at the realization of certain environmental objectives. The problems in this area are comparable to those of collective labour agreements, such as the voluntary nature, non- or limited publicity, limited coverage and continuity, and difficulties related to their enforcement. Some directives provide for the implementation by means of an environmental agreement. In that case, the latter might be accepted by the Court as a valid means of implementation.[92]

In 1996, the Commission adopted a recommendation which sets specific (and rather strict) guidelines for the use of environmental agreements as an instrument for implementation.[93] Like in the case of collective labour agreements, a combination of a strong legislative framework and environmental agreements is indicated.[94]

Finally, another type of agreement that was supposed to serve the purpose of implementation was at issue in *Evans*.[95] In order to give effect to Article 1 of Directive 84/5 (insurance against civil liability—motor vehicles),[96] the Secretary of State for Environment, Transport and the Regions concluded a number of private law agreements with the MIB (Motor Insurers' Bureau, a private-law entity). The MIB

---

[89] That may however be difficult in some Member States. Adinolfi 1988, 305, for instance, reports a judgment of the Italian Constitutional Court which found such an extension to be unconstitutional. A *de facto* extension, on the other hand, is questionable from the point of view of legal certainty.

[90] Cf Case 143/83 *Commission v. Denmark* [1985] ECR 427, Case 235/84 *Commission v. Italy* [1986] ECR 2291. In addition to this there are also problems of continuity, publicity, and enforcement/ judicial protection. Cf Nielsen 2002.

[91] Cf e.g. also Art 2 of Directive 1999/70 (fixed-term work) [1999] OJ L175/43. For a detailed discussion of European collective agreements and their implementation see Franssen 2002, in particular Chs 5, 6, and 7.

[92] Cf Case C–255/93 *Commission v. France* [1994] ECR I–4949, concerning Directive 93/76 (carbon dioxide emissions—energy efficiency) [1993] OJ L237/28. The case law is not entirely clear on this issue. Cf also Case C–340/96 *Commission v. UK* [1999] ECR I–2023. However, see also Case C–96/98 *Commission v. France* [1999] ECR I–8531, in which the contracts between the State and the farmers were not accepted, *inter alia*, for their voluntary character.

[93] Commission Recommendation 96/733 concerning environmental agreements implementing Community directives [1996] OJ L333/59. Cf also Council Resolution on environmental agreements, [1997] OJ C321/6.　　　[94] For a more detailed discussion see Verschuuren 2000 and Jans 2000, 146–8.

[95] Case C–63/01 *Evans*, judgment of 4 December 2003, nyr in ECR.　　　[96] [1984] OJ L8/17.

was under the obligation to pay compensation for injuries caused by uninsured or untraced drivers. Advocate-General Alber found that such an agreement, as a basis for rights of injured persons, is not *per se* objectionable. However, since the rights of these persons were not identifiable, could not be pursued with the requisite clarity and certainty, and, moreover, were not enforceable against the MIB by the victims, the agreement could not amount to proper implementation of the Directive. On the latter point the Court decided otherwise: it accepted the agreement as a proper way of implementing the directive, though under the proviso that adequate judicial protection is guaranteed through the interpretation and application of the agreement.[97]

5.4 The application and enforcement of directives and the requirements resulting therefrom for implementing measures

As explained in Chapter 3, Section 3.3, the obligations imposed upon Member States are not fulfilled by the mere enactment of national rules. The rules must also be applied and enforced in practice.[98]

As regards their application, it is up to the Member States to decide—where appropriate—upon the national body which will be responsible. It goes without saying that the competent national authority must act in conformity with the rules laid down in the directive.[99] In this respect, the requirements, discussed above, of clarity and precision of the implementing measures and their legally binding nature are crucial for avoiding their misapplication and ensuring that the administration *will* apply them. Likewise, with regard to directives (primarily) concerning relationships between private individuals or intended to impose obligations upon individuals, the same requirements are a prerequisite for securing compliance with the terms of the directives which underlie the national implementing measures. Briefly, the requirements imposed by the Court as to the content of the measures and their nature must guarantee the correct application of the directive in practice as well. This will hardly come as a surprise, since the principle of full effect, including actual application of the rules,[100] together with the principle of legal certainty, forms the very basis of these requirements.

As in the case of national rules, in order to compel observance, by natural or legal persons, of the provisions of the directive (as transposed in national law) the State will often be obliged to provide an appropriate system of sanctions,[101] since

---

[97] Cf point 37 of the judgment. For an implementation through a method of undertakings between the Secretary of State and water companies which did not satisfy the requirement of a precise legal framework see Case C–340/96 *Commission v. United Kingdom* [1999] ECR I–2023.

[98] Moreover, in that Chapter, Section 3.2.1, I have also briefly pointed at a new development in the field of enforcement, namely the role which national regulatory authorities play in this respect.

[99] Cf above, Ch 4, Section 4.4.   [100] Cf above, Ch 3, Section 3.3.

[101] 'Sanctions' are interpreted here broadly, namely as legal consequences laid down in a secondary norm for non-compliance with a primary norm of conduct. Similarly, the Member States must ascertain that there exist measures *within* the administration which ensure the observance of the rules at issue. This is primarily an internal matter of the Member State. Cf above, Ch 4, Section 4.3.

otherwise effective enforcement will be unrealistic. With respect to these sanctions three different situations can be distinguished.[102]

Firstly, in some cases, a directive may give specific indications as to the sanctions which should be imposed for non-compliance with the norm resulting from the directive. Under Directive 76/207 (equal treatment at work), for instance, provisions contrary to the principle of equal treatment which are included in individual contracts shall be, or may be declared, null and void.[103] Another form of specific sanction is exemplified by the possible withdrawal of authorization provided for in Directive 73/293 (insurance other than life assurance I),[104] or different measures spelled out in Directive 92/28 (advertising of medicinal products) in the case of misleading advertising.[105]

Secondly, some directives stipulate in fairly general terms that the Member States shall introduce penalties for failure to comply with the provisions adopted pursuant to the directive and that the penalties must be suitable or sufficient to promote compliance with the provisions concerned.[106]

As from the mid-1990s,[107] in its proposals the Commission has tightened up its legislative practice in this respect. It uses either a standard clause (referring to effective, proportionate, and dissuasive sanctions) or a more specific clause, as appropriate, in order to prescribe explicitly that the Member States must introduce certain sanctions.[108] As a rule, the character of the sanctions—civil, administrative, or criminal—is left to the Member States.[109]

In these examples, the requirements relating to sanctions have been a part of the content of a directive and, depending on the terms of the relevant provisions, they entail different margins of discretion for the Member States when transposing them. However, it is the third and still large category of directives which is the most interesting; namely those in which no indications whatsoever are given as to the sanctions to be imposed.

[102] Cf Timmermans (Rapport communautaire) in FIDE Reports 1992, 36–42.
[103] [1976] OJ L39/40, Art 5(2)b.   [104] [1973] OJ L228/3, Art 22(1)c.
[105] [1992] OJ L113/13; e.g. courts or administrative authorities must be able to order the cessation or the prohibition of misleading advertising (Art 12(2)).
[106] Cf Art 16 of Directive 91/477 (arms control) [1991] OJ L256/51, Art 5 of Directive 92/59 (product safety) [1992] OJ L228/24, Art 14 of Directive 91/308 (money laundering) [1991] OJ L166/77, Art 13 of Directive 89/592 (insider dealing) [1989] OJ L334/30, Art 19 of Directive 92/46 (milk products) [1992] OJ L268/1. On the implementation of such an explicit provision see Case C–225/97 *Commission v. France* [1999] ECR I–3011.
[107] Cf in this respect Council Resolution of 29 June 1995 on the effective uniform application of Community law and on the penalties applicable for breaches of Community law in the internal market [1995] OJ C188/1.
[108] Cf Timmermans 1998, 27–8. See e.g. Art 14 of Directive 2003/6 (insider dealing and market manipulation) [2003] OJ L96/16, and Art 15 of Directive 2000/43 (non-discrimination on the ground of race) [2000] OJ L180/22. Cf the proposed directive on criminal protection of the Community's financial interests [2001] OJ C240/125. In 2001 the Commission also attempted to propose a complete directive on the protection of the environment through criminal law ([2001] OJ C180/238). In 2003 the Council did adopt such an instrument, but then in the form of a framework decision ([2003] OJ L29/55). Recently, the Commission has brought an action for annulment of this framework decision. See Case C–176/03 *Commission v. Council*, pending.
[109] Indeed, the character of the sanction is often to be determined more or less by the area of law in which the directives is to be implemented.

The Member States consequently appear to enjoy a considerable margin of discretion in two respects: firstly as to whether they will provide for sanctions at all and secondly, if they do, as to the form and content the sanctions will have. In both of these respects, however, the discretion is becoming less and less unfettered.

As to the question *whether* Member States must provide for sanctions, from their obligation 'to adopt in their national legal systems all the measures necessary to ensure that the directive is fully effective, in accordance with the objective which it pursues'[110] it follows that the answer will depend on the objective of the directive at issue. The Court's case law on this went through an interesting development. This development started in the context of Directive 76/207 (equal treatment at work).[111] With respect to this directive, the Court held that both from its actual purpose, i.e. to establish real equality of opportunity, and from Article 6, which requires that (alleged) victims of discrimination must be able to pursue their claims by judicial process, it follows that the Member States must provide for *an* appropriate system of sanctions.[112] Moreover, the Court also specified the conditions under which the sanction can be considered to be appropriate, in the light of the objective of the directive at issue. In *Von Colson* the Court stipulated that the sanction chosen must be such as to guarantee real and effective judicial protection and it must have a real deterrent effect.[113] If the Member State chooses the award of compensation, the latter must be adequate in relation to the damage sustained. *Marshall II*[114] made clear that 'adequate' means that the loss and damage actually sustained must be made good in full, including the award of interest, which in the Court's view is an essential component of compensation.[115]

Furthermore, as appears from the judgment in the *Dekker* case,[116] the requirement that the sanction must be effective not only concerns the sanction itself and its content, but also has consequences for the substantive conditions which must be fulfilled before the sanction can be imposed. According to the judgment in *Dekker*, the requirements of fault and absence of grounds of exemption applicable under the Dutch rules on civil liability had to be disregarded.

Meanwhile, the Court's case law on sanctions expanded far beyond the area of equal treatment of men and women. There exists now a general requirement that sanctions must be effective, proportionate, and dissuasive.[117]

---

[110] Case 14/83 *Von Colson* [1984] ECR 1891, para 15. This requirement also implies that the Member States are allowed to adopt provisions other than sanctions for which the directive does not provide at all but which are nevertheless useful for ensuring the full effect of the directive: cf Case C–143/91 *Van der Tas* [1992] ECR I–5045.   [111] [1976] OJ L39/40.

[112] The choice whether it should be a sanction under civil law, administrative law, or criminal law was left to the Member States.

[113] Case 14/83 [1984] ECR 1891, confirmed ever since then. See e.g. case C–180/95 *Draehmpaehl* [1997] ECR I–2195.   [114] Case C–271/91 [1993] ECR I–4367.

[115] See, however, Case C–66/95 *Sutton* [1997] ECR I–2163, where national rules which do not provide for the payment of interest were upheld by the Court. On compensation, see also below, Ch 10, Subsection 10.5.2. Cf also Ch 7, Subsection 7.3.4.   [116] Case C–177/88 [1990] ECR I–3941.

[117] Cf Case C–341/94 *Allain* [1996] ECR I–4631, Case C–29/95 *Pastoors* [1997] ECR I–0285, Case C–186/98 *Nunes* [1999] ECR I–4883 and cases referred to in note 113.

In Case 68/88 (Greek maize),[118] in relation to an inadequate enforcement of a regulation, the Court held that where Community legislation does not specifically provide any penalty for an infringement or refers for that purpose to national law, by virtue of Article 10 of the Treaty the Member States are required to take all measures to guarantee the application and the effectiveness of Community law.[119]

This requirement entails in particular that, firstly, breaches of Community law are penalized under conditions, both procedural and substantive, which are analogous to those applicable to infringements of national law of a similar nature; secondly, that penalties and the procedures which result in imposing them are in any event effective, proportionate, and dissuasive, and thirdly, that national authorities must proceed with respect to infringements of Community law with the same diligence as that which they bring to bear in implementing corresponding national laws.[120]

From case law that followed later it appears that these requirements apply equally in the field of directives.[121] Unlike in *Von Colson*, where the requirement of sanctions and their contents was based on the interpretation of Article 249(3) and the terms of the directive, in the more recent cases the basis is Article 10 of the EC Treaty.

Moreover, there are, in more recent case law, two types of requirements; namely the 'comparability' with sanctions for breaches of 'purely' national law and the requirements as to the effectiveness, proportionality, and dissuasive effect. As the second must be satisfied *in any event*, the two types obviously apply in a cumulative way.[122] Accordingly, even if the sanctions are comparable but, from the point of view of Community law, ineffective, disproportionate, or not dissuasive, they do not meet the standard resulting from Article 10.

What the terms effective, proportional and dissuasive imply in a particular set of circumstances is certainly not always clear. Arguably, *effective* should be understood in this context as producing the desired result, which is to compel observance of the terms and spirit of Community law, *proportionate* as referring

---

[118] *Commission v. Greece* [1989] ECR 2965.

[119] Cf also Case 50/76 *Amsterdam Bulb* [1977] ECR 137 in which, however, the Court merely stated that the Member States are competent to adopt such sanctions as appear to them to be appropriate (para 32).

[120] Confirmed also in Case C–326/88 *Hansen* [1990] ECR I–2911 and Case C–7/90 *Vandevenne* [1991] ECR I–4371. The requirement that the national authorities must act with the same care and attention as they exercise in applying national law was already laid down in older case law. See e.g. Joined Cases 119 and 126/79 *Lippische Hauptgenossenschaft* [1980] ECR 1863. For a 'codification' of these requirements, as far as fraud with Community money is concerned, see Article 280 EC Treaty.

[121] Case C–382/92 *Commission v. United Kingdom* [1994] ECR I–2435, Case C–383/92 *Commission v. United Kingdom* [1994] ECR I–2479, Case C–5/94 *Hedley Lomas* [1996] ECR I–2553 (in particular para 19), and Joined Cases C–58/95, C–75/95, C–112/95, C–119/95, C–123/95, C–135/95, C–140/95, C–141/95, C–154/95, and C–157/95 *Gallotti* [1996] ECR I–4345 and Case C–354/99 *Commisson v. Ireland* [2001] ECR I–7657.

[122] Cf the Opinion of AG Van Gerven in Case C–271/91 *Marshall II* [1993] ECR I–4367, para 15.

to the relation between the nature of the offence committed and the sanction imposed laying down both a lower limit and an upper limit, and *dissuasive* as preventing disobedience of the Community law rules.[123] Until now, the application of these criteria translated often into a negative test. However, as has been rightly pointed out,[124] a crucial issue is to formulate positive criteria for determining the adequacy or effectiveness of a remedy or a sanction.

The comparability issue is also relevant in another type of case, decided in a different context and forming in a way a mirror image of the problems at issue here; namely those in which the sanctions for infringement of rules originating in Community law or falling within the scope of Community law are more severe than those for breaches of similar provisions of national law. As long as the two types of provisions and their respective infringements can be compared,[125] the comparability principle, which is often applied together with the principle of proportionality, may function as an *upper* limit to the sanctions.[126]

Finally, the requirements laid down by the Court apparently not only concern the content of the sanctions but also relate to the procedures which result in their imposition. In this respect it should be noted that if national authorities proceed with respect to infringements of Community law with the same *negligence* as with respect to national laws, rather than diligence, Community law may require a higher standard of control and enforcement than that which is common practice in the Member State concerned.[127]

To conclude this Section, a remark should be made regarding judicial protection. Obviously, a system of effective judicial protection is vital for the enforcement of norms resulting from a directive,[128] and it is, as pointed out above, one of the principles underlying the requirements posed by the Court concerning the implementing measures. This principle therefore curtails the freedom of the Member States with respect to form and methods of implementation. This principle will be discussed at greater length in Chapter 7.

---

[123] For a slightly different definition of the terms effective, proportionate, and dissuasive see the Opinion of AG Van Gerven in Case C–326/88 *Hansen* [1990] ECR I–2911, para 8. For a discussion of 'effectiveness' see also Harding 1997.   [124] Cf Van Gerven 2000, 529–35.

[125] Cf Case 8/77 *Sagulo* [1977] ECR 1495 and, although in a slightly different context, Case 299/86 *Drexl* [1988] ECR 1213.

[126] Cf Case 118/75 *Watson and Belmann* [1976] ECR 1185, Case 299/86 *Drexl* [1988] ECR 1213, and Case C–276/91 *Commission v. France* [1993] ECR I–4413.

[127] Cf on this aspect Weatherill 1997, in particular 40–3.

[128] Cf also Timmermans (Rapport communautaire) in FIDE Reports 1992, 21–5 and Mertens de Wilmars 1991, 395–6.

6

Directives as sources of rights

6.1 The place of directives within the national legal system

Behind the austere terms of Article 249(3) there hides a complex reality which the drafters of the Treaty probably never dreamed of. Instead of merely giving general instructions for action, as its name would at first sight suggest, the directive has developed into a fully fledged legislative instrument of the Community. The most essential characteristic distinguishing it from a regulation is the fact that a directive is never self-sufficient. In order to be fully effective, implementing measures have to be enacted at national level. As a rule, the implementation of a directive requires its transposition into national law. In particular, due to the last factor, in the early years of the Community it seemed inconceivable that directives could be of any direct relevance to private individuals.[1] However, reality has proven to be different. Today, directives are invoked by individuals for several purposes and they are frequently applied or, at least, taken into account as legal rules by national courts.

The fundamental choice made by the Court of Justice in *Van Gend en Loos* and *Costa v. ENEL*[2] as to the relationship between Community law and national law in general also determines the place of directives within the legal orders of the Member States. The Community's own legal system is an integral part of the legal systems of the Member States.[3] This means that the whole body of Community law (including directives, which are a component of this law) is as such incorporated within the national legal orders, without measures of transformation, incorporation—or whatever else the terminology might be—being necessary.[4] This *automatic* incorporation was in the past not always readily accepted. While regulations engendered the least discussion in legal writing, since the Treaty provides that they are 'directly applicable' in the Member States,[5] the status of other provisions of Community law, and directives in particular, was regarded as uncertain, to say the least.

---

[1] For a brief overview of the different positions see e.g. Lauwaars 1973, 33–5 and Louis 1993, 501–5.
[2] Case 26/62 [1963] ECR 1 and Case 6/64 [1964] ECR 585.
[3] Confirmed recently in Joined Cases C–6/90 and C–9/90 *Francovich* [1991] ECR I–5357.
[4] For terminology and analysis see e.g. Kovar 1987, 351–62 and Kovar 1983, 130–7.
[5] On the concept of 'direct applicability', which I do not use in the technical sense often attributed to it, namely as not necessitating incorporation, see Ch 9, Subsection 9.3.1.

Today the discussion on the status of directives seems to be outdated and there can be little doubt that in the view of both the Court of Justice and the majority of Community law scholars directives *are* integrated in the national legal systems as from the date of their entry into force.[6] If this were otherwise, there would be no explanation for the fact that individuals can rely on provisions of Community directives before national courts and that the latter must take them into consideration as elements of Community law which they are bound to apply. Indeed, the concept of direct effect of directive provisions is based on the very theory that directives are a part of the national legal order.[7] Similarly, the Court's case law obliging national authorities and, in particular, national courts to interpret national law in conformity with a directive can more readily be understood if one accepts that directives are an integral part of the legal systems of the Member States.[8] Once a directive has entered into force and become a part of the law in the Member States, it should as a rule produce effects since, as is generally assumed, any legal rule is in principle intended to operate effectively.[9] In the vast majority of cases legal rules are designed to be applied in practice. A different question is whether such an application is possible in a concrete case and, if it is, how this application will take shape.[10] The answer depends on several other factors, such as the purpose for which an individual is relying on a provision and whether this can be satisfied by a court, having regard to the terms and content of the relevant provision.

A difference with respect to directives is that they are devised to become fully operative in national law through implementation, and the Member States are given a certain period of time for the purpose of accomplishing this. This is an additional factor to be taken into account when the question of possible modalities of application of directives is addressed.[11] This does not, however, alter the fact that directives *are* a part of the body of law which is valid within the national legal order[12] and may as such produce various kinds of effect.[13]

As was already briefly discussed in Chapter 2, directives may, together with Article 10, produce certain effects between the entry into force of the directive and the deadline for its implementation.[14] Furthermore, as the *Tobacco* case of 2002 made

---

[6] For a brief overview of the discussion and further references see the first edition of this book, 119.

[7] Declaring that Community law is a part of the national legal order is the quintessence of Case 26/62 *Van Gend en Loos* [1963] ECR 1. On this basis the Court was able to develop the doctrine of direct effect. Cf Kapteyn and VerLoren van Themaat 1998, 82–9. See also Mertens de Wilmars 1969, 69 and Everling 1984, 107.   [8] Cf Everling 1984, 107.

[9] Pescatore 1983, 155. Although, as was observed by Emmert 1992, 66, the stepmotherly way in which, in this perspective, Pescatore treats directives is striking. Cf also Mertens de Wilmars 1991, 398.

[10] Very illuminating in this respect is the four-step approach made by Klein 1988, 8–9 who distinguishes 1) the '*Existenz*' and '*Gültigkeit*' of the norm (existence and validity), 2) '*Geltung*' (its force as law to be applied within the State), 3) '*Anwendbarkeit*' (its applicability or its suitability to be applied), and 4) '*Anwendung*' (its actual application in a concrete case). Cf for a similar approach Langenfeld 1992, 955–7, Bach 1990, 1110–11.   [11] Cf Klein 1988, 12, Pescatore 1980, 171.

[12] Cf Everling 1984, 106–7, Kovar 1987, 365.

[13] Cf Langefeld 1992, 957, Timmermans 1979, 534–5.

[14] Section 2.3 and, in particular, Case C–129/96 *Inter-environnement Wallonie* [1997] ECR I–7411.

clear, the very existence of a directive, even during the implementation phase, may produce effects which, as such, may justify preliminary questions as to the *validity* of the directive before the period for its implementation has expired.[15] In that particular case the issue was the authority of the United Kingdom Government to apply section 2(2) of the European Communities Act. On the other hand, since, according to the CFI, a directive cannot of itself, before the adoption of national transposing measures and independently of them, impose obligations on economic operators, it does not affect them directly for the purposes of Article 230(4) EC Treaty.[16]

The theory that directives are, as a part of Community law, integrated into the legal systems of the Member States says nothing as such about their position *vis-à-vis* other national rules. However, from the case law of the Court of Justice it follows unambiguously that directives take precedence over the law of the Member States. Ever since *Costa v. ENEL*[17] the Court has constantly affirmed the supremacy of Community law over national law. This principle holds true for both primary and secondary Community law and, in my opinion, irrespective of whether the provisions at issue are directly effective or not. Although direct effect and supremacy often go hand in hand, they are two separate concepts.[18] The reason why they are often coupled[19] is that, as a rule, national courts encounter supremacy each time an individual relies on a directly effective provision of Community law in order to have contrary provisions of national law set aside and to have the Community provision applied instead, where necessary. However, the principle of supremacy also means that a national court may not review the validity of Community acts in the light of national provisions of (constitutional) law.[20] In such a case the individual does not rely on the provisions of Community law in the sense indicated above. On the contrary, the person then argues that the Community act is invalid, for instance, for reasons of incompatibility with his constitutionally guaranteed rights. Similarly, it is submitted, the national courts may not construe the Community law provision in accordance with national legal rules.

From the point of view of the courts and, arguably, also from the point of view of national administration,[21] supremacy can be conceived as a rule of conflict. For the legislator, the principle of supremacy has more the effect of blocking the enactment of unilateral and contrary national measures[22] and of national legal provisions being brought into line with Community law.[23]

---

[15] Case C–491/01 *British American Tobacco (Investments) Ltd* [2002] ECR I–11453.

[16] Joined Cases T–172/98, T–175/98, T–176/98, and T–177/98 *Salamander and Others v. Parliament and Council* [2000] ECR II–2487. [17] Case 6/64 [1964] ECR 585.

[18] Cf Kovar 1983, 114, Mertens de Wilmars 1969, 71, Lauwaars and Timmermans 2003, 34, Louis 1993, 547, Marescau 1978, 26–7, Langenfeld 1991, 174.

[19] Cf Louis 1993, 546 ff., Marescau 1978, 26–7. See also for a discussion as to the relationship between the two concepts De Witte 1984, 440.

[20] Cf Case 11/70 *Internationale Handelsgesellschaft* [1970] ECR 1125.

[21] Cf Case 103/88 *Costanzo* [1989] ECR 1839.

[22] Cf Case 106/77 *Simmenthal* [1978] ECR 629; national provisions which are not in conflict with Community law are however allowed. Cf Case C–143/91 *Van der Tas* [1992] ECR I–5045.

[23] Cf e.g. Case C–197/96 *Commission v. France* [1997] ECR I–1489.

If the theoretical underpinning of the principle of supremacy is the conception of an autonomous Community legal order involving a transfer of powers to the Community and consequent limitation of Member States' sovereign rights, as is frequently contended,[24] national legal rules which are contrary to a directive cannot apply nor be validly adopted, as they are *ultra vires*.[25] Thus, although the principle of supremacy was not initially conceived as differentiating between legal rules of a lower order (national rules) and higher order (Community rules),[26] in practice the construction often amounts to giving directives and Community law in general a higher ranking in the hierarchy of norms which are valid within a national legal system.[27]

6.2 Directives as (indirect) sources of rights and duties of individuals

As an instrument of Community intervention, the directive imposes upon the Member States the obligation to implement it. This obligation exists primarily *vis-à-vis* the Community and other Member States. However, as was argued in the previous Section, from their entry into force directives form part of the law in the Member States and thus constitute a source of law within the national legal system. Furthermore, as explained in Chapter 3, particularly Section 3.2, the actual content of a directive may aim at establishing different types of legal relationships. In principle, it is designed to result in the creation of a whole conglomerate of rights and obligations between Community institutions and Member States, Member States *inter se*, Member States and individuals, and individuals amongst themselves. For every single case, depending on the terms of the provision concerned or the combination of provisions, an answer must be established to the question of who is obliged or entitled to what or, at least, *will be* obliged or entitled at the end of the day, i.e. once the directive has been transposed.

For the purpose of this Chapter, the focal point is the relationship between the Member State and individuals and individuals *inter se*. With respect to the question of who will be party to the relationship(s) which the directive intends to establish, it should be recalled that the substantive provisions of a directive may formulate obligations for either the Member States or for individuals and, similarly, they may formulate 'rights' for either Member States[28] or for individuals.

For the sake of clarity: the rights and obligations formulated for the respective subjects by the substantive provisions must be distinguished from the obligation

---

[24] Cf Kapteyn and VerLoren van Themaat 1998, 85–7. For a critique of this position see De Witte 1984, 437–8.   [25] Cf Kapteyn and VerLoren van Themaat 1998, 87.

[26] Cf Kapteyn and VerLoren van Themaat 1998, 87, Mertens de Wilmars 1969, 70.

[27] Cf Case 106/77 *Simmenthal* [1978] ECR 629, para 17.

[28] The somewhat unusual term 'rights' denotes in this context the right as the correlative of an individual's obligation. E.g. Member State authorities are entitled to claim certain conduct from the individual, like the payment of VAT. Cf also Joined Cases 66, 127, and 129/79 *Salumi* [1980] ECR 1237, where the Court talks about the rights of public authorities.

of a Member State to implement a directive and from the fact that directives as such cannot impose obligations upon individuals.

The specific nature of the directive as an instrument of two-stage legislation means that a Member State is under two distinct types of obligations. Firstly, it has the obligation to implement the directive and, secondly, it has certain obligations which are imposed on it by the *actual* text of a directive, such as to allow the sale of products when these products satisfy the conditions of the directive, grant exemption from VAT, award public works contracts in accordance with the procedure laid down in the relevant directive, and give social security benefits to men and women on a non-discriminatory basis.

In Chapter 4, I briefly discussed the problem that a directive as such cannot *impose* obligations upon individuals and, consequently, neither the State nor another individual can base a claim against an individual directly on a directive.[29] This in no way precludes that directives may *formulate* the obligations: it is, however, only upon transposition that the obligations become enforceable.

In summary, the substantive provisions may formulate both the persons who will be the beneficiaries and the persons who will be under obligation after the transposition into national law of the directive at issue. The fact that the directive as a whole is binding upon the Member State only, is in this respect immaterial.

As regards the content of the relationship, in some cases the obligations and rights may be laid down in the provisions of the directive very precisely and in concrete terms. In other cases the content and scope must subsequently be defined with more precision by national or—less usually—Community measures. However, even in the latter cases it should be possible, as a rule, to establish whether a directive or particular provisions are aiming to confer rights or impose obligations on individuals, or whether they are rather intended to regulate, for instance, the relations between administrative bodies. The answer to the question will only be facilitated by precision and consequently more concrete wording.

Considered from these two points of view, a directive will often be a source of rights and duties of individuals. In principle, however, it is an *indirect* source in the sense that it is the origin of rights and obligations laid down in national legislation. In other words, it reaches the individuals through implementing measures adopted by the Member States.[30] Yet in some cases it could be considered as a *direct* source of rights (but not obligations), namely where the provisions apply by virtue of 'direct effect', i.e. in cases where provisions of directives can apply and actually are applied without the intercession of national measures implementing the directive at issue.

---

[29] Cf also below, Ch 9, Subsection 9.5.2.
[30] Cf Case 270/81 *Rickmers* [1982] ECR 2771, Case 8/81 *Becker* [1982] ECR 53.

6.3 The conception of rights: the ambiguities

6.3.1 Introduction

Rights, which individuals derive from Community law, directives included, play a central role in both case law and legal writing. In the first place because direct effect of Community law provisions and the creation of rights[31] or obligations[32] with respect to individuals are often regarded as synonyms which can be used interchangeably. The matter is, however, more complicated, not least as a result of a fairly indiscriminate right-talk of the Court of Justice. In addition to denoting direct effect, in the Court's case law the creation of rights appears to have a crucial function both in the context of proper implementation of directives[33] and for the role assigned by the Court to national courts. The latter are required to protect the rights which individuals derive from Community law, including directives. In that context they may be obliged to adapt national procedural rules and remedies.[34] Similarly, one of the central conditions of State liability is that the infringed rule of law must have been intended to confer rights.[35] Yet, the Court has never clearly indicated what it means by the term 'right'.

To a certain extent this is not very surprising. Despite the many learned treatises on the concept of 'rights' in national law, the concept as such is by no means easy to pin down and define. In Community law the concept of a right seems even more ambiguous: 'It refers to the general right, and accompanying remedy concept, to have a court set aside national measures which conflict with the requirements of a directive, but may also refer to a specific right which a directive grants to private parties, and which, together with other conditions, gives a rise . . . to a right and an accompanying remedy for compensation . . . '.[36] The term right here has various meanings which depend on the context in which the term is used. Van Gerven, for instance, provides a very general and, in his words, 'tentative' definition. In his view, 'the concept of rights refers . . . to a legal position which a person recognized as such by the law . . . may have and which in its normal state can be enforced by that person against . . . others before a court of law by means of one or more remedies . . . '.[37]

---

[31] Often called 'Community law rights'. For the sake of clarity it must be observed that wherever I use this term or a similar expression this does not correspond to the term 'enforceable Community right' as employed in the European Communities Act 1972, section 2(1) which, it is understood, relates to directly effective Community law provisions.

[32] Where appropriate. As was explained, directives as such cannot impose obligations upon individuals, but only by virtue of implementing legislation.   [33] Cf above, Ch 5.

[34] Cf below, Ch 7.   [35] Cf e.g. Case C–127/95 *Norbrook* [1998] ECR I–1531.

[36] Van Gerven 2000, 507, referring to the famous point 25 of the *Becker* judgment.

[37] Ibid, 502.

The rather indiscriminate rights language of the Court and the interpretation thereof in legal writing, has hardly contributed to a clarification of the matter. This is not only due to purely doctrinal differences but is also a reflection of divergent national perceptions and divergent jurisprudential traditions. It would seem the catalyst for this confusion lies in the Court's case law on State liability and it is this case law which has triggered a discussion on the concept of a right in Community law, even though the term has been regularly used by the Court prior to the development of this particular line of case law. Interestingly, the intensity of the debate differs between Member States. In Germany, for instance, numerous studies have been devoted to the question of the necessity to rethink traditional national legal concepts of 'subjective public rights' as well as the starting point of '*Individualrechtsschutz*'.[38] Writers based in other legal traditions appear to limit their concerns to the inherent ambiguity of the terms deployed by the Court, discussing, for example, whether the Court indeed refers to the stricter or more narrow concept of a '*droit subjectif*' or whether the protection of a legitimate interest would suffice in the Community context to be labelled as a 'right'.[39] Others have used the Hohfeldian analytical framework in order to clarify the Court's rights terminology and describe more precisely the legal relationships and the specific legal effects involved.[40]

In the present Section, I will, first, briefly discuss the relationship between the concept of a 'right' and the direct effect of a Community law provision. Second, I shall examine the approach of the Court in its case law on State liability in order to establish whether the provision breached confers rights upon individuals or not. Third, I will address the use of the terminology of 'rights' in the case law concerning the implementation of directives and the link between an individual right and infringement proceedings against Member States for non-compliance with the provisions of such directives.

---

[38] Cf e.g. Eilmansberger 1997, Ruffert 1996 and 1998, Winter 1999, Triantafyllou 1997, Schoch 1999.

[39] Often without explaining what the difference between a right and a (legitimate or mere) interest is. Cf Pâques 1996, in particular 199–201, and Léger 1999, in particular 328. On a number of implications Community law may have for the distinction made in Italy between (subjective) rights and legitimate interests, see Caranta 1993, 286–91.

[40] See, in particular, Hilson and Downes 1999, Gilliams 2000 and partly also Coppel 1994. In Hohfeld's analysis, there are in fact four kinds of rights with, similarly, four kinds of correlatives. Namely: *claim* (or *right strictly speaking*) which says something about the existence of duties of others, *privilege*, which says something about the existence of the duties of the person having the 'right', *power*, which says something about the possible alteration of the duties of the persons involved in the relationship, and *immunity*, which says something about the freedom from possible alteration in the duties of the person in which the 'right' is vested. Thus, for instance, Ms Becker's right to exemption from VAT is in this approach rather a *privilege*: she has no duty to pay VAT (Case 8/81 *Becker* [1982] ECR 53); *Faccini Dori* has a *power* to rescind a contract (Case C–91/92 [1994] ECR I–3325) and *Francovich* has a wage *claim* (Joint Cases C–6/90 and 9/90 [1991] ECR I–5357). Cf also AG Van Gerven in C–70/88 *European Parliament v. Council* [1990] ECR I–2041, para 6, who pointed out the necessity to conceive 'rights' in the widest sense of the term, namely as right, power, and prerogative.

6.3.2 Rights and direct effect

The existence of an individual right is often equated to direct effect. The root of the problem lies in the terminology of the Court of Justice.[41] In *Van Gend en Loos* the Court held that 'Article 12 must be interpreted as producing direct effects and creating individual rights which national courts must protect'.[42] The implicit suggestion of this phrase, that rights come into being by virtue of direct effect, seems to be affirmed in cases like *Salgoil* where the Court found that 'Article 31 . . . lends itself perfectly to producing direct effect . . . *Thus* Article 31 creates rights which national courts must protect.'[43] Another example is *Van Duyn*. In this case, after an examination of the conditions to be satisfied by a provision in order to be directly effective, the Court held that 'Article 3(1) of Council Directive No. 64/221 . . . confers on individuals rights which are enforceable by them in the courts of a Member State and which the national courts must protect'.[44] In numerous other, also more recent, cases the Court has used the same or comparable terms to indicate the meaning of the fact that a provision has direct effect.[45]

However, as has been pointed out by several authors,[46] 'direct effect' is a broader concept, in the sense that a directly effective provision of Community law may be relied upon for several purposes. Defining direct effect in terms of the creation of individual or subjective[47] rights as understood in national law will often be, if not impossible, then rather artificial and, moreover, unnecessary.[48]

> For instance, in the case of discriminatory dismissal the person concerned may base her or his claim to compensation on the right to equal treatment as laid

---

[41] Cf Maresceau 1978, 45–7, Mertens de Wilmars 1969, 67. For a more general discussion see also Kovar 1981, 161 and Timmermans 1979, 538–9.   [42] Case 26/62 [1963] ECR 1, 13.

[43] Case 13/68 [1968] ECR 453, 461 (emphasis added).

[44] Case 41/74 [1974] ECR 1337, para 15.

[45] Cf also Case 265/78 *Ferwerda* [1980] ECR 617, para 10, where the Court talks about 'the rights which subjects obtain through the direct effect of Community law'. For more recent cases see e.g. Case C–200/90 *Dansk Denkavit* [1992] ECR I–2217, Case C–236/92 *Comitato* [1994] ECR I–483 and Case C–37/98 *Savas* [2000] ECR I–2927, para 68. This is remarkable since in the same case the Court defines direct effect in much less rights-related language: the provision at issue . . . is sufficiently operational to be applied by a national court and therefore capable of governing the legal position of individuals' (para 54).

[46] Cf Mertens de Wilmars 1969, 67, Maresceau 1978, 49–50, Timmermans 1979, 538–9, Bleckmann 1984, 775 and Bleckmann 1978, 89, Barents 1982, 98, Kovar 1981, 161, Klein 1988, 15 and Prechal 2000, 1049–51.

[47] Or personal rights; the adjectives added vary in legal writing. According to David 1984, 6, the English term 'individual rights' can be used as the equivalent of 'subjective rights' commonly employed in the civil law tradition. The latter term stems from the need to distinguish between 'law' and 'rights' as these two notions have been fused into one single word, e.g. '*droit*' in French or '*Recht*' in German. Hence the distinction between '*droit objectif*' and '*droit subjectif*' or '*objektives*' and '*subjektives Recht*'. Interestingly, in the English version of the Court's judgments the term 'subjective right' may appear from time to time. See e.g. Case C–147/01 *Weber's Wine World*, judgment of 2 October 2003, nyr in ECR, para 95.

[48] Cf Barents 1982, 98 and Pâques 1996, 199. However, some scholars hold a different view. Cf Kovar 1978, 250–1.

down in Directive 76/207 (equal treatment at work).[49] On the other hand an
employer may invoke the provisions of the same directive in his defence in
criminal proceedings brought against him for reasons of employing women at
night, which is prohibited under national law, while no such prohibition exists
with respect to male employees.[50] While in the first situation it is plausible to
speak of a right to equal treatment of men and women, in the latter case it is
difficult to maintain that the directive creates a substantive right for the
employer.

The essential point with respect to direct effect is *the possibility for an individual to
invoke provisions of Community law in order to protect his interests.*[51] If direct effect must
be classified as a right, then this right will be, at the most, *a right to invoke Community
law,*[52] thus a kind of 'procedural' right, with a corresponding obligation for the
national courts to apply it.

The broader concept of the 'invocability' of a Community norm which gradually
emerged in the case law, allows a Community law provision to be relied upon or
invoked for a wide variety of purposes, for example as a defence in criminal
proceedings or as a standard for review of the legality of a Member State's
action in administrative proceedings. The question of whether the provision at
issue confers an individual right is not necessarily relevant. Moreover, since
Community law provisions are relied upon within the context of national proceedings and for various purposes, it is a matter of national law to define the
individual's position.

As regards provisions of directives, the Court's definition of direct effect seems
to take into account the various roles this concept may play in national
procedures when it holds that ' . . . wherever the provisions of a directive appear . . .
to be unconditional and sufficiently precise, those provisions may . . . be relied
upon as against any national provision which is incompatible with the directive or
in so far as the provisions define rights which individuals are able to assert against
the state'.[53]

The discussion about direct effect as creation of rights and direct effect as a
matter of invocability is in fact a very old one. Interesting observations have

---

[49] [1976] OJ L39/40; cf Case 152/84 *Marshall I* [1986] ECR 723 and Case C–271/91 *Marshall II*
[1993] ECR I–4367.   [50] Cf Case C–345/89 *Stoeckel* [1991] ECR I–4047.
[51] Barents 1982, 98 quoting Mertens de Wilmars. Cf also Mertens de Wilmars 1991, 398. For the
question whether the protection of a person's interest is a condition for direct effect see Ch 9,
Subsection 9.3.5.
[52] Cf Bebr 1981, 559, Steiner 1986, 109, Kapteyn and VerLoren van Themaat 1998, 528, Lauwaars
1976, 77, Easson 1981, 35, Everling 1984, 101. Cf also e.g. Case C–431/92, *Grosskrotzenburg* [1995] ECR
I–2189, para 26, Case C–96/95 *Commission v. Germany* [1997] ECR I–1653, para 37, Case C–76/97
Tögel [1998] ECR I–5357, para 26, and Case C–162/00 *Pokrpkowicz* [2002] ECR I–1049, para 30.
[53] Case C–221/88 *Busseni* [1990] ECR I–495, para 22. Since Case 8/81 *Becker* [1982] ECR 53 this
has been consistent case law.

been made in this respect by an 'outsider',[54] who pointed at the fact that, when the doctrine of self-executing treaties—which originates, as is well-known, in the United States—was introduced in Europe, it underwent a conceptual transformation. Under the influence of the advisory opinion of the Permanent Court of International Justice in the *Danzig* case,[55] European scholars regarded as self-executing those treaties which create individual rights that are enforceable in national courts. According to the same writer, this conception was reinforced by the case law of the ECJ in the 1960s.

For Community law in particular, it was, *inter alia*, Bleckman who analysed the two above-mentioned approaches and cogently pointed out that national judges do not solely apply norms which create rights and that the notion of direct effect of a legal norm is much broader than the notion which refers only to creation of rights and duties.[56] Although the debate on direct effect and the nature of the rights created by directly effective provisions of Community law is therefore an old one, the reality shows that certain deep-rooted conceptions die hard. The judgment in *Kraaijeveld*, for instance, appears to have triggered a renewed discussion on the concept of direct effect. The central issue in this discussion is whether a 'legality review' *à la Kraaijeveld* is a form of direct effect or not.[57] It has been contended that since the relevant provisions of the Directive do not necessarily confer rights upon individuals, *Kraaijeveld* is not about direct effect. Yet, the approach taken in *Kraaijeveld* was reconfirmed in, *inter alia*, *Linster*.[58] Similarly, the *Brinkmann* case was argued along the lines of 'creation of rights'.[59] However, the Court reformulated the question into a problem of 'a right to rely' on the directive at issue and approached the problem from a perspective of 'review of legality'.[60]

In brief, to equate the concept of direct effect with the creation of rights does not do justice to the diversity of the effects which directly effective provisions may produce. Nevertheless, despite the introduction of the broader concept of invocability,

[54] Iwasawa 1986, 629–33. Cf also Kapteyn and VerLoren van Themaat 2003, 420–1.

[55] Advisory Opinion on the Jurisdiction of the Courts of Danzig, 1928 P.C.I.J., Ser. B, No. 15.

[56] Bleckmann 1978. Cf also Timmermans 1979.

[57] Cf e.g. Edward 1998 and Scott 1998, 123–4. Also, for instance, Wyatt 1998, 17–18 has obvious doubts as to the extension of direct effect beyond the concept of 'self-standing source of rights'. Cf also below, Ch 9, Subsections 9.3.3. and 9.3.4.

[58] Case C–287/98 *Linster* [2000] ECR I–6917. See also C–435/97 *WWF* [1999] ECR I–5613 and Case C–127/02 *Landelijke Vereniging tot Behoud van de Waddenzee*, judgment of 7 September 2004, nyr in ECR. Cf also below, Ch 9, Subsection 9.3.4.

[59] Case C–365/98 *Brinkmann II* [2000] ECR I–4619, where a preliminary question was referred as to whether a directive conferred 'a direct right to be taxed in accordance with the Directive'. Also the Commission argued, for instance, that the directive at issue confers upon individuals a direct right to be 'subjected either to an *ad valorem* excise duty, or to a specific excise duty, or to a mixture of both . . .'. See the Opinion of AG Mischo, at point 55.

[60] Case C–365/98 *Brinkmann II* [2000] ECR I–4619. At the end of the day, the Court found that there was no 'right to rely', thus no direct effect, at least not for the purposes for which Brinkmann wanted to rely on the directive. See on this also below, Ch 9, Subsections 9.3.4 and 9.4.2.

the problem remains that the Court occasionally still employs the language of 'creating rights' or equivalent formulations in order to determine direct effect. Indeed, the consequence of direct effect may well be that a substantive individual right is created, but this is not always necessarily so. A provision may be directly effective in the sense that it may be relied upon without creating substantive rights.

> Arguably, this proposition is explicitly confirmed in the *Unilever* case.[61] In this case Unilever contended, in a dispute with another firm, that an Italian law on the labelling of olive oil should not be applied. Italy failed to comply with Article 9 of Directive 83/189 (notification of technical regulations) which provides for an obligation to observe a certain period of delay after the Commission has been notified of the national measures, giving the latter the opportunity to form an opinion on their compatibility with Community law. On the basis of the judgment in *CIA Security*[62] Unilever argued that such a failure to observe the requisite procedure rendered the Italian law inapplicable. After having found that this was indeed the case, and such procedures should have been observed the Court addressed the arguments submitted by several Member States who had claimed that if the Court recognized the inapplicability of a national measure in the case at issue this would amount to an implicit recognition of horizontal direct effect. It is established law that a directive cannot of itself impose obligations on an individual and cannot therefore be relied upon in a dispute concerning contractual rights and obligations between private parties.[63] The Court countered this argument by pointing out that Directive 83/189 does not 'define the substantive scope of the legal rule on the basis of which the national court must decide the case before it. It creates neither rights nor obligations for individuals.'[64] Nonetheless Unilever was allowed to rely on the Directive for the purposes of having the Italian law at issue set aside.

In addition, the discussion on the creation of rights and direct effect is complicated by national factors. In some legal systems individual rights may play a pivotal role and have, in that context, a specific—dogmatic—meaning, as in Germany or Italy for example. In other legal systems the term 'right' may be used as a kind of shorthand for a person's legal position, without any specific consequences being attributed to it. In yet other jurisdictions the concept may play a particular role in private law procedures, while in administrative law procedures different concepts are operative, as in France or the Netherlands, for example.

---

[61] Case C–443/98 [2000] ECR I–7535.   [62] Case C–194/94 [1996] ECR I–2201.
[63] Cf Case 152/84, *Marshall I* [1986] ECR I–723 and, in particular, Case C–91/92, *Faccini Dori* [1994] ECR I–3325.
[64] Point 51 of the judgment. However, in order to increase the confusion: in *Wells* (Case C–201/02, judgment of 7 January 2004, nyr in ECR, paras 66–69) the Court has apparently accepted liability for a breach of an essentially procedural obligation, namely the failure to carry out an environmental impact assessment. The question is indeed whether this obligation confers rights upon individuals. This is after all one of the central requirements for State liability.

Thus, for instance, in Italy the modality of protection depends on the notoriously difficult distinction between 'subjective right' and 'legitimate interest'.[65] When this distinction came before the Court of Justice in the *Salgoil* case, the latter found that it was for the national court to classify the position as one of having a subjective right or a legitimate interest or perhaps even a 'diminished right' under national law, provided however that the protection granted was direct and immediate.[66]

In German administrative law treatises dealing with European law it was not unusual, at least until recently, to find arguments to the effect that the creation of an individual right is another (implicit) condition for direct effect.[67] This approach is closely linked to the focus of German law on '*Individualrechtsschutz*', the protection of individual rights. This protection implies a three step scrutiny of the provisions at issue: there must be a generally binding (statutory) provision ('*ein zwingende Rechtssatz des objectiven Rechts*'); the provisions must aim at the protection of individual interests (only those who can avail themselves of such a *Schutznorm* can claim individual rights) and the persons concerned must be given the '*Rechtsmacht zur Durchsetzung*' (power to effectuate/enforce) of their legally protected interests.[68] Only when a person can claim an 'individual right',[69] can she bring an action before an administrative court, for example. From this point of view it is no surprise that German legal literature contains a number of attempts to classify the protection of an individual's position by Community law using, for an outsider, rather sophisticated categories of rights.[70] An illustration of this approach is the opinion of Advocate General Lenz in the *Costanzo* case.[71] In his view, the nature of Article 29(5) of Directive 71/305 (public works contracts)[72] was such as to create rights for individuals. He recalled the *Transporoute* judgment,[73] in which the Court held that 'the aim of the provision . . . is to protect tenderers against arbitrariness on the part of the authority awarding contracts'. The Advocate General continued by saying that 'the obligation to examine the tender, which has the effect of a procedural guarantee, may be construed as a right vesting in the tenderer who submits an obviously abnormally low tender'. To a Dutch lawyer, for instance, it may not be clear why it should be necessary to translate a procedural guarantee into a right.[74]

The German focus on protection of individual rights is also the direct background to the fierce debate in German legal writing on the nature and impact

---

[65] Cf Clarich 1991, 239–41.   [66] Case 13/68 [1968] ECR 453.

[67] Cf however, Winter 2002, 314, referring to a judgment of the Federal Administrative Court, which seems to accept that the creation of rights is a consequence of direct effect.

[68] For a brief discussion see e.g. Hölscheidt 2001.

[69] For as far as these terms can serve as an appropriate translation for the German '*subjektives Recht*'.

[70] Cf Winter 1991b, 659 ff.; cf on this issue also Grabitz 1971, 22.

[71] Case 103/88 [1989] ECR 1839, para 27.   [72] [1971] OJ English Spec Ed (II) 682.

[73] Case 76/81 [1982] ECR 417.

[74] Cf however, Winter 1991b, 662 who criticizes the Court for not having dealt with this issue more carefully and for not giving reasons.

of the Court's case law, which has in turn caused significant conceptual problems. In particular this has resulted in the distinction between 'subjective direct effect', which remains conditional upon the existence of an individual right, and 'objective direct effect', a new form of direct effect which is not conditional upon the existence of an individual right.[75]

In common law systems the language of rights does not seem to have any special technical, dogmatic, or other particular meaning. The use of the term is, as one writer put it, 'popular'.[76] This is understandable since in that system, the emphasis lies on remedies. Not the rights give rise to a remedy, but a cause of action, id est—in brief—the facts that entitle a person to sue. The focus of judicial proceedings is not directed towards the specific interpretation of the provision at issue in order to establish whether an individual right has been granted or not. Since the term 'right' seems to be used rather loosely and the focus is, in the first place, on remedies, it is not surprising that English lawyers have so easily embraced the creation of rights as equivalent to direct effect.[77] Ubi ius, ibi remedium and, after all, does direct effect not imply that there must be a remedy available?[78] Yet, the English approach may also appear strange to some continental lawyers. For instance, it has been argued that in the case of the exercise of statutory powers by public authorities in a way that contravenes a directly effective provision of Community law, the 'Community law right is akin to a right in English law not to be subjected to an ultra vires act'.[79] Moreover, in the United Kingdom another type of classification is crucial for individual protection, namely whether the 'right' at issue can be considered as a public law right or a private law right, since the remedies available differ accordingly.[80]

The French do not seem to be over-concerned as to the concept of 'Community law right'. The reason for this is, that in French administrative law the focus is not the creation of rights, but the question whether the State's or public authorities' behaviour is compatible with Community law, since Community law provisions are often used in the context of the 'contrôle de légalité'.[81] In France, direct effect is usually perceived as either 'l'invocabilité d'exclusion' and 'l'invocabilité de substitution'.[82] The first form of invocability is to be understood as Community law provisions being used as a standard for review and if there is incompatibility,

---

[75] Cf Ruffert 1997, in particular at 320, with further references, and Winter 2002.

[76] Legrand 1996, 70.

[77] Cf e.g. the House of Lords in the Three Rivers Case [2000] 3 CMLR 205, where the two notions of direct effect and creation of rights are conflated. See, however, Hilson and Downes 1999, who demonstrate that direct effect and rights are not synonymous. Cf also Craig and De Búrca 2003, 179–82.

[78] Cf also section 2(1) of the European Communities Act, which stresses the enforceability of the Community law provisions.   [79] Lewis 1992, 457.

[80] For difficulties occasioned by this distinction in relation to the enforcement of Community law see e.g. Steiner 1986 and Ward 1990, 25 ff.

[81] However, in the context of an action for damages, the main concern is the protection of rights.

[82] Cf e.g. Galmot and Bonichot 1988 and AG Léger in his Opinion in Case C–287/98 Linster [2000] ECR I–6917, paras 57–59.

the national rules must be disapplied or set aside. Often, depending on a number of factors, this may suffice. The second form indicates that in certain cases it may be necessary to *apply Community law provisions instead* of national rules which have been found incompatible with Community law provisions.[83]

Equating direct effect with the creation of rights for individuals is also deceptive from another point of view. It is not only incorrect to maintain that only Community law provisions which (are intended to) grant rights to individuals are able to produce direct effect:[84] it is similarly erroneous to argue that *only* directly effective provisions may confer rights upon individuals. In *Waterkeyn*[85] the Court held that the rights accruing to individuals derive from the actual provisions of Community law *having direct effect*. This is, however, certainly in the light of more recent developments, an outdated point of view. The question whether a provision creates individual rights is, in my view, *a matter of its content*; the question whether a provision has direct effect relates to *the quality ascribed to it*, namely whether it can be invoked by those concerned within the national legal system.[86] Moreover, the basis of the two is entirely different. While the 'procedural right' of an individual to rely on a provision of a directive is based on Article 249(3) combined with Article 10 EC,[87] the substantive right which the individual seeks to enforce stems from a particular (provision of a) directive.[88]

---

[83] An intermediate position can be found in, for instance, Belgium. There a distinction is made between direct effect *senso stricto* and direct effect *senso lato*. The last one encompasses the control of legality, without addressing the question whether the provision at issue creates individual rights. Cf Bribosia 1998, 6–10, Wathelet and Van Raepenbusch 1997, 44.

[84] Cf the Opinion of AG Warner in Case 152/79 *Lee* [1980] ECR 1495, 1514: 'a provision in a directive cannot have direct effect unless it is to be inferred from "the nature, general scheme and wording of the provision" that it required Member States to confer, by their own law, rights on private persons'. Cf also his Opinion in Case 131/79 *Santillo* [1980] ECR 1585.

[85] Joined Cases 314 to 316/81 and 83/82 [1982] ECR 4337.

[86] Provided that it meets certain conditions for this purpose; see below, Ch 9, Section 9.4. For a comparable distinction see Grabitz 1971, 22. A good example is provided by Case C–37/98 *Savas* [2000] ECR I–2927. First, the Court decided that Art 41(1) of the Additional Protocol of 23 November 1970, annexed to the Association Agreement between EEC and Turkey has direct effect. Next, it examined the *scope* of the provision and found that it did not confer a right of establishment. However, the provision (standstill clause of that Article) could be relied on in so far as it prohibited new restrictions on the freedom of establishment and the right of residence. For a substantive analysis see also Case C–222/02 *Peter Paul*, judgment of 12 October 2004, nyr in ECR.

[87] Case 190/87 *Moormann* [1988] ECR 4689.

[88] Cf also Case C–208/90 *Emmott* [1991] ECR I–4269. On the one hand the Court found (para 19) that where directives are intended to create rights for individuals clear and precise transposition is necessary since only then can they ascertain the full extent of those rights. On the other hand the Court reiterated in para 20 that where a Member State has failed to take the implementing measures required 'the Court has recognized the right of a person affected thereby to rely . . . on a directive as against a defaulting State'. Cf also Case C–338/91 *Steenhorst-Neerings* [1993] ECR I–5475, where the Court refers on the one hand to the rights stemming from the directive at issue and on the other hand to the right to rely on the directive. Furthermore, it must be observed that the substantive right may, in turn, be procedural in character: e.g. the right to be heard versus the right to an exemption from taxes, social security benefit, etc.

As was already observed above, direct effect and creation of rights may and will often coincide; the provision can thus both have direct effect and define rights, although this is not always necessarily the case. The most obvious example in this respect is the *Francovich* case.[89] In this case the directive was regarded as being designed to create rights for the benefit of individuals but the direct effect doctrine was of no avail for the individuals concerned, since the provisions on the identity of the debtor were not sufficiently clear and unconditional. In other words, they did not meet the classical conditions for direct effect. Consequently, for this reason *and* in the absence of implementing measures, the individuals could not 'enforce the right granted to them by Community law before national courts', as the Court put it.[90]

Another example to indicate that the creation of rights and possible direct effect must be considered separately can be drawn from cases concerning rights of individuals which are to be asserted against other individuals. The content of the relevant provisions may very well confer rights upon a person but since directives do not have horizontal direct effect the person concerned cannot assert them against another individual.[91] This does not mean, however, that no right has been created. It is 'only' not enforceable against the other individual. In principle, of course, there is no point in having a right if a person has no opportunity to enforce it in practice. However, the existence of a right and the ways in which it is protected are two separate issues.[92]

In summary, direct effect and the creation of rights should not be equated. Direct effect refers to the ability to rely on a provision of Community law for a variety of purposes, even where the provision does not confer substantive rights. On the other hand, Community law provisions may confer rights upon individuals, or order Member States to do this, without being directly effective.

6.3.3   Rights and State liability

Although the language of rights is certainly present in the Court's case law on State liability, this same case law has not been particularly helpful in providing the necessary criteria for identifying the existence of an individual right. To a certain extent

---

[89] Joined Cases C–6/90 and C–9/90 [1991] ECR I–5357.

[90] Cf also the Opinion of AG Mischo in Joined Cases C–6/90 and C–9/90 *Francovich* [1991] ECR I–5357, para 60, where he observes that 'the lack of direct effect does not mean that the effect sought by the directive is not to confer rights on individuals but solely that those rights are not sufficiently precise and unconditional to be relied upon and applied as they stand without any action on the part of the Member States to which the directive is addressed'.

[91] Cf Schockweiler 1992, 38 and Case C–91/92 *Faccini Dori* [1994] ECR I–3325.

[92] This might seem peculiar from the point of view of common law where, it is understood, the existence of a remedy at common law or under statute enables the English lawyer to deduce the existence of a right. EC law operates the other way round: it confers rights and national law must supply the remedy. Cf Durand 1987, 43, Van Gerven 1994b, 341. See also on this approach in general MacCormick 1977, 195–9. Cf also below, Subsection 6.4.6.

the issue seemed unproblematic. In *Francovich*[93] the Court has acknowledged that the result required by Directive 80/987 (protection of employees in the event of the insolvency of their employer)[94] entailed the grant of a right to the employees concerned 'to a guarantee of payment of their unpaid wage claims'. Perhaps because the issue was so obvious, the Court did not explain the grounds for its conclusion.

In other cases the Court relies on the terms and/or the aim of the provisions at issue, or on the preamble or on both. The preamble of Directive 85/577 (protection of the consumer in respect of contracts negotiated away from business premises)[95] at issue in *Faccini Dori*[96] made clear, according to the Court, that the directive intended to improve consumer protection. Since the directive was 'undeniably intended to confer rights on individuals', the first condition for liability, namely that the purpose of the directive must be to grant rights to individuals, was fulfilled.

In *Dillenkofer*[97] it was submitted that the main aim of the directive in question, 90/314 (package travel, package holidays, and package tours),[98] was to guarantee the freedom to provide services and fair competition. However, the Court stressed that the preamble repeatedly refers to the purpose of protecting consumers and also the aim and wording of the particular provision, which the Court had to interpret, Article 7 of the directive, was to protect consumers. The fact that the directive intended to ensure other additional objectives could not detract from this finding. Therefore, the purpose of the pertinent provision was 'to grant to individuals rights'.

In *Peter Paul*,[98A] on the other hand, the mere fact that the objective of the directives concerned also includes protection of depositors did not suffice to deduce from it the existence of a right.

In *Norbrook*,[99] where the Licensing Authority has imposed requests and requirements which were allegedly incompatible with the directives at issue, the Court found that Directive 81/851 (veterinary medicinal products)[100] provides that an application for marketing authorization may be refused only for reasons set out therein. Therefore, according to the Court, the directive gives individuals the right to obtain an authorization if certain conditions are fulfilled. These conditions are laid down precisely and exhaustively in Directives 81/851 and 81/852 (on testing of veterinary medicinal products).[101] These directives also provide a basis to identify the scope of the right to obtain a marketing authorization.

In the case law involving State liability for failed or incorrect implementation of directives an additional uncertainty had to be taken into account. In *Francovich* the Court stated that the *result* of the directive must entail the grant of a right, but in *Faccini* it required that it should be the *purpose* of the directive to grant

---

[93] Joined Cases C–6/90 and 9/90 [1991] ECR I–5357.   [94] [1980] OJ L283/23.

[95] [1985] OJ L375/31.   [96] C–91/92 [1994] ECR I–3325.

[97] Joined Cases C–178/94, C–179/94, C–188/94, C–189/94, and C–190/94 [1996] ECR I–4845.

[98] [1990] OJ L158/59.

[98A] Case C–222/02 *Peter Paul*, judgment of 12 October 2004, nyr in ECR.

[99] Case C–127/95 [1998] ECR I–1531.   [100] [1981] OJ L317/1.   [101] [1981] OJ L17/16.

rights.[102] There is of course a difference in these conditions. The first one may be understood more broadly, namely that even in cases where the directive as such does not intend to create rights, an individual provision in the directive may still do so.[103] Put differently, under the first formulation, it is not the objective pursued by the directive but the result that counts. In later cases, the Court has, in the light of *Brasserie du Pêcheur*, reformulated the first condition for liability so that the rule of law infringed must have been intended to confer rights.[104] It would seem to follow that it is sufficient for one or more provisions, where appropriate, to confer or intend to confer rights. The purpose of the directive remains, however, an important aid for interpretation.[105]

In other cases the ECJ merely stated that the relevant provision created rights for the purposes of establishing State liability, because the Court had (previously) found that the provision at issue created rights in the sense of having direct effect.[106] On the one hand, it may be clear that in the light of what was said in the previous Subsection, this link is not necessarily always present. To say that a provision of Community law is directly effective does not automatically imply that it confers individual rights. On the other hand it cannot be denied that there is a link between direct effect and individual rights. This link lies in the traditional conditions for direct effect, namely that the provisions must be clear, sufficiently precise, and unconditional. I will come back to this issue in Section 6.4.5.

6.3.4   Rights and implementation of directives

In the—well-established—case law on the requirements which national measures implementing directives must satisfy,[107] the Court has made plain on several occasions that where directives are intended to create rights and duties for individuals, they must be implemented by legally binding measures. The case law reveals that for individuals the binding quality of the implementing measures is significant in at least two respects: from the point of view of legal certainty, since it enables them to ascertain in a sufficiently predictable way the extent of their rights and duties, and from the point of view of effective judicial protection, since it defines a legal position, on which individuals may rely upon in their national courts.

Not surprisingly, in the context of infringement proceedings the Court has frequently addressed the question of whether a particular directive intends to create

---

[102] Reiterated in Case C–192/94 *El Corte Inglés* [1996] ECR I–1281. However, in *Dillenkofer* (Joined Cases C–178/94, C–179/94, C–188/94, C–189/94, and C–190/94 [1996] ECR I–4845, *inter alia* para 42), it was once more: 'the result prescribed by Article 7 of the Directive entails the grant of rights ...'.

[103] Cf the first edition of this book, 327–8.

[104] Cf Case C–127/95 *Norbrook* [1998] ECR I–1531, C–66/95 *Sutton* [1997] ECR I–2163, and Joined Cases C–94/95 and C–95/95 *Bonifaci* [1997] ECR I–3969.   [105] Cf also below, Subsection 6.4.2.

[106] Cf Joined Cases C–46/93 and C–48/93 *Brasserie du Pêcheur* [1996] ECR I–1029, Case C–5/94 *Hedley Lomas* [1996] ECR I–2553, and Case C–150/99 *Lindöpark* [2001] ECR I–493.

[107] Cf Ch 5, in particular Section 5.2 and Subsection 5.3.1.

rights (and duties) for individuals. In several cases relating to environmental directives it ruled that the latter were intended to create rights and obligations for individuals because the directives at issue were enacted, *inter alia*, with a view to protect human health.[108] If human health is endangered as a result of non-compliance, the persons concerned must be able to rely on mandatory rules and assert their rights. Such a reasoning could suggest that the objective of the protection of human health is as such sufficient to give rise to individual rights. In one such case, the Court did not only focus upon the objective of the directive, but rather upon specific provisions. These provisions required the Member States to adopt a series of prohibitions, authorization schemes, and monitoring procedures 'in order to prevent or limit discharges of certain substances'. The Court concluded that '[t]he purpose of the directive is . . . to create rights and obligations for individuals'.[109]

The first question is indeed what the Court has in mind when it refers, in this context, to rights. Again there is uncertainty here as illustrated, on the one hand, by the approach taken by AG Jacobs who opined, on the basis of this case law, that Directive 80/788 (drinking water) confers rights and that its incorrect implementation may give rise to liability under *Francovich* type principles. Zuleeg, on the other hand, failed to see how an individual right could be construed on the basis of the mere fact that the directive aims at protecting human health.[110] In addition, Schockweiler has pointed out that the requirement of rights in *Francovich* means that the State liability regime is not concerned with breaches where mere interests are protected by the directive at issue, such as in the case of numerous environmental directives.[111] It could well be that each of these authors give a slightly different meaning to the concept of right.

Moreover, if the objective of the directive is the protection of human health and this in turn determines whether a directive gives rise to rights, then it is not readily apparent why, in *Comitato*,[112] no such rights were found to exist. The directive at issue in that case was after all aimed at the protection of human health.

It is submitted that the Court's case law in infringement proceedings should not be interpreted as meaning that the directives give rise to *concrete* individual (environmental or other) rights. Directives, and environmental directives in particular, usually aim at a certain degree of external effect in that they are designed to regulate

---

[108] Cf Case C–361/88 *Commission v. Germany* [1991] ECR I–2567, Case C–58/89 *Commission v. Germany* [1991] ECR I–4983, Case C–59/89 *Commission v. Germany* [1991] ECR I–2607, Case C–13/90 *Commission v. France* [1991] ECR I–4327, Case C–14/90 *Commission v. France* [1991] ECR I–4331, Case C–64/90 *Commission v. France* [1991] ECR I–4335, and Case C–298/95 *Commission v. Germany* [1996] ECR I–6747. These cases concerned directives regulating the quality of water and air quality legislation. Since by setting environmental quality standards the directives aim at protecting, *inter alia*, human health, also other directives could be relevant in this respect. For instance, Directive 90/219 (contained use of genetically modified micro-organisms) [1990] OJ L117/1 and Directive 90/220 (deliberate release of genetically modified organisms) [1990] OJ L117/15.
[109] Case C–131/88, *Commission v. Germany* [1991] ECR I–825.   [110] Zuleeg 1993, 37.
[111] Schockweiler 1992, 44. Cf also Van Gerven 1997, 187.
[112] Case C–236/92 [1994] ECR I–483.

relations between individuals and between individuals and public authorities. They require the Member State to provide at the national level, through the process of implementation, for legally sufficiently defined positions which may be relied upon in the courts, if necessary. These may take the shape of rights, which are then in some way implied in the directive, but they must be given their *final* shape and content in the process of implementation,[113] or, perhaps even require the intervention of the national administration for instance where a licence or authorization should be issued.[114]

This is however not necessarily the only way that the provisions at issue may be implemented and further concretized. Much depends on how the individual's position is perceived and translated in the national legal system. A case in which the Court did *not* use the language of rights clarifies this further. In Case C–433/93[115] the Court held that the rules regarding participation and advertising in public procurement directives[116] are intended to protect tenderers against arbitrariness on the part of the contract-awarding authority. Effective protection implies that a tenderer must be able to rely on those rules as against the procuring authority and, if necessary, to plead a breach of those rules before national courts. This case may be defined in terms of the protection of the bidder's rights. It may, however, also be couched in a system of control of administrative action.

In brief, the main concern of the Court seems to be that the legal position of the individual must be safeguarded and, perhaps even more importantly, that Community law is simply applied. How this position is further qualified under national law (e.g. as one of individual rights or protected interests) is primarily a matter for the national legal order. If this is true, the implication is that where the Court uses, in the context of its 'implementation case law', the term right, it has nothing specific in mind. A more or less automatic transplant of a 'right' labelled as such in infringement proceedings to, for instance, the area of State liability would seem a perilous undertaking.[117]

Comparable concerns seem also to lurk behind the expression of effective protection of rights (and its equivalents), which the Member State and, in particular, national courts must provide under another line of case law, namely where the Court requires, on the basis of Article 10 EC Treaty, that national courts must protect

---

[113] Cf Winter 1999, 470.   [114] Cf Case C–127/95 *Norbrook* [1998] ECR I–1531.

[115] *Commission v. Germany* [1995] ECR I–2303.

[116] Directive 88/295, [1988] OJ L127/1 and Directive 89/440, [1989] OJ L210/1.

[117] Cf also AG Mischo in Case C–340/96 *Commission v. United Kingdom* [1999] ECR I–2023, in particular paras 84–92, who makes a distinction between the question whether a directive confers on a consumer a direct right, enforceable against a water company, to receive 'clean' water on the one hand, and the question whether a Member State has appropriately implemented a directive by providing sufficient legal remedies. On the other hand, a case like C–63/01 *Evans*, 4 December 2003, nyr in ECR, seems to suggest that the Court did accept such a transplant. When dealing with the question of proper implementation, it found that the Second Directive (insurance against civil liability for use of motor vehicles; Directive 84/5, [1984] OJ L8/7) intended to accord rights. When the issue of possible State liability came to the fore, the Court continued tacitly on the basis that the directive intends to confer rights.

the rights individuals derive from Community law.[118] It is more often the case that the full application of Community law provisions as such is what matters, as opposed to the protection of any specific rights. Although for the purposes of the principle of effective judicial protection the Court may refer to the principles enshrined in Article 6 and Article 13 of the ECHR, the scope of the protection required is much broader than (civil) rights.[119]

6.4   Rights for individuals: parameters in the Court's case law?

6.4.1   Introduction

From the case law on implementation as well as on liability, set out above, it may be deduced that as to the question whether rights are (intended to be) created or not, there seem to be two possibilities which correspond with the direct/indirect source scenario: The directive at issue may indicate that rights should be created at national level (implementation/liability case law), or it may be that the rights are directly created by the directive, namely as a result of direct effect (direct effect/liability case law). Unfortunately, the case law does not bring us much further than this: it neither defines or delineates *a priori* when rights will or will not exist, nor what their nature or scope should be. In other words, considerable uncertainty surrounds the concept of rights in Community law.

To a certain extent, this might be less problematic than one would perhaps assume. *For the purposes of direct effect*, understood as the possibility for an individual to rely on Community law provisions in various situations and the corresponding obligation of the courts to apply the provisions, I have argued that the classification is a matter of national law and therefore the question of what is a (subjective) right under Community law, is immaterial.[120] Firstly, many of the preliminary questions submitted to the Court of Justice have been and continue to be worded in terms of whether a provision creates rights, and the Court's answers are couched in the same terms. What the national courts are anxious to know, however, relates to *direct effect* and thus to the questions whether the individual can rely on the provision in question and whether the courts have to apply it. Secondly, in this context to say that the obligation of the courts is to protect the rights which individuals derive from Community law is only another way of saying that the courts must protect the individual's position, whatever the classification of the effects of Community law for this position might be under national law.

---

[118] Cf the case law that started with Case 33/76 *Rewe* [1976] ECR 1989 and Case 45/76 *Comet* [1976] ECR 2043.   [119] For a more detailed discussion see below, Ch 7, Subsections 7.2.2 and 7.4.2.

[120] Yet, also in relation to direct effect it has been submitted that the definition in terms of 'creation of rights' raises the problem of what constitutes a subjective right in Community law. Cf Barents 1982, 98.

The way in which the provisions granting rights under Community law will be treated in the national context depends on the notions used within the various national legal systems and the branch of law—for instance criminal, civil, administrative—in which the provisions will be applied or implemented.

Thus, for instance, while in Germany the entitlement to social security benefits under Directive 79/7 (equal treatment in statutory schemes of social security)[121] will be classified as a '*subjektives öffentliches Recht*' (a public law subjective right),[122] in Dutch law, where the notion of 'subjective right' is often reserved for rights under private law, such a classification will be unusual.[123] This 'reclassification' of legal concepts of Community law into national legal concepts is a consequence of the very fact that the transition from Community law level to national law level entails a certain alteration of the provision at issue.[124]

Nevertheless, all this does not mean that the issue of *what is a right in Community law* can entirely be side-stepped. The main reasons—State liability, the modalities of implementation of the directive in question—have been set out above.[124A] Consequently, the next question to be addressed is that of the circumstances in which provisions of directives confer rights upon individuals, or at least, are intended to confer rights.[125]

Finding the answer is far from simple, for a number of reasons. The Court's 'language of rights' as such is not very helpful in the search for parameters to enable us to identify occasions when a provision gives rise to rights. On the one hand, the inevitable translation of Community law rights into national legal notions is presumably also the reason why the Court of Justice uses the rather neutral term 'rights' and why it is reticent in indicating the nature of the right at issue.[126] The various and often subtle (dogmatic) distinctions and constructions which exist within the national law of the Member States are determined by tradition, the purposes they serve, and the particular structures and organization of the respective legal systems. From this point of view it is understandable and even inevitable that the Court should adopt a somewhat aloof attitude.

---

[121] [1976] OJ L6/24.

[122] More precisely a '*Leistungsrecht*'; cf Winter 1991b, 661. On the theory of 'subjective public rights' ('*subjektive öffentliche Rechte*'; developed in Germany in the 19th century and which still appears to dominate German public law thinking as well as that of other Member States which follow the 'German model', like Austria), in particular, in relation to EU Law see Reich 1995. Interestingly, on the other hand, Community law is also putting this theory under pressure. See e.g. Hölscheidt 2001.

[123] Some efforts have been made however to construe a subjective right also in the public law sphere. Cf Bergamin 1991, Holtmaat 1992, 263 ff.

[124] Mertens de Wilmars 1969, 79. Cf also Mertens de Wilmars 1981, 391.

[124A] Moreover, as Case C–222/02 *Peter Paul* (judgment of 12 October 2004, nyr in ECR) illustrates, for certain purposes of national law the question may be initial.

[125] Namely through implementation. Cf above, Section 6.2.

[126] Cf Case 13/68 *Salgoil* [1968] ECR 453. The issue of classification was recently raised again in Case C–236/92 *Comitato* [1994] ECR I–483, but the Court answered the preliminary question by reasoning purely along the line of direct effect.

On the other hand, as mentioned above, the question whether a provision, a group of provisions, or a directive as a whole confers or intends to confer rights upon individuals plays a vital role in the Court's case law. It would therefore seem that at least some minimum guidelines would be indispensable. The notion of rights, in this context, is a Community law notion: obviously one cannot simply use, for this purpose, the national criteria of what constitutes a right.[127] It has been suggested in this respect that useful criteria could be derived from a comparative legal study.[128] Without excluding the usefulness of such an exercise *a priori*, one may nevertheless wonder whether, given the national differences, this method would be feasible or whether it would lead to satisfactory results. Another possibility is to fall back on legal theory which should, in principle, be less hampered by the peculiarities, technicalities, and vicissitudes of the various national legal systems. However, in this respect one encounters another problem: there is an impressive quantity of treatises on the concept of (subjective) rights but they diverge on the definitive interpretation.[129]

It is certainly not my intention to undertake a comparative study in this respect or to plunge into legal theory: both of these would be quite beyond the scope of this book. However, despite the doubt expressed above, it may be that to a certain extent, in combination with some very basic notions about rights, some useful lessons can be drawn from the case law of the Court of Justice.

6.4.2   Terms and purpose of the provisions

The obvious starting point for analysis is to look at the terms and purpose of the provisions at issue. Community law may grant rights to individuals *expressis verbis*. Furthermore, as was already made clear in *Van Gend en Loos*,[130] the Court made clear that obligations imposed on individuals, on the Member States, and on the Community institutions may also give rise to rights in favour of (other) individuals. It appears that the addressee of the relevant provisions, whether Member State, Community institution, or individual, is not important—the obligation of one subject of Community law is correlative to the right of another.[131]

---

[127] Cf Langenfeld 1992, 962, Winter 1991c, 455. Cf also Caranta 1993, 286 ff.

[128] Cf Langenfeld 1992, 962.

[129] Cf Alexy 1985, 159. Exemplary for the disagreement are e.g. White 1984 and MacCormick 1982.

[130] Case 26/62 [1963] ECR 1. It must be noted that, although the relevant consideration in *Van Gend en Loos* was 'preparing the ground' for the finding that Art 12 EEC was directly effective, in my view, the granting of rights on the one hand and direct effect on the other, as laid down in this judgment, must be distinguished. This is particularly confirmed by *Francovich* (Joined Cases C–6/90 and C–9/90 [1991] ECR I–5357), where the Court reiterated its consideration about the delegation of rights which must be protected while the protection by means of direct effect did not work in this case. Cf also (already) Bleckmann 1978, 116.

[131] Cf Joined Cases C–178/94, C–179/94, C–188/94, C–189/94, and C–190/94 *Dillenkofer* [1996] ECR I–4845, in particular para 34 *et seq.* where the focus is on the obligation of the organizer.

There is, in fact, nothing revolutionary in this approach. The most common attempts to explain the conception of right utilize the notion of a duty or obligation and many jurisprudents assume that one person's duty implies another person's right.[132] With respect to directives, it may seem that matters are complicated in so far as a directive cannot, as such, impose obligations upon individuals. This is, however, as stated above, a problem of enforceability. From the terms of a provision it may very well follow that its purpose is to impose an obligation on an individual, and it is from these terms that another person may derive rights.

The pivotal role the objective or the terms of the provisions at issue can play in relation to the question whether rights are (intended to be) created or not is illustrated by the brief discussion in Subsections 6.3.3 and 6.3.4, on 'Rights and State liability' and 'Rights and implementation of directives'.

In many situations it appears to be easy to see that the terms of the Community law provisions concerned, combined—where necessary—with the purpose of the rules,[133] confer rights; so easy, in fact, that it must be accepted without further ado. The most obvious examples in this respect can be found in the field of free movement of workers or persons in general, freedom of establishment, and freedom to provide services. In the opinion of the Court, both Treaty provisions and secondary legislation enacted in order to facilitate the exercise of these freedoms confer rights upon individuals.

For instance in *Royer*, after having quoted Articles 39(3), 43, and 49 of the EC Treaty, the Court held that 'these provisions, which may be construed as prohibiting Member States from setting up restrictions or obstacles to the entry into and residence in their territory of nationals of other Member States, have the effect of conferring rights directly on all persons falling within the ambit of the above-mentioned provisions . . . '.[134] The same holds true with respect to equal treatment of men and women[135] and most probably with respect to any other rules of Community law in the field of social policy intended to protect the individual, such as Directive 80/987 on the approximation of laws

[132] The system of correlatives has been elaborated in detail by Hohfeld (fundamental legal conceptions), mentioned already above, in note 40. Although his conceptual framework is still used by some, e.g. Alexy 1985, 187 ff., Salmond 1966, 224–33, it has been equally criticized to an extent by others; see e.g. Waldron 1984, 7 ff. and *passim* MacCormick 1977, MacCormick 1982, White 1984.

[133] Sometimes coupled with recitals of the preamble. See Case C–63/01 *Evans*, 4 December 2003, nyr in ECR, para 36. Cf also Case C–222/02 *Peter Paul*, judgment of 12 October 2004, nyr in ECR. In that case, an analysis of the terms, objective, and purpose of the directive resulted in a denial of rights.

[134] Case 48/75 [1976] ECR 497, para 24. It must be observed that here the Court was answering the question whether the provisions were a direct 'source of rights' and that the passage did *not* relate to the question of direct effect. Cf further also Case 222/86 *Heylens* [1987] ECR 4097, Case 29/84 *Commission v. Germany* [1985] ECR 1661, Case C–306/89 *Commission v. Greece* [1991] ECR I–5863, and Case C–340/97 *Nazli* [2000] ECR I–957.

[135] Cf Case 43/75 *Defrenne II* [1976] ECR 455, Case C–208/90 *Emmott* [1991] ECR I–4269.

relating to the protection of employees in the event of the insolvency of the employer, at issue in *Francovich*.[136] The right granted by this directive was the employees' entitlement to a guarantee of payment of their unpaid wage claims. Undoubtedly in many other fields of Community law, on the basis of the terms of the provisions alone, it can be said that they confer rights.[137]

Terms are not however always unequivocal and conversely, of course, even if a provision is couched in clear terms, it does not necessarily imply that rights are granted to individuals. It may therefore be necessary to apply other parameters as well.

6.4.3 Parties to the legal relationship

In the first place, if rights may come into being by virtue of an obligation imposed on another, the relevant question to be considered in this respect relates to the legal relationship laid down in the provision concerned; or, more precisely, it relates to the issue of *who* are the parties to the relationship in the concrete case: *vis-à-vis* whom does the obligation exist?

In *Costa v. ENEL*[138] the Court held that by virtue of Article 102 EEC the Member States have bound themselves to prior consultation with the Commission and have thus undertaken an obligation to the Community. For its part, the Commission is bound to ensure respect for the provisions of the Article. However, according to the Court, these obligations did not create rights in favour of individuals. In *Enichem*[139] the Court found that Article 3(2) of Directive 75/442 (waste),[140] obliging the Member States to inform the Commission in good time of any draft rules within the scope of that provision, had to be construed as concerning relations between the Member States and the Commission only. It therefore did not give rise to any rights for individuals.

---

[136] [1980] OJ L283/23. Cf also with respect to Directive 77/187 (safeguarding employees' rights in the event of transfer of undertakings) [1977] OJ L61/26, Case C–362/89 *D'Urso* [1991] ECR I–4105 and for a right to a 'full pension' (under Regulation 1408/71), and Case C–118/00 *Gervais Larsy* [2001] ECR I–5063.

[137] Cf e.g. Case C–96/95 *Commission v. Germany* [1997] ECR I–1653 concerning directives 90/365 [1990] OJ L180/28 and 90/364 [1990] OJ L180/26, both on the right of residence and Cases C–144/99 *Commission v. the Netherlands* [2001] ECR I–3541 and C–478/99 *Commission v. Sweden* [2002] ECR I–4147, both concerning Directive 93/13 (unfair terms in consumer contracts) [1993] OJ L95/29. With respect to Directive 85/577 (contracts negotiated away from business premises) [1985] OJ L372/31, see Case C–91/92 *Faccini Dori* [1994] ECR I–3325. In relation to Directive 90/313 (access to information on the environment) [1990] OJ L158/56, the Court found that it is the purpose of the Directive to confer a right on individuals and, in this way, assure them freedom of access to information. Cf Case C–217/97 *Commission v. Germany* [1999] ECR I–5087. See further also the brief discussion above, in Subsection 6.3.3.   [138] Case 6/64 [1964] ECR 585.

[139] Case 380/87 [1989] ECR 2491. Cf also Case C–235/95 *Dumon* [1998] ECR I–4531 and Case C–159/00 *Sapod* [2002] ECR I–5031.   [140] [1975] OJ L194/39.

The judgment in *Costa v. ENEL* suggests that if the individual is not a party to the relationship at issue, the provision cannot create rights in his favour.

However, proper regard must be given in this respect to the fact that a provision may give rise to multiple relationships. It is a matter of interpretation whether a particular person in a concrete case is party to one of these or not. In particular, the purpose of the provision concerned is highly relevant in this respect.

In *Enichem* the relevant article was intended, according to the Court, to ensure that the Commission is informed of any plans for national measures in the area of waste disposal. The information should enable the Commission to consider whether Community harmonizing legislation is called for and whether the draft rules are compatible with Community law. The Commission could subsequently consider taking appropriate measures. These aspects are apparently not considered as being of immediate concern to private individuals. It has been suggested that this would be otherwise if the draft measures had to be submitted to the Commission, for instance, for approval, and pending the approval procedure the Member States were precluded from adopting them in a legally valid manner.[141] Yet although the measures thus adopted would be rendered unlawful, this mere fact does not *eo ipso* imply that a right of an individual would have been equally violated. Whether this is the case or not depends, it is submitted, on the question whether or not the approval procedure also served the protection of the individual interest of the person concerned.[142]

The 'notorious' case law on the consequences of non-compliance with the obligations under Directive 83/189 (notification of technical regulations) is causing a lot of confusion in this respect. In fact, this directive was no doubt designed to regulate relations between the Member States and the Commission, or the Member States *inter se* respectively, since the latter may also make observations on proposed measures. The directive's aim is not to regulate behaviour either between private individuals or between individuals and public authorities. This may also explain why the Court held that Directive 83/189 does not define the substantive scope of the legal rule on the basis of which the national court must decide the case before it and that it creates neither rights nor obligations for individuals. Nevertheless, the Court accepted that the sanction of inapplicability of national rules adopted in breach of the Directive could also be relied upon in disputes between two private parties. In my view, this is the consequence of the fact that legal rules may influence in different ways a relationship between legal subjects. Rules may also have a more indirect

---

[141] Opinion of AG Jacobs in Case 380/87 *Enichem* [1989] ECR 2491, para 14.

[142] In the same line it can be argued that where the State is obliged not to effectuate State aid measures until they have been approved by the Commission, this obligation exists not only *vis-à-vis* the Community but apparently also *vis-à-vis* private undertakings. The latter can rely in national courts on the 'blocking provision' of Art 93(3), last sentence. The explanation for this is that the procedure to be followed by the Commission also serves the protection of their individual interests.

impact, which ultimately alters the relationship. This is, in particular, the case where the rules do not themselves regulate the relationship, but where they influence the application of a rule which does directly regulate a parties' relationship. Both in *CIA Security* and *Unilever*[143] it was the status and validity of public law regulatory standards which determined the private law obligations between the parties, either non-contractual (*CIA Security*) or contractual (*Unilever*). The respective obligations were dependent on the lawfulness of national 'technical' standards, which were not notified or adopted, in violation of Article 8, respectively Article 9, of Directive 83/189. These standards then became unenforceable since they were contrary to a Community law rule.[144] Another—additional—explanation could also be that the approval procedure of Directive 83/189 did not serve the protection of the individual interest of the persons concerned. I will come back to this issue in the next Subsection.

Another still somewhat unorthodox but more and more topical example of indirect influence is provided by cases where, before national courts, individuals present an argument that a directive measure is invalid because it has been adopted on a wrong legal basis.[145] On the one hand, legal basis provisions have an important function in protecting at least the public at large against measures which institutions are not competent to take.[146] On the other hand, as such, they are not really intended to govern the position of individuals in relationship with other individuals or with their State authorities. Yet, legal basis provisions may be relied upon by those individuals and produce legal effects in the relationship between individuals or between individuals and a Member State: the invalidity of a directive will have consequences for national law implementing it.

The issue of the legal relationship and the parties involved is by no means a problem of notification obligations only. It is often not explicitly addressed because the issue does

---

[143] Case C–194/94 *CIA Security* [1996] ECR I–2201 and Case C–443/98 *Unilever* [2000] ECR I–7535. Cf also Case C–159/00 *Sapod* [2002] ECR I–5031.

[144] Cf also Prechal 2002, 29–31 and Betlem 2002, 93–6, though the latter discussion focuses primarily on the issue of indirect horizontal direct effect. However, Dougan 2001, 1507 has observed that, in the ultimate analysis, the effect is the same as if the directive did define the substantive scope of the legal rule on the basis of which the national court must decide the case and that it creates neither rights nor obligations for individuals. For a further discussion of this issue see Ch 9, Subsection 9.5.3.

[145] For instance, Case C–331/88 *Fedesa* [1990] ECR I–4023, and Case C–74/99 *Imperial Tobacco* [2000] ECR I–8599, and Case C–491/01 *British American Tobacco (Investments) Ltd* [2002] ECR I–11453.

[146] The position of the Court is not very clear in this respect. In the First *Meroni* case (Case 9/56 [1957–1958] ECR 133) the Court clearly stated that the observance of the balance of power provided a guarantee to the undertakings under the ECS Treaty. This finding is contrasted with the more recent judgment in *Vreugdenhil* (Case C–282/90 [1992] ECR I–1937) where the Court held that the aim of the system of division of powers between the various Community institutions is to ensure that the institutional balance provided for by the Treaty is maintained, and not to protect the individuals. This position has been—in my view rightly—criticized in legal writing. See e.g. Fines 1997a, 24.

not create any particular problems. However, for instance, in her Opinion in Case C–222/02 *Peter Paul*, Advocate General Stix-Hackl explored whether Article 3, Sections 2–5, of Directive 94/19 (deposit-guarantee schemes)[147] regulates the relationship between depositors and their credit institutions, the competent State authorities, or the guarantee scheme, which was, in her opinion not the case: the provision merely regulates a number of competences and obligations of the credit institutions, the competent State authorities, and the guarantee scheme.[148]

In brief, to identify the parties to a legal relationship is not always a problem, particularly not where the addressees of the relevant rules can be directly ascertained on the basis of the directive. Yet, in other cases a considerable interpretative effort may be necessary to find out, also because a single provision may give rise to multiple relationships. For instance, a provision may at first sight appear only to concern the relationship between the Member State and the Commission, or a credit institution and competent State authorities. If, however, the purpose of the provision is to protect the interest of the individual, the individual may become party to a different relationship under the provision at issue, namely the relationship between him and the Member State, or between him and the competent State authorities, with as subject matter the obligation of the Member State or the authorities to act as prescribed by the directive concerned.

6.4.4   Protection of individual interest

At the end of the last Subsection, I came to the second relevant element for the problem under discussion here, namely that the legal rules which are the source of the alleged right must exist to protect the individual interest and not merely to protect the general or public interest.

This view, which is still generally accepted, linking a right to interest,[149] dates back in particular to Jhering, who states:

Zwei Momente sind es, die den Begriff des Rechts konstituieren, ein substantielles, in dem der praktische Zweck desselben liegt, nämlich der Nutzen, Vorteil, Gewinn, der durch das Recht gewährleistet werden soll, und ein formales, welches sich zu jenem Zweck bloss als Mittel verhält, nämlich der Rechtsschutz, die Klage.[150]

For Jhering it is primarily the substantive criterion which is important. This view has strongly marked the general thinking about rights and explains the common thesis that rights are considered to serve the protection of individual interests.[151]

---

[147] [1994] OJ L135/5.   [148] Opinion of 25 November 2003, at paras 75 and 95–96.

[149] Cf White 1984, 79 and 102. See also the Opinion of AG Capotorti in Case 158/80 *Butter-buying cruises* [1981] ECR 1805, para 6. However, for Community law a requirement of interest was denied by Bleckmann 1978, 94.

[150] Jhering, *Geist des Römischen Rechts*, Vol 3, 339, quoted by Alexy 1985, 165.

[151] Cf White 1984, 79, Salmond 1966, 217–21, MacCormick 1977, 192.

The problem is that the distinction between general and individual interest is not black and white but rather a matter of degree. Every legal rule and its correct application can be considered as protecting general interest and as being the concern— in principle—of everybody, or at least, of very large and general groups of persons. Whether over and above that the rule protects the special interest which some individuals might have is a problem of interpretation of the provision at issue.[152] Environmental law directives are often mentioned in this context as examples of Community law rules intended to protect the general interest.[153] For instance, in his discussion of the conditions for State liability as formulated in the *Francovich* judgement[154] Judge Schockweiler explained that the first condition, i.e. that the result prescribed by the directive should entail *the granting of rights to individuals*, must be understood in the sense that the Court wanted to exclude State liability for violation of *'simple intérêts'* which the relevant directive intended to protect. To give examples of directives which most probably do not intend to grant rights to individuals he refers to directives in the field of environmental law.[155] This position is rather surprising, as in the same year that the *Francovich* judgment was rendered the Court found in a number of cases brought under Article 226 and relating to environmental directives that these directives *are* intended to create rights and obligations for individuals.[156]

In Subsection 6.3.4, on 'Rights and implementation of directives', I have already pointed out that the term 'right' in the context of implementation case law may have a loose, a-dogmatic meaning which might explain why Schockweiler's proposition is still valid.[157] The difficulty is indeed that from the point of view of coherence of Community law, a differentiation in relation to the concept of right does not seem to be beneficial, in particular as it causes confusion, in addition to the confusion resulting already from the 'national perceptions'.[158] On the other hand, from a functional point of view, such a differentiation might be unavoidable.

It is undoubtedly true that some directives *as a whole* protect the general or public interest more than other directives. An example can be drawn—again—from environmental directives protecting the general interest in a less polluted environment

---

[152] Cf also what has been said about the provisions on State aids above, in note 142. Undoubtedly, the rules of the Treaty are general rules against distortion. However, at the same time they protect the individual interests of the undertakings affected. Cf also Temple Lang 1992–1993, 33–5.

[153] Cf Temple Lang 1992–1993, 28. See also Case 240/83 *ADBHU* [1985] ECR 531, in particular para 15.   [154] Joined Cases C–6/90 and C–9/90 [1991] ECR I–5357.

[155] Schockweiler 1992, 44. More specifically he mentions as examples Directive 75/440 (surface water I) [1975] OJ L194/56, Directive 79/869 (surface water II) [1979] OJ L271/44, and Directive 80/68 (groundwater) [1980] OJ L20/43. Cf also Gilliams 1991–1992, 19. Cf however also Schockweiler 1993b, 114.

[156] Case C–59/89 *Commission v. Germany* [1991] ECR I–2607, Case C–58/89 *Commission v. Germany* [1991] ECR I–4983, Case C–361/88 *Commission v. Germany* [1991] ECR I–2567, and Case C–131/88 *Commission v. Germany* [1991] ECR I–825. In particular the last case relates to a directive which Schockweiler has given as an example of a 'non rights granting' directive. Cf also Van Gerven 1993, 19.

[157] As already mentioned, others also failed to see how a subjective right can be construed on the basis of the mere fact that the directives concerned aim at protecting human health. Cf Zuleeg 1993, 214. See also Everling 1992a, 384–5 and Everling 1993, 214–15.   [158] Cf above, Subsection 6.3.2.

on the one hand, and directives like Directive 77/187 safeguarding the rights of employees in the case of transfer of an undertaking on the other.[159] However, with a view to realizing the general interest objective pursued by a directive, the directive will often contain more detailed and concrete provisions. These may as such grant rights to (or have the purpose of imposing obligations upon[160]) individuals. This was stated in unambiguous terms by the Court of Justice in Case C–131/88 (groundwater), where it held that the directive at issue

seeks to protect the Community's groundwater . . . by laying down specific and detailed provisions requiring the Member States to adopt a series of prohibitions, authorization schemes and monitoring procedures in order to prevent or limit discharges of certain substances. The purpose of those provisions of the directive is thus to create rights and obligations for individuals.[161]

In brief, it seems that it is not the kind of interest which a directive as a whole intends to protect but the protection sought by its separate provisions that is decisive.

A number of other judgments[162] suggest that the Court is rather easily satisfied that a directive provision also intends to protect individual interests. The mere fact of a directive being enacted—*inter alia*—with a view to protecting human health is sufficient to assume that there is an individual (health) interest of those who are exposed to higher air-quality values than the ones provided for by the directive or of those whose health is endangered because the measures required (surveillance of surface water and of the purification treatment of the water) have not been observed. In other words, a phrase expressed in terms of protection of general (or public) interest is relied upon in order to assert that the directives' provisions protect individual interests as well or even 'in particular'. From this it could be concluded that the 'individual interest requirement' can hardly be considered a serious restriction.[163]

Two cases concerning Germany related to directives laying down air-quality limit values for sulphur dioxide (80/779) and lead respectively (82/884).[164] The relevant articles of the respective directives obliged the Member States to prescribe limit values which must not be exceeded within specified periods and specified circumstances. It likewise appeared from the directives that this

---

[159] [1977] OJ L61/26.   [160] With rights resulting therefrom as 'correlatives'.

[161] *Commission v. Germany* [1991] ECR I–825, para 7.

[162] Case C–361/88 *Commission v. Germany* [1991] ECR I–2567 and Case C–59/89 *Commission v. Germany* [1991] ECR I–2607. These judgments were subsequently confirmed in three judgments brought by the Commission against France: C–13/90 [1991] ECR I–4327, C–14/90 [1991] ECR I–4331, and C–64/90 [1991] ECR I–4335 (summary publications). Cf also Case C–58/89 *Commission v. Germany* [1991] ECR I–4983 and Case C–298/95 *Commission v. Germany* [1996] ECR I–6747.

[163] This does not come as a surprise when one takes into consideration the application of a similar and not very restrictive requirement in cases brought under Art 288 of the Treaty. Cf Grabitz 1988, 6–7. However, this may change under the influence of the *Bergaderm* case law. *Bergaderm* (Case C–352/98 P [2000] ECR I–5291) has introduced the requirement that the infringed legal norm must intend to confer rights on individuals instead of the 'old' requirement that the rule at issue must be a rule of law aiming at the protection of individuals.   [164] [1980] OJ L229/30 and [1982] OJ L378/15.

obligation is imposed on the Member States 'in order to protect human health in particular'[165] or 'specifically in order to help protect human beings against the effects of lead in the environment'.[166] Other objectives of the directive were the elimination or prevention of unequal conditions of competition and the protection of the quality of the environment. Yet, here again the caveat, that those cases have been decided in the context of implementation case law, must be mentioned.[167]

In other cases, the class of protected persons is perhaps still rather broad, but in any case more defined than the very large and general groups of persons concerned in the environmental directives case law. The former include, for instance, consumers which are sufficiently defined by the Directive at issue.[168] In other terms, there was an identifiable class of persons protected.

In *Dillenkofer*,[169] the Court relied on the fact that the preamble repeatedly refers to the purpose of protecting consumers. Moreover, also the aim and wording of the particular provision, which the Court had to interpret, Article 7 of the directive, was to protect consumers. The fact that the directive intended to ensure other additional objectives (freedom to provide services and fair competition) could not detract from this finding. In Case C–144/99 the Court deduced from one of the aims of Directive 93/13 (unfair terms in consumer contracts), set out in the preamble, namely 'to safeguard the citizen in his role as consumer when acquiring goods and services under contracts which are governed by the laws of Member States other than his own', that the directive intended to accord rights to individuals.[170] In Case C–478/99 the Court also accepted that the same directive aims at creating rights for individuals, but this time on the basis of a number of specific provisions.[171]

In her Opinion in *Peter Paul*, on the other hand, the Advocate General found that several banking directives admittedly mention the protection of investors in the preamble, but the recitals as such do not enable individuals to derive rights from them.[172] For that purpose, in her view, a directive must also contain a number of

---

[165] Case C–361/88 *Commission v. Germany* [1991] ECR I–2567, para 16. Other objectives of the directive are the elimination or prevention of unequal conditions of competition and the protection of the quality of the environment.

[166] Case C–59/89 *Commission v. Germany* [1991] ECR I–2607, para 19.

[167] Cf discussion above in Subsection 6.3.4 and the Opinion of AG Mischo in Case C–340/96 *Commission v. United Kingdom* [1999] ECR I–2023, in particular paras 84–92. See also the Opinion of AG Kokott in Case C–127/02 *Landelijke Vereniging tot Behoud van de Waddenzee*, of 29 January 2004, para 143.

[168] Joined Cases C–178/94, C–179/94, C–188/94, C–189/94, and C–190/94 *Dillenkofer* [1996] ECR I–4845, para 44.

[169] Joined Cases C–178/94, C–179/94, C–188/94, C–189/94, and C–190/94 [1996] ECR I–4845.

[170] Case C–144/99 *Commission v. the Netherlands* [2001] ECR I–3541.

[171] Case C–478/99 *Commission v. Sweden* [2002] ECR I–4147.

[172] Opinion of 25 November 2003 in Case C–222/02. Interestingly, national courts in various Member States came to different conclusions on this issue. Cf Andenas and Fairgrieve 2002 and Andenas and Fairgrieve 2000.

specific provisions. Moreover, where Directive 94/19 provides for supervisory measures, before these measures are taken a complex balancing of a number of interests of a different nature must be made, which excludes that the individual interest of depositors should be given priority. Like the Advocate General the Court did not accept that the protection of depositors, mentioned as one of the objectives of the directives at issue, could be a decisive factor.

How strict—in Community law—this requirement of protection of individual interest is, is far from clear and it seems to depend on the various contexts in which until now the cases have been decided. In any case, there is an agreement that the Court's approach is less strict than, for instance, German or Austrian law.[173] In particular in German legal writing it is often pointed out that the Court of Justice is more readily satisfied that a provision is also aiming at the protection of individual interests than a German court would be under the application of the German 'Schutznormtheory'.[174] Until recently it seemed that the very fact that the protective scope of a Community law rule includes individual interest is sufficient. Individual interest as a specific aim of protection was not necessary. However, the judgment in Peter Paul[174A] suggests that the Court is going to tighten the individual interest requirement.

> This also triggers the question whether directives which are 'a first step in a process of harmonisation' and as such concerned with 'the removal of barriers' to the fundamental freedoms guaranteed by the EC Treaty confer rights upon individuals. According to the House of Lords, a directive will be found not to create rights for individuals exactly for these two arguments.[175] However, in the area of public procurement, the Court stressed that Directive 92/50 (public procurement—service contracts)[176] was adopted with a view to eliminating barriers to the freedom to provide services and therefore is intended to protect the interests of traders who wish to offer services to contracting authorities in other Member States.[177] This would rather point in the direction of individual rights.

The example of Directive 92/50 brings me to a specific category of provisions, i.e. essentially procedural rules and the question in how far these rules aim at the protection of individuals. In relation to procedural provisions the latter is often less evident than with respect to substantive rules. In some cases, there can hardly be any doubt. The most obvious examples of this are indeed public procurement

---

[173] Jarass and Beljin 2003, 176–90.

[174] Hölscheidt 2001, 386–9. For a rather reserved position of an English court see e.g. *Bowden v. South West Water Services Ltd* [1999] 3 CMLR 180 (Bathing Water Directive and Waste Water Directive did not entail the granting of rights to shell-fishermen).

[174A] Case–222/02 *Peter Paul*, judgment of 12 October 2004, nyr in ECR.

[175] *Three Rivers Case* [2000] 3 CMLR 205. Cf also Case C–222/02 *Peter Paul* (judgment of 12 October 2004, nyr in ECR) where the Court used comparable arguments.   [176] [1992] OJ L209/1.

[177] Joined Cases C–20/01 and C–28/01 *Commission v. Germany* [2003] ECR I–3609.

directives.[178] However, does Directive 83/189, for instance, aim at the protection of individuals? Its purpose is to protect the free movement of goods by means of a preventive mechanism obliging the Member States to notify national draft measures on technical standards and await the reactions of the Commission or other Member States. Maintaining the free movement of goods, a rather general (Community) interest, includes indeed the interest of traders. But is this sufficient for the purposes at issue here, namely in relation to the question whether a provision of Community law, as a matter of its content, creates individual rights? The Court denied the creation of rights in *Unilever*.[179] Moreover, the cases relating to Directive 83/189 have been decided rather along the *effet utile* line, i.e. the full effectiveness of the preventive system laid down in the Directive, than as a matter of protection of interest of traders.[180]

> However, the issue of protection of individual interest has slipped into the discussion on the level of direct effect, namely in relation to the question *who* is allowed to rely on the inapplicability resulting from the Court's case law. Both the Dutch government before the ECJ and Advocate General Fennelly in the *Lemmens* case[181] argued that only those persons whose interests are intended to be protected by the directive provisions may invoke the directive before the courts. The invocability of the directive is by both reserved for those persons who have an interest in the free movement of goods. The Court, at least in my view, did not decide the latter issue in its judgment.[182]

Similar questions may also arise in relation to the Environmental Impact Assessment Directive.[183] There is no doubt whatsoever that the directive protects the general interest to protect the environment. However, how far does it also protect certain individual interests? It is more or less generally accepted that, for instance, in *Kraaijeveld*, the EIA Directive did not protect the claimant's rights or interests, which were at stake: the access to his harbour.[184] However, could this be different in other circumstances?

---

[178] Cf also Case C–19/00 *SIAC* [2001] ECR I–7725, and Case C–243/89 *University of Cambridge* [2000] ECR I–8035, and the already mentioned (Subsection 6.3.4) Case C–433/93 *Commission v. Germany* [1995] ECR I–2303, where the Court held that the rules regarding participation and advertising in public procurement directives are intended to protect tenderers against arbitrariness on the part of the contract-awarding authority.

[179] Case C–443/98 [2000] ECR I–7535. However, it should be noted that what was at issue there, were the potential rights and obligations between private traders and not rights and obligations between a private trader and the Member State. Interestingly, AG Elmer argued in his Opinion in Case C–194/94 *CIA* [1996] ECR I–2201, in particular paras 62–67, that the same directive did create rights for individuals.

[180] Cf also Case C–253/00 *Muñoz* [2002] ECR I–7289, which was analysed by AG Geelhoed in terms of rights of traders/competitors but decided by the Court as mainly an issue of full effectiveness of the (enforcement of the) rules on fruit standards.

[181] Case C–227/97 [1998] ECR I–3711; see also Timmermans 1997, 22.

[182] For further discussion see below, Ch 9, Subsection 9.3.5.

[183] Directive 85/337 [1985] OJ L175/40.

[184] Edward 1998, 441–2, Prechal 2002, 19. Cf however the effort of AG Elmer in *Kraaijeveld* (C–72/95 [1996] ECR I–5403), to squeeze the legality review at issue in that case into the straitjacket of rights.

This directive has the objective of ensuring that development consent for public and private projects which are likely to have significant effects on the environment is granted only after prior assessment of those effects. Furthermore, it aims at the assessment being conducted on the basis of information supplied by the developer and by the authorities and the people concerned by the project. The information supplied by the developer must be communicated to the authorities concerned and made available to the public. Those authorities and the public are given an opportunity to express their opinion. The authorities which are competent to grant consent for the project must take into consideration all the information gathered in the course of the assessment procedure. Finally, the public must be informed of the decision adopted and of any conditions attached thereto.

Much in this context depends on who are to be considered as the public concerned. Yet, even this term seems to relate to large categories of persons and cover very general interests to be protected.[185]

It could be, that at the end of the day, for the purposes of the question whether certain legal rules, like a directive, create rights for individuals, more specific provisions are necessary, in addition to general dicta in the preamble, which make it possible to identify the persons protected under the rules at issue. According to well-established approaches, the legal subjects who claim a right must also be ascertainable with sufficient precision. Protection of the public at large is too indefinite for these purposes.

6.4.5 Ascertainability

In general it is assumed that a right must be enforceable by some form of legal process by the person concerned;[186] or as White puts it, the 'common jurisprudential definition of a right is that it is a legally enforceable claim'.[187] Indeed, this characteristic can be found in the quotation from Jhering given above ('*der Rechtsschutz, die Klage*') and it has been considered by some as the decisive element for the existence of a right.[188] However, not everyone agrees with this latter requirement, pointing out that in every legal system there are classes of legal rights which are not

---

[185] To an important extent this can be compared to the cases on environmental directives decided in infringement proceedings and discussed before, in Subsection 6.3.4. Moreover, if one has to construe rights under this directive, these are of procedural nature only. Cf AG Cosmas, Opinion in Case C–321/95 *Greenpeace* [1998] ECR I–1651, para 59.   [186] Cf Bergamin 1991, 96.

[187] White 1984, 129.

[188] In fact Jhering's quote reflects the old and still not satisfactorily resolved (cf Alexy 1985, 166–167) discussion between adherents of the 'will theory' and 'interest theory'. Jhering himself was an adherent of the latter and defined rights as '*rechtlich geschützte Interessen*'. For those advocating the 'will theory' the second, formal element was decisive. In this respect it was similarly argued that in cases where the formal criterion, the possibility of enforcement, was lacking but nevertheless the legal rule did protect an interest, there existed the so-called 'reflex right' ('*Reflex Recht*'). Cf also MacCormick 1977.

enforceable by any legal process. Those who contend that rights which are not enforceable are in reality no legal rights at all are, in this view, confusing obligatoriness with enforceability.[189] With respect to the 'enforceability', two different aspects must be distinguished. First, the ascertainability of the content of the right and second, the availability of judicial protection of the right.

As far as ascertainability is concerned, in addition to the persons concerned,[190] it requires that also the subject matter, the content of the right, is sufficiently concrete or delineated. Or, in other—everyday—words, one must know *what* one is claiming *in concreto* and, accordingly, the other party must know *to what* it is obliged *in concreto*. Thus, in the case of directives the content of the right must be circumscribed in the provisions of the directive.

In public law this aspect of ascertainability will often pose problems. Public law rules may impose obligations on public authorities or on the State as a whole, while leaving them a considerable degree of discretion with respect to the concrete fulfilment or realization of those obligations. As the corresponding right of an individual must be ascertainable with sufficient precision, it can only exist as a correlative of the obligation if the latter is sufficiently defined. Whether this is the case will depend on the extent to which the public authority is bound. Thus, while some provisions do not as such give rise to an individual right, they may define the conditions in which rights come to be created. The less discretion is left to the authorities concerned, the more probable it is that the requirement of ascertainability will be satisfied.[191]

In Community law, the prerequisite that (the subject matter of) the right is defined in sufficiently concrete terms is a familiar feature. It is very similar to the requirement for a Community law provision to have direct effect and is therefore frequently encountered in the Court's case law.[192] Similarly, the Court requires, in the context of State liability, that the—allegedly violated—right must be 'determinable with sufficient precision' or similar terminology. Initially, this requirement was laid down in the *Francovich* judgment as a second separate condition for the purposes of State liability in the case of non-implementation of a directive. The Court stated that 'it should be possible to identify the content of [the] rights [at issue] on the basis of the provisions of the directive'.[193] In the meantime, it is generally accepted that this condition has no self-standing meaning and that the requirement of 'identifiability' is a part of the first requirement (the provision infringed must intend to confer rights).

---

[189] Cf Salmond 1966, 234, MacCormick 1977 *passim*.

[190] Cf previous Subsection. Cf also the Opinion of AG Tesauro in Joined Cases C–178/94, C–179/94, C–188/94, C–189/94, and C–190/94 *Dillenkofer* [1996] ECR I–4845, para 18 and Case C–140/97 *Rechberger* [1999] ECJ I–3499, para 22.

[191] Cf Bergamin 1991, 106–7 and Holtmaat 1992, 281 and 283–4.   [192] See Ch 9, Section 9.4.

[193] Joined Cases C–6/90 and C–9/90 [1991] ECR I–5357, para 40. Cf also Case C–91/92 *Faccini Dori* [1994] ECR I–3325. See also Schockweiler 1992, 44 who observed with respect to the second condition: 'cette deuxième condition est intimement liée à la première qu'elle ne semble vouloir que préciser et développer'.

Although this 'identification of the content' from State liability case law and the requirements for direct effect are closely linked, they should not be conflated. In this respect, it is interesting to note that, in legal writing it has been observed that in *Francovich* the Court intentionally did not use the orthodox terms of direct effect conditions 'unconditional and sufficiently precise'.[194]

> The danger of not making the appropriate distinction in this respect is nicely illustrated by the *Three Rivers* judgment of the House of Lords.[195] The case concerned, *inter alia*, a claim for damages, based on Community law, which several thousands of depositors incurred as a consequence of the collapse of the BCCI. The Bank of England, in its capacity of banking supervisor, allegedly acted in breach of the First Banking Directive.[196]
>
> According to the House of Lords, there were two distinct routes which could be followed: one based on the principle of direct effect (the *Becker*-type liability) and one based on the principle of State liability (the *Francovich*-type liability). However, it was not necessary to distinguish between those two. The conditions to be satisfied under both types of liability 'are so closely analogous that they can be taken to be . . . the same'.[197] Next, the Lords proceeded to analyse the two 'critical questions', namely whether the First Banking Directive entails the granting of rights to individual depositors and potential depositors and whether the content of those rights is identifiable on the basis of the provisions of the directive. The Lords found that there was, in the directive, no provision which entailed the granting of rights to individuals.
>
> In addition to the remarkable dicta about two routes by which damages can be claimed which, as a matter of Community law, do not exist, it is highly questionable whether the conditions can be treated as the same, despite the analogy which indeed exists between them.[198]

In my opinion, the conditions for direct effect and for the identifiability of rights for the purposes of State liability are two issues that should be treated separately.[199] In the first place because, as explained above,[200] direct effect should not be equated without qualification to the creation of rights. The creation of rights—as a consequence of direct effect—is only one of the 'manifestations' of this doctrine. In this respect, it is submitted that an affirmative answer to the question whether the test for direct effect, i.e. the conditions of clarity, sufficient precision, and unconditionality, is satisfied will usually also indicate that there is a right conferred upon

---

[194] Cf Gilliams 1991–1992, 879. See also below, Ch 10, Subsection 10.4.2.
[195] [2000] 3 CMLR 205.
[196] Directive 77/780 [1977] OJ L322/30.   [197] [2000] 3 CMLR 2005, at p. 230, No 45.
[198] For a critical comment of the judgment see e.g. Andenas 2000 and Jans and Prinssen 2002, 112–14.
[199] Cf also the Opinion of AG Stix-Hackl of 25 November 2003 in Case C–222/02 *Peter Paul*, in particular para 58.   [200] Subsection 6.3.2.

individuals, provided that the question is indeed raised in a context where a person asserts a positive claim, often a right.[201]

Conversely, as has also been pointed out,[202] Community law provisions may grant rights without being directly effective, for instance, because of the lack of *horizontal* direct effect of directives or because the *concrete identity* of the person at the other end of the relationship is not yet entirely certain, as was the case in *Francovich*. Therefore, the ascertainability (or identifiability) of the subject matter of the right and the test for direct effect will often coincide, but one should bear in mind that the concepts are not interchangeable. A provision may be sufficiently precise to be directly effective *and* to create individual rights, but this is not necessarily always so. Once it has been established that the provisions at issue are not directly effective, one has to proceed with the question whether the content of the right is ascertainable on the basis of the directive of the provisions concerned. Arguably, this condition is different from the precision and unconditionality required for direct effect and seems to be less restrictive.

In relation to the connection between the ascertainability of rights, or, more precisely, of their subject matter and the discretion left to the administration or the legislature—as the case may be[203]—it has been noted that the (potential) creation of rights depends in particular on the degree of discretion left to the administration and the legislature respectively. It is obvious that in Community law, and in particular with respect to directives, this problem is extremely real. The very nature and purpose of directives is to be transposed into national law. The question as to the choice left to the implementing authorities in relation to the *content* of the implementing measures[204] will therefore be decisive for the problem of whether the subject matter of the (alleged) right is defined with sufficient precision. When the test for direct effect—which ultimately also

---

[201] The situation may be different where a person uses Community law provisions in the context of a legality review. Cf the Opinion of AG Léger of 11 January 2000 in Case C–287/98 *Linster* [2000] ECR I–6917. See also the Opinion of AG Stix-Hackl of 25 November 2003 in Case C–222/02 *Peter Paul*. While, on the one hand, she made a neat distinction between the issue of direct effect on the one hand and State liability on the other, in the actual application of the relevant criteria there is a considerable overlap. The latter is in particular due to the fact that already the issue of direct effect was formulated and treated by the AG as a problem of a right which depositors allegedly derived from the directive concerned. An important factor is, in this context, that when a positive claim is asserted, the Community law provisions must be able to be applied *instead of* the national rules which are incompatible with Community law or which do not exist at all, and, therefore, must be sufficiently precise and unconditional *for this very purpose*. See on direct effect as '*Alternativ Normierung*' below, Ch 9, Subsection 9.3.3.

[202] Subsection 6.3.2.

[203] For instance the discretion left to the legislature to substantiate the content in implementing legislation. Cf also Case C–403/98 *Monte Arcosu* [2001] ECR I–103: for reasons of discretion enjoyed by Member States in respect of the implementation of certain provisions of a regulation, individuals could not derive rights from these provisions when no measures of application were taken.

[204] Note that what is at stake here is *not* the discretion in relation to the means to be adopted in order to implement the directive. Cf e.g. the Opinion of AG Tesauro in Joined Cases C–178/94, C–179/94, C–188/94, C–189/94, and C–190/94 *Dillenkofer* [1996] ECR I–4845, paras 15–18.

concerns the issue of discretion[205]—is satisfied, the provision must be considered as being sufficiently precise with respect to the subject matter of the right.[206] However, it seems that also where a provision leaves some choice, as to the content, to the authorities transposing it and which, for that reason, cannot be considered as directly effective, it may, nevertheless, give *grosso modo* sufficient indications as to the subject matter concerned. Therefore, it may, in fact be considered as creating rights or intending to do so.

The case of *Annalisa Carbonari*[207] provides a nice example in this respect. It concerned a situation where the content of the obligation was not defined with sufficient precision in the directive at issue, neither were the institutions named which bore the obligation to pay the relevant remuneration. Under Directive 75/363,[208] as amended by Directive 82/76,[209] trainees in specialized medicine were supposed to get appropriate remuneration. So far there was, according to the ECJ, an unconditional and sufficiently precise obligation imposed upon the Member States. Yet, the Directive did not define what level of remuneration had to be regarded as 'appropriate', neither did it indicate the methods by which that remuneration was to be fixed. Furthermore, the Directive did not enable the national courts to determine what body should be liable to pay the remuneration. This resulted in that direct effect was of no avail. However, the Court went on and recalled the possibility of State liability. One would expect that the Court has done so because, despite the lack of direct effect, there were probably sufficient indications as to the right the trainees could derive from the directive in the context of State liability.

Finally, it should be pointed out that even when Member States are left with quite some discretion as to the exact scope and modalities of the content of the measures to be enacted at national level in pursuance of the directive, this may not lead to the conclusion that a directive is *not intended* to create rights in favour of individuals, with all the consequences for the requirements posed with respect to its implementation.[210] In such a situation, the *actual* rights will result from the national measures, which must, for this very reason, be sufficiently precise. It is then ultimately up to the Member States to create legally defined and enforceable positions.[211]

Arguably, there is some gradation: for the purposes of rights in the context of direct effect the requirements to be satisfied as to the ascertainability are rather strict. The test to be applied for the purpose of ascertainability of the content of the alleged right in the context of State liability is more lenient. The 'implementation case law'

---

[205] Cf e.g. the positive claim to be taxed according to a certain standard laid down in the directive at issue in *Brinkmann II* (Case C–365/98 [2000] ECR I–4619). This claim could not be accepted because the Member States—more precisely the national legislator—had a choice from three different tax formulas. See further also below, Ch 9, Subsection 9.4.3.

[206] Again, provided that a right is asserted.   [207] C–131/97 *Carbonari* [1999] ECR I–1103.

[208] [1975] OJ L167/14.   [209] [1982] OJ L43/21.   [210] See above, Ch 5.

[211] See above, Ch 5, Subsection 5.2.1 and Subsection 6.3.4.

requires merely an indication that the Member States should, in the process of implementation, create sufficiently defined and enforceable positions for individuals.

6.4.6 Judicial protection

The question whether appropriate judicial protection exists for the (sufficiently precisely defined) right is inextricably linked with one of the main concerns of 'subjective rights' theories, namely how to transform legal provisions into legally enforceable entitlements.[212] Rights are usually accompanied by the power to institute legal proceedings for their enforcement. If a breach of an individual right is claimed, in many legal systems, the individual concerned will have guaranteed access to the courts. Furthermore, in relation to the consideration of the merits of the case and the remedial outcomes, a 'bearer of rights' will often be in a more advantageous position than a person who just claims the protection of a (legitimate) interest.[213] In this context, individual rights may appear to have a special normative force, a kind of 'magic'. Also at the level of a concrete dispute, where the judge is often required to balance conflicting interests, rights may override other considerations, such as those of general welfare or considerations of a more general economic character. The position of a person vindicating the protection of 'mere' interests will obviously be different and usually weaker.

In some directives specific provisions are laid down as to the enforceability of the rights which they grant. These types of provisions could—if necessary—be used as an argument for the thesis that the directive intends to create rights. In the majority of cases, however, such provisions are lacking.

In general, in Community law the problem of judicial remedies available for the protection of the rights which this law confers or intends to confer, stands out in particularly sharp relief. The main reason for this is that Community law relies heavily on national legal orders for its enforcement. Thus, where Community law confers rights it is left to national law to supply the remedy. This system of articulation may operate in an imperfect manner with, as a possible consequence the existence of a Community law right without an appropriate remedy at national level. As far as directives are concerned, the most obvious example of the difficulties which may occur is the poor record of their implementation. Even if there are rights which should be conferred upon individuals by a certain directive, in the absence of proper implementation they would not be enforceable in national courts.

---

[212] Cf e.g. on this issue of so-called 'subjectivization' Reich 1995, 167. These efforts may sometimes stretch the concept of rights considerably. See e.g. Gurlit 1997 for an attempt to construe an 'individual right to proper implementation of Community law'.

[213] This holds in particular true for legal systems where this somewhat opaque distinction is used. In Italian law, for instance, an infringement of a rule which generates 'only' a legitimate interest, cannot sound in damages. Also in Belgium, this distinction seems to be common and, like in Italy, it also determines the jurisdiction of ordinary and administrative courts. Cf Pâques 1996, in particular 199–200.

The fact that the situation is otherwise is the consequence of several jurisprudential developments at Community law level which concentrate on the possibilities for individuals to assert their rights and on the obligation in the national courts to protect them. These developments will be addressed in detail in the next Chapters.

Considered against this background, it may be clear that the element of 'judicial protection' (which is necessarily protection through national courts) as an indication for the existence of a right does not work. Where the approach is that enforcement and judicial protection are consequential on the recognition or conferment of rights, and for the reasons just explained this must be the only approach in Community law, one cannot turn things upside down and make the existence of the right depend on whether or not the right is protected in the courts. In other words, in Community law it is not '*ubi remedium ibi ius*' but '*ubi ius ibi remedium*'.

6.4.7   The parameters: a summary

Where do all these reflections lead? Certainly not to an unequivocal answer to the question regarding the circumstances in which a directive confers or is intended to confer rights upon individuals. Nevertheless, some general points can be made. Apart from cases where the answer can be given simply because the terms of the directive are clear, the following issues at least must be taken into consideration. Firstly, there is the question whether an individual can be party to the relationships to which the directive in question gives rise. Secondly, one or more provisions of a directive, where necessary interpreted in the light of one or more of its purposes, must be such that it protects individual interest, along with other things, like general interest. Although it has been argued that the Court is apparently willing to accept readily that this is the case, in my opinion, this is one of the most uncertain elements in the case law. Thirdly, there is the issue of 'concreteness' or 'ascertainability'. Also in this respect some clarification in the case law would be welcome. In my opinion, here the following distinction must be made: if the content of the alleged right is defined in sufficiently precise and concrete terms, then the directive will be a direct source of the right at issue; however, if this is not the case, the directive may still be intended to confer rights, but the actual creation will take place at a later implementing stage. Whether a directive is intended to do this must be decided on the basis of its text and purpose, using the other parameters as well. Finally, the fact that a directive requires appropriate judicial protection will be a useful indication that it creates or is intended to create rights. This is not, however, a condition which must be satisfied.

7

The role of national courts

7.1 National judge made accomplice

The very purpose of directives is their implementation in national law. As a rule, therefore, their provisions should apply within the national legal order in their 'converted' form, i.e. as provisions of national law. Whenever the question of effects of directives is addressed, this should be the point of departure. This normal state of affairs was described by the Court of Justice in very clear terms in *Becker*, where it held that

wherever a directive is correctly implemented, its effects extend to individuals through the medium of the implementing measures adopted by the Member State concerned.[1]

Directives are, however, notorious for not being implemented correctly or not being implemented in due time. In the same judgment the Court expressed this as follows:

. . . special problems arise where a Member State has failed to implement a directive correctly and, more particularly, where the provisions of the directive have not been implemented by the end of the period prescribed for that purpose.[2]

The special problems referred to by the Court in the context of *Becker* related primarily to the questions whether and, if so, to what extent the effect of directives can also reach individuals *without* the mediation of national implementing measures. Directives may and often do create rights for individuals (or, at least, may be of direct concern for them),[3] but in the absence of implementing measures the individual would be deprived of the possibility of asserting those rights and having them protected.[4] The problem is, however, more extensive. It relates to the more *objective* necessity of implementation of directives in a correct way and within the period prescribed as discussed in Chapter 5. In order to counteract, as far as possible, the detrimental effects of inappropriate (i.e. incorrect, belated, or both) implementation of directives, the Court of Justice, assisted by 'vigilant individuals',[5] resorts to its

---

[1] Case 8/81 [1982] ECR 53, para 19.   [2] Ibid, para 20.

[3] Cf the discussion above, in Ch 6. When I use the term 'right', I use it as an umbrella term, in principle to denote a legal position an individual may derive from Community law, whatever its further qualification might be.

[4] As early as 1963 the Court recognized that procedures provided for in Arts 226 and 227 of the Treaty do not guarantee sufficient and direct legal protection of individuals. See Case 26/62 *Van Gend en Loos* [1963] ECR 1.   [5] Ibid, at 13.

natural allies, namely the national courts. These courts are entrusted with the task of protecting the rights which individuals derive from directives and of ensuring the full effect of the latter.

The two intimately linked concerns of the Court, namely the protection of the individual and the full force and effect of Community law, are of course not peculiar to directives but concern Community law in general. Ever since *Van Gend en Loos*[6] the Court has maintained that it is the task of the national court to protect the rights of individuals under Community law without, however, indicating the precise basis of this obligation in the Treaty.

For a long time it was assumed that this task of the national courts stemmed from or was a corollary of supremacy of Community law and, in particular, the doctrine of direct effect.[7] This point of view was confirmed by a sequence of consistent case law where the task of the national courts was always coupled with direct effect of the provisions at issue.[8] In 1976, the Court made explicit the basis of the national court's duty in the *Comet* and *Rewe* judgments, where it held that

... in application of the principle of cooperation laid down in Article 5 [new 10] of the Treaty, the national courts are entrusted with ensuring the legal protection conferred on individuals by the direct effect of the provisions of Community law.[9]

Again in these cases, the protection by the courts was related to direct effect.

The approach of the Court is, viewed from the historical perspective, entirely understandable. For a long time the issue of direct effect was raised only in judicial procedures and the sole interlocutors of the Court of Justice in Article 234 proceedings are the national courts. Likewise, the coupling of direct effect and the task of the national courts can be considered as a way of expressing that the counterpart of the individual's right to rely on directly effective Community law provisions is the courts' duty to apply them. However, in the light of more recent developments, the point of view that the task of national courts derives from direct effect of Community law provisions or relates only to those provisions is too limited. Also— or perhaps *in particular*—where the doctrine of direct effect is of no avail, the need for protection remains. It is therefore not surprising that in *Francovich* the Court modified its position slightly and stated that

the national courts whose task it is to apply the provisions of Community law in cases within their jurisdiction must ensure that those rules have full effect and protect the rights which they confer on individuals.[10]

By deleting the reference to direct effect (and the Court could hardly do otherwise in this case) a more satisfactory solution has been reached, in my view. Apart from

---

[6] Case 26/62 [1963] ECR 1.   [7] Cf Barav 1991, 2, Kapteyn 1993, 39, Kovar 1981, 164.

[8] Cf Case 106/77 *Simmenthal* [1978] ECR 629 and, more recently, Case C–213/89 *Factortame* [1990] ECR I–2433.

[9] Case 45/76 *Comet* [1976] ECR 2043 and Case 33/76 *Rewe* [1976] ECR 1989; quotation is from *Comet*, para 12. Cf also Due 1992, 360–1.

[10] Joined Cases C–6/90 and C–9/90 [1991] ECR I–5357, para 32.

a national court's obligation under Article 10 of the Treaty, the protection of individuals by national courts and, generally, their duty to take Community law into consideration and ensure its full effect, follow from the very fact that Community law is an integral part of the legal systems of the Member States, 'which their Courts are bound to apply'[11] in principle in exactly the same way as they are bound to apply any other rule of national law, irrespective of its 'external' origin.

Another, in my view more cogent, argument than that based on direct effect can be drawn from the fundamental principle of the 'Rechtsstaat', the rule of law. The Court, albeit in a different context, has stressed several times that the Community is a community based upon the rule of law. This entails, inter alia, that neither the Member States nor the national authorities can avoid a review of whether the measures they adopt are in conformity with the law, including Community law.[12] Under the Community law system this control lies partly with the Court of Justice and partly with the national courts. Thus the control required by the rule of law necessarily involves the application of Community law by the national courts. Similarly, the principle of the 'Rechtsstaat' requires that rights of individuals are effectively protected, and this task, in the absence of protection provided directly by the Court of Justice, must be assumed by the national courts.[13]

Thus, anxious both to ensure effective operation of Community law and to safeguard the judicial protection of individuals, the Court entrusted the national courts with an important mission. However, this was not the end of the matter. In Becker, to palliate the effects of the non-implementation of the directive concerned, the Court had recourse to the principle of direct effect, stating that

. . . wherever the provisions of a directive appear . . . to be unconditional and sufficiently precise, those provisions may . . . be relied upon as against any national provision which is incompatible with the directive or in so far as the provisions define rights which individuals are able to assert against the State.[14]

Direct effect proved to be a powerful device, placed at the disposal of national courts to enable them to accomplish their task under Community law. In the meantime, however, it has become clear that direct effect has its limits. Nevertheless, the need for judicial protection remains. In order to complete the system of effective operation of Community law and the judicial protection of individuals, the Court has designed two other tools for national courts, namely the interpretation of national law in conformity with Community law and the principle of liability of the State for harm caused to individuals by breaches of Community law.

These mechanisms do not operate in a vacuum, but within the framework of the national systems of judicial protection. To put this another way, whether Community law can be put into effect by the courts and, accordingly, whether the

[11] Case 6/64 *Costa v. ENEL* [1964] ECR 585, 593.
[12] Cf Case 294/83 *Les Verts* [1986] ECR 1339, Case C–2/88Imm. *Zwartveld I* [1990] ECR I–3365, Opinion 1/91 *EEA* [1991] ECR I–6079.   [13] Cf Klein 1988, 17.
[14] Case 8/81 [1982] ECR 53, para 25.

legal position of individuals under Community law can be protected by means of the three mechanisms depend on the availability and organization of national procedures leading to some form of legal relief. This 'environment' within which the mechanisms can be deployed determines to a large extent the outcome of their operation and, consequently, the extent of the protection afforded. In the following Sections it will become apparent that the articulation between Community law and the national systems of judicial protection poses several problems which often call for a Community law solution.

7.2   Judicial protection under national law and Community law requirements

7.2.1   Principles laid down in early case law

According to the system laid down in the E(E)C Treaty the actual application and enforcement of Community law is, in general, dependent upon the legal systems of the Member States. This dichotomy between the law-making power of the Community institutions and the power of the Member States to apply and enforce Community law entails that the task assigned to the national courts to protect rights which individuals derive from Community law is accomplished within the framework of national procedures.[15] In other words, an individual with a right under Community law or, more generally, an interest in its application, makes use of national procedures and remedies in order to enforce it. It is in the context of proceedings brought before national courts that the need for interpretation of national law in accordance with Community law may arise, directly effective provisions are relied upon and the liability of the Member State for a breach of Community law must be established. The degree of judicial protection afforded therefore depends in the final analysis on national courts, national procedures, and national remedies.

On the one hand, an important merit of this construction is that Community law is enforced in familiar national courts, in accordance with familiar national rules of procedure, and in this way it promotes the actual integration of Community law into the national legal order.[16] Moreover, the construction involves a minimum degree of Community intervention in matters such as the organization of the administration of justice, paying due regard to what is known as 'procedural autonomy'.[17]

---

[15] For this clear assumption compare the definition of regulations in Art 249 and the system of judicial cooperation provided for in Art 234 of the Treaty. Cf also Bridge 1984, 31 and Barav 1989, 369 with further references.   [16] Cf Bridge 1984, 28–9.

[17] Cf Kovar 1978, 248, who considers procedural autonomy as a specific form of institutional autonomy. For the latter see above, Ch 4, Section 4.3. The term 'procedural' must not be understood too strictly in this context. It relates not only to procedural rules *stricto sensu*, but also to 'any rules and principles of organizational or substantive nature which concern actions in law aiming at judicial protection' (see Kapteyn and VerLoren van Themaat 2003, 451; translation is mine). In this sense it includes remedies and sometimes also issues of substance. Cf in the same sense also Mertens de Wilmars 1981, 390.

On the other hand, there are also several disadvantages. Since Community law rules must, in view of their application and enforcement, pass through the national systems, the effect of Community rules may be affected by the particularities of these systems of judicial protection. National rules of procedure relating, for instance, to delays in bringing action or to prescription of action, to *locus standi*, or to burden of proof are unlikely to be uniform within the various Member States. This obviously leads to unequal protection of individuals within the Community. Similarly, the effectiveness of remedies available for enforcement of Community law provisions may differ considerably, as may the powers of the courts. The problems which stem from disparities of this kind could actually be tempered by harmonization. Until now, however, very few measures have been adopted in this respect and the Community has to live with the 'regrettable absence of Community provisions harmonizing procedure . . . [which] entails differences in treatment on a Community scale', as the Court put it in *Express Dairy Foods*.[18]

To describe the problems encountered at this stage, i.e. when addressing the question of how judicial protection of an individual's position under Community law is safeguarded at national level, Mertens de Wilmars has used the imaginative expression 'problems of the second generation'.[19] By now, the Court has found some second generation answers.

Apart from some rather isolated instances of harmonization of different procedural aspects, such as Regulation 2913/92 (Community Custom Code)[20] and Directives 89/665 (public contracts—review procedures) and 92/13 (ibid for excluded sectors),[21] two kinds of situations occur in Community law: either no provisions on procedures and remedies are laid down or the Member States are obliged, by some in principle very generally worded provisions, to provide for judicial protection in the area concerned.

> As examples of this last kind of provision can be mentioned the directives in the field of equal treatment of men and women,[22] all of which contain a provision whereby Member States must introduce into their national legal systems such measures as are necessary to enable all persons who consider themselves to be victims of discrimination to pursue their claims by judicial process. Similarly, Directive 64/221 (public policy and public health)[23] prescribes that

---

[18] Case 130/79 [1980] ECR 1887, para 12. Cf also Langenfeld 1991, 185.

[19] Mertens de Wilmars 1981, 380.   [20] [1992] OJ L302/1 (Title VII).

[21] [1989] OJ L395/33 and [1992] OJ L76/14. Cf further also harmonizing measures in the field of consumer protection such as Directive 2002/8 (access to justice in cross-border disputes—minimum common rules for legal aid) [2003] OJ L26/41. Directive 98/27 (injunctions for the protection of consumers' interests), [1998] OJ L166/51 and the Commission's proposal on unfair business-to-consumer commercial practices, COM (2003) 356 final. In the field of intellectual property, see the recent Directive 2004/48 (enforcement of intellectual property rights) [2004] OJ L195/16.

[22] Directive 75/117 [1975] OJ L45/19, Directive 76/207 [1976] OJ L39/40, Directive 79/7 [1979] OJ L6/24, Directive 86/378 [1986] OJ L225/40, Directive 86/613 [1986] OJ L359/56, and Directive 2002/73 [2002] OJ L269/15. Cf comparable provisions in Directives 2000/31 and 2000/43.

[23] [1963–1964] OJ English Spec Ed 117.

the person concerned shall have the same legal remedies in respect of any decision concerning entry, or the refusal to issue a residence permit, as are available to the nationals of the State concerned in respect of acts of administration.
Article 8 of Directive 89/48 (mutual recognition of diplomas)[24] provides that
a remedy shall be available against a decision on recognition of professional
qualifications, or the absence thereof, before a court or tribunal in accordance
with the provisions of national law.[25] Article 11 of Directive 97/7 (protection
of consumers in respect of distance contracts)[26] or Article 4 of Directive
2002/21 (electronic communications networks and services)[27] provide in general terms for judicial or administrative redress.

In principle, it is not important whether there are some very general provisions or no
provisions at all, as the former are usually rather non-committal.[28] In both situations
it is left to the Member States to determine the competent courts and to lay down
rules for the legal proceedings in which Community law is to be enforced.[29]

A court with appropriate jurisdiction

In the first place, and although, as the Court of Justice has stressed, Community law
was not intended to create new remedies in the national courts to ensure its observance other than those which already exist,[30] the Member States must make sure
that in any case where Community rights are involved there *is a court having
jurisdiction*. Furthermore, the Member States are responsible for ensuring that the
courts provide 'direct and immediate protection'[31] and that the rights are 'effectively
protected in each case'.[32] Yet, it was held to be for the national courts to apply the

---

[24] [1989] OJ L19/16.

[25] Other examples of comparable provisions can be found in Directive 73/239 (insurance other than
life assurance I) [1973] OJ L228/3, Directive 91/533 (conditions applicable to the employment
relationship—information of employees) [1991] OJ L288/32, Directive 92/28 (advertising of medicinal
products) [1992] OJ L113/13, Directive 92/59 (product safety) [1992] OJ L228/24, Directive 92/85
(pregnant workers) [1992] OJ L348/1, Directive 93/13 (consumer contracts) [1993] OJ L95/29,
Directive 92/53 (type-approval of motor vehicles) [1992] OJ L225/1, Directive 2000/43 (race-
discrimination) [2000] OJ L180/22 and Directive 2000/78 (general anti-discrimination) [2000] OJ
L303/16, Directive 2003/4 (information on environment) [2003] OJ L41/26, and Directive 2003/6
(insider dealing) [2003] OJ L96/16. On harmonization of national mechanisms of judicial protection see
also Timmermans 1998, 28 and Barav 1998, 443–58.   [26] [1997] OJ L144/19.

[27] [2002] OJ L108/33. As to the role national regulatory authorities may play in the context of
enforcement and dispute resolution see Ch 3, Subsection 3.2.1.

[28] See however Subsection 7.4.1: explicit provisions may serve as a written basis for national courts
to extend their powers.

[29] Cf Case 33/76 *Rewe* [1976] ECR 1989, Case 45/76 *Comet* [1976] ECR 2043. The approach is
comparable to that with respect to sanctions. See above, Ch 5, Section 5.4.

[30] Case 158/80 *Butter-buying cruises* [1981] ECR 1805. It is, however, doubtful whether this proposition
still holds true nowadays. See below, Subsection 7.3.4. Cf also Schockweiler 1992, 39–40 and Barav 1994, 269.

[31] Case 13/68 *Salgoil* [1968] ECR 453, 463.

[32] Case 179/84 *Bozzetti* [1985] ECR 2301, para 17.

most appropriate of the various measures available under national law in order to protect the individual rights conferred by Community law.[33] In other words, there must be *a* court and *a* procedure available before which and within the context of which an individual can enforce his Community law rights.[34] However, the decision as to which court is competent, what kind of procedure can be used, and how this procedure is organized is in principle left to the discretion of the Member States. The Court refrains, in principle, from getting involved in the resolution of matters of jurisdiction 'to which the classification of certain legal situations based on Community law may give rise in the national judicial system'.[35] Exceptionally this can be otherwise, namely if from Community law itself, for instance from a directive, it follows that there is an obligation to make a certain type of judicial protection available to the persons concerned.[36]

Requirements of equivalence and effectiveness

In the second place, the Court of Justice has curtailed national discretion by formulating two minimum requirements which national procedural law must satisfy. According to the first requirement, which can be called the principle of equivalence,[37] the substantive and procedural conditions governing the respective actions for the enforcement of Community law cannot be less favourable than those relating to similar actions of a domestic nature. The second principle, which is usually designated with the term the principle of effectiveness,[38] requires that the conditions are not framed in such a way as to render virtually impossible the exercise of the rights conferred by Community law. Ever since *Rewe* and *Comet* these two principles have been confirmed in a consistent sequence of cases, using the same or similar language.[39] In *San Giorgio*[40] the Court appeared to have added a new proviso, namely where it held that the conditions should not make the exercise of Community law rights not only virtually impossible but also excessively difficult. In my view, there is a difference in degree between 'virtually impossible' and

---

[33] Cf Case 34/67 *Lück* [1968] ECR 245 and, more recently, Joined Cases C–10–22/97 *IN.CO.GE* [1998] ECR I–6307.

[34] Cf e.g. Case 244/80 *Foglia Novello II* [1984] ECR 3045 and Case C–54/96 *Dorsch Consult* [1997] ECR I–4961.

[35] Cf e.g. Case C–462/99 *Connect Austria* [2003] ECR I–5197, para 35 or Case C–54/96 *Dorsch Consult* [1997] ECR I–4961, para 40.

[36] Cf Case 152/79 *Lee* [1980] ECR 1495. In the absence of specific provisions the obligation to provide judicial protection is based on Art 10 of the Treaty. Cf above, Section 7.1 and Mertens de Wilmars 1981, 392.   [37] Other terms, such as 'non-discrimination' or 'assimilation' are sometimes also used.

[38] Both terms have been more or less officially introduced in Case C–261/95 *Palmisani* [1997] ECR I–4025.

[39] In some cases the terms are, for instance, 'render impossible in practice' or just plain 'render impossible'. Cf e.g. Case C–78/98 *Preston* [2000] ECR I–3201, paras 31 and 34 and Case C–147/01 *Weber's Wine World*, judgment of 2 October 2003, nyr in ECR, para 103.

[40] Case 199/82 [1983] ECR 3595.

'excessively difficult'. In the Court's case law, however, there was for a long time no indication that it wished to broaden the scope of the second requirement accordingly. Only since more recently has case law suggested that meeting the 'lesser' requirement of 'excessively difficult' may suffice.[41]

For a considerable period of time these requirements led a fairly subdued existence. On the one hand, it was clear that the two principles applied both where Community law referred explicitly to national law and where it did not.[42] Furthermore, they applied to all actions, regardless of whether they were brought by a private party or by public authorities.[43] On the other hand, the Court gave little guidance as to the meaning of either of these principles. Moreover, they largely evolved in a rather limited area of Community law, namely in cases concerned with (re)payment of sums of money.[44] The cases concerned matters like the application of national limitation periods,[45] rules on the payment of interest,[46] or on the burden of proof;[47] principles which exist under national law having the effect of limiting the remedial outcomes of full application of Community law rules, such as unjust enrichment[48] and what was called 'the principle of innocent error',[49] were also submitted to the Court. This case law concentrated more on the principle of effectiveness than on that of equivalence.[50]

Furthermore, the case law made clear that the mere equivalence of the applicable rules was as such not a guarantee that the requirements were satisfied. In *San Giorgio* the Court held in unequivocal terms that

the requirements of non-discrimination laid down by the Court cannot be construed as justifying legislative measures intended to render any repayment of charges levied contrary to Community law virtually impossible, even if the treatment is extended to tax payers who have similar claims arising from an infringement of national tax law.[51]

In other words, the requirements are cumulative and not alternative. Even if national procedural rules are applied without distinction, if they render nugatory the exercise of Community law rights the second requirement is clearly not satisfied.[52]

---

[41] Cf Case C–129/00 *Commission v. Italy*, judgment of 9 December 2003, nyr in ECR, Case C–327/00 *Santex* [2003] ECR I–1877, para 61, and Case C–147/01 *Weber's Wine World*, judgment of 2 October 2003, nyr in ECR, in particular para 113.   [42] Cf Case 265/78 *Ferwerda* [1980] ECR 617.

[43] Cf Case 33/76 *Rewe* [1976] ECR 1989 on the one hand and Joined Cases 119 and 126/79 *Lippische Hauptgenossenschaft* [1980] ECR 1863 on the other.

[44] For a detailed discussion see e.g. Bridge 1984.

[45] E.g. Case 45/76 *Comet* [1976] ECR 2043 and Case 386/87 *Bessin and Salson* [1989] ECR 3551.

[46] E.g. Case 130/79 *Express Dairy Foods* [1980] ECR 1887.

[47] E.g. Case 199/82 *San Giorgio* [1983] ECR 3595 and Joined Cases 331, 376, and 378/85 *Bianco* [1988] ECR 1099.   [48] E.g. Case 68/79 *Just* [1980] ECR 501.

[49] Cf Oliver 1987, 887 with respect to Case 265/78 *Ferwerda* [1980] ECR 617.

[50] See, however, Joined Cases 66, 127, and 128/79 *Salumi* [1980] ECR 1237. Also Case 240/87 *Deville* [1988] ECR 3513 was in fact concerned with the application of the principle of equivalence.

[51] Case 199/82 [1983] ECR 3595, para 17. Cf also Case 104/86 *Commission v. Italy* [1988] ECR 1799 and Joined Cases 331, 376, and 378/85 *Bianco* [1988] ECR 1099. See, however, also Case C–231/96 *Edis* [1998] ECR I–4951, briefly discussed below, in Subsection 7.4.2.

[52] Cf also the opinion of AG Van Gerven in Case C–271/91 *Marshall II* [1993] ECR I–4367, para 15.

Once it is established that one or both of the requirements are not satisfied, the case law suggests that the national provisions concerned cannot be applied by the national court.[53]

Parallel to this case law on minimum requirements to be met by national procedural law, which at that stage was rather limited both in scope and in depth of scrutiny, another development took place which provoked some confusion as to the rigour of the requirements posed by the Court.[54]

Rheinmühlen II and Simmenthal

These two cases concerned national procedural obstacles which, in ultimate analysis, were also likely to impair the effectiveness of Community law but which were treated in a different way by the Court of Justice compared to those at issue in the *Rewe/Comet* and related cases.

In *Rheinmühlen II*[55] the Court of Justice turned down a procedural rule which fettered the discretion of the lower national court under Article 234 of the Treaty to request a preliminary ruling. According to the Court, a rule whereby a court is bound on a point of law by the rulings of the court superior to it and which, consequently, is not able to refer matters to the Court of Justice, would compromise the application of Community law at all levels of the judicial system of the Member States. However, *Rheinmühlen II* was different from *Comet* and *Rewe* and related cases because the power limited by the national rule was a power stemming directly from Article 234. The principles defined in *Comet* and *Rewe* therefore did not apply.

Simmenthal,[56] which is usually considered to be a culmination of the doctrines of supremacy and direct effect making plain their ultimate consequences,[57] also concerned a crucial aspect of procedural law of constitutional nature, to say the least. The Court first spelled out that direct applicability means that rules of Community law must be fully and uniformly applied in all Member States, that the provisions are direct sources of rights and duties for all those affected thereby, and that this consequence also concerns any national court in its capacity as an organ of a

---

[53] Cf Case 199/82 *San Giorgio* [1983] ECR 3595 where the Court found that 'once it is established that the levying of the charge is incompatible with Community law, *the court must be free* to decide whether or not the burden of the charge has been passed on . . . to other persons' (para 14, emphasis added). In Case 309/85 *Barra* [1988] ECR 355 the Court held with respect to a limitation period rendering impossible the exercise of Community law rights that 'the national court . . . must not apply such a provision of national law' (para 20).

[54] A second development which was described in more detail in the first edition of this book (154) related to case law which evolved around Art 48 (3) of the Treaty and the provisions of Directive 64/221 (public policy and public health) [1963–1964] OJ English Spec Ed 117. These cases illustrate nicely the Court's willingness to give the provisions on protection of individuals a substantive meaning and to guarantee their effectiveness as much as possible.   [55] Case 166/73 [1974] ECR 33.

[56] Case 106/77 [1978] ECR 629.   [57] Cf Pescatore 1983, 156, Barav 1991, 9.

Member State. Consequently, the Court held, after having also explained the meaning of the principle of supremacy, that the national court must

in a case within its jurisdiction, apply Community law in its entirety and protect rights which the latter confers on individuals and must accordingly set aside any provision of national law which may conflict with it.[58]

The Court next turned to a procedural issue, namely the national judge-made rule reserving to the Constitutional Court the power to set aside provisions of national law contrary to Community law. In this respect it found that any rule

which might impair the effectiveness of Community law by withholding from the national court having jurisdiction to apply such law the power to do everything necessary at the moment of its application to set aside national legislative provisions which may prevent Community rules from having full force and effect [is] incompatible with these requirements, which are the very essence of Community law.[59]

Thus, in *Simmenthal* the Court stated clearly that for the sake of effectiveness of Community law a national rule relating to the power of the national court had to be disregarded by the national court *a quo*.[60] Remarkably, the reasoning of the Court of Justice did not follow the same line as in *Rewe* and *Comet*, leaving domestic procedural law more or less intact and, where necessary, focusing on the minimum requirement of effectiveness, although there was no doubt that the rule laid down by the Constitutional Court made the exercise of Community law rights virtually impossible.[61] Instead, it approached the problem in terms of consequences for the national judge of direct effect and supremacy of Community law, with a considerably more far-reaching outcome, which resulted in empowering the national court to do something it was unable to do under national law.

The judgment in *Simmenthal* is deceptive in that the Court of Justice refers to the national court 'having jurisdiction' or to 'the limits of its jurisdiction' in the *dictum*. At first sight this could suggest that there was jurisdiction to apply Community law but the national rule prevented the court from exercising it. Wyatt, however, has very cogently argued that

the very problem which had arisen in the national court had arisen because national law was withholding jurisdiction from the national court to apply Community law in the case before it.[62]

Therefore the jurisdiction referred to by the Court of Justice is solely subject matter jurisdiction. Jurisdiction, or power, to apply the regulation at issue was lacking.[63] Yet it is difficult to understand how direct effect and supremacy of Community law, or

---

[58] Case 106/77 *Simmenthal* [1978] ECR 629, para 21.

[59] Case 106/77 *Simmenthal* [1978] ECR 629, para 22.

[60] In legal writing this form of supremacy, concerning procedural rules, has been coined as 'structural supremacy'. See De Witte 1999, 191.

[61] Ibid, Report for the Hearing, 633–5, in particular the fact that the 'cumbersome and complex' procedure leads to a declaration of unconstitutionality with an only partial retroactive effect.

[62] Wyatt 1989, 208. Cf also Abraham 1989, 182–3.

[63] Wyatt 1989, 209. For a comparable reference to 'areas within their jurisdiction' see also Joined Cases C–6/90 and C–9/90 *Francovich* [1991] ECR I–5357, para 32.

its full effectiveness, or Article 10 of the Treaty to which the Court implicitly refers[64] can *create powers* for the national courts which did not exist before. However this might be, *Simmenthal* remained an isolated case in this respect for the next twelve years until the judgment in *Factortame* was given, which again raised comparable problems.[65]

Contradictions in the Court's approaches?

Another issue which has not yet been entirely clarified relates to a contradiction, or at least a tension, between cases like *Rewe* and *Comet* on the one hand and *Simmenthal* on the other.[66] In the former type of cases direct effect and supremacy are equally compromised by the application of a rule limiting the power of a domestic court which has to safeguard the full force and effect of Community law.[67] Persons who have not brought action within the period established by national law to seek protection of their Community law rights or who see their action frustrated by the application of the principle of unjust enrichment[68] are *de facto* denied a remedy for breaches of Community law by the Member State or by other individuals, as the case may be. Why in some cases the Court follows the line set out in *Simmenthal* while in other cases it applies the minimum principles laid down in *Comet* and *Rewe* is somewhat puzzling.[69]

One possible explanation for the difference in approach could lie in the fact that the principles underlying *Rewe/Comet* and related cases, i.e. the principle of legal certainty and the principle of unjust enrichment, are to be considered as legitimate limitations to the applications of community law,[70] while there was no such general principle of law at the origin of the rule at issue in *Simmenthal*. Similarly, it can be argued that the national rules under consideration in the *Rewe/Comet* type cases were regarded more as ancillary questions, or rules limiting in certain respects the exercise of the rights.[71] Having merely a 'procedural dimension', therefore, they could in principle be left to national law. The limitation of the power of the national

[64] Case 106/77 *Simmenthal* [1978] ECR 629, para 16.
[65] Case C–213/89 [1990] ECR I–2433. Cf also below, (Sub)sections 7.3.4 and 7.4.
[66] Cf also cases like *Factortame* and *Francovich* where it was pleaded that it was a matter of national law whether and under what conditions a certain type of action can be brought. The Court, however, took a different approach.
[67] Or, in the terms of Mertens de Wilmars 1981, 381, they affect the '*effet utile de l'effet direct*'.
[68] As was, for instance, the situation in Case 68/79 *Just* [1980] ECR 501 and several subsequent cases. Cf also Oliver 1987, 889.
[69] *Rewe* and *Comet* are still 'good' law. See e.g. Joined Cases C–31/91 to C–44/91 *Lageder and Others* [1993] ECR I–1761. See also below, Subsection 7.4.2. In German legal writing, the distinction between 'direct' and 'indirect' conflict is often used in order to clarify the effects (and limits) of supremacy in the procedural context. Cf Jarass and Beljin 2003, 32–43 and 116–17, with further references.
[70] Cf also below, Ch 9, Subsection 9.5.1.
[71] Cf Case 130/79 *Express Dairy Foods* [1980] ECR 1887, para 17. The distinction between the existence of a right, which should be decided under the supremacy doctrine, and its exercise, to which the *Rewe/Comet* mantra applies, reappeared recently in the Opinion of AG Léger in Case C–453/00 *Kühne*, judgment of 13 January 2004, nyr in ECR.

court in *Simmenthal*, however, was considered to be incompatible with the Community legal order as such, since it amounted to an almost absolute bar for national courts to perform the task conferred upon them under Community law.[72] Its application would go so far as to challenge the very principles of supremacy and direct effect. In other words, it was a matter of concern regarding Community constitutional law.

In some cases[73] it seems that the Court of Justice made an attempt to reconcile the *Comet/Rewe* approach and the *Simmenthal* approach, i.e. the principle of structural supremacy. On the one hand it stressed, under reference to *Simmenthal*, that (directly effective) rules of Community law must be fully and uniformly applied in all Member States from the day of their entry into force and for so long as they continue in force. On the other hand it held that the safeguard of the rights conferred upon individuals by those rules does not necessarily require a uniform rule common to the Member States relating to the formal and substantive conditions for the recovery of charges levied in violation of Community law.

> The Court continued by explaining the immense variety of rules governing the recovery within the Member States and wound up with a reference to the *Comet/Rewe* principles. The result of this approach was in fact the acceptance of the 'special features of national laws'[74] which govern the recovery of unduly paid charges. This acceptance can be explained by the fact that the Court found it beyond its jurisdiction to give *positive rules* in this respect.[75]

In the meantime, although structural supremacy reappeared again in a number of cases, in the light of more recent case law it seems that there are limits to this principle. I will come back to this in Section 7.4.

7.2.2   The principle of effective judicial protection

For some considerable time the Court of Justice did not spell out what is meant by the requirements 'not less favourable' or 'virtually impossible' laid down in *Comet* and *Rewe*.[76] Neither did it indicate in more concrete terms what constitutes direct, immediate, and effective protection as required in *Salgoil* and *Bozetti*.[77] The early case law did not extend deeply in these respects. During the mid-1980s, however, national judicial protection and the function assigned in this context to national courts became the focus of particular attention on the part of the Court of Justice.

---

[72] Cf the Opinion of AG Jacobs in Case C–312/93 *Peterbroeck* [1994] ECR I–4599, para 43 and also his Opinion in Joined Cases C–430/93 and C–431/93 *Van Schijndel* [1995] ECR I–4705, para 22.

[73] Cf Case 61/79 *Denkavit* [1980] ECR 1205, Case 826/79 *Mireco* [1980] ECR 2559, and Case 811/79 *Ariette* [1980] ECR 2545.   [74] Case 826/79 *Mireco* [1980] ECR 2559, para 15.

[75] Cf Case 130/79 *Express Dairy Foods* [1980] ECR 1887, in particular para 12.

[76] Case 45/76 [1976] ECR 2043 and Case 33/76 [1976] ECR 1989.

[77] Case 13/68 [1968] ECR 453 and Case 179/84 [1985] ECR 2301.

The new leading principle of the Court's case law seems to be the *principle of effective judicial protection* identified *expressis verbis* in the landmark judgment in the case of Mrs Johnston,[78] following a prelude given in *Von Colson*.[79] In *Johnston* the Court objected to an evidential rule in the Sex Discrimination (Northern Ireland) Order 1976 which rendered judicially unreviewable a decision of the Chief Constable of the Royal Ulster Constabulary and, consequently, deprived Mrs Johnston of any remedy. The central provision of this part of the judgment was Article 6 of Directive 76/207.[80] With respect to this Article the Court of Justice held the following:

The requirement of judicial control stipulated by that article reflects a general principle of law which underlies the constitutional traditions common to the Member States. That principle is also laid down in Articles 6 and 13 of the European Convention for the Protection of Human Rights and Fundamental Freedoms of 4 November 1950. As the European Parliament, Council and Commission recognized in their Joint Declaration of 5 April 1977 (Official Journal, no. C 103, p. 1) and as the Court has recognized in its decisions, the principles on which that Convention is based must be taken into consideration in Community law.

By virtue of Article 6 of Directive no. 76/207, interpreted in the light of the general principle stated above, all persons have the right to obtain an effective remedy in a competent court against measures which they consider to be contrary to the principle of equal treatment for men and women laid down in the directive. It is for the Member States to ensure effective judicial control as regards compliance with the applicable provisions of Community law and of national legislation intended to give effect to the rights for which the directive provides.[81]

The Court's statement that Article 6 reflects a general principle of law proved to be crucial for the further application of the principle in areas of Community law where no such principle existed in a codified form. Moreover, it is similarly important to note in this context that the principle does not apply solely where a person relies *directly* on provisions of a directive, but also where the national law provisions implementing the directive are invoked and applied. In other words, even if a directive which—in contrast to Directive 76/207—does not contain a provision relating to judicial protection, is as such correctly implemented in national law, the Member States must ensure that the rights *under the national implementing measures* can be asserted by judicial process by the individuals concerned. The absence of such a possibility will amount to inadequate implementation.[82]

The principle of effective judicial protection is a *self-standing general principle of law* rather than a corollary to direct effect of Community law provisions.[83] The underlying rationale is the fact that in a Community based on the rule of law everyone must have the opportunity to assert, on his own initiative, his rights before the

---

[78] Case 222/84 [1986] ECR 1651.

[79] Case 14/83 [1984] ECR 1891: sanction chosen by the Member State must be such as to guarantee real and effective judicial protection Cf above, Ch 5, Section 5.4.

[80] [1976] OJ L39/40.   [81] Case 222/84 [1986] ECR 1651, paras 18–19.

[82] Cf above, Ch 5, Section 5.4.

[83] As it was considered in the past. Cf above, Section 7.1. However, Bleckmann 1976, 486 for instance construed the requirement of effective judicial protection on the basis of Art 5 EEC [new 10 EC].

courts.[84] Moreover, the protection provided must be *effective*. From this point of view the new principle can be considered an expansion of the principle of effectiveness as laid down earlier in *Rewe* and *Comet*,[85] which in the *Johnston* case was given a specific basis, namely the constitutional traditions of the Member States and the ECHR. On the other hand, there are grounds for not considering the principle of effectiveness and the principle of effective judicial protection as one and the same thing. In *Verholen*,[86] for instance, both principles figure alongside each other in the judgment. Furthermore, it should be noted that the principle of effectiveness has a much broader scope of application. It may also be relevant for the imposition of sanctions upon individuals,[87] for instance, or for the way in which collection of Community charges from the individual is organized.[88]

In accordance with its *general* nature the principle has now been extended to other areas of Community law, even to those where it does not exist in a codified form, as it does in the area of equal treatment of men and women.[89] A few months after *Johnston*, this newly discovered principle appeared in *Heylens* in the field of free movement of workers, where the Court held, under reference to *Johnston*, that

the existence of a remedy of a judicial nature against any decision of a national authority refusing the benefit of that right[90] is essential in order to secure for the individual effective protection of his right.[91]

The absence of appropriate judicial proceedings would amount to a violation of Article 39 of the Treaty.[92] The principle as applied in *Heylens* was subsequently transposed to other areas of Community law, such as the freedom of establishment.[93]

---

[84] Cf the Opinion of AG Van Gerven in Case C–70/88 *European Parliament v. Council* [1990] ECR I–2041, para 6. On the principle of effective judicial protection in general see also Dubouis 1988.

[85] Cf Kapteyn 1993, 43.

[86] Joined Cases C–87/90, C–88/90, and C–89/90 [1991] ECR I–3757. For a mixture of both approaches see e.g. also Case C–453/99 *Courage* [2001] ECR I–6297.

[87] Cf above, Ch 5, Section 5.4 and, in particular, Case 68/88 *Commission v. Greece* [1989] ECR 2965.

[88] Cf Joined Cases 66, 127, and 128/79 *Salumi* [1980] ECR 1237, para 20, Case 54/81 *Fromme* [1982] ECR 1449, para 6, and Case C–290/91 *Peter* [1993] ECR I–2981, para 8.

[89] Apart from sex-discrimination, there are other areas, like public procurement, where the combination of the requirement of effective judicial protection and specific provisions of a directive gave rise to interesting litigation. See e.g. Case C–54/96 *Dorsch Consult* [1997] ECR I–4961, Case C–76/97 *Tögel* [1998] ECR I–5357, Case C–111/97 *Evobus* [1998] ECR I–5411, and Case C–81/98 *Alcatel* [1999] ECR I–7671.   [90] I.e. free access to employment.

[91] Case 222/86 [1987] ECR 4097, para 14.   [92] Ibid, para 17.

[93] Cf Case C–340/89 *Vlassopoulou* [1991] ECR I–2357, Case C–104/91 *Borrell* [1992] ECR I–3003, Case C–19/92, *Kraus* [1993] ECR I–1663. See also Case C–459/99 MRAX [2002] ECR I–6591 and Case C–226/99 *Siples* [2001] ECR I–277. Furthermore, it should be noted that a comparable development can be found in the Court's case law on free movement of goods, although in this area the Court did not explicitly rely on the principle of effective judicial protection. Here the requirement of judicial protection is construed as stemming from Art 30 of the Treaty and the principle of proportionality. Case 178/84 *Commission v. Germany* [1987] ECR I–1227, Case C–18/88 *RTT* [1991] ECR I–5941, and Case C–42/90 *Bellon* [1990] ECR I–4863. Cf also Jans 1993a, 200.

The principle of effective judicial protection having thus been established in the mid-1980s, it has since been applied by the Court of Justice in different types of cases. Its potential impact and its extension to Community law in general is likewise illustrated by cases concerning the protection of individuals and, where appropriate, even Member States against Community institutions.[94] In particular in the context of the litigation on the restrictive standing rules for individuals under Article 230(4), that principle was one of the central arguments.[95]

As far as its application in the domestic law context is concerned, there is a whole line of cases decided by the Court which illustrate the possible implications of the requirement that the protection should be *effective*.[96] Moreover, more recently also the principle of equivalence became the focus of the Court's attention.

7.3 The shortcomings of the system and the Court's responses

7.3.1 Introduction

The conception of the Court of Justice of the judicial protection of individuals in the national courts has been quite cogently described by Barav[97] as a kind of obligation of result, leaving the courts the choice of the procedures and means by which this result has to be achieved, fully respecting the institutional and procedural autonomy of the Member States. The same author[98] has similarly pointed out that the Court's conception of the task to be assumed by national courts is based upon two presumptions: firstly, the existence of courts having jurisdiction and having the necessary powers to safeguard rights which derive from Community law; and secondly, the availability of appropriate procedures and remedies[99] which offer the

---

[94] Or even in cases involving disputes of institutions *inter se*. Cf the opinion of AG Van Gerven in Case C–70/88 *European Parliament v. Council* [1990] ECR I–2041, paras 3 and 6. For other direct actions in which the requirement of effective judicial protection played a part see e.g. Case 53/85 *AKZO* [1986] ECR 1965, Case C–312/90 *Spain v. Commission* [1992] ECR I–4117, Case 169/84 *Cofaz* [1986] ECR 391, Case C–152/88 *Sofrimport* [1990] ECR I–2477, and Case T–24/90 *Automec* [1992] ECR II–2223.

[95] Cf the litigation that culminated, for the time being, in the Court's judgment in Case C–50/00 P *Union de Pequeños Agricultores* [2002] ECR I–6677.

[96] Moreover, as was already discussed above, in Ch 5, Section 5.4, the principle of effective judicial protection has also strongly influenced the Court's case law on sanctions for breaches of Community law or of rules intended to implement Community law.   [97] Barav 1991, 9.

[98] Barav 1991, 14.

[99] The dichotomy 'procedures and remedies' is used here purposely. The term 'remedies' can basically mean two things. Firstly, the means provided by the law to recover rights or to obtain redress, relief, etc. In this sense the term 'remedies' is usually translated into the French '*voies de recours*'. Cf Case 158/80 *Butter-buying cruises* [1981] ECR 1805, para 44. Secondly, it may denote the (form of) relief or redress given by a court. I will use the term 'remedy' in this latter (narrow) sense.

individuals concerned access to justice and the opportunity to assert in an effective manner the protection of their rights. It is against this background that one must consider the Court's judgment in the *Butter-buying cruises* case, where it held that Community law was not intended to create new remedies, although at the same time every type of action provided for by national law must be available for the purposes of ensuring observance of Community provisions.[100] By now, however, it has appeared on several occasions that the mere reference to national procedures and remedies could be inadequate. The relevant national rules may contain certain lacunas and weaknesses which may preclude the national court from accomplishing the task assigned to it and this may accordingly compromise the effectiveness of the protection of individuals.[101] If this is the case, an adaptation of the existing national rules with a view to giving full and effective protection to the individuals concerned will be indispensable.[102] Moreover, it has been argued that in certain circumstances the ultimate consequence could be the creation of a new remedy.[103]

The shape which this adaptation should take will obviously depend on the concrete circumstances of the case. For this reason, on the basis of cases decided by the Court of Justice, only a number of general indications can be given in this respect. Two features which the cases have in common are the often far-reaching intervention by the Court into what was believed to be the province of the Member States' procedural autonomy and the high quality of the solutions imposed. By analogy with the 'second generation answers',[104] it is very appropriate to call them 'third generation solutions'.[105]

In particular during the last ten years the Court's case law in this area, often nourished by detailed questions from national courts, has expanded very rapidly.[106] What follows are only the main lines of the development, with a focus on, as much as possible, issues that are directly relevant for the enforcement of directives.[107] First, I will briefly discuss the various areas of national procedural law—in the broadest sense

---

[100] Case 158/80 [1981] ECR 1805.

[101] Barav 1991, 14, Simon 1991, 484. For an overview of the development of the Court's case law see also Jacobs 1993.

[102] Cf already in 1969 Mertens de Wilmars, 81. Cf also the Opinion of AG Mischo in Joined Cases C–6/90 and C–9/90 *Francovich* [1991] ECR I–5357, para 49.   [103] See below, Subsection 7.3.4.

[104] See above, Section 7.2.

[105] Cf Curtin and Mortelmans 1994, 433. For the sake of clarity, it must be pointed out that Community law may also interfere with national procedural law through other mechanisms than the requirements of equivalence and effectiveness or effective judicial protection. In a number of cases either the Treaty freedoms or the general prohibition of discrimination laid down in Art 12 had implications for national procedural rules. Cf Case C–336/94 *Dafeki* [1997] ECR I–6761, Case C–43/95 *Data Delecta* [1996] ECR I–4661, and Case C–122/96 *Saldanha* [1997] ECR I–5325. In other cases, it is mainly on the basis of an interpretation of a particular directive that the Court reaches a result with considerable implications for national procedural law. Cf e.g. Joined Cases C–240/98 and C–244/98 *Océano* [2000] ECR I–4941.

[106] And has generated a wealth of literature. My references are limited only to some of the many works.

[107] Obviously, most of the issues discussed here relate to the enforcement of Community law in general, far from being specifically about directives only.

of the term—which have been submitted to the scrutiny of the Court and which illustrate the possible intrusiveness of the principle of effectiveness and, in particular, the principle of effective judicial protection.[108] For the purposes of the discussion I have divided the cases into three groups. In the first place there are cases which relate to the initial stage of a procedure. The central issues here are those concerning different aspects of the *access to judicial process*. The second group of cases concerns the rules applicable *during the proceedings*. Thirdly, there are cases in which the *remedial aspects* are the focus of attention.[109] Next, this Chapter will be wound up with a Section that addresses a number of common features, questions, and problems to which the jurisprudential developments give rise.

7.3.2 Access to judicial process

As regards the first group of cases, it has already been noted that Community law does not interfere with the organization of the courts and the division of the jurisdiction of the judicial bodies within the Member States. Whether the remedy is to be sought from ordinary courts, administrative courts, or otherwise specialized courts is left to the national legal system.[110] On the other hand the access to the courts as such and even the stage before the judicial process starts may be governed by certain requirements imposed by Community law. Thus in *Heylens*,[111] the principle of effective judicial protection produced effects in the prelitigation stage, as the Court obliged the competent authorities to give reasons for the decision at issue, either in the decision itself or subsequently, upon request of the individuals affected. According to the Court, the latter must be able to defend their rights under the best possible conditions and to decide with full knowledge of the relevant facts whether there is any point in bringing a case before a court.[112]

Another issue within the sphere of *conditions* under which the right to access to justice is exercised and on which Community law could potentially have an effect is the availability of legal aid. In the literature it has been suggested that the absence

---

[108] The application of the principle of equivalence that also emerged in some more recent cases will be discussed below, in Subsection 7.4.2.

[109] The subdivision of the case law may actually seem somewhat arbitrary. In my view, however, it helps to present matters in a structured way.

[110] Provided, however, that the protection given is effective. As to the Member States' latitude, see e.g. Case 98/79 *Pecastaing* [1980] ECR 691, para 11. [111] Case 222/86 [1987] ECR 4097.

[112] The obligation to give reasons is also explicitly laid down in a number of directives. See e.g. Directive 64/221 (public policy and public health) [1963–1964] OJ English Spec Ed 117, Directive 92/59 (product safety) [1992] OJ L228/14, Directive 92/50 (public service contracts) [1992] OJ L209/1, Directive 92/53 (type-approval of motor vehicles) [1992] OJ L225/1, Directive 84/532 (construction plants) [1984] OJ L300/111, Directive 2003/4 (information on environment) [2003] OJ L41/26 and Directive 2003/86 (family reunification) [2003] OJ L251/12.

of legal aid or the existence of very strict conditions for allowing legal aid, could *de facto* render nugatory the principle of effective judicial protection.[113]

Access to the courts in the stricter sense of the term usually depends on the satisfaction of a number of requirements, such as *locus standi* on the part of the applicant, i.e. the person's right to bring an action or challenge a decision, which is usually described in terms of the individual's interest in the matter.[114] Similarly, the nature of the decision being challenged is relevant, as are the time limits for bringing proceedings. In principle, these matters are, according to the *Rewe/Comet* case law,[115] governed by national law. Yet, Community law does not leave these matters entirely unaffected either.

Locus standi

In the *Verholen*[116] case one of the questions referred to the Court of Justice asked whether in proceedings before a national court an individual could rely on Directive 79/7 (equal treatment in statutory schemes of social security)[117] if he suffered the effects of a discriminatory national provision regarding his spouse, although she herself was not, and according to national law could not be, a party to the proceedings. The Court answered the question in the affirmative.

It found that persons other than those falling within the personal scope of the Directive may also have a direct interest in ensuring that the principle of non-discrimination is respected as regards persons who are protected, and therefore the former must be able to rely on the Directive in question. In this respect the Court stressed that it was in principle for national law to determine an individual's standing and legal interest in bringing proceedings. Nevertheless, Community law required that national legislation should not restrict the right to effective judicial protection and its application could not render virtually impossible the exercise of the rights conferred by Community law.

The inferences to be drawn from this judgment are that Community law requirements may influence national standing rules and that, in the ultimate analysis, the persons concerned should, under certain circumstances, be given *locus*

---

[113] Cf Herbert 1993, 61–3. Cf also the inclusion of legal aid 'to those who lack sufficient resources insofar as such aid is necessary to ensure effective access to justice' in Art 47, last paragraph, of the EU Charter of Fundamental Rights, which is directly inspired by the judgment of the ECrtHR in the *Airey* case, ECrtHR 9 October 1979, 2 EHRR 305 and Case C–63/01 *Evans*, judgment of 4 December 2003, nyr in ECR, in particular para 77.

[114] Obviously, the interest required and the test applied may vary considerably from Member State to Member State and even between the different types of proceedings within one single Member State.

[115] Case 33/76 [1976] ECR 1989 and Case 45/76 [1976] ECR 2043.

[116] Joined Cases C–87/90, C–88/90, and C–89/90 [1991] ECR I–3757, confirmed in Case C–343/92 *Roks* [1994] ECR I–571.   [117] [1979] OJ L6/24.

standi, even in situations where they have no standing under national law, if this is necessary to safeguard effective judicial protection.[118]

Although until now the question has scarcely been raised, delineating the class of persons who should be allowed to bring an action in pursuance of Community law requirements is not always unproblematic. It will often be possible to establish on the basis of the relevant Community law provisions which persons are to be protected and, consequently, should be able to bring an action.[119] This can be the case because a provision gives an explicit statement in this respect.[120] Similarly, few problems will arise when the personal scope of, for instance, a directive can be deduced from its actual text. As a rule, persons falling within the personal scope of the directive will be sufficiently affected by the misapplication or non-application of the provisions which give them some advantage or right. Since they will then have an interest in the judicial decision which they are striving to obtain, they should be given standing.[121] With respect to some directives, however, it may be quite difficult to establish which (reasons or categories of) persons are protected and should accordingly be able to bring an action or challenge a decision. This is for instance *and* in particular the case with respect to environmental law directives, since these directives often aim at protecting the environment as such rather than being concerned with securing advantages to individual members of given classes separately.[122] Furthermore, if it appears that the directive is

---

[118] On issues related to *locus standi* see, for instance, Oliver 1992, 360, Jans 1993a and Jans 1993b, Kraemer, 1992, 173–6, Geddes 1992, Ward 1993, 232–5, Herbert 1993, 36–48, Harlow and Szyszczak 1995, and Jans 2000, 205–10. Cf also the Opinion of AG Capotorti in Case 158/80 *Butter-buying cruises* [1981] ECR 1805, para 6. A broad interpretation of standing rules is also supported by Case C–459/99 *MRAX* [2002] ECR I–6591, para 101.

[119] And indeed, some directives may themselves provide for standing. See e.g. Art 11 of Directive 97/7 (protection of consumers in respect of distance contracts) [1997] OJ L144/19, and Art 7(2) of Directive 2000/43 (race discrimination) [2000] OJ L180/22.

[120] Cf Article 6 of Directive 76/207 (equal treatment at work) [1976] OJ L39/40: 'all persons who consider themselves wronged by sex discrimination . . . ' and Article 12 of Directive 92/28 (advertising of medicinal products) [1992] OJ L113/13, which provides that persons or organizations regarded under national law as having a legitimate interest in prohibiting any advertisement inconsistent with the Directive must be able to take legal action. A similar provision can also be found in Art 7(2) of Directive 93/13 (consumer contracts) [1993] OJ L95/29. Cf also Directive 2003/4 (information on environment) [2003] OJ L41/26, Art 3 (any legal or natural person must obtain information).

[121] As to the identification of persons falling within the scope of a directive see e.g. Case 115/78 *Knoors* [1979] ECR 399, Joined Cases C–6/90 and C–9/90 *Francovich* [1991] ECR I–5357 and Case C–91/92 *Faccini Dori* [1994] ECR I–3325.

[122] Cf Jans 1992, 6 ff. In particular in relation to the 'air and groundwater' cases (Case C–361/88 *Commission v. Germany* [1991] ECR I–2567, Case C–59/89 *Commission v. Germany* [1991] ECR I–2607, Case C–58/89 *Commission v. Germany* [1991] ECR I–4983), in the literature it has been questioned whether the Court in fact requires an *actio popularis*. Cf Jans 1993a, 205–6, Jans 1993b, 158, Everling 1992a, 384–5 and Everling 1993, 214–15. See also the first edition of this book, at 168.

protecting some interest of the public at large, it is not self-evident that consequently everybody should be given standing.[123]

Be this as it may, the scope of the Court's case law is not limited to those within the personal scope of the directive. In the *Van Duyn*[124] case the Court found in very general terms that *persons concerned* must have the opportunity to rely on (directly effective) provisions of a directive. From *Verholen* it follows that the category of 'persons concerned' includes those who have a direct interest in the application of the rules and not merely those who are directly protected by the rules at issue.[125] Furthermore, in my view, the principles which can thus be deduced from Community law do not apply solely where an individual wishes to rely *directly* on the directive in question but also where the person brings an action under the national law transposing the directive. A different solution would lead to an anomaly, namely, as long as the person was invoking the directive he would have standing, while as soon as he relied on national law (with Community origins) his *locus standi* would potentially be curtailed. When a directive is being implemented, therefore, a part of the implementation process should relate to amendments of national standing rules if this seems necessary from the Community law point of view.

The questions of who should be considered as 'persons concerned' by Community law provisions and, thus, what degree of interest is necessary and what is the appropriate test for standing is a matter to be decided under Community law. Next, the outcome of this exercise should be confronted with the applicable national standing rules. According to the principles rehearsed in *Verholen*, the Member States are left discretion as to the question of an individual's standing. The only provisos are that the applicable rules must not render the exercise of the rights virtually impossible and they must observe the requirement of effective judicial protection. It is submitted that when deciding whether these limits have been transgressed in a particular case, the Court of Justice will take into account the entire system of judicial protection under the national law of the Member State concerned in order to ascertain whether the requirement of effective judicial protection remains safeguarded or not.[126] Moreover, proper account should also be

---

[123] Cf AG Jacobs who remarked in his Opinion in Case C–58/89 *Commission v. Germany* [1991] ECR I–4983, para 34, that 'the public at large, as well as ecologists and environmental pressure groups, have a general interest in water quality and indeed in the respect of Community law. It does not however automatically follow that enforceable rights must be made available to them in national courts'. Arguably, it also does not follow that those having 'general interest' must be given standing.

[124] Case 41/74 [1974] ECR 1337.

[125] Joined Cases C–87/90, C–88/90, and C–89/90 [1991] ECR I–3757. Cf also AG Geelhoed, Opinion of 4 March 2004, in Case C–174/02 and C–175/02 *Streekgewest Westelijk Noord-Brabant*, paras 54–58, who points out that the category of persons who may rely on the provisions at issue is also determined by the consequences attributed, by Community law, to their breach.

[126] The absence of standing in a certain type of procedure does not *eo ipso* mean that there is no effective judicial protection: the individual concerned has for instance standing in another type of procedure. Cf in this sense Case C–13/01 *Safalero* [2003] ECR I–8679. See also below, Subsection 7.4.2, on the content of the whole procedure to be taken into account.

taken of the functions of the respective standing rules[127] and they should be weighed against the two requirements.

The nature of the challenged act

As with the question of the individual's standing, Community law may also have implications for the conditions of admissibility of an action in which a *certain act* is challenged. In other words, the focus of attention in these cases is more the *nature of the act* at issue than the person of the applicant.

In the *Borrelli*[128] case the applicant brought an action for annulment against a decision of the Commission, by which the latter refused to grant the applicant aid from the EAGGF funds. The Commission did this in pursuance of a negative opinion of the Regional Council of Liguria. This negative opinion meant that one of the conditions required under the applicable rules had not been fulfilled: aid can only be granted if the competent national authorities give a favourable opinion. The principal ground of illegality submitted by the applicant was the alleged illegality of the negative opinion of the Regional Council. The applicant argued that if this illegality had no effect on the validity of the Commission's decision he would be deprived of all judicial protection, since the opinion, as a preparatory act, cannot be challenged under Italian law. Obviously the Court held that in Article 230 proceedings it has no jurisdiction as to the legality of an act of a national authority. The mere fact that the 'national' opinion was a part of a process resulting in a Community decision could not alter this conclusion. On the other hand, the Commission was bound by the opinion of the national authorities and was also unable to control the legality. It was against this background that the Court considered that it is for the national courts to decide upon the legality of the act in question under the same conditions as those governing any final act which, when adopted by the same authority, is capable of affecting the interests of third parties. The national court had to consider as admissible the action brought for this purpose, even if the national procedural rules do not provide for this. In other words, an act against which no appeal could be made under national law had nevertheless to be considered as an act which could be appealed. The Court based this decision on the requirement of effective judicial protection as expounded in *Johnston* and *Heylens*.[129] Since the national opinion was integrated in a procedure which ultimately led to a decision under Community law, the Member

---

[127] As to the function of standing rules see Cane 1986, 165–6. Cf also the Opinion of AG Capotorti in Case 158/80 *Butter-buying cruises* [1981] ECR 1805, para 6.

[128] C–97/91 [1992] ECR I–6313.

[129] Case 222/84 [1986] ECR 1651 and Case 222/86 [1987] ECR 4097.

State concerned was obliged to observe the requirement of effective judicial protection.

The more general implications of the judgment in *Borelli* are that under defined circumstances and with a view to safeguarding effective judicial protection a certain type of action must be declared admissible, even if no appeal against a comparable decision is possible under national law alone.[130]

Time limits

The last category of potential obstacles to access to judicial process which up to now have been addressed by the Court of Justice consists of the time limits for bringing action.

In principle, time limits—just like all other conditions governing (national) actions at law in which individuals enforce the rights they derive from Community law—are a matter which is left to national legal systems. The only two conditions to be satisfied are that the time limits are no less favourable than those for similar actions of a domestic nature and that they do not make impossible or excessively difficult the exercise of the rights conferred. In *Rewe* and *Comet* the Court found that 'a reasonable period of limitation within which an action must be brought' in fact satisfies the latter requirement.[131] The Court pointed out in this respect that fixing a period of this kind is actually an application of the principle of legal certainty, which protects both the national authorities concerned and private individuals.[132]

By accepting the existence of reasonable time limits for instituting proceedings in national courts for reasons of legal certainty the Court also accepted the consequences: in certain circumstances the individual will be deprived of the opportunity to enforce the rights which he derives from Community law. However, the Court apparently gave priority to the principle of legal certainty over the need for judicial protection of the individuals concerned *and* the full force and effect which Community law should have in national legal orders. This apparently well-established rule was confirmed in several subsequent cases.[133]

---

[130] Cf also Case 53/85 *AKZO* [1986] ECR 1965 and Case C–459/99 *MRAX* [2002] ECR I–6591, para 101.

[131] Case 33/76 [1976] ECR 1989 and Case 45/76 [1976] ECR 2043. Cf also Case C–208/90 *Emmott* [1991] ECR I–4269, para 16.

[132] The finding that time limits serve the need to respect the principle of legal certainty was scarcely a surprise. See already Case 3/59 *Germany v. High Authority* [1960] ECR 53, 61. Cf also Case 156/77 *Commission v. Belgium* [1978] ECR 1881, para 23. However, the protection of legal certainty does not go so far that infringements of Community law committed over a long period may be justified for the very reason that neither the authorities nor the individuals were aware of the unlawful character of—in that case—the taxes that were levied. Cf Case C–188/95 *Fantask* [1997] ECR I–6783.

[133] Cf Case 826/79 *Mireco* [1980] ECR 2559, Case 811/79 *Ariete* [1980] 2545. Cf also Case 386/87 *Bessin and Salson* [1989] ECR 3551, which concerned time limits for submission of applications for reimbursement with the competent authorities and not time limits for bringing action *stricto sensu*.

Similarly, for considerations of legal certainty, administrative bodies cannot be placed under an obligation to reopen an administrative decision which has become final upon the expiry of reasonable time limits for legal remedies or by exhaustion of the latter. Community law respects, in principle, the finality of an administrative decision.[134] However, the Court has accepted that it may be otherwise in exceptional circumstances.

> In *Kühne*, the Court decided that Article 10 EC Treaty imposes an obligation on an administrative body to review a final administrative decision, where the latter was requested to do so in the light of an interpretation of Community law provisions given by the Court in a situation where: '. . . under national law, it has the power to reopen that decision; the administrative decision in question has become final as a result of a judgment of a national court ruling at final instance; that judgment is, in the light of a decision given by the Court subsequent to it, based on a misinterpretation of Community law which was adopted without a question being referred to the Court for a preliminary ruling under Article 234(3) EC; and the person concerned complained to the administrative body immediately after becoming aware of that decision of the Court'.[135]

This judgment is very much tailored to the specific facts of the case. Nevertheless, it also gives a general indication: where the individual concerned has taken, in procedural terms and in due time, every possible step to defend his or her position and it is the final instance national court that can be blamed for misinterpretation, then the finality of the decision has to yield;[136] all this under the proviso that the national body has the power to reopen the decision and that interests of third parties are not adversely affected.

> In the case of Theresa Emmott[137] the Court seemed to create another important exception to the general acceptance of reasonable time limits. Equally, the judgment caused quite a stir in both academic and legal practice circles.[138] The Court held, in very general terms, that where a directive has not been properly transposed into national law, the Member State may not rely on national time limits for initiating proceedings until the directive has been properly implemented. The period for bringing proceedings also cannot begin to run

---

[134] Cf also the Court's findings in relation to the principle of *res judicata* in Case C–224/01 *Köbler*, judgment of 30 September 2003, nyr in ECR, para 38. However, it must be noted that a decision, even if it became final, which is contrary to Community law, cannot result in imposing a sanction. Cf Case C–224/97 *Ciola* [1999] ECR I–2517.

[135] Case C–453/00, judgment of 13 January 2004, nyr in ECR, para 28.

[136] Comparable considerations can also be found in the judgment of ECrtHR in case *Dangeville v. France*, application 36677/97, judgment of 16 April 2002.

[137] Case C–208/90 *Emmott* [1991] ECR I–4269. For a detailed discussion and further speculations on the impact of the case see the first edition of this book, 171–3.

[138] Cf e.g. Oliver 1992, 367–9 and Hoskins 1996, 367–71.

before that date. The effect of these *dicta* was, potentially, to disrupt various temporal restrictions every time a claim was based on a non- or incorrectly transposed directive, with detrimental consequences for legal certainty and having, in many cases, also a considerable financial impact.

In a line of subsequent cases the Court has curbed the effect of its judgment. The reasoning was often not clear and rather contradictory.[139] In particular, the Court stressed at several instances that the solution adopted in *Emmott* was justified by the particular circumstances of the case, specifying that the time-bar at issue had the result of depriving the plaintiff in the main proceeding—i.e. Ms *Emmott*—of any opportunity of enforcing her rights before national courts.[140] Yet, on the other hand the Court also held that

... it is compatible with Community law for national rules to prescribe, in the interest of legal certainty, reasonable limitation periods for bringing proceedings . . . it cannot be said that [the time limit] makes the exercise of rights conferred by Community law either virtually impossible of excessively difficult, even though the expiry of such limitation periods entails by definition the rejection, wholly or in part, of the action brought.[141]

The ultimate rationale in *Emmott* lay rather in the fact that there was quite some dissuasive correspondence and misleading of the applicant by the competent national authorities and that it was notably their doing that Ms Emmott did not initiate her case within the three-month time limit for bringing an action for judicial review under Irish law. Indeed, in other cases the Court stressed that in the documents before it and the arguments presented it did not appear that the conduct of the national authorities, in conjunction with the existence of the time limit at issue, deprived the plaintiff of any opportunity of enforcing its rights in national courts. In other terms, the Court has introduced an element of obstruction, reproachable behaviour or, where appropriate, deliberate misleading which may result in the non-application of time limits at issue.[142] In case such an element is present, the application of time limits may be qualified as making the enforcement of Community law rights virtually impossible or excessively difficult.[143]

In *Magorian*,[144] the Court has formulated a slightly different exception: a rule which strikes at the very essence of the right conferred by the Community legal order must be considered as a rule which renders any action by individuals

---

[139] For a more detailed account see Prechal 2000a or Shelkoplyas 2003, 85–90.

[140] Cf e.g. Case C–231/96 *Edis* 1998] ECR I–495.

[141] Case C–326/96 *Levez* [1988] ECR I–7835, para 19. Cf also Case C–78/98 *Preston* [2000] ECR I–3201, para 34, and Case C–261/95 *Palmisani* [1997] ECR I–4025, para 28.

[142] Cf Case C–231/96 *Edis* [1998] ECR I–4951 and Case C–326/96 *Levez* [1998] ECR I–7835.

[143] Cf Case C–327/00 *Santex* [2003] ECR I–1877. This line of reasoning, *including Emmott* into the effectiveness test, was already proposed by AG Jacobs in his Opinion in Case C–2/94 *Denkavit* [1996] ECR I–2827, para 74 ff.   [144] Case C–246/96 [1997] ECR I–7153.

relying on Community law impossible in practice.[145] The major difficulty with this test is indeed how to draw the distinction between 'ordinary' procedural limitation and those that strike at the heart of Community law rights.

One issue remains to be addressed briefly here, namely the various kinds of limitation periods.[146] Access to the courts (in the broad sense of the term) in the various Member States and even access to different courts within a single Member State is regulated in different ways. Several types of conditions often have to be satisfied before proceedings can be brought before a court. In administrative law, for instance, the requirement will quite often be posed that the individual concerned first makes a complaint to the competent authority. This complaint usually has to be made within a certain period of time. Similarly, where applications (e.g. for reimbursement or for a social security benefit or unduly paid taxes) to an authority first have to be made, a certain time limit will often apply.[147] In other words, in the prelitigation stage there are already time limits to be observed. The rules governing those time limits obviously do not directly concern a deadline for bringing an action before the courts. Indirectly, however, their expiry may have the same effect as the expiry of time limits for bringing proceedings.

Another common distinction relates to the nature of limitation periods. Some time limits, in particular time limits for bringing action in administrative law (*'délai de recours'*), are considered procedural time limits in the strict sense of the term and they are relatively short. Other—often longer—limitation periods are periods of prescription (*'délai de prescription'*) which are more common in civil law. They may relate to the right of action or to the substantive right itself. Their observance will often not be treated as a matter of admissibility but rather as concerning the merits of the case.[148] Whatever their consequences might be under national law, the effect of the expiry of both types of limitation periods, as regards the possibility of asserting one's right in the courts, is similar.

In the light of all the possible varieties of limitation periods as they exist within the Member States and the differences in their legal classifications and in their application, it is submitted that for the purposes of the application of the principles of effectiveness, equivalence, and effective judicial protection—and indeed, the

---

[145] Cf also Case C–78/98 *Preston* [2000] ECR I–3201. See, in comparable sense also Case C–62/00 *Marks & Spencer* [2002] ECR I–6325 where a retroactive reduction of the period within which reimbursement may be claimed, deprived the individuals of *any* possibility of exercising a right which they previously enjoyed was held incompatible with the principle of effectiveness [emphasis added]. Cf also Case C–255/00 *Grundig* [2002] ECR I–8003.

[146] Other temporal limitation, such as those governing the retroactive scope of a claim for certain benefits, are briefly discussed below, in Subsection 7.3.4.

[147] Cf e.g the application for payments of insolvency compensation in Case C–125/01 *Pflücke* [2003] ECR I–9375 and reimbursement of unduly paid VAT in Case C–62/00 *Marks & Spencer* [2002] ECR I–6325.

[148] Cf as to the classification of the five-year limitation period of an action for damages under the E(E)C Treaty (Art 43 of the Statute of the Court of Justice) Heukels 1988, 97–8.

exception to the rules as it results in the final analysis from the judgments following upon *Emmott*—there is, in principle, from the Community law point of view
no reason to treat these limits differently.

7.3.3   Rules applicable during the proceedings

Evidential rules

On the borderline between the first category of cases and the second category of
cases, which have so far been mainly limited to the rules of evidence, one can situate
the *Johnston*[149] case. As explained above,[150] the evidential rule at issue prevented the
national court from exercising any judicial control. Thus, although Mrs Johnston
was not strictly speaking denied access to the court, her application was aborted at
such an early stage and in such a way that it could be considered as tantamount to
refusing her access to justice.

There are, however, national rules of evidence with less draconian effects; i.e.
they do not as such exclude judicial control but, on the other hand, the burden of
proof falling upon a party may be extremely difficult to satisfy. In principle, in
the absence of relevant rules of Community law,[151] the rules of evidence are
governed by national law. The only requirements to be met are the requirements
of non-discrimination and effectiveness. Already in its 'early case law', as I have
termed it, there are some instances in which the Court disapproved the burden of
proof being placed upon the applicant, since it made the exercise of the rights
derived from Community law virtually impossible or excessively difficult.[152] Ever
since then, national evidential rules are regularly submitted to the Court for
scrutiny.

This case law evolves notably but not only[153] in cases concerning the recovery
of sums paid though not due, often various types of indirect taxes which were
levied contrary to Community law provisions and the question whether the
repayment results in unjust enrichment of the taxpayer. In national law there

---

[149] Case 222/84 [1986] ECR 1651.   [150] See above, Subsection 7.2.2.

[151] However, various directives contain provisions as to the burden of proof. See, for instance,
Directive 85/374 (product liability) [1985] OJ L210/29, Directive 93/13 (consumer contracts) [1993]
OJ L95/29, Directive 97/80 (sex discrimination—burden of proof) [1998] OJ L14/6, Directive 97/7
(protection of consumers in respect of distance contracts) [1997] OJ L144/19, Directive 2000/43 (race-
discrimination) [2000] OJ L180/22 and Directive 2003/86 (family reunifiction) [2003] OJ L251/12.

[152] Cf Case 199/82 *San Giorgio* [1983] ECR 3595, Joined Cases 331, 376, and 378/85 *Bianco* [1988]
ECR 1099. Cf also, more recently, Case C–228/98 *Dounias* [2000] ECR I–577.

[153] Cf Case C–298/96, *Oelhmühle* [1998] ECR I–4767 which concerned the recovery of sums not
due *from* a undertaking. Similarly, from, for instance, Case C–242/95 *GT-Link* [1997] ECR I–440, it
appears that the principles at issue are by no means limited to cases relating to recovery; they are rather
of general application.

often exist *de facto* or statutory presumptions that the taxpayers pass on to third parties the charges at issue and it is for them to rebut this presumption by adducing evidence to the contrary, which often boils down to a requirement of negative proof. Similarly, in certain cases only documentary and no other evidence was allowed. The main line of this case law, which sometimes goes into great detail, is that unjustified presumptions to the claimant's disadvantage fall foul of the principle of effectiveness.[154]

In certain other cases, presumptions or other evidential rules may turn out to be incompatible with Community law for other reasons. In *Skripalle*,[155] for instance, it was the interpretation of the Sixth VAT Directive[156] that brought about such a result. In the area of free movement the problem often lies in the fact that presumptions do not meet the test of proportionality.[157]

In some other cases the Court did not reiterate that evidential rules were a matter to be determined by national law, nor did it focus on the question whether the exercise of the rights was virtually impossible. The focal point was rather the principle of effective judicial protection, as a rule in combination with a written provision of Community law such as Article 6 of Directive 75/117 (equal pay).[158]

Thus in *Danfoss*,[159] for instance, one of the questions submitted to the Court concerned the appropriate burden of proof for proving pay discrimination in a situation where the pay system was 'characterized by a total lack of transparency'. The Court found that in such circumstances the applicants 'would be deprived of any effective means of enforcing the principle of equal pay before national courts if the effect of adducing [the] evidence was not to impose upon the employer the burden of proving that his practice in the matter of wages is not, in fact, discriminatory'.[160] The approach chosen by the Court in *Danfoss* was subsequently confirmed in *Enderby*.[161] Although in this case the Court's starting point was that 'it is normally for the person alleging facts in support of a claim to adduce proof of such facts', it recalled that 'the onus may shift when it is necessary to avoid depriving workers who appear to be the victims of discrimination of any effective means of enforcing the principle of equal pay'.[162]

---

[154] See the more recent cases Case C–343/96 *Dilexport* [1999] ECR I–579, Joined Cases C–192/95 to C–218/95 *Comateb* [1997] ECR I–165, Joined Cases C–441/98 and C–442/98 *Michailidis* [2000] ECR I–7145, Case C–147/01 *Weber's Wine World*, judgment of 2 October 2003, nyr in ECR and Case C–129/00 *Commission v. Italy*, judgment of 9 December 2003, nyr in ECR.

[155] Case C–63/96 [1997] ECR I–2847.   [156] Directive 77/388 [1977] OJ L145/1.

[157] Cf e.g. Case C–250/95 *Futura Participations* [1997] ECR I–2471, Case C–28/95 *Leur-Bloem* [1997] ECR I–4161, and Case C–336/94 *Dafeki* [1997] ECR I–6761.   [158] [1975] OJ L45/19.

[159] Case 109/88 [1989] ECR 3199.   [160] Ibid, para 13.

[161] Case C–127/92 [1993] ECR I–5535.

[162] Cf also Case C–180/95 *Draehmpaehl* [1997] ECR I–2195, where the Court held that it is for the employer to adduce proof that the applicant would not have obtained the vacant position even if there had been no discrimination, since the employer has in his possession all the applications submitted.

Obviously, these cases concerned the interpretation of written provisions of
Community law.[163] However, as the principle of effective judicial protection was
declared by the Court to be a general principle of Community law, it is of general
application. Consequently, it may also have implications for the rules of evidence
applicable with respect to other issues arising under Community law.[164]

Finally, the *Steffensen* case[165] made clear that evidential rules must comply with
the requirements arising from fundamental rights, such as Article 6(1) of the ECHR.
For instance, evidence established in breach of the adversarial principle and, thus,
the right to a fair hearing, must be excluded from the proceedings.

Abuse of rights

A category of national rules which emerged relatively recently in the Court's case
law is the prohibition of abuse of rights and, in particular, the question in how far
a *national* provision on the abuse of rights[166] may be relied upon in order to deny
or, at least, limit the right of an individual to rely on (directly effective) provisions
of a directive in national courts.

In concrete terms, in a number of Greek cases[167] the question was submitted
to the Court whether Article 281 of the Greek Civil Code could be applied
in order to assess whether the exercise of a right that an individual derived from
Article 25(1) of Directive 77/01 (second company law directive)[168] was abusive, with, as a consequence, the rejection of the action. Article 281 of the Civil
Code, which is not a procedural but a substantive rule, provides that

[163] Directive 75/117 (equal pay) [1975] OJ L45/19 and Art 141 EC Treaty. For an obligation of a
national court to interpret national evidential rules in the light of the purpose of a directive although
the directive at issue states explicitly that the national rules concerning the burden of proof are not
affected, see Joined Cases C–253/96 to C–258/96 *Kampelmann* [1997] ECR I–6907.

[164] The interferences of Community law with evidential rules go in fact much further than the
issues discussed briefly in this Subsection. In addition to the free movement mentioned above, one
may also, for instance, add the application of the concept of indirect discrimination. In the field of sex-
discrimination the latter concept has lead, *inter alia*, to rather technical judgments about the use of
statistics. See e.g. Case C–400/93 *Royal Copenhagen* [1995] ECR I–1275 and Case C–167/97 *Seymour-
Smith* [1999] ECR I–623. For an extensive discussion of the various aspects of evidence and Community
law see Prechal and Hancher 2001.

[165] Case C–276/01 [2003] ECR I–3735. For an aspect of fair hearing see also Case C–63/01 *Evans*,
judgment 4 December 2003, nyr in ECR.

[166] Abuse of rights is, as such, not an unfamiliar concept in Community law. Cf e.g. Case 33/74 *Van
Binsbergen* [1974] ECTR 1299 or Case C–148/91 *Veronica* [1993] ECR I–487, where the concept
functions as a limit to free movement. Cf on the broader issues than only those under discussion here
e.g. Schmidt-Kessel 2000.

[167] See, in particular, Case C–441/93 *Pafitis* [1996] ECR I–1347, Case C–367/96 *Kefalas* [1998] ECR
I–2843 and Case C–373/97 *Diamantis* [2000] ECR I–1705. For a comment see e.g. Triantafyllou 1999,
Anagnostopoulou 2001, and Schmidt-Kessel 2000. The approach is, however, more general: see e.g. Case
C–201/01 *Walcher* [2003] ECR I–8827, in particular para 37.   [168] [1977] OJ L26/1.

'the exercise of a right is prohibited where it manifestly exceeds the bounds of good faith, morality or the social or economic purpose of that right'.

Initially, in *Pafitis*, the Court recalled that it is its task to verify whether the judicial protection available under national law is appropriate and *de facto* it prohibited, in that particular case, the application of the national concept of abuse of rights.[169] However, in later cases it moderated its position. The Court stressed that Community law may not be relied upon for fraudulent or abusive ends and it allowed, in principle, the application of national provisions on abuse of rights. Yet, under one proviso: the application must not prejudice the full effect and uniform application of Community law.[170]

Interestingly, the Court chose neither the 'minimalistic' *Rewe* line nor absolute supremacy, as suggested by Advocate General Tesauro,[171] but a standard akin to supremacy. On the other hand, the Court did not formulate a community law standard of 'abuse of rights'.[172]

The question whether conduct amounts to abuse must be assessed by the national court, on the basis of objective evidence and in the light of the objectives pursued by the Community law provisions at issue. When proceeding with the assessment, the national court may not alter the scope of the provision nor compromise the objective pursued by it. As such an assessment of the allegedly abusive exercise of right is tied up with the interpretation of the Community law provision at issue, it may necessitate guidance by the Court. Indeed, the latter did not refrain from providing it by giving an interpretation of the provisions at issue within the particular context of the cases.

> In *Diamantis*, for instance, the Court held that by initiating an action for the declaration of invalidity, the claimant has chosen a remedy that appears to be manifestly disproportionate, in particular, since it will cause serious damage to the legitimate interests of others.

Application of Community law by the national court of its own motion

Is a national court obliged to apply Community law or to take it into consideration for purposes of interpretation of national law in conformity therewith in a case before it where the parties have not presented any arguments drawing upon Community law provisions? The question has been dealt with in *Van Schijndel* which put an end to a number of speculations but, at the same time, gave rise to new and complex issues.[173]

---

[169] Case C–441/93 *Pafitis* [1996] ECR I–1347.
[170] Case C–367/96 *Kefalas* [1998] ECR I–2843.
[171] Opinion of AG Tesauro in Case C–367/96 *Kefalas* [1998] ECR I–2843.
[172] For a brief discussion of these 'minimalist' and 'maximalist' approaches see Triantafyllou 1999, 160–3.   [173] Joined Cases C–430/93 and C–431/93 *Van Schijndel* [1995] ECR I–4705.

Before *Van Schijndel*, some confusion existed about this question of *ex officio* application. In *Verholen*, for instance, the national court asked whether Community law *precludes* the national courts from reviewing (of their own motion) a national legal provision in the light of an EC directive, which was, according to the Court, not the case.[174] Similarly, a case was reported from Germany where a *Finanzgericht* found that the Sixth VAT Directive could only be applied when the claimant relied on it explicitly.[175]

In *Verholen*, Advocate General Darmon also addressed the question whether the national court is *under a duty* to apply Community law of its own motion. The Advocate General gave an affirmative answer. Basically, he referred to the Community law obligation of national courts to apply directly effective provisions of Community law and the obligation to interpret national law in conformity with the latter. Furthermore, in his view 'the primacy of Community law cannot be left to the discretion of the national courts, without the risk of its *uniform* application being seriously compromised'.[176]

In the literature the question has not been addressed in much detail. Several authors have suggested that national courts are under the obligation to apply Community law of their own motion, although the basis for such an obligation is scarcely discussed.[177] Apparently, it is common understanding that since Community law, including directives, forms a part of the legal norms valid within the Member State, the courts must apply it accordingly and where necessary of their own motion. Furthermore, the obligation seems to be reinforced by the principle of supremacy and the need for uniform application of Community law. Another argument has been submitted by Lenaerts, who argues that Community law is 'of public policy' (*'d'ordre public'*) within the legal orders of the Member States and therefore the courts must apply it of their own motion.[178]

There is of course the obligation for the courts to apply directly effective Community law and, furthermore, to interpret national law in conformity with the latter. These obligations have been formulated with respect to cases where at least one of the parties was relying on Community law provisions. However, the question whether a national court must apply Community law of its own motion is a separate issue. It does not automatically follow from the obligations which have just been described that there is a duty for national courts to apply Community law provisions of their own motion. An unqualified obligation to apply Community law *ex officio* would, taken to its ultimate conclusion, entail that in every single case

---

[174] Joined Cases C–87/90, C–88/90, and C–89/90 *Verholen* [1991] ECR I–3757.

[175] See Fischer 1991.

[176] Joined Cases C–87/90, C–88/90, and C–89/90 [1991] ECR I–3757, para 19.

[177] Cf Fuß 1981, 192, Bleckmann 1976, 486, Ress 1993, 360, Grabitz 1971, 21, Jarass 1991, 2669, Winter 1991b, 664, Fischer 1991, 561. On the other hand, the obligation has been denied by Weymüller 1991, 503 or it has been submitted that the case law is not clear in this respect: Classen 1993, 84. As to this issue cf also (already) Kovar 1978, 266.   [178] Lenaerts 1993, 1105.

before it the national court had to examine whether some rule of Community law was applicable to the case or whether some Community provision had been violated.

The first matter which has been clarified in *Van Schijndel* and also in *Peterbroeck* is that the application of Community law by national courts of their own motion is not some kind of sequel to direct effect and, in particular, supremacy, as argued by, for instance, Advocate General Darmon.[179] On the contrary, it is a matter of procedural law and is, as such, subject to the principles enunciated in *Rewe/Comet* and, where appropriate, to the principle of effective judicial protection.

In more concrete terms, in *Van Schijndel* the ECJ had to deal with the question as to whether, first, national courts in the context of civil law proceedings are under the duty to apply Community law *ex officio* and, second, whether such an obligation also exists where it would imply that the court must disregard the principle of judicial passivity in civil matters.[180] Under the Dutch Code of Civil Procedure a judge has to supplement of his or her own motion legal grounds not put forward by the parties. However, in supplementing the legal grounds a judge may neither go beyond the limits of the dispute nor rely on facts and circumstances other than those relied on by the party concerned. This principle of judicial passivity is, indeed, intimately linked to the other fundamental principle of private law: party autonomy or the freedom of disposition.

Under the application of the principle of equivalence, the ECJ required the national courts to apply Community law of their own motion in cases where such an obligation exists under national law. However, it went further and found that the courts are also under obligation to apply Community law of their own motion where domestic law allows such an application and where it is necessary in order to safeguard the legal protection of individuals. Yet, this obligation is not unlimited. In fact, the ECJ also upheld the rule that the national court should not go beyond the ambit of the dispute and asserted facts, the judicial passivity. It found this rule justified by exactly the principle of parties' freedom of disposition, which 'reflects conceptions prevailing in most of the Member States as to the relations between the State and the individual; it

---

[179] Cf above. The Advocate General's point of view is symptomatic for, in particular, French legal writing in this area where all kinds of obstacles to the application of Community law are perceived as a problem of supremacy and where use is often made of the 'supremacy is all argument' (this term is from Hoskins 1996, 376). This conception of supremacy also explains why the French scholars were disappointed by the *Van Schijndel* judgment. Cf e.g. Simon 1996a and 1996b, Boutard-Labarde 1996, 245, Canivet and Huglo 1996. Arguments drawing upon supremacy, *effet utile*, and uniform application of Community law have also been discussed (and refuted) by AG Jacobs in his Opinion in *Van Schijndel*, at paras 24–45.

[180] For the *ex officio* application of Community law in administrative/tax law proceedings see Case C–312/93 *Peterbroeck* [1995] ECR I-4599 and Case C–72/95 *Kraaijeveld* [1996] ECR I–5403. The issue was also raised in a criminal case, namely Case C–226/97 *Lemmens* [1998] ECR I–3711, but neither the Court nor the AG addressed it.

safeguards the rights of defence; and it ensures proper conduct of the proceedings by, in particular, protecting them from delays inherent to examination of new pleas'.[181]

On the one hand, in the Court's solution the judicial protection of the individual relying on Community competition rules was perhaps upgraded in comparison to an individual who would have based his claim on a domestic provision. On the other hand, at the end of the day the Court's interference with the Dutch rules at issue was less dramatic than some might have expected in the light of the firm language about the need to maintain the full force of Community law and to safeguard effective judicial protection.[182]

Van Schijndel concerned, in the context of *ex officio* application, another point: in Dutch civil procedure there is an exception to the principle of judicial passivity as set out above: the courts are not bound to the duty of passivity if the rules at issue may be qualified as pertaining to public policy. Both before the ECJ and the *Hoge Raad*, Van Schijndel argued that Community law competition provisions fall within this exception and, therefore, they should be applied *ex officio*. In the procedure before the ECJ, neither the Court nor the Advocate General paid much attention to this issue. Advocate General Jacobs first discussed a number of differences in the legal systems as to the question when a court may raise a point of law of its own motion. Then he continued by pointing out that there is no agreement on what constitutes a matter of public policy. For Community law he foresaw difficulty in deciding whether all Community law should be applied by the courts of their own motion or only certain parts of it, and if so, which parts. In the Court's judgment there is only a somewhat timid reference to public interest requiring a court's *ex officio* intervention in exceptional cases only.[183] However, two years later, the question of the public policy character of Community (competition) law came before the Court again in *Eco Swiss*.[184]

---

[181] Para 21 of the judgment. See on this justification also below, Subsection 7.4.2. In contrast to *Van Schijndel*, in *Peterbroeck* there was no justification for the provisions of the Belgian Income Tax Code, under which an argument based on Community law could not be considered by the national court if the taxable person has not raised it within a certain prescribed period.

[182] Although the Court's guidelines may seem rather simple, at national level there are quite some difficulties with the application of these principles, last but not least because the *ex officio* application as such is already rather problematic in the national context itself. Cf e.g. Honorat and Schwartz 1991, Sauron 2000, 64 and 67, Stuyck 2001 and Widderhoven 2003.

[183] The *Hoge Raad* did not uphold this argument either. It found that neither the general interest nor fundamental legal principles were involved in Van Schijndel's claim. What he pursued was a matter of mainly individual interest. In his opinion in this case, the Advocate General with the *Hoge Raad*, Koopmans, pointed to the fact that '*ordre public*' is a concept which varies according to the context in which it is used. He also pointed at the principle of parties' freedom of disposition in civil procedure. Only in very exceptional circumstances may a court depart from it. In his view, no such exceptional circumstances were present in the *Van Schijndel* case. NJ 1997, no 117.

[184] Case C–126/97 [1999] ECR I–3055. For a discussion of the 'public economic order' character of the provisions on unfair terms in consumer contracts see the Opinion of AG Saggio in Joined Cases C–240/98 and C–244/98 *Océano* [2000] ECR I–4941 and the comment of Stuyck 2001.

In that case the Court found that where the domestic rules of procedure require a national court to grant an application for annulment of an arbitration award where such an application is founded on failure to observe national rules of public policy, the court must also grant such an application where it is founded on failure to comply with the prohibition laid down in Article 81 EC Treaty. In other words, the ECJ has ruled that the provisions of Article 81 EC are to be regarded as fundamental rules of public policy falling under the substantive scope of the public policy ground for annulment of arbitral awards contained in national law.

It goes far beyond the scope of this book to reflect upon the complex and controversial questions relating to the public policy character of Community law provisions and the scope of the judgment in *Eco Swiss*. However, it is submitted that, for the time being, the finding of the Court in *Eco Swiss* should be restricted to the area of review of arbitral awards and should not be given general application: One of the important considerations in that case was that arbitrators are not in a position to request the Court to give a preliminary ruling on questions of interpretation of Community law. Declaring Article 81 a matter of public policy was the only way to get its interpretation before the Court of Justice.[185]

Finally, it must be briefly mentioned that in two other cases it was on the basis of an interpretation of a particular directive, i.e. in particular Article 6 of Directive 93/13 (unfair terms in consumer contracts),[186] together with the principle of effective judicial protection, that a national court was held to apply the directives' provisions of its own motion.[187]

7.3.4 Remedies

The last category of cases relates to the question: 'What can a court do in a concrete case?' To put it another way, provided that there is a court having jurisdiction, i.e. having the power to hear and decide the case, what can the content of its decision be? What type of remedy can the court grant and what can its substance be?

The substance of remedies and sanctions

In Chapter 5, Section 5.4, where the Community law requirements as to the form and content of sanctions and remedies made available for contraventions of

---

[185] For a detailed discussion of various aspects of public policy in general and in relation to Community law, in particular, see Shelkoplyas 2003, 171–239. Cf also Prechal and Shelkoplyas 2004.

[186] [1993] OJ L95/29.

[187] Joined Cases C–240/98 and C–244/98 *Océano* [2000] ECR I–4941. Cf also Case C–473/00 *Cofidis* [2002] ECR I–10875.

Community law were discussed, it was shown that in order to ensure real and effective judicial protection national courts had to disregard certain limitations, deriving from national rules, to the remedies and sanctions at issue.

Thus, for instance, contrary to what was suggested by other case law,[188] in *Marshall II*[189] interest had to be paid to the applicant. Interest is to be considered an essential part of compensation, since it represents damage on the account of the effluxion of time; and this was despite the fact that the national court had no power to award interest. Similarly, the statutory limitation of the damages to be given was found to be incompatible with Community law.[190]

In *Steenhorst-Neerings*[191] the limitation of the award of social security benefits with only a restricted retrospective effect was at issue. In this case the Court accepted the limitation. It recalled that claims for the social security benefit at issue must be exercised in accordance with the conditions laid down in national law, subject to the two minimum requirements of non-discrimination and effectiveness. The latter were satisfied in this case. In terms of justification of the limitation, the Court found that the rule at issue met the requirement of good administration, in particular the need to control whether the person concerned satisfied the conditions for entitlement. Moreover, it was also necessary for safeguarding the financial equilibrium of the scheme at issue. On the other hand, in *Preston*, a rule which provided that a person's pensionable service is to be calculated only by reference to service completed as from two years prior to the date of the claim, was contrary to the principle of effectiveness, as it rendered any action by individuals impossible in practice.[192]

Even the standard of judicial review is potentially affected by Community law. The *Upjohn* case[193] illustrates this point. Upjohn argued that effective judicial review implied that the national court must be able to review fully the decision taken by the administrative authority and to substitute its assessment of the facts and scientific

---

[188] Cf Case 130/79 *Express Dairy Foods* [1980] 1887, Case 54/81 *Fromme* [1982] ECR 1449: interest is a matter of national law.

[189] Case C–271/91 [1993] ECR I–4367. Cf also Joined Cases C–397/98 and C–410/98 *Metallgesellschaft* [2001] ECR I–1727, where the Court found that the interest constitutes the essential component of the right conferred on claimants and Case C–63/01 *Evans*, judgment of 4 December 2003, nyr in ECR. On the other hand, in *Sutton* (Case C–66/95 [1997] ECR I–2163), the payment of interest on social security benefits which were awarded retroactively was considered a matter of *Rewe* requirements and not a matter of adequate compensation.

[190] Cf also Case C–180/95 *Draehmpaehl* [1997] ECR I–2195.

[191] Case C–338/91 [1993] ECR I–5475. Cf also Case C–410/92 *Johnson* [1994] ECR I–5483 and Case C–394/93 *Alonso-Pérez* [1995] ECR I– 4101.

[192] Case C–78/98 *Preston* [2000] ECR I–3201. The rules at issue made it impossible to take the entire record of service completed into consideration for the purposes of pension and, therefore, at the end of the day, limited the amount to be granted. Cf also Case C–246/96 *Magorrian* [1997] ECR I–7153.

[193] Case C–120/97 [1999] ECR I–223. Cf also Case C–380/01 *Schneider*, judgment 5 February 2004, nyr in ECR, and in particular, the Opinion of AG Alber of 10 December 2002. For a 'reverse' problem in the specific context of competition law see Case C–94/00 *Roquette Frères* [2002] ECR I–9011. For limited judicial review of an arbitral award see Case C–63/01 *Evans*, judgment of 4 December 2003, nyr in ECR, and in relation to penalties Case C–13/01 *Safalero* [2003] ECR I–8679.

evidence for the one made by the administrative authority. In this case, the ECJ pointed to its own limited judicial review in cases where the Community authorities enjoy a wide measure of discretion,[194] and found that national courts cannot be obliged to carry out a more extensive review than that carried out by the Court in similar situations. On the other hand, the Court also held that, in a procedure for judicial review, the national court must be able effectively to apply the relevant principles and rules of Community law when reviewing the legality of a decision. It would seem that the requirement of an effective remedy may also raise the question about the limits of judicial review.[195]

In brief, wherever Community law does not contain an explicit provision, it is common understanding that the Member States are, in principle, free to choose the sanctions and remedies which will apply for the enforcement of Community law in the national legal order. Once the choice has been made,[196] however, the *substance of the remedies and sanctions* chosen is not left entirely unaffected. Yet Community law goes further and influences the *type of remedy* to be made available to aggrieved parties. Consequently, it also interferes in this respect with the principle of procedural autonomy, according to which it is in principle a matter of national law whether a certain type of action aiming at a particular remedy can be brought or not.[197]

Types of remedies which should be available

In its case law the Court has so far defined one general remedy and a number of specific remedies to which individuals are entitled.[198] These remedies have been introduced at different stages of the development of Community law,[199] and sometimes it seems that they simply continue along their own lines, without the necessary coherence one would expect.

The—what is then called—general remedy of setting aside national measures which are incompatible with Community law is in fact nothing else than a consequence of

---

[194] For instance, when it examines the accuracy of the findings of fact and law or when it verifies whether a manifest error occurred, or misuse of powers, clear transgression of the bounds of discretion, etc.

[195] To a certain extent, a parallel may be drawn with comparable problems under the ECHR, namely whether the *Wednesbury* standard of judicial review, as it exists in the UK, satisfies the requirements of Art 13 ECHR. In *Smith and Grady v. UK* (applications no 33985/96 and 33986/96, judgment of 27 September 1999, the ECrtHR found indeed that the review did not meet the requirements of an effective remedy. Cf also *Hatton v. UK*, application no 36022/97, judgment of 8 July 2003. For a (much broader) discussion of these issues see Canor 2002, who in particular focuses on the influence of the principle of proportionality. For a brief discussion of the exercise of judicial discretion in relation to EC law matters see also Jans and Prinssen 2002, 120–2.

[196] Often the 'choice' may be more or less automatic since Community law is integrated into national law for which there already exists a system of enforcement.

[197] Cf the observations of the Member States in cases like *Factortame* (Case C–213/89 [1990] ECR I–2433) and *Francovich* (Joined Cases C–6/90 and C–9/90 [1991] ECR I–5357).

[198] Cf e.g. Van Gerven 2000.

[199] Setting aside in *Simmenthal* (1978; or even earlier), restitution in *Rewe* (1976), interim relief in *Factortame II/Zuckerfabrik* (1990/91) and compensation in *Francovich* (1991).

supremacy of Community law. It is a minimum remedy in the sense that in some cases the disapplication of the conflicting national provisions will suffice to decide the case. In other cases the relevant provisions of Community law have to be applied instead.[200]

Similarly, it is a minimum remedy in the sense that this is what Community law requires. The Court does not usually say what the further consequences should be. From cases like *Lück* and, more recently, *IN.CO.GE*[201] we learn that, apart from the obligation to disapply the national rule which is contrary to Community law, the national court should apply, from among the various procedures available under national law those which are appropriate for protecting the individual rights conferred by Community law. In other words, the issue of further legal consequences shifts to the national legal order. Up until now, the Court has refrained from indicating into which legal category the 'obligation to set aside' falls. The choice of any of the possible concepts—non-existence, invalidity, inopposability, absolute or relative nullity, illegitimacy, voidness, loss of force, or whatever classifications there may exist in national law—as well as their meaning and scope, are left to the national legal system.[202]

At national level, depending on the context, setting aside will usually translate into more specific remedies, such as restitution, compensation, rescission of a contract, interim relief, declaratory relief, order of specific performance, acquittal in criminal proceedings; it may also result in an administrative decision being annulled, entirely or partially, environmental permit being withdrawn or changed, etc., all depending on what is possible under national law.[203]

Considered in this perspective, where Community law stops, i.e. at the point of setting aside, national law takes over. Although as of this point everything seems to be left to the national legal system, there is, as mentioned above, increased EC law intrusion at this stage too. The most obvious examples of this are the specific remedies as defined by the Court, namely restitution (and specific performance), interim relief,[204] and compensation.[205]

---

[200] Cf below, Ch 9, Subsection 9.3.3 on direct effect and '*Alternativ Normierung*'.

[201] Case 34/67 *Lück* [1968] ECR 245; Joined Cases C–10 to 22/97 *IN.CO.GE* [1998] ECR I–6307.

[202] Cf Joined Cases C–10 to 22/97 *IN.CO.GE* [1998] ECR I–6307 and the Opinion of AG Ruiz-Jarabo Colomer in that case. To this one may add that even the meaning and scope of the nullity sanction of Art 81(2) EC Treaty and the consequences it may have for other sanctions is not an entirely clear matter. For a brief overview see Van Gerven 2001.

[203] Cf also Case C–159/00 *Sapod* [2002] ECR I–5031, para 52, where the Court seems to tone down the consequences of its *CIA/Unilever* case law (discussed below, in Ch 9, Subsection 9.5.3) by pointing out that '. . . as regards the severity of the sanction under the applicable national law, such as nullity of unenforceability of the contract [concerned], [it] is a question governed by national law, in particular as regards the rules and principles of contract law which limit or adjust that sanction in order to render its severity proportionate to the particular defect found'.

[204] *Factortame* and *Zuckerfabrik* case law; Case C–213/89 [1990] ECR I–2433 and Joined Cases C–143/88 and C–92/89 [1991] ECR I–415.

[205] Joined Cases C–6/90 and C–9/90 *Francovich* [1991] ECR I–5357, Joined Cases C–46/93 and C–48/93 *Brasserie du Pêcheur* [1996] ECR I–1029, and subsequent case law.

According to well-established case law, the right to a refund of charges levied in a Member State in breach of rules of Community law is the consequence and complement of the rights conferred on individuals by Community provisions as interpreted by the Court.[206] An important limitation to this right lies in the principle of unjust enrichment, which has in the meantime generated rich and detailed case law.[207]

The cases on repayment and restitution were as such not very revolutionary, in the sense that the existence or the availability of the remedies themselves was not at issue. Things were different in other cases, such as *Heylens, Nimz, Factortame, Zuckerfabrik Süderdithmarschen* and *Francovich*.[208]

The judgment in *Heylens* made clear that the individual concerned must be able to bring an action for judicial review even if no specific legal remedy is available against the decision in dispute under national law.

In *Nimz*[209] the Court dismissed the argument of autonomy of the parties to the collective agreement, laid down in Article 21 of the German Basic Law, and the corresponding limitation of the power of the national court. It held that the latter must apply as regards the members of the group which is discriminated against the same arrangements as are applied regarding other employees, without awaiting the solution decided by the parties to the agreements.

From *Factortame*, it follows that an individual has the right to interim relief even if the injunction against the Crown sought by the applicants was unconstitutional under national law.

The action in damages against the State as construed in *Francovich* has deeply affected some Member States' system of State liability.[210] The same can be said of the judgment in *Zuckerfabrik Süderdithmarschen*, which lays down in detail the conditions to be fulfilled for granting interim relief against a national administrative decision taken on the basis of a regulation which is alleged to be invalid.

The remedy of specific performance has not as yet taken shape at Community level.[211] One of the key questions in this respect is whether a court may give an order

---

[206] Cf e.g. Joined Cases C–397/98 and C–410/98 *Metallgesellschaft* [2001] ECR I-1727, para 84.

[207] Cf e.g. Joined Cases C–192 to 218/95 *Comateb* [1997] ECR I–165 and Case C–129/00 *Commission v. Italy*, judgment of 9 December 2003, nyr in ECR. See also, for an atypical situation, Case C–377/89 *Cotter and McDermott II* [1991] ECR I–1155, where the Court found that national authorities could not rely on the (national) principle prohibiting unjust enrichment, since then they would be able to use their own unlawful conduct as a ground for depriving the relevant provisions of the directive of their full effect.

[208] Case 222/86 [1987] ECR 4097, Case C–184/89 [1991] ECR I–297, Case C–213/89 [1990] ECR I–2433, Case C–143/88 [1991] ECR I–415 and Joined Cases C–6/90 and C–9/90 [1991] ECR I–5357.

[209] Case C–184/89 [1991] ECR I–297. Cf also Case C–15/96 *Schöning-Kougebetopoulou* [1998] ECR I–47 and Case C–187/00 *Kutz-Bauer* [2003] ECR I–2741.

[210] Cf below, Ch 10, in particular literature referred to in Section 10.1 and Subsection 10.4.1. Especially the immunity of the State in its capacity as a legislator cannot be raised as a valid argument.

[211] Briefly on this Van Gerven 2000, 521. Van Gerven couples this remedy with restitution. However, in some legal systems, as for instance in the Netherlands, 'specific performance' is to be situated within the context of tort law, i.e. it may be ordered instead of compensatory damages.

to legislate, with an aim to achieving compliance with Community law obligations. An example of the difficulties which may arise in this context can be the *Waterpakt* case as decided relatively recently by the Dutch *Hoge Raad*.[212] In that case several environmental organizations sought, *inter alia*, an order to legislate, before a certain deadline, directed at the State. The substance concerned the non-implementation of Directive 91/676 ('nitrates directive').[213] In 'cassation', the *Hoge Raad* held, *inter alia*, that under Dutch constitutional law the drafting of primary legislation is a political process in which the government and the parliament act together and balance all the interests involved. It is not for the courts to interfere in this process. Even if the legislation has to be adopted in order to comply with a directive, that does not change the matter. According to the *Hoge Raad*, the courts still lack jurisdiction in this respect because the question as to whether legislation should be adopted and, then, what the content of the legislation would be, remains a matter for the political branch. It is also up to that branch to choose for non-implementation and consequently risk an action under Article 226 EC Treaty. As regards the specific question, namely whether Community law dictates a different solution, the *Hoge Raad* referred to the duty of national courts to ensure the full effect of Community law and to protect the rights which individuals may derive from that law. However, it followed from *Van Schijndel* that this duty exists only within the scope of competences and jurisdiction as defined under national law. In Dutch law the limit prescribed was exactly that the courts have no jurisdiction to order the adoption of primary legislation.

From a Community law perspective, this decision is certainly debatable, in particular because the *Hoge Raad* did not make a preliminary reference, against the Advocate General's suggestion. Equally, arguments about the political choice of the legislator—to implement or not—leave a Community law minded reader somewhat perplexed.[214] However, the case also illustrates the difficult position of a national court which is told, on the one hand, that jurisdiction as defined by national law is decisive, provided that the minimum requirements of equivalence and effectiveness are satisfied and on the other hand, in cases such as *Simmenthal*, *Factortame*, and the State liability case law, that the constitutional rules have to yield to the effective application of Community law and that if the courts do not have jurisdiction, they have to assume it.

Different grounds have been presented for this rather far-reaching—though not entirely unexpected[215]—interference by the Court of Justice with the national systems of remedies: in particular, the principle of effective judicial protection, the full effectiveness of Community law and the useful effect of Article 234. The Court did not stop here, however, indicating the appropriate remedies which have to be available.

---

[212] Judgment of 21 March 2003, JB 2003, no 120. It should also be noted that at the origin of Case 71/85 *FNV* [1985] ECR 3855, was the action brought by FNV against the State for non-implementation of Directive 79/7; in this case, the president of the District Court of The Hague issued an order to amend the unemployment benefit law.   [213] [1991] OJ L375/1.

[214] For instance, how to reconcile it with the Court's finding that non-implementation constitutes *per se* a sufficiently serious breach?   [215] Cf Case 106/77 *Simmenthal* [1978] ECR 629.

In *Factortame*, notwithstanding the express question of the House of Lords, the Court side-stepped the issue of the circumstances under which a national court must give interim relief. In *Zuckerfabrik Süderdithmarschen*, however, for the sake of uniform application of Community law it defined uniform conditions under which interim relief must be given and which must be applied by the national courts instead of the conditions existing in national law.[216]

In this respect it must be pointed out that in contrast to *Factortame*, which concerned the compatibility of *national law* with the EEC Treaty, in *Zuckerfabrik Süderdithmarschen* the validity of secondary Community law itself was called into question. Furthermore, in *Factortame* the barrier against the measures which were applied for came from national law, while in *Zuckerfabrik Süderdithmarschen* it was a Community law barrier originating in the Court's earlier case law.[217] Moreover, since the judgment is tailored to the situation of the application of Community law (or, more precisely, a national decision based on it) having to be suspended, it is far from clear whether the conditions laid down in this judgment also apply to the '*Factortame* type' situation.[218]

Be this as it may, that the Court is willing to lay down conditions to be fulfilled where national measures (or the absence of necessary measures) are at issue is clearly apparent in the State liability case law: the Court defined three Community law conditions which—as soon as they are fulfilled—give rise to a right to compensation on the part of individuals for damage suffered as a result of a violation of Community law.[219]

The foregoing clearly suggests that the initial assumption that the national legal systems provide sufficient means of redress for aggrieved parties has apparently been reconsidered by the Court of Justice. The cases decided have shown that the Court may deem it necessary to give strict instructions, with respect to both the types of remedies which should be available and the substantive conditions which must be fulfilled by the remedies applicable. Whether the Court's guidelines amount to an amendment of the existing remedies offered by national law or to creation of new ones is a matter which has given rise to diverging views. In particular with respect to *Factortame* it has been argued that the judgment amounts to an obligation to create a new remedy.[220] *Factortame* can indeed be presented as a case where the national court had no power to grant interim relief against the Crown and therefore, after *Factortame*, there is a new remedy. Yet the problem can also be formulated

---

[216] Case C–143/88 *Zuckerfabrik Süderdithmarschen* [1991] ECR I–415 (concerning suspension), further refined in Case C–465/93 *Atlanta* [1995] ECR I–3761 (concerning injunctive relief), and subsequent cases.

[217] Cf Case 314/85 *Foto-Frost* [1987] ECR 4199: only the Court may declare a Community act invalid.   [218] Cf Oliver 1992, 360; see, however, also Curtin 1992, 42–3.

[219] Cf e.g. the conditions in Joined Cases C–46/93 and C–48/93 *Brasserie du Pêcheur* [1996] ECR I–1029 and Joined Cases C–178/94, C–179/94, C–188/94, C–189/94, and C–190/94 *Dillenkofer* [1996] ECR I–4845. See also below, Ch 10, Section 10.4.

[220] Cf Curtin 1992, 42, Boch and Lane 1992, 173, Toth 1990, 586, Barav 1994, 269, and Lang 2000.

in other terms—as the Court of Justice actually did—namely that the national court may in principle give an interim injunction, but a rule of national (constitutional) law curtails its power: it is prevented from doing this against the Crown.[221] From this perspective it is rather an extension of an existing remedy.

Similarly, *Francovich* and the issue of State liability, can be approached from both angles. It is arguable that it offers a new remedy in the sense that normally the national judiciary has no power to grant damages for breaches committed by the legislature.[222] On the other hand it is equally arguable that *Francovich* implies a (farreaching) amendment of existing national rules on State liability.[223]

> The divergence in approach may be due to conceptual differences between common law and the civil law tradition, and the double meaning of the term 'remedy'.[224] In so far as the term 'remedy' is understood as a form of relief given by the court, the cases can indeed be considered as creating a new remedy. If, however, the term 'remedy' is employed in the broad sense, i.e. as the means provided by law to obtain a certain form of relief, then it is conceivable that under common law it can still be said that a new remedy is created while in the civil law tradition there is no new '*voie de recours*'. The claimant seeks a new form of relief but he does so via an existing procedure which must, however, be adapted for this purpose.

In my view, it does not really matter whether the result of the requirements is called a new remedy or rather the adaptation of an existing system of national procedures and remedies. What *does* matter is the fact that the requirements imposed by the Court *broaden the powers of national courts*. This may be done either by removing restrictions of the existing powers (the *negative* way) or by giving the courts, in a *positive* way, the necessary powers to be able to do something which it is beyond their jurisdiction to do as a matter of national law alone.[225]

7.4   Problems of the third generation

7.4.1   Role of national courts: direct empowerment?

In the foregoing Sections it has been explained that national procedures and remedies which are used as vehicles for the enforcement of Community law and

---

[221] For a critical review of the Court's judgment cf Barav 1994, 274 ff. His main objection is that the Court treated the matter as one of exercise of powers, whereas the crucial issue was the very existence of powers.

[222] Cf Steiner 1993, 12, Craig 1993, 597–601.

[223] Cf Schockweiler 1992, 48, Kapteyn 1993, 45. Obviously, in *Francovich* also the Court assumed as a premise that national rules on State liability exist in the Member States.

[224] Cf above, Subsection 7.3.1, n 99.

[225] This development did indeed not pass unnoted. Cf the literature on the changing position of national courts, like, for instance, Barav 1991, Grevisse and Bonichot 1991, Simon 1991, Schockweiler 1991, Barav 1994.

the protection of the rights which individuals derive from it must satisfy certain requirements. The next issue to be addressed in this context is *which organ* within the Member State is responsible for the appropriate measures being taken in order to guarantee the observance of these requirements.

For a long time it was assumed that it was for the national legislative bodies to secure access to the courts and to provide national courts with the necessary procedures, powers, and remedies to enable them to afford adequate protection of individuals.[226] However, as early as *Simmenthal*[227] the Court had made clear that the national court should ignore national rules precluding it from giving full force and effect to Community law.

Despite the firm language of *Simmenthal*, for a while it was uncertain whether a national court, on its own authority, should disregard national rules on procedures and remedies and, arguably, the rules defining their powers. Matters seem to be relatively uncomplicated in cases where the national court can rely on a written provision of Community law relating to procedural and remedial aspects, such as Article 6 of Directive 76/207 (equal treatment at work)[228] or provisions in public procurement or consumer protection directives.[229] Using the technique of interpretation of national law in conformity with such a provision,[230] or by applying the 'tandem doctrine' of direct effect and supremacy[231] the national court can reach the result desired by Community law. In contrast to these cases, in *Factortame* (and in fact earlier in *Simmenthal*) the Court found that it is a duty of the national court to depart, by disapplication, from the relevant rules defining its powers *without it being possible to indicate an explicit Community law provision* serving as the basis for the power of doing this. Since then, this assignment to the judiciary has been confirmed in an even more vigorous way in the *Francovich* and *Zuckerfabrik Süderdithmarschen* judgments.[232]

Arguably, these developments amount to a *direct empowerment* by Community law—whether written or unwritten—of the national courts to extend their existing powers or to assume, on the basis of Community law alone, new powers which do

---

[226] Cf Wyatt 1989, 205, Lauwaars and Timmermans 2003, 37, Kovar 1978, 248–50. Cf also Case 98/79 *Pescastaing* [1980] ECR 691, in particular paras 10–11, which relate to the obligations of the Member States laid down in Art 8 of Directive 64/221 [1963-1964] OJ English Spec Ed 117.

[227] Case 106/77 [1978] ECR 629.

[228] [1976] OJ L39/40.

[229] E.g. Directive 89/665 (public contracts—review procedures) [1989] OJ L395/33 or Directive 93/13 (unfair terms in consumer contracts) [1993] OJ L95/29.

[230] Cf Case 14/83 *Von Colson* [1984] ECR 1891, Case C–177/88 *Dekker* [1990] ECR I–3941, Joined Cases C–240/98 and C–244/98 *Océano* [2000] ECR I–4941, and Case C–327/00 *Santex* [2003] ECR I–1877.

[231] Cf Case 222/84 *Johnston* [1986] ECR 1651, Case C–271/91 *Marshall II* [1993] ECR I–4367, Case C–327/00 *Santex* [2003] ECR I–1877 and Case C–125/01 *Pflücke* [2003] ECR I–9375; in relation to the EEX Treaty see e.g. Case 288/82 *Duijnstee* [1983] ECR 3663.

[232] Cf also a case like *Union de Pequeños Agricultores* (Case C–50/00 P [2002] ECR I–6677), which clearly suggests that national courts are expected to stretch the provisions of their own legal system, perhaps sometimes even of what is reasonably possible and, moreover, this seems to be based on the erroneous assumption that national courts are perfectly able to deal adequately with Community law matters.

not exist under national law in order to fulfil effectively the task assigned to them by the Court of Justice.[233] However, firstly, the very fact that the national courts have been made accomplices in the enforcement of Community law has led to a situation in which the *formal* source of their power stems from the national legal order, while the *substance* of their function may originate in Community law.[234] In other words, they remain national judges but they have a Community law mission. This mission may imply certain duties for which, in order to accomplish them successfully, the courts do not always have the necessary powers or are even straightforwardly prohibited from taking a certain course of action. An assignment of tasks to the national courts, entrusting them with a Community law mission or giving them a function in the enforcement of Community law, cannot as such create the necessary powers.[235]

Secondly, the bases in Community law having for such empowering effect on which the Court relies, i.e. in particular the principle of effective judicial protection, Article 10, the full force and effect of Community law and the useful effect of Article 234 respectively, are rather tenuous.[236] To this extent, the national courts' Community law mission is in urgent need of obtaining a more solid theoretical underpinning and, in terms of positive law, an explicit basis, preferably in both Community and national law.[237]

7.4.2   Reconciling national procedural autonomy and Community law requirements

In the case law on national procedural and remedial rules two extremes can be ascertained, with many cases pending somewhere between those two. On the one hand, there is the rather 'minimalist' approach ushered in with the Rewe-mantra, on the

---

[233] Cf the Opinion of AG Mischo in *Francovich*, para 53 ('there can no longer be any doubt that in certain cases Community law may itself directly confer on national judicial authorities the necessary powers in order to ensure effective judicial protection of those rights, even where similar powers do not exist in national law'), Curtin 1990b, 736 and Lang 2000. For general (constitutional) implications of these developments Cf De Búrca 1992, 239, Simon 1991, 491–2, Curtin and Mortelmans 1994, 457.

[234] Cf in the same sense Boch 2004, 4.

[235] Neither can eloquent catchwords, like '*juge national en sa qualité de juge communautaire*' (Simon 1991, 484), '*la fonction du juge de l'ordre juridique communautaire*' (Schockweiler 1991, 56), or the Community law mandate of the national judge (Louis 1993, 546, Curtin and Mortelmans 1994, 457) create the necessary powers. The first two merely describe the function of the national court. The second connotes the development brought about by the Court's case law which started to define the national courts' powers. However, the very problem is exactly that the basis for such a mandate is lacking. National courts, as organs of the State and not of the Community, still derive their authority from the State. Cf also Dubouis 1992, 8–9.

[236] Cf with respect to *Zuckerfabrik Süderdithmarschen* Mortelmans 1991, 680, with respect to *Factortame* Lauwaars 1991, 480 and Simon and Barav 1990, 594. Cf also above, Subsection 7.2.1, observations with respect to *Simmenthal*.

[237] Cf for such a combined approach the detailed and thorough study by Claes (2004).

other there are a few more 'radical' cases like *Factortame* and *Francovich*[238] which are based upon another rationale and seem to build upon the supremacy language used in *Simmenthal*.[239] Considerations of full effectiveness of Community law and effective judicial protection make national procedural rules—often fundamental and of (quasi-) constitutional character—yield to Community law.

The difference in approach and outcome of the cases and, in particular, the reasons behind that difference, are difficult to grasp.[240] While, for instance, *Factortame* and *Francovich* were argued along the *Rewe*-line, the Court went much further and decided these two cases in the perspective of full effectiveness and effective judicial protection. By using the firm (*Simmenthal*-like) language of effective judicial protection and, in particular, full effectiveness of Community law, the Court had created a wrong impression that national procedural autonomy did not matter anymore.[241]

There are, however, also signs that national procedural autonomy, together with the 'corrections' it implies,[242] is the main rule and that the full effectiveness of Community law is not an overpowering principle. Moreover, gradually, the Court seems to pay more respect to national procedural rules and the fundamental rationale which is often beyond these provisions. In particular, the assessment of the principles of effectiveness and equivalence mark a slight reorientation.

Community law provisions are a part of the valid law in the Member States and they should in principle be handled in the same way as national law. Theoretically, the whole range of procedural and remedial provisions which exist in every legal system—whether private, administrative or criminal—may be tested against the Community law requirements of equivalence and effectiveness/effective judicial protection. However, this does not imply that those provisions must necessarily yield to Community law. These rules have usually been introduced into the national legal system for certain valid reasons and therefore they should not be dismissed for the simple reason that they seriously hamper the application of Community law provisions. From this perspective, there is nothing so special about Community law provisions that they should be treated differently. It is in certain exceptional rather than common situations that Community law may impose higher standards on procedures and remedies than the existing national ones. The ultimate basis of these

---

[238] Case C–213/89 [1990] ECR I–2433 and Joined Cases C–6/90 and C–9/90 [1991] ECR I–5357, Case C–118/00 *Larsy* [2001] ECR I–5063 and to an extent also Case C–453/99 *Courage* [2001] ECR I–6297. Cf also the contrastive approach of AG Léger, who follows the supremacy argument, on the one hand and the Court, which reasons along a procedural autonomy line, on the other hand, in Case C–453/00 *Kühne*, judgment of 13 January 2004, nyr in ECR.

[239] Case 106/77 *Simmenthal* [1978] ECR 629, discussed above, in Subsection 7.2.1.

[240] Cf Prechal 1998 and De Búrca 1997, 41. Cf also above, Subsection 7.2.1.

[241] In the same vein, some authors deny the existence of procedural autonomy. See, in particular, Kakouris 1997. Cf however also Hoskins 1996 (supremacy is all argument: 375) and Van Gerven 2000, 501.

[242] I.e. the principles of equivalence and effectiveness, as sometimes reinforced by the principle of effective judicial protection.

standards seems to lie in fundamental legal principles, which are, *inter alia*, laid down in Article 6 of the ECHR[243] or they are closely linked to some specific character-istics of the substantive Community law provisions at issue.[244]

The assessment of effectiveness

Under what conditions will the national provision at issue satisfy the effective-ness test?

. . . each case that raises the question whether a national procedural provision renders appli-cation of Community law impossible or excessively difficult must be analysed by reference to the role of that provision in the procedure, its progress and its special features, viewed as a whole, before the various national instances and . . . in the light of that analysis, the basic principles of the domestic judicial system, such as the protection of the rights of the defence, the principle of legal certainty and the proper conduct of procedure, must, where appropriate, be taken into consideration.[245]

In other words, after it has been established, in the context of the whole procedure at issue, that there is a serious limitation to the application of Community law, it is necessary to examine whether it can be justified by fundamental principles of the domestic judicial system.[246] Thus the tension between Community law requirements and national procedural and remedial rules should be resolved by means of a balanc-ing exercise between the interests which are served by the national procedural rules and the (minimum) effectiveness of Community law. Obviously, the principles or aims underlying these rules must, as such, be compatible with the Community legal order.[247] Moreover, the Court seems to find it important that the principle at issue is part of the legal heritage common to the Member States.[248] In a number of ways, this

---

[243] Cf Case 222/84 *Johnston* [1986] ECR 1651. For another example of how Art 6 of the ECHR can be integrated in Community law requirements in relation to procedures see Case C–276/01 *Steffensen* [2003] ECR I–3735. Cf also Haguenau 1995, 327–38 and Prechal 2001.

[244] Cf e.g. Joined Cases C–240/98 and C–244/98 *Océano* [2000] ECR I–4941.

[245] Case C–276/01 *Steffensen* [2003] ECR I–3735. This test was explicitly introduced by the Court in Joined Cases C–430/93 and C–431/93 *Van Schijndel* [1995] ECR I–4705, and Case C–312/93 *Peterbroeck* [1995] ECR I–4599. Interestingly, the approach chosen by the Court is similar to the one of the ECHR when the latter addresses the question as to the compatibility of limitations under domestic law with the right of access to court under Art 6 ECHR. Cf e.g. the judgment in case *Eliazer v. the Netherlands*, application 38055/97, judgment of 16 October 2001.

[246] From Case C–63/01 *Evans*, judgment of 4 December 2003, nyr in ECR, it appears that also con-siderations of speed and economy of legal costs may, under circumstances, serve as a justification. In this case, in contrast to AG Alber, the Court found that the procedures at issue, *taken as a whole*, satisfied the requirement of effectiveness.   [247] Cf Kakouris 1997, 1404.

[248] Cf the Court's reference to 'conceptions prevailing in most Member States as to the relations between the state and the individual', in para 21 of the judgment. Cf also Case C–125/01 *Pflücke*, judg-ment of 18 September 2003, ECR I–9375, para 38, where the Court refers, on the issue of certain time limits, to the situation in other Member States.

exercise greatly resembles the rule of reason developed by the ECJ in the area of free movement of goods and services[249] and is also very close to the proportionality test.[250]

The merit of this case law is that there is a framework in which the question of effectiveness should be resolved. The weakness of this approach is indeed that it requires the assessment of the intrinsic characteristics and effects of the national rule at issue and subsequently a scrutiny of its underlying values which may serve as a justification. The result is a case to case approach which does not provide for much clarity and certainty.

The assessment of equivalence

The principle of equivalence has not generated many spectacular results. Initially, the Court made plain in only a few cases that special (and as a rule less favourable) rules introduced by the Member States for certain Community law claims could not be upheld.[251] Even in more recent case law, there are instances of a relatively low key application of the principle. In *Edis*,[252] the Court analysed the various possible actions under Italian law, but it was finally quite easily—perhaps too easily[253]—satisfied: since the same time limit applied to the repayment of a number of other governmental charges and of certain indirect taxes, the time limit at issue met the principle of equivalence. However, there is apparently also quite some potential in the principle of equivalence. A good example is the *Draehmpaehl* case.[254] In this case the Court found, *inter alia*, that a ceiling on the possible amount of compensation payable for discrimination was unacceptable because there was no equivalent in other rules of German labour law.

Although the question 'what is a similar action of domestic nature?' is an old one,[255] only more recently the Court formulated the relevant criteria for the application of the principle of equivalence.[256] The guidance given reveals that two elements must be taken into account when identifying a similar domestic action: the purpose and the cause of action, and the essential characteristics of the rules at

---

[249] Cf Prechal 1998.

[250] Cf Van Gerven 2000.

[251] Cf e.g. Case 240/87 *Deville* [1988] ECR 3513. This case law has been confirmed since then in a whole line of cases. See e.g. Case C–343/96 *Dilexport* [1999] ECR I–579, Case C–62/00 *Marks & Spencer* [2002] ECR I–6325 and Case C–147/01 *Weber's Wine World*, judgment of 2 October 2003, nyr in ECR. Such a specific limitation is also contrary to Art 10 EC Treaty.

[252] Case C–231/96 [1998] ECR I–4951.

[253] At the origin of the application of the disputed time limits was a remarkable, perhaps even suspicious, change in case law of the *Corte Suprema di Cassazione*.

[254] Case C–180/95 [1997] ECR I–2195.

[255] Cf Steiner 1986, 103. Sometimes, a domestic action of a similar nature just is not found, the consequence being the equivalence test cannot be applied! See e.g. *Matra v. Home Office* [1999] 1 WLR 1646 CA.

[256] Case C–261/95 *Palmisani* [1997] ECR I–4025. The test has been further refined in, for instance, Case C–326/96 *Levez* [1998] ECR I–7835 and Case C–78/98 *Preston* [2000] ECR I–3201.

issue. Furthermore, when comparing the applicable procedural rules, the national courts must 'take into account the role played by [the relevant rules] in the procedure as a whole, as well as the operation and any special features of that procedure before the different national courts'.[257] Moreover, the relevant aspects of the procedural rules must be examined in their general context and in an objective and abstract fashion.[258]

Arguably, these rather abstract and vague guidelines given by the Court do not make the national court's job easier. On some other points the Court was more concrete. In *Edis*, it pointed out that the principle of equivalence cannot be interpreted as obliging a Member State to extend its most favourable rules governing recovery under national law to all actions for repayment of charges (or other amounts) in breach of Community law.[259] From *Levez* and *Preston* it follows that procedural rules would be deemed less favourable if a person, relying on a Community law right, were forced to incur additional costs and delay in comparison with a claimant whose action was based solely on domestic law.[260]

7.4.3   Critique and controversy

There is no doubt that over the years the case law relating to the problems of enforcement of Community law through national procedural and remedial mechanisms has grown increasingly complex. The appreciation ranges from critical comments, blaming the Court for lack of consistency or unnecessary interference with national procedural and remedial law in favour of effectiveness of Community law, to pleas for further uniformity to be introduced, preferably by harmonizing certain parts of national procedures and remedies.[261]

In particular the reactions to the judgments in *Van Schijndel* and *Peterbroeck*,[262] where the idea of balancing the Community law interest of effective protection against the aims pursued by the domestic procedural rule was introduced, show a remarkable disagreement about how this jurisprudential development has to be appreciated. While some authors caught this development in terms of 'striking the balance', others preferred to call it 'tilting the balance'.[263] Some scholars seem to consider the judgments as a too great an intrusion into national procedural autonomy, which unnecessarily complicates the role of national courts in particular as the vast majority of procedural rules can be justified by principles such as legal certainty and the need for proper conducting of the proceedings. Additionally, it

---

[257] Case C–326/96 *Levez* [1998] ECR I–7835, para 44.

[258] Cf Case C–78/98 *Preston* [2000] ECR I–3201, para 62. See also the detailed Opinion of AG Léger in this case.   [259] Case C–231/96 *Edis* [1998] ECR I–4951.

[260] Case C–326/96 *Levez* [1998] ECR I–7835 and Case C–78/98 *Preston* [2000] ECR I–3201.

[261] See, for instance, Biondi 1999, 1271, Hoskins 1996, 365, De Búrca 1997, 37, Ward 2000, Van Gerven 2000, Prechal 2001, Dougan 2002, Girerd 2002, and Hinsworth 1997.

[262] Joined Cases C–430/93 and C–431/93 [1995] ECR I–4705 and Case C–312/93 [1995] ECR I–4599.   [263] Cf Jacobs 1997 and, on the other hand, Hoskins 1996.

does not add much to the predictability of the Court's case law, as it does not really provide any guidance.[264]According to other scholars, the judgments must be accorded positive value since they enhance the application of Community law by national courts.[265] In the opinion of yet others, the judgments result in a 'renationalization' of the Community law functions of national courts and lead to an abandonment of the Community law limits of national procedural autonomy.[266]

In general, the *ad hoc* approach followed by the Court—not concentrating only on the rules in the abstract, but also on the question of how they operate in context[267]—results in dozens of procedural provisions being submitted to the Court for scrutiny, inviting it to plunge into the particularities of national procedural law. In some cases quite some latitude is given to national courts. In others the Court formulates precise prescriptions. As a reaction to the current situation and its inherent weaknesses, in some quarters harmonization of national procedural law was suggested as an alternative.[268] Others admit that, indeed, divergence in the remedial relief available is deplorable from the point of view of uniformity, but unavoidable. In the light of legal and political reality harmonization is not a viable option and one has to look for second best solutions.[269]

In this context Van Gerven[270] has proposed to make the following distinction: the conditions which must be satisfied in order to give rise to the remedy (the constitutive conditions)[271] must be uniform and therefore formulated at Community level. The rules which implement the remedy (the so-called executive rules or remedial rules)[272] are a matter for the Member States. However, they should meet the standard that the remedy must provide adequate judicial protection. The remedy must allow for obtaining redress commensurate with the nature and the degree of interference with the right. Finally, there are procedural rules *stricto sensu*.[273] These rules must satisfy the test of minimum protection and equivalence.

---

[264] Cf Hoskins 1996, De Búrca 1997 and Biondi 1999.

[265] Cf Szyszczak and Delicostopoulos 1997.   [266] Cf Simon 1996a and 1996b.

[267] Where the Court is requiring 'an analysis by reference to the role of the provision at issue in the national procedure, the progress of the procedure and the special features of the procedure taken as a whole' (point 19), it requires a rather detailed and concrete examination. That is at least how I understand this somewhat opaque passage of the judgment.

[268] For a discussion see e.g. Van den Bossche 2001, Chiti 1997, Himsworth 1997, Dougan 2002, and Waelbroeck 2002, 65.   [269] Van Gerven 2000.

[270] Van Gerven 2000.

[271] For instance, the three conditions for liability laid down in *Francovich*.

[272] They concern the form and extent of the remedy, i.e. issues like active and passive legitimation, standard of proof, permissible means to bring evidence, burden of proof, time limits, foreclosures, statutory limitations, etc.

[273] These are practical rules of a rather technical nature, according to which the remedy is to be pursued in a court of law (for instance, formal requirements as to the introduction of proceedings, the practical progress of the procedure, default of appearance, costs, disqualification of judges, calculation of calendar year, month and day, etc.).

This approach results in limited uniformity in application and enforcement of Community law, namely only at the level of rights and constitutive conditions of remedies. On other matters, the Member States must provide for the necessary procedural rules which govern the content and extent (the executive elements) of the remedy. This leads to divergence in the remedial relief available, which is perhaps deplorable, from the point of view of uniformity, but unavoidable, in the light of legal (and political) reality. The requirement to safeguard adequate protection keeps the divergence within certain limits.

There is certainly still room for improvement. In my opinion, what the Court (and sometimes also the Community legislator) should continue doing, is to set standards to be met from the point of view of effective judicial protection of individuals' rights and effective enforcement of Community law.[274] A certain degree of uniformity is a consequence of the judge-made rules, rather than their purpose. The divergence in content and extent of remedial relief is not a serious problem, as long as it is kept within certain limits.[275] The quest for uniformity is not only unrealistic, but it also makes little sense as long as the overall relationship between Community law and national law remains structured as at present.

The majority of Community law rules are integrated into the respective national legal orders of the Member States. In particular directives, if properly transposed, apply in the national legal order in their 'translated' form, i.e. as provisions of national law. Even more importantly, many directives aim at (substantive) harmonization of laws,[276] under which the Member States are required to adapt their laws on certain points only. Similarly, the way in which Community law provisions are relied upon before courts is relevant. On the continent, at least, Community law is usually relied upon in the context of national proceedings in an integrated way, i.e. in the sense that it is not treated as a separate Community law claim. Community law may be brought forward as only one of many arguments. Under such circumstances, a separate set of procedural and remedial rules makes no sense.

Where Community law provisions are applied and enforced in their 'translated' or, at least, in their fully integrated form, the pursuit of uniformity in remedies and procedures may seriously distort the integration of these provisions into national law. At the end of the day, it would lead to two separate pillars: procedures and remedies for 'pure' national law and procedures and remedies for national law of Community law origin. In other terms, real uniform protection of Community

---

[274] As has been already observed (Ch 5, Section 5.4 and above, Subsection 7.2.1) the two do not need to go hand in glove; Community law may also be enforced against individuals. However, it should be noticed that also in this respect the same principles of assimilation and effectiveness and the 'procedural rule of reason' apply. Cf for instance Case C–480/98 *Spain v. Commission* [2000] ECR I–8717 and Case C–110/99 *Emsland-Stärke* [2000] ECR I–11569.

[275] Things may be different if, for instance, the rules cause a distortsion (in terms of the EC Treaty). Cf in this sense the preamble of Directive 2004/48 (enforcement of intellectual property rights) [2004] OJ L195/16.   [276] Harmonization of procedural rules and remedies is still exceptional.

rights and enforcement of Community law in all Member States would only be feasible if we started to work with two parallel systems of enforcement and judicial protection: one for Community law and one for national law.[277] This, however, is difficult to reconcile with the very idea that (substantive) Community law provisions are integrated into national law, and it will make (substantive) harmonization even more problematic than it already is.

---

[277] An ultimate but highly disproportionate solution would indeed be to harmonize procedural rules and remedies for both purposes, Community and national.

8

Consistent interpretation

8.1   The context

Whenever a directive has not been correctly implemented or has not been implemented at all, an individual may find that although a provision exists which should be considered to be a part of the national legal order and which is intended to grant him rights or to allow him to benefit in other ways, his Member State's inadequate action or inaction means he appears to be left empty-handed. The actual situation is, however, less drastic. Apart from the fact that he can nevertheless rely on the directive before national authorities or other bodies which can be considered an 'emanation of the State',[1] an option which will not be elaborated further, he may have resort to a national court with a view to compelling observance of the directive at issue. The courts, which are then called upon to protect the individual concerned, may use one of the three tools designed by the Court of Justice: the doctrine of direct effect, the interpretation of national law in conformity with the directive, and the principle of State liability for harm caused to individuals by breaches of Community law. The interpretation of national law in conformity with the directive constitutes, in general, a relatively mild incursion into the national legal system. In the ultimate analysis, it is then still national law which applies, although its content may be adjusted in the light of the directive. The effects should, in principle, be less radical than the application of a provision of a directive in lieu of national law or the disapplication of the latter.[2] However, as will be demonstrated in Section 8.5, this does not always hold true, as the Court pushes this technique quite far.

In the *Von Colson* case the Court made clear that national courts are under a legal duty to interpret and apply national law and in particular legislation adopted for the implementation of the directive, in conformity with the latter.[3] The obligation is based on the binding nature of Article 249(3) and Article 10 of the Treaty. The national courts, like any other organ of the Member State, are bound by Article 249(3) and they are called upon to help to achieve the result of the directive at issue.

---

[1] Cf Ch 4, in particular Section 4.2.

[2] Cf Case C–125/01 *Pflücke* [2003] ECR I–9375. Interesting material on how national courts cope with consistent interpretation can be found in the reports prepared in the context of the 19th colloquium of the Association of the Councils of State and Supreme Administrative Jurisdictions of the European Union, available at www.raadvst-consetat.be.

[3] Cf Case 14/83 *Von Colson* [1984] ECR 1891. In Case C–373/90 *X* [1992] ECR I–131, para 7: consistent interpretation is labelled 'a line of authority now well-established by the Court'.

Recently, in *Pfeiffer*, the Court added that the requirement of consistent interpretation is inherent in the system of the Treaty. The Court linked the obligation explicity to the need to provide legal protection and to ensure the full effectiveness of Community law.[3A]

The obligation for the national court laid down in *Von Colson* and the subsequent developments of this doctrine have been the subject of many comments and, similarly, many terms are used to denote this phenomenon. Indirect effect, concurring or concurrent interpretation, loyal interpretation, harmonious interpretation, benevolent interpretation, conciliatory interpretation, consistent interpretation, interpretative obligation, principle of purposive interpretation, *Von Colson* principle, uniform interpretation, '*invocabilité d'interprétation*',[4] they all indicate the requirement to interpret national law in conformity with the directive. Although the term 'indirect effect' is most common in the English literature, I prefer to use the term 'consistent interpretation' or simply the terms 'interpretation in conformity with' or 'in accordance with'. In my view, the term 'indirect effect' is not sufficiently clear and precise. It can, for instance, also be used to indicate the effects which application of a directly effective provision might have *vis-à-vis* third parties[5] or any other effects produced by directives other than 'direct effect'.

The basic idea of consistent interpretation is less new than some might assume. As far as traditional international law is concerned, in several Member States national courts attempt by means of interpretation to reconcile two—at first sight—conflicting rules. Often they will do so in order to evade an outright choice of one of the conflicting rules, in so far as such an option is possible,[6] or they will proceed to such an interpretation with a view to helping their State comply with its international law obligations and avoiding their State's liability.

In the Netherlands it is generally accepted that an interpretation of national law in conformity with a provision of an international treaty is one of the methods of resolving a conflict between the two.[7] In several cases the *Hoge Raad* has resorted to this interpretative technique, in particular in cases involving the ECHR.[8]

In the United Kingdom a similar method is applied by the courts, although in a more restrictive way. As Lord Diplock put it: 'It is a principle of construction of United Kingdom statutes, now too well established to call for citation of authority, that the words of the statute passed after the treaty has been signed and dealing with the subject matter of the international obligation of the United Kingdom, are to be construed, if they are reasonably capable of bearing such

---

[3A] Joined Cases C–397/01 to C–403/01, *Pfeiffer*, judgment of 5 October 2004, nyr in ECR. There is a clear parallel with the foundation of State liability, discussed below in Ch 10, subsection 10.2.1.

[4] Cf Shaw 1991, 319, Betlem 1993, 204, Boch and Lane 1992, 181, Dal Farra 1992, 648, Plaza Martin 1994, 31, Curtin and Mortelmans 1994, 463, Simon 1997, 438.

[5] Cf below, Ch 9, Subsection 9.5.3.   [6] In particular from a constitutional point of view.

[7] Cf De Boer 1985a, 84, the Opinion of AG Moltmaker in HR 8 July 1988, NJ 1990, 448, in particular point 4, De Lange 1991, 211.   [8] Cf De Boer 1985b, 215.

meaning, as intended to carry out the obligation, and not to be inconsistent with it.'[9] However, in principle the courts will construe a domestic statute in conformity with an international treaty only where the statute is ambiguous and from the context it clearly appears that the enactment of the statute was intended to meet the government's obligation resulting from the treaty.[10]

In France, if there is a conflict between a statute and a prior international treaty the courts will try to reconcile the two norms by an interpretation of the statute in accordance with the treaty concerned. This approach is based on the presumption that the legislator knows Article 55 of the Constitution[11] and that it wishes to respect the international obligations of the French Republic.[12] For a long time this was the only possibility available to the French courts for resolving a conflict between a statute and a prior treaty as they were not permitted to review the former in the light of the latter. Since the judgment of the *Cour de Cassation* in *Jacques Vabre*[13] and, more recently, the decision of the *Conseil d'Etat* in *Nicolo*,[14] things have radically changed. Both decisions are understood as enabling the French courts to review statutes and to decide that a statute contrary to a prior treaty ought not to be enforced.[15] However, this does not necessarily mean that the courts will no longer have recourse to interpretation of statutes in conformity with a treaty. As the *commissaire du gouvernement* Laroque pointed out in the *Nicolo* case, the judge 'always enjoys the very useful resource of interpretation, which enables him to empty applicable texts of their contradiction'.[16]

In Germany, a current technique of construing national law similar to the interpretation in conformity with a treaty is the '*verfassungskonforme Auslegung*', i.e. interpretation in conformity with the Constitution. As a rule, if the wording of a norm, the genetic history, the coherence of the rules concerned and their sense and purpose allow several interpretations, the court has to follow that method of interpretation which brings the rule to be construed in conformity with the Constitution.[17] The '*verfassungskonforme*' interpretation is

---

[9] *Garland v. British Railway Engineering Ltd* (1982) 2 All ER 402, 415.

[10] Cf De Búrca 1992, 219–20, MacCormick and Summers 1991, 378.

[11] This Article provides as follows: 'Treaties and agreements that have been regularly ratified have, from the date of their publication, an authority superior to that of statutes, provided that for every agreement or treaty, it is enforced by the other party.'

[12] Cf Abraham 1989, 107–8.   [13] *Cour de Cassation* 24 May 1975, CDE 1975, 631.

[14] *Conseil d'Etat* 20 October 1989, RFDA 1989, 813.

[15] Cf MacCormick and Summers 1991, 187–8.

[16] Quoted in MacCormick and Summers 1991, 188.

[17] Cf MacCormick and Summers 1991, 101. Jarrass 1991a, 214 observes that the experience in Germany with '*verfassungskonforme Auslegung*' may be very useful for the doctrine of consistent interpretation. It is noteworthy that in German literature a parallel is drawn between consistent interpretation and interpretation in conformity with the Constitution rather than between the former and the '*vertragskonforme Auslegung*' which does exist as a concept, but which is not well established (cf Ress 1985, 163). For a detailed discussion of the various scholarly positions in, in particular, Germany, see Brechmann 1994, Ch 5.

generally considered a form of judicial self-restraint, a manner to respect, at least on the surface, the choice made by the legislature. It enables the courts to avoid a 'hard clash' between the legal provision and the Constitution which could ultimately result in a declaration of unconstitutionality, or any other consequence possible under German law.[18] However, it has been pointed out that in some situations it may also be an instrument of judicial activism: the consequences, seen from the point of view of the legislature, may be more far-reaching than a declaration of unconstitutionality.[19]

With respect to interpretation in conformity with an international treaty in general, the same could also hold true. In some cases this interpretative technique will be deployed with a view to giving effect to an international treaty, especially when other forms of application are excluded for constitutional reasons, such as maintaining the principle of separation of powers, as was the case in France. From this point of view, interpretation may be considered a form of judicial activism. In other situations, particularly where review in the light of an international treaty is allowed, interpretation in conformity with the treaty may testify to judicial self-restraint.

In Community law, the approach of the Court of Justice is in principle no different. Provisions of secondary law must wherever possible be construed in conformity with the Treaty.[20] Moreover, not only is the Treaty a standard for interpretation, but so too are general principles of Community law: secondary Community law must be construed in conformity with those principles.[21] The same holds true for fundamental rights[22] and for provisions of international law.[23]

As far as the interpretation of *national law* in accordance with Community law[24] and, in particular, with a directive is concerned, in the 'pre-*Von Colson* era' a few cases were brought before the Court of Justice in which the interpretation of national law in conformity with a directive was touched upon in some way by the Court.[25] Moreover, even before *Von Colson* it was suggested that the national

---

[18] Cf Zeidler 1988, 209–14.   [19] Cf Jarass 1991a, 215, Heukels 1991, 128.

[20] Cf Case 201/85 *Klensch* [1986] ECR 3477, para 21, and Case C–12/00 *Commission v. Spain* [2003] ECR I–459, para 97.

[21] Cf Joined Cases C–90 and 91/90 *Neu* [1991] ECR I–3617, para 12.

[22] Cf Case C–465/00 *Rechnungshof* [2003] ECR I–4989, para 68.

[23] Cf Case C–76/00 P *Petrotub* [2003] ECR I–79, para 57.

[24] The obligation of interpretation of national law in accordance with community law in general is, by now, well established. Cf e.g. Case C–262/97 *Engelbrecht* [2000] ECR I–7321 and Case C–327/00 *Santex* [2003] ECR I–1877. For a similar obligation in relation to international law provisions see, for instance, Case C–53/96 *Hermès* [1998] ECR I–3603. For interpretation in the light of a recommendation see Case C–322/88 *Grimaldi* [1989] ECR I–4407. For a critical discussion of the latter see Senden 2003, 400–9.

[25] Cf Case 32/74 *Haaga* [1974] ECR 1201, Case 67/74 *Bonsignore* [1975] ECR 297, Case 111/75 *Mazzalai* [1976] ECR 657. For a more detailed discussion see the first edition of this book, 203–5.

courts are obliged to proceed to consistent interpretation of national implementing measures *and* of national law in general.[26]

In summary, the interpretation of a legal provision, be it of national or of secondary Community law, in conformity with a higher ranking (international) provision is as such nothing new. It is well known within the Member States and in the Community legal order. It can most appropriately be characterized as a judicial technique which is often applied in order to avoid an outright confrontation between the rules involved. Although the concept as such is therefore not unfamiliar, the conditions, modalities, and scope of its application are considerably different. Some of the problems which may arise from these differences will be given further consideration in the Sections below.

8.2   The scope of consistent interpretation: the resolved issues

From the case law of the Court of Justice it appears that for the purposes of consistent interpretation it is immaterial whether the provisions which serve as standards for interpretation are directly effective or not. Thus in *Von Colson*,[27] for instance, the Court formulated the obligation of consistent interpretation of national law on sanctions although, according to the same judgment, the directive did not include any unconditional and sufficiently precise obligations as regards sanctions for discrimination on which individuals could rely directly. In *Johnston*[28] the Court clearly indicated that the conflict at issue could be resolved either by means of consistent interpretation or by means of direct effect.

Likewise, the obligation applies irrespective of the legal relationship at issue in the main proceedings, i.e. whether there is a conflict between a private individual and the State or between two private individuals. In the parallel cases of *Von Colson* and *Harz*, the former involved a State prison while the defendant in the latter was a private undertaking.[29]

Furthermore it must be pointed out that the duty of consistent interpretation is not confined to the wording of the directive. The national court must also construe national legal provisions in the light of the objective of the directive concerned. In other words, national courts are required to proceed to a *purposive interpretation* of national law, giving it a meaning which makes it suitable to achieve the objective of the directive. Thus not only the wording but also the purpose of the directive is an important element to be taken into account.[30]

---

[26]   Cf Timmermans 1979, 536.   [27]   Case 14/83 [1984] ECR 1891.

[28]   Case 222/84 [1986] ECR 1651, in particular paras 53–57. Cf also Case C–91/92 *Faccini Dori* [1994] ECR I–3325.

[29]   Case 14/83 [1984] ECR 1891 and Case 79/83 [1984] ECR 1921. Cf also e.g. Case C–334/92 *Miret* [1993] ECR I–6911, Case C–91/92 *Faccini Dori* [1994] ECR I–3325, Case C–472/93 *Spano* [1995] ECR I–4321, Joined Cases C–240/98 and C–244/98 *Océano* [2000] ECR I–4941, and Case C–63/97 *BMW* [1999] ECR I–905.   [30]   Cf Bleckmann 1992, 365.

Yet, although the precision and unconditionality required for direct effect is by no means necessary for the purposes of consistent interpretation, it should be noted that the terms of the directive at issue must provide for a certain 'minimum to hold on to' for the court concerned. It is, for instance, not for the courts to give effect, through consistent interpretation, to provisions of (frame)work directives which, as such, first require further elaboration by legislative or other measures—Community or national.

A point of slight controversy is still the issue whether the obligation of consistent interpretation already applies during the period between the entry into force and the deadline for implementation of the directive. In Chapter 2, I came to the conclusion that, in principle, there is no such obligation within the period provided for implementation but that, on the other hand, the national court has the faculty to proceed to consistent interpretation.[31]

The main issue to be addressed here concerns the *object* of the obligation of consistent interpretation. For some time disagreement existed with respect to the question of *what* had to be interpreted in conformity with the directive. *Von Colson* was not entirely clear in this respect. While in one paragraph of the judgment the Court referred to 'national law and in particular the provisions of a national law specifically introduced in order to implement Directive No 76/207',[32] according to the operative part of the judgment it was solely the legislation adopted for the implementation of the directive that had to be interpreted in conformity with the directive.

In *Marshall I*, Advocate General Slynn underlined this discrepancy. Subsequently, he argued that the duty of consistent interpretation did not apply where the national legislation pre-dated the directive. The only exception the Advocate General was willing to make was a situation in which it was clear 'that the legislation was adopted specifically with a proposed directive in mind'.[33]

In *Kolpinghuis*,[34] Advocate General Mischo agreed with this point of view, but he formulated another exception. In his opinion the obligation of consistent interpretation also applied to national law which was deemed to satisfy the requirements of the directive even when, for that reason, the Member State considered it unnecessary to adopt implementing measures. In this respect it was cogently argued by Szyszczak that 'it would be absurd to allow legislation predating the directive to be immune from the *Von Colson* principle . . . simply because there was no need for amendment of existing legislation'.[35]

Although, according to some authors, *Kolpinghuis* was already sufficiently clear on the issue as to whether the obligation of consistent interpretation also related to

[31] For a more detailed discussion see Ch 2, Section 2.3.

[32] Cf also Case C–185/97 *Coote* [1998] ECR I–5199, paras 18–19.

[33] Opinion of AG Slynn in Case 152/84 *Marshall I* [1986] ECR 723, 732. For a more detailed discussion of his reasoning see the first edition of this book, 208. See also Tridimas 2002, 347.

[34] Case 80/86 [1987] ECR 3969.

[35] Szyszczak 1990, 485. In Case C–334/92 *Miret* [1993] ECR I–6911, the Court of Justice has stressed that consistent interpretation should in particular be followed in cases where the Member State believed that the already existing provisions of national law satisfied the requirements of the directive concerned (para 21).

pre-existing law,[36] it was in *Marleasing*, that the Court put an end to all speculation and disagreement. It made explicitly clear that the obligation applies to national law irrespective of 'whether the provisions in question were adopted before or after the directive'.[37] The Court apparently proceeded from its theory that Community law is an integral part of the national legal systems: once this has been accepted and Community law must for that reason be taken into consideration by the national courts, it would be paradoxical to restrict the requirement of consistent interpretation only to implementing measures.[38]

Furthermore, it should be noted that the term 'law' covers a broader category than legislation. It may, for instance, also include unwritten principles of law and judge-made law.[39] The judgment in *Pfeiffer* went even a step further: the national courts are required to consider national law as a whole.[39A] In legal writing it has been also suggested that contracts too must be construed in conformity with the relevant directive.[40] This is, in my opinion, certainly true for agreements which are intended to implement the directive.[41] In its judgment in *Evans*, although without using the standard terminology about consistent interpretation, the Court found that the implementation of Directive 84/5 (insurance against civil liability—motor vehicles) was acceptable under the proviso that the agreement implementing the directive is interpreted and applied in conformity with the obligations resulting from the latter.[42] This seems to imply, in my view, an obligation of consistent interpretation. Moreover, the same obligation results from the very fact that the agreement at issue serves as a means of implementing the directive.[43]

A number of problems having thus been resolved, the crucial question concerns the limits of the obligation of consistent interpretation. These limits seem to lie, at least according to the Court, in general principles of law. In legal writing

---

[36] Case 80/86 [1987] ECR 3969. Cf Everling 1993, 212, Richter 1988, 396, Timmermans 1992, 818. Cf also Morris 1989, 241 and Case 125/88 *Nijman* [1989] ECR 3533 where the terms ' . . . and in particular . . . ' were deleted.

[37] Case C–106/89 [1990] ECR I–4135, para 8. Cf also e.g. Case C–76/97 *Tögel* [1998] ECR I–5357, Joined Cases C–240/98 and C–244/98 *Océano* [2000] ECR I–4941 and Case C–63/97 *BMW* [1999] ECR I–905, para 20:' . . . whatever the applicable national law may be, it must be interpreted, as far as possible, in the light of the wording and purpose of the directive . . . '.

[38] Cf also the Opinion of AG Van Gerven in Case C–262/88 *Barber* [1990] ECR I–1889, para 50. In *Marleasing* AG Van Gerven argued that the legal basis of consistent interpretation followed not only from Art 249(3) combined with Art 10 of the Treaty but also from the principle of supremacy: directives, as part of Community law, take precedence over *all* provisions of national law (para 9). Cf also Lutter 1992, 604.

[39] Case C–456/98 *Centrosteel* [2000] ECR I–6007. Cf also Rodriguez Iglesias and Riechenberg 1995, who also point out, at 1230, that under the obligation of consistent interpretation lower courts may be held to overrule well-established case law of the last instance jurisdictions.

[39A] Joined Cases C–397/01 to C–403/01, *Pfeiffer*, judgment of 5 October 2004, nyr in ECR.

[40] Cf Wissink 2001, 302–11.   [41] Cf on implementation by agreements Ch 5, Subsection 5.3.2.

[42] Case C–63/01, judgment of 4 December 2003, nyr in ECR.

[43] Cf however the House of Lords in *White v. White and the Motor Insurers' Bureau* [2001] 2 CMLR I, where the Lords found that the obligation of consistent interpretation did not apply since the agreement at issue was a contract under private law.

and national case law also other possible limits are proposed and sometimes accepted.

For a proper appreciation of these issues it is useful to make a distinction between cases where the directive as such has been correctly transposed into national law and cases where the directive has either not been transposed correctly or not in due time. As will become apparent, in the former type of cases consistent interpretation is relatively unproblematic. It is notably in the latter type of cases that difficult questions as to the limits of the obligation may arise and the potential implications of the obligation of consistent interpretation within the national legal systems are thrown into high relief.

8.3 Consistent interpretation within the context of judicial implementation of directives

Too often the obligation of the courts to interpret national law in accordance with a directive is discussed as a means to counteract inadequate transposition of a directive. This is fully understandable as the cases which have so far been decided by the Court of Justice, dealing with different aspects of the obligation, have, in principle, concerned situations of directives which have not been (correctly or timely) implemented. Moreover, the developments in this area are the most interesting. However, in my view, this is too limited an approach. The obligation in the *Von Colson* judgment is worded in very general terms and clearly implies that the obligation exists irrespective of whether there is a deficiency in the implementing measures or whether implementation took place at all.[44]

As explained in Chapters 2 and 5, directives may be transposed in several ways.[45] Different modalities of transposition can be chosen, with *verbatim* transposition at one end of the spectrum and translation into national legal concepts and terminology at the other. Similarly, it has been observed that both methods have their advantages and disadvantages. From a Community law point of view, as a rule neither method is imperative, provided that the content of the measures adopted to transpose the directive is sufficiently clear and precise. Individuals must be able to ascertain their rights and duties and there must be no risk of the measures being misapplied in practice, judicial practice included. Where it appears that national courts systematically construe provisions of national law aimed at transposing a directive in a way which causes the provisions to be at variance with the directive, it could be an important indication that the directive has not been correctly transposed. If a different wording had been chosen by the legislator the courts would probably also interpret the provision in another fashion, but this may not be so. It is conceivable that a directive as such has been transposed into national legislation in an adequate manner, satisfying the requirements developed by the Court of Justice. However, it may also be the courts

---

[44] This distinction is also observed by e.g. Götz 1992, 1853–4 and Betlem 1993, 212.

[45] See above, Section 2.6 and Section 5.2.

which, when construing the relevant provisions, choose one of the possible options for interpretation and, subsequently, the latter leads to a result inconsistent with the underlying directive. This would result in a sort of 'de-implementation', as one author called it: it is not the statute as such but its construction by the courts which fails to achieve the objective of the directive.[46] Today it is perhaps a truism to say that the application of any legal rule in a concrete case requires its interpretation. However, it is important to realize that legislation, by the nature of things, is cast at a certain level of abstraction. This is equally true with respect to legislative measures transposing a directive. In other words, there will in principle always be a certain margin for national courts when they are applying and thus interpreting a legal rule.

Not surprisingly, several authors have pointed out that, even where the directive is correctly transposed into national law it will remain relevant as a standard for inter-pretation of the implementing measures.[47] In fact, a national court will often first raise a question of interpretation of a directive in order to be able to examine whether the national implementing or other measures are compatible with it or with a view to ascertaining the meaning which should be given to the national provisions concerned. Indeed, national courts have their own specific role in the process of implementation: they must apply the national provisions transposing the directive in a concrete case before them.[48] Whenever the national court is called upon to apply a provision of national law intended to transpose a directive, it will necessarily come across the question of the meaning of the provision. Pursuant to the obligation laid down in *Von Colson*, this meaning must correspond with the meaning of the 'counterpart-provision' of the directive. Obviously, considerable problems may arise in this respect. National legislation may literally just take over the terms of the directive, which could be unfamiliar to the national legal order. Similarly, the 'trans-lation' of the directive into national legal terminology is not necessarily a safeguard for proper interpretation and application by the courts. Neither of the methods of transposition is a watertight guarantee that the provisions will be understood and applied in perfect harmony with the underlying directive. Furthermore, the interpretation by the Court of Justice of the terms of the relevant directive may also evolve over time. Some examples may illustrate the (potential) problems.

In Case C–373/90[49] a 'garagiste' in Bergerac, Mr X, published advertisements with the exhortation:'Buy your new vehicle cheaper.' Mr Richard lodged a com-plaint before the *Juge d'Instruction* against X, together with a claim for civil indem-nity, for untruthful and unlawful advertising, prohibited under Article 44 of Law No 73–1193. This Law transposed Directive 84/450 on misleading advertising.[50] The problem in this case was, *inter alia*, not an incorrect transposition of the

---

[46] Bates 1986, 185. Cf also Everling 1992b, 380 who points out the danger of 'de-harmonization' through interpretation.

[47] Cf Pescatore 1980, 172, Lutter 1992, 598, Everling 1989, 367, and Timmermans 1979, 535. Cf also Case 270/81 *Rickmers* [1982] ECR 2771, para 25.

[48] As to the 'umbrella' use of the term implementation see Ch 1, Section 1.3.

[49] [1992] ECR I–131.   [50] [1984] OJ L250/17.

Directive into national legislation, but rather the question of what constituted a
'new car', since depending on this qualification the advertisement could be considered as misleading. There was a relatively recent judgment of the
Criminal Division of the *Cour de Cassation* in which this court held, in a different but comparable context, that 'to count as new, a vehicle must not only not
have been driven, but must also not yet have been registered'.[51] Both the Advocate
General and the Court of Justice disagreed with the view that for the purposes of
the Directive at issue and, moreover, within the broader context of protection
which parallel imports enjoy to a certain extent under Community law, the cars
should no longer be considered new because they had been registered in Belgium
before importation into France. Therefore the directive had to be construed as
meaning 'that it does not preclude vehicles from being advertised as
new . . . when the vehicles concerned are registered solely for the purpose of
importation [and] have never been on the road . . . '. Furthermore, the Court
made plain to the national judge that he had to interpret national law in
conformity with this interpretation of the Directive.

Another example, taken from the area of sex discrimination, relates to dismissal.
In three very similar cases[52] the Court of Justice drew a sharp distinction between
age limits governing dismissal on the one hand and the pensionable age, i.e. the
age at which a person is entitled to the payment of a retirement pension, on the
other. With respect to the former type of age limits, discrimination between men
and women, i.e. different age limits for men and women, was prohibited by virtue
of Directive 76/207 (equal treatment at work).[53] On the other hand, differences
in pensionable age were allowed, at least as far as statutory pensions were concerned, owing to an exception to that effect in Directive 79/7 (equal treatment
statutory schemes of social security).[54]

Mrs *Beets-Proper* was dismissed at the age of 60 while her male colleagues were
allowed to work until the age of 65. Her employer took the view that the
employment relationship automatically ended, by virtue of an implied condition in the contract of employment, at the moment that she became entitled to
an old age pension under a pension scheme of the employer's pension fund. For
women this was the case at 60, for men at 65. The question in the national courts
was whether such an implied condition was compatible with Article 1637ij of
the Dutch Civil Code. This Article at the material time read as follows:

(1) As regards the conclusion of a contract of employment, staff training, the terms of
employment, promotion and the termination of the contract of employment, an
employer may not make any distinction between men and women . . . The terms of
employment do not include benefits or entitlements under pension schemes. . . .

---

[51] See Report for the Hearing, I–135.
[52] Case 152/84 *Marshall I* [1986] ECR 723, Case 262/84 *Beets-Proper* [1986] ECR 773, and
Case 151/84 *Roberts* [1986] ECR 703.   [53] [1976] OJ L39/40.
[54] [1979] OJ L6/24.

(2) Any clause which is contrary to the first sentence of paragraph 1 shall be void.[55]

In contrast to the *Gerechtshof Amsterdam*, following an unequivocal preliminary ruling by the Court of Justice, the *Hoge Raad* considered in cassation that Article 1637ij of the Civil Code, which implements the Equal Treatment Directive, must be construed in such a manner that a condition in a contract of employment which makes this contract terminate on the date when the employee attains pensionable age, is covered by the first sentence of the first paragraph, which prohibits different treatment of men and women. The condition does not fall within the scope of the second sentence. Consequently, the disputed condition is, by virtue of the second paragraph of Article 1637ij, null and void.[56]

It did not take much effort to decide the case in this way, in conformity with the directive at issue, as the terms of the provision to be construed lend themselves very well to such an interpretation. Accordingly, Article 1637ij could be considered as an appropriate transposition of the directive, even after the judgment of the Court of Justice and there was no need to subsequently amend the provision.

Two general conclusions can be drawn with respect to the interpretation by national courts of the measures intended to implement a directive. Firstly, case law will serve as a yardstick as to whether the implementing measures are sufficient or not. Secondly, national courts have a distinct role in the process of achieving the result prescribed by the directive. As explained in Chapter 3, Section 3.3, in this process it is not sufficient to transpose the directive into national legislative measures. The obligation goes further and involves the realization of the result in practice and *in concreto*. Viewed from this perspective, the national judge must be situated somewhere near the end of the 'chain of implementation', as it is he who will often be called upon to apply the measures of transposition to a concrete case before him. In other words, the court is entrusted with the task of '*judicial implementation*'. In this process the court must often interpret national law, in particular the provisions transposing the directive. That interpretation must be in conformity with the underlying directive.

8.4 Consistent interpretation and inadequately transposed directives: remedial interpretation

Wherever a directive has been correctly transposed into national law, as a rule, consistent interpretation of the national provisions by the courts will not pose particular problems, provided that the courts are aware of the Community origins

---

[55] Case 262/84 *Beets-Proper* [1986] ECR 773, para 10.
[56] Judgment of 21 November 1986, NJ 1987 no 351.

of the rules to be interpreted. Likewise, the courts will achieve the desired result by giving the provisions under consideration a certain meaning without resorting, from the national law point of view, to artificial and strained constructions.

Matters are somewhat different in the case of incorrect implementation.

In the United Kingdom a number of cases have concerned the same problem as in the *Beets-Proper*[57] case discussed in the previous Section, but the outcomes have been entirely different. The relevant national provision, section 6(2)(b) of the Sex Discrimination Act 1975, provided that 'it is unlawful for a person, in the case of a woman employed by him at an establishment in Great Britain to discriminate against her'. Furthermore, section 6(4) of the same Act provided that section 6(2)(b), *inter alia*, 'does not apply to provision in relation to death or retirement'. This latter exception was interpreted by the courts as meaning 'about retirement' with the consequence that dismissal of women at an earlier age than men was allowed since it fell within the scope of section 6(4). After the Court of Justice had made plain that age limits for dismissal and age at which pension becomes payable should be regarded as two separate matters, it was clear that the provision and certainly the construction of the provision by the UK courts was not compatible with Directive 76/207, as interpreted by the Court of Justice. Even then, however, the courts refused to construe the relevant section in another way, although it was argued that another interpretation was not entirely impossible.[58] At the end of the day the Sex Discrimination Act had to be amended in order to bring it into line with the Directive.[59] It is submitted that when one compares the terms of the Dutch provision which had to be interpreted by the *Hoge Raad* and the terms of the provision of the Sex Discrimination Act, it cannot be denied that a consistent interpretation by the English courts would have required more effort and inventiveness and would probably be less obvious than in the Dutch case.[60] The next question to be answered in this respect is: does the obligation of consistent interpretation require such a *special effort*, going further than the national court would be inclined to do under the rules of construction usual in its Member State?

According to the Court's jurisprudence, consistent interpretation also has the function of *temporarily*[61] bridging the gap between national law and the directive which has not been adequately transposed. This function of consistent interpretation can probably best be labelled as '*remedial interpretation*', in order to distinguish it from the consistent interpretation in the context of judicial implementation. The next Sections will mainly concern this type of interpretation, which is only a

---

[57] Case 262/84 [1986] ECR 773.

[58] Cf *Duke v. Reliance Systems Ltd* [1987] 2 CMLR 24.

[59] Section 2(1) of SDA 1986 repealed section 6(4) of SDA 1975.

[60] The reasons for refusing an interpretation consistent with the directive will not be considered here. For a discussion of the UK courts' approach see e.g. Scyczszak 1990, De Búrca 1992. The case law has subsequently evolved in a more 'community friendly' way'. See e.g. Boch 1996. For a brief overview see also Craig 1997 and FIDE 1998—the UK Report by Weatherill.

[61] Cf Case C–338/91 *Steenhorst-Neerings* [1993] ECR I–5475, paras 31–34.

palliative for inadequate implementation and will certainly *not cure* the Member State's non-compliance as such.[62]

Incorrect or inadequate transposition can take various forms. The most blatant is the situation in which the directive has not been transposed into national law at all, while it is plain, and is admitted by the Member State concerned that such a transposition is necessary in order to comply with Article 249(3). These 'pathological' failures can be divided into situations where there is no national legislation covering the subject matter of the directive at all and situations where there is such legislation but it needs further adjustment.

The second type of inadequate transposition concerns a situation where no transposition measures have been adopted as the Member State is of the opinion that the result to be achieved under the directive is already fully realized within the national legal order; but upon further consideration this turns out not to be correct.

In the third type of situation the Member State has enacted the necessary measures but in fact it appears that these do not meet the requirements for correct transposition as developed by the Court of Justice.[63]

Finally, the directive may appear to have been transposed adequately at first sight, for instance by adoption of new legislation dealing fully and correctly with the subject matter of the directive, but the Member State has forgotten to 'clear up' some other provisions which at the end of the day frustrate the application of the measures transposing the directive.[64]

There are of course several other forms of inadequate transposition, such as incorrect transposition of a part of a directive or a specific provision only. It is certainly not my intention to map them all. It is important in the context of the present Section to emphasize that the various categories of inadequate transposition are relevant for the question whether the national courts can proceed to remedial interpretation or not. Obviously, if there is no national law governing the subject matter of the directive then there is also nothing to be interpreted. On the other hand, if national legal provisions exist but do not amount to adequate transposition, the chance that the national judge can temporarily remedy the defect will depend on the degree of variance between national law and the provisions of the directive. In some cases there can be an overt conflict; in other cases there may be merely a minor variance. Likewise, where it is plain that national law must be amended in order to satisfy the directive it will probably be more difficult to bridge the gap than where a directive has been transposed but the national provisions adopted for this purpose are not entirely satisfactory.

To put it differently, the possibility of giving provisions of national law an interpretation in conformity with the directive is closely linked to the terms of those

---

[62] Cf ibid, the opinion of AG Darmon, para 47, Case C–236/95 *Commission v. Greece* [1996] ECR I–4459 and Case C–144/99 *Commission v. the Netherlands* [2001] ECR I–3541.

[63] Cf above, Ch 5.

[64] E.g. amended or newly introduced provisions which do not work within the broader context of the relevant legislation. This was for instance the basic problem in Case C–177/88 *Dekker* [1990] ECR I–3941.

provisions. The 'closer' or the more 'flexible' the terms, the more probable it is that consistent interpretation will be feasible. On the other hand, the greater the variance, the more difficult consistent interpretation will be. The degree of variance will in turn often depend on the type of inadequate transposition at issue.

This is not the end of the story. Whether a certain construction of national law is possible or not will, as already pointed out, to an equal extent depend on the limits of judicial interpretation. As will be illustrated below, from the point of view of national law, remedial interpretation may often result in an artificial or at least unusual construction. The question is indeed: 'Where are the limits?' This question will, as a rule, not occur very often with respect to interpretation within the context of judicial implementation. It should, however, be noted that the distinction in practice between the latter type of interpretation and remedial interpretation, which seems to run alongside the difference between 'usual' and 'unusual' methods of interpretation, is not always easy to make.[65]

8.5 Limits to consistent interpretation

8.5.1 National rules of construction

The national courts are required to construe national law in conformity with a directive 'as far as possible'. How this crucial qualification should be understood is unclear. One of the suggestions sometimes made is that the terms are to be understood as referring to the national methods of interpretation. In fact, this issue goes back to the judgment in *Von Colson*. From that judgment it followed that national courts are under a legal duty to interpret and apply national law in conformity with a directive. However, the national court is obliged to do this '*in so far as it is given discretion . . . under national law*'.[66] This reference to discretion under national law can, within the context of the *Von Colson* judgment, be explained largely by the fact that the German government argued before the Court that the provision on compensation to be paid to a person discriminated against as regards access to employment (the provision was clearly incompatible with the requirements of Directive 76/207) did not necessarily exclude the application of the general rules of law regarding compensation. The Court of Justice held that 'it is for the national court alone to rule on that question concerning the interpretation of its national law'.[67] Nevertheless it went on to lay down the above-mentioned obligation of consistent interpretation.

The orthodox understanding of these references to national law was that it was up to the national court itself to decide whether it will be able to proceed to

---

[65] Cf Jans 1994, 250.

[66] Case 14/83 [1984] ECR 1891, para 28. In the German version: '*unter voller Ausschöpfung des Beurteilungsspielraums den ihm das nationale Recht einräumt*'; in the French version: '*dans toute la mesure où une marge d'appréciation lui est accordée par son droit national*', both of which seem more demanding than the English version.   [67] Para 25 of the judgment.

consistent interpretation or not. Likewise it was assumed that the obligation applied if several alternative interpretations were possible. In such a case the national judge had to choose the interpretation which would be in line with the directive. Whether this was indeed the case, however, was again a matter for the national court to sort out.[68] Moreover, it was argued in legal writing that the Court in no way authorized the national judge to choose an interpretation *contra legem*.[69]

Obviously, as consistent interpretation is interpretation of *national* law, it is within the competence of the national courts and not within that of the Court of Justice. As such it fits entirely within the idea of the division of functions between the national courts and the Court of Justice as laid down in established jurisprudence.[70]

When searching for an answer to the question whether consistent interpretation is possible or not, and thus when addressing the issue of the discretion of the national courts under national law, the crucial factor is the approach, or methods or rules of interpretation or construction prevailing within the Member State concerned.[71] Quite naturally, the national judge will be inclined to hold that consistent interpretation is impossible if it implies a departure from the usual rules of construction.

Soon after the judgment in *Von Colson* it became obvious, particularly from the UK experience, that the national rules of construction may form a very serious and perhaps too far-reaching restriction upon the doctrine of consistent interpretation.

> In a number of cases the UK courts were not prepared to construe domestic legislation in accordance with a directive. One of the main arguments presented in this respect was that the legislation pre-dated the directive and, consequently, was not designed to transpose it.[72] These cases have been severely criticized in the UK in academic writing. According to one author they revealed 'lack of understanding by the House of Lords of the principle of *indirect* effects'.[73] In other cases the House of Lords was more responsive and applied a 'purposive construction' of national legislation in order to bring it into line with the directives at issue.[74] However, the cases concerned interpretation of national legislation purported to transpose the directives. Moreover,

---

[68] Cf Galmot and Bonichot 1988, 22, Jarass 1991a, 218: national rules of construction are decisive.

[69] Cf Galmot and Bonichot 1988, 22.

[70] Cf in particular with respect to interpretation Case C–37/92 *Vanacker* [1995] ECR I–4947. Cf also Case C–60/02 *X*, judgment of 7 January 2004, nyr in ECR.

[71] Cf Everling 1992b, 381. By all these terms I refer to the different principles, rules, canons, etc. which may guide interpretation. In some legal systems they may have more a character of 'real' rules while in others they are rather considered as guidelines. Cf also Marsh 1973, 9.

[72] Cf *Duke v. Reliance System Ltd* [1988] 1 CMLR 719, House of Lords (Sex Discrimination Act 1975 pre-dated Directive 76/207) and *Finnegan v. Clowney Youth Training Programme Ltd* [1990] 2 CMLR 859, House of Lords (Sex Discrimination (Northern Ireland) Order 1976 had been enacted after the Directive 76/207, but in the view of the House of Lords the Order was also not adopted with the intention of complying with the Directive).

[73] Szyszczak 1990, 484. Cf also De Búrca 1992, 219 ff. and Mead 1991.

[74] Ibid. Cf also Boch 1996.

it has been argued that the 'purposive approach' of the UK courts does not correspond with the purposive interpretation desired by the Court of Justice when the latter refers to the purpose of the directive. The UK courts in fact did nothing more than base their interpretation on the (presumed) intent of the legislature behind the enactment of a piece of legislation. In other words, it was rather the purpose of the legislature than the purpose of the directive that played the central role in the UK courts' construction.[75]

Similarly in Germany, the aftermath of the *Von Colson* case illustrated vividly the kind of problems which the obligation of consistent interpretation may present at national level.[76] The central issue in these cases was the limits of judicial law-making in pursuance of the obligations as formulated in *Von Colson*. Article 611a of the Civil Code, which was adopted to implement Directive 76/207, provided for damages as relief in the case of sex discrimination in respect of access to employment. The damages were limited to compensation for frustration of expectations ('*Vertrauensschaden*'), which would, as a rule, amount to indemnification of the costs incurred in relation to the application for a job, like stamps. In the view of the Court of Justice such compensation did not meet the requirements of the directive. It was, however, precisely the intention of the German legislature to limit the right to compensation to such a negligible amount. After *Von Colson*, the German courts had to face the problem whether they could override Article 611a by allowing damages on the basis of general principles of tort law.

The Labour Court of *Hamm*, which referred *Von Colson* to the Court of Justice, considered in this respect that according to the Federal Constitutional Court judges would be exceeding their judicial function if their interpretation contradicted the wording of the provisions at issue, the spirit of the measure, and the intention of the legislature. The Labour Court recalled that, according to the intention of the legislature and the general rules of systemic interpretation, Article 611a of the Civil Code had to be interpreted as limiting the compensation to the very low amount payable in respect of '*Vertrauensschaden*' and as excluding the application of the general principles of tort law. In other words, the Labour Court did not have much discretion in this respect. However, it went on to consider that the interpretation required by the Court of Justice implied that the systemic and historical (i.e. focusing on the intention of the legislature) arguments of interpretation ought to be disregarded.[77] The compensation for '*Vertrauensschaden*' could then on the basis of its wording

---

[75] Cf De Búrca 1992, 222. For a similar approach in Germany see Spetzler 1991, 579. Interestingly, in Case C–334/92 *Miret* [1993] ECR I–6911 the Court introduced a similar fiction by stating that when national courts interpret and apply national law 'every national court must presume that the State had the intention of fulfilling entirely the obligations arising from the directive concerned' (para 20).

[76] Cf for a brief account Roth 1991, 141. For a more detailed discussion see Prechal and Burrows 1990, 255–9, on which the following description is partly based.

[77] Cf also Bleckmann 1984, 776.

be construed as dealing with a specific ground for compensation *without* excluding the application of Article 823 of the Civil Code, the general provision governing compensation. On the one hand, this or a similar line of reasoning was also followed by several other courts. On the other hand, there were courts which were very hesistant. The Labour Court of *Niedersachsen*, for instance, expressed serious doubts as, in its view, it was a task for the legislature to bring national law into conformity with Community law. Another court refused to construe national provisions in accordance with the directive since two initiatives had been taken by the *Land of Hessen* and by the Socialist Party to amend the law. Under these circumstances, in the opinion of the court, there was no place for judicial intervention.[78]

The Supreme Labour Court finally settled the matter, giving the victims of discrimination higher compensation than that available for '*Vertrauensschaden*' only, but at the same time respecting the intention of the legislature.[79] In brief, on the one hand, it pointed out that the clear terms of Article 611a of the Civil Code cannot serve as a basis for a claim in damages in excess of those available for '*Vertrauensschaden*'. It recalled that even interpretation of statutes in conformity with the Constitution reaches its limit at the point where it would conflict with the wording and the evident intention of the legislature. The position can be no different as regards the interpretation of national law in conformity with a directive. On the other hand, it held that the restriction of the liability to pay compensation to damages under Article 611a does not affect the right to compensation for non-pecuniary damage in respect of infringement of rights of personality under Article 823(1) and 847 of the Civil Code. In particular, it referred to the fact that even before Article 611a was adopted, compensation for non-pecuniary damage under the two other articles of the Civil Code was recognized in cases of discrimination. Although the Supreme Court's construction may be in accordance with the requirements laid down by the Court of Justice in some cases, in others the result will be at variance with Directive 76/207. According to the Supreme Labour Court pecuniary damages only arise in the case of a serious infringement of the rights of personality. Whether this is the case depends in particular on the degree of *fault* on the part of the author of the discrimination. This approach, in turn, was at odds with the *Dekker* judgment.[80]

In cases before the Court of Justice after *Von Colson*, it was suggested, perhaps in reaction to the unfortunate UK experience, that national rules of construction should not apply without qualification.

---

[78] Cf Roth 1991, 141 and Prechal and Burrows 1990, 255–9.

[79] Two judgments of 14 March 1989: *Re a rehabilitation centre* and *Re an animal house* [1992] 2 CMLR 21, 29.

[80] Cf above, Ch 5, Section 5.4. In Case C–180/95 *Draehmpaehl* [1997] ECR I–2195 the Court indeed decided that the requirement of *fault* was incompatible with the directive at issue.

In his opinion in the *Barber* case, Advocate General Van Gerven concluded from the manner in which the Labour Court of Hamm interpreted national law, in pursuance of the obligation laid down in *Von Colson*, that 'it would appear that Community law may set limits to certain methods of interpretation applied under a national legal system'.[81] As explained above, this court decided to disregard the intention of the legislature which, in the opinion of the Supreme Labour Court, it was not allowed to do under national rules of interpretation.

Similarly, in *Marleasing* the Commission argued that since the Community legal system is an integral part of national law and the national court is also a Community court, the latter cannot be denied the possibility of interpreting national law in conformity with the directive. According to the Commission this type of interpretation should prevail over the rules of interpretation commonly recognized in the national legal order of the court concerned. In the Commission's view, it is the principle of supremacy of Community law which precludes the application of any rule of interpretation which might frustrate the result intended by the authors of the directive.[82]

The judgment in *Marleasing* suggests that the Court was not entirely insensitive to these arguments. Although it reiterated that according to *Von Colson* 'the Member States' obligation arising from a directive to achieve the result envisaged by the directive and their duty under Article 5 [Article 10] of the treaty . . . is binding on all authorities of the Member States including, for the matters within their jurisdiction, the courts', it held subsequently that 'the national court called upon to interpret [national law] is required to do so, *as far as possible*, in the light of the wording and the purpose of the directive . . . '.[83] In summary, the reference to 'discretion under national law' disappeared and was replaced by the terms 'as far as possible', which has been the standard terminology ever since.[84] For the concrete problem at issue in *Marleasing* the Court found that the requirement of consistent interpretation *precluded* the interpretation of national law in a manner different from interpretation in conformity with the directive.[85]

What conclusions can be drawn from *Marleasing* as to the problem of applying national rules of construction? Several commentators have suggested that since *Marleasing* there has no longer been any scope for limitations resulting from the national methods of interpretation. Community law itself prescribes the methods to be used and that determines the limits of the obligation of consistent interpretation.

[81] Case C–262/88 [1990] ECR I–1889, para 50. Cf also Everling 1992b, 381.

[82] Case C–106/89 [1990] ECR I–4135, Report for the Hearing, I–4142.

[83] Ibid, para 8 (emphasis added).

[84] Cf e.g. Joined Cases C–240/98 and C–244/98 *Océano* [2000] ECR I–4941, Case C–386/00 *Axa Royal Belge* [2002] ECR I–2209 and Case C–462/99, *Connect Austria* [2003] ECR I–5197. Interestingly, in Case C–269/97 *Engelbrecht* [2000] ECR I-7321 and Case C–327/00 *Santex* [2003] ECR I–1877, the standard expression '*dans toute la mesure du possible*' is translated into 'as far as is at all possible' paras 39 and 63 respectively. In Case C–60/02 *X*, judgment of 7 January, nyr in ECR, the terms are entirely omitted and replaced by the following phrase: '. . . national courts are required to interpret their national law *within the limits set by Community law* . . . ' (para 59, emphasis added). See on this below, Subsection 8.5.2.

[85] Case C–106/89 *Marleasing* [1990] ECR I–4135, paras 9 and 13.

The words 'as far as possible' merely refer to the nature of the judicial function as such and no longer to the methods of construction under national law.[86] Similarly, this approach seems to imply that the question whether the national court is still within the boundaries of its judicial role or not would in the ultimate analysis be a matter of Community law as opposed to national (constitutional) law.[87] Others, however, have argued that 'as far as possible' still includes the national rules of construction.[88]

The Court's far-reaching interference with the way national law had to be interpreted by the Spanish court in *Marleasing* militates in favour of the first point of view. The Court specified in very concrete terms the manner in which the national court had to interpret the relevant provisions of national law in order to comply with the directive and it prohibited the national court from choosing another interpretation.[89] The latitude left to the national court was evidently reduced to zero. In my opinion, however, it would be an over-interpretation of *Marleasing* to conclude that the obligation of consistent interpretation is an *absolute* one, requiring national courts to give effect to directives, whatever the terms and context of the national provisions to be interpreted might be.[90] Such a conclusion would plainly be at odds with the 'possibility for interpretation' put forward by the Court in *Marleasing* itself. The Court's strict wording must be seen within the context of the case. As the Opinion of AG Van Gerven shows, the type of construction of national law desired by the Court of Justice was certainly possible.[91]

Spanish law lacked a specific rule as to the nullity applicable to limited companies. Instead, the general rule for the nullity of contracts applied by analogy. Under this rule, contracts lacking cause or having an unlawful cause have no legal effect. In pursuance of the obligation formulated by the Court of Justice the national judge

---

[86] Cf Curtin 1992, 40, Snijder 1993, 43, Prechal 1991a, 1597. Tanney 1992, 1026 also suggests that national rules of interpretation are no longer relevant. 'Wherever possible' should, in his view, be understood as 'where there is no irreconcilable conflict as a matter of language'.

[87] Cf the discussion in German literature (Spetzler 1991, 579, Dänzer-Vanotti 1991, 754, Di Fabio 1990) as to the question whether consistent interpretation prevails over national methods of interpretation in which the limits of the judicial function play a part. On the nature of judicial function as a limit to consistent interpretation see below, Subsection 8.5.2.

[88] Cf AG Lenz in his Opinion in Case C–331/92 *Gestión Hotelera International* [1994] ECR I–1329, para 15, thus after *Marleasing*. See also Jarass and Beljin 2003, 67 and 162. As to a discussion whether the obligation to consistent interpretation changes the existing methods of interpretation or whether it constitutes a new method which should be given priority, see Ehricke 1995 and Wyatt and Dashwood 2000, 93–5.   [89] Cf Stuyck and Wytinck 1991, 210.

[90] Cf De Búrca 1992, 223 and Wissink 2001, 106. See also Case C–334/92 *Miret* [1993] ECR I–6911, para 22 and Case C–91/92 *Faccini Dori* [1994] ECR I–3325, para 27, where the Court clearly accepts that consistent interpretation is not always possible. For more recent cases see for instance, Case C–111/97 *EvoBus* [1998] ECR I–5411, paras 19–20, and Case C–327/00 *Santex* [2003] ECR I–1877, para 64. Interestingly, in Case C–462/99 *Connect Austria* [2003] ECR I–5197, AG Geelhoed was of the opinion that consistent interpetation was impossible (para 55 of the Opinion). The Court, however, started to remind the referring court that it should try to proceed along this way of consistent interpretation first. Only if that would not work out, then there was the option of 'disapplication'.

[91] Cf also Timmermans 1992, 819 and Rodrigues Iglesias and Riechenberg 1995, 1221–2.

had to interpret the concept of 'unlawful cause' as including only the grounds of nullity listed in the directive at issue.

It is undoubtedly true that the Court's reasoning was not entirely satisfactory in this respect as it did not explain why in this particular case the obligation of consistent interpretation was able to preclude any other interpretation. Similarly, it is arguable that the Court was at the boundaries of its own competence under Article 234, interfering perhaps too much with the construction of national law, when it prescribed how the national court must interpret the national provisions. However, if the judgment is placed within its proper context, *Marleasing* is much less revolutionary than would appear at first sight. It is only unfortunate, that the Court has not always been consistent in the choice of language it uses in order to indicate what the concrete obligation for the national court is.[92] Interestingly, in *Pfeiffer* the reference to interpretative methods under national law reappeared. These methods may, for instance, require that a provision of domestic law be construed in such a way as to avoid conflict with another national law provision. Likewise, they may result in restricting the scope of the national provisions in such a way that there is no conflict with the other rule at issue. If such methods exist, national courts are bound to use them in order to achieve the result sought by the directive.[92A] In *Pfeiffer*, the Court seems to make clear what it has forgotten to do in *Marleasing*: to indicate that the seemingly far-reaching solution is a solution which is still allowed as a matter of national law.

Be this as it may, it seems that national courts are no longer entirely free to determine the parameters of what is 'possible' and what is not. The most obvious example in this respect can—again—be found in the *Marleasing* judgment. If, according to the Court, the obligation of consistent interpretation applies with respect to both national law predating the directive and national law enacted after the directive, the UK rule of 'Community law consistent' construction which was restricted to posterior national provisions only, can obviously no longer apply. In so far as national methods of interpretation apply, under circumstances, they have to be adapted in the light of what Community law requires. Similarly, from *Pfeiffer* it follows that the mere option under national law of using a certain interpretative method becomes an obligation where it helps to avoid a conflict with Community law provisions.[92B]

---

[92] Since Marleasing, strong terms, referring to 'preclusion', show up from time to time also in other cases on consistent interpretation. See, for instance, Case C–421/92 *Habermann-Bertelmann* [1994] ECR I–1657, Case C–456/98 *Centrosteel* [2000] ECR I–6007, Case C–386/00 *Axa Royal Belge* [2002] ECR I–2209 and Joined Cases C–397/01 to C–403/01, *Pfeiffer*, judgment of 5 October 2004, nyr in ECR (national courts must prevent the limits laid down in the directive being exceeded). Cf also Betlem 2002, 82–4. In other cases the Court uses a more mild language, like in Joined Cases C–240/98 and C–244/98 *Océano* [2000] ECR I–4941, para 32, where it found that the national court is required 'to favour' the interpretation in accordance with the directive.

[92A] Joined Cases C–397/01 to C–403/01, *Pfeiffer*, judgment of 5 October 2004, nyr in ECR, para 116.

[92B] Cf for similar construction where an option becomes an obligation, Joined Cases C–430/93 and C–431/93 *Van Schijndel* [1995] ECR I–4705 and Case C–453/00 *Kühne*, judgment of 13 January 2004, nyr in ECR, both discussed above, Ch 7, Subsections 7.3.2 and 7.3.3 respectively.

8.5.2   The limits of the judicial function

In legal writing, as was already indicated in the previous Subsection, it was also
suggested that the terms 'as far as possible' refer to the *limits of the judicial function*
rather than to the national methods of interpretation strictly speaking. Such a
distinction must, indeed, be considered in a proper perspective, since there is a close
relationship between the methods of interpretation and the role courts play or are
supposed to play within a legal system. For instance, reference to the intention of
the legislature and interpretation in accordance with such an intention are evidence
of the respect by the judiciary for the legislative power.

In their comparative analysis of judicial interpretation of statutes Summers and
Taruffo[93] identify eleven basic types of arguments given by judges as reasons
for their decision about the meaning of the text concerned. These constitute
a 'common core of good reasons for interpretative decisions' shared by different
legal systems.[94] The authors describe how the different types of arguments
operate in practice, how they may compete with each other and how the
conflicts between arguments are solved.

The relative weight of the arguments comes to light particularly where two
or more arguments conflict. The courts may then deploy several modes of resolution: on further consideration one of the arguments may be deprived of its
prima facie force and consequently be ignored, one of the arguments may be
subordinated pursuant to a rule or maxim of priority, or it may be 'out-
weighed'. Although there are no clearly formulated priority rules in the
event of conflict between the various arguments,[95] MacCormick and
Summers identify a number of values which function as a kind of second-level
or priority criteria guiding the application of the first-level criteria. A crucial
factor which greatly influences the interpretative preference, i.e. the decision
as to the arguments to which priority should be given, is the upholding of the
separation of powers.[96] The relative roles which courts and legislatures play

[93] In MacCormick and Summers 1991, 461 ff. The analysis is based on reports on statutory
interpretations in 9 countries, including Germany, Italy, France, and the UK. Cf also the first edition of
this book, 229–36.

[94] Ibid, 3. This typology of arguments runs partly parallel to what are in some countries known as
canons of interpretation or principles of interpretational method, such as literal/grammatical/semiotic
interpretation, historical interpretation, systemic/schematic intepretation, teleological interpretation on
the one hand, and special types of legal arguments or techniques of interpretation, such as reasoning by
analogy or *a contrario* on the other. The various distinctions and classifications are indeed a matter of legal
methodology which varies between the countries concerned, and even within one single country often
no consensus exists. Cf MacCormick and Summers 1991, e.g. 77, 82, 89, and 179.

[95] Cf also Dänzer-Vanotti 1991 and Spetzler 1991. In some systems, however, there exist some legal
norms which should discipline interpretation. Cf Art 1 of the Spanish Civil Code and the 'preliminary
provisions' of the Italian Civil Code (cf MacCormick and Summers 1991, 231). Cf also for international
law Vienna Convention Arts 31–33.

[96] MacCormick and Summers 1991, 534. Cf also De Lange 1991, Ch 7.

within the constitutional framework have a considerable impact on the outcome of the process of interpretation. While in some countries the courts are prepared to go quite a long way,[97] in other countries they may seek to 'protect and preserve a constitutional balance of powers by generally taking a relatively restrictive approach to statutory interpretation'.[98] It is no exception for the courts to admit in explicit terms that, in certain cases, the limits of their function within the legal system have been reached.[99]

As a matter of principle, national courts are obliged to give effect to the directive through interpretation. No particular problems are to be expected, from the perspective of the separation of powers, where the directive has actually been implemented or where pre-existing legislation is deemed to satisfy the requirements posed by the directive. The obligation of consistent interpretation will 'point in the same direction' as the intention of the legislature or at least the presumption may operate that the legislature intended to comply with the directive. Moreover, there will usually exist a national provision which, from the linguistic point of view, will not be too remote. Matters are different in a situation of conflict, for instance, if it appears from *travaux préparatoires* that the legislature's intention was different from the directive and, moreover, where this difference in views shows clearly from the words employed in the statute.[100] Isn't it after all the legislator who makes and unmakes the law and isn't it the judge's duty to interpret and apply it but not to 'rewrite' it? Interestingly, in a recent judgment the Court pointed out that the obligation to interpret national law so far as possible in the light of the wording and the purpose of a directive applies '. . . notwithstanding any contrary interpretation which may arise from the *travaux préparatoires* for the national rule'.[101]

From the perspective of the *doctrine of separation of powers*, which, indeed, includes the question of the limits of the judicial function under discussion here,[102] the key question can be put as follows: can the interpretative role assigned to the courts under the doctrine of consistent interpretation carry them beyond the judicial function as accepted under national law? The cases decided so far by the Court of Justice are not very helpful in this respect.

Indeed, 'as far as possible' might be read as meaning 'as long as the judge can do that *as judge*', i.e. without becoming a legislator or without usurping the

---

[97] Although this does not always happen in an overt manner. For instance French judges disclaim any interpretative role, as in their view law-making is entirely an issue for the legislature which is the democratically elected organ of the people (MacCormick and Summers 1991, 503); that, however, does not mean that they do not interpret, sometimes even in a manner which may appear to be *contra legem* (ibid, 192).

[98] Ibid, 396 (the quotation relates to the UK).

[99] De Lange 1991, 191–4, Bell and Engle 1987, 22–3.

[100] Cf Galmot and Bonichot 1988, 22 who point out the paradox that incorrect but ambiguous implementation can to a certain extent be corrected by the domestic court whereas in the case of a clear and unambiguous violation the court is powerless; indeed, as long as the deficiency cannot be remedied by direct effect.   [101] Case C–371/02 *Björnekulla*, judgment of 29 April 2004, nyr in ECR, para 13.

[102] And which makes clear that consistent interpretation should be ultimately perceived as a constitutional matter. Cf De Búrca 1992, 240.

powers of the executive.[103] However, it says nothing about the question as to the standards—national or Community—according to which this function must be considered and, moreover, it is common knowledge that the role of the judiciary differs from Member State to Member State.[104]

Another indication might be sought in the terms 'for matters within their jurisdiction'. The *Von Colson* formula, which was reiterated in other cases, holds that 'for matters within their jurisdiction', the national courts are under the obligation of consistent interpretation. This formulation may suggest that reference is made to jurisdiction in the narrow sense, i.e. the competence of the court to hear and decide the case before it.[105] However, the term 'jurisdiction' can also have a wider meaning, connoting the limits of the exercise of a court's power in general, including the fashion in which it is allowed to interpret the law. Furthermore, when one considers versions of *Von Colson* in other languages, the terminology is perhaps even more ambiguous. In German it says '*im Rahmen ihrer Zuständigkeiten*', in Dutch '*binnen het kader van hun bevoegdheden*', in French '*dans le cadre de leurs compétences*'. A more appropriate English translation of these terms would be, in my view, 'within the framework of their competence'. In his Opinion in *Faccini Dori* Advocate General Lenz argued that '*dans le cadre de leurs compétences*' does indeed refer to the limits of interpretation and not merely to jurisdiction in the strict sense of the term.[106] Be this as it may, in my opinion, for the time being, neither the terminology employed nor the context indicate clearly the type of jurisdiction the Court had in mind.

Are there other reasons to believe that the qualification 'as far as possible' does *not* require the national courts to disregard the limits of what is considered to be their judicial function within the national legal order?

The way in which Community law influences the position of national courts and seems to lead to a kind of 'direct empowerment' was described in Chapter 7, Subsection 7.4.1. The advocates of this development tend to employ an argument which can be summarized, in somewhat over simplified terms, as follows: the national judge in his function of Community law judge should be freed of all the constraints resulting from national law which prevent him from giving full effect to Community law. Whatever the merits of this position might be, in my view it is not a matter of course that similar considerations, taking the courts beyond their powers under national law, should apply with respect to consistent interpretation.

---

[103] Cf Curtin 1992, 40. As to the relationship between judicial function and interpretation see also Jarass 1991a, 218.   [104] Cf Mead 1991, 500. See also MacCormick and Summers 1991, 496–508.

[105] As a rule this meaning of 'jurisdiction' refers to four different aspects: authority to deal with the subject-matter of the dispute, authority over the persons, authority *ratione loci*, and power to give the kind of relief sought. Cf De Smith and Brazier 1989, 553 and Stroud's Judicial Dictionary 1986, 1379. Cf also above Ch 7, Subsection 7.2.1, in particular where the *Simmenthal* judgment is briefly commented upon.

[106] Case C–91/92 [1994] ECR I–3325, para 37 of the Opinion. Cf already in 1988 and 1991 Richter, 396 and Jarass 216.

Firstly, the fact remains that what is being interpreted is *still* national law. This is, in my opinion, a different matter from the application of directly effective Community norms, and where appropriate, the setting aside of provisions or principles of national law, as was the issue in cases like *Simmenthal* and *Factortame*.[107]

Secondly, it is highly disputable what the basis of an enlargement of the judicial function should be. Neither Articles 249(3) and 10 of the Treaty, on which the obligation of consistent interpretation is based, nor the principle of supremacy of Community law can, in my view, serve as a basis for extending the interpretative powers of national courts and thus changing their judicial function.

Thirdly, even if one should accept that national courts are empowered on the basis of Community law to transcend the limits of their function, where should the new limits then lie? The answer seems to be simple: in Community law, as laid down by the Court of Justice. However, I wonder whether, in the final analysis, this would make much difference. The 'common core of good reasons for interpretative decisions' is shared equally, for evident reasons, by the Court of Justice itself. Indeed, it is common understanding that the Court, in its interpretative role, often goes considerably further than the courts of the Member States. This is to be attributed to the very nature of Community law.[108] As a consequence the weight given to the distinct arguments differs from that which is usual in national legal systems and may cause a shift of priorities between them.[109] Consequently, it is not self-evident that the same 'dynamic' approach will also hold true for interpretation of national law.

Yet, there are also some indications that the effect of the doctrine of consistent interpretation may go in the direction of requiring national courts to stretch the boundaries of what is considered, under their national law, as a matter of judicial function.[110]

8.5.3   General principles of law

To the possible limits suggested in the literature, the Court has added general principles of law.[111] These principles were referred to in the *Kolpinghuis* judgment where the Court of Justice held that

[the] obligation on the national court to refer to the content of the directive when interpreting the relevant rules of its national law is limited by the general principles of law

---

[107] Case 106/77 [1978] ECR 629 and Case C–213/89 [1990] ECR I–2433.

[108] Cf Brown and Jacobs 2000, 322–4.

[109] On 'dynamic criteria' see Bengoetxea 1990, in particular 251–62.

[110] Cf above, Subsection 8.5.1. Interestingly, in German legal writing a distinction is made between '*richtlinienkonforme Auslegung*', which is a matter of interpretation, and '*richtlinienkonforme Rechtsfortbildung*', which refers to the judicial development of the law, which is within certain limits allowed in Germany and still considered to be within the bounds of the judicial function. Cf on this, e.g. Von Bogdandy 2002, 21, and for a detailed and theoretical discussion, Canaris 2002.

[111] Moreover, according to some, the Court has also accepted in Case C–168/95 *Arcaro* [1996] ECR I–4705 the imposition of an obligation on individuals as another limit to consistent interpretation. See on this below, Section 8.6.

which form part of Community law and in particular the principles of legal certainty and non-retroactivity.[112]

This quotation from the Court's judgment immediately gives rise to two questions: firstly, to what general principles of law is the Court referring, national or Community law principles? Secondly, which general principles of law function as limits to consistent interpretation in addition to the principle of legal certainty and the principle of non-retroactivity?

The answer to the first question is not entirely unproblematic. It has been argued that the principles to which the Court makes reference are Community law principles.[113] This would imply that their content and scope is entirely determined by Community law itself. An argument for this proposition could be that the obligation of consistent interpretation, being an obligation stemming directly from Community law, can only be limited by Community law principles. On the other hand, as was observed in Chapter 2, Section 2.5, according to well-established case law, the Court allows the application of national general principles of law which are deemed to be a part of the legal order of the Community. However, the application of such national principles is not unlimited—they cannot go beyond what that principle requires under Community law. Thus their interpretation and application is ultimately subjected to the control of the Court of Justice. The difference between the application of Community law principles and national principles in their 'curtailed' form is mainly theoretical. The practical implications are rather limited. In the first situation, i.e. the application of general principles of Community law, the national judge has to ascertain the existence of such a principle and, furthermore, how it is to be applied. In the second situation he can take the national principles as a point of departure and should subsequently discern whether the content given to the principle in national law and its way of application is permitted under Community law. The different approaches may often lead to subtle but nonetheless distinct results.

In relation to the second question, the Court's judgment in *Kolpinghuis* clearly suggests that principles other than those of legal certainty and non-retroactivity may also come into play.

It is, indeed, not my intention to review all the principles now accepted by the Court of Justice as general principles of Community law[114] or all the possible candidates for consideration as principles which form part of Community law and which could serve as limits to consistent interpretation. By way of example, I shall mention unjust enrichment, equity, equality, and perhaps also

---

[112] Case 80/86 [1987] ECR 3969, para 13., recently confirmed in Case C–60/02 *X*, judgment of 7 January 2004, nyr in ECR. As such the reference to such principles is nothing revolutionary. On interpretative arguments appealing to general legal principles see Summers and Taruffo 1991, 467–9.

[113] Cf Timmermans 1988, 334.

[114] For a brief overview of general principles of Community law see e.g. Schermers and Waelbroeck 2001, 28–133 or, comprehensively, Tridimas 1999.

proportionality. It should not be excluded *a priori* that consistent interpretation may, under certain circumstances, amount to unjust enrichment of a legal subject or to a result which can be considered inequitable or as violating the principle of equality. Similarly, it is conceivable that the national court, when it proceeds to consistent interpretation, could achieve a result which on further consideration is disproportionate to the objective pursued by the directive or by the specific provision of a directive which serves as a standard for interpretation. Perhaps this case had best be labelled a case of 'consistent over-interpretation'.

In the *Kolpinghuis* judgment itself two other principles were implicitly—and in later case law explicitly—recognized as limiting the obligation of consistent interpretation, namely *nulla poena sine lege* and *nullum crimen sine lege*.[115] Both principles can be regarded as underlying the prohibition of retroactivity of criminal law.[116] The proceedings against *Kolpinghuis* were criminal proceedings. It would be incompatible with both principles if consistent interpretation effectively 'created' a new criminal offence or increased criminal liability.[117] In two later cases the Court added a reference to Article 7 of the ECHR.[118]

The matters are indeed different outside the sphere of criminal law. Although there too the rule is non-retroactivity, the principle is less absolute and under certain circumstances exceptions are allowed.[119]

Another principle of criminal law which could come into play as a limit to consistent interpretation is the presumption of innocence, the principle of *nulla poena sine culpa*.[120] In Chapter 5, Section 5.4, the case of Mrs Dekker[121] was briefly mentioned. In this case, the requirement of fault and absence of grounds of exemption applicable under the Dutch law on civil liability had to be disregarded as a direct consequence of the interpretation of Directive 76/207 (equal treatment at work)[122] given by the Court of Justice. Theoretically, in

---

[115] Cf Joined Cases C–74/95 and C–129/95 *X* [1996] ECR I–6609 and Case C–60/02 *X*, judgment of 7 January 2004, nyr in ECR.

[116] Cf Case 63/83 *Kent Kirk* [1984] ECR 2689 and the Opinion of AG Jacobs in Joined Cases C–206/88 and C–207/88 *Vessoso and Zanetti* [1990] ECR I–1461, para 25. Cf also Art 7 of the ECHR.

[117] Cf Case 80/86 [1987] ECR 3969, para 13, confirmed in Case C–168/95 *Arcaro* [1996] ECR I–4705 and Joined Cases C–74/95 and C–129/95 *X* [1996] ECR I–6609.

[118] Joined Cases C–74/95 and C–129/95 *X* [1996] ECR I–6609 and Case C–60/02 *X*, judgment of 7 January 2004, nyr in ECR.. Cf also Case C–58/02 *Commission v. Spain*, judgment of 7 January 2004, nyr in ECR, where the Court pointed out that the interpretation of the Spanish criminal code in accordance with the directive cannot fill the gaps in implementation without breaching the principles of legality and legal certainty.

[119] Cf Case C–331/88 *Fedesa* [1990] ECR I–4023. Moreover, not in every criminal case does the issue of '*nulla poene/nullum crimen*' arise. See e.g. Case C–373/90 *X* [1992] ECR I–131, discussed briefly hereabove in Section 8.3, where consistent interpretation worked out more in favour of the suspect than to his disadvantage.   [120] Cf Art 6(2) ECHR.

[121] Case C–177/88 [1990] ECR I–3941.   [122] [1976] OJ L39/40.

criminal proceedings the same may occur as well: the requirement of proof of
fault on the part of the person concerned may, through the interpretation in
conformity with a directive, turn into a system of strict criminal liability.
Whether this is allowed or not will in the final analysis depend on the question
as to how far certain restrictions of this principle are admitted.[123]

Returning to *Kolpinghuis*, the Court's explicit reference to legal certainty did not
just appear out of the blue. On the one hand, to put it simply, interpretation is about
giving a meaning to a legal provision which the judge applies to a particular situation.[124] On the other hand, the concept of legal certainty implies that the application of the law to a specific situation must be predictable.[125] This implies that,
depending on the circumstances and, in particular, on its wording, a rule cannot be
construed as bearing a meaning which would fly in the face of the meaning one
may expect the rule to have.[126]

This is perhaps somewhat oversimplified: firstly, because construction of rules
may be a rather complicated operation; secondly, because the concept of legal
certainty is very wide and encompasses various sub-concepts, such as
non-retroactivity, vested rights, and legitimate expectations. For these reasons, the
search for an appropriate meaning of a provision which does not offend against
legal certainty is anything but unproblematic. To gain a more precise impression
as to the manner in which legal certainty could limit consistent interpretation
would require a study of the application and interpretation of the concept in all
its various manifestations. However, this would be fairly beyond the scope of the
present book. Suffice it to observe that, in any case, one cannot just transplant
the interpretation and application of the concept in a certain context to another
one. For example, what legal certainty requires in the area of implementation of
directives[127] is not equally valid for the purposes of consistent interpretation,
since there the function of legal certainty is different. Similarly, while in the case
law on proper implementation of directives and on horizontal direct effect there
exists a fiction that individuals are not aware of their existence, in other cases and
situations the existence of a directive is considered a relevant element.[128]

[123] Cf Prechal 1991b, 669. As to strict criminal liability see the Opinion of AG Van Gerven in
Case C–326/88 *Hansen* [1990] ECR I–2911.   [124] Cf Marsh 1973, 20.
[125] Cf Schermers and Waelbroeck 2001, 64. Cf also with respect to Community legislation Case
70/83 *Kloppenburg* [1984] ECR 1075: 'Community legislation must be unequivocal and its application
must be predictable for those who are subject to it' (para 11).
[126] Cf AG Van Gerven who wondered in Joined Cases C–63/91 and C–64/91 *Jackson and Creswell*
[1992] ECR I–4737, para 29, whether the obligation of consistent interpretation also applies to a national
rule which is clear and, as such, not susceptible to differing interpretations. However, in his Opinion in
Case C–271/91 *Marshall II* [1993] ECR I–4367, para 10, he disapproved of such an obligation as it would
amount to an interpretation *contra legem* and, consequently, as I will argue below, infringe the principle
of legal certainty.   [127] Cf Ch 5, Sections 5.2 and 5.3.
[128] In *Barber* (Case C–262/88 [1990] ECR I–1889), for instance, the existence of the relevant directive
played a role in accepting that the legal certainty of the parties concerned as to the scope of Art 119

Another implication of the principle of legal certainty is that no interpretation of national law in accordance with the directive can take place if the facts of the case at issue are situated within a period *before* the relevant directive was adopted.[129]

One of the limitations of consistent interpretation which is usually brought forward is the prohibition of interpreting national law *contra legem*.[130] Interpretation *contra legem* in this context seems to denote giving national provisions a meaning which clearly deviates from an initial (literal) reading of the provisions concerned. As a rule, in a case of this kind the wording as such cannot be stretched sufficiently far, but nevertheless the courts choose the deviating meaning. This prohibition can also be considered as deriving from the principle of legal certainty. Interpretation *contra legem* affects, almost by its very nature, legal certainty in the sense of predictability of the law, and from this point of view it is fully understandable that the prohibition should in principle apply as a limitation in the field of consistent interpretation. Yet, in my view, the categoric manner in which this argument is generally presented is slightly surprising. Although within the national legal systems *contra legem* interpretation is certainly not a daily occurence, there are instances where the national courts arrive at such a result.[131] The prohibition is apparently not sacrosanct. Moreover, in the same line of argument, it should be observed that—in practice—legal certainty is a rather flexible principle which may, depending on the circumstances, allow various interpretations and which does not have to be safeguarded at all costs. Therefore, in my opinion, the possibility that in certain (exceptional) circumstances consistent interpretation will amount to or will require interpretation of national law *contra legem* should not be excluded.[132]

deserved protection and in *Fedesa* (Case C–331/88 [1990] ECR I–4023) the probable knowledge of those concerned regarding the content of the directive at issue blocked their argument drawing on the principle of protection of legitimate expectations. Cf also the Opinion of AG VerLoren van Themaat in *Kloppenburg* (Case 70/83 [1984] ECR 1075, 1093). In a judgment of 20 May 1992 the Court of Appeals in Brussels interpreted national law in conformity with a directive 86/653 (self-employed agents) [1986] OJ L382/17. The Court dismissed an argument drawing on legal certainty. In its view the parties concerned could have had knowledge of the changes to be introduced in national legislation, since the first draft of the directive dated from 1977 and the final text was adopted in 1986. Cf Devloo 1993–1994, 380.

[129] Cf Van Gerven 1993, 11. For this very reason the *Hoge Raad* refused to interpret the *Benelux Merkenwet* in conformity with Directive 89/104 (trade mark) [1989] OJ L40/1, in *Michelin v. Michels*, 17 December 1993, Rechtspraak NJB 1994/2, 14. A case where a national court (*Rechtbank van Koophandel Namen*) did interpret the *Benelux Merkenwet* in accordance with the directive is briefly discussed by Devloo 1993–1994, 380.

[130] Cf Galmot and Bonichot 1988, 22, Van Gerven 1993, 10, Curtin 1992, 40, Wissink 2001, 201, 206, Jann and Schima 2003, 285. See, for instance, also AG Saggio in Joined Cases C–240/98 and C–244/98 *Océano* [2000] ECR I–4941, para 28 and AG Jacobs in Case C–456/98 *Centrosteel* [2000] ECR I–6007, para 32.   [131] Cf MacCormick and Summers 1991, 93, 181 and 191.

[132] Cf also Timmermans 1997, 23. In academic writing the question has been raised whether the obligation of consistent interpretation as laid down by the Court of Justice in Marleasing in fact interferes with the principle of legal certainty or results in interpretation *contra legem*, as the case may be. Cf Betlem 1993, 250, Stuyck and Wytinck 1991, 211, Keus 1993, 65, De Búrca 1992, 229. For a brief discussion of this point see the first edition of this book, at 228.

Legal certainty as a limitation to the obligation of consistent interpretation is certainly not surprising. The maintenance of the principle of legal certainty is undoubtedly one of the major concerns of courts when interpreting the law.[133] As was already pointed out, the incorporation of this concept by the Court of Justice into the doctrine of consistent interpretation consequently means that the ultimate boundaries of the concept and its application are under the control of the Court of Justice.

The final subject which I would like to address briefly in the present Subsection is the following: as a rule, general principles of law constituting limitations to consistent interpretation are discussed in relation to the *obligation* of the domestic court. Viewed from this perspective, they are a kind of 'safety net' which should prevent the courts being forced to go to unacceptable lengths. A related question is whether the principles can also forbid the domestic courts to arrive at a certain interpretation which is still within the limits of their respective national legal systems and which they believe to be a consistent interpretation under Community law, but which, from a Community point of view, would not be acceptable. It is submitted that the answer to this question should be affirmative. The domestic courts are here operating within the context of Community law. For this very reason Community law, and especially Article 10 of the Treaty, may not only require them to do something positive but may also stop them if they should transcend the limits of what is considered as acceptable under Community law. This is, in my opinion, also the consideration behind the—at first sight—somewhat surprising phrase of the Court in Case C–60/02, where it held that '. . . national courts are required to interpret their national law *within the limits set by Community law* . . . '.[134] When proceeding with consistent interpretation in a criminal case, the national court must observe the limit imposed, in that particular case, by the principle of non-retroactivity of penalties, as enshrined in Article 7 ECHR.[135]

8.5.4   Limits: a summary

If the national court is under the obligation to proceed 'as far as possible' with consistent interpretation, the minimum that should and certainly can be required is that judges *must under all circumstances take due account* of the relevant (provisions of the) directive.[136] In this way the directive becomes one of the—rather compelling—

---

[133] Ultimately, the issue of legal certainty can also be linked to the rule of law, as MacCormick and Summers do, in so far as the rule of law requires reasonable generality, clarity, and constancy in the law; a rational and reasonably well-informed citizen should be able to understand it. See MacCormick and Summers 1991, 535.

[134] Case C–60/02 *X*, judgment of 7 January 2004, nyr in ECR, para 59 (emphasis added).

[135] This is perfectly in line with well-established case law according to which Member States must observe fundamental rights when implementing Community law or acting within its scope.

[136] Cf also Everling 1992b, 381 and Wissink 2001, 143 ff.

arguments available for giving a certain meaning to the national text at issue. Likewise, the argument drawing on the directive can be deployed to raise an issue of interpretation or to undermine other possible interpretations of the law. Although this may in fact seem rather obvious, giving consideration to the directive is already an achievement when one realizes that, for instance in the UK, courts do, in principle, not look beyond the statute unless the text is ambiguous. There is an important difference between, on the one hand, looking to see whether national law is ambiguous and only in the case of an affirmative answer turning to the directive, and, on the other hand, giving proper consideration to the directive first and then seeking to interpret national law accordingly.[137]

The matters become more complicated where consistent interpretation has to compete with other possible interpretations. How strong is the 'fire-power'[138] of the argument based on the directive and the obligation to proceed to consistent interpretation? In other words, how much weight does the argument that a certain interpretation would bring national law in line with the directive, carry? The national court should make a special—maximum—effort: it should go as far as possible. Yet, 'as far as possible' remains an intriguing concept in this respect. It may require to depart, to a certain extent, from national rules of construction. It may imply for the national court to 'stretch' the limits of its judicial function as it exists in the national legal system. It should, in any case, be understood as *within the limits of the general principles of law*', in particular legal certainty. In other words, although what is possible and what not lies primarily in the hands of national courts, they are not totally free, but operate under the control of—or it is perhaps better to say in the context of dialogue with—the Court of Justice, which may be quite demanding.[139]

The limits to consistent interpretation discussed in the present Section are interrelated. Obviously, the need for safeguarding legal certainty will stand out wherever the terms of the national provision to be interpreted are clear. If constraints are imposed by clear language, a statute cannot be interpreted in terms of a meaning which its words do not sustain. This factor must be respected by the Court if it wishes to uphold legal certainty.[140] Linguistic arguments are then likely to take priority over arguments based on the directive. However, even when the 'sparkling clarity' is missing, other arguments, such as legislative intention (however conceived) and the legislative context, are highly relevant elements for the predictability of the law and

---

[137] Cf also Curtin 1990a, 222.   [138] MacCormick and Summers 1991, p 511.

[139] Cf also Wissink 2001, 106, who points out that the Court requires, from the national courts, an 'active attitude' and efforts to explore new ways of interpretation of national law.

[140] As MacCormick and Summers 1991, 481–2, 533, 464, 466 have made clear, legal certainty will often militate in favour of a linguistic approach to the text. In particular, linguistic arguments in particular seem to be relatively more difficult to set aside, or relatively less frequently subordinated by virtue of a rule of priority, or relatively more difficult to outweigh than other arguments. Cf also Case 80/76 *Kerry Milk* [1977] ECR 425: 'the elimination of linguistic discrepancies by way of interpretation may . . . run counter to the concern for legal certainty, in as much as one or more texts involved may have to be interpreted in a manner at variance with the natural and usual meaning of the words' (para 11).

they must therefore be taken into account when considering the question of legal certainty. Similarly, the usual methods of construction and 'what one may expect from a court' within a given legal system may, in turn, also play a part in this context.

Apart from some broad and not always very helpful *dicta*, the appropriate answer regarding possibility and impossibility can only be given in the context of a concrete case. Legal certainty as an abstract concept has no reality. Its content must be attributed in every concrete case. In order to do this, on the one hand, the Court of Justice must give proper consideration to the issues arising under national law.[141] Comparable considerations hold equally true for the limits of the judicial function within a certain context and the methods of interpretation. On the other hand, there is also an important task for the referring court. As it is national law which must be interpreted, the national court is in a better position than the Court of Justice to oversee the possibilities offered by the text and context. Therefore, in order to get helpful guidance, the court should explain clearly and in detail the problems it is facing and all the other relevant factors involved.

8.6   Effects of consistent interpretation

The most obvious effect of consistent interpretation is that a provision of national law is given a meaning which it would not necessarily have had but for the directive.

In certain situations, which I have described as judicial implementation, the result achieved by consistent interpretation will be more or less 'natural'; i.e. the domestic court's approach will follow the normal methods of construction accepted under its national law. This process can perhaps be described as rendering explicit a meaning which was already implicit.

In cases of consistent interpretation in the sense of remedial interpretation, the interpretation must bridge the gap between national law and the directive. In this process, the meaning or scope of an application of the relevant provisions of domestic law may be extended or, to the contrary, it may be narrowed down, sometimes almost to zero. The very nature of this activity is attributing a meaning and scope to a provision of national law which it did not have before or which it certainly would not have had if only considerations of national law were taken into account. It is in this second type of situation in particular that the concerns for legal certainty and, where appropriate, separation of powers, will emerge most sharply.

Furthermore, it must be stressed that consistent interpretation in the context of judicial implementation and remedial interpretation, when considered from the point of view of the interpretative efforts to be made by the domestic court, is not a matter of black and white. There is a large grey area in between.

Be this as it may, it is important to point out that in all situations it is *national law* that will be applied to the case concerned at the end of the day and not

---

[141] Cf also Rodriguez Iglesias and Riechenberg 1995, 1221–9, and Jann and Schima 2003, 284.

Community law. The latter merely gives direction to the meaning of national provisions.[142]

One of the major concerns which can be discerned in both academic writing and legal practice as to the effects produced by consistent interpretation relates to the question whether interpretation of a national provision in conformity with the directive can amount to *de facto* (horizontal) direct effect of the directive.[143] In particular, the main issue is whether national law, interpreted in accordance with the directive, can impose obligations upon individuals. The considerations underlying this discussion are clearly prompted by the paradox that, on the one hand, according to the Court of Justice, directives cannot impose obligations upon private persons, while, on the other hand, this result would be reached through interpretation of national law. Some authors have suggested in this respect that if interpretation in conformity with the directive amounts to such a result, the limits of consistent interpretation have been reached.[144] The same idea can also be found in national case law.[145] Other authors, however, consider consistent interpretation as a judicial technique which can help to overcome the limitations of the Court's case law on (horizontal) direct effect of directives,[146] while yet others warn against considering consistent interpretation a viable alternative for the absence of horizontal direct effect or inverse vertical direct effect of directives.[147]

Certainly, it cannot be denied that there is something rather hypocritical about obliging a domestic court to secure by interpretation a result which cannot be achieved owing to the Court's own case law. However, this is not necessarily in itself a decisive argument against consistent interpretation of national law which amounts to imposing obligations upon individuals.

In Chapter 4, Section 4.1, it was briefly mentioned that it is not entirely clear what the Court means by stating that 'a directive may not of itself impose obligations on

---

[142] Cf the Opinion of AG Van Gerven in Case C–106/89 *Marleasing* [1990] ECR I–4135 and Timmermans 1997, 23. In this respect it seems that there is still a lot of misunderstanding. See e.g. Rodière (1991, 575) who argues on the basis of the *Dekker* judgment: '*L'employeur est considéré par la Cour de justice comme tenu de respecter les impératifs de la directive*' which was obviously not the case. The employer was bound by the provisions of the Civil Code. Cf also Langenfeld 1991, 179.

[143] Cf De Búrca 1992, 231, Stuyck and Wytinck 1991, 210, Coppel 1994, 878, Swaak 1996, Craig 1997, 526–8, Tridimas 2002, 346–53 and Betlem 2002, 88–90 and 96–8. Cf also Gilliams 2000, 228 who points out that in the context of consistent interpretation it is *de facto* the directive that is relied on and national law is merely the instrument to impose the obligation.

[144] Cf Lauwaars 1993, 707, Keus 1993, 60.

[145] Cf e.g. *Finnegan v. Clowney Youth Training Programme Ltd*, House of Lords [1990] 2 CMLR 859 and reference in the Dutch FIDE Report 1998, at 343–5.

[146] Cf Curtin 1992, 40–1, Prechal 1990, 470, Wissink 2001, 216. Moreover, I cannot resist mentioning another, highly paradoxical, advantage of consistent interpretation pointed out by *commissaire du gouvernement* Hagelsteen in the case of '*Cercle militaire mixte de la caserne Mortier*', 22 December 1989, AJDA 1990, 328. Mrs Hagelsteen, in trying to convince the *Conseil d'Etat* to interpret Art 256B of the *Code générale des Impôts* in accordance with the Sixth VAT Directive, referred to the notorious *Cohn-Bendit* case law and said: '*Mais, précisément, le fait que votre jurisprudence ne reconnaisse pas un tel effet* [i.e. direct effect] *aux directives constitue une raison de plus . . . de faire l'effort d'interprétation . . .*'.

[147] Cf Timmermans 1992, 820. For the two concepts see below, Chapter 9, Subsection 9.5.2.

an individual'. Moreover, as will be discussed in more detail in relation to direct effect, the Court seems to accept that a directive may affect the position of a private party, although the exact scope of such a 'permitted' negative effect is far from plain.[148]

Comparable considerations arise in the context of consistent interpretation. Also in this area the same questions arise, namely what is the difference between the 'imposition of obligations' and negative or detrimental effects for a person's legal position and, further, whether it is feasible to distinguish between the two.[149]

> For instance, it has been pointed out that in *Marleasing*,[150] on the one hand, the directive did not impose any positive obligation on the company concerned,[151] but, on the other hand, the judgment resulted in an indirect enforcement of the directive against it.[152]
>
> A few years later, in *Arcaro*, the Court suggested that '[the] obligation of the national court to refer to the content of the directive when interpreting the relevant rules of its own national law reaches a limit where such an interpretation leads to the imposition on an individual of an obligation laid down by a directive which has not been transposed . . .'.[153] Although, at first sight, this case could be understood as a recognition by the Court of Justice of *de facto* horizontal effect being the limit to consistent interpretation, such a reading of the case goes too far. In the first place, *Arcaro* must be put in the limited context of criminal liability and should therefore be interpreted restrictively.[154] More importantly, cases decided after *Arcaro* make plain that consistent interpretation may still result in imposing obligations on individuals or, at least, adversely affect their legal position, as was, for instance, the case in *Océano* and *Centrosteel*.[155]

In *Pfeiffer*, while referring to the interpretative methods under national law, the ultimate result sought by the Court was a disapplication of the national rules which were contrary to the directive. Indeed, this boils down to an exclusionary direct effect in the context of private litigation which is, as such, highly disputed, if not prohibited.[155A]

---

[148] See below, Ch 9, Subsection 9.5.3.

[149] Cf Wissink 2001, 217–18, Tridimas 2002, 348–9. See for a more detailed discussion Ch 9, Subsection 9.5.3.   [150] Case C–106/89 [1990] ECR I–4135.

[151] See the Opinion of AG Van Gerven, para 8: the problem in *Marleasing* concerned the exclusion of the grounds of nullity as they existed in national law and not an imposition of nullity.

[152] Cf Stuyck and Wytinck 1991, 214. See also Curtin 1992, 40–1.

[153] Case C–168/95 *Arcaro* [1996] ECR I–4705, para 42.

[154] Cf Tridimas 2002, 349 and AG Jacobs in Case C–456/98 *Centrosteel* [2000] ECR I–6007, para 34.

[155] Joined Cases C–240/98 and C–244/98 [2000] ECR I–4941 and Case C–456/98 [2000] ECR I–6007. Cf also Betlem 2002, 88–90 and Case C–386/00 *Axa Royale Belge* [2002] ECR I–2209. Indeed, the same was the case in several cases decided before *Arcaro*, like, for instance, *Harz* (Case 79/83 [1984] ECR 1921), once it had been decided by the competent Labour Court. Cf *Arbeitsgericht Hamburg*, 7 March 1985, DB 1985, 1402. Cf also Jarass 1991a, 222, Langenfeld 1991, 183, and Case C–421/92 *Habermann-Bertelmann* [1994] ECR I–1657, in particular paras 8 and 9.

[155A] Joined Cases C–397/01 to C–403/01, *Pfeiffer*, judgment of 5 October 2004, nyr in ECR. For a discussion of the exclusionary effect, see below, Ch 9, Subsection 9.5.3.

Attempts to redefine the effect of consistent interpretation in terms of direct effect and subsequently to see whether the limits of the doctrine of direct effect of directives have been transgressed, pay insufficient attention to the fundamental difference between direct effect and consistent interpretation. While in the former case it is the provision of the directive that applies directly to the facts of the case, in the latter it is the provision of national law which governs the situation concerned. To this one may add that if the *de facto* horizontal effect as a limit to consistent interpretation would be accepted, it will considerably reduce the potential of this technique to be used as a substitute for horizontal effect of directive provisions, whenever necessary and possible.

Therefore, in my view, national law interpreted and, next, applied in accordance with the directive can, as a matter of principle very well affect the legal position of an individual, as well as impose an obligation upon him.[156] This 'position of principle' is, however, qualified: it should not imply that individuals will be confronted with different types of obligations for which they were in no way prepared.[157] A crucial safeguard is provided in this respect by the general principles of law which serve as a limit to consistent interpretation, and notably by the principle of legal certainty.

Thus the permissibility of the effects of consistent interpretation and, by implication, the permissibility of this interpretative technique itself depends on the interpretation and application of the general principles of law and not on the fact that consistent interpretation may come close to or amount to direct effect of directives. For the time being, the only clear guidance provided so far by the Court concerns the limits of consistent interpretation in criminal proceedings: it may not result in the imposition or aggravation of criminal liability.[158] Similar considerations which militate in favour of restrictive interpretation, thus leaving little space for consistent interpretation, will probably also apply in the field of tax law.[159]

In other branches of law, however, such as general administrative law and civil law, matters are different. No constraints similar to those in criminal or tax law apply here.

As regards civil law, in *Zanetti* Advocate General Jacobs made a distinction between criminal law and civil law.[160] In his view, consistent interpretation 'may have the result that obligations may arise and be enforceable in civil proceedings between private parties which would not result from an interpretation of

---

[156] See also e.g. Timmermans 1997, 23, Jann and Schima 2003, 285.

[157] To a large extent matters are not much different from overruling established case law by the courts. In these cases the courts may provide for some form of protection of legitimate expectations of the persons concerned who relied on a certain meaning of the provisions at issue. This, however, does not preclude that for the future the provisions will bear the 'new' meaning. Cf Everling 1992b, 384.

[158] Cf above, Subsection 8.5.3.

[159] Cf MacCormick and Summers 1991, 474. See, however, *Conseil d'Etat* 22 December 1989, AJDA 1990, 328 (*Cercle militaire mixte de la caserne Mortier*): the *Cercle militaire* had to pay VAT at the end of the day by virtue of the *Code générale des impôts* construed in accordance with the directive. Though in this case, the *Conseil d'Etat* did not need to do violence to the language. For a brief discussion see Dal Farra 1992, 665.

[160] Joined Cases C–206/88 and C–207/88 [1990] ECR I–1461, paras 24–26. Cf also Betlem 1993, 222 ff.

the national legislation taken in isolation'. He points out in particular that in civil law the *nulla poena* rule does not apply. Similarly, in *Centrosteel*, he found that, while consistent interpretation cannot have the effect of determining or aggravating criminal liability, 'it may well lead to the imposition upon an individual of civil liability or a civil obligation which would not otherwise have existed'.[161] On the other hand, in the Opinion of Advocate General Van Gerven, for instance, consistent interpretation could not result in the imposition of a civil sanction such as nullity.[162] Another much discussed case in this respect was *Dekker*.[163] *Dekker* produced a stricter liability for the private employer involved, which differed from liability under national law alone. Therefore, it is perhaps debatable whether the final national judgment is not beyond the limits set by the principle of legal certainty or the principle of equity.[164]

All this should, however, not be understood as implying that in civil law there are no safeguards. Legal certainty and the other principles, depending on the modalities of their interpretation and application, may indeed, also in this area of law, block consistent interpretation.

The last issue to be addressed briefly here is the question as to whether a distinction should be made between, on the one hand, the situation in which an individual invokes the directive for the purposes of consistent interpretation in a dispute with another individual and, on the other hand, the situation in which it is the State that relies on the directive for the purposes of consistent interpretation against a private person. In both situations an obligation may be imposed by national law as the result of consistent interpretation. However, in the first situation it is an individual who seeks to compel obedience, while in the second situation it is the State.

It has been submitted in legal writing that the principle of estoppel which has been introduced by the Court of Justice as a rationale for direct effect of directives[165] should apply in this respect as well.[166] Thus, a State authority may wish to rely on the directive in order to have national law interpreted in a way which will result in affecting the legal position of an individual or imposing an (additional) obligation

---

[161] A–G Jacobs in Case C–456/98 *Centrosteel* [2000] ECR I–6007, para 35. Interestingly, in Case C–60/02 *X*, judgment of 7 January 2004, nyr in ECR, which did not concern a directive but a regulation, the Court transposed explicitly its reasoning from the area of directives; it distinguished, like AG Jacobs in *Centrosteel*, consistent interpretation in the context of civil law, on the one hand, and in the context of criminal law, on the other, and made clear that what was allowed under civil law was not necessarily allowed in the field of criminal law.

[162] Opinion in Case C–106/89 *Marleasing* [1990] ECR I–4135, para 8.

[163] Case C–177/88 [1990] ECR I–3941.

[164] Cf Keus 1993, 67. Furthermore, it should be noted that several authors read in *Dekker* things which, however, upon proper consideration, did not come into play at all before the Court of Justice and, therefore, cannot be considered as decided by the Court. For a more detailed discussion see the first edition of this book, at 243. Another judgment that is going rather far is the one in Joined Cases C–240/98 and C–244/98 *Océano* [2000] ECR I–4941 and, indeed, the judgment in Joined Cases C–397/01 to C–403/01 *Pfeiffer*, judgment of 5 October 2004, nyr in ECR. See Océano Stuyck 2001, in particular 734–5.   [165] Cf below, Ch 9, Subsections 9.2.2 and 9.2.3.

[166] Cf Betlem 1993, 227–9 and Betlem 2002, 96–8.

upon him. This possibility, however, should be blocked for the very reason that the Member State concerned cannot rely for any purposes whatsoever on the directive which it has failed to implement correctly or in time. The same reasoning would probably *mutatis mutandis* hold true in a situation where a State authority, for instance the tax inspectorate, would try to enforce a directive, such as one of the VAT directives, against another national authority, for instance a municipality, or another 'emanation of the State'.

I have doubts about this line of reasoning. Obviously, in cases where consistent interpretation serves as a means of judicial implementation this argument can certainly not hold true. As a rule, in such a case the directive has been implemented correctly and in time. However, even in the case of incorrect implementation or complete non-implementation, some considerations may militate against this suggestion.

Firstly, it is not always obvious whether the measures adopted by the Member State amount to correct implementation or whether they must be dismissed as incorrect. It is, however, only in the latter situation that the Member State should not be allowed to rely on the directive for the purposes of consistent interpretation.

Secondly, the *Kolpinghuis* judgment is so ambiguous in relation to this issue that it may be read as suggesting that such an interpretation of national law in conformity with the directive is allowed in principle, provided that the limits which lie in the general principles of law are observed.

Thirdly, this line of reasoning puts too much emphasis on the role the principle of estoppel plays in the Court's case law. In my opinion, as I will explain below,[167] this role is overestimated.

Finally, this approach overlooks the fact that consistent interpretation means interpretation in the light of the wording and the purpose of the directive. Both the wording and, in particular, the purpose of the directive may intend to impose obligations upon individuals. It has already been noted[168] that Community law is not only concerned with the protection of the rights which individuals derive from it, but also with giving full effect to the rules in question.[169] Often, as has been the situation in the majority of cases decided up to now by the Court, protection and full effect are two sides of the same coin. In some cases, however, the concern for protection of the individual and that for full effect of the rule at issue may lead in opposite directions.[170] In my view, it should not automatically be assumed that the choice made by the Court of Justice will always be to the advantage of the individual. If the terms of national law can bear the meaning construed with the aid of the directive and the general principles of law are observed, there are no grounds for denying an interpretation in conformity with the directive. Consistent interpretation should not *a priori* be excluded for the sole reason that it is public authorities which are relying on the directive for this purpose.

---

[167] Ch 9, Subsection 9.2.3.   [168] Cf above, Ch 7, Section 7.1.

[169] Cf also Langenfeld 1992, 964: '*richtliniekonforme Auslegung . . . dient . . . in hohem Maße der Effektuierung der gemeinschaftlichen Vorgaben*'.   [170] For instance in the field of VAT.

9

Direct effect of directives

9.1 Introduction: a glance at past discussions

Soon after the case law of the Court of Justice on direct effect of Treaty provisions started to develop, the question was raised as to the possible direct effect of directives.[1] As is often the case in any doctrinal controversy, there were opponents of direct effect of directives, as well as advocates thereof and those taking an intermediate position, allowing some sort of 'restricted direct effect' (particularly in order to maintain the distinction between regulations and directives) or, at least, not excluding such an effect *a priori*.[2] Nowadays, it is often forgotten that the case law of the Court on direct effect of directives was preceded by an intensive controversy in academic writing which more or less 'prepared the ground' for the Court's decisions.[3]

The main arguments were as follows:[4] The principal argument of those who denied the possibility of direct effect of directives was primarily based on the text of Article 249 of the Treaty. Firstly, they pointed out that according to paragraph 3 of this Article directives are only binding upon the Member States, which can thus be the only addressees of a directive. Moreover, directives are only binding with respect to the result to be achieved, leaving the choice of form and methods to national authorities. From these elements it would clearly follow that effects for individuals could only arise from the implementing measures. Secondly, they drew attention to the distinction, laid down in Article 249, between regulations and directives. Only the former are directly applicable in each Member State. A recognition of direct effect of directives would blur the distinction between regulations and directives, which would lead to legal uncertainty, affect the principle of special powers, and upset the system of Community acts as laid down in the Treaty.[5]

---

[1] Strictly speaking, it would be more appropriate to speak of 'direct effect of a provision or a number of provisions of a directive', since it is usually not the directive as a whole that has direct effect. Yet, for reasons of convenience, I use the term 'direct effect of directives'.

[2] For overviews of the discussions see e.g. Lauwaars 1973, 32–5, Oldenbourg 1984, 215 ff., Oldenkop 1972, 100, De Ripainsel-Landy and Gérard 1976, 55 ff., Gilsdorf 1966, 163–9, Maresceau 1978, 137–40.

[3] Everling 1984, 97–8.

[4] Cf also the observations of the Commission in Case 9/70 *Grad* [1970] ECR 825, 831–3.

[5] According to some, direct effect of directives amounted to '*application abusive du traité de Rome au profit d'une quasi-législation communautaire*'. Foyer, quoted by Everling 1984, 96.

An additional argument drew on the fact that directives do not have to be published. Direct effect would therefore depend on the chance of whether an individual wishing to invoke the directive was aware of the existence of the directive. This would have repercussions for equality before the law and, again, for legal certainty.

The advocates of direct effect of directives dismissed the above-mentioned arguments as formalistic. They referred to the Court's case law on direct effect of Treaty provisions and argued that it is the nature and the content of the provision concerned which is decisive and not the addressee of the act. They also argued that simply from the fact that Article 249 defines regulations as directly applicable it cannot be deduced that directives cannot have direct effect. Paragraph 3 of Article 249 does not say this explicitly. Moreover, acceptance of direct effect of directives would, in their view, both strengthen the legal protection of individuals and promote integration.

In 1970 the Court delivered judgment in the *Grad* case[6] which, seen in retrospect, decided the issue of direct effect of directives in a positive way. The approach seemed to be confirmed in *SACE*,[7] a few months later. With respect to directives, however, neither *Grad* nor *SACE* clarified the problem entirely. Both cases related to the combined effect of directives and other provisions, namely a decision (*Grad*) and a Treaty provision together with the *Acceleration Decision 66/532*[8] (*SACE*). Moreover, the judgments concerned direct effect of a provision of a directive fixing a deadline. For these reasons they could be considered special cases.

However, from the *Van Duyn* judgment it was deduced that both substantive provisions of directives and directives standing alone may also have direct effect.[9] In this case, the Court reasoned as follows:

If . . . by virtue of the provisions of Article 189 [249] regulations are directly applicable and, consequently, may by their very nature have direct effects, it does not follow from this that other categories of acts mentioned in that Article can never have similar effects. It would be incompatible with the binding effect attributed to a directive by Article 189 [249] to exclude, in principle, the possibility that the obligation which it imposes may be invoked by those concerned. In particular, where the Community authorities have, by directive, imposed on Member States the obligation to pursue a particular course of conduct, the useful effect of such an act would be weakened if individuals were prevented from relying on it before their national courts and if the latter were prevented from taking it into consideration as an element of Community law. Article 177 [234], which empowers national courts to refer to the Court questions concerning the validity and interpretation of all acts of the Community institutions, without distinction, implies furthermore that these acts may be invoked by individuals

---

[6] Case 9/70 [1970] ECR 825, which concerned the direct effect of decisions directed to Member States.   [7] Case 33/70 [1970] ECR 1213.

[8] [1966] OJ 2971.

[9] Case 41/74 [1974] ECR 1337. According to Bebr 1981, 586 this was the decisive case in this respect. Yet, in my opinion, it is arguable that also in *Van Duyn* there was still a link to Article 48 [39] of the E[E]C Treaty. Cf the opinion of AG Mayras, 1355–6.

in the national courts. It is necessary to examine, in every case, whether the nature, general scheme and wording of the provision in question are capable of having direct effects on the relations between Member States and individuals.[10]

The Court thus dismissed the *a contrario* argument and it gave three arguments in support of the thesis that directives may have direct effect: the binding effect attributed to directives in Article 249(3), the useful effect ('*effet utile*') of directives and an argument based on Article 234 of the Treaty. Not surprisingly, the soundness or otherwise of these arguments and, indeed, the further implications of this case law have been discussed at length in legal writing.[11] Whatever the merits of the discussions may have been, the binding nature of directives and *effet utile* remained the leading arguments for direct effect of directives.[12] Moreover, and leaving aside—for the moment—the discussion about the possible horizontal direct effect of directives,[13] ever since *Van Duyn* the question has been no longer whether directives *can* have direct effect but rather *under what circumstances* this may be the case.

   In the next Sections four central issues of the doctrine of direct effect of directives will be discussed, including the developments which have taken place since *Van Duyn*.

9.2   Basis of direct effect of directives

9.2.1   Binding nature of directives

Although the wording of Article 249 is in no way revealing as to the possible direct effect of directives, it is this provision which serves as the basis for such an effect. More particularly, the very fact that Article 249(3) provides that directives are binding made the Court decide to attribute direct effect to directives, provided that certain conditions are met.

   Considered in isolation, it is not self-evident that the binding nature should entail the possibility of direct effect. After all, as pointed out by Hartley,[14] a measure can be fully binding at an inter-State level without being enforceable in national courts by individuals. However, from the Court's conception of Community law as articulated in *Van Gend en Loos* it follows that directives are considered an integral part of the legal systems of the Member States.[15] Seen against this background, the Court's position, according to which 'the binding nature of a directive . . . constitutes

---

[10]   Case 41/74 [1974] ECR 1337, para 12.
[11]   Cf Hartley 2003, 207–9, Dashwood 1978, 240–2, Grabitz 1971, 7–14 (on *Grad*), Bebr 1981, 586 ff., Easson 1979, 325 ff.
[12]   The not very convincing Art 234 argument disappeared quickly. See e.g. Case 51/76 *VNO* [1977] ECR 113.   [13]   See below, Subsection 9.5.2.
[14]   Hartley 2003, 207.   [15]   Cf above, Ch 6, Section 6.1.

the basis for the possibility of relying on the directive before a national court . . .',[16] is easier to understand.

Moreover, the Court added another important argument, namely the useful effect or effectiveness of directives.[17] Often, the—what is often called—'principle of useful effect' is considered as a basis of direct effect of directives. It must be noted, however, that useful effect is not a substantive principle. It is merely a rule of interpretation which requires that 'preference should be given to the construction which gives the rule its fullest effect and maximum practical value'.[18] Seen against this background it is not useful effect as such which is the basis of direct effect of directives but rather Article 249(3) interpreted according to the interpretational rule of useful effect. As Grabitz put it, useful effect means in this context '*das den Rechtsakten der Gemeinschaften derjenige Grad und derjenige Umfang an Rechtswirksamkeit beigemessen werden muss der den Zielen der Integration am besten gerecht wird*'.[19]

In summary the *legal basis* of direct effect of directives is Article 249(3), since it provides that directives are binding. In 1988 the Court of Justice added another ground to the legal basis of direct effect, namely the obligation of cooperation laid down in Article 10 of the Treaty.[20]

Although the legal basis of direct effect of directives seems to be one of charming simplicity, the theoretical underpinning is more complex. Apart from the necessity of giving an interpretation to Article 249(3) such that it will secure as far as possible the practical and effective operation of the instrument, several other arguments have been put forward in this respect in legal writing. According to some, the principal motive for the Court's acceptance of direct effect of directives is the concern for judicial protection.[21] Another more practical consideration behind the Court's case law is the important role of citizens as vigilant individuals who contribute in this way to the practical operation of Community directives[22] or to the need to combat inertia on the part of the Member States.[23]

There is a general consensus among scholars that all these arguments constitute very important elements of the doctrine of direct effect of directives. Since the *Ratti* case,[24] however, many authors and Advocates General have argued that the quintessence of the Court's case law on direct effect of directives is an estoppel-like notion, according to which a Member State should not be able to rely on its own failure to implement the directive. This—what has been called—'*motif véritable*'[25] of the attitude of the Court with respect to direct effect of directives is far from

---

[16] Cf Case 152/84 *Marshall I* [1986] ECR 723, para 47.

[17] Cf Case 41/74 *Van Duyn* [1974] ECR 1337 and Case 148/78 *Ratti* [1979] ECR 1629.

[18] Kutscher 1976, 41. Cf also Bengoetxea 1990, 254 (functional criterion for interpretation).

[19] Grabitz 1971, 10.

[20] Case 190/87 *Moormann* [1988] ECR 4689. For a more detailed discussion of this case see below, Subsection 9.2.2.   [21] Cf Everling 1984, 108, Jarass 1990, 2422, Mertens de Wilmars 1991, 389.

[22] Cf Curtin 1990a, 196.

[23] Cf Galmot and Bonichot 1988, 13. For a brief overview see also Klagian 2001, at 338–46.

[24] Case 148/78 [1979] ECR 1629.   [25] Pescatore 1980, 175.

uncontroversial and, moreover, if it is to be considered as the ultimate theoretical basis for the doctrine of direct effect of directives, it has considerable consequences for, in particular, the possibility of horizontal direct effect.[26] It will therefore be discussed in some detail in the next two Subsections.

9.2.2 'Estoppel' proposed as the basis

Although the idea of estoppel did not appear in the Court's case law until the *Ratti* case, an early signal for the development of the 'estoppel theory'[27] as the basis for direct effect of directives could be found in Advocate General Warner's Opinion in the *Enka* case:

A Member State that fails fully to give effect to a directive is in breach of the Treaty, so that to allow it (through its executive or administrative authorities) to rely upon that fact as against a private person in proceedings in its own Courts would be to allow it to plead its wrong.[28]

In the Advocate General's view this factor 'makes a provision of a directive have direct effect'.[29] There is undoubtedly a good deal of common sense in these considerations. However, I fail to see why this reasoning was necessary, as the main arguments for direct effect had already been formulated in previous case law. The Court of Justice did not take up the Advocate General's argument. It simply reiterated that the effectiveness of a directive would be weakened if individuals could not rely on it and domestic courts were prevented from taking it into consideration as an element of Community law.

In *Ratti* the Court, addressing 'the general problem of the legal nature of the provisions of a directive adopted under Article 189 [249] of the Treaty', simply recalled three arguments already mentioned in *Van Duyn*, namely the untenability of the *a contrario* argument about direct applicability of regulations, the binding effect which Article 249 ascribes to directives and the necessity of the effectiveness of directives. Thereupon the Court held:

Consequently a Member State which has not adopted the implementing measures required by the directive in the prescribed period may not rely, as against individuals, on its own failure to perform the obligations which the directive entails.[30]

Judgments rendered by the Court since *Ratti* present a varied picture as to the basis of direct effect of directives. In some cases the Court has only recalled the

---

[26] See below, Subsection 9.5.2.

[27] I use this term for reasons of convenience. It must be observed that the Court has never used the term 'estoppel' nor '*nemo auditur*' nor '*venire contra factum proprium*'. It simply says that the Member State may not rely on its own failure.

[28] Case 38/77 [1977] ECR 2203, 2226. Cf also already in 1978 Dashwood, 241 and 243.

[29] Cf the Opinion of AG Warner in Case 131/79 *Santillo* [1980] ECR I–1585, 1609.

[30] Case 148/78 *Ratti* [1979] ECR 1629, para 22.

'effectiveness argument',[31] in other cases the argument of the binding nature of direct-ives,[32] and in yet other cases both arguments appear.[33] Similarly the Court frequently reiterates that a Member State may not plead its own wrong, sometimes as the sole argument,[34] sometimes in combination with one or both of the other arguments mentioned above.[35] It is difficult to decide on the basis of this case law how much importance the Court attaches to the 'estoppel theory'. Although some have observed that the principle of estoppel has displaced the requirement of '*effet utile*' which should be given to directives as the theoretical underpinning of their direct effect,[36] in other cases '*effet utile*' has reappeared.[37] Moreover, it would appear that the general tendency is to present this 'estoppel-like notion' as a *consequence* of rather than as a basis for direct effect of directives.[38]

In the past, it was academic writing which especially raised this 'consequence' to the rank of the ultimate rationale of direct effect of directives, the main proponent of this theory being the former Judge of the Court of Justice Pescatore.[39] It is strik-ing how many other authors adhered to this theory,[40] as did several Advocates General.[41] In Germany the 'estoppel-doctrine' was generally considered an '*Ausprägung des Grundsatzes von Treu und Glauben*', an utterance of the principle of good faith.[42] From there it is only a small step to consider direct effect of directives as a sanction upon the failure of the Member State to comply with its obligation.[43] This same 'sanction rationale' was ultimately also an important argument in a judgment of the German Constitutional Court which brought to an end domestic controversies about direct effect of directives.[44]

---

[31] Cf Case C–221/88 *Bussenni* [1990] ECR I–495, Case C–188/89 *Foster* [1990] ECR I–3313.

[32] Cf Case 80/86 *Kolpinghuis* [1987] ECR 3969, Case 152/84 *Marshall I* [1986] ECR 723.

[33] Cf Case 8/81 *Becker* [1982] ECR 53.

[34] Cf Joined Cases C–6/90 and C–9/90 *Francovich* [1991] ECR I–5357, Case C–91/92 *Faccini Dori* [1994] ECR I–3325.

[35] Cf Case 8/81 *Becker* [1982] ECR 53, Case 71/85 *FNV* [1986] ECR 3855, and Case C–157/02 *Rieser*, judgment of 4 February 2004, nyr in ECR.

[36] Cf Curtin 1990, 196, Morris 1989, 310, 312, and 313, Schockweiler 1993c, 1205.

[37] Cf Schockweiler 1993c, 1205.

[38] Cf Case 152/84 *Marshall I* [1986] ECR 723, para 47('. . . from that the Court deduced that . . .') and Case C–157/02 *Rieser*, judgment of 4 February 2004, nyr in ECR. Also according to Schockweiler 1993c, 1205 both in *Ratti* and *Becker* binding force and '*effet utile*' remained the basis for direct effect.

[39] Cf, in particular, Pescatore 1980, 176.

[40] Cf Easson, 1979, 342, Galmot and Bonichot 1988, 12, Leitao 1981, 437, Isaac 1992, 6, Oldenbourg 1984, 224–5, Hartley 2003, 208–9. Cf also Emmert 1992, 64.

[41] E.g. AG Slynn (Case 8/81 *Becker* [1982] ECR 53, Case 152/84 *Marshall I* [1986] ECR 723), AG Mischo (Case 80/86 *Kolpinghuis* [1987] ECR 3969, Case C–221/88 *Busseni* [1990] ECR I–495), AG Lenz (Case 103/88 *Costanzo* [1989] ECR 1839), AG Darmon (Case 190/87 *Moormann* [1988] ECR 4689). Cf also the Opinion of AG Van Gerven in Case C–188/89 *Foster* [1990] ECR I–3313 who used this theory as basis for giving a broad interpretation to the concept of 'the State'.

[42] Cf Nicolaysen 1984, 386, Oldenbourg 1984, 224.

[43] Cf Jarass 1990, 2422, Winter 1991b, 659, Emmert 1992, 57.   [44] Cf Hilf 1988, 1.

In the *Moormann* case[45] the Court expanded the legal basis of direct effect of directives by combining Article 249 with Article 10. This step was probably not entirely unrelated to the German reasoning that the principle of good faith was the basis of individuals' entitlement to rely before a court on a directive where the State has failed to meet its obligations. In this respect, the referring court indicated explicitly in its judgment the German principle of '*Treu und Glauben*' contained in the German Civil Code. Similarly, in his opinion in *Moormann*, Advocate General Darmon argued that allowing the Member State to rely on its own failure would amount to allowing it to disregard the principle of good faith and the duty not to adopt conflicting provisions as laid down in Article 10 of the Treaty.

The reasoning of the Court of Justice in this case is less explicit. The Court recalled that according to Article 249(3) directives are binding and that Article 10 requires the Member States to take all appropriate measures to ensure the fulfilment of their obligations. Subsequently, the Court considered that

[i]t follows from the binding effect which the third paragraph of Article 249 ascribes to directives and the obligation of cooperation laid down in Article 5 [10] that the Member State to which the directive is addressed cannot evade the obligations imposed by the directive in question.[46]

Furthermore the Court pointed out that whenever the provisions of an unimplemented directive are unconditional and sufficiently precise they may be relied upon as against the State and the national court must give precedence to the provisions of the directive. Accordingly, the right of an individual to rely on a directive 'is based on the combined provisions of the third paragraph of Article 189 [249] and Article 5 [10] of the Treaty'.[47]

Briefly put, Article 10 is deployed here in order to *reinforce* the obligation which already follows from Article 249(3). The combination of Article 249 and Article 10 can, in a way comparable to cases on consistent interpretation, be understood as the basis for the obligation of the national court to give precedence to (and, where appropriate, apply) the provisions of the directive to which the individual's right to rely on it corresponds.

In some other cases, however, the Court has been more explicit. In the judgment in *McDermott and Cotter I*, for instance, the Court held that the possibility for individuals to rely on a directive

is based on the fact that directives are binding on the Member States and on the principle that a Member State which has not taken measures to implement the directive within the prescribed period may not, as against individuals, plead its own failure to fulfil such obligations.[48]

---

[45] Case 190/87 [1988] ECR 4686.

[46] Case 190/87 [1988] ECR 4686, para 22.

[47] Ibid, para 24. Cf also, with respect to a decision, Case 249/85 *Albako* [1987] ECR 2345. In this case, however, no reference is made to Art 10.   [48] Case 286/85 [1987] ECR 1453.

In *Marshall I*[49] and, in particular, in *Faccini Dori*[50] the Court went a step further. In the latter case it held that the case law on direct effect of directives 'seeks to prevent "the State from taking advantage of its own failure to comply with Community law" '.[51] It would seem that what was initially conceived as a consequence of direct effect of directives has become its purpose.

In summary, initially the Court merely said in the majority of cases that from the binding effect of the directive and the necessity of giving it useful effect it *followed* that a Member State may not rely, as against individuals, on its own failure to perform the obligations which the directive entails. Undoubtedly under the influence of doctrine and several opinions of Advocates General the desire to prevent the State from taking advantage of its own failure was transformed into the purpose of the Court's case law. Although a few cases may suggest that the concept of estoppel is the ultimate theoretical basis for direct effect of directives, in my opinion, the Court's case law in its totality does not justify such a conclusion.

9.2.3 Disqualifying the 'estoppel theory'

The 'estoppel theory' has never been entirely uncontroversial.[52] It came under fire particularly in the context of the discussion about the horizontal direct effect of directives, since a theoretical underpinning by way of the principle of estoppel constitutes a serious obstacle to the recognition of such an effect. Those who advocate the latter effect question usually also the 'estoppel theory'.[53]

It has been suggested by Pescatore[54] that the emergence of this theory, or what he calls 'a clarification by the Court', must be placed against its proper historical background. Then, however, it appears that the real reasons for explaining direct effect of directives by the 'may not plead its own wrong' prohibition were political rather than legal ones;[55] or, alternatively, the theory was at best an additional '*ex post facto* rationalisation designed to beg the question already resolved by the Court *sub silentio* on other grounds'.[56]

A few years after the case law on direct effect of directives started to develop, two prominent courts of Member States openly showed their disagreement with the Court's approach. The French *Conseil d'Etat*,[57] basing itself on a

---

[49] Case 152/84 [1986] ECR 723.   [50] Case C–91/92 [1994] ECR I–3325.

[51] Ibid, para 22. Cf also Case C–343/98 *Collino* [2000] ECR I–6659 and Case C–157/02 *Rieser*, judgment of 4 February 2004, nyr in ECR.

[52] Cf e.g. Schockweiler 1993c, 1205, Royla and Lackhoff 1998, 1117, and Winter 2002, 313–14.

[53] Cf Emmert 1992, Manin 1990, Van Gerven 1994b, Boch and Lane 1992. Cf also the opinion of AG Jacobs in Case C–316/93 *Vaneetveld* [1994] ECR I–763.   [54] Pescatore 1983, 169–71.

[55] Cf also Nicolaysen 1984, 388.   [56] Wyatt 1983, 246.

[57] *Cohn-Bendit*, 22 December 1978 [1980] 1 CMLR 543.

strictly literal interpretation of Article 249(3), denied the possibility for an individual to invoke a directive with a view to challenging an administrative decision which is addressed to him. Some three years later, the German *Bundesfinanzhof*[58] held, under explicit reference to the above-mentioned decision of the *Conseil d'Etat*, that there could be no reasonable doubt that a directive was incapable of creating legal rules directly applicable in a Member State.

These hostile attitudes of the two influential national supreme courts certainly constituted a considerable danger to the Court's own 'construction of Europe'. However, in my opinion it is questionable whether the Court consciously deployed the 'may not plead its own failure' prohibition as an argument to persuade the two national judiciaries. The judgment in *Ratti* was rendered only some three months after the decision of the *Conseil d'Etat*. The judgment in *Becker*, where the Court reiterated its earlier 'estoppel-finding' in Ratti, was indeed given '*en connaissance de cause*'.[59] However, whether the Court really wanted to clarify the basis for direct effect of directives by reference to the principle of estoppel will remain a secret of the Court's deliberations.

In my view, with all respect to the eminent scholar, it should not be ruled out that Pescatore in his '*tentative de démythification*' and later in his famous article in the European Law Review[60] was making a personal attempt, by expounding a particular theory, to get the mutinous courts into line. It cannot be denied that, at the end of the day, his attempt was rather successful.[61]

The major objection against the 'estoppel-theory' as a theoretical basis for direct effect of directives is that it does not fit within the conception of a Community legal order which is integrated within the legal order of the Member States. If the principle that a Member State may not rely on its own failure to comply with the obligations imposed by the directive is considered as the basis for direct effect of directives, this direct effect is reduced to a sort of 'side-effect', a 'reflex' or a 'corollary' of the failure on the part of the Member State concerned.[62] In other words, the very existence of direct effect, which has been described as a capacity of the legal norm,[63] is made dependent on the failure of the Member State. This is in sharp contrast to the Court's conception of the Community legal order. In this view, as explained above,[64] Community law, of which directives are a part, is integrated in the national

---

[58] 16 July 1981, EuR 1981, 442.

[59] Pescatore 1983, 170.   [60] Pescatore 1980 and Pescatore 1983.

[61] As to the developments in Germany see Hilf 1988 (*Bundesverfassungsgericht* had accepted direct effect of directives). In France the situation remains unsatisfactory in that a review of an individual administrative decision in the light of a directive is not allowed if no implementing measures have been taken. Cf Kovar 1992, Simon 1992, Sauron 2000, 58–61 and Cassia 2002, in particular at 30–2. Interestingly, the *Conseil d'Etat*'s stubborn refusal to fully accept direct effect of directives was indirectly at the origin of a censure by the ECrtHR in case *Dangeville v. France*, application 36677/97, judgment of 16 April 2002.

[62] Cf the Opinion of AG Reischl in Case 148/78 *Ratti* [1979] ECR 1629, 1650, Galmot and Bonichot 1988, 12–13, Pescatore 1980, 176, Leitao 1981, 433.   [63] Cf Timmermans 1979, 538.

[64] See above, Chapter 6, Section 6.1.

legal order from the moment of its entry into force. As a part of Community law, directives are considered as sources of law and, where appropriate, as sources of rights and duties of individuals who are subjects of the Community legal order.[65] Although directives are primarily conceived as indirect sources, this does not alter the fact that they are a part of a system of legal norms valid within a Member State and should accordingly be given practical effect, as this is the purpose of any legal rule.[66] Direct effect of directives as a reflex of a Member State's failure does not fit within this conception. It amounts to a misunderstanding of their legal nature as binding rules of Community law. As such, they are capable of producing direct effect in their own right, provided that certain conditions are satisfied.[67]

In my opinion, the Member State's failure to comply with its obligations is at the utmost a condition or a trigger for direct effect of directives. The possibility for the individual to rely on a directive and the corresponding duty of the courts to apply it presupposes, in particular, that the directive has not been transposed in due time or has not been transposed correctly.[68] Similarly, as it transpires from more recent case law, even in the case of adequate transposition there may be a need for an individual to rely on the directive, for instance, whenever the implementing measures are not observed or enforced by national authorities.[69] Yet, such a condition of a practical nature cannot amount to transforming the Member State's failure into the very basis of direct effect of directives.

Apart from these considerations which draw on the tension caused by, on the one hand, linking direct effect to the behaviour of the Member State and, on the other hand, considering directives as an integral part of the norms valid within the national order, there are other arguments which militate against the 'estoppel theory' as the basis for direct effect of directives.

Several authors have submitted that this theory does not explain other instances of reliance by individuals upon Community law provisions, such as those of the Treaty,[70] and, in particular, of Article 141. To this one may add that the 'estoppel theory' seems to fail in cases where a public authority of the defaulting Member State is allowed to rely on a directive against another authority or the Member State itself.[71]

In another line of argument, it has been pointed out that owing to the extensive interpretation of the concept of 'the State'[72] the theory has been 'denatured and

---

[65] Cf in this respect Green 1984b, 308, who remarks that under the 'estoppel-theory' 'it is unfortunate that individual rights exist as the fortuitous consequence and not the direct object of a legal rule'.

[66] Cf Everling 1984, 104, who denies the idea of 'reflex' since '*Vielmehr treffen den Einzelnen die Wirkungen der Richtlinie . . . direkt weil es sich bei der Richtlinie um eine Norm des Gemeinschaftsrecht handelt die Verwirklichung beansprucht.*' Cf also Mertens de Wilmars 1991, 398.

[67] Cf Curtin 1990a, 197. Cf also Manin 1990, 692 who fails to see how a principle like estoppel could determine the legal nature of a unilateral act.   [68] Cf Case 8/81 *Becker* [1982] ECR 53.

[69] Case C–62/00 *Marks & Spencer* [2002] ECR I–6325.

[70] Wyatt 1983, 246.   [71] Cf Winter 1991b, 663. See also below, Subsection 9.3.5.

[72] Cf above, Ch 4, Section 4.2.

deprived of its substance'. Individuals are now allowed to rely upon the failure of the State as against persons 'exceedingly remote from and in all reasonableness not responsible for the failure'.[73]

This contradiction was in fact present in the 'estoppel-theory' from the very beginning. The primary responsibility to implement the directive will usually lie with the legislature or the executive in its legislative capacity. The directive will not, however, actually be relied upon against the legislator, but against other bodies, which cannot, as such, be held responsible for the non-implementation and cannot be considered as the defaulting authority. In strict terms, therefore, the prohibition of 'not pleading their own failure' already made little sense. Initially, however, several types of organs, owing to their close link, organic or otherwise, with the State, were obliged to bear the failure of those responsible for implementation. The Court of Justice has subsequently extended the ambit of the estoppel principle considerably, far beyond personal default and beyond any form of reasonable imputability.[74]

These practical and doctrinal developments show clearly the serious shortcomings of the 'may not plead its own wrong' prohibition as a theoretical underpinning of direct effect of directives. In my opinion it can be submitted without any exaggeration, and irrespective of the cases which may suggest otherwise, that the 'estoppel theory' has lost all its explanatory force and should therefore be rejected as a theoretical basis for direct effect of directives.

9.3   Content of the concept of direct effect of directives

9.3.1   Direct effect versus direct applicability

It is no secret that there is no entirely uniform terminology in the literature, and to some extent in the case law of the Court of Justice as well, to denote the special character of Community law which is often called 'direct effect'. The matter is further complicated by the multilinguism of Community law.[75] Whatever the merits of the different terminological distinctions might be (and by saying this I am certainly not denying the need for a settled terminology, as it may at least help to avoid misunderstandings), there is one distinction which deserves particular attention since it has been argued that the distinction goes beyond the mere question of 'labelling', and denotes two different conceptions in Community law. This

---

[73] Boch and Lane 1992, 184.

[74] Cf also the Opinion of AG Jacobs in Case C–316/93 *Vaneetveld* [1994] ECR I–763, para 20. For a skilful effort to redefine the problem and, moreover, to give the principle of estoppel another content, i.e. it must be understood as a means of protecting legitimate reliance on the part of the plaintiff and not as a sanction against the Member State's failure, see Van Gerven 1994b.

[75] Cf Kovar 1983, 137 and 1981, 151, Klein 1988, 3 ff., Easson 1979, 319–21, Oldenbourg 1984, 14.

distinction concerns the terms 'direct effect' and 'direct applicability'. Moreover, it has played an important part in the discussions about direct effect of directives.

According to some authors, the terms direct effect and direct applicability can be used interchangeably, while according to others the terms must be carefully distinguished.[76] A third group admits that there is a distinction but the difference must not be dramatized.[77]

The origin of the confusion lies in Article 249(2), which provides with respect to regulations that they are *directly applicable* in the Member States. As mentioned in Section 9.1, the Court held in *Van Duyn* that regulations are directly applicable and, consequently, may by their very nature have direct effect. The Court's reasoning suggested that direct applicability is in this context not the same as direct effect: direct applicability *may lead to* direct effect. The central question is then: what is the difference between the two, particularly if one takes into consideration that with respect to Treaty provisions the Court uses the terms direct effect and direct applicability indiscriminately?[78]

A well-known and influential discussion of this distinction is Winter's classic article in the Common Market Law Review.[79] According to his thesis 'direct applicability', on the one hand, is used in Article 249(2) to make clear that, as far as regulations are concerned, the traditional requirement of incorporation by the Member States of legal rules stemming from an external (i.e. international) source into their national legal order is superseded. Incorporation is superfluous and even forbidden.[80] Winter refers in this respect to the German version of the Treaty which 'seems to express this idea unambiguously'. In this version a regulation '*gilt unmittelbar*' in the Member States (is a part of the law valid within the Member States) instead of '*ist unmittelbar anwendbar*' (which corresponds better with 'is directly applicable'). Direct effect (in German often called '*unmittelbare Wirkung*'), on the other hand, should be reserved to indicate the capacity of a provision to create individual rights which must be enforced by the domestic courts.[81]

Those adhering to this theory correctly point out that regulations often contain provisions which are not meant to give private individuals enforceable rights or which are too vague and incomplete to make judicial application

---

[76] Cf Pescatore 1980, 155, Dashwood 1978, 229–30, Easson 1979, 319–21, Hartley 2003, 203–4.

[77] Cf Bebr 1981, 560, Louis 1993, 494. For a more detailed account of these discussions see the first edition of this book, at 260–3.

[78] Cf e.g. Case 2/74 *Reyners* [1974] ECR 631, Case 43/75 *Defrenne* [1976] ECR 455.

[79] Winter 1972. Cf also already in 1970 the observations of the Commission in Case 9/70 *Grad* [1970] ECR 825, 832.

[80] Cf Bebr 1981, 560. See also Case 34/73 *Variola* [1973] ECR 981 and Case 50/76 *Amsterdam Bulb* [1977] ECR 137.

[81] My own translations, making an effort to explain 'the point' in English. See for terminological confusion Klein 1988, 3–7, Oldenbourg 1984, 14–18. Cf also Winter 1972, 436. For a critique of this thesis see e.g. Eleftheriadis 1996.

possible.[82] As 'every provision of every regulation is directly applicable' by virtue of Article 249(2) 'but not every provision of every regulation has direct effect, in the sense of conferring on private persons rights enforceable by them in national courts',[83] the two concepts cannot be equated. A comparison is often drawn with a national statute, which is undoubtedly 'directly applicable' in the sense of being part of the law valid within the national legal order but does not necessarily give rights to individuals, or is even entirely irrelevant for them.[84]

Some writers hold a slightly different opinion. In their view, legal norms which are a part of the national legal system must in principle also have the capacity to be applied, since that is the normal state of the law.[85] The terms 'directly applicable' must in their view be understood as embracing both concepts: being part of the law valid within the national legal order and having the capacity to be applied; the former is the condition for the latter and the latter is immanently linked with the former.[86] Yet the capacity to be applied must in turn be distinguished from the question whether the provisions concerned can *actually* be applied in a concrete case. The answer will depend on several other factors, like the precision of the drafting of the provision and its content. It is this actual application which they denote by the term 'direct effect'.

Yet, other scholars have argued that direct effect and direct applicability coincide.[87] They point out that if direct effect is defined in terms of 'invocability' of the provision at issue, i.e. the possibility of relying on the provision before a national court and the corresponding duty of the latter to apply the provision, there is no distinction between direct effect and direct applicability of regulations. Every provision of a regulation can be relied upon by an individual and the domestic court is obliged to apply it. Whether the court will be able to do this in the concrete case before it, however, depends on the content of the relevant provision.[88] This latter approach corresponds best with the manner in which the Court of Justice handles regulations: regulations are presumed[89] to be directly effective because Article 249(2) says they are directly applicable in the Member States. The individual may as a rule rely on their provisions without further ado. A test as to whether the conditions of direct effect are satisfied is applied in exceptional situations only.[90]

---

[82] Cf Winter 1972, 435, Easson 1979, 321, Hartley 2003, 204–5, Leitao 1981, 429.

[83] Opinion of AG Warner in Case 131/79 *Santillo* [1980] ECR 1585, 1608.

[84] Cf the Opinion of AG Warner in Case 31/74 *Galli* [1975] ECR 47, 71 and Easson 1979, 322.

[85] Cf Klein 1988, 8 (*Anwendbarkeit, Anwendungsfähigkeit* of the norm), Pescatore 1980, 177.

[86] Cf Klein 1988, 10–11.   [87] Cf Lauwaars 1973, 14, Lauwaars and Timmermans 2003, 107–8.

[88] Cf Lauwaars and Timmermans 2003, 108, with further references.

[89] Cf Dashwood 1978, 241, Bebr 1981, 582.

[90] See Case 9/73 *Schlüter* [1973] ECR 1135 and Case C–403/98 *Monte Acrosu* [2001] ECR I–103. However, also note that legal certainty requires that those concerned must be able to know the exact scope of their obligations. This means , *inter alia*, that the provisions must be sufficiently clear. It also means that the rules concerned must be brought to their knowledge by adequate publicity. Cf Case C–108/01 *Parma* [2003] ECR I–5121.

What is the relevance of this excursion into problems related primarily to regulations for directives? Several points can be made in this respect.

Firstly, as I explained in Chapter 6, Section 6.1, in the Court's conception it is the whole body of Community law which is as such incorporated within the national legal system. Thus, if the term 'directly applicable' in Article 249(2) is understood to refer to the automatic incorporation of regulations into the domestic legal order, directives are also directly applicable in this sense. In other words, what is provided in Article 249(2) for regulations *expressis verbis* also holds true for other provisions of Community law, including directives.[91] Several writers have pointed out that the Court has been careful never to say that directives are directly applicable.[92] The Court's reticence from qualifying directives as directly applicable was probably prompted by the fear of blurring the distinction between regulations and directives, a danger which is not entirely imaginary, certainly as long as there is no clarity about the meaning of direct applicability. Moreover, an explicit statement that directives are directly applicable would be a welcome argument for those who still have difficulties with accepting direct effect of directives, and it could lead to a new wave of criticism.

Secondly, it was explained above that if direct effect is defined as 'invocability' of the provision at issue,[93] direct effect and direct applicability are the same thing. In principle, I see no reason why the same should not also hold true for directives. Like any other provision of Community law, a provision of a directive is also directly applicable in the sense that an individual may rely on it and that the national court is obliged to apply the provision in the concrete case before it. Yet, in contrast to regulations, directives cannot impose obligations upon individuals. For some this is an argument for denying direct applicability of directives.[94]

Given the pitfalls which attend deploying the term 'direct applicability' in connection with directives, it should be noted that whenever in the forthcoming Sections I employ the term 'apply directly', or similar terms, these terms have no special technical meaning but merely indicate the activity of the courts in doing what is part and parcel of their task: applying legal norms in the case before them.

9.3.2 'Direct effect' and 'similar effect'

In *Van Duyn* and subsequent cases the Court held that since regulations are directly applicable and 'may by their very nature have direct effect, it does not follow from this that other categories of acts . . . can never have similar effects'.[95] Several authors have suggested that the Court uses the term 'similar effects' on purpose and

---

[91] Cf Timmermans 1979, 534, Louis 1993, 503.
[92] Cf Usher 1979, 269, Pescatore 1980, 174.
[93] Subsection 9.3.1. See also below Subsection 9.3.3.
[94] Cf AG Reischl in Case 148/78 *Ratti* [1979] ECR 1629, briefly discussed below, in Subsection 9.3.2.
[95] Case 41/74 [1974] ECR 1337, para 12.

consciously avoids the term 'direct effect'.[96] Some have even argued that direct effect of directives would be an inappropriate term, since the real issue is the mere possibility that an individual may *rely on the provision of the directive in question*.[97]

> Thus, for instance, in *Becker* both the German government and the Commission argued that the case did not concern a question of examining the 'direct applicability' or 'direct effect' of the directive concerned. The crucial question was, in their view, whether an individual may rely on its provisions in proceedings before national courts.[98]
>
> Similarly, in *Ratti*, when commenting on the formulation of the preliminary question of the referring judge, AG Reischl found that 'it is certainly not appropriate to speak of the direct applicability of a directive'. He pointed out that this term is used only for regulations, 'that is to say, for directly applicable Community legislation, which may also create legal relationships between individuals'.[99] Directives, however, create obligations only for Member States and, in his view, they can produce at the most *similar* effects. The main point of the Advocate General's analysis seems to be that regulations can both confer rights and impose obligations upon individuals. However, the Advocate General accepted that individuals can rely on the directive concerned against the defaulting Member State.

It has been argued, *inter alia*, that by using the term 'similar effects' the Court was indicating that, in contrast to regulations which are directly applicable and will therefore as a rule have direct effect, directives do not have such direct effect 'by their very nature' and an examination of certain conditions must first take place. With these carefully chosen words the Court wished to express that the result brought about by directives can be the same as that brought about by directly applicable provisions of a regulation. Its cautiousness could then be explained by its concern for maintaining the distinction between regulations and directives.

The thesis that directives do not have direct effect, but a 'similar effect' only, seems just another of the myths surrounding them. In *Van Duyn* and, since then, also in other cases, the Court actually did use the term 'direct effect' in both its reasoning[100] and, more recently, also in the *dicta*.[101]

---

[96] Cf Pescatore 1983, 167, Oldenbourg 1984, 151.

[97] Cf Pescatore 1980, 174. According to some authors, however, this has to be considered as *a limited form of direct effect*. See e.g. Everling 1984, 106, Mertens de Wilmars, 1991, 389.

[98] Case 8/81 [1982] ECR 53, Report for the Hearing, at 59 and 65.

[99] Case 148/78 [1979] ECR 1629, 1650.

[100] Cf Galmot and Bonichot 1988, 13 and Schockweiler 1993c, 1205 who observe that the term 'direct effect' disappeared at a certain point from the case law on directives. Yet it reappeared again in Case C–188/89 *Foster* [1990] ECR I–3313, para 20. Similarly several 'titles' within judgments use the term. See e.g. Joined Cases C–19/90 and C–20/90 *Karella and Karrellas* [1991] ECR I–2691, Case 50/88 *Kühne* [1989] ECR 1925, Joined Cases 231/87 and 129/88 *Carpaneto I* [1989] ECR 3233.

[101] Cf Joined Cases C–465/00, C–138/01, and C–139/01 *Rechnungshof* [2003] ECR I–4989 and C–157/02 *Rieser*, judgment of 4 February 2004, nyr in ECR.

9.3.3   Direct effect as 'invocability'

The problem of whether direct effect should be regarded as the capacity to confer rights or rather as the capacity to be relied upon is an old one and concerns not only Community law and certainly not only directives. In Chapter 6, in Subsection 6.3.2, I have discussed this issue in detail and came to the conclusion that direct effect and the creation of rights should not be equated. Direct effect refers to the ability to rely on a provision of Community law for a variety of purposes, even where the provision does not confer substantive rights. In other words, I agree with those who argue that direct effect is a broader concept than the notion of direct effect understood in the sense that it merely refers to the creation of rights.

The what may be called 'doctrinal divide' is also mirrored in the Court's case law.[102] In some cases the Court of Justice finds, when considering the direct effect of a provision, that the provision confers on individuals rights which are enforceable by them in the national courts and which the national courts must protect (or other equivalent terms).[103] In other cases it is said that the provision may be relied upon by individuals and must be applied by national courts.[104]

While the question of 'creation of rights' was discussed at length in Chapter 6, at this point, the invocability of directives for other purposes deserves some more attention.

The first point to be made concerns the terms 'to invoke the directive' or 'to rely on the directive'.[105] These terms, used in the ordinary sense, could give rise to a good deal of confusion. An individual may rely on a directive in order to ask the national judge to interpret national law in conformity with the directive. Similarly, since the judgment in *Francovich*[106] it has been clear that an individual may invoke a directive when claiming damages for its non-implementation. However, these two situations are outside the scope of the doctrine of direct effect. Thus 'invocability' or 'reliance on' used as the description of direct effect has a more specific meaning which must be carefully kept in mind.[107]

Second, in order to grasp what invocability in the context of direct effect means, it may be useful to have a brief look at the significance of direct effect in a concrete

---

[102] It must, furthermore, also be noted that this divide also runs, to an important extent, along certain 'national lines'. As I have argued elsewhere, the discussion about direct effect is also influenced by 'national perceptions of direct effect' with as a result a Community law concept coloured by national legal thinking. Cf Prechal 1990, 1053–5.

[103] Cf Case C–236/92 *Comitato* [1994] ECR I–483, paras 14–15.

[104] Cf Case 8/81 *Becker* [1982] ECR 53, paras 25 and 27.

[105] As a rule the Court uses the term 'rely'. I will use the terms interchangeably.

[106] Joined Cases C–6/90 and C–9/90 [1991] ECR I–5357.

[107] Cf Manin 1990. In particular the French doctrine has developed several forms of invocability: *l'invocabilité d'interprétation conforme, l'invocabilité d'exclusion, l'invocabilité de prévention, l'invocabilité de réparation, l'invocabilité de substitution.* Cf e.g. Simon 2001, p 438–47.

dispute before a domestic court. On several occasions I have already stressed that
directly effective provisions are invoked and applied within the framework of
national procedures. The way in which the directive will be deployed depends on
the character and the subject matter of the proceedings in the national court, and
also on the content and 'structure' of national rules involved.

In some cases an individual may assert that he has a positive claim based on
Community law, for instance, an amount of money as compensation by virtue
of the product liability directive or the payment of arrears of wages under the
Directive relating to the protection of employees in the event of the insolvency
of their employer.[108] In such cases it will be necessary for the provisions of the
directive to be applied to the facts of the case in order to achieve the situation
desired. The orthodox understanding of direct effect was, indeed, that the relevant Community law provisions must provide an '*Alternativ-Normierung*':
whenever national rules are incompatible with Community law (or where
there are no national rules at all), the Community law provisions must be able
to be applied instead.[109] This happened, for instance, when Ms Becker was basing her exemption from VAT under the Sixth VAT Directive.[110] National legislation exempted only the granting of credit, but not the negotiation of credit,
as the Directive does. Other examples of an attempt to make a positive claim
are the *Carbonari* and *Gozza* cases, where trainee medical specialists claimed
'appropriate remuneration' under Directive 75/362 or the *Silhouette* case, in so
far as a basis for a prohibitory injunction was sought under Directive
89/104.[111] Also the way in which the ECJ handled the *Faccini Dori* case is an
example of positive application of a directive's provisions: the Court examined
whether Ms Dori could claim the right of cancellation provided under
Directive 85/577.[112]

However, judicial activity is not limited to the 'positive' application of
Community law provisions to the facts of the case. Often, the courts may confine themselves to reviewing national law in the light of Community law provisions and, where appropriate, disapplying the national provisions, without it
being necessary to apply the Community law provision instead. Thus, in some
cases the provisions will serve as a touchstone for reviewing the legality of

---

[108] Directive 85/374, [1985] OJ L210/29 and Directive 80/987 [1980] OJ L238/23. For a somewhat
peculiar application of the doctrine see Case 96/84 *Slachtpluimvee* [1985] ECR 1157: the national court
wanted to know whether a private party could rely on a directive against its Member State, in order to
establish whether there was a case of '*force majeure*', relied upon in a civil procedure against another private
party.   [109] Kapteyn and VerLoren van Themaat 2003, 425–6.

[110] Case 8/81 *Becker* [1082] ECR 53.

[111] Case C–131/97 [1999] ECR I–1103, Case C–371/97 [2000] ECR I–7881, and Case C–355/96
[1998] ECR I–4799.

[112] Case C–91/92 [1994] ECR I–3325. In fact, Ms Dori relied upon the directive to protect herself
against national provisions, which were incompatible with the former.

national measures, for instance where an exception of illegality is raised in criminal or administrative proceedings. The same holds true *mutatis mutandis* where the applicant merely seeks a declaration, for instance that a Member State acted contrary to Community law.[113] In fact, quite a few cases, which reached the Court, concerned such a legality control rather than the positive, '*subsumption-like*', approach.

In *Badeck*,[114] it was the Law of the *Land* of Hesse 'on equal rights for women and men and the removal of discrimination against women in the public administration' which was tested, in a '*Normenkontrollverfahren*' (a proceedings for a control of legality) against the provisions of Community law, in particular Article 2(4) of Directive 76/207. In the (British) *EOC* case, after an examination on its substantive merits, the House of Lords granted a declaration that certain provisions of the Employment Protection (Consolidation) Act 1987 were incompatible with Article 119 [141] of the EC Treaty.[115] In *MRAX*,[116] the Movement to combat racism etc. started a proceedings for annulment of a ministerial circular dealing, *inter alia*, with the procedure for publication of banns of marriage and the documents necessary for obtaining a visa for the purpose of reuniting a family on the basis of a marriage contracted abroad. According to MRAX the circular was not compatible with a number of Community law directives in the area of free movement of persons. In *Skandia*,[117] the national provision on the 5 per cent limitation of all the voting rights in a domestic or foreign public limited company was incompatible with Directive 73/239 and Directive 79/267 and therefore had to be disapplied. In *CIA-Security*,[118] national measures on technical standards, which had been enacted without notification under Directive 83/189, were held 'inapplicable'. In criminal cases, Community law is usually relied upon in order to deprive the charges of their legal basis: the relevant national provisions, defining the (criminal) offence remain inapplicable.[119] In certain cases it may suffice to disapply a derogation to the main rule which is, as such, compatible with Community law and it is the derogation which amounts to a violation. This was for instance the case in the Dutch Law on Unemployment Benefit, at issue in *FNV*,[120] which excluded married women from the scheme.

In the context of all these type of cases—and many other examples could be added to these—the question as to which rules must be applied instead does not even occur. The 'negative sanction' of disapplication suffices to achieve the

[113] Cf Case 71/85 *FNV* [1986] ECR 3855.   [114] Case C–158/97 [2000] ECR I–1875.

[115] Judgment of March 3, 1994, *R. v. Secretary of State for Employment, ex parte Equal Opportunities Commission and Another* [1994] 2 WLR 409.   [116] Case C–459/99 [2002] ECR I–6591.

[117] Case C–241/97 [1999] ECR I–1879.   [118] Case C–194/94 [1996] ECR I–2201.

[119] Cf Case C–319/97 *Kortas* [1999] ECR I–3143, Case C–230/97 *Awoyemi* [1998] ECR I–6781, C–345/89 *Stoeckel* [1991] ECR I–4047, and Case C–69/91 *Decoster* [1993] ECR I–5335.

[120] Case 71/85 *FNV* [1986] ECR 3855.

result prescribed by Community law and there is no need for applying an alternative provision.[121]

Yet, again in other cases, in particular if the disapplication results in a gap, it may be necessary for the domestic court to be able to apply a Community law provision instead in order to resolve the case before it.[122]

The judicial practice in which directives may play a part and are relied upon is in fact much more complex than the few examples I have just given. Yet in my view, at least as far as the use of a directive is concerned, two basic formulas can be distinguished.[123] On the one hand, there is the possible *application of the provisions of the directive to the facts of the case.* This application may often result in the creation of rights.[124] On the other hand, there is the *review of legality* of national rules or individual decisions made under national law. Here the directive serves as a touchstone, as a standard in the light of which the legality of the measures at stake must be reviewed. In some cases the control of legality, often with the inapplicability of the contrary national rules as a sanction, thus by way of *exclusion,* may suffice to achieve the result the directive is aiming at. In other cases it may be necessary for the domestic court to apply the provisions of the directive *instead of* the national provisions, by way of *substitution.* This will be necessary in particular where the mere disapplication results in a lacuna or where there are no national legal provisions at all.

9.3.4   Review of legality as a separate category?

The distinction between direct effect in the sense of application of the provisions of a directive to the facts of the case—and in the slipstream of that the creation of individual rights—on the one hand, and the review of the legality of national measures on the other, is not new.

This distinction has been made for instance by Timmermans. In his view, direct effect comprises two elements: the possibility of relying on the provision at issue in order to oppose the application of national law contrary to it *and* the direct application of the directive to the facts of the case.[125] On the other hand, legal review implies that the national courts are under a duty to review the lawfulness of national law with regard to the directive, without the possibility of the directive itself being directly applied instead. His analysis was based on the cases *VNO, Enka,* and

---

[121] Cf e.g. Case C–462/99 *Connect Austria* [2003] ECR I–5197, in particular para 41. Interestingly, the AG comes to another conclusion in this respect.

[122] In certain cases, where such an alternative is not possible, the fall back option, to fill the gap, is indeed consistent interpretation. See, again, Case C–462/99 *Connect Austria* [2003] ECR I–5197, paras 39 and 40, and Case C–365/98 *Brinkmann II* [2000] ECR I–4619.

[123] For a brief discussion of these two formulas see also AG Kokott, Opinion in Case C–127/02 *Landelijke Vereniging tot Behoud van de Waddenzee,* of 29 January 2004, paras 139–143.

[124] Whether rights are created or not depends, it is submitted, on the qualification under national law. See above, Ch 6, Subsection 6.3.2.   [125] Timmermans 1979, 543–4.

Delkvist,[126] where the Court found that national courts must determine whether the competent national authorities in adopting the disputed measures have observed the limits of their discretion as set out in the relevant directives. From the cases, in particular from the fact that there was discretion left to the Member States, it was clear that for the purposes of application of a rule to the facts of the case further implementation was needed first. Nevertheless, the national court was obliged to review the legality of the measures concerned in the light of the provisions of the directive.

In German legal writing[127] a similar distinction is made, namely between '*Wirkung als Maßstabsnorm*' (directive as a gauge for legal review) and '*unmittelbare subjektieve Wirkung*' (direct effect, used in the sense of creation of individuals' rights). Often, '*Wirkung als Maßstabsnorm*' and '*Wirkung als Auslegungsnorm*' (directive as an aid to interpretation) are taken together under the heading '*objektieve Wirkung*'.[128]

French scholars also distinguish between the review of legality, which they call '*invocabilité d'exclusion*', and direct effect in the sense of positive application, which they indicate with the term '*invocabilité de substitution*'.[129] This distinction between 'substitution effect' and 'exclusion effect' has, in the meantime, also gained ground in English legal writing.[130]

Others, however, have argued that legal review is more a form of direct effect and not a distinct concept.[131] Even before the judgments in *VNO, Enka*, and *Delkvist*, Bleckmann, for instance, argued that individuals should be able to rely on provisions of Community law limiting discretionary powers, in order to enable judicial review of national measures.[132]

For a long period of time, cases like *VNO, Enka*, and *Delkvist* have remained somewhat isolated at Community level.[133] It took until 1996 for the Court to explicitly reaffirm the approach, in *Kraaijeveld*.[134] This case triggered a renewed discussion on the concept of direct effect and, in particular, on the question whether the legality review *à la Kraaijeveld* was a form of direct effect or not.[135]

---

[126] Case 51/76 [1977] ECR 133, Case 38/77 [1977] ECR 2203, Case 21/78 [1978] ECR 2327.

[127] Cf Langenfeld 1992, Bach 1990, Klagian 2001.

[128] Others make a distinction in this respect between 'direct effect in the broad sense' and 'direct effect in the narrow sense'. Cf Winter 1991b. For a comparable distinction in Belgium see Pâques 1996, Gilliaux 1998 and Bribosia 1998, 6–10.

[129] Cf Galmot and Bonichot 1988, Simon 2001, 441 and 445, Wathelet 2004, and the Opinion of AG Léger in Case C–287/98 *Linster* [2000] ECR I–6917.   [130] Cf e.g. Tridimas 2002.

[131] Cf Mertens de Wilmars 1980b, 665. Cf also already in 1969 and 1978 Mertens de Wilmars 76, Lauwaars 837–8, and Lauwaars and Timmermans 2003, 29.   [132] Bleckmann 1978, 102 and 125.

[133] Cf also the somewhat peculiar judgment in Case 126/82 *Smit* [1983] ECR 73 and, more recently, Case C–156/91 *Mundt* [1992] ECR I–5567 (in particular the Opinion of AG Jacobs, para 11).

[134] Case C–72/95 [1996] ECR I–5403.

[135] Cf Edward, 1998 and Wyatt 1998. Similarly, some French authors consider the review of legality of national rules rather as a matter of supremacy than direct effect. Cf Simon 1997, 95–9. For a similar line of thinking see the Opinion of AG Léger in Case C–287/98 *Linster* [2000] ECR I–6917. Another important issue raised by *Kraaijeveld* was that the directive concerned does not necessarily confer rights upon individuals. For a discussion of that aspect see Ch 6, Subsection 6.3.2.

A feature which was probably particularly puzzling in these cases was that the existence of discretion did not block the possibility to rely on the directive since, traditionally, the existence of discretion was believed to exclude direct effect.[136] However, if one considers the way in which directly effective provisions are deployed at national level, *Kraaijeveld* is not that revolutionary. It appears that quite often the method actually applied is the control of legality of national rules, whatever might be the formulation adopted by the Court of Justice when answering the question whether a provision has direct effect or not. Many of the examples given in the previous Subsection were about this type of control in which discretion is involved. Indeed, to these one may add others. A whole line of cases dealing with the restriction to movement and residence of foreign nationals based on grounds of public policy, to start with *Van Duyn*,[137] concerned the question whether the Member States or their competent authorities remained within the limits drawn by directive 64/221. *Johnston*[138] was about the question whether national derogation of the principle of equal treatment did not exceed the limits of Article 2(2) of the same directive. While in *Von Colson*[139] no specific sanction could be asked for on the basis of Article 6 of Directive 76/207 since Member States had room for manoeuvre in this respect, it was possible to establish that the sanction chosen by the German legislator did not satisfy the minimum requirements which are implicitly present in that article. *Leur-Bloem*[140] raised, *inter alia*, the question whether certain Dutch tax provisions, aiming at prevention of tax evasion or tax avoidance, remained within the limits set out in Article 11 of Directive 90/434. What the courts, in co-operation with the ECJ, are doing here is to control the use of the margin of discretion the Member States enjoy.

In *Kraaijeveld*, the Court first reiterated the binding nature of a directive, according to Article 243 (3) and then it held:

In particular, where the Community authorities have, by directive, imposed on Member States the obligation to pursue a particular course of conduct, the useful effect of such an act would be weakened if individuals were prevented from relying on it before their national courts, and if the latter were prevented from taking it into consideration as an element of Community law in order to rule whether the national legislature, in exercising the choice open to it as to the form and methods for implementation, has kept within the limits of its discretion set out in the directive.[141]

This type of legality review of national implementing measures and the explicit task for the courts to review whether the competent national authorities did not exceed

---

[136] On this see below, in Subsection 9.4.2.
[137] Case 41/74 [1974] ECR 1337. See also, for instance, Case 36/75 *Rutili* [1975] ECR 1219.
[138] Case 222/84 [1986] ECR 1651.   [139] Case 14/83 [1984] ECR 1891.
[140] Case C–28/95 [1997] ECR I–4161.   [141] Case C–72/95 [1996] ECR I–5403, para 56.

the bounds of their permitted discretion, was subsequently reconfirmed in, *inter alia*, *Linster*.[142] Moreover, in a recent judgment in the *Waddenzee* case, the Court has confirmed that the review is not necessarily limited to national implementing legislation, as is sometimes believed. Its scope is broader and it may relate to any measure. The case at hand concerned the review of an authorization for fishing of cockles issued by the competent Secretary of State, while the relevant provision of the directive has not been transposed in national law at all.[143]

Another interesting example is provided by the *Brinkmann* case.[144] Here the Court made clear that German taxation of cigars and cigarillos was incompatible with Directive 92/80 (taxation of manufactured tobacco)[145] in that the tax formula chosen by the German legislature went beyond the discretion conferred by Article 3(1) of the directive.[146]

In my view, policing the use of discretion by the Member States is just a species of the review of legality. In turn, the review of legality of national measures is merely a form of judicial activity which takes place *within* the concept of direct effect. As was explained in the previous Subsection, the way in which Community law provisions are deployed in a concrete case depends on various factors, such as the type of proceedings, the purpose of a claimant's action, and the 'state' of national law. In such a context it is not very practicable and makes little sense to distinguish between direct effect in the strict sense and review of legality of national measures. To this one might add that the Court does not make such a distinction either, at least not with respect to directives.[147]

9.3.5 Two different perspectives: the individual and the Court

The legal reality behind the definition of direct effect as the capacity of a provision to be invoked by individuals in national courts which are bound to apply it, is extremely varied. This was already illustrated by the previous two Subsections, where the meaning of 'direct application by the national court' was explored and which made clear that this 'application' involves more than the basic Aristotelian syllogism of subsuming the facts under the general rule of the directive. There are still some further issues that deserve attention and which relate to the 'subjects'

---

[142] Case C–287/98 *Linster* [2000] ECR I–6917. See also Case C–435/97 *WWF* [1999] ECR I–5613.

[143] Case C–127/02 *Landelijke Vereniging tot Behoud van de Waddenzee*, judgment of 7 September 2004, nyr in ECR.   [144] Case C–365/98 *Brinkmann II* [2000] ECR I–4619.

[145] [1992] OJ L316/10.

[146] However, at the end of the day, this was not of much help for the claimant since the Court, in contrast to the AG, denied that Brinkmann could rely directly on the directive for the purpose aimed at by Brinkmann, namely to have only an *ad valorem* tax levied. See also below, Subsection 9.4.2.

[147] See, however, cases in which obligations under international law, in particular the WTO, are at stake, for instance Case C–94/02 *P Biret* [2003] ECR I–10565.

involved in the definition of direct effect. As a rule, these are the individuals who may rely on the provisions concerned and the court which is bound to apply them.

First of all some brief remarks must be made regarding the question of '*who*' may actually be concerned by the definition, in addition to courts and individuals. First, as explained in Chapter 4, not only the courts are obliged to apply directly effective provisions but so too are all national authorities upon which the provisions are binding.

Second, there is a common understanding that 'individuals' in this context are not only natural persons but also legal persons.[148] However, the persons who may rely on a directive form a much broader category, namely 'all those concerned'.[149] Thus the ECSC or a body governed by public law, such as a municipality,[150] can also be considered a person concerned for the purposes of direct effect. In *SACE*[151] it was even suggested that another Member State 'concerned' in the performance of the Community law obligation may avail itself of the directly effective provision. For the time being it seems that any legal subject, whether private or public, may rely on a directive if it is 'concerned' by its provisions.[152]

In the aftermath of the *CIA-Security* judgment,[153] a sort of *Schutznorm* requirement has slipped into the discussion about the question who are 'the persons concerned' and, consequently, who may rely on a directive. According to some,[154] only those persons whose interests are intended to be protected by the directive provisions may invoke the directive before the courts. The Court has not as yet clarified this matter. The judgment in *Lemmens*,[155] for instance, is particularly obscure on this point and can be interpreted in many ways. While some read it as a confirmation of linking invocability to an interest requirement,[156] others find that the Court's judgment is not conclusive in this respect.[157]

In my opinion, introducing an interest requirement of this type for the 'invocability' of Community law provisions would amount to an unnecessary and

---

[148] Cf Case 31/87 *Beentjes* [1988] ECR 4635, Case 138/86 *Direct Cosmetics* [1988] ECR 3937.

[149] Cf Case 41/74 *Van Duyn* [1974] ECR 1337, para 12, Case 148/78 *Ratti* [1979] ECR 1629, para 20.

[150] Cf Case C-221/88 *Busseni* [1990] ECR I-495, Joined Cases 231/87 and 129/88 *Carpaneto I* [1989] ECR 3233 and Joined Cases C-487/01 and C-7/02, *Gemeente Leusden*, judgment of 29 April 2004, nyr in ECR.

[151] Case 33/70 [1970] ECR 1213.

[152] As to the question whether somebody is concerned, see above, Ch 7, Subsection 7.3.2.

[153] Case C-194/94 [1996] ECR I-2201.

[154] For instance the Dutch government before the ECJ and AG Fennelly in Case C-226/97 *Lemmens* [1998] ECR I-3711. See also Hilson and Downes 1999, 131 ff., who are also 'smuggling' an interest requirement into the concept of direct effect, and Timmermans 1997, 22.

[155] Case C-227/97 [1998] ECR I-3711.

[156] Cf Van Gerven, 2000, 508 and Lenaerts 1998, 269.

[157] Cf Koopmans 1999, 338 and Jans *et al.* 2002, 108–11. In my view, the ECJ delimited the scope of the consequences of the violation at issue, i.e. the non-applicability, rather than the circle of persons who may rely on the directive. On the lack of clarity of this judgment see also the comment by Streinz 1999 and Abele 1998.

incomprehensible restriction, adding in fact a new condition for direct effect. By this, I am not denying that the matter of interest does not play a role. It does, but at national (procedural) level. The interest requirement, for instance, plays a part in relation to *locus standi*, as a condition in action for damages and as a condition for the '*recevabilité des moyens*'.[158] These are matters which are governed by provisions of national (procedural) law. From a Community law point of view, these national procedural provisions are subject to the well-known principles of equivalence and effectiveness.[159] As these national provisions as such already limit either the access to the courts or the admissibility of certain submissions, I see no need to introduce an additional limitation at the level of direct effect. Moreover, direct effect is a quality that pertains to the provision at issue and not to the person that relies on it.

As regards the reliance by individuals on the one hand and the application by courts on the other, the Court's case law contains three basic modalities. In some cases the Court makes plain the meaning of direct effect if considered *from the point of view of the individual*: for instance, individuals may demand the application of the directive, they may rely on it before national courts, etc.[160]

In other cases the Court's findings relate explicitly to both perspectives, i.e. the *implications both for the individual and the court concerned* are addressed: for instance, in the classic *Van Duyn* formula it was held that the relevant article 'confers on individuals rights which are enforceable by them in the courts of a Member State and which the national courts must protect'.[161]

Indeed, many more examples of both categories could be added. It is, however, striking that only rarely does the Court confine itself to stating the meaning of direct effect if considered *from the perspective of the court alone*. One of those rather exceptional cases is *Verholen*.[162] In this case the Court of Justice made clear that if the national court considers 'either that Community law must be applied and, if necessary, national law disapplied, or that national law must be interpreted in a way that conforms with Community law' it may do so of its own motion,

---

[158] For the purposes of this Subsection this should be understood very broadly, as relating to the requirement that, if somebody in a proceedings relies on a provision in order, for instance, to defend himself, the provision at issue should also aim at protecting his interests.

[159] Cf also on a comparable problem AG Geelhoed, Opinion of 4 March 2004, in Case C–174/02 and C–175/02 *Streekgewest Westelijk Noord-Brabant*, paras 51–61 and AG Kokott, Opinion in Case C–127/02 *Landelijke Vereniging tot Behoud van de Waddenzee*, of 29 January 2004, paras 138–43. On the other hand, see however also Case C–157/02 *Rieser*, judgment of 5 February 2004, nyr in ECR, paras 43 and 44, which seems to limit the circle of persons who may rely on the directive at issue.

[160] Cf Case 222/84 *Johnston* [1986] ECR 1651, Case 31/87 *Beentjes* [1988] ECR 4635.

[161] Case 41/74 [1974] ECR 1337, para 15. Cf also Case 38/77 *Enka*, [1977] ECR 2203, Case 126/82 *Smit* [1983] ECR 73.

[162] Joined Cases C–87/90, C–88/90, and C–89/90 [1991] ECR I–3757. Cf also Case C–158/91 *Levy* [1993] ECR I–4287 and Case 36/75 *Rutili* [1975] ECR 1219, (in particular para 16).

thus irrespective of whether or not (one of) the parties involved has relied on the directive.[163]

The Court's emphasis on direct effect as a matter of invocability can be explained by the way preliminary questions are posed, as their formulation may often determine the way in which the answer is phrased; or perhaps by the initial formulation of direct effect, namely the creation of rights for individuals. Equally the Court often has recourse to a number of well-established formulas which are reiterated as magic spells on any occasion. The main point is, however, that in the ultimate analysis direct effect is, in my opinion, not so much concerned with the issue of what an individual can do with a provision of a directive but rather *whether the national court can apply it or not*.[164] In this respect I fully agree with Hilf, who has pointed out that the invocability of a directive is too narrow a concept since a directive may equally be applied by the domestic court of its own motion, as illustrated above by the *Verholen* case.[165] Moreover, as mentioned above, the term 'invocability' is as such misleading in that it may also refer to reliance on the directive for purposes other than direct effect. To this one may add that, as will be explained in Section 9.4, the conditions for direct effect developed by the Court are intimately linked to the judicial function and its limits. This may be considered a further indication that the important point is whether the court can apply the provision at issue.

In brief, for all these reasons and in contrast to the definitions presented above, the definition of direct effect would, in my opinion, be more appropriately phrased in terms of the obligation of the national court to apply the provisions of the directive concerned.[166]

9.3.6   Redefining direct effect?

In the foregoing Subsections the concept of direct effect was scrutinized, to a large extent in the light of its practical operation. The definition of direct effect as the creation of rights for individuals which the national courts must protect was rejected as being too narrow.

Subsequently it appeared that the other (and more appropriate) definition of direct effect, namely the capacity of the norm to be invoked by individuals in national courts which are bound to apply the provisions, was not entirely satisfactory either. Firstly, I pointed out that the term 'to invoke' is rather misleading since a directive may also be invoked for purposes other than direct effect. Moreover, even where the directive is not invoked as such, a national court may apply the relevant

---

[163] Cf also Case C–72/95 *Kraaijeveld* [1996] ECR I–5403. As to the question whether national courts must apply Community law of their own motion see above, Ch 7, Subsection 7.3.3.

[164] Cf Timmermans 1979, 540–1, Pescatore 1983, 176.   [165] Hilf 1993, 9.

[166] And, indeed, under the proviso that 'to apply' is understood broadly.

provisions of its own motion. Thus, invocability as a central element of the definition is not entirely satisfactory. Secondly, I have argued that the term 'to apply' is misleading to the extent that it suggests that what is at stake is the subsumption of the facts under the rules of the directive. I tried to make clear that the deployment of a directive in a national procedure amounts to something more, and will often also include the control of legality of the national measures. Thirdly, another argument can be added: the definition consists of the description of the consequences of direct effect for individuals (to invoke/to rely on) and for the courts (to apply). However, as pointed out briefly in Subsection 9.3.5 and discussed in detail in Chapter 4, national authorities other than the courts are equally obliged to apply the directive.[167] Moreover, the category of subjects who may rely on a directive is very broad.

For these reasons it may be asked whether there is not a necessity to redefine the concept of 'direct effect' in terms which take it a stage beyond invocability by individuals and which correspond more closely to what is really important. In my view, a more appropriate definition would run as follows: *Direct effect is the obligation of a court or another authority to apply the relevant provision of Community law, either as a norm which governs the case or as a standard for legal review.* Directly effective provisions are then provisions having the quality to be applied accordingly.

9.4   Conditions for direct effect of directives

9.4.1   Introduction

Whatever the most apt definition of direct effect might be, the central concern of this doctrine is that the provision at issue must lend itself to being applied (in the broad sense of the term) in a concrete case, by a court of law.[168] Perhaps it is more appropriate to say in *the* concrete case before the court since, as discussed above, the mode of application will depend on several factors and, it is submitted, so too will the content of the conditions to be met by the relevant provision.

The conditions for direct effect of directives as formulated by the Court of Justice have gone through a process of development, the main issue being whether the conditions laid down by the Court for direct effect of Treaty provisions also applied in the field of directives.[169]

---

[167] Cf Case 103/88 *Costanzo* [1989] ECR 1839 and subsequent case law, discussed in Section 4.3 and Section 4.4, in particular.

[168] Cf Case 158/80 *Butter-buying cruises* [1981] ECR 1805, para 43. The same holds true, where appropriate, for other authorities whenever these are called upon to apply directly effective provisions of a directive. However, in the present Chapter the focus is on the courts.

[169] For a more detailed discussion and further references see the first edition of this book, 277–80.

In *Van Duyn*,[170] on the one hand, the Court relied partly on the criteria laid down for direct effect of Treaty provisions. On the other hand, the test was more tailored to the specific provision at issue and therefore it did not provide clear guidelines as to the question of the more general circumstances under which the 'nature, general scheme and wording' of a provision will bring about direct effect.

The next three cases decided by the Court in which the question as to the direct effect of a directive was again raised,[171] namely *VNO, Enka*, and *Delkvist*,[172] did not illuminate the matter either. On the contrary, they caused quite some confusion in that, firstly, the Court did not examine whether the relevant provisions met the usual requirements for direct effect; nevertheless, it held that the national measures had to be reviewed in the light of the provisions in question. Secondly, such a review was held to be possible despite the clear margin of discretion in two of those three cases, while as regards direct effect, it was precisely the existence of discretion which usually blocked direct effect.[173]

The two elements which, considered retrospectively, became the test for direct effect of directives appeared for the first time in *Ratti*,[174] but it was not until *Becker* that the Court, in its famous 'lecture' on the effects of directives in general, explained that provisions of directives are directly effective whenever they '*appear, as far as their subject-matter is concerned, to be unconditional and sufficiently precise*'.[175] As a rule, since the *Becker* judgment the Court has referred to these conditions whenever the question of direct effect of directives arises.[176]

The next question is then: under what circumstances does a provision meet these criteria? I shall deal with this in the next Subsection. However, it is first necessary to point out that the question as to direct effect of provisions arises only if two other conditions are satisfied. Firstly, it must be established that the Member State concerned has not transposed the directive at all, or in time, or that it has done so incorrectly,[177] or that the rules which have, as such, adequately implemented the directive, are not

---

[170] Case 41/74 [1974] ECR 1337.

[171] In a number of cases following *Van Duyn* and concerning equally free movement of persons, direct effect of directives as such was not explicitly considered by the Court. Though there was hardly any doubt that the relevant provisions were directly effective. Cf Case 67/74 *Bonsignore* [1975] ECR 297, Case 36/75 *Rutili* [1975] ECR 1219, Case 118/75 *Watson and Belmann* [1976] ECR 1185.

[172] Case 51/76 [1977] ECR 133, Case 38/77 [1977] ECR 2203, and Case 21/78 [1978] ECR 2327, respectively.   [173] Cf also above, Subsection 9.3.4.

[174] Case 148/78 [1979] ECR 1629, para 23. See also Case 88/79 *Grunert* [1980] ECR 1827. However, in other cases a slightly different terminology was used. Cf Case 131/79 *Santillo* [1980] ECR 1585, para 13.

[175] Case 8/81 [1982] ECR 53, para 25.

[176] Cf e.g. Case C–134/99 *IGI* [2000] ECR I–7717, Case C–157/02 *Rieser*, judgment of 5 February 2004, nyr in ECR, and Case C–150/99 *Lindöpark* [2001] ECR I–493 where, however, slightly different terms are used: 'sufficiently clear, precise and unconditional' (para 31).

[177] Case 8/81 *Becker* [1982] ECR 53. Cf also Case 270/81 *Rickmers* [1982] ECR 2771.

correctly applied.[178] The latter results, indeed, in an important extension of situations in which a directive may be relied on. Secondly, the period for implementation must have expired. National courts are, in principle, not allowed to apply the directive before the expiry of this period.[179] There are some exceptions, though. Some may be closely linked to national law, for instance where national (criminal) law requires the application of the most favourable rules.[180] Furthermore, in exceptional circumstances, a directive may be relied upon where, during the implementation period, a Member State takes measures which are liable to gravely jeopardize the attainment of the result prescribed by the directive at issue.[181]

9.4.2 The meaning of 'unconditional and sufficiently precise'

Although since *Becker* the test for determining direct effect of directives focuses on the unconditional and sufficiently precise nature of the provisions involved, this does not mean that in every single case the Court scrutinizes explicitly and separately whether the two conditions are satisfied.

In some cases the Court confines itself to quoting or describing the relevant provision and subsequently simply finds that the provision is precise and unconditional.[182] Similarly, in some cases a different phrasing is chosen; such as in *Kühne*, where the Court held that the prohibition at issue is 'complete, legally perfect and consequently capable of producing direct effects in the legal relations between Member States and persons within their jurisdiction'.[183]

In other cases the Court examined more closely the relevant provisions, checking whether they are sufficiently precise and unconditional. The difference in approach may, first of all, be explained by the rather pragmatic way in which the Court deals with the question as to the direct effect of provisions at issue. Moreover, it is not possible in every case to distinguish clearly between the two elements of the test, as the distinction is often rather fluid and both elements are interlinked by another condition of direct effect emerging from the Court's case law, namely the absence of discretion in the application of the provisions at issue. Finally, when

---

[178] Cf Case C–62/00 *Marks & Spencer* [2002] ECR I–6325, in particular para 27.

[179] Cf Case 148/78 *Ratti* [1979] 1629 and Case C–157/02 *Rieser*, judgment of 5 February 2004, nyr in ECR.   [180] See Case C– 319/97 *Kortas* [1999] ECR I–3143.

[181] Cf Case C–129/96 *Inter-Environnement Wallonie* [1997] ECR I–7411 and Case C–14/02 *ATRAL* [2003] ECR I–4431. Cf also Kaczorowska 1999.

[182] Cf Case C–38/88 *Siegen* [1990] ECR I–1447, Case 103/88 *Costanzo* [1989] ECR 1839, Case 96/84 *Slachtpluimvee* [1985] ECR 1157, Case 301/82 *Clin-Midy* [1984] 251, Case C–76/97 *Tögel* [1998] ECR I–5357, Case C–347/96 *Solred* [1998] ECR I–937, and Case C–438/99 *Melgar* [2001] ECR I–6915.

[183] Case 50/88 [1984] ECR 1925, para 26. Cf also Case 271/82 *Auer II* [1983] ECR 2727 and Case 5/83 *Rienks* [1983] ECR 4233.

addressing the question as to the meaning of 'unconditional and sufficiently precise' one must keep in mind the purpose of these requirements, which is judicial application: provisions must be unconditional and sufficiently precise to enable them to be applied by a court of law, which is the quintessence of direct effect.[184]

Sufficiently precise

The condition of a sufficient degree of precision is primarily concerned with the *wording* of the provision at issue. Several features are relevant in this respect. The Court may find that the provision is unequivocal and therefore sufficiently precise.[185] However, this does not imply that ambiguous or unclear provisions are incapable of being directly effective. Problems of ambiguity and lack of clarity can be resolved by interpretation by the courts and where necessary, by the Court of Justice in a preliminary procedure.[186] Similarly, the fact that a provision may require the evaluation of issues, economic or otherwise, does not preclude their direct effect, provided that the courts are able to make this evaluation themselves or to review the assessment required.[187]

The question of sufficient precision seems to correspond with justiciability: the national court must be able, equipped with the provision at issue, to deal with the problem before it. Specific, clearly defined, or detailed provisions will satisfy this requirement.[188] On the other hand, when the provisions are so vague and general that for their application in a concrete case further measures must be adopted in order to 'furnish workable indications for the national court',[189] they obviously cannot be applied by the court, as the latter would run into the limits of its judicial function.[190]

The major difficulty with respect to a sufficient degree of precision lies in vaguely worded concepts. In some cases it will, after interpretation, appear that they are still capable of judicial adjudication.[191] In other cases, however, behind

---

[184] Several authors have pointed out in this respect that the same problem also occurs under national law: some legal norms may necessitate further elaboration by subordinate legislation before they can be applied by the courts. Cf Louis 1993, 545, Abraham 1989, 21.

[185] Cf Case 71/85 *FNV* [1986] ECR 3855, Case C–236/92 *Comitato* [1994] ECR I–483, Case C–157/02 *Rieser*, judgment of 5 February 2004, nyr in ECR, Case C–276/01 *Steffesen* [2003] ECR I–3735 (referring to 'clear language').

[186] See the clear reference in Case 41/74 *Van Duyn* [1974] ECR 1337, para 14. See also the Opinion of AG Jacobs in Case C–150/99 *Lindöpark* [2001] ECR I–493, who points out that what matters is that '. . . the provision must be capable of clear and precise interpretation and of direct application by the courts' (para 44).   [187] Cf Joined Cases 231/87 and 129/88 *Carpaneto I* [1989] ECR 3233.

[188] Cf Case 131/79 *Santillo* [1980] ECR 1585, Case 103/88 *Costanzo* [1989] ECR 1839, Joined Cases 231/87 and 129/88 *Carpaneto I* [1989] ECR 3233.

[189] Cf Pescatore 1983, 175. See also e.g. Joined Cases 372 to 374/85 *Traen* [1987] ECR 2141, Case 14/83 *Von Colson* [1984] ECR 1891 and Case 31/87 *Beentjes* [1988] ECR 4635.

[190] Cf Bleckmann 1978, 99–100, Timmermans 1979, 541, Pescatore 1983, 176–7.

[191] E.g the so-called 'indefinite legal concept' ('*unbestimte Rechtsbegriffe*'). See also below in this Subsection.

the vague terms will hide discretion, allowing several choices for the administration or the legislator, where appropriate. This will either make judicial application impossible or it will at least considerably restrict the possibilities of adjudication by the courts.[192]

Unconditional

According to Pescatore,[193] the determination of the unconditional character of the provisions involved is a relatively easy task. In his view, in every single case one has to consider whether there may be some reservation with a view to further implementing measures in respect of which discretion is left to the competent authorities. The reservation may be either inherent in the provision itself or in the system of which the provision is part. Whether such a reservation exists is a matter of legal analysis. Although this is undoubtedly true, in practice matters may be rather complicated. The requirement of unconditionality may relate to several issues.

Firstly, a provision will be conditional if its implementation is made dependent upon the *expiry of a certain period*. This may be, indeed, the period provided for its implementation and, moreover, also for instance the period within which other legal subjects in the Member States must comply with the directive, which may be later than the date of implementation.[194]

Secondly, the application of a provision of a directive will usually depend upon the *fulfilment of certain (factual) conditions*, although as long as these are ascertainable by the judge the conditions do not preclude direct effect. The latter is not always a clear matter. Article 4(5) of the Sixth VAT Directive, for instance, requires certain activities to be treated as taxable if their treatment as non-taxable would lead to a significant distortion of competition. According to Advocate General Mischo,[195] this provision implied discretion for the Member States and could not be relied upon before a court. The Court of Justice admitted that the application of this provision involves an assessment of economic circumstances, but, nevertheless, it found that this assessment is not exempt from judicial review.[196]

Thirdly, the possible application of a provision of a directive may seem to be *made dependent on the adoption of certain further implementing measures*, such as the establishment of guarantee funds under Directive 80/987 (protection of workers—insolvency of employers),[197] the introduction of a certain, though

---

[192] See further below in this Subsection.   [193] Pescatore 1983, 174–5.

[194] Cf above, Ch 2, Section 2.3.

[195] Joined Cases 231/87 and 129/88 *Carpaneto I* [1989] ECR 3233 (Opinion, paras 22–24).

[196] Ibid. Cf also Case 27/67 *Fink-Frucht* [1968] ECR 223 for Treaty provisions.

[197] [1980] OJ L283/23. Cf Joined Cases C–6/90 and C–9/90 *Francovich* [1991] ECR I–5357. See, however, also Case C–441/99 *Garehveran* [2001] ECR I–7687.

unspecified, type of sanction under Directive 76/207 (equal treatment at work),[198] or the definition of 'building' land under Article 4(3)b of the Sixth VAT Directive.[199] Yet, whether or not provisions of this type will block direct effect will depend on a number of factors. For instance once the necessary measures have been adopted, the provision can no longer be regarded as conditional and a court may proceed to the application of its terms. Thus, for instance, once a Member State has made its choice as to the type of sanction to be imposed in the case of discrimination, the court may review whether the sanction is effective or not.[200] Similarly, not every provision prescribing further implementing measures will make the application of another provision conditional in the sense that without the measures the latter would be inoperative. As a rule this will only be the case when the competent authorities are left discretion with respect to the further implementing measures to be adopted and this discretion affects the result prescribed.[201] Moreover, it may happen that the further implementing measures are not relevant to the case at issue,[202] or that they are merely intended to facilitate the application of the provision concerned.[203]

Fourthly, where the issue of the possible conditionality of the relevant provision arises, the Court often looks into the 'derogations, exceptions, reservations', etc.[204] provided for in the directive to the rule invoked by the person concerned.[205] Derogations may take different forms. Sometimes they are laid down as an obligation for the Member States,[206] in other cases they take the form of an option.[207] Making use of the option is indeed a matter within Member States' discretion.[208] Once the choice has been made, matters may be

---

[198] [1976] OJ L39/40. Cf Case 14/83 *Von Colson* [1984] ECR 1891. See, however, also Case C–271/91 *Marshall II* [1993] ECR I–4367.

[199] [1977] OJ L145/1. Cf Case C–468/93 *Gemeente Emmen* [1996] ECR I–1721.

[200] Cf Case C–271/91 *Marshall II* [1993] ECR I–4367.

[201] Cf Joined Cases C–6/90 and C–9/90 *Francovich* [1991] ECR I–5357 (discretion as to the organization of the guarantee funds), Case 71/85 *FNV* [1986] ECR 3855 (discretion as to the methods but not as to the result to be achieved), and Case C–276/01 *Steffesen* [2003] ECR I–3735.

[202] Cf Case C–221/88 *Busseni* [1990] ECR I–495 (adequate legal safeguard, by means of appropriate transitional provisions, for the rights of other creditors did not apply, as it referred to the protection of rights of creditors other than the two parties involved, namely the ECSC and the State), Case 8/81 *Becker* [1982] ECR 53 (discretion in other areas was not relevant for the application of Art 13B).

[203] Case 8/81 *Becker* [1982] ECR 53.

[204] Note that the procedure under Art 95(4) EC Treaty does not affect the possible direct effect of a directive. Cf Case C–319/97 *Kortas* [1999] ECR I–3143.

[205] Conversely, an individual may of course also rely on a derogation.

[206] E.g. exemptions under the Sixth VAT Directive [1977] OJ L145/1.

[207] The Member States *may* do something (cf Art 25(2) of Directive 77/91 (second company law directive) [1977] OJ L26/1) or the Directive will be 'without prejudice to the right of the Member States to exclude . . .' (cf Art 2(2) of Directive 76/207 (equal treatment at work) [1976] OJ L39/40).

[208] Cf Case 51/76 *VNO* [1977] ECR 113.

different. As far as the content of derogations is concerned, they may be precisely drafted,[209] but they may also leave discretion to the Member States as to their material content.[210] Equally, a derogation may in turn be conditional.[211]

However, derogations as such do not necessarily amount to a condition, in the sense of rendering the provision to be applied conditionally and, consequently, blocking its direct effect. It could be that the Member State has not availed itself of the option to derogate or that, for the case to be decided, the derogation is not relevant.[212] Indeed, if the derogation is relevant to the case, whenever it is precisely drafted the national court can verify whether and to what extent the derogation may apply. However, the matter is less unproblematic where the derogation as such applies, for instance because the Member State has made use of its option, but the derogatory provision leaves the Member States discretion as to its actual operationalization. Here again discretion may block or restrict direct effect. The scope of direct effect of the provision to be applied will then depend on the degree of judicial control that is possible.[213]

Discretion

In the foregoing discussion on the sufficient degree of precision of a provision and its unconditional character it was apparent that a constantly recurring question relates to discretion on the part of the Member States. In legal writing it has been observed that the absence of discretion of the Member States with regard to the implementation of the directive provision is the common denominator of both conditions for direct effect or, in other words, that it is the basic condition to which the other various criteria can be reduced.[214]

A crucial issue which must be kept in mind, particularly with respect to directives, is that the discretion must exist in respect of the content of the provision at issue.[215] The fact that the provision is an integral part of a directive which, taken in its

---

[209] See e.g. 'precise, concrete derogations' in Joined Cases C–19/90 and C–20/90 *Karrella and Karellas* [1991] ECR I–2691, para 22.

[210] Cf Case 51/76 *VNO* [1977] ECR 113, Case 184/83 *Hofmann* [1984] ECR 3047, Case 222/84 *Johnston* [1986] ECR 1651.   [211] Cf Art 9 of Directive 86/378, [1986] OJ L225/40.

[212] Cf the Opinion of AG Mischo in Joined Cases 231/87 and 129/88 *Carpaneto I* [1989] ECR 3233, para 15 ('obligation is unconditional in so far as a given activity can in no case come within the scope of the exception'). Cf also Case 152/84 *Marshall I* [1986] ECR 723, para 54, and Case C–157/02 *Rieser*, judgment of 4 February 2004, nyr in ECR, para 37.

[213] Cf Case 51/76 *VNO* [1977] ECR 113, Case 222/84 *Johnston* [1986] ECR 1651 and Joined Cases C–358/93 and C–416/93 *Bordessa* [1995] ECR I–361.

[214] Cf Kapteyn and VerLoren van Themaat 2003, 424–5, Timmermans 2003, 26–7, Maresceau 1980a, 276, Lauwaars and Timmermans 2003, 27.

[215] Cf Case 8/81 *Becker* [1982] ECR 53, para 25: '. . . as far as their subject-matter is concerned . . .'.

entirety, reserves to the Member States a margin of discretion in various respects, is not an obstacle to direct effect of the provision. As long as the latter can be severed from the general body of provisions and applied separately it may, on its own, be directly effective.[216]

As was already discussed in Chapter 5, Member States enjoy a degree of freedom as to the forms and methods of implementation of a directive. In some cases this freedom has been invoked to deny direct effect of a provision of a directive. However, such an argument confuses the issue of direct effect of a particular provision with that of the discretion available to Member States with regard to the choice of form and methods for implementation of the directive into national law.[217]

> The question as to whether or not discretion is left to the Member States is a matter of interpretation of the relevant provision or set of provisions. Sometimes matters may be quite straightforward. In other cases, however, things are less certain. In particular, provisions using vague concepts which have to be substantiated in the light of the facts of the case are notoriously difficult. A theoretical distinction often referred to in this respect is that between indefinite legal concepts and discretion. The former imply that there are several possible views as to their interpretation but only one is right; discretion means not only that a choice of different views is possible but also that it is lawful to follow any of them.[218] It is only the latter form, which some call 'real discretion',[219] which seems to preclude direct effect. In practice, however, it is not always an easy task to decide whether such 'real discretion' exists or not. This is confirmed, for instance, by the different views of Advocates General on the one hand and the Court of Justice on the other with respect to the same provision.[220]

Originally the mere existence of discretion was generally considered to be an obstacle to direct effect[221] and today, under certain circumstances it still is, in particular where the discretion may be labelled as 'very broad'.[222] However, the case law of the

---

[216] Ibid, para 29. Cf also Joined Cases C–465/00, C–138/01, and C–139/01, *Rechnungshof* [2003] ECR I–4989, para 100 and C–157/02 *Rieser*, judgment of 4 February 2004, nyr in ECR, where one provision of the directive had direct effect but another not.

[217] Cf e.g. Case 71/85 *FNV* [1986] ECR 3855 and the Opinion of AG Mancini, at 3867. For a comparable line of reasoning see also Case C–157/02 *Rieser*, judgment of 4 February 2004, nyr in ECR, para 32.

[218] Definition by Kapteyn and VerLoren van Themaat 1998, 532.

[219] Cf Timmermans 1979, 540.

[220] Cf Joined Cases C–6/90 and C–9/90 *Francovich* [1991] ECR I–5357, Case C–221/88 *Busseni* [1990] ECR I–495, Joined Cases 231/87 and 129/88 *Carpaneto I* [1989] ECR 3233.

[221] Cf the judgment in *Kaefer and Procacci* (Joined Cases C–100/89 and C–101/89 [1990] ECR I–4647), where the Court held that 'an unconditional provision is one which leaves no discretion to the Member States' (para 26).

[222] Cf Case C–157/02 *Rieser*, judgment of 4 February 2004, nyr in ECR, para 40. See, however also Case C–441/99 *Gharehveran* [2001] ECR I–7687.

Court has evolved considerably in this respect. In *Francovich*[223] the Court admitted that several Articles of Directive 80/987 (protection of workers—insolvency of employers)[224] left the Member States discretion in determining the content of the guarantee to be paid to the employees concerned. Nevertheless it found that as it was possible to determine the minimum guarantee provided for on the basis of the terms of the directive as such, the provisions in question were unconditional and sufficiently precise. This approach was confirmed in a rather puzzling *obiter dictum* in *Marshall II* and in *Faccini Dori*.[225] Thus, discretion on the part of the Member States with respect to the content of the measures to be taken does not necessarily seem to be an obstacle to direct effect as long as the national court can itself construe the content of the provision to be applied on the basis of the terms of the directive.[226] In *Francovich* it was still the 'minimum default option' that had to be applied.

Interestingly, the broad discretion that, ultimately, blocked direct effect in *Francovich*, namely with regard to determining the person liable to pay the claims guaranteed by the directive at issue, did not work out in the same way in *Gharehveran*.[227] The Court found that since that discretion was fully used by the Member State concerned, it could no longer be invoked validly for the purposes of preventing Ms Gharehveran from relying on the directive in national courts.

Another important tendency in the Court's case law which implies that the mere existence of discretion does not necessarily prevent direct effect, has already been alluded to above.[228] In *VNO*[229] and its progeny[230] the Court recognized the possibility for the individual to invoke a provision of a directive to make the national court rule whether the competent national authorities have kept within the limits of their discretion as set out in the directive.

Indeed, conceptually it may seem difficult to reconcile the two approaches of the Court of Justice. The first, despite the concession made in *Francovich*, still focuses on the absence of discretion, while the second takes discretion as a starting point, and, subsequently, allows judicial control.[231] The crux of the matter is that direct effect must be considered within the context of the concrete case.

---

[223] Joined Cases C–6/90 and C–9/90 [1991] ECR I–5357.   [224] [1980] OJ L283/23.

[225] Case C–271/91 [1993] ECR I–4367, para 37 and Case C–91/92 [1994] ECR I–3325, para 17. More recently, see Case C–303/98 *Simap* [2000] ECR I–7963, paras 68–69.

[226] This was, for instance, not possible in Case C–403/98 *Monte Arcosu* [2001] ECR I–103 (which related to a regulation) or in Case C–365/98 *Brinkmann II* [2000] ECR I–4619.

[227] Case C–441/99 [2001] ECR I–7687.   [228] See Subsections 9.3.4 and 9.4.1.

[229] Case 51/76 [1977] ECR 113. Cf also the Opinion of AG Jacobs in Case C–164/90 *Muwi* [1991] ECR I–6049, para 25.

[230] Cf Case C–72/95 *Kraaijeveld* [1996] ECR I–5403, Case C–435/97, *WWF* [1999] ECR I–5613, and C–287/98 *Linster* [2000] ECR I–6917.

[231] A kind of mixture of the 'orthodox' approach to direct effect, i.e. taking unconditionality and sufficient degree of precision as a starting point, and the control of the observance of the limits laid down in a directive can be found in Case 126/82 *Smit* [1983] ECR 73.

9.4.3   Direct effect and the context of the case

The question whether the conditions for direct effect of a particular provision are satisfied cannot be separated from the concrete case to be decided and the answer will vary accordingly. The context of the case and, in particular, the way in which the national court deploys the directive will also determine the issue of direct effect.

The understanding of direct effect as '*Alternativ-Normierung*',[232] also explains the conditions of sufficient precision and unconditionality. The existence of discretion is hardly compatible with this idea, since the court is then unable to know what the applicable rules should be. Discretion implies certain choices, either by the legislator or by the executive, which cannot be made by a court.[233] Yet, what the court can do, is to control whether the authorities have kept within the limits Community law imposes. As explained in Subsection 9.3.3, judicial activity is not limited to the positive application of the provisions of a directive to the facts of the case. In several cases the court confines itself to reviewing the national law in the light of the directive and, where appropriate, disapplying the national provisions, without it being necessary to apply the directive instead. In such an event, the existence of discretion as such is not an obstacle to direct effect, provided that the limits of the discretion are sufficiently clear to serve as a standard for judicial review.[234] Whatever a Member State does *within* those limits is as such not submitted to judicial review. However, once the limits are exceeded, it is up to the courts to intervene. The result may then indeed be that a provision has direct effect in some cases, but not in others.[235]

> The requirements for direct effect must be considered against this background of all the possible ways in which Community law provisions can be used. In a concrete case, the answer to the question whether the national court, equipped with the provision at issue, will be able to deal with the problem before it, will depend on what the party, which relies on Community law, is seeking.
>
> Where a person uses Community law to assert a 'positive' claim, the appreciation of the unconditional and sufficiently precise character of the provisions at issue may differ from a situation where one seeks, for instance, the annulment of an individual decision or where Community law is raised as a defence in

---

[232] I.e. legal norms which can be applied by national courts, where appropriate, instead of national rules which are incompatible with Community law provisions. Cf above, Subsection 9.3.3.

[233] Cf Case C–365/98 *Brinkmann II* [2000] ECR I–4619, para 38 and C–157/02 *Rieser*, judgment of 4 February 2004, nyr in ECR, para 40.

[234] Cf Maresceau 1980a, 276. The same is perhaps an even more important issue in cases where a court has to assess whether, during the implementation period, a Member State has taken measures which are liable gravely to jeopardize the attainment of the result prescribed by the directive. Cf Case C–129/96 *Inter-Environement Wallonie* [1997] ECR I–7411.

[235] Cf Kapteyn and VerLoren van Themaat 1998, 532, Lauwaars and Timmermans 2003, 28. Cf also the discussion of Case 14/83 *Von Colson* [1984] ECR 1891, Case 222/84 *Johnston* [1986] ECR 1651 and Case C–271/91 *Marshall II* [1993] ECR I–4367 in the first edition of this book, 289–90.

criminal proceedings. Arguably, for positive application, thus for a fully fledged alternative, the national court will need 'more' and another type of guidance from the provisions at issue than when it is asked to proceed to review of legality.[236] In the first situation discretion will block application. The court cannot make this choice, which is up to the legislator or the executive. In the second situation, discretion will not block the possibility of review.[237] Moreover, an important consideration in this context may be that in many cases, also those involving discretion, there is no need for the courts to proceed with 'positive application' and risk doing things they are not allowed to do. After the decision of the administration has been, for instance, annulled, it is usually not up to the courts but up to the competent authorities to take a fresh decision. In this process, the latter may very well take into account the limits set out in Community law.[238]

A case like *Comitato*,[239] may illustrate how things may differ. The case started with the national court asking the question as to whether Article 4 of the Waste Directive does grant individuals 'subjective rights'.[240] The Court responded that Article 4, which 'indicates a programme to be followed and sets out the objectives which the Member States must observe in their performance of the more specific obligations imposed on them [by the directive]',[241] does not require, in itself, the adoption of specific measures or a particular method of waste disposal. Therefore, it is 'neither unconditional nor sufficiently precise and thus is not capable of conferring rights on which individuals may rely as against the State'.[242] As long as this case is understood as saying that individuals cannot claim the adoption of specific measures or a particular method of waste disposal from the competent authorities, there is no problem. In this respect it is not directly effective. However, this does not exclude that the court may be called upon to review whether the measures taken by the authorities are in conformity with the objectives and, thus, within the limits drawn by that Article. A later judgment in an infringement proceedings has confirmed that the latter option is open.[243] After having stated that the provision at issue does not specify the actual content of the measures which must be taken, the Court pointed out that, whilst it leaves to the Member States a margin of discretion in assessing the need for such measures, it is binding on them as to the objective to be achieved. Then the Court continued by saying that if a situation

---

[236] Or in the words of AG Léger in his Opinion in Case C–287/98 *Linster* [2000] ECR I–6917: 'When reviewing the compatibility of a subordinate rule, the need to ensure that the directive is precise is less important . . .' (para 74). Cf also Gilliaux 1998, 118–21 and Wathelet 2004.

[237] Cf also e.g. Case C–365/98 *Brinkmann II* [2000] ECR I–4619, where the directive did not confer right to be taxed according to a certain type of duty on products, but, on the other hand, it was possible to establish that the German legislator went beyond the discretion conferred by the directive.

[238] Cf an indication in this respect in Case C–435/97 *WWF* [1999] ECR I–5613.

[239] Case C–236/92 [1994] ECR I–483.   [240] Directive 75/442 [1975] OJ L194/47.

[241] Para 12 of the Judgment.   [242] Para 14 of the Judgment.

[243] Case C–365/97 *Commission v. Italy* [1999] ECR I–7773.

which is not in conformity with the objectives laid down in the first paragraph of Article 4 of the Directive 'persists and leads in particular to a significant deterioration in the environment over a protracted period without any action being taken by the competent authorities, it may be an indication that the Member States have exceeded the discretion conferred on them by that provision'.[244]

In brief, the conditions for direct effect cannot be separated from the context of the concrete case. Therefore, the answer to the question whether they are satisfied will vary accordingly. For a positive application of a directive the conditions of sufficient precision and unconditionality may often have a different content when compared to the degree of precision and unconditionality required for judicial review.[245] The result of this *contextual approach*, i.e. testing the conditions *in concreto* and for the specific purposes of the case, is that the conditions for direct effect are of a relatively limited value only. Considered against this background, the proposal of Advocate General Léger not to examine anymore whether the conditions of direct effect are satisfied, at least not in a situation where a directive is relied on 'where they are invoked for the purposes of reviewing the legality of rules of domestic law',[246] is neither surprising nor revolutionary. In the final analysis the ultimate test is to be found in the doctrine of separation of powers and the place attributed therein to the courts. Pescatore has pointed out in this respect that direct effect 'depends less on the intrinsic quality of the rules concerned than on the *possumus* or *non possumus* of the judges'.[247] The reality is that even the question of what the national court as a court of law can and cannot do is no longer entirely a matter of national law.

As is well-known, in discrimination cases[248] and, more recently, even in certain cases involving 'mere' restrictions,[249] the Court has provided the national courts with an aid to fill the gap, if it occurs: the same rules must be applied to the disadvantaged group as those which are applicable to the persons which are 'better off'. Such an approach is in sharp contrast with how national courts

---

[244] Para 68 of the Judgment. See for a comparable line of argument AG Kokott, Opinion in Case C–127/02 *Landelijke Vereniging tot Behoud van de Waddenzee*, of 29 January 2004, paras 132–137.

[245] However, Galmot en Bonichot 1988, 17, for instance, argue that review of legality and direct effect in the sense of 'substitution' are two different problems which have to be resolved in accordance with different criteria.

[246] Opinion in Case C–287/98 *Linster* [2000] ECR I–6917, para 82. See also Wathelet 2004. After having compared how courts proceed in similar situations in the context of *national* law (no preliminary question as to whether the provisions at issue are unconditional and sufficiently precise) I have suggested to take the argument a step further and proposed to drop the examination of the conditions altogether. Cf Prechal 2000, 1064. For differing national approaches see also Jans & Prinssen 2002.

[247] Pescatore 1983, 177. Cf also in the same sense AG Van Gerven, Opinion in Case C–128/92 *Banks* [1994] ECR I–1209, para 27, and Kapteyn and VerLoren van Themaat 2003, 427.

[248] Cf Case C–184/89 *Nimz* [1991] ECR I–297 and Case C–15/96 *Schöning-Kougebetopoulou* [1998] ECR I–47. See also Case C–360/97 *Nijhuis* [1999] ECR I–1919, in particular paras 30–31.

[249] Case C–18/95 *Terhoeve* [1999] ECR I–345.

may see the things. The Dutch *Hoge Raad*,[250] for instance, refused to apply Article 26 (prohibition of discrimination) of the International Covenant on Civil and Political Rights because the solution for the inequality at issue[251] was not a matter for a court but for the legislature. It is up to the latter to decide how equality must be realized in this respect. Apparently, what seems to be a justiciable matter in the eyes of the Court of Justice is often, for reasons of judicial restraint, not necessarily considered to be justiciable in the purely national context; or, as was pointed out by Mertens de Wilmars, 'false' discretion may come into being through the powerlessness of the courts, which may fear the accusation of '*gouvernement des juges*'.[252]

9.5   Limits to direct effect of directives

9.5.1   Obligations under international agreements and general principles of law

Although direct effect of Community law is considered to be one of the twin pillars of the Community legal system,[253] or one of its essential characteristics,[254] it is not sacrosanct. Direct effect of Community law and thus also direct effect of directives has its limits. The most important and controversial limitation is, indeed, the denial of horizontal direct effect of directives which is the main topic of the present Section. However, before turning to this '*plat de résistance*', I would like to briefly discuss two other limits.

The first limitation results from the application of the conflict rule laid down in Article 307 of the EC Treaty. In two French cases[255] the Court came to the conclusion that the national court was not obliged to disapply the national provision which was contrary to the directive at issue in so far as the application of the provision concerned was necessary to ensure the performance by the Member State concerned of obligations arising from an agreement anterior to the Treaty in the sense of Article 307. It was for the national court to verify the concrete obligations under the agreement, in order to determine the extent to which these obligations constitute an obstacle to the application of the provision of the directive. Similarly, the national court had to verify whether the national provisions in question were designed to implement the above-mentioned obligations.

General principles of law and, in particular, the principle of legal certainty, may under particular circumstances also entail that directly effective provisions of

---

[250] *Hoge Raad* 12 October 1984, NJCM-Bulletin 1985, 32.
[251] A woman could, upon marriage with a Dutch citizen, opt for Dutch citizenship while a man could not.   [252] Mertens de Wilmars 1969, 78.
[253] Cf Wyatt and Dashwood 2000, 62.   [254] Opinion 1/91 *EEA* [1991] ECR I–6079, para 21.
[255] Case C–345/89 *Stoeckel* [1991] ECR I–4047 and Case C–158/91 *Levy* [1993] ECR I–4287.

Community law cannot be relied on.[256] Establishing the direct effect of a provision is a matter of interpretation. As a rule, interpretation of a Community law provision by the Court of Justice has retroactive effect, i.e. the provision *as interpreted by the Court* applies from its entry into force.[257] For direct effect of directives this implies, for reasons particular to directives,[258] that the provision which is declared to be directly effective produces this effect from the end of the period provided for its implementation, even if the judgment making this plain is rendered at a later stage. However, in exceptional cases the Court has been prepared to limit the general retroactive effect of its ruling. The basis for such a limitation is 'important considerations of legal certainty'.[259]

This limitation of direct effect as such must be carefully distinguished from the situation where the Court allows the application of national principles within the framework of national procedures used for the enforcement of Community law. As was already discussed in Chapter 7, in particular Subsection 7.3.3, in a number of cases the Court of Justice did not object to the application of the principle of unjust enrichment[260] or the principle of legitimate expectations.[261] The difference is, in my view, that in the first situation direct effect itself is restricted, while the second type of cases limits the—what one may call—'effects of direct effect'. Or, as the Court put it in *Edis*, whenever national courts apply Community law to the facts of the case,

. . . it is . . . necessary . . . for the detailed procedural rules governing legal proceedings under national law to have been complied with as regards matters both of form and of substance.

The application of those detailed rules must not . . . be confused with a limitation on the effects of a judgment of the Court ruling on a request for interpretation of a provision of Community law. The consequence of such a limitation is to deprive litigants, who would normally be in a position, under their national procedural rules, to exercise the rights conferred on them by the Community provision concerned, of the right to rely on it in support of their claims.[262]

Admittedly, the distinction is very subtle and may in some cases be extremely difficult to make. The link between direct effect of the relevant provision and the 'effect of its direct effect' may be so close that one may wonder whether the limitation of the immediate consequences does not amount to a limitation of the direct effect itself.

---

[256] For an example of how legal certainty may block direct application of a regulation see Case C–108/01 *Parma* [2003] ECR I–5121.   [257] Cf Case 61/79 *Denkavit Italiana* [1980] ECR 1205.

[258] Cf Ch 2, Section 2.3. As to entry into force of directives, see n 47 in that Section.

[259] Cf e.g. Case 43/75 *Defrenne II* [1976] ECR 455, Case 24/86 *Blaizot* [1988] ECR 379, Case C–262/88 *Barber* [1990] ECR I–1889, and Joined Cases C–197/94 and C–252/94 *Bautiaa and Société Française Maritime* [1996] ECR I–505. As is well-known, it is solely for the Court of Justice to determine whether the circumstances are such that the principle of legal certainty would be compromised.

[260] See e.g. Case 68/79 *Just* [1980] ECR 501.

[261] See e.g. Case 265/78 *Ferwerda* [1980] ECR 617.

[262] Case C–231/96 *Edis* [1998] ECR I–4951, paras 17–18.

9.5.2   Horizontal direct effect of directives

Arguments pro and contra

As was already observed, the most important limitation of direct effect of directives is the absence of horizontal direct effect, as decided by the Court of Justice in the *Marshall I* case and confirmed in *Faccini Dori*.[263] By the terms 'horizontal direct effect' I understand that the relevant provision can be invoked and enforced by an individual *vis-à-vis* other individuals. For reasons to be explained later,[264] this concept must be distinguished from the concept of 'inverse vertical direct effect'[265] which means that a Member State can rely on a provision against a private individual. As far as directives are concerned, such an effect has equally been denied by the Court of Justice.[266] Thus, also in this situation direct effect is limited: the application of a directive may not amount to the State imposing an obligation upon private individuals and subsequently enforcing it against them.

The issue of horizontal direct effect has generated considerable literature, both before and after the *Marshall I* judgment. By now, all the possible arguments *pro* and *contra* horizontal direct effect seem to be on the table: some are more convincing than others, but not one of them is entirely decisive. They can be summarized as follows.[267]

The *first argument* against horizontal direct effect of directives draws upon the definition of directives in Article 249(3). According to this definition directives are binding upon the Member States and therefore not upon private individuals. For this reason they cannot impose obligations on individuals but only on Member States. In its judgment in *Marshall I* the Court found in favour of this textual argument, keeping close to the terms of Article 249(3). This approach is, however, difficult to reconcile with the Court's case law on direct effect of, notably, Treaty provisions. From this case law it appears, firstly, that direct effect is not conditional upon the addressee of the relevant provision[268] and that the nature of the legal relationship involved plays no part in the matter at all.[269] Further, the case law on direct effect of Treaty provisions has made clear that in determining the legal effects it is the content of the measure rather than its form which is decisive. There has been no indication

---

[263] Case 152/84 [1986] ECR 723 and Case C–91/92 [1994] ECR I–3325, respectively.

[264] See further below in this Subsection.

[265] For the same distinction (which is, however, not made by everybody) cf also Arnull 1988, 44, Langenfeld 1992, 958, Nicolaysen 1984, 390, Schilling 1988, 659, and Betlem 2002, 96–8.

[266] Cf Case 80/86 *Kolpinghuis* [1987] ECR 3969 and Case C–168/95 *Arcaro* [1996] ECR I–4705.

[267] For the various arguments (and often further references) see e.g. Timmermans 1979, Easson 1979b, Wyatt 1983, Nicolaysen 1984, Schockweiler 1993c. Craig 1997, Mastroianni 1999, Dougan 2000a, Colgan 2002, and Tridimas 2002. For certain further details see also the first edition of this book, 295–305.

[268] Cf Barents, 1992, 98, Easson 1979b, 71.   [269] Barents 1982, 101.

that direct effect is dependent on the legal character of the act in which the relevant provision has been laid down.[270] According to some, the mere fact that Member States are obliged, under Article 249(3), to implement the directive does not as such decide the question as to the potential legal effects of the *substantive* provisions.[271]

The *second argument* against horizontal direct effect of directives refers to the difference between regulations and directives. Only the former are, according to Article 249, directly applicable and may, for that reason, impose obligations on private individuals.[272] Accepting horizontal direct effect of directives would amount to assimilating directives to regulations. This argument was embraced by the Court in *Faccini Dori* when it held that the acceptance of horizontal direct effect would mean 'to recognize a power in the Community to enact obligations for individuals with immediate effect, whereas it has competence to do so only where it is empowered to adopt regulations'.[273] This argument of— no doubt—constitutional character is often also considered an expression of the rule of law or, more precisely, of the 'principle of legality'.[274] Yet, with respect to the distinction between regulations and directives, it has been observed that such an argument is the same as that put forward against direct effect of directives in general, which has, however, been dismissed by the Court.[275] Moreover, allowing horizontal direct effect of directives would change nothing with respect to the obligation to implement them,[276] nor would it alter the choice of form and methods left to the Member States.[277] To this one may add that 'the directive', as an instrument of Community law, has undergone an important development to which, however, Article 249 has not been adapted.[278]

The *third argument* relates to legal certainty. It comprises two distinct elements. Firstly, there was no legal requirement to publish directives in the Official Journal.[279] This rather formalistic argument according to some,[280] is considered by certain other scholars to be an important one. Advocate General Lenz made

---

[270] Cf Barents 1982, 102.

[271] Cf AG Jacob's Opinion in Case C–316/93 *Vaneetveld* [1994] ECR I–763, para 20. Cf also Wyatt and Dashwood 2000, 99–102 and Richter 1988, 397–8.

[272] Case C–108/01 *Parma* [2003] ECR I–5121.

[273] Case C–91/92 [1994] ECR I–3325, para 24.

[274] The German '*Gesetzmäßigkeitsprinzip*'. Cf Royla and Lackhoff 1998, who in this respect point out the fact that any intervention by the public authorities at the detriment of individuals needs a valid legal basis. [275] Cf Case 41/74 *Van Duyn* [1974] ECR 1337.

[276] Cf the Opinion of AG Jacobs in Case C–316/93 *Vaneetveld* [1994] ECR I–763, para 25.

[277] Cf the Opinion of AG Lenz in Case C–91/92 *Faccini Dori* [1994] ECR I–3325, para 59. Cf also Emmert 1992, 64–5 and Barents 1982, 103.

[278] Cf Opinion of AG Jacobs in Case C–316/93 *Vaneetveld* [1994] ECR I–763, para 28. In contrast to what the terms of Art 249(3) suggest, the choice of form and methods has been curtailed, directives may be precise and exhaustive etc.

[279] According to Art 191 of the EEC Treaty, thus before its amendment by the EU Treaty.

[280] Cf Timmermans 1979, 542, Barents 1982, 97, and Schilling 1988, 63. According to Richter 1988, 402, what really matters is that the law is accessible.

a distinction in this respect between publication with a 'constitutive' effect and a merely declaratory publication. In his opinion '[t]he basic condition for a burden imposed on the citizen by legislative measures is their *constitutive publication in an official organ*'.[281] The entry into force of directives is, under the 'old' EEC Treaty, made dependent upon their notification and not their publication. This is now different under Article 254 EC Treaty.

Secondly, it was maintained that to allow directives to be pleaded against individuals would create a situation of considerable legal insecurity. In principle, certainly as far as obligations are concerned, individuals must be able to rely on national law. If horizontal direct effect were accepted, individuals would be required to scrutinize both national law and the relevant Community directives, which would impose a heavy burden on them. This argument has been countered that neither the situation under national law nor the situation with respect to regulations is much different.[282] However this might be, the Court seems to attribute quite some weight to this argument. In a recent case it held that 'the principle of legal certainty prevents directives from creating obligations for individuals'.[283]

However, even with the issue of legal certainty which lies at the heart of the entire discussion, there are at least two scenarios. On the one hand, there is the legal certainty of those who are entitled to expect that their position as safeguarded by the directive will be protected. On the other hand, there is the legal certainty of those who would be confronted with an obligation which is not laid down in national law. The ultimate question is: whose legal certainty deserves protection? In my view, this question cannot be answered once and for all, and in general terms. Depending on the context of the case the outcome may differ. As a rule, for the reasons already presented above, an individual should be able to rely on and enforce a provision of a directive against another individual.[284] The latter may raise in his defence that he was not and in all reasonableness could not have been acquainted with the obligations resulting from the directive at issue. Whether this defence will succeed depends on several factors, such as the publication of the directive, the experience and vigilance of the defendant etc.[285]

The *fourth argument* against horizontal direct effect of directives appeared in *Ratti*[286] where the Court held that a Member State which has not adopted the implementing measures required by the directive at issue may not rely, *vis-à-vis* individuals, on its own failure to perform the obligation which the

---

[281] Opinion in Case C–91/92 *Faccini Dori* [1994] ECR I–3325, para 64.

[282] Cf Emmert 1992, 65, Richter 1988, 402, Van Gerven 1994b, 352, Craig 1997, 542.

[283] Cf Case C–201/02 *Wells*, judgment of 7 January 2004, nyr in ECR, para 56.

[284] Cf, however, Langenfeld 1992, 960 who makes a choice in favour of the person who will be confronted with a new obligation.

[285] Cf also Emmert 1992, 65, Wyatt 1983, 246, as well as the Opinion of AG Jacobs in Case C–316/93 *Vaneetveld* [1994] I–763, para 34.   [286] Case 148/78 [1979] ECR 1629.

directive entails. It has been reiterated in other cases, such as *Faccini Dori*,[287] where the Court maintained that its case law on direct effect of directives seeks to prevent the State from taking advantage of its own failure to comply with Community law and thus depriving the individuals of the benefit of the rights which directives may confer on them. This so-called 'principle of estoppel' has already been discussed at length in Subsection 9.2.2. The most obvious counter-argument is indeed that the Court of Justice has never attached much importance to the principle of estoppel as a conceptual basis. It was rather doctrine which declared this principle to be the ultimate rationale of direct effect of directives.[288]

An important argument in favour of horizontal direct effect draws upon the need for uniform application and the '*effet utile*' of Community law.[289] To allow horizontal direct effect of directives would increase their effectiveness, and would constitute a further incentive for the Member States to implement directives in time and safeguard as far as possible uniform application of Community law and the protection of rights which individuals derive from it.[290] The latter would be compromised not only by a denial of horizontal direct effect as such but also by fresh discriminations to which such a denial would lead. The anomalies to which the denial of horizontal direct effect of directives would lead,[291] was particularly conspicuous after the *Marshall I* judgment, where the Court introduced an unfair distinction between private employees and State employees: the latter may rely on a directive while the former may not. Such a distinction may vary over time, as in the case of privatization of nationally run businesses, and from Member State to Member State, with as a consequence discriminations and inequalities in conditions of competition, which can hardly be considered compatible with Community law as such.[292] In other—general—terms, both from the perspective of the functioning of the internal market as from the perspective of equality as a fundamental right, the Court's approach is deemed highly unfortunate.[293]

---

[287] Case C–91/92 [1994] ECR I–3325. It should be noted that in this case the Court invited the Member States to give their opinions as to the possible horizontal direct effect of directives. By many, this case was considered a test case.

[288] Cf above, Subsections 9.2.2 and 9.2.3. See also e.g. Emmert, 1992, 66 and Colgan 2002, 563–64.

[289] It has even been submitted that to deny horizontal direct effect of directives would amount to a denial of supremacy of Community law. Cf Barents 1982, 103, Boch and Lane 1992, 179–80, Manin 1990, 690.

[290] Cf Emmert 1992, 63 ff., Curtin 1990, 197, Schockweiler 1993c, 1213 ff., Easson 1979b, 75, the Opinion of AG Jacobs in Case C–316/93 *Vaneetveld* [1994] ECR I–763, and Dougan 2000a, 588–9 who links the existence of exactly the same rights and obligations to the status of Union citizenship.

[291] Already pointed out before *Marshall* by e.g. Easson 1979b, 76.

[292] Cf e.g. the opinion of AG Van Gerven in Case C–271/91 *Marshall II* [1993] ECR I–4367, para 12.

[293] Cf Dougan 2000a, 587–9 and Mastroianni 1999, 432–5, who indicates the risk that, under the constraints of the fundamental principle of equality, national courts may opt for a unilateral extension of horizontal effect.

The evolution after *Marshall I*

The *Marshall I* judgment indeed marked an important departure from the Court's usual approach to interpretation, which had often been inspired by '*effet utile*' (and thus the concern to make provisions of Community law as effective as possible) and concern with uniform application of Community law. According to some authors an argument of a political rather than a legal nature played an important part in this decision, namely the difficulty which some national courts had in accepting direct effect of directives at all.[294]

In contrast to what might perhaps be expected, the evolution of the case law after *Marshall I* saw to it that the discussion did not quieten down.[295]

Firstly, the Court has stretched the concept of 'the State' to all public authorities and equally to some public enterprises.[296] All these bodies, even if they could not be held responsible for the non-implementation of the directive at issue, have nevertheless been prevented from raising 'their' Member State's failure as a defence. This development clearly undermined the principle of estoppel, in so far as the latter could be considered to be the basis of direct effect of directives.[297]

Secondly, the obligation of consistent interpretation[298] imposed upon national courts has placed considerable constraint upon the latter, forcing them to operate at the edges of their competences in order to give the fullest possible effect to Community law. In some cases, consistent interpretation comes very close to giving horizontal direct effect to directives. However, at the same time this doctrine cannot be considered to be a fully fledged alternative for the absence of horizontal direct effect, since it also has its limits.

The third element to play a part in the issue is the Court's judgment in the *Francovich* case,[299] according to which the Member State is liable, under certain conditions, for damages incurred by an individual in the case of non-implementation of a directive. However, *Francovich* is only a second best solution. It cannot satisfactorily replace the direct application of a directive and, in particular, it does not remedy the unequal conditions under which the various legal subjects have to operate.[300]

[294] Cf Wyatt and Dashwood 2000, 99, Morris 1989, 314. For severe criticism of the judgment see e.g. Nicolaysen 1986, Richter 1988, Curtin 1990, 196–7, Boch and Lane 1992, 179–80. More recently, in the same sense Colgan 2002, 564–7, indicating, as many others, the fact that in *Faccini Dori* all but one of the Member States that made submissions were against horizontal direct effect.

[295] For discussion of this evolution see e.g. Van Gerven 1994, Boch and Lane 1992, Emmert 1992, Grabitz 1993 and the Opinion of AG Jacobs in Case C–316/93 *Vaneetveld* [1994] ECR I–763.

[296] Cf above, Ch 4, in particular Section 4.2.

[297] See above, Subsection 9.2.3.

[298] Discussed *in extenso* in Ch 8. To this one may also add the disadvantageous effects which vertical direct effect may have for third parties. See above, Ch 4, Subsection 4.1.

[299] Joined Cases C–6/90 and C–9/90 [1991] ECR I–5357.

[300] As to the shortcomings of *Francovich* in this context, see e.g. the Opinion of AG Van Gerven in Case C–271/91 *Marshall II* [1993] ECR I–4367, para 12 and the Opinion of AG Jacobs in Case C–316/93 *Vaneetveld* [1994] ECR I–763, para 30.

Fourthly, the Court's more recent case law has been strongly influenced by the desire for national courts to give full and effective protection to the rights which individuals derive from Community law.[301] However, this full and effective protection is at the same time seriously compromised by the Court's refusal to give horizontal direct effect to directives.[302]

To this one may add the sometimes perplexing cases in which the Court accepts horizontal effects which result from the application of a directive in 'vertical situations'.[303]

In summary, the Court's legal construction regarding the internal effects of directives is considered to be extremely complex, both for the national courts and the individual. It involves heavy burdens for national courts,[304] it may lead to considerable confusion,[305] and there is the intrinsic risk that, due to the case-to-case solutions, it may result in new inconsistencies and inequalities.[306] According to some, the system has become so extremely complicated and opaque,[307] that it is itself at odds with the principle of legal certainty.[308] It is against the background of these more general considerations that some scholars advocate the recognition of (some kind of) horizontal direct effect of directives. Such a recognition would, to a large extent, counter the disadvantages I have just described and would contribute to more complete, coherent, and equal judicial protection of individuals.[309]

Inverse vertical direct effect?

If horizontal direct effect were to be accepted, at the end of the day, should this also imply that under certain circumstances a Member State may rely on an obligation in a directive against a private individual? Arnull[310] has rightly remarked that the question whether a directive may ever impose obligations on private individuals is broader than the question whether it can produce horizontal direct effect. The Court answered the first question in the negative in *Marshall I* and it is this judgment which is often cited as an argument in cases concerning inverse vertical direct effect.[311] For both horizontal direct effect and inverse vertical direct effect the underlying principle, i.e. the binding nature of directives *vis-à-vis* the state, is the

---

[301] Cf above, Ch 7, Subsection 7.2.2 and Section 7.3 .

[302] Cf Boch and Lane 1992, 172. Cf also the Opinion of AG Jacobs in Case C–316/93 *Vaneetveld* [1994] ECR I–763, para 29.   [303] For a more detailed discussion see below, Subsection 9.5.3.

[304] Cf Van Gerven 1994, 349.   [305] Cf Boch and Lane 1992, 183.

[306] Cf the Opinion of AG Van Gerven in Case C–271/91 *Marshall II* [1993] ECR I–4367, para 12.

[307] Cf Emmert and Pereira de Azevedo 1993, 17.

[308] Cf the Opinion of AG Jacobs in Case C–316/93 *Vaneetveld* [1994] ECR I–763, para 31.

[309] Cf Van Gerven 1994 and Grabitz 1993. Grabitz (71) takes the arguments even further and argues that for reasons of '*Lastengleichheit*' inverse vertical direct effect should be accepted as well.

[310] Arnull 1988, 44.

[311] Cf Case 80/86 *Kolpinghuis* [1987] ECR 3969 and Case C–168/95 *Arcaro* [1996] ECR I–4705. See further also Joined Cases C–74/95 and C–129/95 *X* [1996] ECR I–6609.

same. However, to allow horizontal direct effect of directives does not necessarily mean that inverse vertical direct effect is allowed as well. Reliance by a Member State on an unimplemented or not correctly implemented directive against a private individual may after all be precluded by the principle of estoppel,[312] brought down to its proper proportions, without making it the ratio of direct effect of directives. Yet, as will be discussed below, certain lines taken in more recent case law may have a limited inverse vertical direct effect as a final consequence.

9.5.3 Horizontal side effects of direct effect

Just like *Marshall I*, *Faccini Dori*[313] did not stop the debate about horizontal direct effect of directives. Apart from the rather hostile reactions to the judgment,[314] it is in particular what appears to be a slight form of schizophrenia on the Court's part following *Faccini*, that gives rise to new criticism. On the one hand, on several occasions the Court has firmly confirmed its denial of horizontal direct effect.[315] On the other hand, in a whole line of cases it has accepted some kind of horizontal side effects.[316] In a few of the cases the Court simply ignored the possible detrimental effect of its judgment on the position of private individuals, although in some of them it was brought to its attention.[317] Arguably, the Court just left it to the national court to sort out how to give effect to the preliminary decision.[318] In other cases it just repeated that directives, as such, cannot by themselves impose obligations upon individuals, without such questions about the issue being referred by the national courts involved.[319] In yet other—relatively rare—cases it said a bit more.[320]

In legal writing, considerable effort has been put into systematizing, analysing, and explaining what is perceived as a complex, ambiguous, and inconsistent body of case law.[321] On the other hand, it is interesting to note that these efforts and critique

---

[312] Or its equivalents (*nemo auditur/non venire*). Cf Wyatt 1983, 247 and the opinion of AG Jacobs in Case C–316/93 *Vaneetveld* [1994] ECR I–763, para 33. Nicolaysen 1984, 389 and Langenfeld 1992, 959 would appear to see this rather as a consequence of the Court's case law in Art 226 proceedings: no excuses for non-implementation drawing upon direct effect.   [313] Case C–91/92 [1994] ECR I–3325.

[314] Cf e.g. Tridimas 1994 and Emmert and Pereira de Azevedo 1995.

[315] Cf Case C–192/94 El *Corte Inglés* [1996] ECR I–1281, Case C–97/96 *Daihatsu-Händler* [1997] ECR I–6843, and Case C–456/98 *Centrosteel* [2000] ECR I–6007.

[316] Sometimes also called 'incidental' effects. Cf Arnull 1999.

[317] Cf Case C–103/88 *Costanzo* [1989] ECR 1839, Case C–201/94 *Smith & Nephew* [1996] ECR I–5819, Case C–441/93 *Pafitis* [1996] ECR I–1347, Case C–129/94 *Ruiz Bernáldez* [1996] ECR I–1829, Case C–194/94 *CIA Security* [1996] ECR I–2201, and Case C–180/95 *Draehmpaehl* [1997] ECR I–2195.   [318] Indeed, in some cases consistent interpretation might have been an option.

[319] Cf Case C–2/97 *Borsana* [1998] ECR I–8597, Case C–185/97 *Coote* [1998] ECR I–5199, and Case C–386/00 *Axa Royale Belge* [2002] ECR I–2209.

[320] Cf Case C–443/98 *Unilever* [2000] ECR I–7535 and Case C–201/02 *Wells*, judgment of 7 January 2004, nyr in ECR.   [321] Cf e.g. Dougan 2000a, Colgan 2002, Craig and De Búrca 2003, 226–7.

are in particular of German and UK origin. Other legal systems, such as France, have less difficulty with understanding and accepting the Court's approach.[322]

So, Dougan,[323] for instance, has tried to explain the case law by introducing, *inter alia*, the distinction between unimplemented remedial provisions and unimplemented substantive provisions, directives harmonizing individual rights and dealing merely with inter-institutional relations, directives concerning relations between Member States and individuals, and those regulating purely private relationships as well and, finally, by looking at the type of breach by the Member State concerned: breach of the obligation to transpose or breach of a substantive provision. His notion of 'disguised vertical direct effect' precludes an individual from benefiting from a substantive breach of a directive by the State.

In an incisive study, using the Hohfeldian analytical framework,[324] Gilliams[325] comes to the conclusion that a distinction should be made between directives which are designed to govern vertical legal relationships and those which are intended to apply to relationships between private parties. The first category may be relied upon against a broad category of legal subjects and also against individuals.

Others have tied up with the generally emerging distinction in the Court's case law between 'exclusion effect' and 'substitution effect' which was prompted by the explicit recognition of the review of legality as a form of direct effect.[326]

Until now, all these efforts have not led to a satisfactory result, as most scholars admit. Therefore, quite unsurprisingly, many of them advocate full horizontal direct effect. In my opinion, an effort to explain and rationalize the case law *ex post facto* is perhaps also doomed to fail because the Court itself is searching for a method how to cope with the horizontal side effects. Looking into the details of the cases may be helpful to get straight what is going on in the case law. However, what is needed next, is to develop one common approach. It is submitted that, in the meantime, the latter is taking shape. The cases can be divided into two main categories, which I will discuss in turn.

Multi-angular relationships

In contrast to the situation of private individuals, directives impose obligations on the Member States and their authorities which are binding upon them *without* an

---

[322] Cf Simon 2001, 400–2, Demazières de Sechelles 1998, 242–3. The way in which national courts deal with the horizontal side effects give a varied picture. See e.g. Jans and Prinssen 2002, 116–19, Pâques 1996, 165–79.   [323] Dougan 2000a.

[324] Cf also Hilson and Downes 1999.   [325] Gilliams 2000.

[326] Tridimas 2002. Cf also Lenz, Sif Tynes, and Young 2000 and Hilson and Downes 1999, who use the sword and shield analogy. For a detailed analysis, including an overview of the discussion in Germany, see also Jarass and Beljin 2004.

intercession of national implementing rules. Provided the relevant provisions of the directive meet the requirements of direct effect, an individual may compel the State or competent authorities to comply with the provision, although compliance by the authorities with this obligation may entail consequences to the detriment of another individual. This state of affairs will particularly occur in triangular (or multi-angular) relationships.[327]

> The most obvious examples of such relationships occur under the public works and environmental directives.[328] For instance, a public authority may award a contract of work to a private undertaking in accordance with national rules which are, however, incompatible with the directive. A subsequent claim by another undertaking which argues that the authority has violated the provisions of the directive may result in the work being given to the claimant, to the detriment of the first undertaking.[329] Similarly, an environmental interest group or another person with standing under national law may rely on the provisions of a directive against a national authority, often resulting, at the end of the day, in the withdrawal of a permit given to an undertaking in accordance with national rules but in violation of the rules laid down in the directive at issue.[330] This problem is, however, not confined to the area of public procurement or environmental law, as *Smith & Nephew*[331] illustrate. In this case, the claimant challenged, on the basis of a directive, the validity of a marketing authorization issued by the Medicines Control Agency to one of its competitors. Similarly, in the area of, for instance, telecommunications the same problems are likely to occur in the triangular relationship between the newcomer, the national regulatory authority and the incumbent.

The possibility for an individual to press claims based directly on the directive against a public authority may detrimentally affect another individual. Nevertheless, negative consequences of this kind did not prevent the Court from acknowledging the right of the claimant to rely on the directive, and the obligation of the national authorities to apply the directive and disapply national rules which were in conflict with it. However, since the Court did not accept such negative effects explicitly and,

---

[327] For an analysis see Lackhoff and Nyssens 1998 and Colgan 2002.

[328] Cf Jans 2000, 198–200. In German literature this problem is often discussed under the heading 'Doppelwirkung' of directives. Cf e.g. Classen 1993, 84–5, Langenfeld 1992, 960–1, Jarass 1991, 2667–8. Some authors even make a further subdivision of these triangular situations. See Lackhoff and Nyssens 1998, 401–2.

[329] Cf in particular Case 103/88 *Costanzo* [1989] ECR 1839. Further in the area of public procurement, see e.g. Case C–143/94 *Furlanis* [1995] ECR I–3633, Case C–304/96 *Hera* [1997] ECR I–5685, Case C–76/97 *Tögel* [1998] ECR I–5357, Case C–470/99 *Universale Bau* [2002] ECR I–11617, and Case C–327/00 *Santex* [2003] ECR I–1877.

[330] Cf in particular Case C–201/02 *Wells*, judgment of 7 January 2004, nyr in ECR. Yet, the problem was already implicitly present in, for instance, Case C–435/97 *WWF* [1999] ECR I–5613 and Case C–231/97 *Van Rooij* [1999] ECR I–6355.

[331] Case C–201/94 [1996] ECR I–5819.

more importantly, since it was not made clear which effects were still acceptable and which not,[332] this case law was rather controversial.

In January 2004 the Court broke the silence in *Wells*,[333] an environmental case in which Ms Wells relied on the EIA Directive.[334] This would result, for the quarry owners concerned, in suspending the mining operations while awaiting the results of an environmental impact assessment which did not take place when the permission for mining was issued.

The Court reminded first that directives can only create rights but no obligations for individuals and went on stating:

Consequently, an individual may not rely on a directive against a Member State where it is a matter of a State obligation directly linked to the performance of another obligation falling, pursuant to that directive, on a third party. . . .[335]

The Court continued by pointing out that 'mere adverse repercussions on the rights of third parties' could not prevent an individual from invoking the provisions of a directive against the Member State concerned. In the case before the Court, the obligation for the Member State to ensure that an environmental impact assessment will take place was not directly linked to the performance of any obligation which would fall, pursuant to the directive, on the quarry owners. The fact that the mining operations must be halted was considered as a 'mere adverse repercussion' and not as an obligation for the quarry owners.

What lessons can be learned from this? First, negative consequences for third parties ('mere adverse repercussions on the rights of third parties' in the terminology of the Court) are no obstacle to direct effect.[336]

There is a certain parallel with the old and somewhat controversial *Busseni* case.[337] In this case, the Court has restricted the possibility for the ECSC to press a claim in respect of a preferential debt directly on the basis of certain provisions of ECSC recommendation 86/198,[338] according to which the ECSC should have the same privileged creditor status as national tax authorities. According to the Court, the ECSC's claims could be in competition not only with those of the Member State concerned but also with those of other

---

[332] Cf Timmermans 1997, 18–19. For another effort to make some sense from this case law see also the first edition of this book, at 65–8.

[333] Case C–201/02, judgment of 7 January 2004, nyr in ECR.

[334] Directive 85/337, [1985] OJ L175/40.   [335] Para 56 of the judgment.

[336] Cf also, in the same sense, AG Kokott, Opinion in Case C–127/02 *Landelijke Vereniging tot Behoud van de Waddenzee*, of 29 January 2004, points 148–150 implicitly confirmed by the court in its judgment of 7 September 2004. For an analysis of this case see also Jarass and Beljin 2004, 731–3.

[337] Case C–221/88 [1990] ECR I–495. The case is controversial in that it was not evident how to reconcile it with other 'triangular' cases decide by the Court. Cf Timmermans 1997, 18–19.

[338] [1986] OJ L144/40. The Court treated the recommendation in the same way as an EEC directive. Cf. paras 21–22 of the judgment.

creditors of the undertaking. The application of the recommendation, far from operating solely against the Member State to which it is addressed, may also reduce the prospects of payment for some of the other creditors. The rights of all the other creditors would be directly affected if the preferential status were conferred on certain debts owed to the ECSC. In other words, a directive cannot prejudice a person's rights, at least not *directly*. On the other hand, indirect consequences (i.e. 'mere adverse repercussions'?) were not excluded.

Secondly, if the State would be obliged, by the individual who relies on the directive, to make a third individual comply with *another* obligation under the directive, direct effect is excluded. Here we are apparently not anymore in a situation of 'mere adverse repercussions' but of direct interference, in a negative and specific way, with a person's legal position, including his or her rights.

So in *Dahaitsu*,[339] for instance, the applicant relied against a German authority (which happened to be an *Ambtsgericht*) on Article 6 of Directive 68/151,[340] in order to achieve the imposition of a penalty on the respondent company and to force it to disclose its balance sheets. This latter (i.e. *the other*) obligation followed from Article 2(1) of the Directive.

The guidance provided on the question of how to establish whether there are indirect negative consequences or not is indeed welcome. On the other hand, it also seems to make the outcome rather contingent upon the formulation of the directive's provision and on the question in how far can the obligations of the State and the obligations of a third (private) party be separated.

For instance, a directive may make the granting of an authorization by a national authority to undertake certain activities dependent upon certain substantive requirements which must be met by the applicant. A claim by a third party against the competent national authorities which have, in the opinion of the former, granted the authorization to a company which meets the requirements under national law but not the (stricter) requirements of the directive concerned, aims at the withdrawal of the authorization by virtue of the application of the directive. Under *Wells* this should be possible, since it is an obligation of the Member State authorities which the 'third party' relies on and which is arguably not 'directly linked to the performance of *another* obligation' of the company under the directive involved. However, from the perspective of the latter this does not amount to anything other than imposing an obligation upon them, namely to meet the requirements of the directive provision at issue.

---

[339] Case C–97/96 *Daihatsu-Händler* [1997] ECR I–6843. This case is quoted as an example by the Court itself. The other reference, namely to *Busseni*, fits less well as an example for the 'constellation' presented by the Court.   [340] [1968] OJ English Spec Ed (I), 41.

Despite the clarification given in *Wells*, the horizontal effects in 'triangular situations' will remain a haphazard matter which is, from the point of view of legal certainty unsatisfactory.[341]

To this one may add another consequence of *Wells*, going beyond the multi- or triangular relationships. As was pointed out above,[342] direct effect involves that national authorities other than the courts are equally obliged to apply the directive. And this, more or less naturally, irrespective of whether an individual has relied on it or not.[343] The limit of such an application lies in the prohibition of inverse vertical direct effect. In my opinion, the judgment in *Wells* brings about that as long as the application of a directive by the competent authorities results in 'mere adverse repercussions' in the sense (and including all the difficulties) as set out hereabove, they should proceed with it. After all, and also from the perspective of the individual or companies involved, the application of a directive—for instance concerning the issue of environmental permits—cannot be made dependent on a fortuitous claim brought by a (third) interested party. In other words, such limited inverse vertical direct effect should be accepted. Negative consequences for one should not be considered as mere correlatives of the right to rely on a directive in proceedings against State authorities by another.

Collateral challenge in private litigation

The judgments in *CIA Security* and, in particular, *Unilever*,[344] have received considerable attention since while both concerned litigation between private parties, Directive 83/189 (notification of technical standards)[345] was invoked in order to preclude the application of divergent national law. In other words, one private party used the directive against another private party as the root of defence to an action based on national law, which was, however, not in conformity with the directive and had to be held inapplicable. This collateral challenge like use of the directive had as a result that the directive determined the legal position of the parties involved and worked to the detriment of the claimant. In some quarters it was argued that such a use of a directive should be restricted to Directive 83/189. The latter is an unconventional directive in the sense that it lays down a *procedure* for the notification, etc. of technical standards. Its aim is not to regulate behaviour either between private individuals or between individuals and public authorities and, therefore, it does not contain obligations for individuals.[346] Indeed, the Court

---

[341] Note that in *Wells* (para 56) the Court recalled that it is exactly the principle of legal certainty which prevents directives from creating obligations for individuals.

[342] Cf in particular Subsection 9.3.6.

[343] Cf Case C–431/92 *Commission v. Germany* [1995] ECR I–2189. Cf also on this Lackhoff and Nyssens 1998, 401, Barav 1998, 429, and Klagian 2001, 352.

[344] Case C–194/94 [1996] ECR I–2201 and Case C–443/98 [2000] ECR I–7535.

[345] [1983] OJ L109/8.

[346] Jarass and Beljin 2004, 722–3.

itself held that case law, denying horizontal direct effect, was not applicable in *Unilever*, since

... Directive 83/189 does not in any way define the substantive scope of the legal rule on the basis of which the national court must decide the case before it. It creates neither rights nor obligations for individuals.[347]

However, there are other instances of using a directive by way of a collateral challenge or, to use another common term, an exception of illegality or an incidental plea, while the directive at issue is not merely procedural but contains 'substantive' rules. The two *Piageme* cases,[348] just like the *CIA* case, were brought under the Belgian Law on Commercial Practices. Under this law, injunctive relief may be sought against a 'seller' if he acts in breach of good commercial practice and the conduct is likely to cause harm to other businessmen or consumers.[349] In these cases, the 'sellers' relied in their defence on the fact that the allegedly infringed provisions of national law ran counter to Directive 79/112 (labelling and presentation of foodstuffs)[350] and therefore could not be applied as basis for the claim brought by the plaintiffs. Other cases too, which were brought in the context of similar unfair trading proceedings, for instance in Austria or Germany, operated in a similar way.[351]

Moreover the idea is certainly not new. In the past some authors have suggested that a form of mitigated horizontal direct effect could be allowed, which would consist of a review of legality of national measures within the context of a dispute between two private parties. Thus, without asking for the application of the provision of the directive to the facts of the case, the persons concerned could nevertheless invoke that provision in the national courts in order to oppose the application of national law which does not conform to it, even in a 'horizontal' legal relationship.

Timmermans, who—as was observed—made a distinction between direct effect and legal review as two different concepts, concluded that even a mitigated horizontal direct effect is hardly acceptable.[352] The outcome of such a

---

[347] Para 51 of the judgment.

[348] Case C–369/89, [1991] ECR I–2971 and Case C–85/94, [1995] ECR I–2955, also known as *Peeters I* and *Peeters II*.

[349] Breach of good commercial practice exists, *inter alia*, if the seller infringes, in the exercise of an economic activity, any duty imposed by law and regulation which may relate to any area of law, be it tax law, criminal law, social law, competition law, etc., EC law included. For an EC wide introduction of such a mechanism see Commission's proposal on unfair business-to-consumer commercial practices, COM (2003) 356 final.   [350] [1979] OJ L33/1.

[351] Cf e.g. Case C–77/97 *Smithkline Beecham* [1999] ECR I–431 and Case C–220/98 *Estée Lauder* [2000] ECR I–117.

[352] Timmermans 1979, 543 (with respect to direct effect). However, at 551 (with respect to the control of legality) the author takes a slightly different view.

construction would be that the national court could apply neither national law because of its incompatibility nor the relevant provision of the directive because the latter cannot have horizontal direct effect. In his view, legal certainty would then be seriously compromised. Moreover, the solution would also not result in uniform application of Community law.

According to Louis, on the other hand, such an effect is possible. In his view, what happens is to be considered as the '*jeu normal de l'exception de l'illégalité*' which should not be equated to imposing obligations upon individuals.[353]

It is submitted that, in private proceedings, a directive may not be relied upon and used as rules to be applied to the facts of the case and on the basis of which the case has to be decided. In other words: not 'substitution'[354] or 'positive'[355] effects. On the other hand, directives may be relied upon in the context of a proceedings between private individuals in order to have the conformity reviewed of the applicable national rules with the directive at issue. The incompatibility of the applicable national rules with the directive entails the disapplication of the former. Such an 'exclusion'[356] or 'negative'[357] effect should, in principle, be allowed.[358]

What is then going on, is indirect impact by the provisions of the directives on a legal relationship between two individuals, i.e. a relationship of mutual rights and obligations. In other terms, the provisions of the directive do not themselves regulate the relationship, but they merely influence the application of a rule which does directly regulate the parties' relationship. Both in *CIA Security* and *Unilever*[359] it was the status and validity of public law regulatory standards which determined the private law obligations between the parties, either non-contractual (*CIA Security*) or contractual (*Unilever*). These standards then became unenforceable since they were contrary to a Community law rule.[360]

---

[353] Louis 1993, 512. This possibility is apparently also accepted by Manin 1990, 690. A very similar approach has been suggested by Stuyck and Wytinck 1991, 212 which they have termed 'passive' horizontal direct effect: the application of a directive does not entail a 'positive obligation' on an individual but only obliges him to respect the right which another individual derives from a directive.

[354] Cf Tridimas 2002, 346.   [355] Cf Jarass and Beljin 2004, 717 and 721.

[356] Cf Tridimas 2002, 346.

[357] Cf Jarass and Beljin 2004, 717 and 722–5. These authors, however, limit the exclusionary effect to cases concerning substantial procedural defects, such as those in *CIA Security* or *Unilever*.

[358] In *Pfeiffer* (Joined Cases C–397/01 to C–403/01, judgment of 5 October 2004, nyr in ECR), which concerned the issue of collateral challenge, the Court held that '… even a clear, precise and unconditional provision of a directive seeking to confer rights or impose obligations on individuals cannot of itself apply in proceedings exclusively between private parties' (para 109). This may be understood as excluding a collateral challenge in private proceedings, but the language is not crystal clear. It may also be understood as referring to the substitution effects. However this may be, the Court decided the case along the line of consistent interpretation with, at the end of the day, the same result as a simple disapplication. An important element is, indeed, that the national methods of construction are used here as a vehicle for the disapplication. Cf above Ch 8, Subsections 8.5.1 and 8.6.

[359] Case C–194/94 [1996] ECR I–2201 and Case C–443/98 [2000] ECR I–7535.

[360] See for a more detailed discussion Betlem 2002, 93–6. Cf also Prechal 2002, 27–31 and 34–9.

Perhaps also such consequences can be considered as allowable 'mere adverse repercussions on the rights of [private] parties' instead of prohibited direct interference with their rights and obligations.

By its very nature, such an approach has its limits and will often depend on the constellation of the case and on the remedies and procedures available.[361] As was already explained before,[362] review of legality and the disapplication which should, in principle, follow thereupon may result in a gap. As long as the gap can be filled by the technique of consistent interpretation, there is no problem.[363] However, if the lacuna would require the application of the directive instead, which boils down to a substitution effect and thus a direct imposition of an obligation, then the limits are reached.

Interestingly, in *Faccini Dori*,[364] for instance, Ms Dori relied upon the Directive to protect herself against national provisions, which were incompatible with the former. Nevertheless, the Court treated it as a sort of positive claim, based on the directive. It is submitted that even if it had been treated as a matter of collateral challenge, the outcome would not have been any different, exactly for the reasons just given.

Mitigation of the effects through national law?

In both situations just described, the Court seems to stick to the basic distinction of rights and obligations versus mere legal advantages and disadvantages. Or, differently put, exclusionary effect (advantages and disadvantages) and substitution effect (rights and obligations). Whatever the merits might be of this approach,[365] from the point of view of individuals involved, in particular, from the point of view of legal certainty,[366] the effects of unimplemented or incorrectly implemented directives may be considerable. Some relatively recent cases suggest, however, that these effects may be mitigated through the application of national law.

---

[361] Cf the unfair trading proceedings discussed above.   [362] Cf Subsection 9.3.3.

[363] Cf what happened first in Case C–215/97 *Bellone* [1998] ECR I–2191 (directive 'precluded' national legislation) and, next, Case C–456/98 *Centrosteel* [2000] I–6007 (consistent interpretations). Cf also Joined Cases C–240/98 to C–244/98 *Océano* [2000] ECR I–4941. AG Saggio was in favour of disapplication as such, while the Court gave preference to consistent interpretation. Cf also Joined Cases C–397/01 to C–403/01, *Pfeiffer*, judgment of 5 October 2004, nyr in ECR, where the possible gap was more or less automatically filled by the application of national rules in so far as these were compatible with the directive.

[364] Case C–91/92 [1994] ECR I–3325.

[365] Indeed, in particular the distinction between obligations and mere disadvantages needs further elaboration.

[366] On this see in particular the Opinion of AG Jacobs in C–443/98 [2000] ECR I–7535 and Weatherill 2001.

First, in *Wells*[367] when addressing the question of how to remedy the failure to carry out an environmental impact assessment, the Court referred the matter to the realm of national procedural autonomy. The national court had to establish whether it is possible under domestic law for a consent for exploitation which has already been granted, to be revoked or suspended or whether compensation for the harm suffered would provide an alternative. In other words, it was in the context of national law to find an appropriate solution, with the principles of equivalence and effectiveness as the only two provisos.[368]

Second, an interesting and comparable approach results from the Court's judgment in *Sapod*.[369] The Court first confirmed that according to its settled case law, the failure to observe the obligation to notify under Directive 83/189 renders the national provisions in question unenforceable against individuals and that this may be invoked in private proceedings concerning, *inter alia*, contractual rights and duties. However, as to the question what conclusions had to be drawn from the inapplicability, this was again a question governed by national law. As long as the principles of equivalence and effectiveness were observed, national rules and principles of contract law which limit or adjust the sanction under national law (for instance, the nullity or unenforceability of the contracts) and aim at rendering its severity proportionate to the defect found should apply. In other words, the issue of further legal consequences of the inapplicability shifts to the national legal order.[370] It is at this level that the effects of inapplicability which are too harsh, can be toned down on grounds of various considerations, such as general principles of law or other common sense requirements, for instance reasonableness and equity.[371]

---

[367] Case C–201/02, judgment of 7 January 2004, nyr in ECR.

[368] For a discussion of these principles see Ch 7, Section 7.2 and Subsection 7.4.2.

[369] Case C–159/00 [2002] ECR I–5031.

[370] Which is in line with settled case law. Cf Case 34/67 *Lück* [1968] ECR 245 and Joined Cases C–10 to 22/97 *IN.CO.GE* [1998] ECR I–6307. See on this also Prechal 2002, 34–9.

[371] Cf for comparable considerations Tridimas 2002, in particular 336–40 and Prechal 2002, 39–40.

10

Liability of the State in cases of inadequate implementation of directives

10.1 Liability before *Francovich*

Non-implementation or incorrect implementation of a directive amounts to a breach of Community law. In so far as this or any other breach of Community law causes loss and damage to individuals, they should be able to bring an action for damages against the Member State concerned in national courts. Yet, State liability in relation to directives has an extra dimension. First, exactly for reasons of being an instrument which in principle needs implementation, the risk that something 'goes wrong' is certainly not negligible. Second, the denial of horizontal direct effect of directives poses additional problems to their enforcement and to the judicial protection which liability may palliate to a certain extent.

The idea that infringement of Community law by a Member State should be actionable under national regimes of public non-contractual liability is as such not new.[1] In 1975, in its suggestions on European Union, the Court of Justice proposed that persons affected by a failure of a Member State to fulfil an obligation under Community law should obtain redress before their national courts.[2] Moreover, as regards the infringement of Article 234 of the Treaty, the Court suggested as one of the remedies an action for damages against the Member State concerned at the suit of the party adversely affected.[3] During the preparation of the Treaty on European Union, and still prior to the *Francovich* judgment, the Commission proposed to insert into the Treaty a provision stipulating that the Member States should be obliged to make good the consequences of infringements of Community law; and furthermore, if necessary, the institutions should enact harmonizing or coordinating measures for that purpose.[4] Ultimately, however, such provisions were not included in the EU Treaty.

In earlier literature this option was similarly discussed and accepted as one of the remedies available for breaches of Community law.[5] Yet in general it was assumed that action for damages was entirely governed by national law.[6]

---

[1] For a more detailed discussion see the first edition of this book, 306–12.

[2] Bull EC Supp 9/75, 18. From other language versions it appears that the Court had in mind particularly damages.   [3] Ibid.

[4] Bull EC 2/91, 152–3. Prieß 1993, 125 reports that the Court of Justice was also in favour of such a provision and stressed equally the need for harmonization.

[5] Cf Karpenstein 1977, 65–8 (with further references), Pescatore 1972, 21, Kovar 1978, 271–5. Cf also FIDE Reports 1980.   [6] Cf Karpenstein 1977, 65 ff. and Millarg 1977, 225–6.

In fact several cases involving breaches of Community law were decided by national courts in the 'pre-*Francovich*' era under the relevant national rules of non-contractual liability, although with varying degrees of success for the applicants.[7]

In so far as the cases have been given attention, their discussion reveals divergence in approach and in outcome.[8] Although the legal systems of all the Member States now recognize the principle of public non-contractual liability, the conditions under which this liability gives rise to compensation and the types of acts or activities which give rise to liability differ considerably. A serious obstacle to employing the national systems of non-contractual liability lies especially in the impossibility of bringing an action for normative injustice, certainly as far as primary legislation is concerned.[9]

Not surprisingly, both doctrine and legal practice searched for Community law arguments to overcome real or imaginary hurdles in national non-contractual liability law. The case law of the Court of Justice provided some elements which could be used for this purpose.[10]

Judgment under Article 226 as argument for liability

The indications given in the Court's case law as to the consequences which a judgment under Articles 226–228 has within the national legal order were interpreted as entailing the reparation of damages.

In a number of cases the Court has clearly indicated that the Member States are under the obligation to draw the necessary inferences from a judgment in an Article 226 proceedings or to take appropriate measures to remedy the default.[11] These 'inferences' or 'measures' to be taken may indeed include making reparation for the damage which the Member State has caused to individuals by its unlawful conduct. Procedure under Article 226 is not only

---

[7] Cf Huglo 1993, 79, Schockweiler 1992, 38.

[8] Cf e.g. for cases decided in different Member States Barav 1988, 156–65, Barav 1997, 376–406 (an updated version, after the Court of Justice has established State liability as a matter of Community law), Taylor 1985, 479–86; for a brief discussion of some French cases Simon 1992, Kovar 1992, Moreau 1991; for English cases cf Oliver 1987, 899–906, Green 1984a, Ward 1990, Steiner 1986. Bok 1993, 48–50 discusses a number of Dutch cases. For an interesting effort to fit the problem of directives which have not been (adequately or timely) implemented into the Dutch regime of non-contractual liability see Dekker 1991.

[9] Cf Schockweiler 1990, 73, Arts 1993, 504, Karl 1992, 440 and 442 as well as FIDE Reports 1992.

[10] Cf Barav 1988, 150–6, Barav and Simon 1987, 166–7, Schockweiler 1992, 36–40. Cf also the Opinion of AG Mischo in Joined Cases C–6/90 and C–9/90 *Francovich* [1991] ECR I–5357, paras 34–68.

[11] Cf Case 48/71 *Commission v. Italy* [1972] ECR 527, Joined Cases 24 and 97/80 R *Commission v. France* [1980] ECR 1319, Joined Cases 314 to 316/81 and 83/82 *Waterkeyn* [1982] ECR 4337, para 14. Cf also Pescatore 1972, 15–16, and the judgment in Case C–101/91 *Commission v. Italy* [1993] ECR I–191.

concerned with elimination of the infringement in the future but also in the past.[12] In particular, where it is no longer possible physically to comply retroactively with the obligations, reparation will often provide a partial remedy at least. Further authority for this was also drawn from the old *Humblet* case where the Court obliged the Member States 'to make reparation for any unlawful consequences which may have ensued'.[13]

An even clearer indication that such a judgment under Article 226 may provide a basis for an action for damages by the individual concerned was given by the Court in Case 39/72 (*premiums for slaughtering cows I*). The Court held that the Commission may have interest in pursuing infringement proceedings, even though the national legislation complained of had been amended, because a judgment may be of interest

as establishing the basis of a responsibility that a Member State can incur as a result of its default as regards other Member States, the Community or private parties.[14]

Since then, this finding has been reiterated in other cases, though sometimes in slightly different terms which do not, however, change the basic idea.[15] Some of the cases concerned the non-implementation of a directive.[16]

The exact basis of this liability remained controversial. Essentially, two interpretations were possible. According to the first, the basis of liability is a matter to be decided under national law. According to the second interpretation, the Court recognized the existence of non-contractual liability as a matter of Community law, but the terms 'can incur' indicated that some other—as yet not established—conditions had to be satisfied first.[17]

Need for effective judicial protection as argument for liability

The approach which takes the requirement of effective judicial protection as the point of departure[18] has one important merit: the action for damages is then not made dependent upon a judgment of the Court under Article 226.[19]

The development of the Court's case law as to the requirement of effective judicial protection was described in detail in Chapter 7. Initially, the Court entrusted

---

[12] Cf Case 70/72 *Commission v. Germany* [1973] ECR 813.
[13] Case 6/60 [1960] ECR 559. The basis for this was Art 86 of the ECSC Treaty, which is equivalent to Art 10 EC Treaty.   [14] *Commission v. Italy* [1973] 101, para 11.
[15] Cf e.g. Case 309/84 *Commission v. Italy* [1986] ECR 599, Case C–249/88 *Commission v. Belgium* [1991] ECR I–1275, Case C–287/87 *Commission v. Greece* [1990] ECR I–125.
[16] Case C–287/87 *Commission v. Greece* [1990] ECR I–125.
[17] Cf the Opinion of AG Mischo in Joined Cases C–6/90 and C–9/90 *Francovich* [1991] ECR I–5357, para 57.   [18] Cf e.g. Barav 1988, Barav and Simon 1987, Prechal 1990, Curtin 1990b.
[19] Cf Joined Cases 314 to 316/81 and 83/82 *Waterkeyn* [1982] ECR 4337, where the Court held that the rights which individuals derive from Community law emanate from the provisions of Community law themselves.

the national courts with the task of protecting the rights which individuals derive from Community law, although it was left for the national system of judicial protection to provide an appropriate remedy. Yet the protection had to be 'direct and immediate'[20] and 'effective',[21] and it has to satisfy the requirements of equivalence and effectiveness. *Simmenthal*[22] added to the requirement of legal protection the principle of full effectiveness of Community law, which may not be impaired, and the judgment in *Johnston*[23] introduced the principle of effective judicial protection as a general principle of law. Finally, *Factortame*[24] required the national court to grant interim relief, even where it was impossible as a matter of national law, in order to ensure the full effectiveness of Community law and to provide the necessary protection to the individuals affected.

As regards non-contractual liability, actions for damages in fact already existed in all the Member States. Yet the crucial question was whether a Member State can be held liable for breaches of Community law under the national rules of non-contractual liability and, if so, under what conditions. Not surprisingly, the more the Court substantiated *and* tightened the requirements as to the judicial protection to be afforded, the more compelling was the argument that effective judicial protection required the availability of an action for damages against the defaulting State whenever the payment of damages was the appropriate means to provide effective protection.

    The only authority to deal explicitly with the question of damages was the judgment in *Russo*. The Court held that

[i]t is for the national court to decide on the basis of the facts of each case whether an individual . . . has suffered . . . damage. If [the] damage has been caused through an infringement of Community law the State is liable to the injured party [for] the consequences in the context of the provisions of national law on the liability of the State.[25]

Although this finding was—again—not entirely uncontroversial,[26] it was understood by some as an acceptance by the Court of a non-contractual liability based in Community law. The reference to the context of national liability law then merely meant that it governs the conditions of liability.[27]

    Obviously, the main disadvantage of this construction remains that the divergent and, as far as State liability is concerned, often strict national conditions of non-contractual liability apply. Under certain circumstances, the conditions may be set aside or adapted in pursuance of the requirements of effectiveness or effective judicial protection, as the case may be. This involves, however, a case to case approach and, moreover, the exact scope of these principles is rather uncertain. Furthermore, it should be pointed out that the case law on which the principle of effective judicial

---

[20] Case 13/68 *Salgoil* [1968] ECR 453.   [21] Case 179/84 *Bozzetti* [1985] ECR 2301.
[22] Case 106/77 [1978] ECR 629.   [23] Case 222/84 [1986] ECR 1651.
[24] Case C–213/89 [1990] ECR I–2433.   [25] Case 60/75 [1976] ECR 45, para 9.
[26] Cf Bebr 1992, 572.
[27] Cf Barav 1988, 156, Curtin 1990b, 732 as well as the opinion of AG Mischo in Joined Cases C–6/90 and C–9/90 *Francovich* [1991] ECR I–5357, para 44.

protection drew was only concerned with breaches of directly effective provisions of Community law. The question whether damages as a remedy should be made available in the case of infringements of non-directly effective provisions was either not addressed at all or it was cautiously suggested that such a possibility was tenable.[28]

10.2 The principle of State liability as a matter of Community law

10.2.1 The construction of the Court of Justice in *Francovich*

The judgment of the Court in *Francovich* ended the speculation as to the legal foundation of State liability. The judgment has correctly been described as one 'of principle'.[29] The Court did not limit itself to the concrete problem of that case, which related to a non-transposed directive, but addressed the question of State liability for breaches of Community law in general. It found that

it is a principle of Community law that the Member States are obliged to make good loss and damage caused to individuals by breaches of Community law for which they can be held responsible.[30]

The Court's main argument for this view was that such a liability is inherent in the system of the Treaty. The Court identified two grounds in this respect. Firstly, there is the Community legal order's 'own character', as defined in *Van Gend en Loos* and *Costa v. ENEL*.[31] Secondly, as the Court reiterated, referring to *Simmenthal* and *Factortame*,[32] national courts must ensure the full effectiveness of Community rules and the protection of the Community rights of individuals.

   Up to this point there was in fact nothing new in the Court's judgment. However, the Court then took its reasoning a stage further, explaining the requirements of those principles if a Member State is in breach of Community law provisions. According to the Court, individuals must be in a position to obtain redress when their rights are infringed. Next, the Court stressed that the possibility of obtaining redress is in particular indispensable where the full effectiveness of Community rules depends on prior action of the Member States and where, consequently, in the absence of such action, individuals cannot enforce their Community rights.

   An additional argument[33] was found in Article 10 of the Treaty, which requires, as had already been spelled out in *Humblet*,[34] that the Member States nullify the

---

[28] Cf Curtin 1990b, 739.   [29] Cf Gilliams 1991–1992, 877.
[30] Para 37 of the judgment.   [31] Case 26/62 [1963] ECR 1 and Case 6/64 [1964] ECR 585.
[32] Case 106/77 [1978] ECR 629 and case C–213/89 [1990] ECR I–2433.
[33] Many scholars consider this as reinforcing the former arguments. Cf Bebr 1992, 573, Barav 1994, 286, Schockweiler 1992, 42, Simon 1993, 237.   [34] Case 6/60 [1960] ECR 559.

unlawful consequences of a breach of Community law. One of the means to achieve this is indeed making good loss and damage which individuals have incurred as a consequence of the breach.

It is striking that the Court did not refer in the judgment to its position in the infringement proceedings discussed above, namely that a judgment under Article 226 may establish the basis of liability of the defaulting Member State *vis-à-vis* private individuals. The Court apparently wished to avoid any suggestion that for the existence of State liability a judgment under this Article was necessary. In the *Francovich* judgment itself the Court merely observed that the breach of Community law by Italy 'has been confirmed by a judgment of the Court',[35] without any suggestion that such a judgment should constitute a condition for State liability.

The interesting consequence of not making liability dependent on a judgment under Article 226 is, *inter alia*, that the national courts are called upon to apply the requirements for proper implementation of directives developed by the Court of Justice in infringement proceedings.[36] It may be questioned whether the courts are adequately equipped to do this. In some cases the breach may be obvious. However, as experience in Article 226 proceedings shows, this is not always the case. In particular, the crucial role played by the Commission in infringement proceedings has to be played in national courts by private parties. Indeed, unless a reference under Article 234 is made.

In brief, just as the Court found some three decades previously in *Van Gend en Loos*[37] that the Community autonomous legal system entailed that its provisions have, *as a matter of Community law*, direct effect, provided that certain conditions are satisfied, in a very similarly structured reasoning it found in *Francovich* that the existence of State liability in the case of breaches of Community law is rooted in Community law itself.

In general, the *Francovich* judgment has been warmly welcomed as the most important constitutional judgment since *Van Gend en Loos*, completing the system of judicial protection of individuals and strengthening considerably the possibilities of enforcement of Community law.[38]

10.2.2 *Francovich* as a particular modality of the liability regime

On the one hand, in *Francovich*, the Court recognized the Community law principle of State liability in fairly general terms. On the other hand, the Court made clear

---

[35] Para 44 of the judgment. The case at issue was Case 22/87 *Commission v. Italy* [1989] ECR 143.

[36] For a detailed discussion, see above, Ch 5. See also Joined Cases C–178/94, C–179/94, C–188/94, C–189/94, and C–190/94 *Dillenkofer* [1996] ECR I–4845 and Case C–140/97 *Rechberger* [1999] ECR I–3499.   [37] Case 26/62 [1963] ECR 1.

[38] As is well known, this jurisprudential line has generated rather voluminous literature, including, indeed, also critical comments. Cf e.g. Dänzer-Vanotti 1992 and Detterbeck 2000, 230–2.

that the very existence of the principle is, as such, not sufficient to give rise to a right to reparation. For this purpose certain conditions must be satisfied. What these conditions are, depends 'on the nature of the breach'.[39] In the *Francovich* judgment the Court gave only the conditions to be fulfilled in the case of a Member State's failure under Article 249(3) of the Treaty and, moreover, in the particular situation of a non-transposed directive. Another factor of importance was also that, in *Francovich*, direct effect was of no avail to the claimants. Not surprisingly, the question was raised to what extent the principle of State liability applied in other situations and what the conditions will be with respect to other types of breaches.[40]

The Court clarified a number of these matters in *Brasserie du Pêcheur*.[41] It confirmed that the principle of State liability also applies in relation to breaches of all other provisions of Community law, so not merely in the case of non-implementation of directives and that a judgment under Article 226 was not a preliminary condition for liability. Furthermore, it made clear that direct effect of the relevant provisions is not an obstacle to liability. To the contrary, the Court pointed out that the right of individuals to rely on directly effective provisions is only a minimum guarantee and is not sufficient to ensure the full and complete implementation of the Treaty. The right to reparation is in fact the necessary corollary of direct effect of the provisions which have been breached. The Court also ruled that the State will be liable irrespective of which organ of the State is responsible for the breach and regardless of the internal division of powers between constitutional authorities.

Another crucial element was the restatement of the conditions for liability, in particular by adding a new one, the sufficiently serious breach. In an effort to align the liability of the Member States and the liability of the Community, the Court ruled that where a Member State acts in a field where it has wide discretion, the breach must be sufficiently serious.[42] This, indeed, gave rise to the question whether there are two different liability regimes, the 'simple one' under *Francovich*, and a more stringent one expounded in *Brasserie*.

After two rather confusing judgments,[43] the Court consolidated its case law in *Dillenkofer*.[44] In that case it ruled that the judgment in *Francovich* had implicitly

---

[39] Para 38 of the judgment.

[40] A distinction was made, in this respect between breaches of 'substantive' Treaty provisions and the 'definitional' provisions of Art 249(3). Cf also the Opinion of AG Van Gerven in Case C–128/92 *Banks* [1994] ECR I–1209, and Van Gerven 1994a. Similarly, some discussion evolved as to the meaning of 'the nature of the breach'. For a brief overview see the first edition of this book, 315–16.

[41] Joined Cases C–46/93 and C–48/93 [1996] ECR I–1029.

[42] I will come back to the *Francovich* conditions and the *Brasserie* condition and the issue of discretion in Subsections 10.4.1 and 10.4.3. On the not entirely self-evident alignment see, for instance, Fines 1997b, 84–7 and Van Gerven 1996, 525–7. For a detailed comparison see Goffin 1997.

[43] Case C–392/93 *British Telecom* [1996] ECR I–1631 (sufficiently serious test was applied in a case of incorrect implementation of a directive) and Case C–5/94 *Hedley Lomas* [1996] ECR I–2553 (sufficiently serious test was applied in a case where there was hardly any discretion). Cf also Hilson 1997 and Wathelet and van Raepenbusch 1997, 46–8.

[44] Joined Cases C–178/94, C–179/94, C–188/94, C–189/94, and C–190/94 *Dillenkofer* [1996] ECR I–4845, in particular paras 21–26.

established that a non-transposition of a directive is a *per se* sufficiently serious breach. The result of this is that there is one single liability regime, with as conditions those laid down in *Brasserie*. *Francovich* has to be considered *ex post facto* as an application of these rules.

10.3   Liability for breach of Article 249(3): types of breaches

The *Francovich* case was concerned with one particular kind of breach of Article 249(3), namely the non-transposition of a directive into national law. However, the words 'where a Member State fails to fulfill its obligations under the third paragraph of Article 189 [249] of the Treaty to take all the measures necessary to achieve the result prescribed by a directive'[45] suggested that the principles laid down in the judgment may relate to any possible breach of Article 249(3). Only the conditions for liability or their application might differ. Indeed, in the meantime it was made clear that the liability regime also applies to incorrect or incomplete transposition.[46] After all, the failure to transpose a directive properly affects adversely the full effectiveness of Article 249(3) and may also affect the protection of individuals' rights, in exactly the same way as non-implementation.

> As was discussed at length in Chapter 2 and, in particular, Chapter 5, adequate transposition requires that the *content* of the transposition measures corresponds to the content of the directive to be implemented and they must meet a sufficient degree of clarity and precision. Similarly, the *nature* of the implementing measures is not a matter for the Member States alone. As a rule, the implementing measures must be legally binding.
>
> Moreover, as also appears clearly from Chapters 3 and 5, the obligations of the Member States under Article 249(3) go far beyond the mere (timely and correct) transposition of a directive into national law. Member States are often obliged to take implementing measures which go beyond the actual text of the directive. Especially, they may be required to provide for an appropriate system of sanctions, even if the directive is silent on this point. To this one may add that the Court not only stipulates that there must be a sanction, it may also interfere with the form and content of the sanction.

There are, however, more obligations which result from Article 249(3). Firstly, transposition of a directive into national law, even if the transposition is as such correct, does not suffice. The obligation under Article 249(3) requires full application and enforcement of the directive concerned.[47] Thus, the measures transposing the

---

[45]   Para 39 of the judgment.

[46]   Cf Case C–392/93 *British Telecom* [1996] ECR I–1631, Joined Cases C–283/94, C–291/94, and C–292/94 *Denkavit* [1996] ECR I–5063 and Case C–140/97 *Rechberger* [1999] ECR I–3499.

[47]   Cf above, Ch 3, Section 3.3 and Ch 5, Section 5.4.

directive must be applied and enforced in practice. Whenever national authorities *and* national courts do not apply and enforce the directive, or, more properly speaking, the national measures implementing it, there is a violation of Article 249(3). Similarly, national courts and authorities are also under the obligation to construe national law in conformity with the directive, even in the case of correct implementation.[48]

Secondly, one has to consider the possible content of the obligation to be fulfilled. In Chapter 3 a distinction was made between the 'hard core rules' of the directive, i.e. the rules relating to the legal and factual situation which the Member States are required to bring about in their legal orders, and the ancillary obligations for the Member States. The latter obligations are just as binding as the 'hard core rules', although they are of a different character. However, since provisions relating, for instance, to notification of measures, informing and consulting with the Commission and/or other Member States, or to periodical assessment of the operation of the directive's rules are part and parcel of the obligations resulting from Article 249(3), non-compliance with these provisions will as such amount to a breach of this Article.[49]

Thirdly, where the Member State or the body primarily responsible for the transposition (i.e. as a rule, the legislator) has not transposed the directive or has not done so properly, by virtue of the Court's theory that the Member State's obligation arising from a directive to achieve the result envisaged by the directive is binding on all authorities of the Member State, including the courts, the obligation under Article 249(3) entails that those authorities are called upon to apply—if possible—the directive in lieu of national law or to proceed to interpretation of national law in conformity with the directive, both by way of an 'emergency measure'.[50] To this one may add, as was already pointed out, that the Member States are liable irrespective of which organ of the State is responsible for the breach, whether the legislator, the administration, or the judiciary.[51] Similarly, the Court's case law on the concept of 'the State' is of particular relevance. Although this case law is to be situated primarily within the context of direct effect, the approach is in principle not different for the purposes of State liability. Central, decentralized, or otherwise distinct public law bodies may commit a breach of Community law, Article 249(3) included.[52]

---

[48] Cf above, Ch 4, Section 4.4. Cf. also Pieper 1990, 2456.

[49] See, however, below, Subsection 10.4.2.

[50] For bodies bound and the consequences of the Court's construction, see in particular Ch 4, Sections 4.2 and 4.4. Cf also Case C–319/96 *Brinkmann* [1998] ECR I–5255.

[51] Cf Case C–140/97 *Rechberger* [1999] ECJ I–3499 (the legislator), Case C–424/97 *Haim II* [2000] ECR I–5123 or Case C–127/95 *Norbrook* [1998] ECR I–1531 (the administration), and Case C–224/01 *Köbler*, judgment of 30 September 2003, nyr in ECR (the judiciary).

[52] Cf Case C–424/97 *Haim II* [2000] ECR I–5123, Case C–302/97 *Konle* [1999] ECR I–3099, and Case C–118/00 *Larsy* [2001] ECR I–5063. See also Ch 4, Section 4.2 and Schockweiler 1993a, 15. Coppel 1993, 25–6, however, has argued that *Foster* is not an appropriate test in this context. For a broader discussion of these issues see Tridimas 2001, 319–20, Anagnostaras 2001, Leclerc and Mondésert 2002.

Arguably, all these types of breaches of Article 249(3) give rise to the obligation on the part of the State to pay damages, provided that the conditions for liability are satisfied. The discussion which follows will mainly focus on situations of incorrect or non-transposition of directives and, as far as relevant, breaches by the administration. Breaches by the judiciary will only cursorily be touched upon.[53]

10.4   Community law conditions for liability

10.4.1   Introduction

In *Francovich* the Court held that in the case of non-fulfilment of the obligations under Article 249(3) there should be a right of reparation if three conditions are fulfilled. According to the Court these three conditions 'are sufficient to give rise to a right on the part of individuals to obtain reparation'.[54]

The necessity to lay down Community law conditions which are as such sufficient to give rise to State liability is fully understandable if one takes into consideration the differences in State liability regimes as they exist in the Member States. In particular, the non-existence of public liability for legislative action and inaction in the majority of the Member States[55] would make illusory any right to reparation if the conditions were left to the national legal systems. Although some other conditions are still left to the Member States,[56] once the Community law conditions have been satisfied, the right to reparation can apparently not be denied.

The most evident precedent for such far-reaching interference with the 'reme-dial autonomy' of the Member States was undoubtedly the Court's judgment in *Zuckerfabrik Süderdithmarschen*.[57] In this case the Court held that, for the sake of coherence of the system of interim protection, national courts must order suspension of the enforcement of national measures based on a Community measure whose legality is contested, under the same conditions as those which are applied by the Court for the suspension of Community measures themselves. Initially, in *Francovich* the Court did not go as far as was proposed by Advocate General Mischo. Following the solution found in *Zuckerfabrik Süderdithmarschen*, the Advocate General suggested that the liability of the Member States for breaches of Community law should be subject to the same conditions as those developed for the purposes of non-contractual liability of

---

[53] On the old and precarious constitutional issue of liability for loss and damage caused by judicial decisions see, after *Francovich*, Steiner 1993, 11, Szyszak 1992a, 696, and Pieper 1990, 2456. After *Brasserie* see e.g. Toner 1997. In the meantime, the Court has recently also accepted liability for judicial decisions in the context of an Art 266 proceedings: Case C–129/00 *Commission v. Italy*, judgment of 9 December 2003, nyr in ECR. See for an early discussion of this issue Barav 1975, 379 and Nicolaysen 1985.

[54] Para 41 of the judgment.   [55] Cf Schockweiler 1990, 73, Bell and Bradley 1991, 6.

[56] See below, Section 10.5.   [57] Case C–143/88 [1991] ECR I–415.

the Community under Article 288.[58] However, the Court apparently changed its mind in *Brasserie*, where it sought to relate the conditions for liability of the Member States to the conditions applicable in case of liability of the Community.

As is well known, in the meantime both the Member States' and Community liability regimes have been more or less unified. After having first introduced the condition of 'sufficiently serious breach' from the field of liability of the Community legislature regarding normative acts or omissions into the State liability regime in general, *Bergaderm*[59] has established that this condition is now also generally applicable in the area of Community liability. Similarly, the same judgment also introduced the requirement that the infringed legal norm must intend to confer rights on individuals instead of the 'old' requirement that the rule at issue must be a rule of law aiming at the protection of individuals.[60]

It cannot be denied that there are some forceful arguments for the convergence of the liability regimes and requirements. In the first place, according to Article 288, the requirements are based on the principles in the legal systems of Member States governing public non-contractual liability.[61] In the second place, it seems difficult to understand why a Member State should be held liable for breaches under conditions which are less severe than those applicable in the case of non-contractual liability of the Community itself. However, for the time being, for the individual, unification does not seem a step forward as far as the liability of the Community is concerned: the requirements under Article 288 became, from the individual's perspective, more stringent.[62]

The Court's effort in *Brasserie*,[63] to align the liability regime, in particular the conditions, for the Member States and that for the Community, was certainly not an unqualified success. Its transplant of the degree of discretion as a decisive criterion for the application of similar criteria has caused quite some confusion. The Court held that

[58] A position with which another AG disagreed, since, in his view, in contrast to the Community, Member States are subject to a hierarchy of legal norms. See the Opinion of AG Léger in Case C–5/94 *Hedley Lomas* [1996] ECR I–2553. For an early analysis of the developments in the case law see, for instance, Caranta 1995.

[59] Case C–352/98 P [2000] ECR I–5291. Cf also Case T–178/98 *Fresh Marine Company* [2000] ECR II–3331 and Case C–312/00 P *Camar and Tico* [2002] ECR I–11355.

[60] Which reappeared, however, again in the CFI judgment in Case T–56/00 *Dole* [2003] ECR II–577, para 71.

[61] Although this argument must be used with a great deal of caution. In fact, there is much less in common to the Member States in the area of liability for legislative wrongs than the Court has sometimes suggested. Cf Van Gerven 1996, 508–13. For a more general overview see e.g. Lee 1999, Sections 2B and 2C and Larouche 2001, in particular 114–17. For detailed reports see Vandersanden and Dony 1997.

[62] In the same sense already in 1996 AG Léger in Case C–5/94 *Hedley Lomas* [1996] ECR I–2553. For a more optimistic view, see Tridimas 2001, 327.

[63] Joined Cases C–46/93 and C–48/93 [1996] ECR I–1029.

. . . where a Member State acts in a field where it has a wide discretion, comparable to that of the Community institutions in implementing Community policies, the conditions under which it may incur liability must, in principle, be the same as those under which the Community institutions incur liability in a comparable situation.[64]

According to the Court, in such a situation, three conditions must be met: the infringed rule of law must be intended to confer rights on individuals, the breach must be sufficiently serious and there must be a direct causal link between the breach of the obligation and the damage sustained. However, the Court also pointed out that the national legislature does not systematically have a wide discretion when it acts in a field governed by Community law and that Community law may considerably reduce this margin of discretion. This is, for instance, the case when Member States are required, under Article 249(3), to implement a directive. Indeed, this was exactly the situation at issue in *Francovich*, to which the Court referred. From that case it transpired that a mere breach would suffice. Therefore, the question arose whether the existence of 'wide discretion' or not had to be established in every single case first; and next, depending on the outcome, what requirement applied: the one of a sufficiently serious breach or the one of a simple breach.

The next two judgments did not clarify the matter, on the contrary. In *British Telecom*, concerning incorrect implementation of a directive, the Court did not inquire whether the State had wide discretion or not. It just simply looked into the question whether the breach was sufficiently serious.[65] In *Hedley Lomas* the Court admitted that the UK ' . . . was not called upon to make any legislative choices and had only considerably reduced, or even no, discretion . . . '.[66] Nevertheless, the three conditions from *Brasserie* were declared applicable, including the one of the sufficiently serious breach. It was only at the stage of the assessment whether the breach was sufficiently serious, that the mere infringement of Community law satisfied the requirement, exactly because there was hardly any discretion.

From the judgment in *Dillenkofer*,[67] it appears that the existence of discretion is not a criterion to decide whether the requirement of a sufficiently serious breach should be imposed or not. Since *Dillenkofer*, this is a requirement that applies in every case. It is the assessment that may differ and discretion became an element in the context of the assessment whether the breach committed is to be qualified as a serious one or not.[68]

---

[64] Para 47 of the judgment. As is well known, reference is made here to the case law on non-contractual liability of the Community, according to which, in case of legislative measures involving choices of economic policy, the Court takes into account the wide discretion available to the institutions. The Community cannot incur liability unless the breach is sufficiently serious. This is in particular the case where the institution concerned has manifestly and gravely disregarded the limits on the exercise of its powers.   [65] Case C–392/93 *British Telecom* [1996] ECR I–1631.

[66] Case C–5/94 *Hedley Lomas* [1996] ECR I–2553, para 28. Cf also Deards 1997, in particular 128, and Goffin 1997, at 532–7.

[67] Joined Cases C–178/94, C–179/94, C–188/94, C–189/94, and C–190/94 [1996] ECR I–4845.

[68] For a discussion see below, Subsection 10.4.3.

The three conditions laid down in *Brasserie* apply irrespective of which body—the legislator, the administration, or the judiciary[69]—has committed the breach. Especially as far as directives are concerned, the liability the Member States may incur is primarily linked to their failure to meet their obligations under Article 249(3). However, this Article says nothing about the content of the Member State's obligations in a concrete case, i.e. about the result which the Member State was supposed to achieve. Yet, for any reparation it is crucial to know what has to be repaired and, therefore, what the content of the obligation was. For that purpose, the Court has linked the breach of Article 249(3) to the content of the directive at issue.[70] That means that in every single case the content of the directive has to be analysed.

10.4.2   Granting rights to individuals

The first condition, namely that the rule of law infringed must be intended to confer rights on individuals, is a matter of content of the relevant provisions and, indeed, of their interpretation.[71] As I have discussed this topic at length in Chapter 6, it should suffice here briefly to recall that, contrary to what the Court's case law may sometimes suggest, the creation of rights and direct effect should not be conflated. Directly effective provisions may but do not necessarily confer rights.[72] I have, however, pointed out that there is a certain link between direct effect and the creation of rights, namely in the sense that rights—more precisely, their content and the beneficiaries of the rights[73]—must be determinable with sufficient precision, i.e. they must be ascertainable.[74] Here, again, the test for direct effect and the ascertainability may coincide, but cannot be equated. Furthermore, one has to bear in mind that directives may intend to create rights for individuals but that further substantiation of the rights, the elaboration of their exact scope, is left to the Member States. Obviously, a right laid down in the directive in a rudimentary form will make it impossible to determine the loss and damage incurred by the individual. A directive must therefore provide sufficient guidance in this respect. If necessary, the national court may call upon the Court of Justice for this purpose.

Since for the purposes of liability it is sufficient that the provisions *intend* to confer rights, it may be tempting to rely on the case law of the Court in the context of correct implementation of directives. However, here too a more or less automatic transposition is unwise. By using the term rights in the implementation context the

---

[69] In particular for the judiciary see Case C–224/01 *Köbler*, [2003] ECR I–10239, para 52.

[70] Cf Van Gerven 1994a, 25.

[71] Cf e.g. Joined Cases C–178/94, C–179/94, C–188/94, C–189/94, and C–190/94 *Dillenkofer* [1996] ECR I–4845, paras 33–46 and Case C–222/02 *Peter Paul*, judgment of 12 October 2004, nyr in ECR.

[72] See in particular Subsections 6.3.2 and 6.3.3.

[73] Cf the Opinion of AG Tesauro in Joined Cases C–178/94, C–179/94, C–188/94, C–189/94, and C–190/94 *Dillenkofer* [1996] ECR I–4845, para 18 and Case C–140/97 *Rechberger* [1999] ECR I–3499, para 22.   [74] Cf Subsection 6.4.5 for a detailed discussion.

Court may merely indicate that the Member States must, through implementing measures, create a legally sufficiently defined position which may be enforced in the courts, if necessary.[75]

Finally, in Section 6.4 I have made an effort to lay down some guidelines as concerns the question when Community law creates or intends to create rights and when not.

> In addition to this, in the context of the present discussion, it should be pointed out that the Court seems to employ a slightly different formulation of the conditions when a case is concerned with a non-implemented directive: the result prescribed by the Directive entails the grant of rights to them and the content of those rights must be identifiable on the basis of the directive.[76] This formulation is, in my opinion, merely a modality of the first condition.[77]

In formulating the first condition the Court was apparently aiming to introduce the concept of 'relative unlawfulness',[78] a *Schutznorm*, which is common to the non-contractual liability regimes of several Member States:[79] only a breach of a rule creating rights for individuals concerned or intended to create rights or, at least, protecting their interests can give rise to a right to reparation. Although, formally, the Member State commits a breach of Article 249(3) by not implementing a directive, *de facto* it is the violation of an individual right under the directive that really matters. The quintessence of this requirement is to prevent excessive damages by demanding a connection between the infringement of the rule and the interest affected.[80] It is striking that, in contrast to its case law under Article 288 of the Treaty, the Court did not merely require that the provisions of the directive be given to protect the individual.[81] On the contrary, it has imported the requirement of 'a right' into the Community liability regime and, arguably, made this more stringent.[82]

The conferral of rights on individuals referred to in the case law will primarily relate to the 'hard core rules', which have to be transposed into national law.[83] This

---

[75] Cf Subsection 6.3.4.

[76] Joined Cases C–178/94, C–179/94, C–188/94, C–189/94, and C–190/94 *Dillenkofer* [1996] ECR I–4845, para 27. See also for some incoherence in the case law as to whether the grant of rights must be the purpose or the result of the directive Ch 6, Subsection 6.3.3.

[77] Cf also the Opinion of AG Jacobs in Case C–150/99 *Lindöpark* [2001] ECR I–493, para 51.

[78] Cf Van Gerven 1993, 19.

[79] Cf Simon 1993, 237, Van Gerven 1994a, 16. Cf also Ross 1993, 62 who points out that in English law the norm violated must impose a duty which is owed to the claimant. For a different opinion see Barav 1994, 291.

[80] Cf Prieß 1993, 121. See also the Opinion of AG Darmon in Case C–282/90 *Vreugdenhil* [1992] ECR 1992, I–1937, para 53–58.   [81] Cf Bebr 1992, 575.

[82] Cf Case C–352/98P *Bergaderm* [2000] ECR I–5291 and the other cases referred to above, in Subsection 10.4.1. As to the more stringent character, see, for instance, Nettesheim 1992, 1002 and Schockweiler 1992, 44. In addition to that, in Ch 6, Subsection 6.4.4, it was suggested that the Court may be tightening the individual interest requirement as an element of the concept of a right. Cf case C–222/02 *Peter Paul*, judgment of 12 October 2004, nyr in ECR, in particular para 40.

[83] Cf above, Ch 3, Subsection 3.2.1.

actually suggests that the non-compliance of a Member State with one of its 'ancillary obligations',[84] obligations of a more procedural character, cannot give rise to a right of reparation, although it amounts to a breach of Article 249(3). It is undoubtedly difficult to imagine how an obligation of, for instance, notification could give rise to a right of individuals.[85] However, it is not entirely self-evident that liability must be excluded *a priori* for this type of breach. Whether or not there should be such a liability may depend on the legal consequences of such a notification and their objective.[86]

> In any case, in relation to Directive 83/189 (notification of technical standards),[87] the Court pointed out that this Directive does not 'define the substantive scope of the legal rule on the basis of which the national court must decide the case before it. It creates neither rights nor obligations for individuals'.[88]
>
> On the other hand, in *Wells* the Court has apparently accepted liability for a breach of an essentially procedural obligation, namely the failure to carry out an environmental impact assessment.[89]

10.4.3   Sufficiently serious breach

Clearly inspired by the case law under Article 288, in *Brasserie* the Court held that a breach is sufficiently serious when the Member State concerned manifestly and gravely disregarded the limits on its discretion.[90]

> It should be noted, that the introduction of this requirement was preceded by a doctrinal debate. From *Francovich* it was not entirely certain whether a breach *simpliciter* of Community law is sufficient to give rise to liability or whether the breach must be a serious one. According to some authors, a breach of Article 249(3) can as such be considered a serious breach and consequently there is no need for the Court to qualify this requirement further. Similarly, other scholars have pointed out that both in Community law and under certain non-contractual liability regimes of Member States the illegality of an act as such is often not sufficient to give rise to liability. In particular where the public bodies concerned have to interpret complex legal rules or have to intervene in complex subject matters and, moreover, where they possess discretionary powers, not every misconstruction of the rules or other miscalculation (such as errors in the evaluation of a situation) automatically gives rise to liability in

---

[84] Ibid, Subsection 3.2.2.
[85] Cf Case 380/87 *Enichem* [1989] ECR 2491 or Case C–159/00 *Sapod* [2002] ECR I–5031.
[86] Cf Ch 3, Subsection 3.2.2. Cf also Ch 6, Subsection 6.4.3 and 6.4.4.   [87] [1983] OJ L109/8.
[88] Case C–443/98 *Unilever* [2000] ECR I–7535, para 51.
[89] Case C–201/02 *Wells*, judgment of 7 January 2004, nyr in ECR, paras 66–69.
[90] Joined Cases C–46/93 and C–48/93 [1996] ECR I–1029, para 55.

damages.[91] Often some form of further qualification of the breach is imposed in order to limit the potential scope of liability and thus leave the public authorities sufficient room for manoeuvre.

The way in which the Court linked discretion and sufficiently serious breach was, and arguably still is, rather unfortunate and confusing.[92]

In *Dillenkofer* it reiterated that a breach of Community law is sufficiently serious if a Member State, in the exercise of its rule-making powers, manifestly and gravely disregards the limits of those powers.[93] The point is, that, first, also in the area of non-legislative powers, i.e. where the administration takes a decision, for instance, there may exist discretion. Somewhat remarkably, in *Larsy*, which concerned the application of the Regulation 1408/71 by a social security institution, the Court observed that the institution concerned did not have legislative choices.[94] Second, rule-making powers do not *eo ipso* imply that there is a (broad) margin of discretion. Exactly in the context of Community law, the Member States may be called upon to legislate while having no or only very limited latitude. This was, for instance, the case in *Rechberger*,[95] *Denkavit*,[96] and *Lindöpark*.[97]

In *Dillenkofer* the Court indeed pointed out that if, at the time of the breach, the Member State concerned was not called upon to make any legislative choices and it had only considerably reduced, or even no, discretion, the mere infringement of Community law may be sufficient to establish the existence of a sufficiently serious breach.[98] The Court also found that failure to implement a directive in time constitutes *per se* a sufficiently serious breach.[99] However, not, as one would assume, because there is no discretion as to the

---

[91]   Cf Jarass 1994, 883, Craig 1993, 611, Bell and Bradley 1991, 8 and 12–13.

[92]   In addition to the initial confusion as to the question whether there is one single or two separate liability regimes, discussed hereabove, in Subsection 10.4.1. Cf on the problems raised by the reference to discretion Simon 1996c, at 494–6 and Fines 1997b, 93–4.

[93]   Joined Cases C–178/94, C–179/94, C–188/94, C–189/94, and C–190/94 *Dillenkofer* [1996] ECR I–4845, para 25, confirmed in, *inter alia*, Joined Cases C–283/94, C–291/94, and C–292/94 *Denkavit* [1996] ECR I–5063, para 50, Case C–140/97 *Rechberger* [1999] ECR I–3499, para 50, and Case C–150/99 *Lindöpark* [2001] ECR I–493, para 39.

[94]   Case C–118/00 *Larsy* [2001] ECR I–5063, para 41. Even more remarkable is that the English version used the term 'substantive choice', while the French (and its Dutch equivalent) speak of '*choix normatif*'.

[95]   Case C–140/97 *Rechberger* [1999] ECR I–3499, para 51: no margin of discretion.

[96]   Joined Cases C–283/94, C–291/94, and C–292/94 *Denkavit* [1996] ECR I–5063, para 39: the provision breached left certain latitude.

[97]   Case C–150/99 *Lindöpark* [2001] ECR I–493, para 40: no legislative choices and only a reduced or even no discretion.

[98]   Cf Joined Cases C–178/94, C–179/94, C–188/94, C–189/94, and C–190/94 *Dillenkofer* [1996] ECR I–4845, para 25. Cf also Case C–5/94 *Hedley Lomas* [1996] ECR I–2553, para 28, Case C–127/95 *Norbrook* [1998] ECR I–1531, para 109, and Case C–424/97 *Haim II* [2000] ECR I–5123, para 38.

[99]   Cf Joined Cases C–178/94, C–179/94, C–188/94, C–189/94, and C–190/94 *Dillenkofer* [1996] ECR I–4845 and Case C–319/96 *Brinkmann* [1998] ECR I–5255.

question whether a directive must be implemented. Rather, the Member State is said to manifestly and gravely disregard its limits.

In addition to this dichotomy of 'discretion/manifest and grave disregard of the limits' on the one hand and 'reduced or no discretion/mere infringement' on the other, the Court has introduced a third set of criteria which is of relevance.

In order to determine whether the breach is sufficiently serious, there is a whole range of factors which the national courts may take into account when assessing the issue. The factors include the clarity and precision of the rule breached, the measure of discretion left by that rule to the authorities,[100] whether the infringement and the damage caused was intentional or involuntary, whether any error of law was excusable or inexcusable, the fact that the position taken by a Community institution may have contributed towards the omission, and the adoption or retention of national measures or practices contrary to Community law.

In any case, a breach of Community law will clearly be sufficiently serious if it has persisted despite a judgment finding the infringement in question to be established, or a preliminary ruling or settled case law of the Court on the matter, indeed, provided that they make clear that the conduct in question constituted an infringement.[101]

Although it is for national courts to determine whether the breach at issue can be characterized as sufficiently serious, the Court may lend a hand in this respect, at least if it has all the information necessary. In *British Telecom*, for instance, the Court found that Directive 90/531 (procurement in water, energy, transport, and telecommunication sectors)[102] lacked precision and was reasonably capable of bearing the interpretation given to it by the UK in good faith, on the basis of arguments which were not 'entirely devoid of substance'. Although the interpretation was wrong, it was not manifestly contrary to the wording of the Directive and it had also been adopted in other Member States. Moreover, there was no guidance from the case law of the Court, nor has the Commission clarified the matter.[103]

In a number of subsequent cases, in particular the 'clarity and precision' condition was the focus of the Court's attention.[104] For a clear understanding of the matter, this 'clarity and precision' condition should not be equated with the conditions for direct effect, i.e. that the provisions must be clear, precise,

[100] If there is any discretion worth speaking of. In Case C–424/97 *Haim II* [2000] ECR I–5123 and Case C–118/00 *Larsy* [2001] ECR I–5063, para 39, for instance, the reference to the measure of discretion disappeared.

[101] Cf Joined Cases C–46/93 and C–48/93 *Brasserie du Pêcheur* [1996] ECR I–1029, paras 56 and 57, confirmed in subsequent cases.   [102] [1990] OJ L297/1.

[103] Case C–392/93 *British Telecom* [1996] ECR I–1631, paras 43 and 44. See also Joined Cases C–283/94, C–291/94, and C–292/94 *Denkavit* [1996] ECR I–5063, paras 50–52.

[104] Cf Case C–319/96 *Brinkmann* [1998] ECR I–5255, paras 30–32, Case C–140/97 *Rechberger* [1999] ECR I–3499, paras 50–51 and Case C–150/99 *Lindöpark* [2001] ECR I–493, paras 39–41.

and unconditional. Clarity and precision in the liability context means that the meaning of the Community law provisions was reasonably beyond dispute and that it does not give rise to various interpretations. For direct effect, this issue is less relevant since the need to get further clarification of the content does not, as such, block direct effect.[105] So, in *Brinkmann*, for instance, the provisions were sufficiently precise and unconditional to be applied by the competent authorities, but they have misinterpreted them. Yet, this interpretation was defensible.

The Court refers to these factors in various situations. In some cases after having remembered first that a breach is sufficiently serious if a Member State has manifestly and gravely disregarded the limits of its powers.[106] In other cases it recalls that, in case of no or limited discretion, a mere infringement may constitute a sufficiently serious breach, but this is not always necessarily the case. For this purpose, the above-mentioned factors have to be taken into account.[107] Similarly, the factors are relevant irrespective of the question whether the breach is caused by national legislation,[108] or acts of the administration,[109] or judicial decisions.[110]

In case of liability for loss and damage caused by a judicial decision in last instance the Court has underlined that regard must be given to the specific nature of the judicial function.[111] Liability in such a case can be incurred only in the exceptional case where the court has manifestly infringed the applicable law. A specific fact to be taken into account in this context is indeed, in addition to the above-mentioned ones, whether the court in question has complied with its obligation to make a reference under Article 234 EC Treaty. To a certain extent, the way in which the Court treats breaches by supreme courts is comparable to a situation where the body concerned has a wide margin of discretion.

In brief, discretion or its absence is not the decisive factor and neither is the capacity in which the Member State breaches Community law—legislative, administrative, or judicial. It would rather seem that what really matters is whether the legal provision the Member State has to comply with is sufficiently clear and certain. In the more specific context of implementation of directives this means whether the legal

---

[105] Cf Ch 9, Subsection 9.4.2. Cf also the Opinion of AG Jacobs in Case C–150/99 *Lindöpark* [2001] ECR I–493, para 62.

[106] Cf Joined Cases C–283/94, C–291/94 and C–292/94 *Denkavit* [1996] ECR I–5063, para 50 and Case C–140/97 *Rechberger* [1999] ECR I–3499, para 50.

[107] Cf Case C–424/97 *Haim II* [2000] ECR I–5123, paras 41–42.

[108] Cf Joined Cases C–283/94, C–291/94, and C–292/94 *Denkavit* [1996] ECR I–5063 and Case C–140/97 *Rechberger* [1999] ECR I–3499.

[109] Cf Case C–319/96 *Brinkmann* [1998] ECR I–5255, para 30 and Case C–424/97 *Haim II* [2000] ECR I–5123, paras 37–43.   [110] Cf Case C–224/01 *Köbler* [2003] ECR I–10239, paras 54–55.

[111] The special responsibility of courts adjudicating at last instance was also stressed in Case C–129/00 *Commission v. Italy*, judgment of 9 December 2003, nyr in ECR, para 32 and by AG Geelhoed in his Opinion in this case, in paras 58–59.

situation to be realized by the Member State through implementation was sufficiently clear.[112] If the sufficient degree of clarity in what Community law requires does not exist beforehand, the breach or, where appropriate, the incorrect implementation, will be 'excusable' or not 'clear-cut'.[113] This is what the above-mentioned factors are all about.

Most of the cases until now focused on these factors of clarity and precision. It must be noted, however, that the range of possible factors mentioned by the Court is broader and that it constitutes a mixture of objective and subjective elements.

Discretion, in the sense that either the Member State was allowed to make further choices at the moment of implementation or that it had a margin of appreciation, comes in, in my view, as one of the elements for assessment. The broader the discretion or margin of appreciation, the more difficult it is to pin the Member State down on a sufficiently serious breach.[114]

> It should be noted that, in addition to the confusion already set out, it is far from clear what the Court means, in this liability context, by discretion. According to some scholars, discretion must be understood here as 'the legal power to choose between two or more alternatives'.[115] In other words, this would correspond to the German '*Ermessensspielraum*' the term which is as such used by the Court in the German versions of the case law. This again would correspond with the Dutch concept of '*beleidsvrijheid*'. However, the Dutch versions of the case law refer to '*beoordelingsmarge*', a sort of equivalent of the French '*marge d'appréciation*', which in turn is something else than '*pouvoir discrétionnaire*' or what should be in German '*Beurteilungsraum*'. In other words, the various versions use partly different, partly equivalent concepts, without it being clear how to understand these. Some guidance could be provided from the context in which this notion was imported into the State liability regime, namely the analogy with Article 288. In the area of liability for legislative measures involving choices of economic policy, the Court took into account the wide discretion the institutions enjoyed. The problem is, however, that the Member States' position under Community law is considerably different from this and, moreover, the liability regime of the Community too has evolved in another direction.[116]

In any case, in *Haim II* the Court confirmed what was already implicitly made clear in previous cases, namely that the discretion at issue and its scope is to be determined

---

[112] As to the difficult questions and complicating factors Member States may be facing see the discussion above, Ch 2, Section 2.6 and Ch 5, *passim*. The Court takes these fully into account in liability cases, as appears from the factors to be taken into account listed hereabove.

[113] Terminology of AG Jacobs, from his Opinion in Case C–150/99 *Lindöpark* [2001] ECR I–493, paras 59–60. In the same vein, Case C–140/97 *Rechberger* [1999] ECR I–3499, para 51: implementing measures at issue were manifestly incompatible, and Case C–319/96 *Brinkmann* [1998] ECR I–5255, para 31: interpretation was not manifestly incompatible with the directive at issue.

[114] Cf also in this respect the 'sliding scale' introduced by Van Gerven 1996, 521.

[115] Cf Köck and Hinstersteininger 1998, 25.   [116] See Subsection 10.4.1, hereabove.

by reference to Community law and not by reference to national law.[117] This clarification is important because *Brasserie* might have been understood as referring to the subject matter area in which the legislator, under national law, enjoyed wide discretionary powers.[118]

> Finally, the requirement of sufficiently serious breach implies that the Court's case law under Article 226, which makes clear that any excuses, whatever their nature, offered by the Member States for their non-compliance with the obligations resulting from a directive are in principle not accepted, does not as such apply in the context of State liability.[119] The infringement procedure aims, after all, at an objective finding of a failure of the Member State, without any additional requirements as to the gravity of the breach or culpability being imposed.[120] In the context of liability, the assessment may indeed differ. For instance, it would be highly paradoxical to argue that the Member State is liable in damages for the simple reason that it is formally under the obligation to implement the directive at issue, while there are clear indications in the Court's case law that the directive, or at least certain parts of it, are incompatible with primary Community law but the directive has not been annulled or declared invalid.[121]

10.4.4 Causal link

The third condition is the existence of a direct causal link between the breach of the State's obligation and the loss and damage suffered by the injured parties. As causation is largely a question of fact, i.e. it must be assessed in the light of the facts of the case, it is difficult to say in general terms what the exact content of the condition is. For the same reason, it is, in principle, a matter to be determined by the national court.[122] However, since causation is one of the three Community law conditions, it is ultimately for the Court of Justice to indicate its main elements. Similarly, this implies that it is not the national rules governing causation that should be applied.[123]

Despite the fact that causation is a matter for the national court, as in relation to the other conditions, in two cases, where there was sufficient factual evidence, the Court provided some further indications.

---

[117] Case C–424/97 *Haim II* [2000] ECR I–5123, para 40. See, however, also already Case C–140/97 *Rechberger* [1999] ECR I–3499, para 51.

[118] Joined Cases C–46/93 and C–48/93 [1996] ECR I–1029, paras 47–51.

[119] As was sometimes suggested after *Francovich*. Cf Nettesheim 1992, 1002, Temple Lang 1992–1993, 41, Ross 1993, 57, Huglo 1993, 82, Coppel 1993, 23–4.

[120] Cf above, Ch 2, Section 2.4. There I have also argued that in certain exceptional circumstances the Member States may be released, at least temporarily, from the obligation to implement the directive. Cf also Wathelet and van Raepenbusch 1997, 46.

[121] See above, Ch 2, Section 2.7. Cf also Jarass 1994, 882 and Tridimas 1999, 328–30.

[122] Cf Joined Cases C–46/93 and C–48/93 *Brasserie du Pêcheur* [1996] ECR I–1029.

[123] However, the question of causation will be strongly influenced by the evidence available and in the context of State liability, it is in principle the national evidential rules that apply. See Case C–228/98 *Dounias* [2000] ECR I–577. See also Subsection 10.5.2.

In *Brinkmann*, the chain of causation was severed by conduct of the national tax authorities.[124] The relevant Articles of Directive 79/32 were not transposed into Danish law. This amounted to a *per se* sufficiently serious breach. However, the Danish authorities attempted to cover this failure. They directly applied the provisions at issue and, therefore, the causal link between the non-transposition and the damage suffered by *Brinkmann* was breached. The second violation, namely the incorrect application of the provisions of the Directive, was excusable and at the end of the day, *Brinkmann* remained empty-handed.

In *Rechberger* Austria argued that there was no direct causal link.[125] The plaintiffs' loss was not only due to inadequate transposition of the directive at issue, but also to the imprudent conduct on the part of the travel organizer and exceptional and unforeseeable events, that is the overwhelming interest for the offer which had led to logistical and financial difficulties for the travel organizer. The Court did not take this argument on board. It held that the very guarantee laid down in the Package Travel Directive[126] is specifically aimed at arming consumers against the consequences of the bankruptcy of the travel agent, whatever the causes of it may be.

The judgment in *Rechberger* very much focuses on the specific directive at issue. The question is indeed, for instance, whether in another context a Member State may successfully defend itself by arguing that even if the directive had been (correctly and timely) implemented, there would be no guarantee that the (private) party under obligation would behave according to the terms of the implementing measures.[127] Similarly, another of the many issues not yet addressed by the Court in the context of State liability is under what circumstances the chain of causation can be severed by conduct of the party claiming compensation.[128]

10.5   State liability and the context of national law

10.5.1   Introduction

On the one hand, the three above-mentioned conditions are 'necessary and sufficient to found a right in individuals to obtain redress'.[129] On the other hand,

---

[124] Case C–319/96 *Brinkmann* [1998] ECR I–5255.
[125] Case C–140/97 *Rechberger* [1999] ECR I–3499.   [126] Directive 90/314, [1990] OJ L158/59.
[127] Case like C–91/92 *Faccini Dori* [1994] ECR I–3325 would suggest that the causal link may be established in such a situation even though the final obligations are imposed on a private individual. Cf also the Opinion of AG Mischo in Joined Cases C–6/90 and C–9/90 *Francovich* [1991] ECR I–5357, paras 67–68.
[128] Cf Case 26/81 *Oleifici Mediterranei* [1982] ECR 3057 in liability under Art 288 EC Treaty. See, however, also the remarks below, in Subsection 10.5.2 on mitigation.
[129] Joined Cases C–46/93 and C–48/93 *Brasserie du Pêcheur* [1996] ECR I–1029, para 66.

the action for damages is in other regards governed by the national rules on liability. The Court pointed out that

> ... the State must make reparation for the consequences of the loss and damage caused in accordance with the domestic rules on liability, provided that the conditions for reparation of loss and damage laid down by national law must not be less favourable than those relating to similar domestic claims and must not be such as in practice to make it impossible or excessively difficult to obtain reparation.[130]

This reference to national rules merits some further attention. In some cases it may be somewhat difficult to identify the conditions of national law which the Court is aiming at. Apparently, the conditions at issue are those which complement the Community law conditions discussed in the preceding Subsections. In any case, conditions which would interfere with the Community law ones such as, for instance, additional requirements whenever regulatory acts are at stake, are not allowed.

> In *Brasserie* the Court pointed out explicitly that certain restrictions which exist in domestic legal systems as to the non-contractual liability of the State-legislator may be such as to make it impossible or excessively difficult in practice for individuals to exercise their right to reparation. In particular the German requirement of *Drittbezogenheit*, a condition imposed by German law which makes reparation dependent upon the legislature's act or omission being referable to an individual situation (the 'third party'), or the condition in English law requiring proof of misfeasance in public office, were dismissed by the Court as making it in practice impossible or excessively difficult to obtain reparation.[131]
>
> Similarly, the reparation cannot be made conditional upon the existence of fault (whether intentional or negligent) on the part of the organ of the State to which the infringement is attributable, at least not in so far the concept of fault would go beyond that of a sufficiently serious breach of Community law.[132] Such a supplementary condition would not only make the reparation impossible in practice or excessively difficult, but it will ' . . . be tantamount to calling in question the right to reparation founded on the Community legal order'.[133]

As stated above, the fulfilment of the three conditions is as such *sufficient* to give rise to a right to reparation. In other words, conditions of national law which govern the *coming into being* of the right to reparation seem to be excluded.[134] This issue

---

[130] Joined Cases C–46/93 and C–48/93 *Brasserie du Pêcheur* [1996] ECR I–1029, para 67.

[131] Joined Cases C–46/93 and C–48/93 [1996] ECR I–1029, paras 69–73.

[132] Cf also Case C–424/97 *Haim II* [2000] ECR I–5123, para 39. In *Brasserie*, the Court noted that certain objective and subjective factors connected with the concept of fault under a national legal system may be relevant for the purpose of determining whether or not a given breach of Community law is serious. See para 78 of the judgment. As to the discussion about a fault requirement after *Francovich* but before *Brasserie*, see the first edition of this book, 322–5.

[133] Joined Cases C–46/93 and C–48/93 [1996] ECR I–1029, para 79.

[134] Cf also Karl 1992, 446, Schockweiler 1993a, 19.

must be distinguished from questions relating to procedural conditions *stricto sensu*, from evidential rules, and from substantive conditions such as rules concerning the content or form of the reparation to be given to the alleged victim. It is these latter issues which are governed by the relevant rules of national law.[135] However, the dual character of the liability regime, partly Community law conditions, partly referral to the national remedial framework, does not make it easy to draw a clear line.

10.5.2 'Communautorization' of other conditions?

In so far as certain conditions and rules are left to the Member States, they do not escape the influence of Community law either. In Chapter 7 the expanding implications of, in particular, the principle of effectiveness and, to the extent that it can be separated from the former, the principle of effective judicial protection were discussed. These principles also influence the remaining national procedural and substantive rules governing an action for damages. Thus rules relating to the admissibility of an action, *locus standi* of the applicant, time limits for bringing action, evidential rules,[136] nature or categories of damage to be compensated, its assessment, the calculation of compensation to be paid, the form of redress, the award of interest, or any other relevant matter may, under certain circumstances, be modified by virtue of the above-mentioned principles.[137] It is not my intention to discuss all the possible influences *in extenso*. Such a discussion would require a stock-taking of all the possible obstacles within the Member States, which is quite beyond the scope of this book.[138] Nevertheless, some general remarks can be made here on the basis of some lessons which can be drawn from the Court's case law, in particular from cases decided in the area of State liability.

Reparation

According to the Court, reparation must be commensurate with the loss or damage sustained by the individuals, so as to ensure effective protection of their rights. Indeed, when determining the extent of reparation, the principles of equivalence and effectiveness apply fully in this respect as well.[139] Total exclusion of loss of profits

---

[135] Cf also Jarass 1994, 882. For problems that this delimitation may pose see, *inter alia*, Detterbeck 2000, 239–40.   [136] Cf Case C–228/98 *Dounias* [2000] ECR I–577.

[137] For Belgium, for instance, it has been argued that the requirements may imply doing away with the 'execution immunity', i.e. that no forcible execution is possible against public authorities. Cf Arts 1993, 509.

[138] For an overview see for instance Deckert 1997, 229 ff. Indeed, as was to be expected, fresh questions will be submitted to the Court on various aspects of this 'procedural and remedial autonomy'. Cf e.g. Case C–438/03 *Cannito* [2004] OJ C47/13 and Case C–439/03 *Murgolo* [2004] OJ C47/13. In the meantime, both cases have been dismissed as 'manifestly inadmissible' by Order of 11 February 2004, nyr in ECR.

[139] Cf Joined Cases C–46/93 and C–48/93 *Brasserie du Pêcheur* [1996] ECR I–1029, paras 81–82, confirmed in Case C–373/95 *Maso* [1997] ECR I–4051, para 36, Case C–261/95 *Palmisani* [1997] ECR I–4025, para 26 and Joined Cases C–94/95 and C–95/95 *Bonifaci* [1997] ECR I–3969, para 48.

would fall foul of the latter principle. However, how far loss of profits may be excluded and, arguably, also the broader issue of which economic losses must be compensated for and which not, is apparently left to the national court to decide, subject to the two well-known principles.[140]

Furthermore, the principle of equivalence may require the award of exemplary damages,[141] and, finally, the individual is entitled to recover interest on any damages awarded since that is to be considered as an essential component of the compensation.[142]

By stating that the reparation must be commensurate or adequate,[143] the Court does not necessarily require compensation in full.[144] Whether that will be the case depends on the particular context and circumstances. Some indications in this respect can be found in *Von Colson* and, in particular, in *Marshall II*,[145] both decided in the particular context of sex discrimination and the requirements laid down in those cases are the result of interpretation of Directive 76/207 (equal treatment at work).[146] In *Von Colson* the Court stipulated that the compensation awarded for the breach of the prohibition of discrimination 'must in any event be adequate in relation to the damage sustained'.[147] In *Marshall II*, in contrast to the Advocate General who argued that 'adequate' does not necessarily mean 'equal',[148] the Court found that in the particular circumstances of the case adequate reparation means that the loss and damage must be made good in full. An upper limit, restricting the amount of compensation *a priori*, was not allowed.[149]

Also, as to the question what categories of damage are to be taken into consideration for compensation, the Opinion of Advocate General Van Gerven in *Marshall II* is still helpful. He submitted that a national court, when considering the compensation to be awarded, must heed each of the components of damage that are traditionally taken into account in rules governing non-contractual liability, namely loss of physical assets, loss of income or profit,

---

[140] Cf the brief remark of AG Jacobs in his Opinion in Case C–150/99 *Lindöpark* [2001] ECR I–493, para 80. For a detailed analysis of the various factors that may constitute loss for an undertaking, although in a different context, see also the Opinion of AG Geelhoed in Case C–129/00, of 3 June 2003, nyr in ECR.

[141] Joined Cases C–46/93 and C–48/93 *Brasserie du Pêcheur* [1996] ECR I–1029, para 87 and 89.

[142] Cf Joined Cases C–397/98 and C–410/98 *Metallgesellschaft* [2000] ECR I–1727, paras 93–95, in which the Court makes an affort to distinguish the case from *Sutton* (C–66/95 [1997] ECR I–2163) where the claimant was denied the award of interest. Cf also the Opinion of AG Jacobs in Case C–150/99 *Lindöpark* [2001] ECR I–493, para 81 and already in 1993 Case C–271/91 *Marshall II* [1993] ECR I–4367.

[143] In the French version of *Brasserie* for instance and also, alternatively, in Case C–373/95 *Maso* [1997] ECR I–4051, para 41.   [144] Cf Van Gerven 1994a, 17.

[145] Case 14/83 [1984] ECR 1891 and Case C–271/91 [1993] ECR I–4367. For a discussion of these aspects of the cases see Ch 5, Section 5.4.

[146] [1976] OJ L39/40. On the specific context see also Van Gerven 1996, 524.

[147] Para 23 of the judgment.   [148] Para 17 of the Opinion.

[149] Para 30 of the judgment. For a different and more general approach to limitations to compensation see also the Opinion of AG Van Gerven in *Marshall II*, para 14 ff.

moral damage like injury to feelings, and damage on account of the effluxion of time.[150]

In determining the loss or damage for which reparation may be granted, a national court may, as a matter of Community law, inquire whether 'the injured person showed reasonable care so as to avoid the loss or damage or to mitigate it'.[151] According to the Court, it is a general principle common to the legal systems of the Member States that the injured party must show reasonable diligence in limiting the extent of the loss or damage.[152] In this context it is particularly important whether the claimant availed himself in time of all the legal remedies available to him.[153]

> This issue is closely related to the question concerning the relationship of direct effect and liability as a means of enforcement or protection of rights which individuals derive from a directive, in particular the question of which mechanism should be used first. Arguably, where the provisions concerned have direct effect, the claimant should bring an action and rely on the provisions first.[154] Yet, in *Metallgesellschaft* the Court found that, for the purposes of reparation, the company could not be obliged to take steps to obtain a tax advantage which national law denied it before seeking compensation for breach of Community law.[155]

Similarly, on the basis of the judgment in *Kühne*[156] it could be argued that the individual concerned has to ask first for a revision of a final administrative decision by the competent administrative body. However, in the light of the narrow and exceptional circumstances under which the administration is obliged to proceed with such a review, such a proposition goes, in my view, too far. The other side of the *Kühne* case is, that if the exceptional circumstances are not present, the fact that the decision became final may block an action for State liability. This is indeed a matter of national procedural law, to be judged in the light of the principles of equivalence and effectiveness.

---

[150] Case C–271/91 [1993] ECR I–4367, para 18 of the Opinion.

[151] Joined Cases C–178/94, C–179/94, C–188/94, C–189/94, and C–190/94 *Dillenkofer* [1996] ECR I–4845, para 72, referring to *Brasserie*, para 84. Note that here the Court is conflating two distinct legal concepts: contributory negligence, which is a matter of causation, and mitigation of the loss once it occurred.

[152] Cf Joined Cases C–46/93 and C–48/93 *Brasserie du Pêcheur* [1996] ECR I–1029, para 85. The Court established no negligent conduct in Joined Cases C–178/94, C–179/94, C–188/94, C–189/94, and C–190/94 *Dillenkofer* [1996] ECR I–4845, para 73.

[153] Cf Joined Cases C–46/93 and C–48/93 *Brasserie du Pêcheur* [1996] ECR I–1029, para 84.

[154] Comparable questions may indeed also arise in relation to consistent interpretation.

[155] Cf Joined Cases C–397/98 and C–410/98 *Metallgesellschaft* [2000] ECR I–1727, paras 105–107. See also the somewhat curious observations in Case C–150/99 *Lindöpark* [2001] ECR I–493, para 35.

[156] Case C–453/00, judgment of 13 January 2004, nyr in ECR, briefly discussed in Ch 7, Subsection 7.3.2.

The form of redress

The majority of cases before the Court until now were concerned with pecuniary compensation for the loss and damage sustained. One might ask, however, whether other forms of redress should also be made available to plaintiffs, in particular in cases where these seem more adequate and where the full effect of the directive is better safeguarded.[157]

> Still pecuniary but different in character was the reparation provided in Italy in the wake of *Francovich*.[158] It took the form of retroactive application of the—belatedly adopted—measures transposing Directive 80/987 (protection of workers—insolvency of employers).[159] The unpaid wage claims were still to be paid by the INPS, the national social service authority, subject to certain restrictions. The Court was satisfied with such a solution. It found that such a retroactive application enables in principle the harmful consequences of the breach of Community law to be remedied. The effect is, after all, to guarantee the employees concerned the rights from which they would have benefited if the directive had been transposed in due time. In deciding this, the Court also accepted a number of limitations which were part and parcel of the transposition measures.[160] However, the Court also added that where the existence of complementary loss sustained can be established, the result of such a loss must also be made good.[161]

One of the—relatively unproblematic—options seems to be a reparation in kind. Whenever a plaintiff prefers such reparation, and it is physically possible, it is submitted that the principles developed in the Court's liability case law pose no obstacles. The same considerations apply when the plaintiff merely seeks a declaration. Much less certain is whether a court may give an injunction, the content of which may, moreover, vary depending on the case. It may, for instance, contain a prohibition, an order to refrain from certain behaviour, possibly from the application of national rules, but it may equally contain a positive order, an order of specific performance. In particular in the case of an omission to implement a directive, the order could, theoretically, take the form of an order to legislate.[162] From a constitutional point of view this is indeed a very sensitive issue.[163]

[157] A positive reply is given by Temple Lang 1992–1993, 23 and 25, Bok 1993, 52, and Van Gerven 1993, 15.   [158] Joined Cases C–6/90 and C–9/90 *Francovich* [1991] ECR I–5357.

[159] [1980] OJ L283/23.

[160] In particular rules against aggregation and limitations on the guarantee institution's liability.

[161] Cf Case C–373/95 *Maso* [1997] ECR I–4051 and Joined Cases C–94/95 and C–95/95 *Bonifaci* [1997] ECR I–3969. For a detailed discussion see Anagnostaras 2000 and Dougan 2000b, 108–13.

[162] Not excluded by Langenfeld 1992, 961–2. Cf also Triantafyllou 1992, 568 (*Normenersatzklage*) and Lewis and Moore 1993, 168. This for some perhaps odd reasoning, placing other remedies in the line of liability, can be explained by the fact that in Dutch law, tort liability provisions of the Civil Code may be relied upon for various purposes and not only to ask for damages.

[163] Cf Lewis 1992, 451 and Lewis and Moore 1993, 169.

An—unsuccessful—example of such an action is provided by the Dutch *Waterpakt* case, decided in 2003 by the *Hoge Raad*,[164] and already discussed above, in Chapter 7, Subsection 7.3.4. In that case a number of environmental organizations sought, *inter alia*, an order to legislate, before a certain deadline, directed at the State. The substance of the case concerned the non-implementation of Directive 91/676 ('nitrates directive').[165] The *Hoge Raad* held, *inter alia*, that under national constitutional law, the courts lack the necessary jurisdiction to give such an order. The question as to whether legislation should be adopted and, next, what the content of the legislation should be, is a matter for the political branch and, more particularly, for the legislator. Neither the risk of an infringement proceedings under Article 226 EC, nor the Community law requirements of full effectiveness and effective judicial protection change this. According to the *Hoge Raad*, it follows from *Van Schijndel*[166] that the duty of national courts to give full effect to Community law and to ensure the protection of the rights which individuals may derive from that law, exists only within the scope of competences and jurisdiction as defined under national law. Since under Dutch consitutional law the courts have no jurisdiction to order the adoption of primary legislation, the action of the environmental organizations could not succeed.

As was already observed in Subsection 7.3.4, from a Community law perspective this decision and, in particular, the arguments used by the *Hoge Raad*, are less obvious than the *Raad* would like the audience to believe. Indeed, it must be regretted that, in contrast to what the Advocate General at the *Hoge Raad* suggested, the last instance judges did not make a preliminary reference.

In brief, it is far from clear what, in terms of the form of redress, the broader implications of the State liability case law are. The latter concentrates on the reparation *a posteriori* of loss and damage already suffered. These must be 'made good'.[167] However, it is conceivable that, in the future, the courts will be required to offer protection against any consequences of a breach of Community law, thus not only to give redress for breaches which have already occurred but also to prevent unlawful consequences which are likely to occur in the future.[168] Moreover, in some cases where damages *a posteriori* cannot fully make good the loss and damage sustained, a

---

[164] Judgment of 21 March 2003, NJ 2003, no 691. Cf also Case 71/85 *FNV* [1985] ECR 3855. This case concerned in fact an action brought by FNV against the State for non-implementation of directive 79/7; the president of the District Court of The Hague issued an order to amend the unemployment benefit law. In appeal, however, the order was annulled.   [165] Directive 91/676 OJ 1991, L375/1.

[166] Joined Cases C-430/93 and C-431/93 *Van Schijndel* [1995] ECR I-4705.

[167] Cf e.g. Case C-373/95 *Maso* [1997] ECR I-4051, para 35.

[168] Cf Bok 1993, 52.

judicial order seems to be the most appropriate remedy, offering the best protection of the rights which individuals derive from Community law and safeguarding the full effectiveness of Community rules.[169]

Who can sue?

Like other matters under discussion here, *locus standi* in an action for damages under the Community liability regime is primarily a matter of national law. However, it follows from the liability cases decided and, furthermore, from, for instance, *Verholen*[170] that if the standing rules are, from the Community law point of view, such as to undermine the right to effective judicial protection and to render the exercise of the right to obtain reparation virtually impossible or excessively difficult, by virtue of these principles the national rules concerning *locus standi* cannot be decisive. This could imply that not only the—fairly obvious—category of persons to whom the directive or other provisions intended to grant rights will be entitled to bring action, but also those who, for instance, incur damage as a consequence of the breach of Community law by the Member State concerned while themselves not being within the category of persons to whom the directive intends to confer rights.

In relation to the identity of plaintiffs, complications will arise if it seems impossible to identify, on the basis of the directive, the persons who are within the category of the potential beneficiaries.[171] Whether or not the persons are ascertainable may indeed be ultimately resolved by the Court in a preliminary ruling. In *Francovich*, for instance, matters were straightforward.[172] Yet, as I have argued hereabove, it is part and parcel of the first condition, i.e. the (intended) grant of rights, that the identity of the beneficiaries of the rights must also be ascertainable.[173]

Who can be sued?

Although it is primarily the Member State which is liable for loss and damage caused by a breach of Community law, it is not necessarily the central State as such which is the proper defendant and, therefore, should be sued in national courts. The question of which body of the State will be the appropriate defendant is again a matter of national law. At first sight, it seems logical that the body which is responsible *within the Member State* for the breach committed, i.e. to which the breach can be attributed, is the one to be sued.[174]

---

[169] Cf Case C–213/89 *Factortame* [1990] ECR I–2433.

[170] Joined Cases C–87/90, C–88/90, and C–89/90 [1991] ECR I–3757, discussed above in Ch 7, Subsection 7.3.2.   [171] Cf also Jarass 1994, 883 and Geiger 1993, 470.

[172] Cf paras 13–14 and 45 of the judgment. Cf also Case C–334/92 *Miret* [1993] ECR I–6911 and Case C–91/92 *Faccini Dori* [1994] ECR I–3325.

[173] Cf Subsection 10.4.2 and also Barav 1994, 290 and 291 and Fines 1997b, 97.

[174] Cf also Temple Lang 1992–1993, 37, Schockweiler 1993b, 117.

In the cases decided until now, the Court laid down a sort of minimum guarantee. In *Konle* it pointed out that it is for each Member State to ensure that individuals obtain reparation for damage sustained, whichever public authority is responsible for the breach and whichever public authority is, under domestic law, responsible for the reparation.[175] A Member State cannot free itself from liability by pleading the internal distribution of powers and responsibilities. In other words, there must always be a body to make the reparation and if there is not, in the ultimate analysis the central State should be held liable.[176] On the other hand, in the same judgment the Court emphasized that, subject to that reservation, 'Community law does not require Member States to make any change in the distribution of powers and responsibilities between the public bodies which exist on their territory'.[177] Indeed, all this under the proviso that the procedural arrangements comply with the principles of equivalence and effectiveness.

While *Konle* was concerned with liability and reparation in a federal context, the solution is in principle also applicable to geographically or otherwise decentralized bodies. In *Haim II* the Court built upon *Konle* and found that if in a Member State certain legislative or administrative tasks are devolved to territorial bodies with a certain degree of autonomy or to any other public law body legally distinct from the State, the reparation may be made by that body.[178]

In addition to this 'vertical' dimension, there is also a 'horizontal' one: to whom should the responsibility be allocated? Legislature? Administration?[179] In cases of non-transposition or incorrect transposition matters seem to be relatively transparent, as it is the legislature that is to be blamed. However, there exists an independent obligation for the administration to apply Community law provisions or to proceed with consistent interpretation whenever the legislator has failed to transpose the directive or to do so correctly.[180] In such cases it may be difficult to sort out which body exactly has caused the harm, in particular because it may often be a combination of the conduct of both the legislator and the administration. Here again it seems to be a matter for national law.

> Such a dual breach existed in *Haim II* and in *Brinkmann*. In the first case, the Court left it to the national courts to find a way out of the 'institutional imbroglio'.[181] The *Brinkmann* case was 'resolved' by the Court in the sense that the chain of causation between the damage and the non-transposition was said to be broken by the conduct of the national tax authorities which directly

---

[175] Case C–302/97 [1999] ECR I–3099. Cf also Case C–118/00 *Larsy* [2001] ECR I–5063, para 35.
[176] Cf in the same sense already in 1994 Jarass 884 and Jans *et al.* 2002, 376–7. This holds true even if the central State does not have the necessary powers to control the other national authorities.
[177] Para 63 of the judgment.   [178] Case C–424/97 *Haim II* [2000] ECR I–5123.
[179] For a detailed discussion of both aspects see Anagnotaras 2001. Cf further also Leclerc and Mondésert 2002, and Tridimas 2001, 317–21.
[180] Cf hereabove, Section 10.3 and also Ch 4, Section 4.4. Indeed, this reasoning may be extended to the judiciary as well.   [181] Term used by Hessel and Mortelmans 1993, 929.

applied the provisions at issue.[182] They did so wrongly, but this second violation did not amount to a sufficiently serious breach.

Limitation periods

All the Member States have some types of limitation period with respect to actions under the relevant non-contractual liability rules. The nature of these limitation periods may differ. They can be time limits for bringing action as they exist in administrative law. They can also be periods after which the right of action or the substantive right itself is prescribed (prescription periods).[183]

One of the issues raised in *Brasserie* was that the Court did not follow the German Government which requested to limit the judgment in time.[184] The Court's refusal was explained by the fact that under national law substantive and procedural conditions apply which take into account concerns of legal certainty. In other words, at a certain moment, the action for damages will be time-barred or prescribed.

Finally, in *Palmisani*,[185] which concerned the same (retroactive) rules as those at issue in *Maso*,[186] the question was whether the limitation period of twelve months from the entry into force of the legislation at issue for bringing a reparation claim was compatible with the principle of equivalence. For 'ordinary' actions for damages against public authorities the limitation period was five years. In contrast to its acceptance of the national legislation as a viable alternative for the action for non-contractual liability, the Court suggested that, depending on a number of factors,[187] the period of five years might be the correct point of reference for the application of the principle of equivalence.

10.6   Liability of the State: a tailpiece to effective judicial protection

The *Francovich* judgment and its progeny clearly illustrates the way of pushing the limits of remedies available in the case of failure of the Member States in their oblig-ations under Article 249(3) and, indeed, under Community law in general. Where for a long period direct effect of directives was considered to be the last resort,[188]

---

[182] Case C–319/96 *Brinkmann* [1998] ECR I–5255. See also hereabove, Subsection 10.4.4.

[183] See on the various types also above, Ch 7, Subsection 7.3.2.

[184] Joined Cases C–46/93 and C–48/93 [1996] ECR I–1029, paras 97–98. Cf also the Opinion of AG Mischo in Joined Cases C–6/90 and C–9/90 *Francovich* [1991] ECR I–5357, para 87.

[185] Case C–261/95 *Palmisani* [1997] ECR I–4025. For the detailed criteria for the application of the principle of equivalence developed in *Palmisani* see Ch 7, Subsection 7.4.2.

[186] Case C–373/95 [1997] ECR I–4051, discussed above.

[187] In fact, the Court left the issue open as it felt it did not have all the information necessary.

[188] Cf the Opinion of AG Darmon in Case C–177/88 *Dekker* [1990] ECR I–3941, para 10.

today the non-contractual liability of the State for breaches of Article 249(3) has taken over, extending the possibilities of judicial protection a stage further, beyond what seemed for many years to be the ultimate limit.[189]

On the one hand, non-contractual liability of the State seems to be a safety net in cases where other devices designed by the Court fail. On the other, one may wonder whether the Court is not too easily inclined to accept liability as a panacea for various problems in the area of judicial protection, with the result of, ultimately, lowering the effectiveness of the latter.[190] Liability may often seem to be an elegant way out. Yet, it also implies that the rather onerous conditions must be fulfilled such as, in particular, the sufficiently serious character of the breach.

> In this respect one may add that the concern for mitigation of liability is understandable. However, simultaneously, great care must be taken not to open the gates to all sorts of excuses for incorrect implementation or other breaches of Community law. After all, the problems which arise can partly be imputed to the Member States themselves, especially since they participate in the elaboration and adoption of directives. Similarly, under certain circumstances the requirements of equity should be taken into consideration: should the Member State bear the consequences of its unlawful conduct or should these be passed on to private individuals?[191] The fact that the State can incur liability under less strict conditions on the basis of national law, provides some consolation.[192]

Compared with the instruments of direct effect or consistent interpretation, non-contractual liability is, in my opinion, of a *subsidiary character*: liability arises in principle only if the injured party has been unable to safeguard his rights by means of direct effect or consistent interpretation.[193] To put this in a different way, liability is a supplement to direct effect and consistent interpretation, and not a substitute for them.[194] I therefore cannot agree with suggestions that the plaintiff has the choice of which avenue he will follow.[195] Neither can I agree with scholars who seem to prefer State liability to direct effect and consistent interpretation. In this view, liability is 'more legitimate' than the other two instruments, as it lays the sanction directly at the door of the defaulting Member State. Direct effect and consistent interpretation were, in this view, 'simply expedients designed to secure the enforcement of Community law precisely because the State has failed to fulfill its obligations'.[196] In my opinion, liability of the Member States is equally nothing

---

[189] Cf the Opinion of AG Van Gerven in Case C–128/92 *Banks* [1994] ECR I–1209, para 38.

[190] For this critique see in particular Dougan 2000b.

[191] As to this question see also Craig 1993, 618–19.

[192] Cf Joined Cases C–46/93 and C–48/93 *Brasserie du Pêcheur* [1996] ECR I–1029, para 66.

[193] Cf Ossenbühl 1992, 994, Schlemmer-Schulte and Ukrow 1992, 89, Schockweiler 1993b, 120. Cf, however, also Joined Cases C–397/98 and C–410/98 *Metallgesellschaft* [2000] ECR I–1727, paras 105–107 and the not very conclusive para 35 in Case C–150/99 *Lindöpark* [2001] ECR I–493.

[194] Cf Duffy 1992, 135.   [195] Cf e.g. Ross 1993, 59.

[196] Cf Steiner 1993, 9. In the same sense also Schermers 1997, 539.

more than another—and to my mind second-rank—'expedient'. Community law is primarily interested in its application, for which, in the case of a Member State's failure, consistent interpretation and direct effect are the 'second best' solutions, and not the third best solution of 'buying off' the failure. Similarly, an individual may be more favoured by the application of national law in conformity with the directive or by its direct application, than by a sum of money.

The *subsidiary character* of liability seems to be confirmed in a whole line of judgments of the Court, like *Miret, Faccini Dori, Carbonari*, and *Dorsch Consult*,[197] which show that only if direct effect or consistent interpretation are not possible and, therefore, cannot bring sufficient relief does State liability come into consideration.

This said, liability of the State may also function as a *complement to* the other two methods. Under certain circumstances, direct effect or consistent interpretation as such do not suffice to achieve a situation which entirely corresponds with the result which had to be achieved *and* which would have been achieved if the directive had been correctly transposed (or transposed in due time, as the case may be) into national law. In other words, the full effectiveness of the directive is not necessarily always safeguarded by direct effect and consistent interpretation. Similarly, the individual may still be left with additional damage which is not remedied by direct effect or consistent interpretation. In particular, where the national court reviews the legality of national measures and subsequently disapplies them, the result may be a lacuna.[198] Payment of damages to the persons affected may seem to be the appropriate complementary remedy. Thus, neither of the devices guarantees that the individual will be put in the position in which he would have been had the breach not occurred nor that he will be fully compensated for the damage he has actually sustained, including, for instance, legal costs.[199]

As far as the liability of the State is concerned, it is in principle immaterial which of the three State powers commits the breach. The Member State cannot escape liability for the very reason that it was, for instance, the legislator or the judiciary. Yet, in the meantime, the Court has also made certain incursions into the realm of liability of private individuals for breaches of Community law.[200] In relation to directives, the combination of liability of private persons with the Court's *dicta* in *Muñoz*[201] may

---

[197] Case C–334/92 [1993] ECR I–6911, Case C–91/92 [1994] ECR I–3325, Case C–131/97 [1999] ECR I–1103, and Case C–54/96 [1997] ECR I–4961.

[198] See above, Ch 9, Subsection 9.3.3. Cf also Arts 1993, 501.

[199] As examples of such a 'complementary function' of liability can be mentioned Case C–66/95 *Sutton* [1997] ECR I–2163, Joined Cases C–192/95 to C–218/95 *Comateb* [1997] ECR I–165, and to an extent also Case C–90/96 *Petrie* [1997] ECR I–6527. Also note that in *Wells* (Case C–201/02, judgment of 7 January 2004, nyr in ECR) compensation was suggested as an alternative if revocation or suspension of a consent for the working of a quarry were not possible as a matter of national law. Cf also Case C–373/95 *Maso* [1997] ECR I–4051 and Joined Cases C–94/95 and C–95/95 *Bonifaci* [1997] ECR I–3969, for reparation of complementary loss in case the retroactive application of the transposition measures would not suffice to cover the loss or damage actually sustained.

[200] Cf C–453/99 *Courage* [2001] ECR I–6297. See also on this issue the Opinion of AG Van Gerven in Case C–128/92 *Banks* [1994] ECR I–1209 and Van Gerven 1996, 530–2.

[201] Case C–253/00 [2002] ECR I–7289, concerning private enforcement of a regulation.

seem to open up prospects for private enforcement of directives. It has been suggested that, while using domestic tort law, a private individual can enforce his right against another private individual (who is then under an obligation).[202] Thus, for instance, a competitor will try to force a café owner to stop selling tap water as mineral water because it does not meet the requirements laid down in a directive which has not yet been implemented in national law,[203] or he will at least claim damages.

As was already discussed in the previous Chapter,[204] to a certain extent directives are already used in a comparable way, but until now it was always in the context of a defence against claims based on national law, which was, however, incompatible with a directive.[205] In other words, in a 'negative' way. As such, this is already a highly debatable use of a directive. It is submitted that the 'positive' private enforcement as proposed by some is just a bridge too far, having regard to the persistent prohibition of horizontal direct effect of directives.[206]

The final potential problem which I would like to address briefly is State liability for breaches of Article 249(3), while the plaintiff would be better off under national law as such. Put differently, the individual suffers some disadvantage through the doctrine of direct effect or consistent interpretation. Can State liability be of any help? The *Francovich, Miret,* and *Faccini Dori* cases related to a situation where (potential) direct effect, consistent interpretation, and the right to damages concerned the protection of rights which the directive intended to grant to individuals. However, it could be that, while there has been no transposition or only incorrect transposition of a directive, either direct effect or consistent interpretation is to the disadvantage of the individual. As discussed above,[207] the application of directly effective provisions may affect the position of a private individual, in particular in multi-angular relationships. Similarly, interpretation of national law in conformity with the directive may create or at least change obligations for a private party. If the directive did not exist, such effects would not occur.[208] The question is then indeed whether the individuals concerned may bring an action for damages against the Member State which has failed to meet its obligations under Article 249(3).

In the light of the conditions as laid down in the Court's case law, the answer seems to be negative. As explained above, in Subsections 10.4.1 and 10.4.2, the first condition especially links the breach of Article 249(3) to the content of the directive and, in particular, to the existence of a right which would have been granted to the individuals concerned if the directive had been correctly transposed. Furthermore, it may be argued that the adversely affected individual would have

---

[202] Cf Betlem 2004.

[203] Indeed, as was the case in *Kolpinghuis* (Case 80/86 [1987] ECR 3969), only then in a criminal law context. [204] Ch 9, Subsection 9.5.3.

[205] Cf Case C–369/89 *Piageme I* [1991] ECR I–2971, Case C–85/94 *Piageme II* [1995] ECR I–2955, Case C–77/97 *Smithkline Beecham* [1999] ECR I–431, Case C–220/98 *Estée Lauder* [2000] ECR I–117, and Case C–443/98 *Unilever* [2000] ECR I–7535.

[206] See Ch 9, Subsection 9.5.2.   [207] Ch 8, Section 8.6 and Ch 9, Subsection 9.5.3.

[208] An obvious example of such a situation is Case C–177/88 *Dekker* [1990] ECR I–3941.

been affected anyway if the directive had been implemented.[209] In other words, where the directive intends to create obligations for individuals, it is difficult at first sight to understand how they can incur damages by the non-implementation or incorrect implementation. However, it is equally true that by not implementing the directive, the Member State did not enable the individuals to ascertain the full scope of the obligations upon which they would have been able to act. For the time being, the Court's case law does not provide a satisfactory answer to this problem. In my view, in the ultimate analysis, the problem boils down to the tension, already observed, which may occur between the desire to give full effect to Community rules and the need for effective judicial protection.[210]

---

[209] Cf the Opinion of AG Lenz in Case C–91/92 *Faccini Dori* [1994] ECR I–3325, para 62. Cf also Prechal 1991, 602–3.   [210] Cf also above, Ch 8, Section 8.6, *in fine*.

11

Drawing the lines together

11.1 Introduction

In the foregoing Chapters a detailed account has been given of the main characteristics of directives, the main problems related to their implementation, and the difficulties caused by their non-implementation or incorrect implementation. The role played by the national courts in enforcing directives and, in particular, in providing judicial protection has also been extensively discussed. Finally, the case law of the Court of Justice on consistent interpretation, direct effect of directives, and the liability of the State in cases of breach of Article 249(3) in particular, has been analysed and discussed in depth. An attempt has been made to elucidate the numerous questions which this complex subject 'Directives' raises and to bring together its many facets within one treatise.

The purpose of the present Chapter is not to rehearse *in extenso* the findings of the previous Chapters. It will rather focus on a number of salient issues and, where possible, tie them together. Following an overview of how the Court has stretched, on the basis of the definition of directives in Article 249(3) EC Treaty, the obligations resulting from a directive (11.2), I will turn to the problem of the directive as an incomplete legislative act (11.3). Next the relationships between the central and decentralized levels of enforcement (11.4) and the mechanisms of enforcement at decentralized level (11.5) will be addressed. In Section 11.6 I will briefly look into a few issues that the Article 226 procedure and direct effect, consistent interpretation, and State liability have in common and that are closely connected with the application and enforcement of directives. The effects of the application and enforcement of directives for the so-called 'national institutional autonomy' will be critically reviewed in Section 11.7. I will wind up this Chapter with a few brief remarks on the outlook for the future of directives (11.8).

11.2 Article 249(3): reinforcing the binding force

The Court's case law relating to directives is characterized by, on the one hand, an effort to maintain the limitations resulting from the definition of directives in Article 249(3), while, on the other hand, it tries, often in combination with Article 10 of the EC Treaty, to increase the effectiveness of directives and the protection of rights which individuals derive from them. In this process the Court has made a considerable effort to make the most of the binding obligations for the Member States resulting from Article 249(3) and, more concretely, from directives themselves.

The Court has expanded the obligations arising from a directive with respect to the subjects actually bound. It is not only the Member State as such, or their central governments which are bound by the obligations at issue. The Court spelled out that directives are binding upon all the authorities of Member States, including local or regional authorities, constitutionally or otherwise independent bodies, and nationalized industries. It has stretched the concept of 'the State' to entities which cannot, in all reasonableness, be held responsible for the failure to implement the directive and to do so correctly.

The doctrine of consistent interpretation has exemplified outstandingly that the binding effect of directives reaches further than the mere obligation of implementation by the Member State: the obligation to achieve the result envisaged by the directive is binding on all national authorities, including the courts, and not only on those responsible for its implementation.

Within the doctrine of direct effect the Court has merged the various types of obligations which a directive may contain for the State: the obligation to implement the directive and the obligations resulting for the Member States and their 'emanations' from the actual text and particularly from the substantive provisions of the directive.

The consequences of the binding force of the directive were again brought a stage further in *Francovich*[1] and its progeny: another dimension of the binding obligations is the liability for damages in the case of their non-fulfilment or incorrect fulfilment; this irrespective of which State authority is responsible for the breach.

To a certain extent, the Court has also extended the 'temporary element' of directives. It does not only uphold the deadlines for implementation very strictly, accepting, in principle, no excuses whatsoever for belated implementation. Even before the deadline has expired, the Member States must refrain from taking any measures liable seriously to compromise the result prescribed by the directive.[2]

The obligations arising from a directive with respect to the form and methods of implementation have been considerably tightened. The case law on the requirements that adequate transposition of directives must satisfy, is marked by a strong emphasis on the binding elements within the definition of a directive. The preponderant concern with the result to be achieved has resulted in curtailing considerably what is left to the Member States: the choice of form and methods.

On the basis of the combination of the content of the directive in question, on the one hand, and the principles of full effectiveness, legal certainty and

---

[1] Joined Cases C–6/90 and C–9/90 [1991] ECR I–5357.
[2] Case C–129/96 *Inter-environnement Wallonie* [1997] ECR I–7411.

effective judicial protection, on the other, the Court has laid down strict requirements which must be satisfied by the implementing measures.

Apart from the obvious requirement that the content of the measures must correspond to the content of the directive, it must be clear and precise in order to guarantee an unambiguous legal situation. As far as their legal nature is concerned, the implementing measures must in principle be legally binding, particularly but not exclusively where the directive aims at creating rights and duties for individuals.

Since directives must be fully effective in everyday practice, the implementing measures must often be accompanied by an appropriate system of sanctions in order to compel obedience. In this respect the principle of full effectiveness and, where appropriate, the principle of effective judicial protection require that national rules aiming at enforcement of the directive, particularly the sanctions, are provided for.

This tendency has been further reinforced by the shift in attention from adequate transposition of directives into national law to their application and enforcement in practice. The requirement that directives are fully effective may entail additional obligations for the Member States which are beyond the actual text of the directive at issue.

The concern about *de facto* effectiveness is furthermore also underlined by some less orthodox cases. For instance, even if directives are fully and correctly transposed, they may be relied upon if the implementing measures are not correctly applied.[3] Similarly, the failure to notify national measures to the Commission may result in the unenforceability of the latter.[4]

Yet, this process of 'reinforcing the binding force' of directives has an important limit: a directive cannot bind individuals.

11.3   The weakness: general validity with a reservation

Directives are, like any other rule of Community law, integrated within the national legal orders of the Member States. As such they are law-creating and can, in principle, be considered as law generally valid in the Member States.

Most EC directives also aim at the creation of rights and obligations for private individuals. These rights and obligations may exist *vis-à-vis* other individuals or *vis-à-vis* the State authorities. In contrast to what the definition of directives in Article 249(3) may suggest, there is nowadays little doubt that directives are to be considered as Community legislation and as a source of rights and duties. Whether a directive, or one or more of its provisions, creates or is intended to create individual

---

[3] Cf Case C–62/00 *Marks & Spencer* [2000] ECR I–6325.
[4] Cf Case C–194/94 *CIA Security* [1996] ECR I–2201.

rights and obligations is a matter of the *substance* of the directive and must be decided on the basis of the concrete text of the relevant directive provisions.

The specific characteristics of directives are that they provide for legislation in two stages: directive provisions lay down the norms which must be given full effect through the intercession of national law. The conception of the directive entails that only after they have undergone this process should the rights and obligations provided for by the directive become fully binding on the individuals within the Member States. Seen in this perspective, directives are indirect sources of rights and obligations for individuals, since the rights and obligations under national law have their origin in the directive.

Under certain circumstances, directives are direct sources of rights, i.e. they confer rights without the intercession of national implementing measures. This is a vital issue, since, as is well known, the process of transforming the directive provisions into national law has proved to be rather cumbersome. Often, the step required to give them full effect has not been taken, or has been wrongly executed.

However, in contrast to rights, directives cannot impose obligations upon individuals directly. Indeed, this has consequences for the full effectiveness and for the protection of rights of others. Namely, in so far as the enforcement of a right of one requires to comply with an obligation by another. In this sense, there exists an important limitation to the validity of directives as generally binding rules in the Member States.

Yet, also in this respect the Court is exploring and sometimes also pushing the limits of this—in other respects persistently upheld—limitation. The various techniques to bypass the limitations resulting from the denial of horizontal and inverse vertical direct effect of directives have sparked off a lively debate and controversy which is still not settled. It centres on the Court's case law, which seems to accept certain side effects of vertical direct effect and the very fact that consistent interpretation may also result in imposing a burden upon individuals.

As to the latter, I have argued that the obligation to interpret national law in conformity with the directive at issue may result in imposing a new obligation on individuals or otherwise affect their position.[5] At the end of the day, these effects are produced by national law and should not be equated to horizontal or inverse vertical direct effect of a directive. The protection of the individual concerned lies in the general principles of law and, in particular, the principle of legal certainty.

It is in particular the horizontal side effect in multi-angular relationships and the effects produced by collateral challenges in private litigation which give rise to much criticism.[6] From this complex and often not consistent case law it transpires that, according to the Court, the term 'impose obligations' should be understood as having a strict meaning in this context. The mere negative repercussions on an individual's legal position are to be accepted. Similarly, certain harsh consequences of the collateral challenge for an individual's position may be toned down under

---

[5] Cf Ch 8, Section 8.6.   [6] Cf Ch 9, Subsection 9.5.3.

national law. However, the fact remains that the line between mere adverse repercussions on the one hand and obligations for individuals on the other is not easy to draw and will generate new questions and further discussion. In this sense, there is a double weakness: first, over time, directives have been equated in various respects to rules generally valid in the Member States but not as far as the imposition of obligations on individuals is concerned. Second, it is exactly this exception that renders rather complex and controversial the application of directives in the domestic legal order of the Member States.

11.4 Central enforcement and decentralized enforcement: an interaction

The case law on directives in general and their application in domestic legal orders in particular, takes shape in the context of the Article 226 proceedings, the central level of enforcement, and in the context of the cooperation between the national courts and the Court of Justice under Article 234 EC Treaty. I have labelled this as the decentralized level of enforcement.[7]

The Community level of enforcement focuses on the general and uniform observance of Community law rather than protection of rights or of the legal position of individuals. In the past the Court has divorced the two levels of enforcement and found that no parallel may be drawn between them.[8] However, the Court merely wished to separate the two types of procedures. In fact there exist various 'passerelles' between the two.[9]

The case law developed at central level contains several elements which are also relevant within the context of decentralized enforcement and *vice versa*. Some of these can be mentioned briefly.

First, one of the questions in the context of an Article 226 proceedings concerning an implementation problem is whether the directive intends to create rights. Whenever a directive does so, the Court requires implementation, such that the legal position of the individuals concerned is sufficiently precise and clear to enable them to ascertain fully the extent of their rights and, where appropriate, to rely on them before a court. Indeed, such a finding may also have relevance in the context of protection to be given by a national court, in particular for the purposes of liability. Yet caution is required in this respect: the assessment of 'rights' in the context of liability and Article 226 may differ.[10]

Second, a judgment of the Court under Article 226 declaring that the Member State has not fulfilled its obligations resulting from Article 249(3) will

---

[7] Cf Ch 1, Section 1.4.   [8] Case 28/67 *Molkerei-Zentrale* [1968] ECR 211.
[9] Moreover, by creating national regulatory authorities and entrusting them with the enforcement of directives, the Community legislator is equally creating new links between the two levels. Cf Chapter 4.
[10] Cf Ch 6, Subsection 6.3.4.

be an important—although not necessary—indication that the Member State is in breach of this Article and the national court may be required to continue the examination in order to establish whether the State should be held liable in damages. In so far as a case of non-implementation is at issue, matters are straightforward: this amounts to a sufficiently serious breach. Where the individual argues that the directive has not been implemented correctly, the national court must undertake further examination into the existence of a sufficiently serious breach. An objective finding in an infringement proceedings cannot be transposed here as a matter of course, since this proceeding is not concerned with the question of fault or the existence of grounds of justification on the part of the Member States. On the other hand, a breach of Community law is deemed to be sufficiently serious if it has persisted despite a judgment finding the infringement in question to be established.

Third, the Court's case law on full effectiveness of directives, involving the requirement of an appropriate system for enforcement of the measures transposing the directive, was mainly developed in the context of preliminary proceedings. The requirement of effective judicial protection may entail, for instance, that compensation must be full and adequate. These standards are, however, also to be applied in an Article 226 proceedings where the adequate implementation of the directive is addressed.[11]

On the other hand, judgments given by the Court in the framework of decentralized enforcement or in infringement proceedings do not necessarily always translate into consequences on the other level. For instance, a finding of the Court that the directive at issue is directly effective or the possibility that the national court can remedy inadequate implementation or non-implementation by means of consistent interpretation does not release the Member State from its obligation of (correct) implementation. Neither are direct effect and consistent interpretation accepted as valid arguments of defence in infringement proceedings.

As has been noted,[12] there exists some ambiguity with respect to consistent interpretation, on the one hand, and correct implementation, satisfying the requirements of precision and clarity in particular, on the other. According to the Court, the question whether a directive has been implemented correctly has to be considered in the light of the interpretation and application of the implementing measures by the national courts. When the courts are under the obligation to interpret national (transposition) measures in conformity with the directive and they do so by giving the relevant provisions a somewhat strained meaning in order to meet their obligation, can it still be maintained that the directive has been implemented correctly? Put differently, there is a certain tension between the requirement of clear and precise implementation and the way in which the fulfilment of these requirements is assessed: this assessment takes into account the interpretation by the national courts while, at the same time, interpretation

---

[11] Cf Ch 5, Section 5.4.   [12] Cf Ch 5, Subsection 5.2.2 and Ch 8, Sections 8.3 and 8.4.

presupposes a certain degree of flexibility of the terms and must in any case be performed in conformity with the directive.

11.5 Direct effect, consistent interpretation, State liability, and their mutual relationship

Concerned about both the full effectiveness of the norms laid down in directives and the protection of the rights which a directive may intend to grant to individuals, the Court of Justice entrusted the national courts, in accordance with Article 10 of the Treaty, with the protection of the individuals concerned. The Court enabled the national courts to do this by using three mechanisms: consistent interpretation of national law, direct effect and liability of the State for damage caused by incorrect implementation, or non-implementation of the directive concerned.

An important effect of the development of the separate mechanisms is the weakening of the 'monopolistic position' of the doctrine of direct effect. For a long time the orthodox view was that only directly effective provisions can produce effects within the legal orders of the Member States without an intercession of national measures. However, consistent interpretation and State liability have shown that there are also other ways of giving effect to unimplemented or incorrectly implemented directives.

Differences and commonalities

Direct effect and consistent interpretation have in common that the legal consequences they entail are the consequences as determined by national law. In other words, in the case of consistent interpretation, the content of the national provision is adjusted, in accordance with the directive, but after such an adjustment it still applies as a rule of national law. In the case of direct effect, the directive provision is used directly, though as if it were a provision of national law. Basically, direct effect either amounts to application of the provision to the facts of the case or it is used as a standard for review of national measures. However, the consequences, such as the remedies to be given, remain those as defined by national law.

The situation is different in the case of the third device, State liability. Whenever the Member State does not comply with its obligations under Article 249(3) and certain conditions formulated by the Court are satisfied, the consequence, i.e. the right to damages, is determined by Community law. Furthermore, it should be noted that this mechanism operates at a different level from the previous two. While the techniques of interpretation and direct effect operate at primary level, in simple terms, the level of imposing a rule of conduct, liability operates at secondary level, i.e. the level of sanctions for the breach of a rule of conduct. Damages to be paid are, in this context, not based on the directive as such but are the consequence of the breach of a Community law obligation by a Member State. This does not, however, alter the fact that this latter mechanism also serves to protect individuals.

There are also other commonalities and differences between the three mechanisms. First, in contrast to consistent interpretation, direct effect and State liability can operate irrespective of the existence of provisions of national law which (should) apply to the case. Consistent interpretation presupposes that there are national provisions to be interpreted.

Second, the mechanisms of direct effect and, by its very nature, the liability of the State, can operate only against the State. This is not so in the case of consistent interpretation.

Third, while direct effect is limited to sufficiently precise and unconditional provisions of directives in the sense that the national court has at its disposal judicially manageable standards to decide the case before it, no such limitation exists with respect to consistent interpretation. Obviously, the terms of the directives must provide for some guidance as to the meaning and the objective of the directive concerned. However, this is not the same as the conditions of precision and unconditionality for the purposes of direct effect.

For the purposes of liability, the condition to be satisfied is the intended creation of rights. At several points in this book I have stressed that direct effect and creation of (substantive)[13] rights must be distinguished. Direct effect relates to the quality ascribed to the provision in question, i.e. to be invoked by the persons concerned for different purposes and to be applied by the national courts. The creation of rights is a matter of its content. Upholding the distinction is especially important in two respects: equating them does not do justice to the concept of direct effect, which is broader than the creation of rights. On the other hand, it is a misconception to argue that only directly effective provisions can create rights. Often, direct effect and creation of rights will coincide. However, this is not necessarily always the case.

All this having been said, there exists also a close link between the two issues. The (intended) creation of rights involves, in particular, the ascertainability of the content of the right on the basis of the directive and also of the identity of the potential beneficiaries. Ascertainability will often come close to the requirement of a sufficient degree of precision. Yet, these requirements too cannot be equated since liability has a different function from direct effect. This latter topic brings us to another often recurring theme: discretion.

Discretion

Although in many respects it has taken centre stage, the notion is not defined, neither by the Court, nor, as a rule, by legal scholars. The Court does not distinguish

---

[13] As opposed to the 'procedural' right to rely on the directive.

between legislative discretion and administrative discretion. It also seems to paste together the power of appraisal and discretionary power properly speaking. The latter may perhaps be loosely described as the latitude on the part of the Member States to act according to their own judgement, leaving them a number of choices as to what they will do, while it is lawful to choose any of them. Since in several respects the Court gives weight to this notion, it is to be deplored that it does not provide guidance on how to understand it.

The existence and scope of discretion has implications for the intensity of judicial review in general[14] and for the assessment, in the context of State liability, whether a breach of Community law should be considered sufficiently serious or not, in particular. The more discretion there is the smaller the chance that a breach will be considered sufficiently serious. Only a manifest and grave disregard of the limits on discretion will do. Initially, the case law even suggested that the test to be applied in the context of State liability ('sufficiently qualified' versus 'normal' violation of EC law) was dependent on the existence of discretion.[15]

Similarly, the existence of discretion is highly relevant when addressing the question whether a provision gives rise to rights: existence of broad discretionary powers will not allow ascertainment of the content of the right. In different and oversimplified words: discretion can be contrasted with duties; the latter in principle allow no choice as to what the duty-bearer has to do. Now, since rights are conceived as correlatives of a duty, where there is no duty there can be no right. This is also the quintessence of the requirement laid down in State liability case law, namely that the content of the rights must be identifiable on the basis of the provisions of the directive. Existence of (too much) discretion will make such an identification impossible. If the Court finds the provisions relating to the content of the right sufficiently precise and unconditional, the right will be identifiable.

The step to direct effect seems then merely a matter of course: existence of (too much) discretion will, under circumstances, also amount to denying direct effect. As has been observed, the absence of discretion is considered to be the basic condition for direct effect. However, it has equally been explained that, depending on the purposes for which the Community norm is deployed, existence of discretion does not necessarily block direct effect: the national court may be called upon to control whether the Member State or the national authority, as the case may be, has remained within the limits of the discretion that is left. Whenever the court is able to perform such review using the directive as a standard, the directive has direct effect.

One may take this reasoning a stage further: if the Court of Justice is able to examine in infringement proceedings whether a Member State, in the exercise of its discretion as regards implementation, has remained within the limits of the directive, without a problem of direct effect being raised, there are no fundamental reasons why a national court could not do the same. The characteristic which the two courts have in common is that they are courts of law.[16]

---

[14] Cf Case C–120/97 *Upjohn* [1999] ECR I–223.   [15] Cf Ch 10, Section 10.2.2.

[16] Cf also below, Section 11.6.

Complementarity and priority

All three mechanisms have their specific limits. In the case of consistent interpretation the most important limits lie in the principle of legal certainty and, arguably, the judicial function as such. In the case of direct effect the main limits lie in the justiciability of the case, i.e. whether the national court is able, equipped with the directive provisions, to deal with the problem before it, and, as already observed, in the possibility of using the directive solely against the State. The limits of State liability lie in the conditions to be satisfied in order to give rise to a right to damages.

These specific characteristics of the separate mechanisms allow them to operate in a complementary fashion: one takes over where another leaves off. To a considerable extent they constitute a coherent system which comes into operation as a palliative or remedy whenever a directive has not been implemented or has not been implemented correctly. However, due to the limitations of the three mechanisms which, moreover, may have the same cause, such as the indeterminateness of the relevant provisions, the risk of lacunas in the judicial protection will remain.

In a situation where the one does not take over from the other but where theoretically all three mechanisms could be deployed, is there any preference as regards their use?

In the *Johnston*[17] case the Court of Justice suggested that the national court should try first to reconcile the national provision and the provision of a directive through interpretation. Only if such an interpretation is impossible should the court have recourse to direct effect. In my opinion, this is a logical approach. Especially in the case of alleged inadequate transposition the court must interpret relevant provisions of national law first in any event, in order to determine whether inadequate transposition actually exists; and after all, why should a court seek a harsh confrontation with Community law if the matter can be settled in a 'softer' fashion? Consistent interpretation constitutes, in general, a less drastic incursion into the national legal system than direct effect. In the ultimate analysis, it is then still national law which applies, although its content may be adjusted in the light of the directive. The effects should, in principle, be less radical than the application of a provision of a directive in lieu of national law. However, where consistent interpretation will come close to distorting the meaning of national provisions, direct effect may be preferred and will perhaps even be dictated by legal certainty.

By the nature of things, the liability of the State should come in the third position.[18] As was already observed, by comparison with consistent interpretation or direct effect, liability operates at a different level. While these two latter devices should as far as possible remedy the consequences of non-implementation or incorrect implementation at the level of the applicable norm itself, liability

---

[17] Case 222/84 [1986] ECR 1651. Cf more recently, for instance Case C–327/00 *Santex* [2003] ECR I–1877 and Case C–125/01 *Pflücke* [2003] ECR I–9375.   [18] Cf also Ch 10, Section 10.6.

constitutes a 'second rank device'. It originates from the breach of a Community law obligation and not from the directive itself. Seen in this perspective, liability comes into operation only if and in so far as the party concerned cannot sufficiently safeguard its rights by means of consistent interpretation or direct effect. Indeed, under certain circumstances only liability makes sense for the claimant. The availability of the direct effect or consistent interpretation avenues do not, as such, 'block' liability, as the Court makes patently clear in *Brasserie*.[19] However, they may play a role in the context of the mitigation of damage.

11.6   Common preliminary issues, options for the domestic court as tailpiece

A point to be addressed briefly relates to two preliminary issues which must be addressed first, whatever the level of enforcement is, central or decentralized, or whatever mechanism of enforcement at domestic level is relied upon, consistent interpretation, direct effect, or State liability.

The very first question to be dealt with in any concrete case is the interpretation of the provisions of the directive itself. This issue was not addressed in the present study and, indeed, it is a part of a much larger topic, the interpretation of EC law provisions in general. However, it must be underlined that, in contrast to other provisions of Community law, such as the Treaty Articles and regulations, the interpretation of directives has a special dimension. It will also (continue permanently to) determine the meaning of national law, which has been specifically enacted or is deemed to implement the directive concerned.[20]

After the meaning of the relevant provisions is clarified, there is the second common issue: often,[21] it must be established whether there is a conflict, an incompatibility between national law and the provisions of the directive. In the context of an Article 226 proceedings, this will be established by the Court of Justice directly. At the national level, it is up to the national court to look into the issue. Traditionally, when the problem of compatibility was raised at national level, the question as to the direct effect of the relevant provisions was more or less raised automatically as well. Nowadays, this has changed. For the purposes of State liability, national courts have to establish that there was a breach of Community law and they do so irrespective of the direct effect of the provisions at issue. In fact, the domestic courts may be called upon to apply the requirements for proper implementation of directives developed by the Court of Justice in infringement

---

[19] Joined Cases C–46/93 and C–48/93 [1996] ECR I–1029, paras 20–22.

[20] I have touched briefly on this aspect in Ch 2, Section 2.6, Ch 5, Section 5.2 and Ch 8, Sections 8.3 and 8.4.   [21] This problem may be less pronounced in the context of consistent interpretation.

proceedings. Similarly, for the purposes of a deliberate 'remedial' consistent interpretation,[22] the incompatibility will usually be established. Without, however, necessarily deciding the question of direct effect first.

The incompatibility being established, what is next? According to the Court, the finding in infringement proceedings that a Member State has failed to fulfil its obligations under Community law entails for both judicial and administrative authorities a prohibition having the full force of law against applying the national measures incompatible with Community law, as well as the obligation to take all appropriate measures to enable Community law to be fully applied.[23] If this type of prohibitions and obligations is transposed to the national level of enforcement, it will, in the first place, result in the disapplication of contrary national rules.

Here the effects of an Article 226 judgment are very similar to the consequences of direct effect, in particular, direct effect in the form of legal review. They also pose similar problems.

> Disapplication may often result in a lacuna: it may be that there are then no applicable rules at all if the relevant provisions of Community law lack the direct effect for the purpose of being applied and if there is also no possibility of filling the gap by means of consistent interpretation. Furthermore, disapplication of national provisions may under certain circumstances result in affecting the position of private individuals. Here exists a clear parallel between the effects of an Article 226 judgment and the hotly debated collateral challenge in private litigation.[24]

Arguably, when giving effect to a judgment of the Court in infringement proceedings or when deciding on how to follow up a self-established incompatibility, the domestic court has one obligation and a number of choices. The obligation is not to apply the national rules which are incompatible with Community law obligations. Next, the national court may continue to examine the possibility of State liability if that is what the claimant has asked for. The domestic court may also try, if that would be the most appropriate way, to interpret the national rules at issue in conformity with the directive and palliate temporarily the Member State's failure or to apply the provisions of the directive to the facts of the case. That is to say, provided this leads to the desired outcome and that the provisions allow such application. Finally, the court may also stop at the most basic—though sometimes sufficient—level, the disapplication.

However, here too the options for the national court continue: it should apply, from the various procedures available under national law those which are appropriate for protecting the individual rights conferred by Community law. Similarly, as to the conclusions to be drawn from the inapplicability, this is a

---

[22] For 'normal' consistent interpretation as opposed to 'remedial' consistent interpretation see Ch 8, Section 8.4.   [23] Cf Case C–101/91 *Commission v. Italy* [1993] ECR I–191.
[24] Cf Ch 9, Subsection 9.5.3 for further discussion, which has by no means crystallized out yet.

question governed by national law. The ultimate limits to the choices lie in the principles of equivalence and effectiveness.[25]

11.7 Semi-concealed incursions in national autonomy

A principle ostensibly maintained by the Court of Justice is the principle of institutional autonomy: it is a matter for the Member States to decide which bodies will be entrusted with the fulfilment of obligations resulting from Community law, including directives, and to give them the necessary powers for this purpose. The same also holds true for the courts: it is for the Member States to decide which court will have jurisdiction in matters involving Community law and to invest it with the necessary powers enabling it to provide effective judicial protection.

The central question remains: how much is left of this professed non-interference with the institutional structure of the Member States when it is considered in the light of the developments in case law?

National administration

An obvious interference with the domestic institutional structure exists where a directive requires the setting up of special or independent bodies to be entrusted with the rules resulting from the directive, such as is the case in the area of telecommunication. However, there are also more subtle and therefore less visible ways in which Community law and Community law directives may influence the internal (administrative) structure of the Member States.

Community law requirements relating to the nature of implementing measures also determine the body which has to implement the directive concerned. In order to compel national authorities, which are competent *ratione materiae* but independent from the central government, the Member States seem to be required to provide for a mechanism safeguarding that the authorities satisfy the obligations resulting from a directive. For instance, if the subject matter of a directive is within the autonomous legislative powers of the regions, the central government must nevertheless be able, by some means, to induce the regions to implement the directive and to do so correctly.

According to the Court *all* national authorities are bound by the obligation to achieve the result prescribed by a directive, not merely the legislature, which is primarily responsible for the implementation. Particularly for administrative authorities, this binding force entails that they are, where necessary, obliged to apply directly effective provisions of a directive and disapply national measures incompatible with it.

---

[25] Cf also Ch 7, Subsections 7.3.4 and 7.4.2.

Where, for instance, a local authority is, in pursuance of national law, empowered to grant authorizations for certain industrial activities under conditions laid down in national law and, by virtue of direct effect of a directive, the authority grants the authorization required under different conditions, namely those of the directive, the authority is clearly doing something which it is not allowed to do under national law. The possibility should also not be excluded that the obligation for national authorities to interpret national law in conformity with the directive could lead to similar results.

This indeed amounts to a blow to the traditional subordination of the executive to the legislature. It may grant them powers they do not have as a matter of national law and, moreover, it does not make the disapplication of national provisions dependent upon a decision of a court. This is the more remarkable if one takes into consideration the Court's case law according to which a Community measure must be held to be valid and applied accordingly as long as it has not been declared invalid by the Court. Apparently, the same standards do not apply at national level.

National courts

As regards the principle of institutional autonomy with respect to national courts, it would appear that the case law results in the creation of autonomy for the courts instead of respecting the principle, despite the emphasis put upon reference and deference to national procedures and remedies which should apply. The very fact that the national courts have been made accomplices in the enforcement of Community law has led to a situation in which the *formal* source of their power stems from the national legal order, while the *substance* of their function may originate in Community law. In other words, they remain national judges but they have a Community law mission. This mission may imply certain duties for which, in order to accomplish them successfully, the courts do not always have the necessary powers or are even straightforwardly prohibited from taking a certain course of action. The articulation between the two is not always perfectly organized. Partly for this reason, and partly because the Community standards of judicial protection differ from the national standards, the Court of Justice poses certain requirements as to the quality of judicial enforcement which must be available, with the ultimate consequence of requiring national courts to do something they are not necessarily empowered to do as a matter of national law.

The catchwords here are 'procedural and remedial autonomy', a kind of species of the institutional autonomy, which is, however, not entirely unrestricted. National procedural and remedial law has to satisfy, at least, the requirements of equivalence and minimum effectiveness. In some cases the general principle of effective judicial protection serves as a ground for considerably curtailing the Member States' autonomy with respect to procedures and remedies to be made available for breaches of Community law or of national law which originates in Community law provisions. And again in other cases the Court just dictates the remedies to be made available.

The orthodox understanding was that it was up to the legislature within the Member States to provide the courts with the necessary powers to enable them to safeguard rights deriving from Community law in an effective manner. However, after a prelude in *Simmenthal*, the Court's case law suggests clearly that it is the national judiciary itself that should extend its own powers. Either in a negative way, by disapplying the existing restrictions or, where necessary, in a positive way, by assuming powers which do not exist as a matter of national law.

In terms of inroads into the national institutional autonomy, it should be noted that national—constitutional, or other, for instance, procedural—rules, principles, notions, and doctrines often reflect the position of the national courts within the national constitutional context, i.e. *vis-à-vis* the other State organs. The arguments against far-reaching intrusion by the courts in the process of effective application of Community law often relate to the separation of powers and the limits of the judicial function in the constitutional setting.

In general, national courts have a considerable scope for manoeuvre to satisfy the requirements of the ECJ, while relying on their national rules and principles. However, as was already pointed out above, the limit is reached where a court is required to do something which is beyond its competence, i.e. beyond the rules—constitutional or otherwise—defining its powers. This process brings about a change as to the place of the courts within the Constitutional structure of the State.

> In fact, this change initially became visible in the wake of the doctrine of direct effect: national courts were required to disapply national law or to review it in the light of Community law and, where appropriate, to apply norms stemming, from a constitutional perspective, from an external source. What else does this amount to than changing the subordination of the judiciary to the legislature which was, in varying degrees, the common model in many Member States? The tendency did not, however, stop at this point. Firstly, in particular the type of relief to be made available in order to safeguard effective judicial protection, culminating in the liability of the State for breaches of Community law, results in shifting the constitutional balance existing in many Member States. Secondly, the same can be said of the ultimate effects of consistent interpretation: while under national law a court may refrain from giving the relevant provisions a certain meaning since it believes it is reaching the limits of its judicial function, Community law seems to require that these limits are pushed a stage further. In other words, the separation of powers as an important element in the context of judicial interpretation also comes under pressure.

The Court's case law is in many respects somewhat ambiguous. By referring, for instance, to the jurisdiction of national courts and thereby suggesting that they are still acting within their competence, the Court is concealing the real scope of its case law, while, for the time being, a solid basis is lacking.

11.8   An outlook for the future

Despite all the problems discussed—sometimes in great detail—in the previous Chapters, 'the directive', as an instrument of EC intervention and the concept it embodies, has proved its usefulness.

It functions as a crucial element in giving shape to the *sui generis* Community legal order. By its character of two stage legislation it forms an important transmission belt between the European and domestic level. The directive also entails close involvement of the national courts in its application and enforcement and, therefore, in the protection of rights which individuals may derive from it. The national courts, frequently assisted by the Court of Justice, are called upon to strike a balance between the interests of the Community, the Member States, and the individuals. Their task is often a complex one, requiring a lot of creativity.

The directive is certainly not going to be abolished. On the contrary: it survives gloriously all discussions and measures concerning the quality of EC legislation,[26] the hierarchy of norms, the classification of acts, the perceived need for less and better legislation and alternative means of EC regulation.[27] What is more, the main characteristics of the directive were captured in a new instrument under the Third pillar, the framework decision.

Neither the IGC and the Treaty of Amsterdam nor the next IGC and the Treaty of Nice resulted in any changes with respect to the existing instruments. The issue of hierarchy and in that context, the distinction of legislative and executive acts, was put back on the agenda in the Laeken Declaration of 15 December 2001. In the Draft Constitutional Treaty,[28] in Article 32, the directive again survives, though under a new name: framework law.[29]

---

[26] Cf on this topic, for instance, Kellermann 1998 and Xantaki 2001. Obviously, requirements as to the drafting quality, need for consolidation, etc. are highly relevant for directives as well. Furthermore, there is indeed also an important connection between the quality of European legislation and its implementation and application in the Member States. A wealth of (comparative) material on this issue is provided in the context of the 19th colloquium of the Association of the Councils of State and Supreme Administrative Jurisdictions of the European Union, available at www.raadvst-consetat.be.

[27] On the last two aspects, which are part of the so-called 'new legislative culture', see e.g. Senden 2003, Sections 1.5–1.6, with further references. On directives and the hierarchy of norms see, *inter alia*, Timmermans 1997, 3–4. For a general discussion of legal instruments in the EC see Bast 2003.

[28] Treaty Establishing a Constitution for Europe, version of 20 June 2003.

[29] Curiously, the English version states that the framework law leaves the national authorities '*entirely*' free to choose the form and means of implementation. No such an addition exists in, for instance, the French or Dutch versions.

This said, it should not be excluded that the Constitutional Treaty, provided it will enter into force, will have an influence on the character of these framework laws. By introducing the distinction between legislative acts and non-legislative acts, the drafters also intended to entrench the idea that a legislative instrument should be limited to the main, essential, elements to be regulated. The more detailed—executive—rules should be left to non-legislative measures.[30] These indications as to the content of framework laws could indeed counter the often bemoaned detailedness of directives.

There is one issue that may be considered a missed opportunity: the problem of horizontal direct effect is not addressed in the Constitutional Treaty, the definition of the directive, i.e. the framework law, remained the same. In *Faccini Dori*, the Court gave a clear signal that the question of horizontal direct effect is to be considered a problem of powers and, therefore, a constitutional problem.[31] As the drafters of the Constitutional Treaty did not clarify this matter, is this a signal to the Court to find a way out of its own jurisprudential *imbroglio*?

---

[30] Cf the Final report of Working Group IX on Simplification, CONV 424/02, 8–13. Cf also the terms of Art 35 of the Draft Constitutional Treaty. As to the need to distinguish better between essential principles to be captures in basis legislation on the one hand and implementing rules on the other see also the Final Report of the Committee of Wise Men on the Regulation of European Securities Markets (Lamfalussy Report), Brussels, 15 February 2001. The European Commission made, in its White Paper on European Governance, COM (2001) 428 final, 20, comparable distinctions, but then in relation to the so-called framework directives. Cf also above, Ch 2, Section 2.1.

[31] Case C–91/92 [1994] ECR I–3325. Cf also Ch 9, Subsection 9.5.2.

Bibliography

Abele (1998) comment on Case C–227/97 Lemmens, EuZW 1998, 571–2.

Abraham (1989) *Droit international, droit communautaire et droit français*, (Paris: Hachette).

Adinolfi (1988) The Implementation of Social Policy Directives through Collective Agreements? CMLRev 291.

Alberton (2002) L'applicabilité des normes communautaires en droit interne. Les autorités administratives françaises: obligations de faire et de ne pas faire RFDA 2002/dossier, 1–19.

Alexy (1985) *Theorie der Grundrechte* (Baden-Baden: Nomos).

Anagnostaras (2000) State liability v. Retroactive application of belated implementing measures: Seeking the optimum means in terms of effectiveness of EC law, Web Journal of Current Legal Issues 2000.

—— (2001) The allocation of responsibility in State liability actions for breach of Community law: a modern gordian knot? ELR 139.

Anagnostopoulou (2001) Do Francovich and the principle of proportionality weaken Simmenthal (II) and confirm abuse of rights? CMLR 767.

Arnull (1988) Having your Cake and Eating it Ruled Out ELR 42.

—— (1999) The incidental effect of directives ELR 1.

Arrowsmith (1998) An Assessment of the Legal Techniques for Implementing the Procurement Directives, in Craig and Harlow, *Lawmaking in the European Union* (London: W.G. Hart legal workshop series, Kluwer).

Arts (1993) Het Francovich arrest en zijn toepassing in de Belgische rechtsorde TBP 495.

Azzi (2000) The Slow March of European Legislation: The Implementation of Directives, in Neunreither and Wiener (eds), *European Integration After Amsterdam: institutional dynamics and prospects for democracy* (Oxford: Oxford University Press).

Bach (1990) Direkte Wirkungen von EG-Richtlinien JZ 1108.

Barav (1975) Failure of Member States to Fulfil Their Obligations under Community Law CMLRev 369.

—— (1988) Damages in the Domestic Courts for Breach of Community Law by National Public Authorities, in Schermers, Heukels, Mead (eds), *Non-Contractual Liability of the European Communities* (Dordrecht: Nijhoff).

—— (1989) Enforcement of Community Rights in the National Courts: the Case for Jurisdiction to Grant Interim Relief CMLRev 369.

Barav (1991) La plénitude de compétence du juge national en sa qualité de juge communautaire, in *L'Europe et le droit. Mélanges en hommage à Jean Boulouis* (Paris: Dalloz).

—— (1994) Omnipotent Courts, in Curtin and Heukels (eds), *The Institutional Dynamics of European Integration. Liber Amicorum Henry G. Schermers* (Dordrecht: Nijhoff).

—— (1997) State Liability in Damages for Breach of Community law in the National Courts, in Heukels and McDonnell (eds), *The Action for Damages in Community Law* (The Hague: Kluwer).

—— (1998) Rapport général, Community Directives: effects, efficiency, justitiability, FIDE reports Eighteenth FIDE Congress, Stockholm, 417.

Barents (1982), Some Remarks on the—Horizontal—Effect of Directives, in O'Keeffe and Schermers (eds), *Essays in European Law and Integration* (Deventer: Kluwer).

—— (1994) The Quality of Community Legislation MJ 101.

Basedow (2001) Codification of Private Law in the European Union: the making of a Hybrid ERPL 35.

Bast (2003) On the grammar of EU Law: Legal Instruments, Jean Monnet Working Paper 9/03.

Bates (1986) The Impact of Directives on Statutory Interpretation: Using the Euro-meaning Statute Law Review 174.

Bavasso (2004) Electronic communications: A new paradigm for European regulation CMLRev 87.

Bebr (1981) *Development of Judicial Control of the European Communities* (The Hague: Nijhoff).

—— (1992) Comment on Joined Cases C–6/90 and C–9/90 *Francovich* CMLRev 557.

Bell and Bradley (1991) (eds), *Governmental liability: a comparative study*, United Kingdom National Committee of Comparative Law, London.

Bell and Engle (1987) *Cross Statutory Interpretation*, 2nd edn (London: Butterworths).

Bengoetxea (1990) *The Justification of Decisions by the European Court of Justice* (Oxford: Clarendon Press).

Bergamin (1991) Publieke subjectieve rechten, in Holtermann (ed), *Algemene begrippen staatsrecht*, 3rd edn (Zwolle: Tjeenk Willink).

Betlem (1993) *Civil Liability for Transfrontier Pollution* (London: Graham & Trotman, Nijhoff).

—— (2002) The Doctrine of Consistent Interpretation—Managing Legal Uncertainty, in Prinssen and Schrauwen (eds), *Direct Effect of European Law* (Groningen: European Law Publishing).

—— (2004) Environmental Liability and the Private Enforcement of Community Law, in Hessenlink et al. (eds), *Towards a European Civil Code*, 3rd edn (Nijmegen Ars Aequi Libri and The Hague etc.: Kluwer Law International).

Beyerlin (1987) Umsetzung von EG-Richtlinien durch Verwaltungs- vorschriften EuR 126.

Bijl (1986) Directe werking van EG-richtlijnen inzake omzetbelasting ten nadele van de burger WFR 285.

Biondi (1999) The European Court of Justice and Certain National Procedural Limitations: Not Such a Tough Relationship CMLRev 1271.

Bleckmann (1976) Art. 5 EWG-Vertrag und die Gemeinschaftstreue DVBl. 483.

—— (1997) *Europarecht*, 6th edn (Köln: Carl Heymanns Verlag).

Boch (1996) noot onder zaak Case C–92/93, Webb CMLRev 547.

—— (2004) *UK Courts and EC Law*, Dissertation, University of Amsterdam.

Boch and Lane (1992) European Community Law in National Courts: a Continuing Contradiction LJIL 171.

De Boer (1985a) Procederen wegens discriminatie, in *Staatkundig Jaarboek 1985* (Amsterdam: Kobra).

—— (1985b) Omgangsrecht, omgaan met het EVRM, de HR gaat om NJCM-Bulletin 211.

Von Bogdandy (2002) in Grabitz/Hilf, Das Recht der Europäischen Union, Kommentar, Beck'sche Verlagsbuchhandlung, München (loose-leaf).

Von Bogdandy, Bast, Arndt (2002) Handlungsformen in Unionsrecht— Empirische Analysen und dogmatische Strukturen in einem vermeintlichen Dschungel ZaöRV 77.

Bok (1993) Het Francovich arrest en onrechtmatige wetgeving naar Nederlands recht TPR 37.

Van den Bossche (2001) *Europees recht in de kering: over winterbedding, potpolder en schorre* (oratie KU Nijmegen) (Antwerpen: Kluwer).

Boulouis (1975) Sur une catégorie nouvelle d'actes juridiques: les 'directives', in *Recueil d'études en hommage à Charles Eisenmann* (Paris: Cujas).

—— (1979) L'applicabilité directe des directives. A propos d'un arrêt Cohn-Bendit du Conseil d'Etat RMC 107.

—— (1990) *Le droit institutionnel des Communautés Européennes*, 2nd edn (Paris: Montchrestien).

Boutard-Labarde (1996) Chronique droit communautaire, La Semaine Juridique 245.

Brechmann (1994) *Die richtlinienkonforme Auslegung* (München: Beck).

Brent (2001) Directives: Rights and Remedies in English and Community Law (London, Hong Kong: LLP).

Bribosia (1998) Report on Belgium, in Slaughter *et al.* (eds), *The European Courts and National Courts—doctrine and jurisprudence: legal change in its social context* (Oxford: Hart Publishing).

Bridge (1984) Procedural Aspects of the Enforcement of European Community Law through the Legal System of the Member States ELR 28.

Brown and Jacobs (2000) *The Court of Justice of the European Communities*, 5th edn (London: Sweet & Maxwell).

De Búrca (1992) Giving Effect to European Community Directives MLR 215.

De Búrca (1997) National procedural rules and remedies: The changing approach of the Court of Justice, in Lonbay and Biondi (eds), *Remedies for Breach of EC Law* (Chichester: John Wiley & Sons).

Canaris (2002) Die richtlinienkonforme Auslegung und Rechtsfortbildung im System der juristischen Methodenlehre, in Koziol (Hrsg.), *Im Dienste der Gerechtigkeit: Festschrift für Franz Bydlinski* (Wien: Springer Verlag).

Cane (1989) *Administrative Law* (Oxford: Clarendon Press).

Canivet and Huglo (1996) L'obligation pour le juge judiciaire d'appliquer d'office le droit communautaire au regard des arrêts Jeroen van Schijndel et Peterbroeck, Editions du Jurisclasseur, Revue Europe 1.

Canor (2002) Harmonizing the European Community's Standard of Judicial Review? EPL 135.

Capotorti (1988) Legal Problems of Directives, Regulations and their Implementation, in Siedentopf and Ziller (eds), *Making the European Policies Work: the Implementation of Community Legislation in the Member States* (IEPA) (London: Sage).

Caranta (1993) Governmental Liability after Francovich CLJ 1993, 272.

—— (1995) Judicial Protection Against Member States: a New Jus Commune Takes Shape CMLRev 703.

Cassia (1999) Le juge administratif français et la validité des actes communautaires RTDE 409.

—— (2002) L'invocabilité des directives communautaires devant le juge administratif: la guerre des juges n'a pas eu lieu, RFDA, Dossier, 20.

Chiti (1997) Towards a Unified Judicial Protection in Europe? European Review of Public Law 553.

Claes (2004) *The National Court's Mandate in the European Constitution* (Oxford: Hart publishing).

Clarich (1991) The Liability of Public Authorities in Italian Law, in Bell and Bradley (eds), *Governmental liability: a comparative study* (London: United Kingdom National Committee of Comparative Law).

Classen (1993) Zur Bedeutung von EWG-Richtlinien für Privatpersonen EuZW 83.

Colgan (2002) Triangular situations: The Coup de Grâce for the denial of Horizontal Direct Effect of Community Directives EPL 545.

Colloque des Conseils d'Etat (1996)—*XVe Colloque des Conseils d'Etat et des juridictions administratives suprêmes de l'Union européenne, La transposition en droit interne de directives de l'Union européenne*, Bruxelles.

Colloquium of Councils of State (2004)—*19th colloquium of Councils of State and Supreme Administrative Jurisdictions of the European Union, The Quality of European Legislation and its Implementation in the National Legal Order*, The Hague.

Constantinesco (1977) *Das Recht der Europäischen Gemeinschaften*, (Baden-Baden: Nomos).

Constantinesco (1985) Division of Fields of Competence between the Union and the Member States in the Draft Treaty Establishing the European Union, in Bieber, Jacqué, Weiler (eds), *An Ever Closer Union* (Luxembourg: Office for Official Publications of the EC).

Coppel (1993) *Individual Enforcement of Community Law: The Future of the Francovich Remedy*, EUI Working Paper No 93/6, Badia Fiesolana 1993.

—— (1994) Rights, Duties and the end of Marshall MLR 859.

Craig (1993) Francovich, Remedies and the Scope of Damage Liability LQR 595.

—— (1997) Directives: Direct Effect, Indirect Effect and the Construction of National Legislation ELR 519.

—— (1998) Indirect Effect of Directives in the Application of National Legislation', in Andenas and Jacobs (eds), *European Community Law in the English Courts* (Oxford: Clarendon Press).

Craig and De Búrca (2003) *EU Law: Text, Cases and Materials*, 3rd edn (Oxford: Oxford University Press).

Curtin (1990a) The Province of Government: Delimiting the Direct Effect of Directives in the Common Law Context ELR 195.

—— (1990b) Directives: the Effectiveness of Judicial Protection of Individual Rights CMLRev 709.

Curtin and Mortelmans (1994) Application and Enforcement of Community Law by the Member States: Actors in Search of a Third Generation Script, in Curtin and Heukels (eds), *The Institutional Dynamics of European Integration. Liber Amicorum Henry G. Schermers* (Dordrecht: Nijhoff).

Dashwood (1978) The Principle of Direct Effect in European Community Law JCMS 229.

David (1984) Sources of Law, *International Encyclopedia of Comparative Law* (II–3) (Tübingen, The Hague: Mohr, Nijhoff).

Deards (1997) 'Curioser and Curioser'? The Development of Member State Liability in the Court of Justice EPL 117.

Deckert (1997) Zur Haftung des Mitgliedstaates bei Verstößen seiner Organe gegen Europäisches Gemeinschaftsrecht, *Europarecht* 203.

Dekker (1991) Diagonale werking van Europese richtlijnen SEW 782.

Desmazières de Sechelles (1998) Rapport français, Community Directives: effects, efficiency, justiciability, FIDE reports Eighteenth FIDE Congress, Stockholm 1998, 237.

Detterbeck (2000) Haftung der Europäischen Gemeinschaft und gemeinschaftsrechtlicher Staatshaftungsanspruch AöV 2000, 202.

Devloo (1993) Richtlijnconforme interpretatie: een bron van recht RW 1993–1994, 377.

Dommering-van Rongen (1991) *Produktenaansprakelijkheid* (Deventer: Kluwer).

Donner (1998) Rapport neérlandais, Community Directives: effects, efficiency, justiciability, FIDE reports Eighteenth FIDE Congress, Stockholm 1998, 333 (also published in SEW 1998, 122).

Dougan (2000a) The 'Disguised' Vertical Direct Effect of Directives? CLJ 586.

—— (2000b) The Francovich Right to Reparation: Reshaping the Contours of Community Remedial Competence EPL 103.

—— (2001) Comment on Case C-443-/98, Unilever CMLRev 1503.

—— (2002) Enforcing the Single Market: The Judicial Harmonisation of National Remedies and Procedural Rules, in Barnard and Scott (eds), *The Law of the Single European Market: unpacking the premises* (Oxford: Hart).

Dubouis (1988) A propos de deux principes généraux du droit communautaire RFDA 691.

—— (1992) La responsabilité de l'Etat pour les dommages causés aux particuliers par la violation du droit communautaire RFDA 1.

Due (1992) Artikel 5 van het EEG-Verdrag. Een bepaling met een federaal karakter SEW 355.

Duffy (1992) Damages against the State: a New Remedy for Failure to Implement Community Obligations ELR 133.

Durand (1987) Enforceable Community Rights and National Remedies, The Denning Law Journal 43.

Easson (1979a) The Direct Effect—of EEC Directives ICLQ 319.

—— (1979b) Can Directives Impose Obligations on Individuals? ELR 67.

—— (1981) EEC Directives for the Harmonization of Laws: Some Problems of Validity, Implementation and Legal Effects YEL 1.

Edward (1998) Direct Effect, The separation of powers and the judicial enforcement of obligations, in *Scritti in onore di Giuseppe Federico Mancini* (Vol II) (Milano: Guiffrè).

Egger (1998) Die Durchführung von EU-Recht durch die Bundesländer in Österreich ZÖR 443.

Ehlermann (1987) Ein Plädoyer für die dezentrale Kontrolle der Anwendung des Gemeinschaftsrechts durch die Mitgliedstaaten, in: Capotorti, Ehlermann et al. (eds), *Du droit international au droit de l'intégration. Liber Amicorum Pierre Pescatore* (Baden-Baden: Nomos).

Ehricke (1999) Die richlinienconforme Auslegung nationalen Rechts vor Ende der Umsetzungsfrist einer Richtlinie EuZW 553.

—— (2001) Vorwirkungen von EU-Richtlinien auf Gesetzgebungsvorhaben ZIP 1311.

Eilmansberger (1997) *Rechtsfolgen und subjektives Recht im Gemeinschaftsrecht: zugleich ein Beitrag zur Dogmatik der Staathaftungsdoktrin des EuGH* (Baden-Baden: Nomos-Verlagsgesellschaft).

Eleftheriadis (1996) The Direct Effect of Community Law: Conceptual Issues YEL 205.

Van Emde Boas (1965) in Droit Communautaire et Droit National, Semaine de Bruges, Collège d'Europe 1965, 148–9.

Emmert (1992) Horizontale Drittwirkung von Richtlinien EWS 56.

Emmert and Pereira de Azevedo (1993) L'effet horizontal des directives. La jurisprudence de la CJCE: un bateau ivre RTDE 503.

—— (1995) Les jeux sont fait: rien ne va plus ou une nouvelle occasion perdue par la CJCE RTDE 20.

Everling (1984) Zur direkten innerstaatlichen Wirkung der EG-Richtlinien: Ein Beispiel richterlicher Rechtsfortbildung auf der Basis gemeinsamer Rechtsgrundsätze, in Börner *et al.* (eds), *Einigkeit und Recht und Freiheit. Festschrift für Karl Carstens* (Köln: Carl Heymann).

—— (1989) Zur Funktion des Gerichtshofs bei der Rechtsangleichung in der Europäischen Gemeinschaft, in Lessman (ed), *Festschrift fur Rudolf Lukes* (Köln: Carl Heymann).

—— (1992a) Umsetzung von Umweltrichtlinien durch normkonkretisierende Verwaltungsanweisungen RIW 379.

—— (1992b) Zur Auslegung des durch EG-Richtlinien angeglichenen nationalen Rechts ZGR 376.

—— (1993) Durchführung und Umsetzung des Europäischen Gemeinschaftsrechts im Bereich des Umweltschutzes unter Berücksichtigung der Rechtsprechung des EuGH NVwZ 209.

Di Fabio (1990) Richtlinienkonformität als ranghöchstes Normauslegungsprinzip NJW 947.

FIDE Reports (1980) *Remedies for Breach of Community Law*, FIDE, Ninth Congress, London 1980.

—— (1992) *La sanction des infractions au droit communautaire*, FIDE, Fifteenth Congress, Lisbonne.

—— (1998) Community Directives: effects, efficiency, justiciability, FIDE reports Eighteenth FIDE Congress, Stockholm.

Fines (1997a) A General Analytical Perspective on Community liability, in Heukels and McDonnel, *The Action for Damages in Community Law* (The Hague/London/Boston: Kluwer)

—— (1997b) Quelle obligation de réparer pour la violation du droit communautaire? RTDE 69.

Fischer (1991) Sind Vertragswidrig nicht umgesetzte Richtlinien innerstaatlich nur auf Antrag anwendbar? EuZW 557.

—— (1992a) Staatshaftung nach Gemeinschaftsrecht EuZW 41.

—— (1992b) Zur unmittelbaren Anwendung von EG-Richtlinien in der öffentlichen Verwaltung NVwZ 635.

Franssen (2002) *Legal Aspects of the Social Dialogue*, (Antwerpen/Oxford/New York: Intersentia).

Fuß (1965) Die Richtlinie des Europäischen Gemeinschaftsrechts DVBl. 378.

—— (1981) Die Verantwortung der nationalen Gerichte für die Wahrung des Europäischen Gemeinschaftsrechts, in Bieber, Bleckmann, Capotorti *et al.* (eds), *Das Europa der zweiten Generation (I). Gedächtnisschrift für Christoph Sasse* (Baden-Baden: Nomos).

Gaja, Hay and Rotnda (1986) Instruments for Legal Integration in the European Community, in Cappelletti, Seccombe and Weiler, *Integration Through Law*, Vol 1: Methods, Tools and Institutions, Book 2 (Berlin/New York: De Gruyter).

Galmot (1990) Directives et règlements en droit communautaire CJEG 73.

Galmot and Bonichot (1988) La Cour de Justice des Communautés européennes et la transposition des directives en droit national RFDA 1.

Geddes (1992) Locus Standi and EEC Environmental Measures, Journal of Environmental Law 29.

Geiger (1993) Die Entwicklung eines Europäisches Staatshaftungsrechts DVBl 465.

Van Gerven (1993) Bescherming van individuele rechten op basis van normatieve aansprakelijkheid in het Europese Gemeenschapsrecht TPR 6.

—— (1994a) Non-Contractual Liability of Member States, Community Institutions and Individuals for Breaches of Community Law with a View to a Common Law of Europe MJ 6.

—— (1994b) The Horizontal Direct Effect of Directive Provisions Revisited: The Reality of Catchwords, in Curtin and Heukels (eds), *The Institutional Dynamics of European Integration. Liber Amicorum Henry G. Schermers* (Dordrecht: Nijhoff).

—— (1996) Bridging the unbridgeable: Community and national tort laws after Francovich and Brasserie ICLQ 507.

—— (1997) The ECJ's Recent Case-Law in the Field of Tort Liability, towards a European Ius Commune? in Reich and Heinz-Marnik (eds), *Umweltverfassung und nachhaltige Entwicklung in der Europäischen Union* (Baden-Baden: Nomos).

—— (2000) Of rights, remedies and procedures CMLRev 501.

—— (2001) A Common Law for Europe: The Future Meeting the Past? ERPL 485.

Gilliams (1991–1992) Overheidsaansprakelijkheid bij schending van Europees recht RW 877.

—— (2000) *Horizontale werking van richtlijnen: dogma's en realiteit, Liber Amicorum Walter van Gerven* (Deurne: Kluwer).

Gilsdorf (1966) Rechtlicher Mittel zur Umsetzung von Gemeinschaftsrecht in nationales Recht durch Legislative und Executive der Mittgliedstaaten EuR 162.

Girerd (2002) Les principes d'équivalence et d'effectivité: encadrement ou désencadrement de l'autonomie procédurale des Etats membres? RTDE 75.

Goffin (1997) A propos des principes régissant la responsabilité non-contractuelle des Etats membres en cas de violation du droit communautaire CDE 335.

Grabitz (1971) Entscheidungen und Richtlinien als unmittelbar Wirksames Gemeinschaftsrecht EuR 1.

—— (1988) Liability for Legislative Acts, in Schermers, Heukels, Mead (eds), *Non-Contractual Liability of the European Communities* (Dordrecht: Nijhoff).

—— (1993) Die Wirkungsweise von Richtlinien, in Everling (ed), *Europarecht, Kartellrecht, Wirtschaftsrecht: Festschrift für Arved Deringer* (Baden-Baden: Nomos).

Green (1984a) The Treaty of Rome, National Courts and English Common Law RabelsZ 509.

Green (1984b) Directives, Equity and the Protection of Individual Rights ELR 295.

Grévisse and Bonichot (1991) Les incidences du droit communautaire sur l'organisation et l'exercice de la fonction juridictionelle dans les Etats Membres, in *L'Europe et le droit. Mélanges en hommage à Jean Boulouis* (Paris: Dalloz).

Van de Gronden (1997) Nationale overgangstermijnen en EG-Richtlijnen, Regelmaat 119.

Gurlit (1997) Umsetzungsverpflichtung der Mitgliedstaaten und subjektive Rechte der Gemeinschaftsbürger—subjektives Recht auf Umsetzung?, in Krämer, Micklitz and Tonner (eds), *Law and Diffuse Interests in the European Legal Order: Liber Amicorum Norbert Reich* (Baden-Baden: Nomos).

Harding (1997) Member State Enforcement of European Community Measures: The Chimera of 'Effective' Enforcement MJ 5–25.

Harlow and Szyszczak (1995) comment on R. v. Secretary of State for Employment ex Parte Equal Opportunities Commission and Another CMLRev (2003) 641.

Hartley (2003) *The Foundations of European Community Law*, 5th edn (Oxford: Oxford University Press).

Haslach (2001) *Die Umsetzung von EG-Richlinien durch die Länder* (Frankfurt am Main: Peter Lang).

Hecquard-Theron (1990) La notion d'Etat en droit communautaire RTDE 693.

Herbert (1993) L'accès au juge: qui peut agir, in Verwilghen (ed), *Access to Equality between Men and Women in the European Community* (Louvain-la-Neuve: Presses Universitaires de Louvain).

Hessel and Mortelmans (1993) Decentralized Government and Community Law: Conflicting Institutional Developments CMLRev 905.

Heukels (1988) The Prescription of an Action for Damages under Article 215(2) EEC, in Schermers, Heukels, Mead (eds), *Non-Contractual Liability of the European Communities* (Dordrecht: Nijhoff).

—— (1991) *Intertemporales Gemeinschaftsrecht* (Baden-Baden: Nomos).

—— (1993) Alternatieve implementatietechnieken en art. 189 lid 3 EEG: grondslagen en ontwikkelingen NTB 59.

Hilf (1988) Der Justizkonflikt um EG-Richtlinien: gelöst EuR 1.

—— (1993) Die Richtlinie der EG—ohne Richtung, ohne Linie—EuR 1.

Hilson (1997) Liability of Member States in Damages: The Place of Discretion ICLQ 941.

Hilson and Downes (1999) Making sense of Rights: Community Rights in E.C. Law ELR 121.

Himsworth (1997) Things Fall Apart: The Harmonisation of Community Judicial Procedural Protection Revisited ELR 291.

Hölscheidt (2001) Abschiedt vom subjektiv-öffentlichen Recht? EuR 376.

Holtmaat (1992) *Met zorg een recht* (Zwolle: Tjeenk Willink).

Honorat and Schwartz (1991) comment on case Société Morgane, C.E 11 janvier 1991 AJDA 111.

Hoskins (1996) Tilting the balance: Supremacy and national procedural rules ELR 365.

Huglo (1993) La responsabilité de l'Etat pour la violation de ses obligations communautaires: l'arrêt Francovich du 19 novembre 1991, in Pappas (ed), *Tendances actuelles et évolution de la jurisprudence de la Cour de Justice des Communautés européennes*, Vol. I (Maastricht: EIPA).

Ipsen (1965) Richtlinien-Ergebnisse, in Hallstein and Schlochauer (eds), *Zur Integration Europas. Feschrift für Carl Friedrich Ophüls* (Karlsruhe: Müller).

—— (1972) *Europäisches Gemeinschaftsrecht* (Tübingen: Mohr).

Isaac (1992) Effet direct du droit communautaire, in *Répertoire Dalloz de Droit Communautaire* (Paris: Dalloz).

Iwasawa (1986) The Doctrine of Self-Executing Treaties in the United States: A Critical Analysis, Virginia Journal of International Law 627.

Jacobs (1993) Remedies in National Courts for the Enforcement of Community Rights, in Perez Gonzalez *et al.* (eds), *Hacia un nuevo orden internacional y europeo. Estudios en homenaje al profesor Don Manuel Díez de Velasco* (Madrid: Tecnos).

—— (1997) Enforcing Community rights and obligations in national courts: Striking the balance, in Lonbay and A. Biondi (eds), *Remedies for Breach of EC Law*, (Chichester: John Wiley & Sons).

Jacqué (1985) The Draft Treaty Establishing the European Union CMLRev 19.

Jann and Schima (2003) Bemerkungen zum Gebot der Richtlinienkonformen Auslegung des nationalen Rechts, in Colneric, Edward, Puissochet, Ruiz-Jarabo Colomer (Hrsg.), *Une communauté de droit, Festschrift für Gil Carlos Rodríguez Iglesias* (Berlin: Berliner Wissenschafts-Verlag).

Jans (1992) *Over de grenzen van Europees milieurecht* (Zwolle: Tjeenk Willink).

—— (1993a) Het belanghebbende-begrip in het licht van het Europees recht, in Boxum *et al.* (eds), *Aantrekkelijke gedachten: beschouwingen over de algemene wet bestuursrecht* (Deventer: Kluwer).

—— (1993b) Legal Protection in Environmental Law EELR 151.

—— (1994) Rechterlijke uitleg als implementatie-instrument van EG-richtlijnen: spanning tussen instrument en rechtszekerheid, in Hoogenboom and Damen (eds), *In de sfeer van administratief recht* (Utrecht: Lemma).

—— (2000) *European Environmental Law*, 2nd edn (Groningen: European Law Publishing).

Jans *et al.* (2002) De Lange, Prechal and Widdershoven, *Inleiding tot het Europees bestuursrecht*, 2nd edn (Nijmegen: Ars Aequi Libri).

Jans and Prinssen (2002) Direct effect: Convergence or Divergence? A Comparative Perspective, in Prinssen and Schrauwen (eds), *Direct effect of European law* (Groningen: European Law Publishing).

Jarass (1990) Voraussetzungen der innerstaatlichen Wirkung des EG-Rechts NJW 2420.

Jarass (1991a) Richtlinienkonforme bzw. der EG-rechtskonformen Auslegung EuR 211.
—— (1991b) Folgen der innerstaatlichen Wirkung von EWG-Richtlinien NJW 2665.
—— (1994) Haftung für die Verletzung von EU-Recht durch nationale Organe und Amtsträger NJW 881.
Jarass and Beljin (2003) Casebook Grundlagen des EG–Rechts (Baden-Baden: Nomos).
—— (2004) Grenzen der Privatbelastung durch unmittelbar wirkende Richtlinien EuR 714.
Jeffreys (1991) The Role of Legislative Draftsmen in the UK in Making and Implementing EC Law RegelMaat 39.
Jung (2001) Das Verhältnis der gesellschaftrechtlichen Richtliniengebung zur deutschen Zivilrechtdogmatik, in Hohloch (Hrsg.), *Richtlinien der EU und ihre Umsetzung in Deutschland und Frankreich*, (Baden-Baden: Nomos).

Kaczorowska (1999) A New 'Right' Available to Individuals under Community Law EPL 79.
Kakouris (1997) Do the Member States possess judicial procedural 'autonomy'? CMLRev 1389.
Kapteyn (1993) De organisatie van de rechtsbescherming van particulieren in de EG NTB 38.
Kapteyn and VerLoren van Themaat (1998) *Introduction to the Law of the European Communities*, 3rd edn (ed Gormley) (Deventer: Kluwer).
—— (2003) *Het recht van de Europese Unie en van de Europese Gemeenschappen*, 6th Completely Revised Edn (Deventer: Kluwer).
Karl (1992) Die Schadenersatzpflicht des Mitgliedstaaten bei Verletzungen des Gemeinschaftsrechts RIW 440.
Karpenstein (1977) Zur Wiedergutmachung von Vertragsverstoßen der Mitgliedstaaten gegen Gemeinschaftsrecht DVBl 61.
Kellerman *et al.* (1998) (eds), *Improving the Quality of Legislation in Europe* (The Hague: Kluwer Law International).
Keus (1993) Europees privaatrecht. Een bonte lappendeken, *Preadviezen voor de Vereniging voor Burgelijk Recht en de Nederlandse Vereniging voor Europees Recht* (Lelystad: Koninklijke Vermande).
Klagian (2001) Die objektiv unmittelbare Wirkung von Richtlinien ZÖR 305.
Klein (1988) *Unmittelbare Geltung, Anwendbarkeit und Wirkung von Europäischen Gemeinschaftsrecht*, Vorträge, Reden und Berichte aus dem Europa Institut Nr 119, Saarbrücken.
Klindt (1998) Die Zulässigkeit dynamischer Verweisungen auf EG-Recht aus verfassungs- und Europarechtlicher Sicht DVBl 373.
Köck and Hinstersteininger (1998) The Concept of Member State Liability for Violation of Community Law and Its Shortcomings, Austrian Review of International and European Law 25.

Kooijmans (1967) De richtlijn van het Europese gemeenschapsrecht—karakter, functie en rechtsgevolg SEW 122.

Koopmans (1995) Regulations, directives and measures, in Due *et al.* (Hrsg.), *Festschrift für Ulrich Everling* (Baden-Baden: Nomos).

—— (1999) comment on Case C–227/97 Lemmens SEW 337.

Kortenaar (1985) Een gemiste kans voor Europa WFR 1272.

Kortmann (1991) De vorm van implementatie van EEG-recht, RegelMaat 47.

Kovar (1978) Voies de droit ouvertes aux individus devant les instances nationales en cas de violation des normes et décisions du droit communautaire, in *Les recours des individus devant les instances nationales en cas de violation du droit européen* (Bruxelles: Larcier).

—— (1981) L'intégrité de l'effet direct du droit communautaire selon la jurisprudence de la Cour de Justice de la Communauté, in Bieber, Bleckmann, Capotorti *et al.* (eds), *Das Europa der zweiten Generation (I). Gedächtnisschrift für Christoph Sasse* (Baden-Baden: Nomos).

—— (1983) The relationship between Community law and national law, in *Thirty Years of Community Law*, Office for Official Publications of the European Communities, Luxembourg.

—— (1987) Observations sur l'intensité normative des directives, in Capotorti, Ehlermann *et al.* (eds), *Du droit international au droit de l'intégration. Liber Amicorum Pierre Pescatore* (Baden-Baden: Nomos).

—— (1992) Le Conseil d'Etat et le droit communautaire: des progrès mais peut mieux faire, Dalloz (Chronique) 207.

Kraemer (1992) *Focus on European Environmental Law* (London: Sweet & Maxwell).

Krislov, Ehlermann and Weiler (1986) Ehlermann and Weiler, The Political Organs and the Decision-making Process in the United States and the European Community, in Cappelletti, Seccombe and Weiler, *Integration Through Law*, Vol. 1: Methods, Tools and Institutions, Book 2 (Berlin/New York: De Gruyter).

Kutscher (1976) Methods of Interpretation as Seen by a Judge at the Court of Justice, *Judicial and Academic Conference, 27–28 September 1976*, Luxembourg.

Lackhoff and Nyssens (1998) Direct effect of Directives in Triangular Situations ELR 397.

Lang (2000) The principle of effective protection of Community law rights, in O'Keeffe and Bavasso (eds), *Liber Amicorum in Honour of Lord Slynn of Hadley* (The Hague: Kluwer Law International).

De Lange (1991) *Publiekrechtelijke rechtsvinding* (Zwolle: Tjeenk Willink).

Langenfeld (1991) Die dezentrale Kontrolle der Anwendung des europäisches Gemeinschaftsrechts im innerstaatlichen Rechtsraum—dargestelt am Beispiel der Richtlinie, in Siedentopf (ed), *Europäische Integration und nationalstaatliche Verwaltung* (Stuttgart: Steiner).

—— (1992) Zur Direktwirkung von EG-Richtlinien DöV 955.

Larouche (2001) The Brasserie de Pêcheur puzzle, in Wouters and Stuyck (eds), *Principles of Proper Conduct for Supranational, State and Private Actors in the European Union: Towards a Ius Commune, Essays in Honour of Walter van Gerven* (Antwerpen: Intersentia).

Lasok (2001) *Law & Institutions of the European Union*, 7th edn (London: Butterworths).

Lauwaars (1973) *Lawfulness and Legal Force of Community Decisions* (Leiden: Sijthoff).

—— (1976) Comment on Case 41/74 *Van Duyn* SEW 78.

—— (1978) Het voorbehoud voor de openbare orde als beperking van het vrije verkeer van personen in de EEG SEW 329.

—— (1983) Implementation of Regulations by National Measures LIEI 41.

—— (1991) Comment on Case C–213/89 *Factortame* SEW 478.

—— (1993) 'Voor elck wat wils' ofwel de vertraagde uitvoering van EEG-richtlijnen FED 705.

Lauwaars and Maarleveld (1987) *Harmonisatie van wetgeving in Europese organisaties* (Deventer: Kluwer).

Lauwaars and Timmermans (2003) *Europees recht in kort bestek*, 6th edn (Denenter: Kluwer).

Leclerc and Mondésert (2002) Vers une responsabilité des collectivités territoriales en cas de violation du droit communautaire AJDA 201.

Lee (1999) In Search of a Theory of State Liability in the European Union, Harvard Jean Monnet Working Paper 9/99.

Léger (1999) Libres propos sur l'application effective du droit communautaire de l'environement, in Rodriguez Iglesias (ed), *Mélanges en hommage à Fernand Schockweiler* (Baden-Baden: Nomos).

Legrand (1996) European Legal Systems are not Converging ICLQ 52.

Leitao (1981) L'effet direct des directives: une mythification—RTDE 425.

Lenaerts (1998) Redactionele Signalen SEW 269.

Lenaerts and Desomer (2003) Simplification of the Union's Instruments, in De Witte, *Ten reflections on the Constitutional Treaty for Europe*, Robert Schuman Centre for Advanced Studies and Academy of European Law (Florence: European University Institute).

Lenz (1990) Entwicklung und unmittelbare Geltung des Gemeinschaftsrechts DVBl 908.

Lenz, Sif Tynes, and Young (2000) Horizontal What? Back to Basics, ELR 509.

Lewis (1992) *Judicial Remedies in Public Law* (London: Sweet & Maxwell).

Lewis and Moore (1993) Duties, Directives and Damages in European Community Law, Public Law 151.

The Liability of the State (1981) *The Liability of the State*, Proceedings of the Ninth Colloquium on European Law, Madrid 1979, Council of Europe, Strasbourg.

Louis (1976) L'effet direct des directives, in *Mélanges en hommage au Professeur Jean Baugniet*, Bruxelles.

Louis, Vandersanden, Waelbroeck and Waelbroeck (1993) *Commentaire Megrèt*, Vol 10, La Cour de justice. Les actes des institutions (Bruxelles: Editions de l'Université de Bruxelles).

Lutter (1992) Die Auslegung angeglichenen Rechts JZ 593.

MacCormick (1977) Rights in Legislation, in Hacker and Raz (eds), *Law, Morality and Society: Essays in Honour of H.L.A. Hart* (Oxford: Clarendon Press).

—— (1982) Rights, Claims and Remedies, Law and Philosophy 337.

MacCormick and Summers (1991) (eds), *Interpreting Statutes* (Darthmouth: Aldershot-Brookfield).

Macrory (1992) The Enforcement of Community Environmental Laws: Some Critical Issues CMLRev 347.

Manin (1990) L'invocabilité des directives: Quelques interrogations RTDE 669.

Maresceau (1978) *De directe werking van het Europese Gemeenschapsrecht* (Antwerpen: Kluwer).

—— (1980a) De directe werking in het Europese gemeenschapsrecht RBDI 265.

—— (1980b) Het verbindend karakter van richtlijnen volgens de rechtspraak van het Hof van Justitie SEW 655.

Marsh (1973) *Interpretation in a National and International Context*, UGA, Heule (Bruxelles: Namur).

Mastenbroek (2003) Surviving the deadline: The Transposition of EU Directives in the Netherlands, European Union Politics 371.

Mastroianni (1999) On the Distinction Between Vertical and Horizontal Effect of Community Directives: What Role for the Principle of Equality? EPL 417.

Mead (1991) The Obligation to Apply European Law: Is Duke Dead? ELR 490.

Mertens de Wilmars (1969) De directe werking van het Europese recht SEW 62.

—— (1981) L'efficacité des différentes techniques nationales de protection juridique contre les violations du droit communautaire par les autorités nationales et les particuliers CDE 377.

—— (1991) Réflexion sur le système d'articulation du droit communautaire et du droit national, in *L'Europe et le droit. Mélanges en hommage à Jean Boulouis* (Paris: Dalloz).

Millarg (1977) Keine Staatshaftung für gemeinschaftswidrige Gesetzgebung ZRP 224.

Monaco (1987) Problèmes des directives communautaires dans l'ordre juridique italien, in Capotorti, Ehlermann *et al.* (eds), *Du droit international au droit de l'integration. Liber Amicorum Pierre Pescatore* (Baden-Baden: Nomos).

Moreau (1991) L'influence de développement de la construction européenne sur le droit français de la responsabilité de la puissance publique, in *L'Europe et le droit. Mélanges en hommage à Jean Boulouis* (Paris: Dalloz).

Morris (1989) The Direct Effect of Directives—Some Recent Developments in the European Court JBL 233 and 309.

Mortelmans (1991) Comment on Case C–143/88 *Zuckerfabrik Süderdithmarschen* SEW 670.

Nettesheim (1992) Gemeinschaftsrechtliche Vorgaben für das deutsche Staatshaftungsrecht DöV 999.

—— (2002) in Grabitz/Hilf, *Das Recht der Europäischen Union, Kommentar* (München: Beck'sche Verlagsbuchhandlung) (loose-leaf).

Nicolaides (2003) Preparing for Accession to the European Union: How to Establish Capacity for Effective and Credible application of EU Rules, in Cremona (ed), *The Enlargment of the European Union* (Oxford: Oxford University Press).

Nicolaysen (1984) Richtlinienwirkung und Gleichbehandlung von Männer und Frauen beim Zugang zum Beruf EuR 380.

—— (1985) Vertragsverletzung durch mitgliedstaatliche Gerichte EuR 368.

—— (1986) Keine horizontale Wirkung von Richtlinien-Bestimmnungen EuR 370.

Nielsen (2002) Implementation of EC Directives in Denmark, The International Journal of Comparative Labour Law and Industrial Relations 459.

Oldenbourg (1984) *Die unmittelbare Wirkung von EG-richtlinien im innerstaatlichen Bereich* (Müchen Florentz).

Oldenkop (1972) Die Richtlinien der Europäischen Wirtschaftsgemeinschaft JöR 55.

Oliver (1987) Enforcing Community rights in the English Courts, MLR 881.

—— (1992) Le droit communautaire et les voies de recours nationales CDE 348.

Ophüls (1966) Les règlements et les directives dans les Traités de Rome CDE 3.

Ossenbühl (1992) Der gemeinschaftsrechtliche Staatshaftungsanspruch DVBl 993.

Pâques (1996) Trois remèdes à l'inexécution du droit communautaire: utilité pour l'environnement? Revue de droit international et de droit comparé 135.

Pescatore (1971) *L'ordre juridique des Communautés Européennes, Etude des sources du droit communautaire* (Liège: Les presses universitaires de Liège).

Pescatore (1972) Responsabilité des Etats membres en cas de manquement aux règles communautaires, Il Foro Padano 9.

—— (1980) L'effet des directives communautaires: une tentative de démythification, Dalloz (Chronique) 171.

—— (1983) The Doctrine of 'Direct Effect': an Infant Disease of Community Law ELR 155.

Pfeiffer (2001) Richtlinien der EU und ihre Umsetzung: Umsetzungstreue und Harmonie der Richtliniengebung mit zivilrechtlicher Dogmatik, in Hohloch (Hrsg.), *Richtlinien der EU und ihre Umsetzung in Deutschland und Frankreich* (Baden-Baden: Nomos).

Pieper (1990) Die Direktwirkung von Richtlinien der Europäischen Gemeinschaft—Zum Stand der Entwicklung, DVBl 684.

Plaza Martin (1994) Furthering the Effectiveness of EC Directives and the Judicial Protection of Individual Rights Thereunder ICLQ 26.

Prechal (1990) Remedies After Marshall, CMLRev 451.

—— (1991a) Richtlijnconforme uitleg: Alice in Wonderland WFR 1596.

—— (1991b) Comment on Case C–177/88 *Dekker* SEW 665.

—— (1992a) Comment on Joined Cases C–6/90 and C–9/90 *Francovich*, Aktualiteitenkatern Nemesis 10.

—— (1992b) Comment on Case C–374/86 *Commission v. Belgium*, CMLRev 371.

—— (2000) Does Direct Effect still Matter? CMLRev 1047.

Prechal (2000a) Commentaire sur l'affaire C-326/96 Levez, Rec I–7835, Revue des Affaires Européennes 167.

—— (2001) Judge-made harmonisation of national procedural rules: a bridging perspective, in Wouters and Stuyck (eds), *Principles of Proper Conduct for Supranational, State and Private Actors in the European Union: Towards a Ius Commune, Essays in Honour of Walter van Gerven* (Antwerpen/Groningen/Oxford: Intersentia).

—— (2002) Direct effect reconsidered, redefined, rejected, in Prinssen and Schrauwen (eds), *Direct Effect. Rethinking a Classic of EC Legal Doctrine* (Groningen: European Law Publishing).

Prechal and Burrows (1990) *Gender Discrimination Law of the European Community* (Aldershot: Dartmouth).

Prechal and Hancher (2001) *Individual Environmental Rights: Conceptual Pollution in EU Environmental Law?*, Yearbook of European Environmental Law, Vol 2 (Oxford: Oxford University Press).

Prechal and Shelkoplyas (2004) National Procedures, Public policy and EC Law. From Van Schijndel to Eco Swiss and beyond ERPL 589.

Prieß (1993) Die haftung der EG-Mitgliedstaaten bei Verstößen gegen das Gemeinschaftsrecht, NVwZ 118.

Reich (1995) System der subjektiven öffentlichen Rechte, in the Union: A European Constitution for Citizens of Bits and Pieces, Collected Courses of the Academy of European Law (The Hague/Boston/London: Martinus Nijhoff) Vol. VI, book 1.

Ress (1985) Die Kontrole internationaler Verträge und der Akte der Europäischen Gemeinschaften durch das Bundesverfassungsgericht, in Koening (ed.), *Die Kontrolle der Verfassungsmäßigkeit in Frankreich und in der Bundesrepublik Deutschland* (Köln: Carl Heymann).

—— (1993) Die Direktwirkung von Richtlinien: Der Wandel von der prozessrechtlichen zur materielrechtlichen Konzeption, in Leipold, Lüke, Yoshino (eds), *Gedächtnisschrift für Peter Ahrens* (München: Beck).

Richter (1988) Die unmittelbare Wirkung von EG-Richtlinien zu lasten einzelner EuR 394.

Riechenberg (1999) Local Administration and the Binding Nature of Community Directives: A Lesser Known Side of European Legal Integration, Fordham International Law Journal 696.

De Ripainsel-Landy and Gérard (1976) La notion juridique de la directive utilisée comme instrument de raprochement des législations dans la CEE, in *Les instruments de raprochement des législations dans la Communauté Economique Européenne* (Bruxelles: Editions de l'Université de Bruxelles).

Rodriguez Iglesias and Riechenberg (1995) Zur richtlinienkonformen Ausleggung des nationalen Rechts, in Due *et al.* (Hrsg.), *Festschrift für Ulrich Everling* (Baden-Baden: Nomos).

Ross (1993) Beyond Francovich MLR 55.

Roth (1991) The Application of Community Law in West Germany: 1980–1990 CMLRev 137.

Royla and Lackhoff (1998) Die innerstaatliche Beachtlichkeit von EG-Richtlinien und das Gesetzmäßigkeitsprinzip DVBl 1116.

Ruffert (1996) *Subjektive Rechte im Umweltrecht der Europäischen Gemeinschaft: unter besonderer Berücksichtigung ihrer prozessualen Durchsetzung* (Heidelberg: Decker).

—— (1997) Rights and Remedies in European Community Law: a comparative view CMLRev 307.

—— (1998) Dogmatik und Praxis des subjektiv-öffentlichen Rechts unter dem Einfluss des Gemeinschaftsrecht DVBl 69.

Salmond (1966) *Salmond on Jurisprudence*, 12th edn (by Fitzgerald) (London: Sweet & Maxwell).

Samuels (1998) Incorporating, Translating or Implementing European Union Law into UK Law, Statute Law Review 80

Sauron (2000) *L'application du droit de l'Union Européenne en France* (Paris: Documentation Française).

Schermers (1997) No Direct Effect for Directives EPL 527.

Schermers and Waelbroeck (2001) *Judicial Protection in the European Union* (The Hague: Kluwer).

Scherzberg (1991) Verordnung—Richtlinie—Entscheidung, zum System der Handlungsformen im Gemeinschaftsrecht, in Siedentopf (ed), *Europäische Integration und nationalstaatliche Verwaltung* (Stuttgart: Steiner).

Schilling (1988) Zur Wirkung von EG-Richtlinien. Versuch einer völkerrechtlichen Betrachtung ZaöRV 637.

Schlemmer-Schulte and Ukrow (1992) Haftung des Staates gegenüber dem Marktburger für gemeinschaftsrechtswidriges Verhalten EuR 82.

Schmidt (2004) Gemeinsame Vorschriften für mehrere Organe, in Von der Groeben, Schwarze (Hrsg.), *Vertrag über die Europäische Union und Vertrag zur Gründung der Europäischen Gemeinschaft*, 6th edn, Vol IV (Baden-Baden: Nomos).

Schmidt-Kessel (2000) *Rechtsmißbrauch im Gemeinschaftsrecht—Folgerungen aus den Rechtssachen Kefalas und Diamantis, Prinzipien des Privatrechts und Rechtsvereinheitlichung*, Jahrbuch junger Zivilrechtswissenschaftler 2000 (Stuttgart: Richard Booberg Verlag).

Schoch (1999) Individualrechtsschutz im deutschen Umweltrecht unter dem Einfluss des Gemeinschaftsrechts NVwZ 457.

Schockweiler (1990) Le régime de la responsabilité extra-contractuelle du fait d'actes juridiques dans la Communauté européenne RTDE 27.

—— (1991) L'emprise du droit communautaire sur les pouvoirs du juge national, Bulletin du Cercle Francois Laurent 1991/III, 51.

—— (1992) La responsabilité de l'autorité nationale en cas de violation du droit communautaire RTDE 27.

—— (1993a) *Die Haftung der Mitgliedstaaten bei vertragswidrigem Verhalten*, Zentrum für Europäisches Wirtschaftsrecht, Vorträge und Berichte Nr 24, Bonn.

—— (1993b) Die Haftung der EG-Mitgliedstaaten gegenüber dem einzelnen bei Verletzung des Gemeinschaftsrechts EuR 107.

Scott (1998) *EC Environmental Law* (London: Longman).

Seidel (1983) *Direktwirkung von Richtlinien*, Vorträge, Reden und Berichte aus dem Europa-Institut, nr 14, Saarbrücken.

Senden (2003) *Soft Law in the European Community Law* (Oxford: Hart Publishing).

Sévon (2003) Inter-Environnement Wallonie—What are the Effects of Directives and from When?, in Colneric, Edward, Puissochet, Ruiz-Jarabo Colomer (Hrsg.), *Une communauté de droit, Festschrift für Gil Carlos Rodríguez Iglesias* (Berlin: Berliner Wissenschafts-Verlag).

Shaw (1991) Pregnancy Discrimination in Sex Discrimination ELR 313–20.

Shelkoplyas (2003) *The Application of EC Law in Arbitration Proceedings* (Groningen: Europa Law Publishing).

Siedentopf and Ziller (1988) (eds), *Making the European Policies Work: the Implementation of Community Legislation in the Member States* (IEPA) (London: Sage).

Siems (2002) Effektivität und Legitimität einer Richtlinienumsetzung durch Generalklauseln ZEuP 747.

Simon (1991) Les exigences de la primauté du droit communautaire: continuité ou métamorphoses-, in *L'Europe et le droit. Mélanges en hommage à Jean Boulouis* (Paris: Dalloz).

—— (1992) Le Conseil d'Etat et les directives communautaires: du gallicisme à l'orthodoxie RTDE 265.

—— (1993) Droit communautaire et responsabilité de la puissance publique. Glissements progressifs ou révolution tranquille AJDA 235.

—— (1996a) Comment on Case C–312/93 Peterbroeck and Joined Cases C–430/93 and C–431/93 Van Schijndel, Journal du droit international 468.

—— (1996b) Comment on Joined Cases C–430/93 and C–431/93 Van Schijndel, Editions du Juris-Classeur, Revue Europe No 57, 10.

—— (1996c) La responsabilité de l'Etat saisie par le droit communuataire AJDA 489–99.

—— (1997) *La directive européene* (Paris: Dalloz).

—— (2001) Le système juridique communautaire, 3rd edn (Paris: PUF droit).

Simon and Barav (1987) La responsabilité de l'administration nationale en cas de violation du droit communautaire RMC 165.

—— (1990) Le droit communautaire et la suspension provisoire des mesures nationales RMC 591.

Slot (1996) Harmonisation ELR 378.

De Smith and Brazier (1989) *Constitutional Law and Administrative Law* (London: Penguin Books).

Snyder (1993) The Effectiveness of European Community Law: Institutions, Processes, Tools and Techniques MLR 19.

Somsen (2003) Discretion in European Community environmental law: An analysis of ECJ case law CMLRev 1413.

Spetzler (1991) Die richtlinienkonforme Auslegung als vorrangige Methode steuerjuristische Hermeneutik RIW 579.

Steiner (1986) How to Make the Action Suit the Case ELR 102.

—— (1993) From Direct Effects to Francovich: Shifting Means of Enforcement of Community Law ELR 3.

Steyger (1991) De directe toepassing van EG-Richtlijnen door anderen dan de staat, RegelMaat 10.

—— (1996) Wringend recht, VAR Preadvies Tjeenk Willink, Alphen a/d Rijn.

Streinz (1999) Comment on Case C–227/97 Lemmens, JuS 599–600.

Stuyck (2001) Comment on Joined Cases C–240/98 to C–244/98, Océano Grupo Editorial SA v. Rocio Murciano Quintero and Salvat Editore v. José M. Sànchez Alcón Prades *et al.* CMLRev 719.

Stuyck and Wytinck (1991) Comment on case C–106/89 *Marleasing* CMLRev 205.

Swaak (1996) Consistent interpretation of National Law: Dutch Courts on the Wrong Track? EPL 219.

Szyszczak (1990) Sovereignty: Crisis, Compliance, Confusion, Complacency ELR 480.

Szyszczak and Delicostopoulos (1997) Intrusions into national procedural autonomy: The French paradigm ELR 141.

Tanney (1992) Comment on *Webb* v. *EMO Air Cargo (UK), Ltd.* (Court of Appeal of England and Wales) CMLRev 1021.

Taylor (1985) Damages as a Remedy for the Breach of Provisions of the EEC Treaty Having Direct Effect, in Jagenburg *et al.* (eds), *Festschrift für Walter Oppenhof*, München 475.

Temple Lang (1992–1993) New Legal Effects Resulting from the Failure of States to Fulfill Obligations under European Community Law: the Francovich Judgment, Fordham International Law Journal 1.

—— (1998) The Duties of National Authorities Under Community Constitutional Law ELR 109–31.

Timmermans (1971) De harmonisatie van nationale voorschriften op het gebied van het vennootschapsrecht SEW 608.

Timmermans (1979) Directives: their Effect within the National Legal Systems CMLRev 533.

—— (1988) Comment on Case 80/86 *Kolpinghuis*, AA 330.

—— (1992) Comment on Case C–106/89 *Marleasing* SEW 816.

—— (1997) Community Directives Revisited YEL 1–28.

Toner (1997) Thinking the Unthinkable? State Liability for Judicial Acts after Factortame (III) YEL 165.

Toth (1990) Comment on Case C–213/89 *Factortame* CMLRev 573.

Triantafyllou (1997) Zur Europäisierung des subjektiven öffentlichen Rechts DÖV 192.

—— (1999) Abuse of rights versus primacy? CMLRev 157.

Tridimas (1994) Horizontal effect of directives: a missed opportunity? ELR 621.

—— (1999) The General Principles of EC Law (Oxford: Oxford University Press).

—— (2001) Liability for breach of Community law: growing up and mellowing down? CMLRev 301.

—— (2002) Black, White and Shades of Grey: Horizontality of Directives Revisited YEL 327.

Usher (1979) The Direct Effect of Directives ELR 268.

Vandamme (2005) *The Invalid Directive, Legal Questions on the Disqualification of a Union's Act requiring Domestic Lawmaking*, Dissertation University of Amsterdam 2005 (Groningen: European Law Publishing).

Vandersanden and Dony (1997) (eds), *La reponsabilité des Etats members en cas de violation du droit communautaire* (Bruxelles: Bruylant).

Verschuuren (2000) EC Environmental Law and Self-Regulation in the Member States: In Search of a Legislative Framework, in Yearbook of European Environmental Law (Oxford: Oxford University Press).

Waelbroeck (2002) Vers une harmonisation minimale des règles procédurales nationales?, in Dony and Bribosia, *L'avenir du système juridictionnel de l'Union européenne* (Brussels: Editions de l'Université de Bruxelles).

Waldron (1984) Introduction, in Waldron (ed), *Theories of Rights* (Oxford: Oxford University Press).

Ward (1990) Government Liability in the United Kingdom for Breach of Individual Rights in European Community Law, Anglo-American Law Rev 1.

—— (1993) The Right to an Effective Remedy in European Community Law and Environmental Protection, Journal of Environmental Law 221.

—— (2000) *Judicial Review and the Rights of Private Parties in EC Law* (Oxford: Oxford University Press).

Wathelet (2004) Du concept de l'effet direct à celui de l'invocabilité au regard de la jurisprudence récente de la Cour de Justice, in Hoskins and Robinson (eds), *A True European. Essays for Judge David Edward* (Oxford: Hart Publishing).

Wathelet and Raepenbusch (1997) La responsabilité des États Membres en cas de violation du droit communautaire. Vers un alignement de la responsabilité de l'État sur celle de la Communauté ou l'inverse? CDE 13.

Weatherill (1997) Reflections on EC Law's 'Implementation Imbalance' in the Light of the Ruling in Hedley Lomas, in Krämer, Micklitz and Tonner (eds), *Law and Diffuse Interests in the European Legal Order: Liber Amicorum Norbert Reich* (Baden-Baden: Nomos).

—— (1998) Rapport britannique, Community Directives: effects, efficiency, justitiability, FIDE reports Eighteenth FIDE Congress, Stockholm 1998, 123.

—— (2001) Breach of directives and breach of contract ELR 177.

Weymüller (1991) Der Anwendungsvorrang von EG-Richtlinien—Eine Diskussion ohne Ende RIW 501.

White (1984) *Rights* (Oxford: Clarendon Press).

Widdershoven (2003) Geploeter bij de amtshalve toepassing van EG-recht, Tijdschrift voor Omgevingsrecht 178.

Winter (1972) Direct Applicability and Direct Effect. Two Distinct and Different Concepts in Community Law CMLRev 425.

—— (1991a) Gevolgen van het Gemeenschapsrecht voor de lagere overheden in Nederland, RegelMaat 52.

—— (1991b) Direktwirkung von EG-Richtlinien DVBl 657.

—— (1991c) Rechtsschutz gegen Behörden die Umweltrichtlinien der EG nicht beachten, NuR 453.

—— (1996) The Directive: problems of construction and directions for reform, in Winter (ed), *Sources and Categories of European Union Law* (Baden-Baden: Nomos).

—— (1999) Individualrechtsschutz im deutschen Umweltrecht unter dem Einfluâ des Gemeinschaftsrechts, NVwZ 467.

—— (2002) Die Dogmatik der Direktwirkung von EG-Richtlinien und ihre Bedeutung für das EG-Naturschutzrecht, Zeitschrift für Umweltrecht 313.

Wissink (2001) *Richtlijnconforme interpretatie van burgerlijk recht* (Deventer: Kluwer).

De Witte (1984) Retour à Costa. La primauté du droit communautaire à la lumière du droit international RTDE 425.

—— (1999) Direct Effect, Supremacy, and the Nature of the Legal Order, in Craig and De Búrca, *The Evolution of EU Law* (Oxford: Oxford University Press).

Wyatt (1983) The Direct Effect of Community Social Law—Not Forgetting Directives ELR 241.

—— (1989) Enforcing EEC Social Rights in the United Kingdom ILJ 197.

—— (1998) Litigating Community Environmental Law—Thoughts on the Direct Effect Doctrine, Journal of Environmental Law 9.

Wyatt and Dashwood (2000) *European Union Law*, 4th edn (London: Sweet & Maxwell).

Xanthaki (2001) The Problem of Quality in EU Legislation: What on Earth is Really Wrong? CMLRev 651.

Zeidler (1988) Die Verfassungsrechtsprechung im Rahmen der Staatlichen Funktionen, Bundesrepublik Deutschland EuGRZ 207.
Zuleeg (1993) Umweltschutz in der rechtsprechung des Europäischen Gerichtshofs NJW 31.

Index

Printed in the United Kingdom
by Lightning Source UK Ltd.
117788UK00001B/73